HOW TO PLAY THE 200 BEST-EVER

CARD GAMES

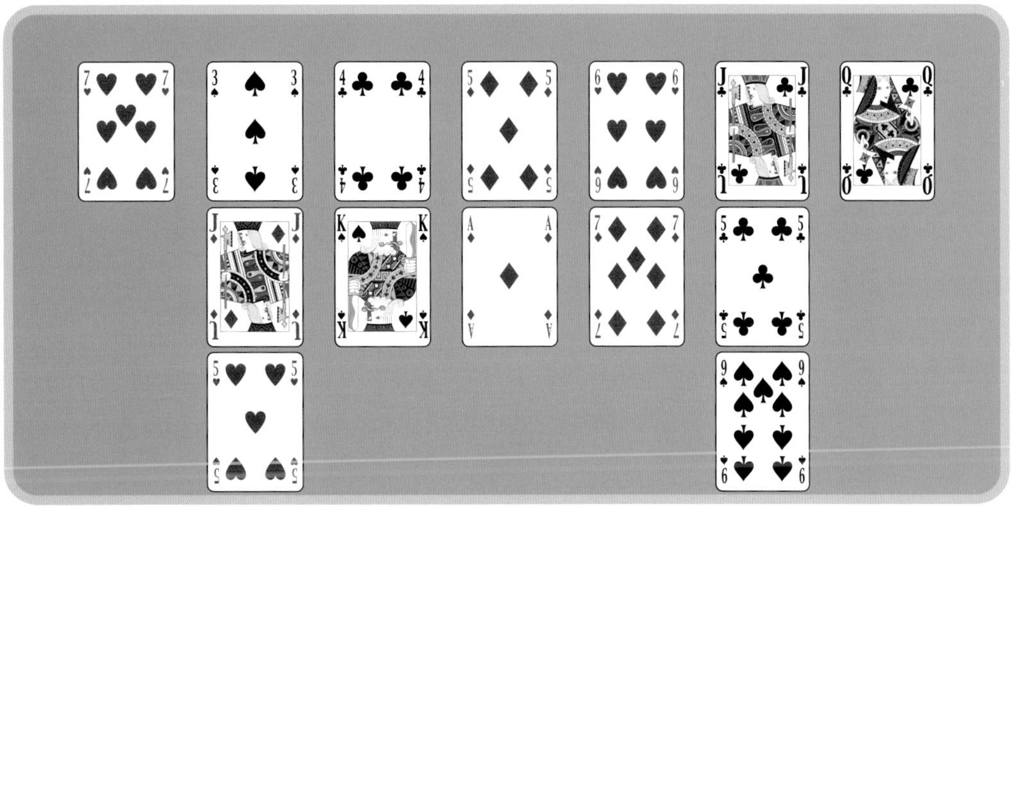

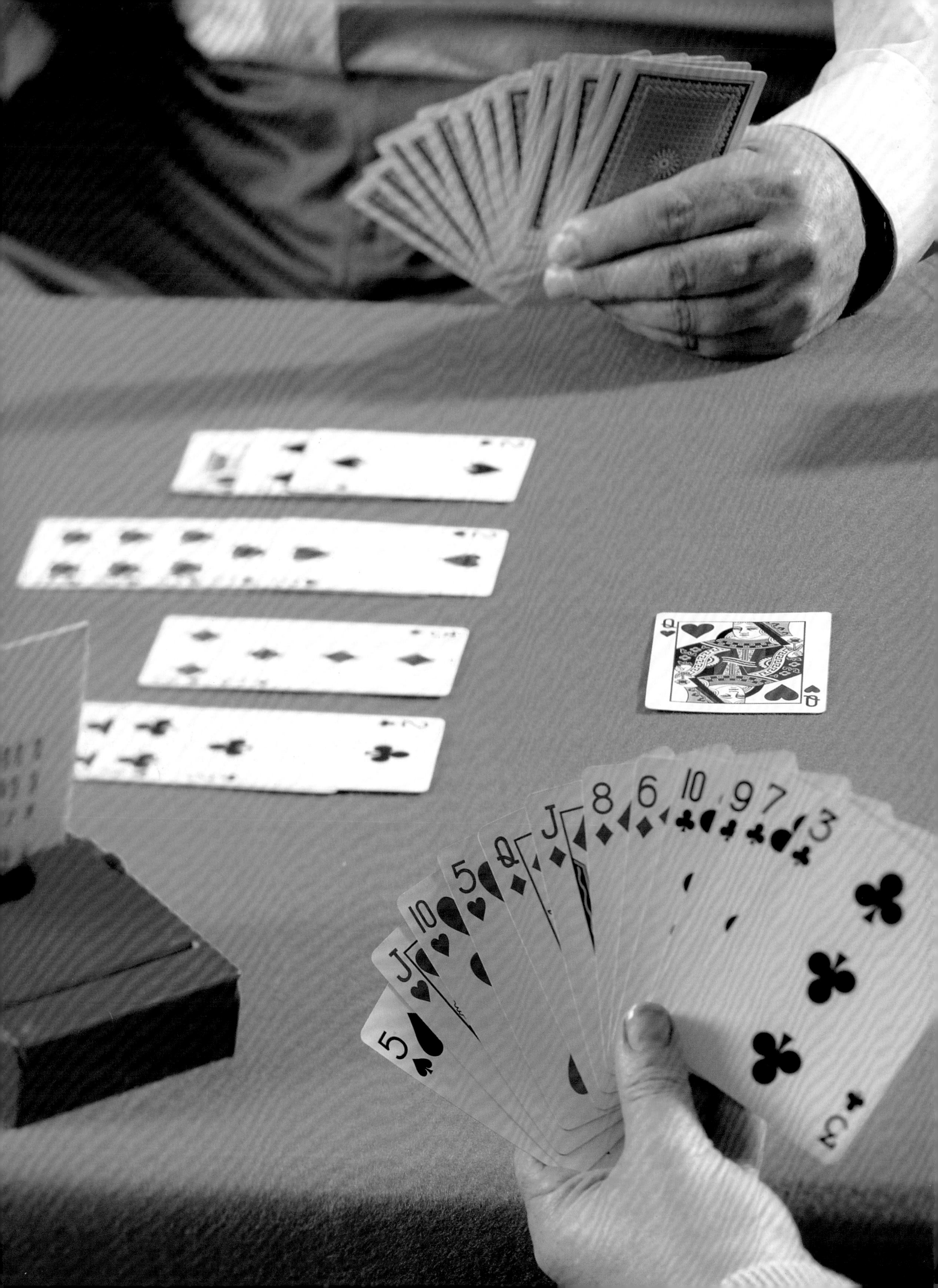

HOW TO PLAY THE 200 BEST-EVER

CARD GAMES

A FANTASTIC COMPENDIUM OF THE GREATEST CARD GAMES FROM AROUND THE WORLD, INCLUDING THE HISTORY, RULES, AND WINNING STRATEGIES FOR EACH GAME, WITH MORE THAN 400 COLOUR IMAGES

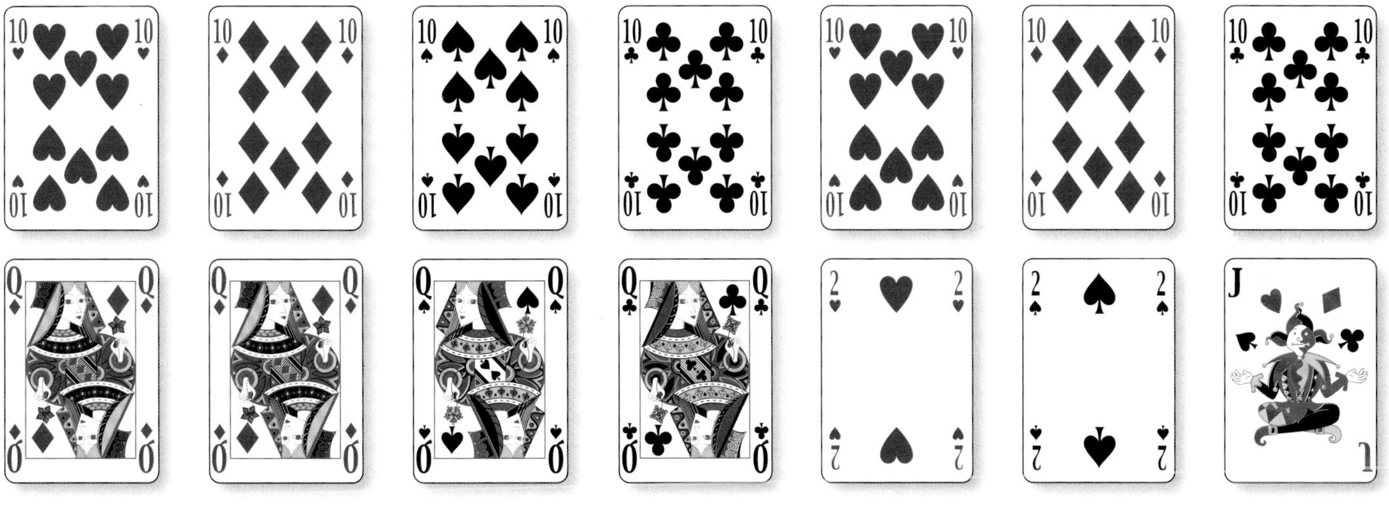

EVERYTHING FROM FUN GAMES AND SIMPLE WAYS TO GET STARTED FOR BEGINNERS AND FAMILY PLAYERS, TO PROFESSIONAL TIPS AND EXPERT GUIDANCE FOR ADVANCED PLAY IN SERIOUS GAMES OF CHANCE

JEREMY HARWOOD

LORENZ BOOKS

This edition is published by Lorenz Books

Lorenz Books is an imprint of
Anness Publishing Ltd, Hermes House,
88–89 Blackfriars Road, London SE1 8HA
tel. 020 7401 2077; fax 020 7633 9499
www.lorenzbooks.com; info@anness.com

UK agent: The Manning Partnership Ltd
6 The Old Dairy, Melcombe Road
Bath BA2 3LR
tel. 01225 478 444; fax 01225 478 440
sales@manning-partnership.co.uk

UK distributor: Grantham Book Services Ltd
Isaac Newton Way, Alma Park Industrial Estate
Grantham, Lincs NG31 9SD
tel. 01476 541080; fax 01476 541061
orders@gbs.tbs-ltd.co.uk

North American agent/distributor:
National Book Network
4501 Forbes Boulevard, Suite 200
Lanham, MD 20706
tel. 301 459 3366; fax 301 429 5746
www.nbnbooks.com

Australian agent/distributor: Pan Macmillan Australia
Level 18, St Martins Tower
31 Market St, Sydney, NSW 2000
tel. 1300 135 113; fax 1300 135 103
customer.service@macmillan.com.au

New Zealand agent/distributor: David Bateman Ltd
30 Tarndale Grove, Off Bush Road
Albany, Auckland
tel. 09 415 7664; fax 09 415 8892

A CIP catalogue record for this book is available from the British Library.

Designed and produced for Anness Publishing by
THE BRIDGEWATER BOOK COMPANY LIMITED
Publisher: Joanna Lorenz
Editorial Director: Helen Sudell
Project Editor: Rosie Gordon
Editorial Readers: Molly Perham and Jay Thundercliffe
Production Controller: Don Campaniello
Editor: Nick Fawcett
Project Manager: Polita Caaveiro
Designers: Stuart Perry & Sylvia Tate
Art Director: Lisa McCormick

10 9 8 7 6 5 4 3 2 1

CONTENTS

Introduction: Playing Cards 8

GAMES FOR FRIENDS AND FAMILY 12

1 PATIENCE AND SOLITAIRE GAMES 14
Klondike 15
Accordion, Aces Up 16
Labyrinth 17
Spite and Malice 18
Spit 19
Nerts 20
Poker Patience 21

2 POINT-TRICK GAMES 22
Manille 23
Spanish Solo 24
Fifteens, Forty for Kings 25
Tressette 26
Terziglio 27
Ciapanò 28
Da Bai Fen 29

3 CATCH AND COLLECT GAMES 30
Snap, Beggar-My-Neighbour, Slapjack, Memory 31
Gops 32
Schwimmen 33
Whisky Poker 34
Go Fish, Authors 35

4 Fishing Games 36
Casino 37
Zwicker 38
Cuarenta 39
Scopa 40
Scopone 41
Cicera, Cirulla 42
Basra 43
Chinese Ten 44
Laugh and Lie Down 45

5 Adding Games 46
Noddy 47
Six-Card Cribbage 48
Five-Card Cribbage 50
Costly Colours 51
Ninety-Eight, Ninety-Nine 52
One Hundred, Jubilee 53

6 Shedding Games 54
Domino 55
Michigan 56
Crazy Eights 58
Switch 59
Eleusis 60
Pope Joan 62
President 63
Zheng Shangyou 64
Tieng Len 66

7 Beating Games 68
Rolling Stone, Sift Smoke 69
Durak 70
Svoi Kozyri 72
Dudak 73
Mustamaija 74
Kitumaija 75
Hörri 76
Skitgubbe 77
Shed 78
Paskahousu 79
Cheat 80
Verish' Ne Verish' 81

8 Rummy Games 82
Rummy 83
Block Rummy, Boathouse Rum, Call Rummy 84
Skip Rummy, Wild-Card Rummy, Krambambuli, One-Meld and Two-Meld Rummy 85
Gin Rummy, Two-Player Gin 86
Three- and Four-Player Gin 87
Loba 88
Thirty-One 89
Three Thirteen 90
Conquian 91
Contract Rummy 92
Push 94
Kaluki 96
Vatican 97

9 Banking Games 98
Pontoon 99
Blackjack 100
Baccarat 102
Yablon 103
Speculation 104
Let it Ride 105

10 ALL FOURS GAMES 106
All Fours 107
Pitch 108
Smear 109
Cinch 110
Don 111

11 SOLO GAMES 112
Solo Whist 113
Belgian Whist 114
Crazy Solo, Knockout Whist 115
Boston 116
Quadrille 117
Ombre 118
Preference 120
Asszorti 122
Oh Hell! 123
Ninety-Nine 124

12 PIQUET GAMES 125
Piquet 126
Imperial 128
Gleek 129

ADVANCED CARD GAMES 130

13 BRIDGE AND WHIST GAMES 132
Contract Bridge 133
Auction Bridge, Chicago Bridge 136
Pirate Bridge, Cut-Throat Bridge, Towie, Booby 137
Whist 138
Bid Whist 140
Spades 141
Kaiser 142
Forty-One 143
Vint 144
Quinto 145
Widow Whist 146
German Whist 146
Calypso 147

14 QUICK TRICK GAMES 148
Euchre 149
Pepper 150
Five Hundred 151
Ecarté 152
Twenty-Five 153
Auction Forty-Fives 154
Napoleon 155
Brandeln, Rödskögg 156
Bourré, Julep 157
Five-Card Loo 158
Norrlandsknack, Femkort 159
Three-Card Loo 160
Tomato, Zwikken 161
Toepen, Agurk 162
Truc 163
Treikort, Put 164
Aluette 165

15 HEARTS GAMES 166
Hearts 167
Jacks, Polignac 168
Barbu 169
Tëtka 170
Schieberamsch 171
Bassadewitz 172
Coteccio 173

16 ACE-TEN GAMES	174
Schafkopf	175
Skat	176
Doppelkopf	178
Avinas	179
Six-Bid Solo	180
Haferltarock	181
Einwerfen, Yukon	182
Scotch Whist, Reunion	183
Madrasso	184
Briscola	185
17 KING-QUEEN GAMES	186
Sechsundsechzig (Sixty-Six)	187
Bondtolva	188
Tute	189
Tysiacha	190
Gaigel	191
Mariás	192
18 QUEEN-JACK GAMES	194
Bezique	195
Marjolet	196
Pinochle	197
19 JACK-NINE GAMES	198
Klaberjass	199
Belote	200
Coinche	201
Boonaken	202
Klaverjas	203
Handjass	204
Schieber Jass	205
20 CANASTA GAMES	206
Samba	207
Canasta	208
Hand and Foot	210
Pennies from Heaven	212
Pináculo	214
Continental Rummy	216
500 Rum	217
21 VYING GAMES	218
Poker	219
Wild-Card Poker	221
Draw Poker	222
Five-Card Stud	224
Seven-Card Stud	225
Texas Hold 'em	226
Pai Gow Poker	228
Freak-Hand Poker	229
Fifty-Two, Forty-Two, Razz and Chicago, No Peek Stud	230
Follow the Queen, Three-Card Drop, Guts	231
Brag	232
Mus	234
Primero	236
Poch	237
Bouillotte	238
Seven Twenty-Seven	239
22 QUASI-TRUMP GAMES	240
Watten	241
Karnöffel	242
Brus	243
Alkort	244
23 TAROT GAMES	245
French Tarot	246
Ottocento	248
Glossary	250
Index	253
Recommended Books/Picture Credits	256

Introduction: Playing Cards

Today, playing cards are used all over the globe and are everyday objects that we all take for granted. But there is much more to these cards than the 52-card deck most of us are familiar with: there are variations in suit systems, patterns and even the number of cards in a pack, depending on where you are in the world and the game you are playing.

Exactly where, when, how and why playing cards originated is still a matter of considerable historical controversy. The current consensus is that they were first devised in China. For some time though, many playing card authorities rejected the theory, largely because traditional Chinese cards are so unlike Western ones in their appearance. This led to both India and Persia being suggested as likelier alternatives.

What is now known for certain is that on New Year's Eve 969, the Chinese Emperor Mu-tsung enjoyed a game of 'domino cards' with his favourite wife. It has also been discovered that what the Chinese called 'money cards', which seem to have originated around the same time as 'domino cards', did bear a close resemblance to their later Western counterparts.

Onwards to Europe

Whatever the exact circumstance of their origins, it is clear that the knowledge of playing cards spread gradually westwards – either across Central Asia and through Persia or, according to some scholars, via India – to reach the Islamic world. It was from there, probably from Egypt, that knowledge of cards eventually crossed the Mediterranean to reach Spain and Italy at about the same time in the late 1300s.

As far as is known, the first brief mention of playing cards comes in a Catalan document dating from 1371, where they are termed *naip*. In 1377, the Italian city of Florence passed a statute regulating the playing of 'a certain card game called *naibbe*, which has been recently introduced into these parts'. That same year, Johannes van Rheinfelden, a monk based in Basle, described playing cards in more detail, writing of a deck of 52 cards. Each of the deck's four suits consisted of 10 numbered cards from One to Ten and three court cards – a King and two Marshals and no Queen or Jack. The suits were not specifically identified, and Johannes confined himself to the remark that 'some of these signs are considered good, but others signify evil'.

Although no physical evidence of it survives, the card deck Johannes was describing had more than a passing resemblance to the decks the Egyptians devised. These consisted of 52 cards, divided into four suits – swords, polo sticks, cups and coins. Each suit consisted of 10 'spot' cards from One to Ten, which were identified by the number of suit symbols or 'pips' on each one, plus three court cards: *Malik* (King), *Na'ib Malik* (Viceroy or Deputy King) and *Thani Na'ib* (Second Under-Deputy). Authorities on early playing card history consider the

Left: The Death tarot card, from the Gringonneur pack, a 15th-century Italian set of tarot cards. Tarot cards were originally simply regular playing cards, and were not used as fortune-telling aids until at least the 18th century.

Centre: The Moon, an Italian tarot card, *c.*1490. Italy has a long-standing reputation for beautiful tarot decks derived from the first models of the 15th century.

Far left: The Page of Coins, from a pack of tarot cards (*c.*1483). Traditional Italian playing cards of the 15th century used swords, batons, cups and coins.

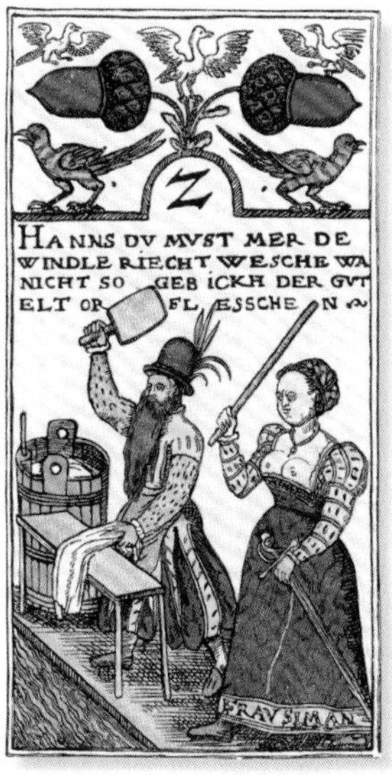

Left: 16th-century European playing card designs featuring acorns and trees. The four suits (Spades, Hearts, Diamonds and Clubs) used in most of the world today originated in France in 1480. The *trèfle* (Club) was probably copied from the acorn; the *pique* (Spade) from the leaf.

Bottom: Various cards from a Chinese game, featuring a fish and a stiltwalker. Chinese playing cards are thin and long so that several cards can be held at the same time, overlapped in a vertical arrangement.

resemblance between these Egyptian cards and early Italian examples as being too great to be coincidental. The only major difference seems to be that the Italians substituted batons for polo sticks (knowledge of polo had not yet reached the West from the East).

Suits and Suit Systems

The composition and design of playing cards varied as knowledge of them spread across Europe. Although the number of cards in a deck was not a constant, the inclusion of numbered cards and court cards plus the division into different suits were standard features from early on.

Early Italian decks contained 56 cards, including four types of court cards – King, Queen, Knight and Knave – and were split into suits of swords, cups, batons and coins. For a newly devised game called Tarocco, they added a wild card, the Fool, and 21 special cards bearing mystical symbols that served as trumps. Such were the origins of the game that German-speakers called Tarock and the French Tarot. In fact, it was not until the 1750s that tarot cards themselves became linked with fortune telling and divination.

The Spanish soon replaced Queens with *Caballeros* (mounted knights), while the Germans dropped the Queen in favour of *König* (King), *Obermann* (Upper Man) and *Untermann* (Lower Man). The Germans also replaced the Italian suit symbols with bells, hearts, leaves and acorns. In fact, they went on to experiment with a wide variety of suit symbols, including wine flagons, drinking cups, books, printers' pads and animals, well into the 16th century and beyond.

By around 1500, three main suit systems had evolved – Latin (Italian, Spanish and Portuguese), Germanic (German and Swiss) and French, the latter of which reinstated the Queen into the ranks of the court cards. As far as the suits were concerned, the French adopted the Germanic hearts and leaves, turning the leaves upside down to become the present-day Spade symbol. Acorns became Clubs, while Diamonds replaced bells. Some card historians believe the suits were representations of the different strata of medieval society: Spades symbolized the nobility, Hearts the church, Diamonds betokened wealth and Clubs represented the peasantry.

Although card games were well established in England by around the same time, it is not known what sort of cards were employed. Card authorities believe the probability is that the earliest English cards were Latin suited, and that French-suited cards were adopted later on. The oldest surviving English cards date from 1590.

Naming the Court Cards

The French paid particular attention to the design and naming of the court cards, often giving them the names of specific heroes and heroines from history and fable. In Rouen, a major centre of French card manufacture until this was moved to Paris, early choices for the identities of the Kings included King Solomon, the biblical ruler of the Israelites; the Roman emperor Augustus; Clovis, ruler

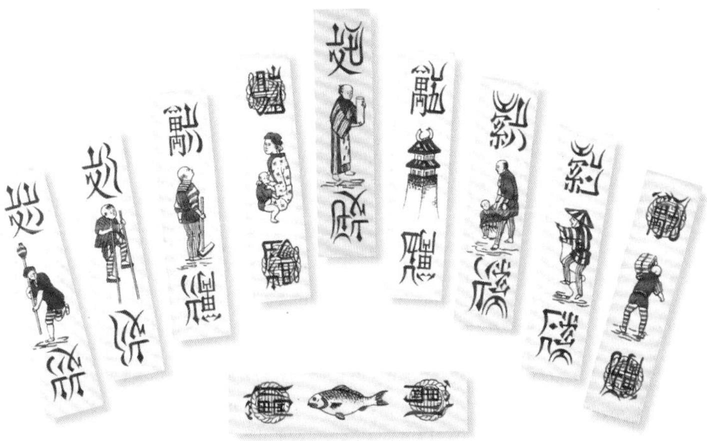

of the Franks; and the Byzantine emperor Constantine the Great. By the time of Henri IV (1557–1610), the Kings were widely considered to be representations of King David, Alexander the Great, Julius Caesar and the Holy Roman Emperor Charlemagne.

The Knaves, or Jacks, as they were eventually to become, were the Trojan hero Hector; *La Hire* (Etienne de Vignolles), comrade-in-arms of Joan of Arc; Ogier, one of Charlemagne's knights; and Sir Lancelot from Arthurian legend. The Queens were the warrior-goddess Minerva (who was thought to represent Joan of Arc); Rachel, Joseph's biblical mother; Argine, which is an anagram of Regina (the Latin for 'queen'); and the Old Testament prophetess Judith.

The assignation of identities to the court cards continued until the last decade of the 18th century, when the practice was brought to an end by the French Revolution. Court cards were briefly eliminated from the deck until reinstated in the Napoleonic era, but not as representations of specific figures.

Card Painting and Engraving

One of the reasons for the relatively swift emergence of the French as Europe's most influential card makers was their technological improvements on card manufacture. The earliest European cards were hand-crafted one-offs. According to contemporary accounts, they were painted by hand 'in gold or various colours' or 'painted and gilded'. Of course, this made playing cards far too expensive for ordinary folk to contemplate buying, even if they had been readily available. However, the development of woodcuts as well as the invention of the printing press markedly transformed this situation and enabled the mass-production of cards. Playing cards ceased to be hand-painted luxuries that only the wealthy could afford. Now, designs for entire sheets of cards could be drawn and carved on wood-blocks, inked, printed on paper, separated and finally glued on cardboard.

At first, it was the Germans in places such as Ulm, Nuremberg and Augsburg who took the lead, but the French were soon challenging them for supremacy. The suit symbols the latter employed were straightforward to stencil, which made their cards far quicker and cheaper to produce. At about the same time, French card makers realized that it was unnecessary to engrave each court card separately, as was the practice of their German competitors. Instead, they created a single printing block or plate for each of the three Royals, printed the cards that they required and stencilled in the suits later.

The Anglo-American Deck

The French suit system became the standard in England, from where it was exported to the British colonies in America, and is thus the ancestor of the 52-card deck that is in international use today. Modern card players know these as Anglo-American cards. The simplest in design and the cheapest to manufacture, they are the cards used in such universally popular games as Whist, Bridge, Poker, Rummy and Canasta.

Left: *Minerva and the Centaur* (*c.*1480) by Botticelli. The French gave court cards the names of specific heroes and heroines. An image of Minerva, the goddess of wisdom and war, depicted here, was often used for the Queen of Spades playing card.

Far left: A 17th-century painting of Joan of Arc (1412–31), artist unknown. Although early French cards depicted Minerva as one of the Queens, she was thought to symbolize the heroine Joan of Arc.

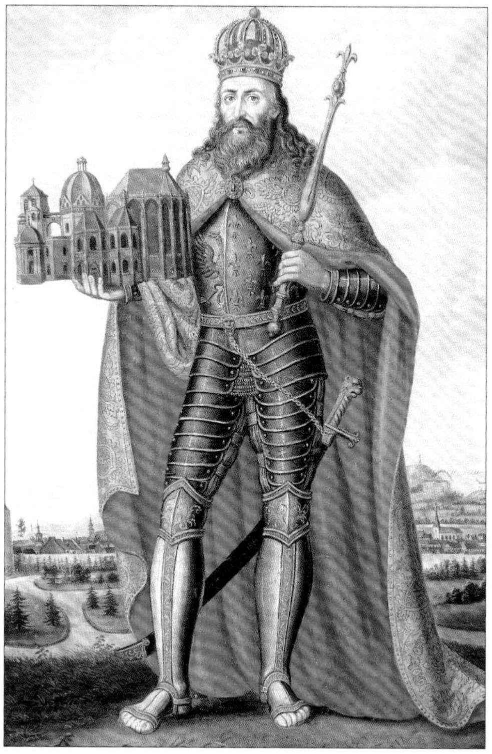

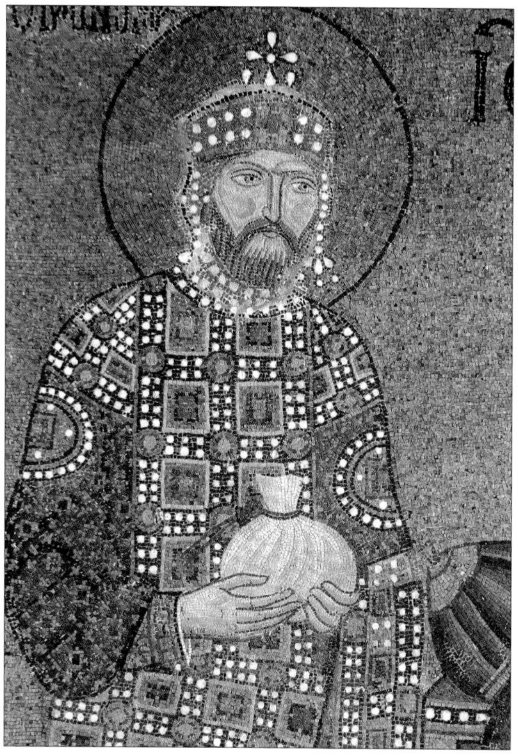

Far left: *Charlemagne with model of Aachen Cathedral* by J.P. Sheuren, 1825. The King of the Franks and Holy Roman Emperor was identified as the King of Hearts in the French deck.

Left: An 11th-century mosaic of the Byzantine emperor Constantine (980–1055), artist unknown. In some French decks, the King of Clubs was supposed to be a representation of him.

The Anglo-American deck consists of 13 ranks of each of the four suits – Spades, Hearts, Diamonds and Clubs. The court cards are modelled on the ones first produced by the celebrated French card makers in Rouen of the late 16th and early 17th centuries. Each suit includes an Ace, King, Queen and Jack with the remaining cards in each suit being numbered from Ten down to Two. The court cards bear single pips (symbols of their suit) while the numbered cards carry the appropriate number of pips. Originally, Kings were always the highest cards in a suit, but, by the late 1400s, the previously lowest cards – the Aces – ranked over them (although in some games, players can specify whether Aces are high or low).

Two Jokers complete the standard deck. These were a 19th-century innovation, which card historians believe were devised by Euchre players – Euchre was thought to have originated in Alsace and been brought to America during the 1860s. In some games, the joker serves as a 'wild card' (which can be used to represent any other card) or as an additional trump (card of a suit nominated to be of higher value). Most card games, however, require one or both Jokers to be removed from the pack before play can start. Other 19th-century practical refinements introduced by the Americans include corner and edge indices (identifying marks), which enabled players to hold their cards close together in a fan in one hand as opposed to two; varnished surfaces, for ease of shuffling; and rounded corners, to reduce wear and tear. Finally, court cards became reversible and Knaves became Jacks.

How to Use this Book

Apart from instruction, the book contains a summary of each of the types of games available to play, as well as their conventional rules, along with some exceptions and variations. Card game rules and strategies are clearly explained and regularly illustrated with diagrams showing example hands in various states of play. Where relevant, there will be a 'D' button, which indicates the position of the dealer in relation to the rest of the players, who are referred to in the diagrams and text as 'Player A' and 'Player B' etc. With each game, there is also a handy information box that provides a general overview of what you will need to play the game, be it a score sheet or gambling chips, as well as information on how many and what kind of cards are used, an age level for each game and the ranking of the particular cards.

Below: An 18th-century woodblock used for printing tarot cards and playing cards.

Games for Friends and Family

The world of card games is endlessly fascinating. There are games available to suit practically any taste or age. Some are intuitive; others are intellectually challenging. What the majority of them have in common is that they are action-packed and speedy. Unlike board games, card games do not keep their players hanging on in suspense waiting for their turn to come around.

Patience and Solitaire Games

Card games for a single player are generically termed Patience in Europe and Solitaire in America. Playing them successfully demands clear thinking and concentration during play. David Parlett, the British card authority, described such games as 'the mental equivalent of jogging'.

Typically, the aim in solitaire games is to play out all the cards in the pack by arranging them in a specific order – usually in suit sequences, starting with the Ace and leading up to the King – with the aid of a preset layout. This acts as a workspace for the cards so that they can be sorted. When this is accomplished, the game is said to have 'come out'.

Trick-taking Games

For many people the attraction of cards lies in playing against other players. Outplay games, as they are termed by experts, make up by far the largest category of card games. Each player is dealt a hand of cards and each in turn plays one or more cards to the table. The game ends when one or all players run out of cards to play.

Above: A 17th-century French painting (artist unknown) depicting the making of playing cards, reproduced by means of hand-coloured woodcuts.

Above: A child turns up a card in the hope of finding a match in the Memory game, a quintessential family game that tests card-recall skills.

Most outplay games are trick-taking games, in which each player in turn plays a card face up to the table. This round of cards is called 'making a trick', and playing the first card is termed 'leading'. The card that wins the trick is either the highest of the suit originally led, or, if 'trumps' (cards of a suit nominated to be of higher value) are played, the highest card of that trump suit. Winning a trick often wins that round of cards and allows that player to choose which suit to lead next.

The way in which the trump suit is selected varies. In some games, the choice of trumps is random. They are selected by cutting the deck and exposing a card, usually at the end of the deal. In other games, the winner of the auction – in which the players bid against each other to make a certain number of tricks or points – decides what the trump suit is to be. Winning the right to choose trumps is therefore a powerful incentive in encouraging players to bid.

There are two ways of scoring such games. In what are termed point-trick games, the value of the tricks is affected by which cards they contain. The players are rewarded or penalized for capturing certain cards, each one of which has a pre-assigned value. This type of game includes Manille. In plain-trick games such as Ombre, on the other hand, it is only the number of tricks taken that matters. Play ends when some or all of the players run out of cards, at which point scores are totalled. The winner places the trick face down on the table and leads to the next trick. In games such as Piquet, the aim is both to win tricks and to score for card combinations.

Non-trick Games

Many card games are based on principles other than the taking of tricks. Some are children's classics, passed down through generations, and many are for adults, but they are all worth investigating. For example, Cribbage, an adding-up game in which the aim is to score or avoid scoring certain totals, is generally thought to date from the early 17th century.

In catch and collect games, the objective is to capture all the cards. Games such as Snap and Happy Families are simple children's games, while others such as Gops are far more complex. Fishing games such as Casino are particularly appealing. They are matching games in which each player competes to match the cards in hand with the ones laid out face up on the table. If the cards match, they are placed face down in front of the player who captured them. If there is no match, the card that was played is added to the layout on the table.

In shedding games, such as Michigan, the object is to get rid of all the cards as quickly as possible or to avoid being the last player holding cards. In collecting games, the object is to collect sets of matched cards (melds). The most popular of such games is undoubtedly Rummy – specifically, Gin Rummy, whose enormous popularity stems from the fact that, while it is simple to pick up, play can become very skilled and challenging. Rummy-type games are also known as draw and discard games, because each player has a hand of cards which he tries to improve through drawing and discarding. The player can either draw a card from the face-down stock of cards or from the face-up discard pile, and ends his turn by placing a card on the discard pile.

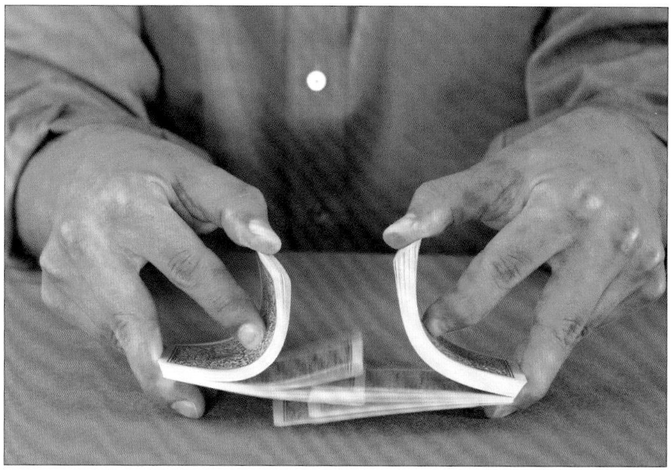

Above: Card play has a long-established set of procedures amounting almost to ritual. The shuffle is among them – it cannot be taught in words, only copied from watching good practitioners.

In banking games, such as Blackjack and Baccarat, an element of gambling is introduced. One player, the banker, takes on each of the other players individually to see who has the best hand.

Playing the Game

Card-playing involves many rituals and conventions, but they are worth following because they are mostly designed to stop anyone having an unfair advantage. You should establish whether you're playing for money or not, what the penalties are for cheating, and at what point the game will cease (after a target score is reached or after a number of deals, for example). When choosing a game to play, look for one that suits the number of players and their card-playing abilites. It is customary to shuffle and cut the cards before each deal.

Far left: A 19th-century playing card trimmer (*c.*1870). Early playing cards were printed on uncoated stock and were occasionally trimmed to eliminate the frayed edges.

Left: *The Illustrated Book of Patience Games* by Angelo Lewis (a.k.a. Professor Hoffman), published in 1917 and reprinted several times.

1 | Patience and Solitaire Games

Patience games, known as Solitaire games in the USA, fall into two main categories. Some are devised for a single player, the aim generally being to sort cards into suit sequences on a layout or tableau. In competitive patience, several players compete to be the first to complete a game. Specific rules govern how the cards can be arranged and rearranged. These solitary games are especially suitable for play against a computer.

Since the first Patience games were devised in the mid-19th century, they have mushroomed. When Britain's Lady Cadogan produced her *Illustrated Games of Patience* in 1874, she was able to list only 24 of them. In contrast, what is generally regarded as today's standard reference, David Parlett's *Penguin Book of Patience,* covers over 250 forms (500, with variations). Even that is not the end of the story. The *Solitaire Central Rulebook* on the Internet currently offers 1,713 different games, and although the list includes some duplication, its compilers conservatively estimate there to be around 1,500 different types of patience.

The aim of the game is to change the position of the cards by 'building' – that is, transferring cards around the tableau. Some can be played immediately, others not until certain blocking cards have been removed. In most games, play starts by placing the cards known as 'foundations', generally the four Aces, into position. After this, the aim is to build on each foundation in sequence and in suit from the Ace through to the King. The gap that is created by moving cards is called a 'space' and knowing how to take advantage of this is a major factor in manipulating the tableau to best advantage. If a player is successful in building the entire pack on to the foundations, the patience 'comes out' and the game is won. If it becomes impossible to sort the cards further, the game is lost and must be abandoned.

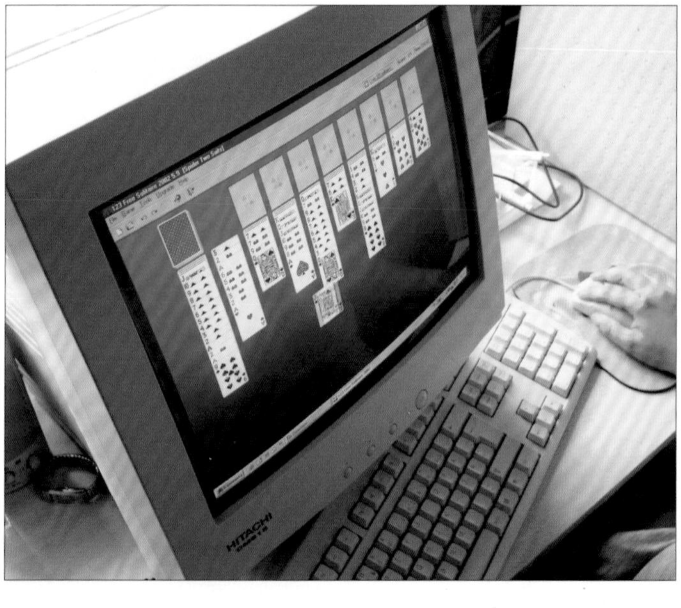

Above: Solitaire is particularly suitable for play against a computer. Many software Solitaire programs can be downloaded from the Internet at no charge.

Klondike

This is probably the best-known game of its ilk in the world, so much so, that many people simply call it Patience or Solitaire without realizing that it has its own name.

You will need: 52-card deck; no Jokers
Card ranking: None
Players: One
Ideal for: 4+

Object

To build all four 'suit stacks' from Ace to King.

The Deal

Deal seven cards in a row, left to right, upturning the first card. Beginning one place along each time, deal another row, again exposing the first card, until you end up with a 'tableau' (see below) of seven columns, the first comprising a single card, the second two, the third three and so on up to seven. Each column should end with an upturned card. The remaining cards are left face down to form the 'stock pile'.

Play

Three cards are turned face up from the stock, but only the top one can be played. If this can be used, the second of the three cards becomes available for play, and so again with the final one. Any exposed Aces from the tableau or at the top of the three cards are removed and placed above the tableau to form the foundation of a suit stack.

Cards that are within the tableau may be built down numerically, although they must alternate in colour – a black Five may be played on a red Six, for instance – while a sequence of cards can be moved in its entirety from one pile to another. Each time a face-up card (or sequence) is moved, the next face-down card is turned over and becomes available for play, with the proviso that in the event an empty space is created on the tableau, only a King can fill it. Exposed cards can be laid in sequence on top of a stacked Ace provided that they are of the same suit.

When all options have been exhausted, any card or cards remaining from the three taken from the stock are placed face up on a 'waste pile' and another three cards turned up, this process being repeated until the stock is exhausted. At any point, the lowest exposed card in a column can be played onto the foundations, or another pile. If the stock becomes exhausted, the waste pile can replace it, but this can happen only twice.

Conclusion

The game ends when either all the suits are stacked – the chances of this happening are 1 in 30 – or when no more moves are possible.

Below: In the layout shown, the A♠ should be moved above the tableau to begin a suit stack, with the 2♠ placed on top of it. The card that was under the 2♠ is then turned face upwards. The 9♠ is placed on the 10♦. The card under the 9♠ is then turned face upwards.

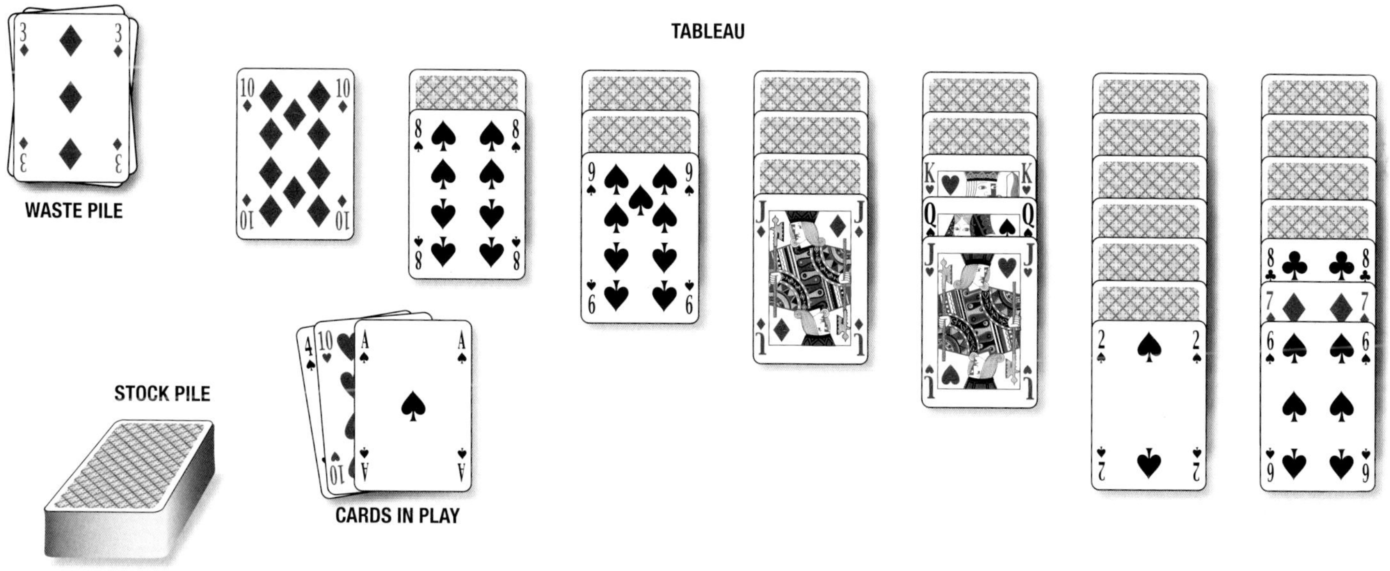

Accordion

It requires persistence to play Accordion successfully, as it takes quite a few deals for the game to come out.

You will need: 52 cards; no Jokers
Card ranking: None
Players: One
Ideal for: 7+

Below: The cards have been dealt in a line from left to right. The repositioned cards, after the moves (King on King, Heart on Heart etc.) have been taken, are shown underneath.

Object

To finish with all the cards in one pile.

The Deal

Unlike other games of this genre, there is no tableau – the player simply deals cards singly face up to form a long line from left to right. There is no maximum or minimum number, but experts favour dealing no more than 13 cards at a time.

Play

Whenever a card matches the suit or rank of the card immediately to the left of it, it is put on top of the card it matches. This is termed 'packing', after which all the cards to the right are squeezed up to close the gap. Cards can also be moved three places to the left. Packing continues until there is nothing left to pack, at which point more cards are dealt on to the end of the line. Multiple cards must be moved as a complete pile, since matching is limited to the top card. A pile may never be split or separated.

Conclusion

The game is won if all the cards can be reduced to a single stack. If not, shuffle the cards and try again.

Aces Up

Somewhat unfairly also known as Idiot's Delight, this is a fast-moving game that requires more skill to play than may be apparent at first glance.

You will need: 52 cards; no Jokers
Card ranking: None
Players: One
Ideal for: 10+

Below: On the left are the four cards dealt at the start of the game. On the right are the two cards left after the lowest two Diamonds have been discarded.

Object

To end up with all four Aces face up in a row and all the other cards discarded in the waste pile.

The Deal, Play and Conclusion

Four cards are dealt face up in a row. Any card of lower rank and the same suit of another top card can be removed from play. Aces are the highest rank. When all possible cards have been removed, four more cards are then dealt, on top of the remaining ones or on any spaces created. The process continues until all the top cards are of different suits. Four more cards are then dealt on top of these.

If one of the four piles becomes empty, the player can move any top card from any of the other piles into the empty space to create more possible plays. The objective is to remove all cards except for the Aces. The exposed cards precipitate the removal of others as play progresses. The only way to get at cards beneath an Ace is to move the Ace to an empty pile.

Aces Up is easy to play, but it is not easy to win. It all comes down to deciding which card to play into an empty space. To win, you need to end up with just the four Aces face up. If there are any other cards left on the table once the last set of four has been dealt, the game is lost.

Labyrinth

This is an unusual game in that players are allowed to take the top card of each column as well as the bottom for building on the Ace piles. There may be many gaps in the tableau, giving it the appearance of a labyrinth, as spaces are not filled, except in the first row.

You will need: 52 cards; no Jokers
Card ranking: None, but they are stacked in ascending order
Players: One
Ideal for: 10+

Object

The aim of this game is to build each Ace up into a pile of 13 cards that are arranged in ascending rank order and all in the same suit.

The Deal

The four Aces are laid out face up in a row at the top of the table. The rest of the pack is then shuffled and a row of eight cards is dealt face up just below the Aces. Further rows are dealt out during the course of the game.

Play

All the cards in the first row are available to start building on the Aces, with new cards being dealt to replace them as needed. When as many cards as possible have been played and any spaces filled, another row of eight cards is dealt. Play proceeds as before, but with one important exception: it is against the rules of the game to fill any more spaces. Instead, once play can go no further, a new row of eight cards must be dealt across the columns underneath the previous row before any further building can take place. All deals must be made in the same direction, usually from left to right.

The last row may consist of fewer than eight cards if cards were used to fill the first row. Strictly speaking this row should be dealt, as far as it can go, in the same direction, but many players prefer to choose which columns to deal the cards to in order to increase the chances of getting the game to come out.

Only the cards in the bottom and top rows are strictly playable. If one can be played from the top row of cards, the card in the bottom row can be played and so on.

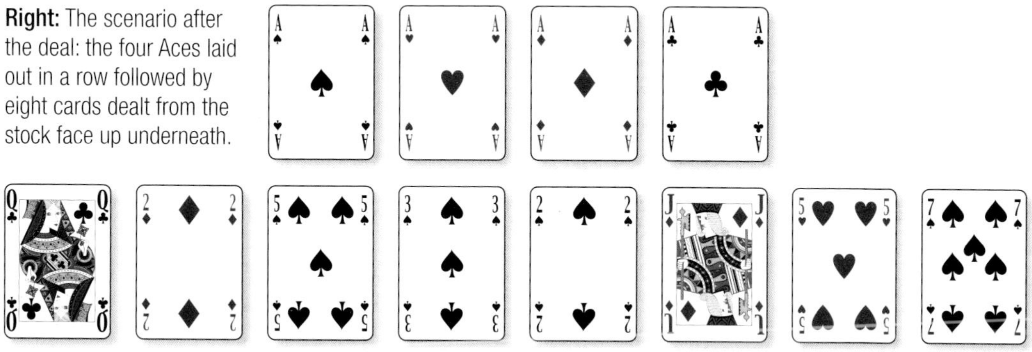

Right: The scenario after the deal: the four Aces laid out in a row followed by eight cards dealt from the stock face up underneath.

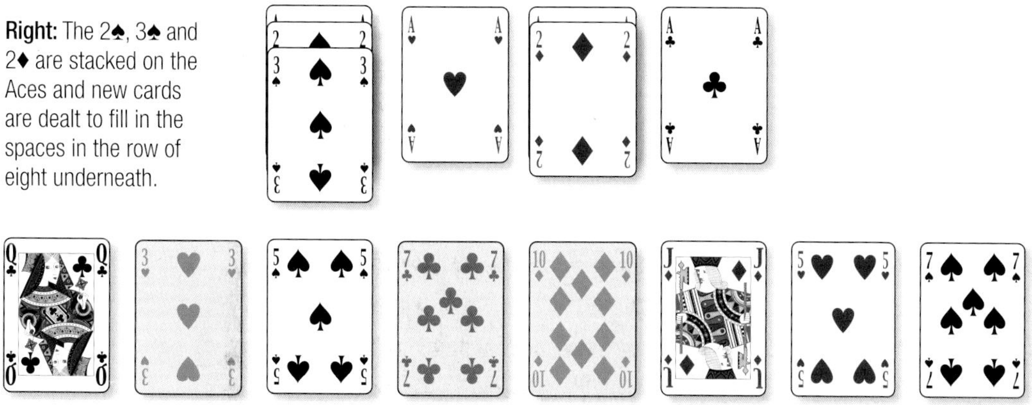

Right: The 2♠, 3♠ and 2♦ are stacked on the Aces and new cards are dealt to fill in the spaces in the row of eight underneath.

Conclusion

The game ends when the stock has been exhausted and every possible move made. If each stack is complete up to Kings, the player has won. If not, better luck next time.

Spite and Malice

This is a competitive Patience game, sometimes known as Cat and Mouse. It is a variation of the late 19th-century Continental game known as Crapette, Cripette, Robuse and Rabouge.

You will need: Two 52-card decks – one without Jokers and another with four Jokers added as wild cards

Card ranking: None, but cards must be stacked in succession; e.g. Two on Ace, Three on Two

Players: Two

Ideal for: 10+

Object

To be the first to get rid of what is termed a 'riddance pile' of 26 cards by playing them to eight piles that are gradually built up in the centre of the table, starting with an Ace and ending with a King. Suits are irrelevant.

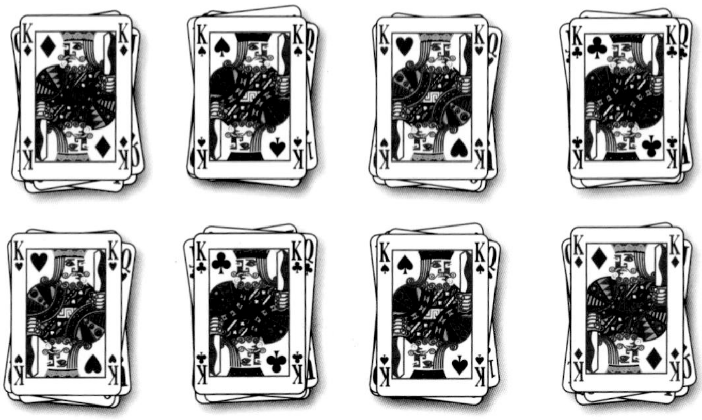

Above: Success – the eight piles from Ace to King are complete. In the game, each stack is turned face down after it is finished.

The Deal

After it has been shuffled thoroughly, each player receives 26 cards from the 52-card pack without Jokers. These are placed face down to form a riddance pile, and the top card (the 'up-card') of each is turned face up. Both players are then dealt five cards from the second 56-card pack (with Jokers), the remainder forming the stock to be used during the course of play and placed face down between the two players. Jokers can represent any card.

Play

A turn consists of a choice of moves. If the up-card is an Ace, the card must be played to start a centre pile. If it is any Two and an Ace has been played, it must be played to that Ace. Playing to a centre pile entitles you to another turn. So does playing off all five cards in one's hand, after which you draw five more from the stock pile. Cards in a riddance pile can be played only to one of the centre piles. Once a pile is completed (i.e. up to King), it is turned face down and set aside.

The alternative to playing to the centre is to play any card from your hand to a discard pile, except an Ace, replacing it with a card from the stock pile. Up to four such piles may be started by the same player, otherwise players may add to the top of an existing discard pile, if the rank of the discard matches or is one below that of the current top card. The top discard can be played off at any time to a centre pile. If a player cannot make a move, the opposing player plays alone until such time as the frozen player can play again. If both players freeze, all the cards in play except for those in the riddance piles are shuffled and redealt.

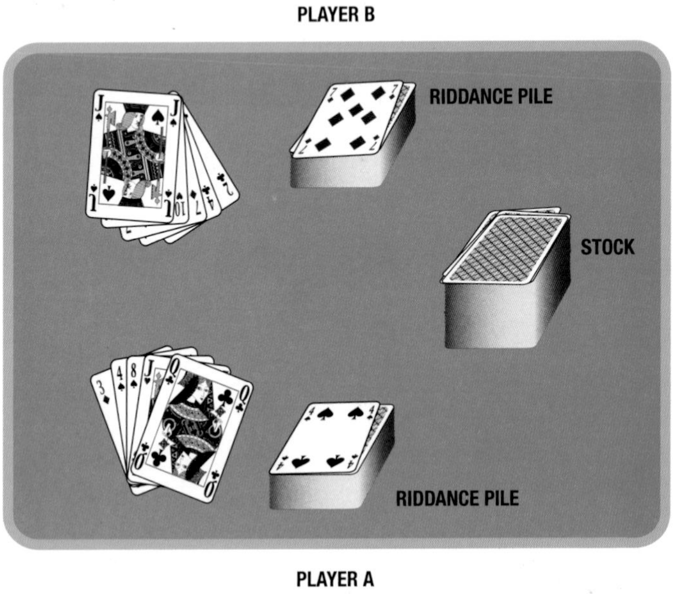

Above: The scenario at the beginning of Spite and Malice. Both players have 26 cards in their riddance piles, the top card turned up, plus five cards in their hands. The remaining stock pile is placed between the two players.

Scoring and Conclusion

The winner scores five points, plus a point for every card the loser has not played from his riddance pile.

When the stock is down to 12 cards, all the completed centre piles are combined with it to form a new one. Play continues until one player succeeds in playing off the last card from his riddance pile.

SPIT

Also known as Speed, there are no turns in this game – opponents play simultaneously. This puts a premium on physical speed and mental agility, both of which are essential if one player is to succeed in playing faster than the other.

You will need: 52 cards, divided equally between the two players
Card ranking: None, but cards can only be played to piles in a certain order (see below)
Players: Two
Ideal for: 10+

OBJECT

The object of the game is to get rid of all your cards faster than your opponent.

THE DEAL

Deal 26 cards to two players from a well-shuffled 52-card pack. Each player deals a layout of five stock piles arranged in a row. The first contains a single card, the second two cards and so on up to five.

All the cards are dealt face down, and the top card of each pile is then turned face up. The 11 remaining cards are the 'spit' cards. These must not be examined before they are played.

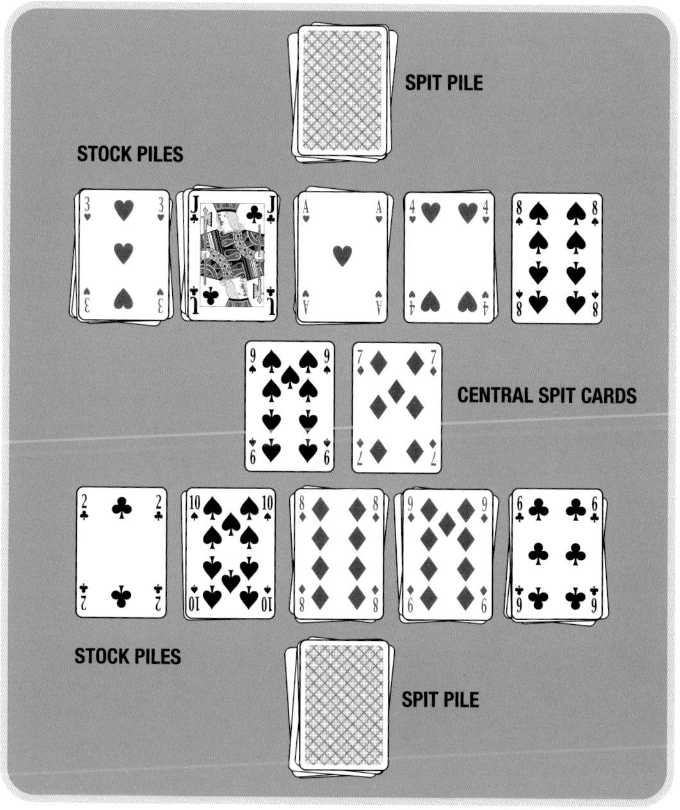

Above: Player A can play the 8♦, 9♦ and 10♠ on to the 7♦, but he needs to be quick, as Player B might try to play the 8♠ on to the 7♦.

PLAY

Both players call 'Spit' while turning over the first spit card in their hands. The two cards are placed side-by-side between the players' respective stock piles to form two spit piles. Players now play simultaneously as fast as they can. They can play the turn-up from any of the stock piles on to either spit pile, provided that the card being played is one rank higher or lower than the turn-up. Suits are irrelevant. Alternatively, if one or more of the stock piles have their top cards face down, these can be turned up, while a turn-up can be moved into an empty stock pile space.

A card counts as played as soon as it touches a pile or space. The opposing player can play on it immediately. If neither player can play, both spit again, turn up the next spit card and place it on top of the particular spit pile they started. Play then continues as before. If neither can play and one player has run out of spit cards, the other spits alone on to either pile.

If one player gets rid of all the stock cards or both of them run out of spit cards, a new layout is dealt. Both players choose a spit pile, ideally the smaller one, by slapping it with their hands. If both choose the same one, the player hitting it first has preference.

Both players then add any remaining spit or stock cards to their respective piles, shuffle their cards and deal new layouts. When the players are ready, they call 'Spit' and play again. If one of the players has fewer than 15 cards, he should deal them into five piles as far as he can and turn each top card over. As this player is unable to spit, there will be only one spit pile, started by the other player.

CONCLUSION

When one spit pile remains and a player runs out of stock cards, the other plays on until he gets stuck. He collects all the cards from the table, deals and spits again. The first to run out of stock and spit cards wins.

Nerts

Also known as Pounce, Racing Demon, Peanuts and Squeal, this is a competitive Patience game that can be played by more than two players if you have enough packs of cards.

You will need: Two (or more) different 52-card packs; no Jokers
Card ranking: None, but piles must be built in order
Players: Two (or more)
Ideal for: 7+

Object

To be the first player to play all the cards in his 'nerts' pile on to four foundation piles.

The Deal

Each player plays with his own pack. Both players deal a nerts pile, 12 cards face down and the last face up, with four more placed face up to form a row of work piles. The remaining cards are kept face down as a stock.

Play

Players use the work piles to sort their cards. They are built in descending order and alternating in colour so, for example, a red Six would be placed on a black Seven. The lowest-ranked cards are available to be played on to the foundations. Players may transfer any card from one work pile to another, together with all the cards on top of it. Foundation piles, each of which must be started with an Ace, are built upwards in suit and sequence. Any player can play to any pile when they hold the next card in the sequence. If two players choose the same pile, the fastest one wins and the other player has to take his back. Foundation cards are communal, with all players having access. Cards from nerts piles can be played to empty spaces in work piles, on to existing work piles, or on to foundation piles. As soon as the top card of a nerts pile is played, the next is turned face up. When a player's pile is exhausted, he can call 'Nerts', stopping play. Players, if stuck, are allowed to turn over stock pile cards three at a time and place them in a waste pile, from which the top card can be played. If every player gets stuck, each waste pile is turned to form a new stock, the top card of the stock being transferred to the bottom.

Scoring and Conclusion

One point is scored for each card played to a foundation pile. Two points are deducted for each card left in a player's nerts pile. Deals are played up to an agreed target.

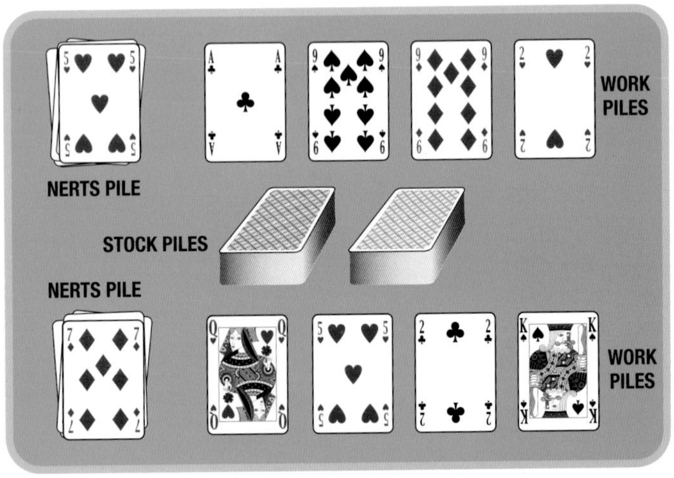

Above: Each player has a nerts pile. The top card is face up and there are four face-up cards that form the work piles.

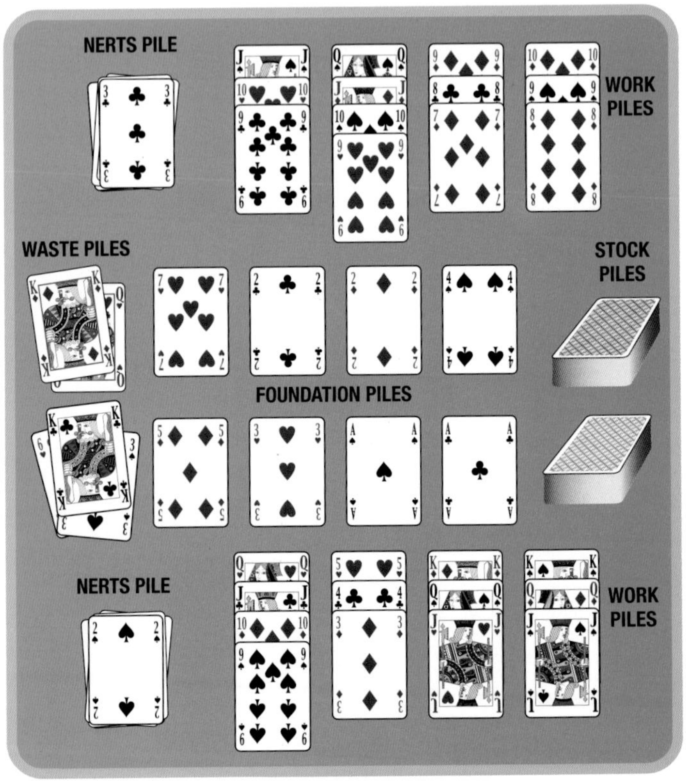

Right: Player A can play the 2♠ from his nerts pile on to the Ace in his foundation pile and the 3♦ from his work pile on to his opponent's foundation pile. Player B can also play the 3♣ from his nerts pile on to his foundation pile.

Poker Patience

Also known as Poker Solitaire and Poker Squares, this game is unusual because only 25 cards are actively employed. Unlike most solitaire games, where the aim is to put cards into a preset order, the aim here is to put the cards into certain combinations that correspond to standard Poker hands.

You will need: 52 cards; no Jokers
Card ranking: See 'Scoring and Ranking', below
Players: One (or can be played competitively)
Ideal for: 14+

Object

To move cards one at a time out of the stock pile and position them anywhere on a 'grid' of five cards by five cards, so that each of the latter's rows and columns forms the best possible Poker hand ranking. The better the hands that can be created, the higher the score. To win the game, a player needs to score at least 200 points in the American system or 70 points in the English one. The game can be played competitively, in which case the highest score wins.

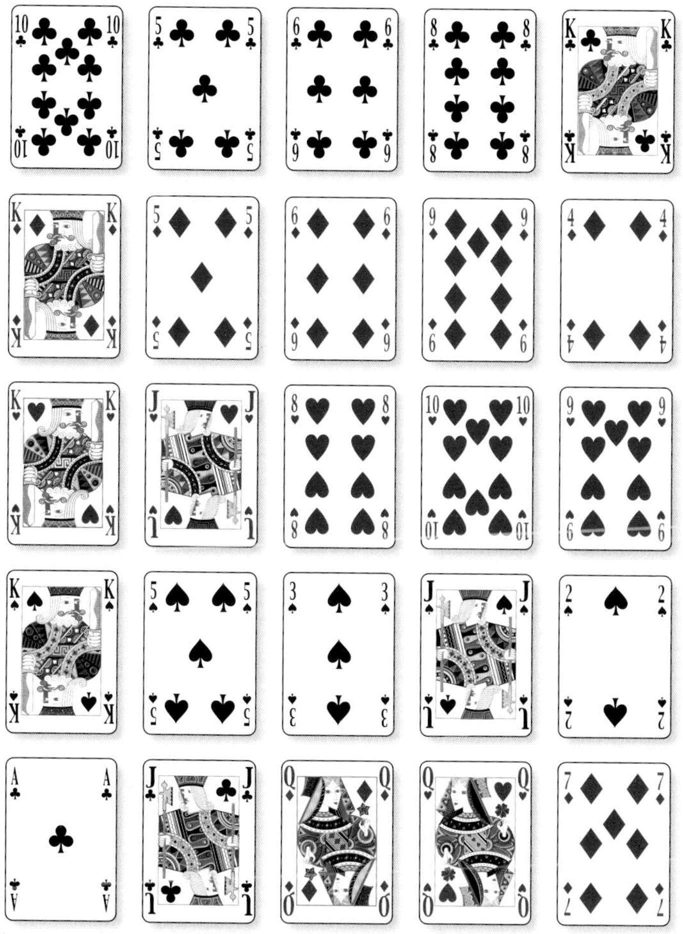

Above: The first four rows here all show a Flush while the final row has a Pair (of Queens). The first column has Three of a Kind (Kings), the second a Full House, the third a Pair (two Sixes), and the fourth a Straight.

The Deal

The player shuffles the pack and deals the first 25 cards face up into a pile to become the stock for the first grid. The remaining cards are kept in reserve for a second one.

Play

A typical strategy is to try to establish Flushes on the first four rows and Full Houses, Fours of a Kind, or Straights on the columns. The last row is often used as a dumping ground for cards that do not fit elsewhere in the layout.

Straights are high scoring but are the hardest to create. The alternative is to settle for lower-scoring, but safer, hands, such as Pairs and Three of a Kind. Even the best plans can be spoilt by bad luck. Once a card has been placed, it cannot be moved, nor may the next card in the stock be examined until the turn-up is placed.

Scoring and Ranking

There are two scoring systems – American and English (given in brackets). Cards are also ranked as follows:

- 100 (30) points for a Royal Flush: A Straight Flush (see below) up to Ace.
- 75 (30) for a Straight Flush: Five cards in sequence and of the same suit.
- 50 (18) for Four of a Kind: Four cards of the same face value.
- 25 (10) for a Full House: Three of a Kind and a Pair.
- 20 (five) for a Flush: Five cards of the same suit.
- 15 (12) for a Straight: A sequence of five cards in any suit.
- 10 (6) for Three of a Kind: Three cards of the same face value.
- 5 (3) for Two Pairs of the same face value.
- 2 (1) for One Pair of the same face value.

Conclusion

The game is finished when all the cards have been laid out on to the grid.

2 | Point-trick Games

Winning and losing point-trick games depends on the point values of individual cards taken within tricks and not on the actual number of tricks won or lost. A trick is a round of cards, where one card is played by each player in the game. A trick is won with the highest card of the suit led or by highest trump. Many games include bidding, in which some bids have aims such as losing all the tricks.

The games range from France's Manille, which originated as Malilla in Spain, to Stovkahra, the only surviving descendant of a strange Italian game called Trappola, first played in Venice in 1524. Stovkahra is a rare Romanian game, in which the aim is to be the first partnership to win 100 points. On its home turf, it is played with a 32-card German-suited pack (the German suits of Acorns, Leaves, Hearts and Bells correspond to Clubs, Spades, Hearts and Diamonds, repectively). Players score by declaring card combinations, such as Three or Four of a Kind, other than Eights and Nines, taking card points in tricks and winning any trick with a Seven. Winning the first and the last trick with a Seven is worth bonus points – 52 points and 26 points, respectively.

Point-trick games have not just been confined to the West, and many games not mentioned in this book are popular in the East. In Japan, Etoni, or 'capturing pictures', originated in the early 1900s, while Napoleon (not the British game of the same name) is one of the country's most popular games. Mighty, played mostly in Korea, is a related game in which Aces, Kings, Queens, Jacks and frequently Tens are worth a point each. The A♠, which is known in Japanese as *ohrumaita* or simply *maita* ('almighty' or 'mighty'), enjoys a special status. It can beat any other card, including trumps.

Above: Japanese women playing cards (*c.*1867). The concept of card games was introduced in Japan as early as the 16th century by Portugese traders.

Manille

There are a number of versions of this partnership game, of which the most popular are Manille Muette, which is played in silence; Manille Parlée, in which partners are permitted to share a single piece of information about their cards, or suggest what card or suit to lead; and Manille à l'Envers (Reverse Manille). Manille was France's national card game from around 1870 until the end of the Second World War, when Belote finally eclipsed it in popularity.

You will need: 52 cards; no Jokers

Card ranking: The Ten ranks highest, followed by Ace, King, Queen, Jack and Nine to Two

Players: Four

Ideal for: 10+

Object

The aim is to be the first to win two successive deals, or to secure an agreed number of points.

The Deal

Each player is dealt eight cards, four at a time, with the dealer turning his last card up to establish the trump suit – that is, the suit of cards that outranks all others – laying it on the table until the first card is led.

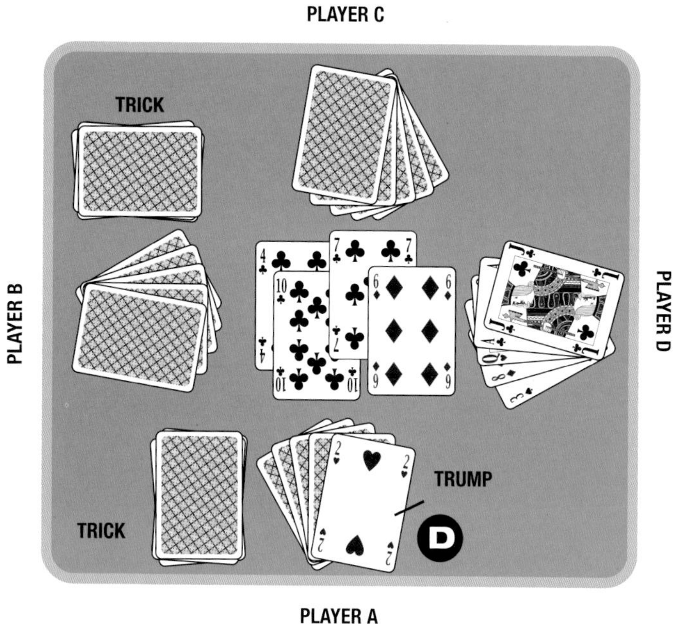

Above: Player D discards, as his partner is winning the trick with the 10♣. He could have followed suit with the A♣ or J♣, or played a trump with the Q♥, but since his partner is winning, he can hold on to his better cards.

Play

The player to the dealer's left leads to the first trick. Players have to follow suit if they can; if not, they can play a trump. The highest card of the suit led takes the trick, or the highest trump, if trumps are played. If a player's partner is winning a trick, that player is not obliged to follow suit or trump. If an opponent is winning, however, suit must be followed or a trump played. The highest card of the suit led or the highest trump takes the trick and the winner leads to the next.

Scoring

Each trick taken is worth a point. Five extra points are scored for a trick containing a Ten (*Manille*), four for an Ace (*Manillon*), three for a King, two for a Queen and one for a Jack. If a trick contains more than one of these, points are scored for each.

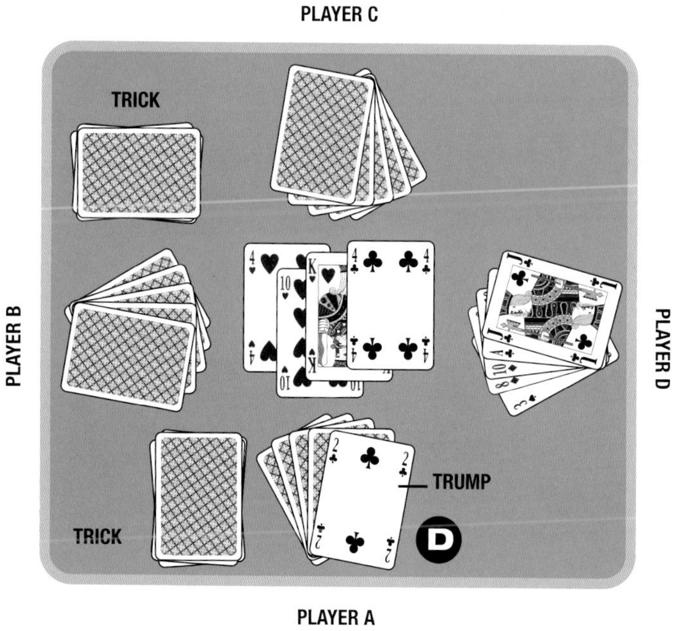

Above: Unable to follow suit in this trick, Player D has played the trump (4♣), thus winning it. Player D's partnership scores an extra three points for the King and an extra five for the Ten.

Conclusion

To win a hand, a partnership needs to score a minimum of 35 points. Convention has it that the target score for game is either 100 or 200 points.

Spanish Solo

Widely popular in Spanish-speaking South America as well as in Spain, this game is a cross between Tresillo, the modern form of Ombre, and Manille. Unlike the latter, it includes bidding. Each player puts one of their chips, coins or counters into the pool before starting.

You will need: 36-card pack, Tens, Nines, Eights and Twos having been removed; gambling chips/counters

Card ranking: Seven is highest, then Ace, King, Queen, etc.

Players: Three

Ideal for: 14+

Object

The aim of the game is to fulfil a specified contract and/or score the most points in a hand.

The Deal

Each player is dealt 12 cards, four at a time.

Bidding

There are three bids, which rank in the following order:

- *Juego* (Solo) – a bid to win at least 37 points (36 points if the bidder is the player to the dealer's left). It is worth two game points or four in Diamonds.
- *Bola* (Slam) – a bid to win every trick, having named wanted card and exchanged an unwanted one for it. Its value is eight game points, 12 in Diamonds.
- *Bola sin Pedir* (No-call Slam) – the highest bid, contracting to take every trick without exchanging a card. Its value is 16 points, or 20 in Diamonds.

The Auction

Starting with the player to the dealer's left, each player in turn must either bid or pass. If the former, the bid must be higher than the one preceding it. If a player passes, he puts another chip into the pool and sits out the rest of the auction. The successful bidder becomes the soloist and announces trumps. If these are Diamonds, the value of the bid increases, as shown above. If everyone passes, it is down to the dealer to choose trumps. The hand is still played.

Play

The player to the dealer's right leads. The other players must follow suit if possible. Otherwise, they may play a trump or, failing that, any card. The highest card of the suit led wins the trick, or the highest trump if any are played. The most valuable cards in each suit are the Seven (*Malilla*), followed by the Ace, King, Queen and Jack. The soloist now tries to fulfil the bid and other players try to score as many points as they can.

Scoring

- Five points for a trick containing a Seven.
- Four points for a trick containing an Ace.
- Three points for a trick containing a King.
- Two points for a trick containing a Queen.
- One point for a trick containing a Jack.

The winner of each trick scores an extra point.

Conclusion

The player scoring the most card points wins the hand. He then receives two chips from the player with the fewest number of points and one chip from the player with the second lowest score. If a soloist's contract is successful, he receives the appropriate number of chips from each opponent, two chips for a successful *Juego*, for instance, and wins the pool. If not, he pays the value of the failed bid to the opposing players and doubles what is in the pool.

Left: With a long strong suit in Diamonds, the natural bid for this player is *Juego* (Solo), naming Diamonds as trumps.

...rward to
...cerning

...d the game

...t trick, and
...f that first
..., playing his
...est card. The next person to win the lead does the same. If he holds no cards of that suit, he must revert to the suit played to take the previous trick or, if still void, the one before that. The next to play also does the same.

You will need: 32-card pack, those below Seven having been removed; no Jokers; gambling chips/counters

Card ranking: Standard

Players: Four

Ideal for: 10+

A King and Queen of the same suit in a hand is known as a *Zwang* (force). A player holding one declares it upon leading the Queen. This forces the holder of the Ace to play it, leaving the King high. Otherwise, the Ace's holder is free to underplay in the hope of winning the King later.

Scoring and Conclusion

Aces score five, Kings four, Queens three, Jacks two and Tens one. Each player calculates the value of the cards taken in tricks and pays a chip to the pot for every point he is short of 15, or wins a chip for every point that exceeds 15. Players settle up chips at the end of the game.

Forty for Kings

You will need: 32-card pack, the lowest card is Seven

Card ranking: King, Queen, Jack, Ace, Ten, Nine, Eight, Seven

Players: Four, in partnerships of two

Ideal for: 10+

This 18th-century partnership game was played in France and Germany, where it was known as Quarante de Roi and Vierzig von König respectively.

Object

The aim is to score points for *Cliques* (three or four court cards of the same rank) and for tricks (a round of cards) containing court cards (Kings, Queens, Jacks).

The Deal

Players are dealt eight cards in packets of three, two and three face down.

Play

The dealer shows his last card to set trumps. Each player then announces and scores for any *Cliques* held. The player to the left of the dealer leads. Players must follow suit or otherwise play any card. The highest card of the led suit or the highest trump takes the trick. The winner leads to the next. Each partnership scores for all the court cards it captures, adding this to its score for *Cliques*.

Scoring and Conclusion

Four Kings score 40 and three score 10, while Queens score 20 and eight, and Jacks score 13 and six. The court cards are worth five, four and three points each when they are captured in tricks. At the end of a trick, the partnerships score all the court cards they have taken and add the total to their scores for *Cliques*. Game is 150 points.

A running total of points is kept, and the first partnership with 150 points (or an agreed amount) wins.

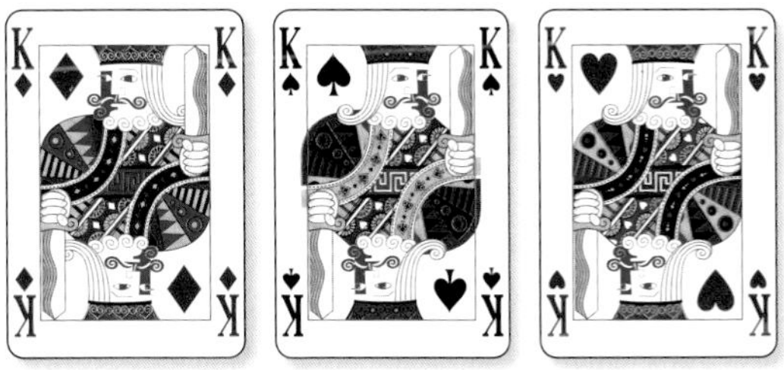

Left: A *Clique* of three Kings is 10 points in Forty for Kings.

Tressette

One of Italy's most popular card games, Tressette, unlike most positive point-trick games, is played without trumps. It is characterized by a distinctive signalling system between partners.

You will need: 40-card pack, the Eights, Nines and Tens having been removed

Card ranking: Three, Two, Ace, King, Queen, Jack, Seven, Six, Five, Four

Players: The standard version is a game for four, playing in partnerships of two, but it can be played by up to eight players

Ideal for: 14+

Object

To score as many points in each hand as possible, until you have reached the winning total, usually 21.

The Deal

Each player is dealt 10 cards face down, five at a time.

Signalling

When leading to a trick, three verbal or physical signals are allowed. A call of '*Busso*' is a signal to the caller's partner to play the highest card of the suit that has been led, the sign being to tap the card or the table with a fist. Saying '*Volo*' means that the caller has no more cards of the suit led, the sign being to glide the card slowly across the table. '*Striscio*' means that the lead is the caller's strongest suit, in which case the sign is to flick the card quickly on to the table.

Play

The player to the left of the dealer leads. Players must follow suit or otherwise play any card. There are no trumps. The highest-ranking card of the suit led wins the trick, the winner leading to the next trick. The cards rank and count in descending order from Three, Two, Ace, King, Queen and Jack to Seven, Six, Five and Four.

Scoring

Only Aces and court cards have individual point values, but certain card combinations also score. Each Ace is worth a point and each Three, Two or court card scores one-third of a point. The winner of the last trick gets a further point. Any fractions in the end totals are ignored. Scores are rounded down to the nearest whole number.

Certain card combinations must be declared and scored at the end of the first trick. A player holding four Aces, Threes or Twos (Four of a Kind) scores four points, and holding three (Three of a Kind) scores three. A *Napoletana*, when a player holds a Three, Two and Ace of the same suit, is three points. When declaring a *Napoletana*, its suit must be specified. So, too, must the missing suit be specified when declaring Three of a Kind otherwise it is invalid. There are several ways to win more points. When a partnership takes all 10 tricks, the points are doubled. This is termed *Cappotto*. When a partership wins all the points, but not all the tricks, the points are trebled (known as *Stramazzo*). *Cappottone*, which occurs when a single player takes all the tricks, wins sixfold. *Strammazzone*, which occurs when one player wins all the points and the opposing partnership wins at least one trick, wins eightfold. *Collatondrione*, which occurs when a single player declares all 10 cards of a suit, wins 16-fold.

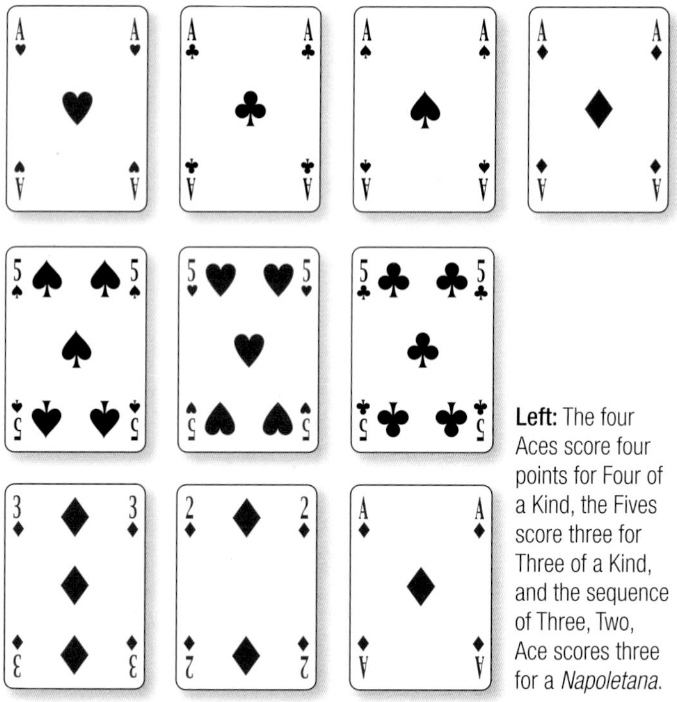

Left: The four Aces score four points for Four of a Kind, the Fives score three for Three of a Kind, and the sequence of Three, Two, Ace scores three for a *Napoletana*.

Conclusion

Once all 10 tricks have been played, each partnership scores the value of the cards it has taken in tricks, plus, if applicable, the point for taking the final trick. The partnership that scores 21 points first wins.

Terziglio

Also known as Calabresella, this well-established Italian game is notable, like Tressette, for its unusual card rankings and lack of trumps. Unlike Tressette, there is a round of bidding, and card combinations are ignored and do not score.

You will need: 40-card deck (Eights, Nines and Tens removed from a standard pack)

Card ranking: A Three ranks as highest followed by Two, Ace, King, Queen, Jack and Seven to Four

Players: Optimally three players, although four can play if the dealer sits out the hand

Ideal for: 14+

Object

The overall aim is to be the first player to reach 21 points by capturing tricks containing valuable cards.

The Deal

Each player is dealt 12 cards four at a time. The remaining four cards, the *Monte*, are placed face down on the table.

Bidding and Exchanging

Starting with the player to the dealer's left, each player bids or passes, and a player who has passed may not come in again. Each successive bid should improve on the last. The bids from low to high are:

- *Chiamo* (Call) – if successful, the bidder is entitled to ask if any of the other players is holding a specific card. If one is, he hands it over, getting a card back from the bidder in exchange. If not, the bidder picks up the *Monte*, discarding four cards face down to form a new one. Whoever wins the last trick will win the *Monte* and benefit from any card-points it may contain.
- *Solo* – same as above, but the bidder does not ask the others for a card.
- *Solissimo* – the player plays with the cards as dealt, does not call a card, takes the *Monte* and discards as above.
- *Solissimo Dividete* – here, the player may choose to increase the stakes by calling '*Dividete*' (Half each), whereby the opposing players each take two cards from the *Monte* and discard two.
- *Solissimo Scegliete* – here, by calling '*Scegliete*' (You choose), the four cards of the *Monte* are turned face up and the opposing players agree on the split, 2–2, 3–1, or 4–0, each discarding as many as they take accordingly.

Play

The player to the dealer's right leads to the first trick, unless *Solissimo* was bid, in which case the bidder leads. Players must follow suit if possible, otherwise they may play any card. There are no trumps. The person to place the highest card of the suit led wins the trick. The winner of each trick leads to the next one. To win the hand, the bidder must score at least six points, in which case each opponent loses points, depending on what was bid.

Scoring

Each Ace scores a point and each Three, Two or court card one-third of a point. The winner of the final trick not only scores a point for being last but also wins a bonus point for the *Monte*. This counts as an extra trick. *Chiamo* is worth one point, *Solo* two, *Solissimo* four, *Solissimo Dividete* eight and *Solissimo Scegliete* 16. Should the bid fail, the bidder's opponents score the points. If the bidder wins or loses every trick, the amount won or paid to their opponents is doubled. If he wins or loses all the points, the amount won or paid out is trebled.

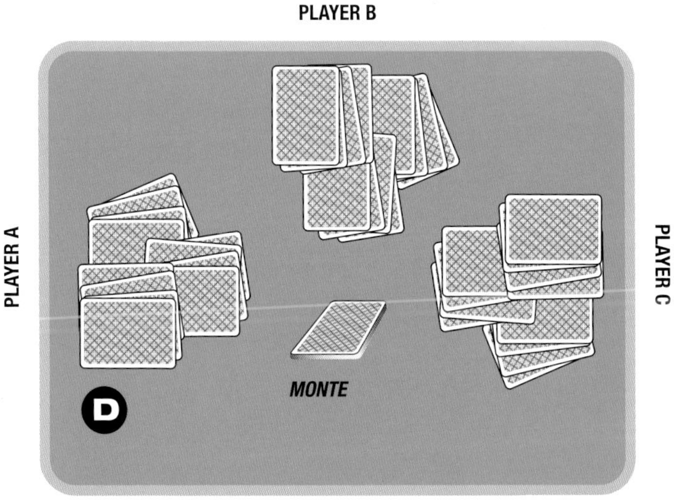

Above: Cards are dealt to each player in three packets of four, the remaining cards forming the *Monte*. Player B will be first to start the bidding, after which Player C leads to the first trick, unless Player B bids *Solissimo*.

Conclusion

The game ends when a player scores 21 points, but a target of 31 or 51 may be agreed.

Ciapanò

This intriguing game originated in Milan and is the reverse of Tressette. It is also known as Rovescino, Traversone, Tressette a non Prendere, Perdivinci and Vinciperdi.

You will need: 40-card pack, Eights, Nines and Tens having been removed

Card ranking: Threes rank highest, followed by the Twos, the Aces, the court cards, Sevens, Sixes, Fives and Fours

Players: Three, four or five

Ideal for: 14+

Object

To avoid taking any trick containing valuable cards, or winning the final trick, which carries an extra penalty.

The Deal

Each player is dealt the same number of cards – eight if there are five players, 10 for four, and 13 for three. In the last case, the dealer takes 14 cards and discards one, which is given to the winner of the last trick.

Play

The player to the dealer's right leads. Any card may be led, the other players following suit if they can. If not, they can play any card. There are no trumps. The highest card of the suit led takes the trick, the winner leading to the next.

Scoring

In this game, each Ace is worth a point and Threes, Twos and court cards score one-third of a point each. When all the tricks have been played, each player, with the exception of the player who took the final trick, adds up the value of the cards he has taken as penalty points. If there are any fractions left over once the points have been added up, these should be discounted. For instance, a player with three-and-a-third points would score only three points. A player with less than one point would score nothing.

The winner of the last trick scores the total of the other players' scores minus 11. The penalty for winning the last trick varies. It can count for one, two or three points depending on how the other tricks are distributed among the players. If one player wins all the points, this is termed *Cappotto*. He scores zero and the other players score 11 penalty points each. Once a player's cumulative score reaches 31 points or more, he drops out of the game, although by prior agreement this can be raised or lowered by 10 points.

Conclusion

When only two players are left in, the one with the lower score wins.

Left: 18th-century French playing cards. Originating in Milan and played widely in France, Ciapanò is typically played with Italian- or French-suited packs.

Below: The 3♠ and 3♥ are the highest cards in this hand, followed by A♠, K♦, Q♦, J♠, the 7♥ and 7♣, the 6♣ and the 2♥.

Da Bai Fen

Roughly translated, Da Bai Fen means 'competing for 100 points', which is the total number of card points in the pack. In China, where the game was invented, there are other versions.

You will need: 52-card pack with the addition of two Jokers as extra trumps

Card ranking: See 'Trumps and Ranks', below

Players: Four players, in partnership

Ideal for: 14+

Object

To win tricks containing counting cards (Kings, Tens and Fives, worth 10, 10 and five points respectively), and to take the last trick of a hand, until your partnership has won a hand of every trump rank, finishing with Aces.

Trumps and Ranks

There are 18 trumps: the two Jokers, the cards of the suit elected trump during the deal, plus the other three cards of a particular rank (which at the start of the game is the Two). From highest to lowest, trumps rank as follows: red Joker, black Joker, the card of the trump rank and trump suit (2♠ initially, if Spades are trump), the other three cards of the trump rank (2♥, 2♣, 2♦) and then the remaining cards of the trump suit from Ace down to Two.

At the start, Two is always the trump rank, so the player who first draws a Two in the deal and his partner become the declarers and play first. The player who drew the Two also has the right to declare its suit as trumps. The two players stay declarers until they lose a hand, when their opponents take over. Afterwards, the declarers' current score determines the trump rank. If, for example, they have 10 game points, the trump rank is Tens, 11 means that it is Jacks, 12 Queens, 13 Kings and 14 Aces.

The Deal

Players sit crosswise in agreed partnerships. One player at random is designated the 'starter', who shuffles the cards. They are then cut by either opponent before being placed face down on the table. The starter draws first, followed by the next player to the right and so on around the table. The draw continues until everyone has 12 cards in hand, with six remaining on the table.

Once a trump suit has been declared, the player who declared it picks up the six table cards and discards six cards face down. If no trumps are declared, the six table cards are turned up one at a time. The first card of the trump rank to appear determines the trump suit. If none of the trump rank appear, the trump suit is the highest of the exposed cards (other than Jokers).

Play

In the first hand, the player who declared trumps starts; subsequently, each trick's winner leads. The leader can lead one card or several cards of the same suit with the proviso that the latter must all outrank any cards of the same suit held by the other players. If this is not the case, a 'revoke', or penalty, is declared. This stops play and the offended opposing partnership scores as though it had won every trick.

The other players must play as many cards as were led. Suit must be followed if possible, otherwise trumps may be played. The highest card of the suit led or the highest trump wins. As play progresses, all players extract the Kings, Tens and Fives from the tricks they have won and place them face up on the table. Other cards are put face down into a waste pile.

Scoring and Conclusion

At the end of play, the six discards are turned up and its counting cards scored, along with the counting cards the players have won. The number of card points won by the opposing partnership determines the result. This decides who scores how many game points and who will be the declarers for the next hand.

If the opposers score between zero and five card points, the declarers score two game points. However, if the opposers score between five and 35 card points, the declarers score one game point. If the score is between 40 and 75 card points, no game points are scored. In all three instances, the declarers remain the declarers. If, however, the opposers score between 80 and 95 or more than 100 card points, they win one or two game points and become the declarers.

In each hand, a partnership's score is determined by the trump rank when they become declarers. If, for example, a side with a score of nine gains two game points in a hand, their score goes up to 'Jack'. The first partnership to reach Aces (i.e. 14 game points) and win a hand with Aces as the trump rank, wins the game.

3 | Catch and Collect Games

Catching games – card games in which the objective is to capture all the cards – are extremely old. Although many of them are classic children's games, this does not preclude them from being games of skill. As the name implies, collect games revolve around collecting cards. These can be pairs of cards of matching ranks or sets of cards that are matched in rank or by suit.

These types of games can be as simple as Snap (although success here still involves speeds of recognition and reaction), Happy Families (the American version of which is Go Fish) and Authors. The latter is an American game for children, but there is an adult version of the game, called Literature, which is a partnership card game for six or eight players. It revolves around the players questioning their opponents about the cards in their hands and acquiring cards accordingly.

Some more obscure games have their own endearing features. In Pig, players signal the end of a game by touching their noses – the last player to do so is the 'pig' – while in Spoons, they grab for a spoon. Other games, such as Gops or Schwimmen, are more complex. The former is an acronym for 'Game of Pure Strategy', reflecting the tactical skill needed to play the game well. In Schwimmen, the idea is for players to improve their hands in turn by swapping a card at a time for a face-up card on the table. It is particularly popular in Germany and in some parts of Austria.

Whisky Poker was invented in the USA, where it was given its name for fairly self-evident reasons. It was played widely in the late 19th and early 20th centuries, and it still has an American following today. Despite its name and the fact it uses ranking, it is played in an entirely different way to Poker: the chief difference is that no betting is involved.

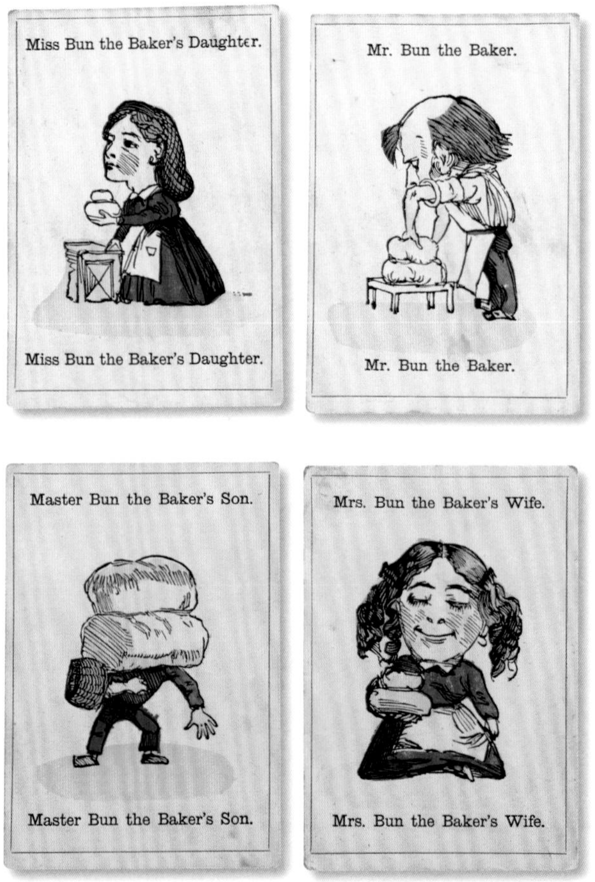

Above: 19th-century playing cards showing the Baker family from the game Happy Families. The aim is to collect families of four.

Card-Catching Games

The simplest and possibly best-known game of this type is Snap, followed by Beggar-My-Neighbour, also known as Beat Your Neighbour Out of Doors. Slapjack is a fun game, which revolves around physically slapping a Jack whenever it appears, while Memory is just what its name implies – a real test of card recall.

Snap

Players hold their cards face down. Each in turn plays their top card face up to the middle of the table as quickly as possible. When the card played matches the rank of the preceding card, the player who calls 'Snap' first wins the central pool of cards. As players run out of cards, they drop out of play.

If someone calls 'Snap' by mistake – or if two or more players call simultaneously – the pool is placed face up to one side and a new one started. When a card played to the new pool matches the top card of the old one, the player to call 'Snap pool' first wins both pools.

Above: Memory involves turning up two pairs from cards scattered face down on the table. Whether through good luck or memory, this player turns up a matching pair, and so keeps the cards.

Beggar-My-Neighbour

Players take it in turns to turn over their top cards and place them face up in the middle of the table. There are two types of card: Ace, King, Queen and Jack are paying cards and the others are ordinary ones.

When a player places a pay card, the opponent has to place four cards for an Ace, three for a King, two for a Queen and one for a Jack. If these cards are all ordinary, the player of the pay card scoops the pool. But if the opponent plays a pay card, the reverse applies. The player who runs out of cards first loses.

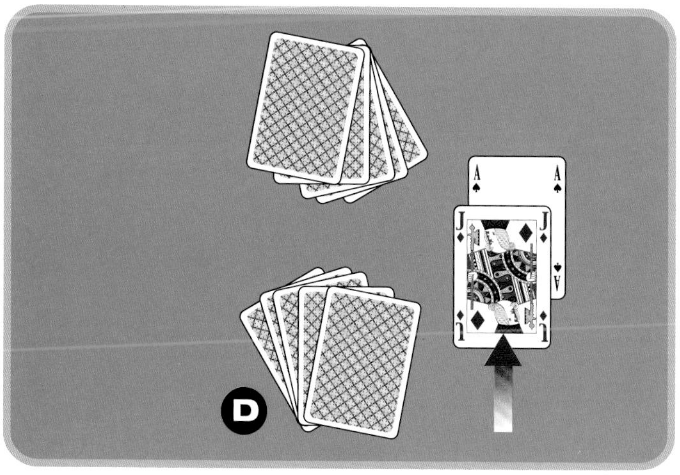

Left: In this example of Beggar-My-Neighbour, Player A has laid a Jack, and so does not have to place four cards. This means that Player B has to place one new pay card.

Slapjack

Players hold their cards as face-down piles, each in turn playing the top card face up to the centre of the table. When a Jack is played, the first player to slap it wins the central pile. The winner is the player ending up with all the cards.

In another version, the aim is to lose cards, not win them. Players try to predict what card they are playing by calling out a rank. If card and call match, all the players race to slap the pile. The last one to do so adds the pile to the cards he is holding.

Memory

The cards are dealt at random face down over the table, after which each player in turn picks up and announces two of them. If the cards form a pair, that player wins them and has another go; if not, they are replaced face down in the same position and it is the next player's turn. The player with the sharpest memory normally wins.

Gops

This strange game is a test of strategy – its name is an acronym of the term Game of Pure Strategy. It is very popular among game theorists as it is susceptible to logical mathematical analysis. It is also known as Goofspiel.

You will need: 52 cards for three players, but with one suit taken out when there are two players

Card ranking: Standard, Aces low

Players: Two to three

Ideal for: 14+

Object

To win the greatest value of Diamonds, or whichever is the chosen suit, until reaching the required point total.

The Deal

The pack is split into its suits, with one – usually Diamonds – being singled out as the so-called competition suit. The remaining suits are divided between the players. If only two are playing, one suit is discarded. The competition suit is shuffled and placed face down on the table, to form the competition stack.

Play and Scoring

Play begins with the top card of the competition suit being turned face up. Players then bid for the card in turn by choosing any card from their hands and placing it face down on the table. When all the cards have been placed, they are turned over. Whichever player has played the highest one wins the competition card. The bid cards, as they are termed, are put aside and the next turn is played.

In the event of a tie between the bidders in a two- or three-player game, the competition card is either discarded or rolled over to the next round, to be taken by the next competition card winner. If there are three players and two tie for best bid, the card goes to the third player.

Gops is difficult to master, since it presents its players with a series of dilemmas that have to be resolved. The skill comes from gauging correctly when to bid high for a card and when to bid low, forcing the opposing players to bid more than they need to take a certain card.

Aces count as one, numbered cards at their face values, Jack 11, Queen 12 and King 13.

Conclusion

The game is over once all 13 cards from the competition stack have been taken. In a two-player game, the player scoring 46 points or more wins; in the three-player version, the target score is 31 points.

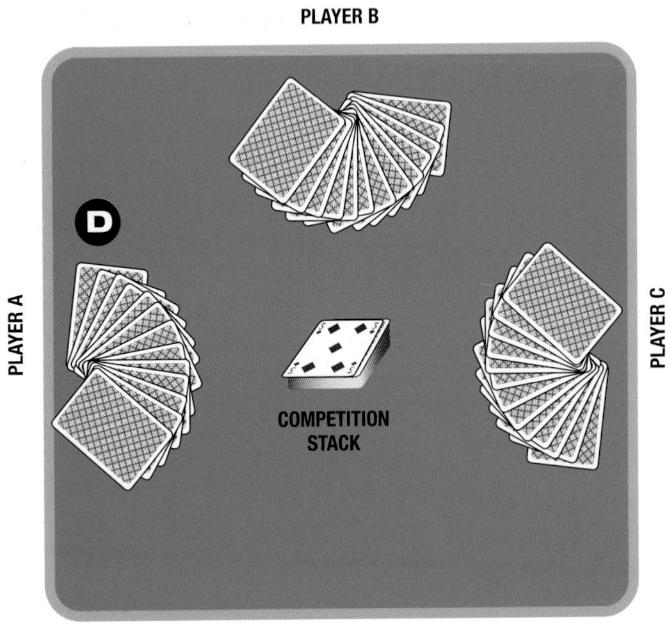

Above: After the deal, the top card of the competition stack is turned over. Players then bid on it by placing one card face down in front of them.

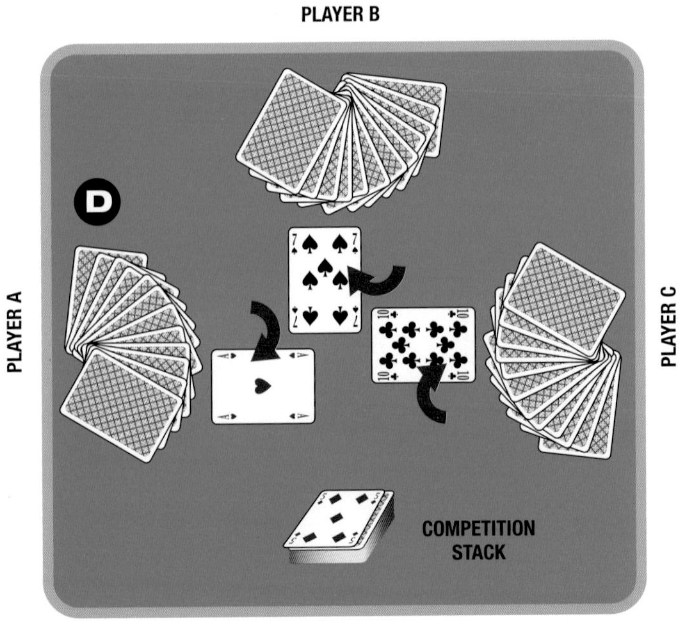

Above: After the deal, all players turn over their bid cards at the same time, and Player C's 10♣ wins over the 5♦.

Schwimmen

Known in English-speaking countries as Thirty-One, Schwimmen is also called Schnautz, Knack and Hosen'runter in Germany and western Austria. Players improve their hands by exchanging cards into a central pool of turned-up cards.

You will need: 32-card pack created by removing the cards from Two to Six; gambling chips/counters

Card ranking: See 'Scoring and Conclusion', below

Players: Two to eight

Ideal for: 10+

Object

To score nearest to 31 or 32 points by collecting cards of the same suit or holding three cards of the same rank.

The Deal

Each player receives an equal number of chips and then is dealt three cards face down, with an extra three being dealt on to the table. The dealer decides whether to play with his dealt hand or exchange it sight unseen with the spare one. The rejected cards are then turned face up.

Play

The player to the left of the dealer plays first, the turn to play passing clockwise around the table. Each player is entitled to exchange a card for one of the cards face up on the table, or pass.

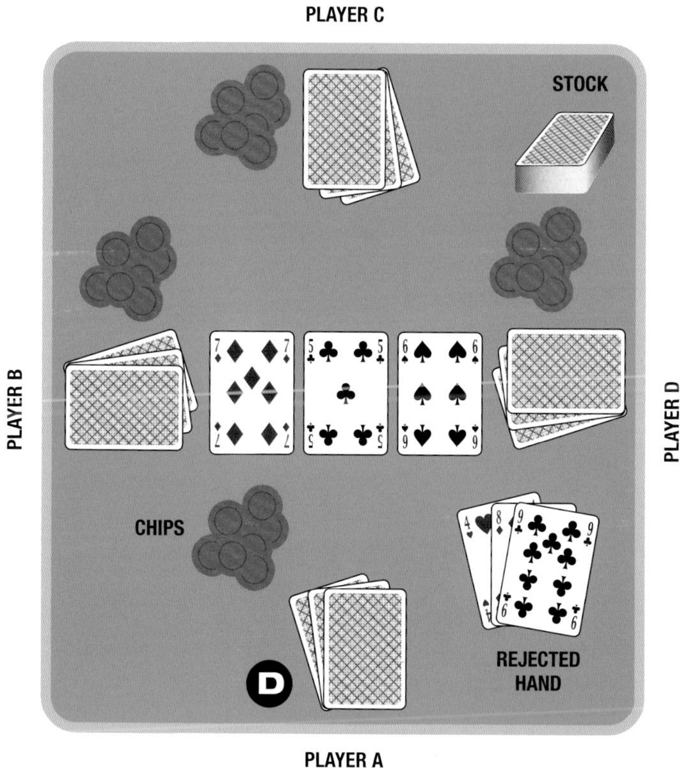

Above: After the cards are dealt, each player has the opportunity to exchange one of his cards with the cards face up on the table. Here, the four players have passed, so the face-up cards are replaced by three new ones.

Above: The game ends if a *Feuer* (three Aces) is declared by a player.

If all of the players pass in succession, the face-up cards are then replaced with new ones from the stock pile, and the game continues.

Any player can decide to 'close' at the end of his turn, after which the others have one more chance to play before the hand is over. The hand also ends if certain sets of cards are disclosed. There are two of these: *Feuer* (fire), comprising three Aces (32 points), and *Schnautz*, featuring three cards of the same suit, worth 31 points. Both of them must be declared as soon as they are made.

To score, all player's cards are exposed and the values of cards in any one suit calculated. If play ends because a player closes or declares *Schnautz*, the player with the worst hand loses a chip. If *Feuer* is declared, all the players except the declarer lose a chip. Once a player has lost all his chips, he is said to be 'swimming'. Although he can continue to play, he may do so only until he loses another hand, when he must drop out of the game.

Scoring and Conclusion

Aces are worth 11 points and the court cards 10 each, while the numbered cards count at face value. Only cards of the same suit are scored. Thus, a hand containing the K♣, 7♥ and 9♥ is worth 16 points for the two Hearts – the King does not score. Three cards of the same rank (Three of a Kind) other than Aces score 30.5 points. If scores are tied, a higher Three of a Kind beats a lower one, as does a higher suit, ranked Clubs, Spades, Hearts and Diamonds. The last player in the game is the winner.

Whisky Poker

In this one-time American favourite, players have the chance to improve their hands by exchanging cards with a spare hand, known as the widow, which is dealt to the table.

You will need: 52 cards, no wild cards; gambling chips/counters
Card ranking: Standard. Hands are also ranked (see below)
Players: Two to nine players
Ideal for: 14+

Object

To collect the best five-card poker hand, the player with the highest hand scooping the pool.

The Deal

Before choosing the dealer for each round, every player puts a chip into a communal pot. They draw to decide who deals first, the player with the lowest card having the honour. Five cards are dealt to each player, starting with the player to the dealer's left, with the widow being dealt immediately before the dealer's own hand. The widow is kept face down in the centre of the table. After the first hand, the deal passes to the left around the table.

Play

The player to the dealer's left starts by deciding whether to exchange his hand as dealt for the widow. If not, the next player is given the same opportunity and so on round the table. If no one exchanges, the widow is turned face up and play begins.

Each player in turn now has one of three options. He can exchange one card (discarding a card face up and taking a replacement from the widow), exchange all five cards, or knock, signalling the imminent ending of play. The other players have one more turn, after which there is a showdown with the best hand winning the pot.

Above: After the deal, no one has exchanged his hand for the widow, so it is turned face up for all players to see before play begins.

Scoring and Ranking

From lowest to highest, the ranking of hands are:

- High card – a hand with no combinations, but with the highest-ranking card among the hands in play.
- One Pair – two cards of the same value; e.g. 3♦, 3♥ or Q♠, Q♣. If another player holds a Pair of the same value, then whoever holds the highest card in the two hands (called the 'kicker'), wins.
- Two Pairs – two sets of Pairs; e.g. 3♦, 3♥ and Q♠, Q♣. Again, whoever holds the 'kicker' wins if two players hold matching Pairs of the same value.
- Three of a Kind – three cards of the same face value (this is also known as 'trips'); e.g. Q♠, Q♣, Q♥.
- Straight – a sequence of five cards in any suit; e.g. 5♦, 6♣, 7♠, 8♥, 9♣. The highest Straight is one topped by Ace, the lowest starts with Ace. Should two players hold a Straight the one with the highest cards wins.
- Flush – five cards of the same suit. If another player holds a Flush, whoever holds the highest card wins.
- Full House – Three of a Kind and a Pair. When two players hold a Full House, the one with the highest ranking trips wins.
- Four of a Kind – four cards of the same face value (known as 'quads').
- Straight Flush – a combined Straight and Flush, which contains cards in sequence and of same suit.
- Royal Flush – a Straight Flush up to Ace.

The player with the highest-ranking hand takes the pot of chips. Alternatively, each player can start with five chips and the player with the weakest hand forfeits one of these, the first to lose all five chips becomes the overall loser.

Conclusion

Depending on the scoring method agreed, a game ends when one player has won all or an agreed number of the chips, or has lost the five chips with which he started.

Other Collecting Games

Games such as Go Fish and Authors are closely related. Their simplicity makes them ideally suited to children. In each, the aim is to collect 'books' – that is, sets of four cards of the same rank – by players asking each other for cards they think might be held. Whoever collects the most books wins the game. The American game Authors gets its name from the fact that, in the 19th century, children played it with cards depicting famous authors. The idea has been extended to include inventors, US presidents, and even well-known baseball players. It is played like Go Fish, but without the stock pile.

Go Fish

You will need: 52 cards
Card ranking: None
Players: Three to six
Ideal for: 4+

Object

To get rid of all of one's cards, by collecting books of four cards of the same rank (i.e. four Tens, Aces or Jacks), or to score more books than any other player.

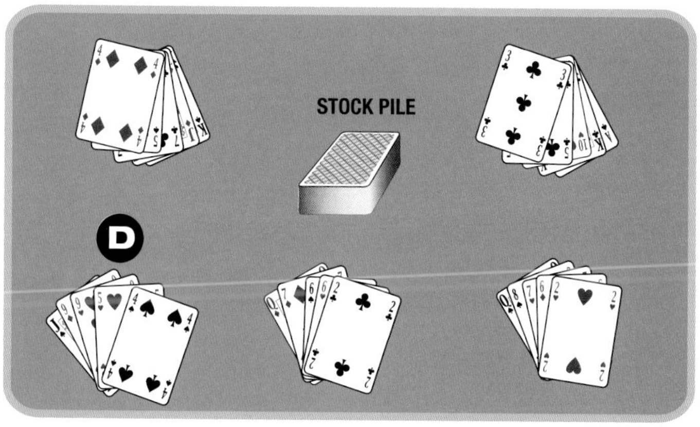

Above: After the deal, Player A asks Player D for a Seven, as he holds one in his own hand and wishes to collect a 'book'. Player D must surrender his 7♦.

The Deal

Although special packs of Go Fish cards are available, a standard card pack may be used as a substitute. Five cards are dealt face down to each player, the remainder being placed face down to form a stock.

Play

The player to the dealer's left starts the game by asking another player for a card of the same rank as one that appears in his hand. If the player asked does hold such a card (or cards), he must give it (or them) to the asking player, who then gets another turn. If the responding player does not hold any cards of the requested rank, he responds with 'Go Fish!'

The asking player than draws the top card of the stock. If this card matches his initial request, the asking player shows it and gets another turn. If not, the turn passes to the player who said 'Go Fish!', although the asking player must keep his new card. When a player has a book, this must be shown and put aside.

Conclusion

The game ends when a player has no cards left and therefore wins, or the stock runs out, in which case, the player who has collected the most books wins.

Authors

You will need: 52 cards
Card ranking: None
Players: Three to six
Ideal for: 4+

Object

To get rid of all one's cards or score more books than any other player.

The Deal

The entire pack is dealt singly as far as it will go. Some players will therefore have more cards than others.

Play and Conclusion

Each player in turn asks any other player for all the cards they have of a specific rank, or alternatively for a specific card, such as the 7♣. The player who asks must have at least one card of the solicited rank in his own hand. If the player who is asked holds the card, he surrenders it to the asking player, who then gets another turn. If not, he replies 'None' and takes over the turn. When a player gets all four of a given rank, he lays the cards down in a won trick to show the other players.

The game ends when all cards are formed into books. The player with the most books wins. Alternatively, players score a point per book and play to a target score.

4 | Fishing Games

Fishing games probably originated in China, spreading from there to Japan and Korea, where they remain popular. They are also widely played in Turkey, Greece and Italy, although, for some reason, they have generally failed to catch on in the rest of the world. The idea is to match the cards held in the players' hands with those turned face up in a layout on the table.

There is a straightforward difference between Eastern and Western games of this ilk. In the Eastern games (a classic example being Go Stop, a Korean game that is played with flower cards), there is generally a face-down stock, from which players draw. In Western games, cards are played only from players' hands, although a single card can be used to 'capture' several cards simultaneously if their ranks add up to the rank of the card that was played. If a player cannot match a card or cards, he has to add a card to the layout, or to those cards that are already on the table. This card is now ready for the next player to capture or 'catch' it.

Casino is probably the best known fishing game, and is played particularly in the USA and parts of Scandinavia as well as southern Africa, where specific variations have developed in South Africa, Swaziland and Lesotho. In all these variations however, captured cards remain in play and so can be recaptured and used in 'builds'. Builds are the most complex features of both Eastern and Western fishing games. They take advantage of the rule that a numbered card can capture its fellows on the table, if they are all of the same rank as the card being played. The intention to play such a card must be announced in advance, with its number specified; after this, the cards can be placed together to form the build. Only by playing a numbered card of the rank that was announced when the build was made can another player capture it.

Above: Flower cards are used in Japan and Korea for games of the fishing group. There are 48 cards in a pack, four for each month of the year.

Casino

Although Casino is generally thought to have originated in Italy, the first evidence of it being played comes from late 18th-century London and subsequently from Germany.

You will need: 52 cards, but only part of the pack is used in any one deal

Card ranking: None

Players: Best with two to four people, the latter playing in opposing partnerships

Ideal for: 10+

Object

To capture opponents' cards by playing a card matching a layout card's number (pairing) or by playing a card that matches the sum of several such cards (summing).

The Deal

Each player is dealt four cards, two at a time, with a further four being dealt face up. The dealer sets aside the remaining cards for use in subsequent deals, but no more cards are dealt to the table.

Play

Above: In Casino, the 10♦ is known as the Big Casino and the 2♠ as the Little Casino.

Each player in turn, starting with the one to the dealer's left, plays a card to the table, either capturing one or more table cards or building a combination for capture on a subsequent turn. There are three options during play: to capture, build or trail.

- Capturing – if a player plays a King, Queen or Jack that matches the rank of a card on the table, he can capture that card. If there is more than one matching card on the table – two Queens, say – only one may be captured. A numbered card can capture cards of the same rank and any sets of cards that add up to the rank of the card played. Capturing all the cards on the table is a sweep, which is worth a point to the player making it.
- Building – there are two kinds of build – single and multiple. If a player adds a Three to a Three on the table and announces, 'building Threes' for instance, this is a single build. A multiple build is when more than one card is added. If a player holds two Sixes and there are two Sixes on the table, he plays a Six to the table, puts all three Sixes together, announces 'building Sixes' and captures the combination with the fourth Six on the next turn. The danger of building combinations of cards to be captured subsequently is that an opponent may capture the combination first.
- Trailing – playing a card without building or capturing, when a player can't match any cards in the layout.

Scoring

Only captured cards score. The most valuable are Spades, Aces, the 10♦ (Big Casino) and the 2♠ (Little Casino). At the end of a hand, whoever has the most Spades wins a point. Aces are worth one point each, while Big Casino is worth two points and Little Casino one point. Capturing more than half the pack is worth three points.

The simplest way of scoring is to treat each deal as a separate game. Alternatively, the first player to score 11 points wins a single game, the total being doubled if it takes two deals and quadrupled if this score is accomplished in only one deal.

A third method is known as 21 Up, which is to agree that the first player to win 21 points wins the game, regardless of how many deals it takes.

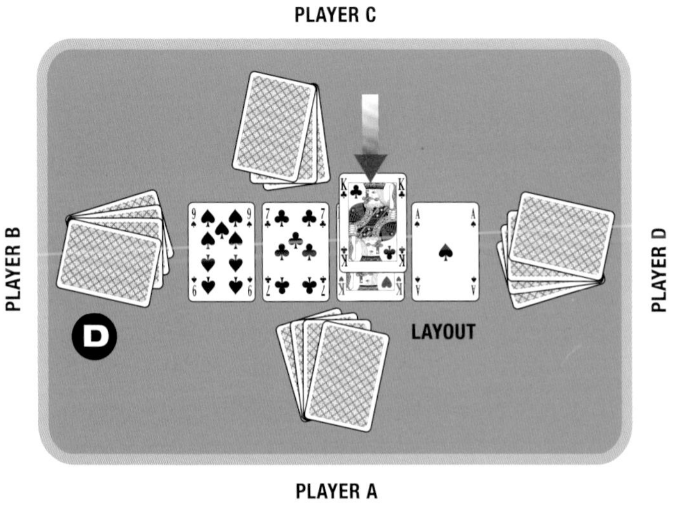

Above: Player C matches the King in the layout, and so captures it.

Conclusion

The game ends when all cards have been played with none remaining in stock, and scores are totalled.

ZWICKER

This popular fishing game from northern Germany originated in the area of Schleswig-Holstein, close to the Danish border. The *Zwick* is the name given to a sweep capturing all the cards on the table.

You will need: 52-card pack, to which it is customary to add three (or sometimes four) Jokers

Card ranking: None

Players: Two to four – ideally four playing in partnerships of two

Ideal for: 10+

OBJECT

To capture cards from the layout on the table by playing a card of matching value, and whenever possible score bonus points for *Zwicks* – sweeps that clear all the cards on the table.

MATCHING VALUES

Fixed matching values determine which cards can capture which. Cards from Two to Ten rank at face value, but Aces, Jacks, Queens and Kings have two possible matching values of one or 11, two or 12, three or 13 and four or 14, respectively. The player who captures such a card, plays it to capture other cards, or makes it part of a build, decides the value. If a Queen counts as 13, it can be used to capture a Six and a Seven or a Two, Three and Eight and so on. The three Jokers – Small, Middle and Large – are valued at 15, 20 and 25, respectively. Players agree in advance which Joker is which.

THE DEAL

To start the game, four cards are dealt singly to each player, plus two face up on the table.

PLAY

The player to the dealer's left starts by playing one card face up, next to the two face-up cards on the table. When everyone has played, the dealer deals another four cards to each player, none to the table, and so on until a final deal of five cards each exhausts the pack.

If a player plays a card that matches a card on the table, that card may be captured. Two or more such cards can be captured by 'summing', that is, taking cards that have matching values adding up to the matching value of the card being played. To form a build, a player announces its value and then places his card half over the layout card.

Any build counts as though it is a single card – hence, a Five and Seven makes a build of 12, which can be captured by a Jack. No build can be higher than 14. A build's player is obliged to capture the build eventually, unless another player captures or modifies it first.

SCORING

The values used in scoring differ from those used in matching. The small, medium and large Jokers gain five, six and seven points, respectively; the 10♦ is worth three; and the 10♠, 2♠ and each Ace are worth one. These are the only cards that score. A player capturing more than half the cards in the pack scores three points, and each *Zwick* is worth a point. The highest score wins.

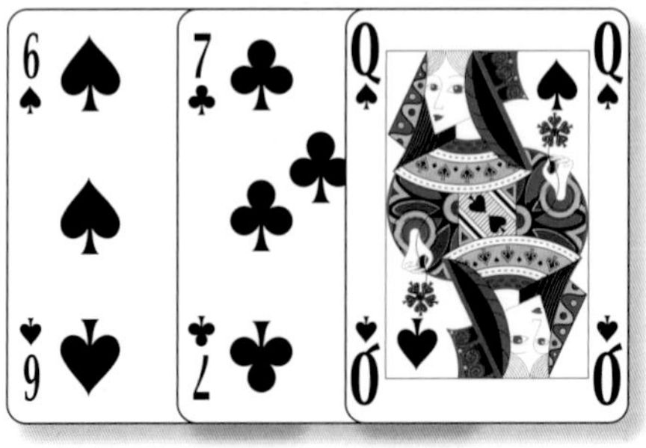

Left: Here, a player captures the 6♠ and 7♣, matching their combined total with the Q♠, which has a matching value of three or 13.

CONCLUSION

Once the final deal (of five cards) has been played, the hand is scored.

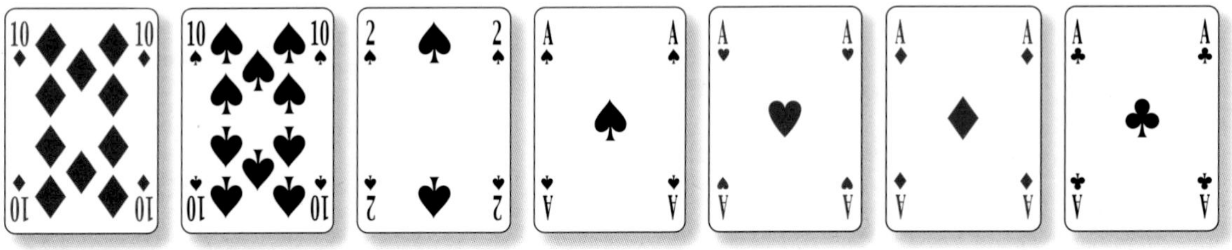

Left: The 10♦ is worth three points; the 10♠, 2♠ and each Ace are worth one point.

Cuarenta

In Spanish, *cuarenta* means 'forty'. And it is also the number of cards in the deck used in this game and the number of points needed to win it. What distinguishes Cuarenta from most other fishing games is that matching a card also allows cards in sequence with it to be captured.

You will need: 40 cards (Eights, Nines and Tens having been removed froma standard pack)

Card ranking: None

Players: Two or four in two partnerships. In the latter case, one partner keeps score while the other stores the won cards

Ideal for: 10+

Object

To capture cards by matching them. Alternatively, in the case of numbered cards, to capture them by addition, or by forming an unbroken ascending sequence.

The Deal

To choose the first dealer, the cards are shuffled and then dealt face up singly to each player. The first player to be dealt a Diamond becomes the dealer. Five cards are then dealt to each player, the remaining cards being stacked face down on the table.

Play

After a deal, a player can make an announcement. If a player is dealt four cards of the same rank (Four of a Kind), the cards are shown (announced) and that partnership wins the game immediately. If a player is dealt three cards of the same rank (Three of a Kind), he calls '*Ronda*' and the declaring partnership scores four points. Although the *Ronda's* rank need not be declared, if one of its cards can be captured by *Caida* – by matching it immediately after it has been played – the opposing partnership scores 10 points if they can remember the event and the rank of the cards at the end of the hand, which is when the bonus can be claimed.

At the start of play, or in the case of *Limpia*, a clean sweep of the table, there is obviously nothing to be captured. The card that was played, either at the start of play or to make *Limpia*, simply remains on the table, as do subsequent cards if no capture is made. *Limpia* is worth two points to the side that is making it.

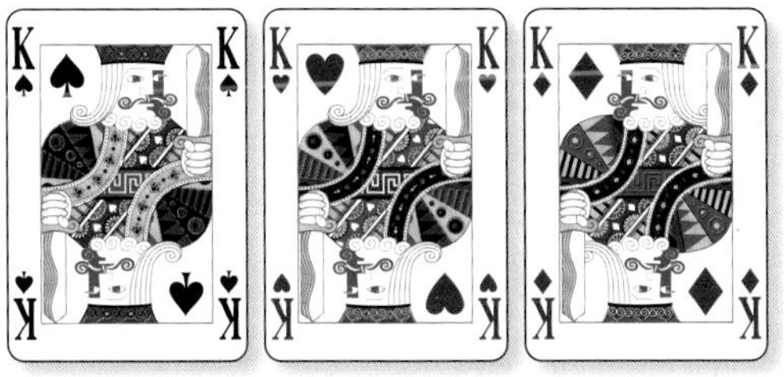

Left: Three of a Kind is called *Ronda* and scores four points for the declaring partnership.

Scoring

The practice is to use the Eights, Nines and Tens to mark scores – these cards otherwise have no function in the game. When face up, each card represents two points; a face-down card, a *Perro* (dog), represents 10 points. Scoring combinations and card plays are:

- *Ronda* (Three of a Kind) – four points to the declaring partnership.
- *Caida* (capturing a card from *Ronda* by matching it immediately after it has been played) – 10 points to the opposing partnership, claimed at the game's end.
- *Limpia* (a clean sweep of the table) – 2 points to the side making it.
- A team with 20 captured cards scores six points (if there is a tie, only the non-dealing partnership scores).
- If more than 20 cards have been captured, each extra card is worth another point, the total being rounded up to the nearest even number.
- If neither partnership captures 20 cards, the one with the greater number scores two points.
- A partnership with 30 or more points cannot score for *Rondas* or *Caidas*, while one that has 38 points cannot collect for *Limpia*. Game is 40 points.

Above: In Cuarenta, the partnership with Four of a Kind wins immediately.

Conclusion

At the end of a hand, each partnership counts its collected cards and scores are calculated.

Scopa

Originating in Italy around the 18th century, *scopa* means 'sweep' or 'broom'. It is still one of the country's major national card games.

You will need: Italian 40-card pack or standard pack with Eights, Nines and Tens removed

Card ranking: None

Players: Scopa started off as a game for two, but can be played by three or four

Ideal for: 10+

Object

To capture as many cards as possible, particularly Diamonds and high-numbered cards.

The Deal

Starting with the player to the dealer's right, each player is dealt three cards face down, after which the dealer deals four cards face up to the table. If the table cards include two or more Kings, it is usual to deal again.

Play

Each player in turn, starting with the player to the right of the dealer, attempts to capture one or more of the cards on the table. Only one capture may be made in a turn. If there is no capture, the card played becomes part of the layout and may be captured. There is no obligation to play a card that makes a capture. It is sometimes better to simply add a card to the table. If, however, the card that is played does make a capture, the captured cards must be taken. When everyone has played out their three cards, they are dealt three more, and so on, throughout the game, as long as any cards remain.

Capturing

The simplest form of capturing is 'pairing', where one card matches another – a Five and another Five, for example. The second form is 'summing', where the value of the card played is the same as the sum of two or more cards on the table. A Seven can capture a Five and a Two. If there is a card on the table which has a value that is the same as the card being played, only that card may be captured. Only one combination may be captured at a time.

A *Scopa* (sweep) is made when only one card is on the table and a player captures it by pairing, or when all the cards are captured by summing. Although a *Scopa* is worth only one point, its additional value is that it leaves the table empty of cards, so forcing the next player to trail (place a card down without matching it). This leaves the way open for another sweep. The 7♦ is the most important card to capture, as it is worth one point and features in the other three points that may be won.

Scoring

Players sort through their won cards and count their scores. A *Scopa* is worth one point. Single points are also awarded for capturing the most cards, for winning the most Diamonds, capturing the 7♦ – the *Sette Bello* (Best Seven) – and for building the best *Primiera*, in which each player extracts from his won cards the highest-valued card he has taken in each suit.

In order to establish which player's *Primiera* is best, the cards are given special values for this particular purpose. Sevens, the most valuable cards, are worth 21 points, Sixes 18, Aces 16, Fives 15, Fours 14, Threes 13 and Twos 12. The three court cards count for 10 points each. The winner of the point is usually the player with the most Sevens in his *Primiera*.

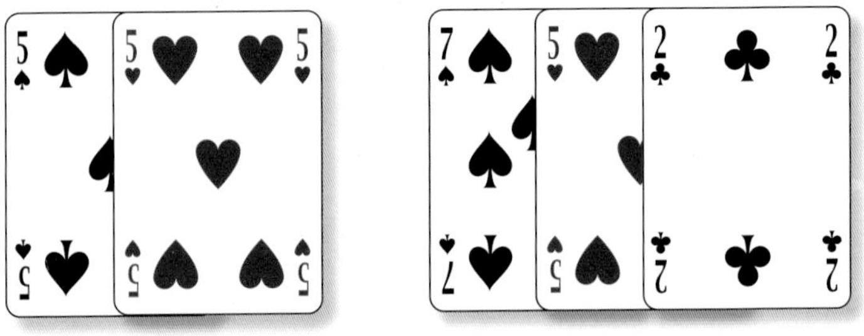

Above: Cards can be captured by pairing, or by summing, the Seven corresponding to the combined value of the Five and Two.

Conclusion

Play continues until no cards remain in hand and the stock is exhausted. Any cards left on the table go to whichever player made the last capture, although this does not count as a *Scopa*. The winner is the first player to score 11 points, or the highest score if more than one player has exceeded that figure. If the scores are tied, the points made on the last deal are counted in strict order, starting with cards and then continuing with points for Diamonds, *Sette Bello*, *Primiera* and *Scopa*.

Scopone

This partnership version of Scopa also emerged some time in the 18th century, and is recommended to players seeking something different to the standard trick-and-trump games.

You will need: Italian 40-card pack or standard pack with Eights, Nines and Tens removed
Card ranking: None
Players: Four, in partnerships of two
Ideal for: 10+

Object

To capture as many cards as possible, particularly Diamonds and high-numbered cards, within partnerships.

The Deal

Four players sit crosswise, in partnerships. Nine cards are dealt to each player in three batches of three, four cards for the table being dealt two and two after the first and second batches. In Scopone Scientifico (Scientific Scopone), each player is dealt 10 cards, in which case the game has to start with a discard.

Play

The rules governing playing, capturing and scoring are broadly the same as in Scopa (see opposite). Partners are not allowed to let each other know which cards they hold in hand, although they can try to signal their intentions by making specific discards in certain situations, such as deciding it is best to avoid capturing a card in favour of trailing one to the table. Captured cards and the cards that captured them are conventionally kept face down in a single pile in front of one of each partnership's players. The first to play – the player to the dealer's right – has to choose the value of the card he plays carefully so as to reduce the chances of it being captured.

Scoring

If a partnership captures more than 20 cards, it wins a point. If the scores are tied, the point is not given. A partnership with five or more Diamonds also gains a point, with an extra point being awarded for the capture of the 7♦. Each *Scopa*, or sweep of the table, is worth a point, while the partnership with the best *Primiera* (the highest-valued card taken in each suit from the won cards) also scores one for it. The first partnership to score 11 or more points wins the game.

In Scientific Scopone, the target is 21 points. Other differences are that a partnership with the A♦, 2♦ and 3♦ scores *Napoli*, a bonus equal to the value of the highest Diamond in the sequence. A partnership that captures all 10 Diamonds – termed *Cappotto* – wins the game outright.

Conclusion

The game is over when a partnership scores the specified number of points, according to the version being played.

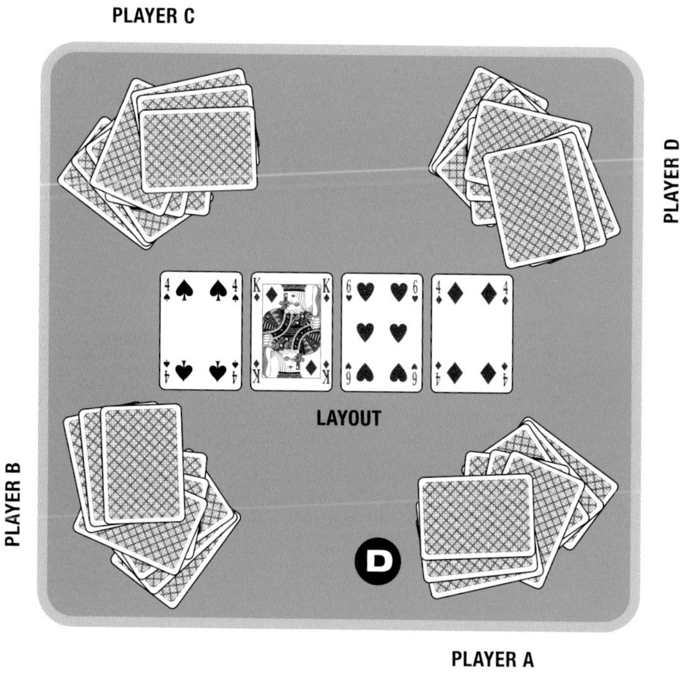

Left: In Scopone, three cards are dealt to each player, two to the table, or layout, then three more to each player, two more to the table and finally three more to each player. The player to the dealer's right is first to play.

Above: In Scientific Scopone, a partnership that succeeds in capturing all 10 diamonds scores *Cappotto* and wins the game outright.

Cicera

Scopa and Scopone have spawned varying rules and options over the years. Cicera, from the Italian province of Brescia, is the most notable variation to have developed.

You will need: Brescian 52-card pack
Card ranking: None
Players: Four, in partnerships of two
Ideal for: 10+

Object

To capture as many cards as possible, aiming to be the first partnership to score 51 points.

The Deal

Each player receives 12 cards, with four being dealt face up to the table.

Play

Each player in turn plays a card to the table and makes a capture or leaves it on the table. Capturing is by pairing or summing numbered cards (one to 10 at face value), or pairing court cards.

Making a capture is optional, while if the card played matches a single card and the sum value of several cards, its player can choose which to capture. Once all the cards have been played, the last to capture takes any remaining cards.

Scoring

Points can be scored by *Scúa* (a sweep that captures all the cards on the table in one turn), *Picada* (matching the card previously trailed or left on the table), by an opponent, *Simili* (capturing a card of the same suit) and *Quadriglia* (capturing a set of three or more cards). The side with the majority of cards scores two points, as does the one with the most Spades.

Napula, which is *Napoli* in Scientific Scopone, scores three points, while capturing the 2♣, the 10♦ and the J♥ is worth a point for each capture. Game is 51 points.

Conclusion

The game ends when a partnership scores 51 points.

Cirulla

The preferred version of Scopone in the Ligurian region around Genoa, Cirulla has several quirks.

You will need: Italian 40-card pack or standard pack with Eights, Nines and Tens removed
Card ranking: None
Players: Four, in partnerships of two
Ideal for: 10+

Object

To capture as many cards as possible, aiming to be the first partnership to reach the agreed target score.

The Deal

Each player is dealt three cards, and four are dealt face up to the table.

Play

Each player in turn plays a card to the table and makes a capture or leaves it to trail. As well as pairing and summing, cards can be captured by 'fifteening' (capturing with a card that makes 15 when added to the cards it captures).

Scoring

If the four cards dealt by the dealer total 15, the dealer scores for a sweep. If they total 30, the score is two sweeps. If the cards dealt to a player total less than 10, the player knocks by showing them. This counts as three sweeps or 10 points if they are three cards of the same rank. The 7♥ may be used as a wild card, which can replace any card.

Players score a point for each sweep, for most cards and most Diamonds. Capturing the 7♦ is worth a point, as is *Primiera* (won by the player with the highest-valued cards taken in each suit in his won cards). *Scala Grande*, the King♦, Queen♦ and J♦, scores five, and *Scala Piccola*, the A♦, 2♦ and 3♦, scores three. If the 4♦ is also held, the score is the value of the highest Diamond held in unbroken sequence. Target scores can be 26, 51 or 101.

Conclusion

Capturing all the Diamonds wins the game. The game ends when the agreed target score is reached.

Basra

This fishing game is widely played in coffee houses throughout the Middle East, sometimes under different names. There are Lebanese, Iraqi and Egyptian versions – the last is described here.

You will need: 52 cards
Card ranking: None
Players: Two; or four, in partnerships of two
Ideal for: 10+

Object

To capture as many table cards as possible, aiming to be the first partnership to reach the agreed target score.

The Deal

Each player is dealt four cards. Four more cards are dealt face up to the table. These are the 'floor' cards and must not include any Jacks or the 7♦. If they do, the offending cards are buried in the pack and replacements are dealt.

Play

The player to the dealer's right plays first. Each player in turn plays a card face up to the table, the aim being to capture some of the cards that have already been exposed. When the players have all played their first four cards, they are dealt another batch of four each (no more are dealt to the table) and so on until the entire pack has been dealt. The hand is then scored.

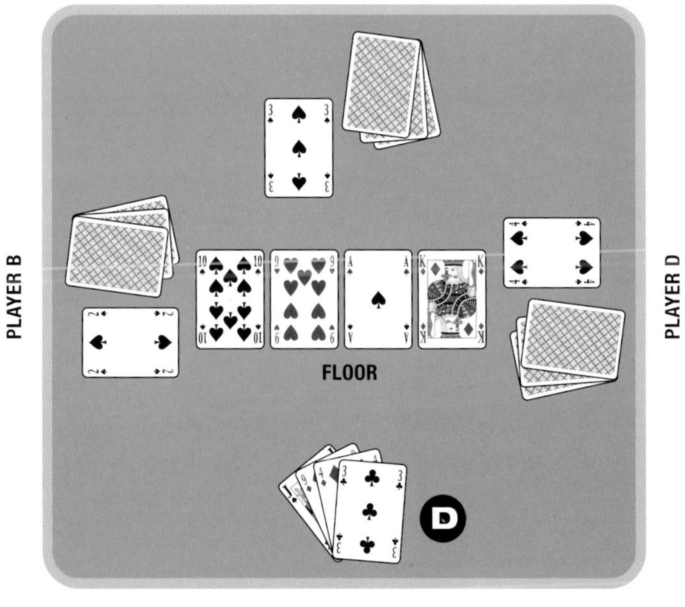

Above: Player A, the last to lay to this trick, could play the 4♦, matching Player D's 4♠, or the 3♣, matching Player C's 3♠. Playing his Jack, he would be able to sweep all the cards from the floor, but this would not count as a *Basra*.

Capturing

A player can capture by pairing (matching one card with another) or summing (capturing two or more number cards which have a combined value that is the same as that of the card being played).

As Kings and Queens have no numerical value, only pairing may capture them. If a card is able to capture, a capture must be made, but there is no obligation to play such a card.

Capturing all the cards from the floor at once is a *Basra* and scores a bonus 10 points. Playing a Jack also sweeps the table, but does not count as a *Basra* and therefore no bonus is awarded.

If a 7♦ is played, however, it does count as a *Basra*, provided that all the cards on the table are number cards with a combined value of 10 or less. If it is more than 10, or if there are court cards on the table, the Seven still captures all the cards, but there is no bonus.

Scoring and Conclusion

After the last card has been played, any remaining cards are taken by the last player to have made a capture. Each team counts its cards. A team with 27 or more scores 30 points. If there is a tie, the points are carried forward.

Each Jack and Ace is worth one point, the 2♣ scores two and the 10♦ scores three. Generally, whichever side scores 101 or more points first wins the game. If the score is tied, the convention is to play the final game up to a total of 150 points. The game ends when a partnership wins a rubber (five games), or at an agreed time or points total.

Right: Neither the 7♦ nor the J♣ may be among the face-up cards on the table at the start of the game, but they are both useful during play for capturing cards.

Chinese Ten

No coverage of fishing games would be complete without an Eastern example such as Chinese Ten. The way a card is flipped from the face-down deck after each play is typical.

You will need: 52 cards; no Jokers
Card ranking: None
Players: Two to four
Ideal for: 10+

Object

To achieve as high a score as possible, before all the cards on the stock pile are exhausted.

The Deal

Depending on the number of players involved, the number of cards dealt varies. If there are two players, they receive 12 cards each; three players receive eight cards each and four players receive six cards. The next four cards are dealt face up to the table and the rest are stacked face down to form the stock.

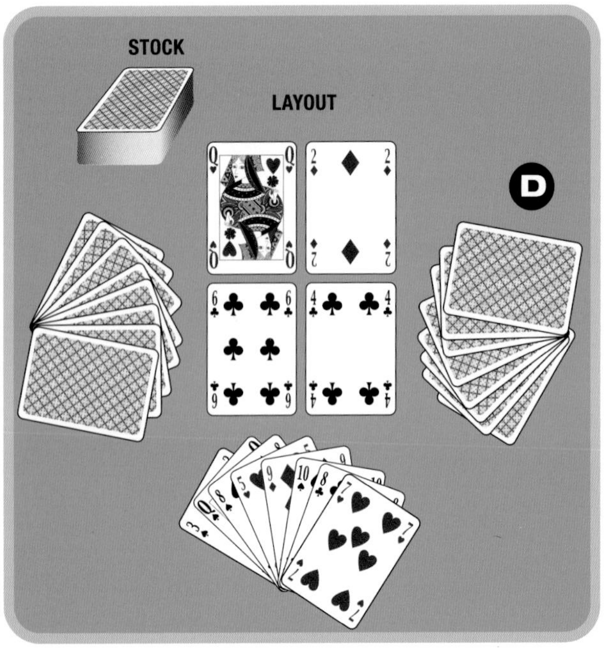

Above: In this three-player hand of Chinese Ten, Player A (Player C having dealt) can play either the 8♠ or 8♣ to make a value of 10 when added to the 2♦. Alternatively, the Q♠ could be paired with the Q♥.

Play

Each player in turn, starting with the player to the left of the dealer, plays a card to the table. To capture a number card, the card played must make up a value of 10 when added to it. For example, an Ace captures a Nine, or a Nine an Ace, and so on. Only pairing can capture Tens and court cards – Ten takes Ten, Jack takes Jack, and so on. At the end of a turn, having either captured a card or trailed, which is to simply place a card on the table, a player then turns the top card of the stock face up. If this captures a card, both cards are taken. If not, it is left on the table for subsequent capture. You can only play one card per turn. Upon making a capture, you place both cards face down in front of you.

Scoring

Players sift all the red cards from their winnings. Low red number cards score at face value, red Nines to Kings score 10 points each, and red Aces score 20. Black cards do not count when two people play. When three or four play, the A♠ counts 30 extra points and the A♣ scores 40 points.

The score is the difference between points taken and the predetermined 'tie' score, which is set at 105 for two players, 80 for three, and 70 for four. For example, in a game between two players, if the points taken are 119 and 90, the former scores +14 and the latter scores -15.

Conclusion

The last card from the pack should always capture the last card from the layout. All 52 cards should end up distributed among the players' winning piles.

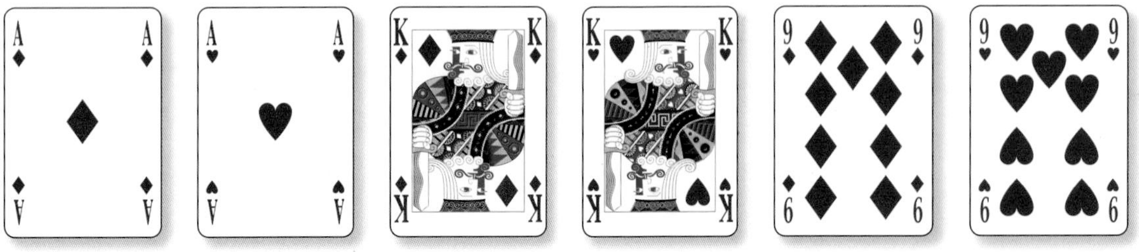

Left: The red cards in Chinese Ten score at face value, except for Aces (which score 20) and Nines to Kings (which score 10).

Laugh and Lie Down

A real oddity, Laugh and Lie Down is the oldest fishing game on record and the only one from English sources. Its name is attributed to players laughing at those who must 'lie down'.

You will need: 52 cards; gambling chips/counters
Card ranking: None
Players: Five
Ideal for: 10+

Object

To make Pairs and Mournivals (Four of a Kind) by matching the cards lying face up on the table.

The Deal

Before the deal, each player stakes two chips to the pot and the dealer three chips. Each player receives eight cards, and the remaining 12 are dealt face up to the table. The dealer takes any Mournivals among them.

Play

Any player with a Mournival in hand 'wins' those cards and places them face down on the table in front of him. If a player holds a Prial (Three of a Kind), he can do the same with two of the cards. The third is retained in hand.

In turn, each player plays a card to the table to make a capture by pairing. This can also be done by spotting other players' oversights. If, for instance, a player captures only one table card when there are three available, the first opposing player to spot this can take the other pair. If a player cannot make a capture he places his hand face up and drops out of play. This is called 'lying down'.

Scoring

The last player left in a hand wins five chips. A player capturing fewer than eight cards pays a chip for every two cards of the shortfall to the pot. However, a player with more than eight cards receives a chip for every two cards he has gone over.

Left: A Mournival (Four of a Kind). After the deal, any Mournivals found among the table cards are promptly won by the dealer.

Conclusion

Play continues until only one player has any cards left in hand, after which chips are settled.

Below: Player D holds a Prial (Three of a Kind) and can place it on the table at the start of play, placing two of the cards face down, and keeping the third card in hand. Player C makes a Mournival of Queens from the two in his hand and two on the table.

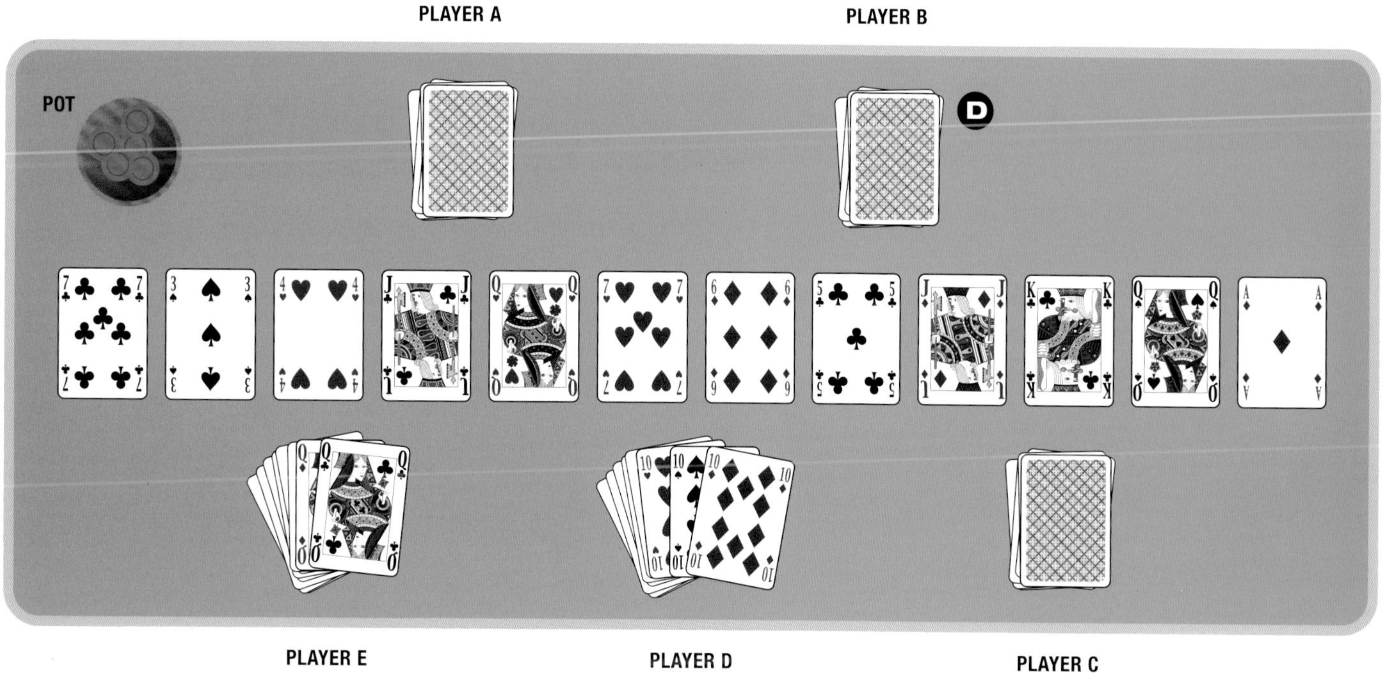

5 | Adding Games

These are arithmetical games, where the aim is to reach or avoid specific point totals. In a variation of Ninety-nine, players are penalized if they play a card that crosses one of the three 'borders' – 33, 66 and 99. Historically, such games have been more popular in Eastern Europe than the West, the exception being Cribbage, Britain's national card game.

Cribbage's history dates back to at least 1630, if not before. Although its invention was, for a long time, credited to Sir John Suckling (1609–42), a notable poet, playwright and wit of the day, there is now little doubt that it actually derived from a game called Noddy, which was popular in the previous century.

The game's fame quickly grew and spread as it was taken up by monarchs and their courtiers. Catherine the Great of Russia, for one, was an enthusiastic Cribbage player, until Whist and then Bridge supplanted it in aristocratic favour. However, it still flourishes in British pubs and clubs; it is estimated that, in Britain alone, there are two million active tournament players. There are two main versions – Six-card Cribbage, which is the standard, and Five-card Cribbage, a game that is older and now far less widely played. They count as adding games because, in their initial stages, the value of the cards played by both players cannot exceed 31.

Ninety-eight, Ninety-nine and One Hundred are similar adding games. In them, the values of the cards are added together as they are played, the aim being to avoid exceeding the target score.

Noddy and Costly Colours are both curiosities. The former appears to date from Tudor times, although the first descriptions date from more than a century later. And, even in its heyday, Costly Colours seems to have been played only in a fairly limited area in Britain.

Above: Russian Empress Catherine II, also known as Catherine the Great, who ruled from 1762–96, was an enthusiastic cribbage player.

Noddy

The undisputed ancestor of Cribbage, dating back to the 16th century, Noddy is so called after the title given to the Jack of the suit turned up at the start of play. 'Noddy' means a fool or simpleton – one who tends to 'nod' off at any opportunity.

You will need: 52 cards; no Jokers; Cribbage board
Card ranking: Standard, Ace low
Players: Two
Ideal for: 7+

Object

To score 31 points over as many deals as necessary, scores being pegged on a board, just as in Cribbage.

The Deal

Players cut for the deal, the one with the lower card dealing first. It then alternates. Each player receives three cards singly, the rest of the pack being placed face down on the table, and the top card is turned up. If it is a Jack, the non-dealer pegs two points for 'Jack Noddy'.

Play and Scoring

After the deal, each player in turn announces and scores for (but does not reveal) any combinations that can be made up from his three cards and the turn-up. A Pair pegs two points, a Pair Royal (three of the same rank) pegs six and a Double Pair Royal (four of the same rank) scores 12. Two or more cards totalling 15 points pegs a point for each constituent card, as does three or more cards totalling 25 and four cards totalling 31, known as Hitter.

PLAYER B

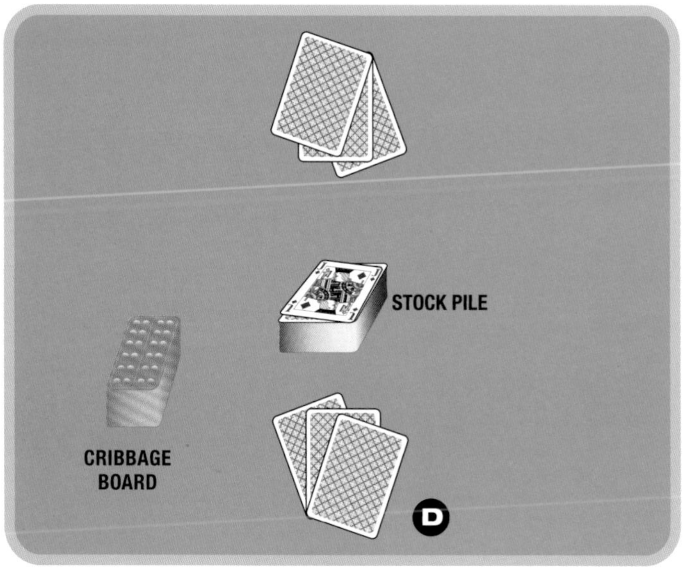

PLAYER A

Above: Non-dealer, Player B, scores two points for the Jack Noddy having been turned up.

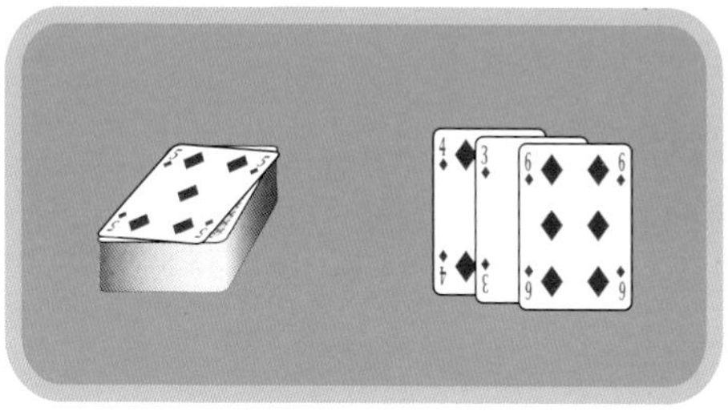

PLAYER A

Left: Here, the turn up card of the 5♦ means that player A not only completes a run of four (worth three points) but also pegs four more points for a four-card flush.

Three consecutive cards, such as Two, Three and Four, peg two, and four consecutive cards peg three. Flushes – three or more cards of the same suit – peg a point per card. If the Jack was not turned after the deal, then Jack Noddy is the Jack of the same suit as the turn-up card, and its holder (if any) pegs a point for it.

Any card can be counted more than once, provided that it forms part of a separate combination on each occasion. If either player reaches 31 points from the combination of cards that he holds in his hand, then the game ends and there is no play-off.

If neither player attains 31 points, then the game proceeds to a play-off. The non-dealer plays a card to the table, announcing its face value. The dealer plays in turn, announcing the combined value of the two cards. In the play-off, Aces count for one point, numbered cards count at face value, and court cards score 10 points each. The process continues until 31 points have been pegged, or until neither player can continue without busting (exceeding 31 points).

If one player can continue to play while the other cannot, he plays on alone. If 31 is exceeded, the player who last kept it under 31 pegs one point.

Conclusion

Once 31 has been scored – which can happen before a card has been played, when the players announce their combinations – the game is over. Any cards left in hand do not score.

Six-Card Cribbage

Whether Six-Card or Five-Card, Cribbage stands out as a unique game. A special Cribbage board is required to play, which uses pegs to record scores. Much of its terminology is also quaint, examples including phrases such as 'one for his nob' and words like 'skunked', used to describe a losing player.

You will need: 52 cards; Cribbage board
Card ranking: Standard, Ace low
Players: Two
Ideal for: 7+

Object

To score as many points as possible in each hand, being the first after several hands to peg out (complete two circuits of the Cribbage board).

The Deal

Both players cut for the deal, the one with the lower card dealing first – Aces are low. Both players, starting with the non-dealer, receive six cards singly. The remaining cards are stacked face down on the table as the stock.

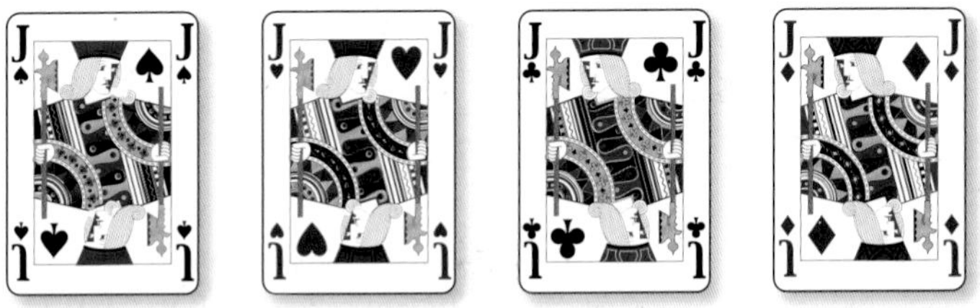

Above: If any Jack is turned up after cutting the pack, the dealer immediately pegs two points 'for his heels'. If a player has a Jack in their hand that is the same suit as the turned-up card, they peg one point 'for his nob' when hands are shown.

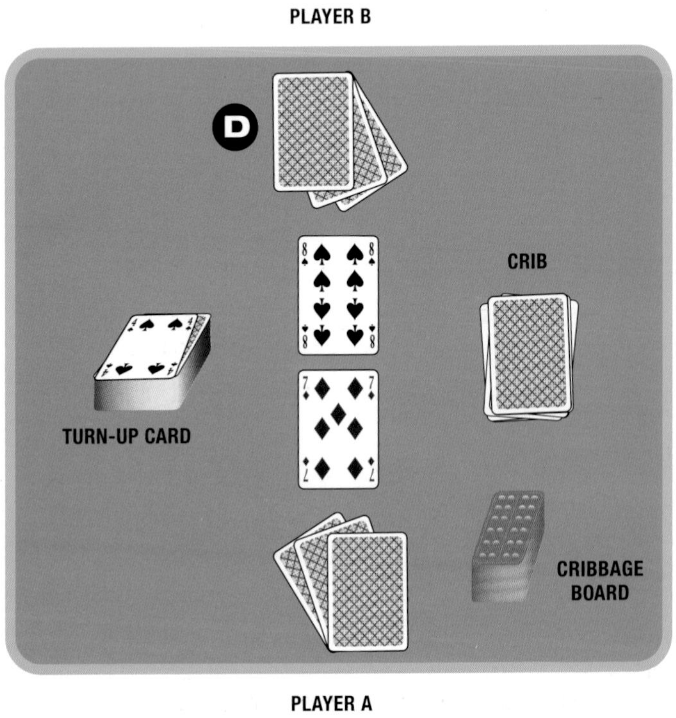

The Discard

After the deal, both players discard two cards face down to form the crib of four cards, aiming to keep a hand that forms scoring combinations. The four crib cards are put aside until the end of the hand, when the cards in it count for the dealer.

The non-dealer cuts the stock. The dealer takes the top card of the bottom half and puts it face up on the top of the pack. This card is the start card. If it is a Jack, the dealer can peg two points, known as 'two for his heels'.

Play

Starting with the non-dealer, each player takes it in turn to play a single card, placing the cards in separate face-up piles. They score a running total, the value of each card being added as it is played.

Each time 31 is reached (players must not go above this), the score goes back to zero and another round starts. When a player plays a card that brings the total exactly to that figure, he claims 'thirty-one for two' and pegs two points. If a player cannot play without going over the total, he says 'go' and allows the opposing player to continue. If neither can play, the last player to do so pegs 'one for the go and one for last'. Play goes on until all the cards in hand have been played.

Above: This hand pegs 22 points. There are seven combinations of Fifteen (three times with each Jack, and all the Fives added together), making 14 points, together with a Pair and a Pair Royal (giving two and six points respectively).

Left: Player B lays an Eight after the initial lead of a Seven. The two cards add up to 15, so Player B calls 'fifteen for two' and is able to peg two points.

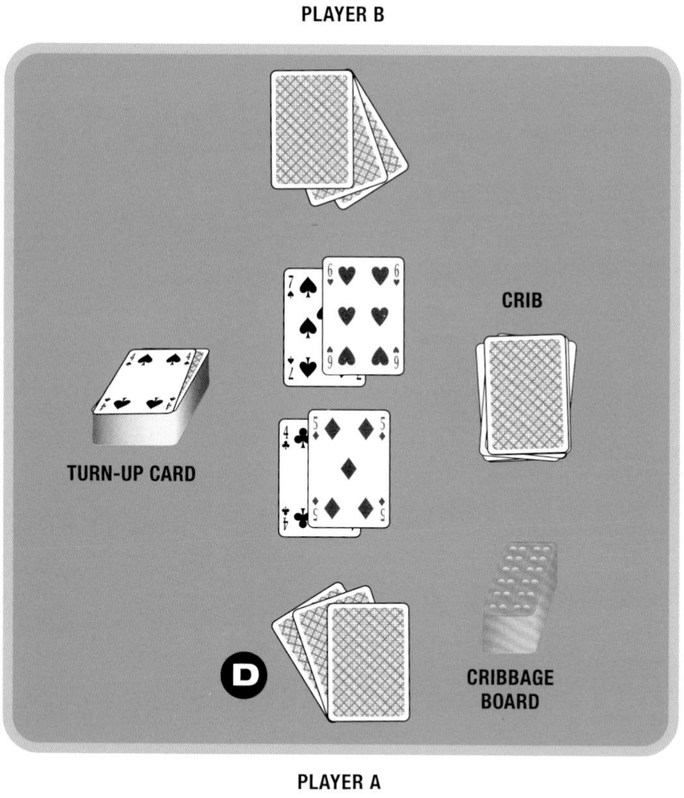

Left: Player B played first here, laying the 7♠. Player A responded with the 4♣. Player B then played the 6♥, allowing Player A to lay the 5♦ and peg four points for a run of Four, Five, Six, Seven.

Pairs and Runs

If a player makes any of the following scores in addition to the ones that have already been described, he can peg them immediately. If a card is played that brings the total to 15, its player claims 'fifteen for two' and pegs two points. If a card of the same rank as the previous one is played, the score is 'two for the pair'. If a third card of the same rank is played immediately after this, it is a Pair Royal and its player pegs six points. A 'Double Pair Royal' is awarded if a fourth card of the same rank is played, its player pegging 12 points.

A run is a sequence of three of more cards of consecutive ranks, irrespective of their suits. A player completing a run pegs for the number of cards in it. If, for instance, a Four, Two, Six, Five and Three are played, the player of the Three scores five for a five-card run.

Above: This hand pegs 18 points. There are four combinations of 15, making eight points, together with a run of four yielding four points and a flush, giving five points. Finally, there's another point 'for his nob'.

The Show (Scoring)

Once all the cards have been played, each player picks up the cards they have played and scores them, the start card being counted as part of the hand for both players.

The combinations and scores (shown in brackets) are:

- Fifteen (2): two or more cards totalling 15, counting Ace as one, numbered cards at face value, court cards as 10.
- Pair (2): two cards of the same rank.
- Prial or Pair Royal (6): three of the same rank.
- Double Pair Royal (12): four of the same rank.
- Run (1 per card): three of more cards in ranking order.
- Flush (4 or 5): four or more cards of the same suit.

The same card can be counted as part of different combinations. If a hand contains a Jack of the same suit as the start card, one 'for his nob' is pegged. Finally, the dealer turns over the crib – the four cards the players discarded between them after the deal – and scores it as a five-card hand, exactly as above.

Conclusion

The first player to peg out – to exceed 121 points – wins the game. This can happen at any time during play as long as the opposing player's pegs are still on the board. It is usual to play the best of three. If the losing player's score is less than 91, he is 'lurched' or 'skunked' and forfeits double. If it is under 60, it is a 'double lurch' or 'skunk' and he forfeits triple.

Above: A special Cribbage board and pegs are needed to record the scores in Cribbage. There are two pegs – the forward one showing a player's current score and the rear peg the previous score.

FIVE-CARD CRIBBAGE

Five-card Cribbage was, for a long time, the standard version of the game and it still features in club, tournament and championship matches, probably because it is partner-friendly.

OBJECT

To be the first to peg 61 points. A player pegging fewer than 45 points is 'in the lurch'.

You will need: 52 cards; Cribbage board

Card ranking: Standard, Ace low

Players: Two

Ideal for: 7+

THE DEAL, PLAY AND SCORING

Four players play as partners, each being dealt five cards and discarding one to the crib. The player to the dealer's left leads first and makes the first show.

At the start of play, the non-dealing partnership pegs 'three for last' as compensation for not having the benefit of the crib.

Hands are played only once until 31 has been reached. Any cards left over remain unplayed.

Four cards of the same suit (a Flush) in hand pegs four – five with the turn-up card. A Flush in the crib (the four cards discarded by players after the deal) only pegs five if it matches the turn-up card's suit.

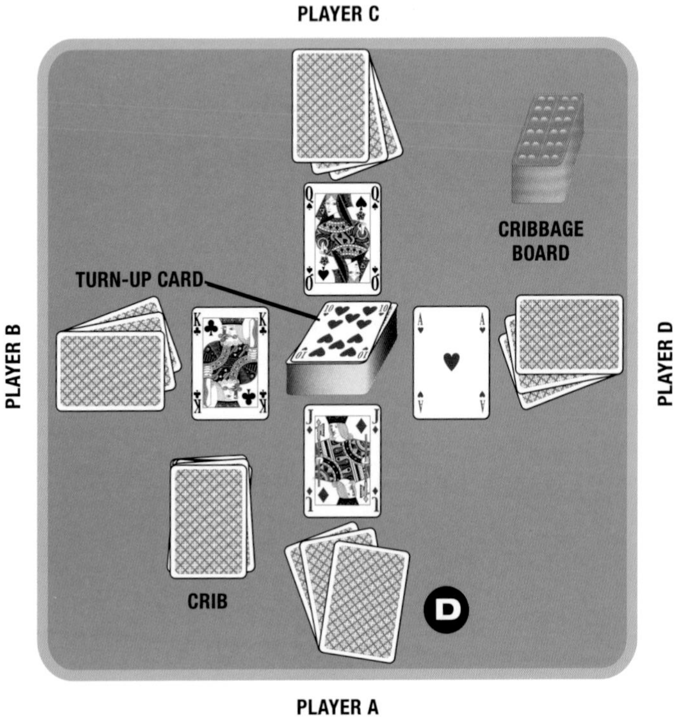

Above: In Five-Card cribbage, if 31 points have been reached, no more cards are laid. Hand points are now calculated.

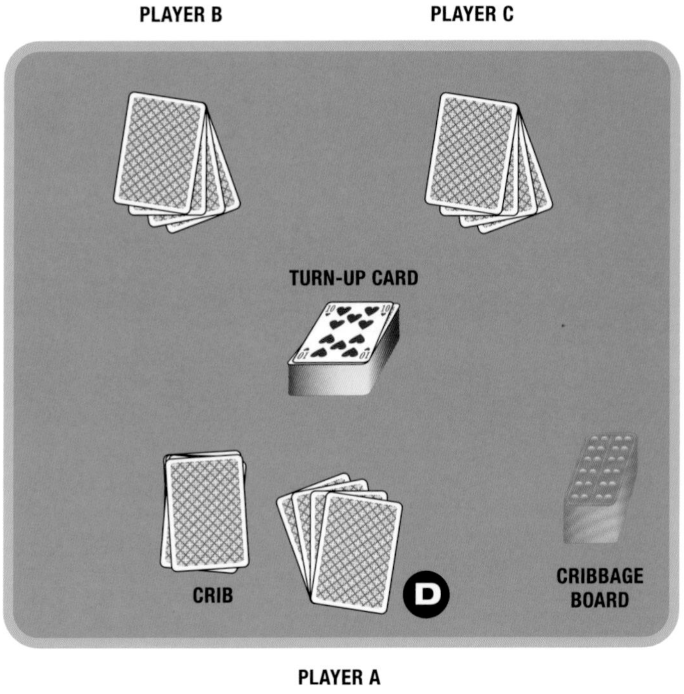

Above: In Three-Handed Cribbage, each player receives five cards and one is dealt for the crib. Players must each make one discard, bringing each hand, including the crib, up to four cards.

VARIANTS

In the cut-throat version of Three-Handed Cribbage, each player receives five cards, followed by one to the crib. Players then discard a card each to the crib, after which the player to the dealer's left cuts the pack to reveal the turn-up and plays first. He also shows and counts first, the last player to do so being the dealer. Each player scores for himself.

In the solo version, the dealer's two opponents play as a partnership, each receiving five cards. The dealer takes six cards. Both partners then pass a card to the dealer, who discards four cards to the crib. Play is the same as in the cut-throat game, the one main difference being that each partner scores the amount made by them both. The same applies in Four-Handed Cribbage.

Losing Cribbage is a two-handed six-card game. It is played as the standard version, but the main difference between the two is that every score a player makes is credited to their opponent. The first to score – or rather not to score – 121 points, wins.

In Auction Cribbage, each player states how many points he will subtract from his score in return for the crib, before the starter is turned. The highest bidder deducts that amount and play proceeds as usual.

Costly Colours

Noted for its complex scoring, Costly Colours is probably a cousin of Cribbage, but relatively little is known about it. Charles Cotton was the first to describe it in his *Complete Gamester*, of 1674. It seems to have survived up to Victorian times, but is no more than a historical curiosity.

You will need: 52 cards; Cribbage board
Card ranking: Standard, Ace low or high
Players: Two
Ideal for: 10+

Object

To be the first player over a series of games to reach 121 points, by making sequences, combinations and other scoring card plays.

The Deal

Both players receive three cards singly, the next card – the deck card – being turned up. Both players use it to help to make sequences and combinations. If it is a Jack or a Two, the dealer pegs four points 'for his heels'.

Play

Before play, each player can 'mog', that is, pass a card from his hand face down to the other player. If a player refuses, the other pegs a point for the refusal. If a player mogs (gives away) a Jack or Two, he may first peg two points for it, or four if it is the same suit as the deck card.

The non-dealer plays a card face up to the table, followed by the dealer, who then announces the combined value of the two cards. Play continues until 31 points are scored, or either player cannot play without exceeding that total. This is termed 'busting'. The first player unable to play without doing this has to say 'go', after which the opposing player may add as many cards as possible before he, too, busts. He scores an extra point for the go, plus a point per card if he manages to score 31 exactly. Both players then reveal their cards and peg the value of their scoring combinations, the non-dealer pegging first. The convention is for declarations to be made in the following order – points, Jacks and Twos, Pairs and Prials, Colours and Flushes (see Scoring).

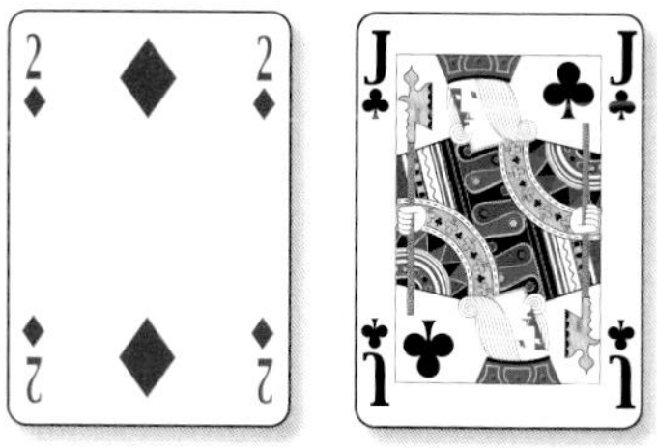

Left: If a Jack or Two is turned up as the deck card, the dealer pegs four points.

If either player is left holding cards in hand, the cards played so far are turned down and removed from play. The next in turn to play then starts a new series.

Scoring and Conclusion

Fifteen, 25 and 31, scored in play or in hand, are one point each, a Pair pegs two points, a Prial (Three of a Kind) pegs nine and a Double Prial (Four of a Kind) pegs 18. A Jack or Two of the turned-up suit pegs four; any other Jack or Two pegs two.

Sequences count only in play (one point per card) while Colours (reds or blacks) count only in hand. Three in Colour pegs two; Three in Suit pegs three; Four in Colour, Two in Suit pegs four, Four in Colour, Three in Suit pegs five, Four in Suit – Costly Colours – pegs six. The first to reach 121 points wins.

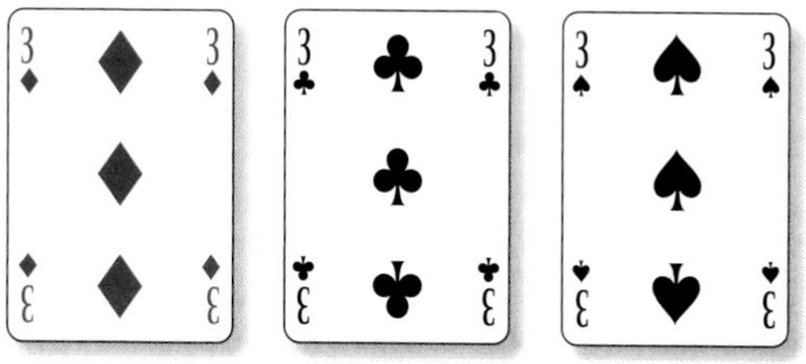

Left: Three of a Kind (a Prial) is worth nine points and Four of a Kind (a Double Prial) 18 points.

Below: With all four cards the same colour, and three of the same suit, this combination would score five points (Four in Colour, Three in Suit). Had the 9♦ been a 9♥, this would have made Costly Colours (four cards of the same suit), scoring six points.

Ninety-Eight

This is the first of a set of games known as Adders, in which the card values are added together during play. The aim is to score a set number of points, or to avoid specific totals.

You will need: 52 cards
Card ranking: See 'Play and Scoring', below
Players: Two or more
Ideal for: 7+

Object

To avoid taking the value of the pile above 98.

The Deal

Each player receives four cards dealt singly, the remainder being placed face down on the table to form a stock. Players play their cards face up to the table to create a pile alongside the stock.

Play and Scoring

The player to the dealer's left plays first, with play continuing clockwise around the table. At the moment a card is played to the pile, its player calls out the pile's cumulative value and then draws the top card of the stock to replace the card that was played.

Certain cards change the value of the pile. Playing a Ten reduces its value by 10 points. If a Jack or Queen is played, the value stays the same, whereas playing a King immediately sets the value at 98. All other cards simply add their face value.

Left: In Ninety-eight, if a King is played, the value of the pile is immediately set at 98.

Conclusion

The first player to take the pile above 98 is the loser and, according to convention, has to buy the other players a round of drinks or do a forfeit.

Ninety-Nine

Said to be a Gypsy game, Ninety-Nine is played along similar conventions to its sister game Ninety-Eight, with some notable exceptions.

You will need: 52 cards; gambling chips/counters
Card ranking: See 'Play and Scoring', below
Players: Up to four
Ideal for: 7+

Object

To avoid taking the value of the pile above 99.

The Deal

Up to four players start with five chips each and receive three cards from a standard 52-card pack. The remaining cards are placed face down on the table to form a stock.

Play and Scoring

The player to the dealer's left plays first and play proceeds clockwise. Each player plays a card face up to a pile on the table, calling out the cumulative value of the pile as they do so. They each then draw the top card of the stock as a replacement.

For each card played, the pile's value goes up by the value of the card, Jacks and Queens counting for 10 points each. An Ace increases the pile's value by one or 11 points, as decided by its player. If a Four is played, the pile value stays the same, but the direction of play reverses. A Nine is worth nothing.

After a Four or Nine, the player calls out the existing value of the pile, saying 'pass to you' or 'back to you', respectively. Playing a Ten increases or decreases the pile's value by 10 points at its player's discretion. Playing a King immediately makes the pile's value 99. Each player loses a point every time they play a card that crosses one of the three 'borders' – 33, 66 and 99.

Conclusion

A player unable to play without taking the pile's value above 99 lays down his hand and tosses a chip into the centre of the table. A player with no chips left drops out of the game. The last player left with any chips, wins.

One Hundred

In certain variations of Adders games, there are individual cards that have special effects; in One Hundred, for instance, playing the A♠ doubles the value of the card pile.

You will need: 52 cards; gambling chips/counters
Card ranking: See 'Play and Scoring', below
Players: Three to six
Ideal for: 7+

Object

To get rid of all your cards without taking the value of the pile above 100.

The Deal

Three cards are dealt one at a time to each player. The remainder is placed face down on the table to form a stock.

Play and Scoring

Play starts with the player to the dealer's left and proceeds clockwise around the table. Cards are played singly face up to form a pile, each player calling out its cumulative value as they play, before drawing the top card of the stock to replenish their hands.

A King is worth nothing. The Queens are worth 10 – except for the Q♥, which sets the pile value at zero. Playing a Jack reduces the pile value by 10. Playing a Ten raises the pile value to 100. Most number cards count at face value. Playing a 2♠ doubles the pile value; playing a Four reverses the direction of play. Playing a red Five decreases the pile value by five points. Playing an Ace from a black suit means that its player can set the pile value at any figure between 0 and 100.

If a player makes the pile value equal 100, the only cards the next player can play are black Aces, Fours, red Fives, Tens, Jacks, the Q♥ or Kings.

Conclusion

A player unable to play without taking the pile's value above 100 lays down his hand and tosses a chip into the centre of the table. Players drop out if they lose all their chips; the last with any chips is the winner.

Jubilee

In this Czech game, played with a 61-card pack, the cards in the black suits score positive points, while those in red suits count as minus points.

You will need: A 61-card pack, containing one full Hearts suit, two Spades suits, two Clubs suits from Ace to Nine (Tens and court cards discarded) and four Jokers
Card ranking: See above, and under Play, below
Players: Two to seven
Ideal for: 10+

Object

To win the most of the 189 points available.

The Deal

Each player is dealt eight cards, the remainder of the pack being placed face down on the table to form a stock.

Play

Starting with the player to the dealer's left, each player in turn plays a card to a common waste pile. The first to play must play a black card and announce its value. As the players play more cards, they must announce the total value of all the cards that have been played so far in the game. Once they have played a card, they draw replacement cards from the stock, and the procedure continues until the stock is exhausted. No one may bring the total score down to zero. Any player unable to make a legal play must show his hand and pass.

Scoring

Any player who is able to make the running total an exact multiple of 25, by addition or subtraction, scores 10 for a 'Jubilee'. If the total is also a multiple of 100, this score is doubled to 20. But, if a player causes the total to 'jump' a Jubilee rather than hitting it exactly, whether by addition or subtraction, he is penalized five points. It is against the rules of the game to bring the total to below zero.

Conclusion

The game ends when the last card has been played. The final total should be 189 points.

6 | Shedding Games

The aim of these games is to get rid of cards and to be the first player to go out. In some, cards must be played in ascending sequence, usually in suit. In others, players must match the rank or suit of the previous card played. Eleusis, devised by games inventor Robert Abbott in 1956, is unique. Players shed cards by matching, but the rules governing this process, known to only the dealer, must be deduced by other players.

Games belonging to the 'Stops' group require that cards be played in ascending order, but also that there is no set order of play. Whoever holds the best card plays it. The 'stops' are the cards that are left undealt and never drawn. This obviously makes it harder to play, since it stops the sequence from following its logical course. In such games, all players are trying to get rid of cards from their hands by playing one or more cards to a discard pile, aiming to match or beat the previous card played.

The oldest of such games is Huc, which was around in the 16th century, followed by Comet a century later. The curiously named Pope Joan game was a middle-class Victorian favourite. The most popular modern game is Michigan, as it is called in the USA. It started off life in Britain as Newmarket.

There are many games within the specific group of shedding games known as 'eights games', but their fundamental objective is the same – to match the rank and suit of the previous card played. Some games are more elaborate than others. In Bartok, for example, the rules about which cards count for what vary from hand to hand. In Eleusis, the dealer invents the rules governing play and the other players try to deduce what it is by noting which plays the dealer rules are legal and which are illegal.

Other games in this group such as Zheng Shangyou and President are known as 'climbing games', as each player in turn tries to play a higher-ranked card than preceding players.

Above: American games inventor Robert Abbott devised the game of Eleusis, which he described as a 'game of inductive reasoning', in 1956.

Domino

This long-established game goes by various names, including Card Dominoes, Fan Tan, Parliament and Spoof Sevens.

You will need: 52 cards; no Jokers; gambling chips

Card ranking: None

Players: Any number, but ideally six or seven

Ideal for: 7+

Object

To be the first player to get rid of all one's cards by playing them to a layout on the table.

The Deal

Dealer cuts the pack, dealing all the cards out singly to the players. Play starts clockwise from the dealer's left.

Play

Before play starts, each player pays an agreed number of chips into the pot. The first to play must then play a Seven – the suit does not matter – or pass. In the latter case, the penalty is a chip to the pot and the turn passes to the next player. Assuming a Seven has been played, that player must play the Six of the same suit to the left of the Seven, the Eight of the same suit to the right, or any other Seven above or below it. The next to play must play another Seven, or the next higher or lower card of the suit sequence. The aim is to end up with four rows of cards, each consisting of 13 cards of the same suit, with the Ace at the far left and the King at the far right. It is best to play Aces or Kings as soon as possible. At each point, if a player cannot go, he must pass and pay a chip.

Scoring

Anyone who fails to play when able to do so, forfeits three chips to the pool. A player who fails to lay a card when he could have played a Seven, forfeits three chips to the pool and five to the holder of the Six and Eight of the suit in question. The first player to get all their cards out scoops the pool. He also collects a chip for each card left in hand from all the other players.

Conclusion

The game ends when a player lays the last of his cards.

Above: After players have paid an agreed number of chips into the pot, each game has to begin with a Seven being played.

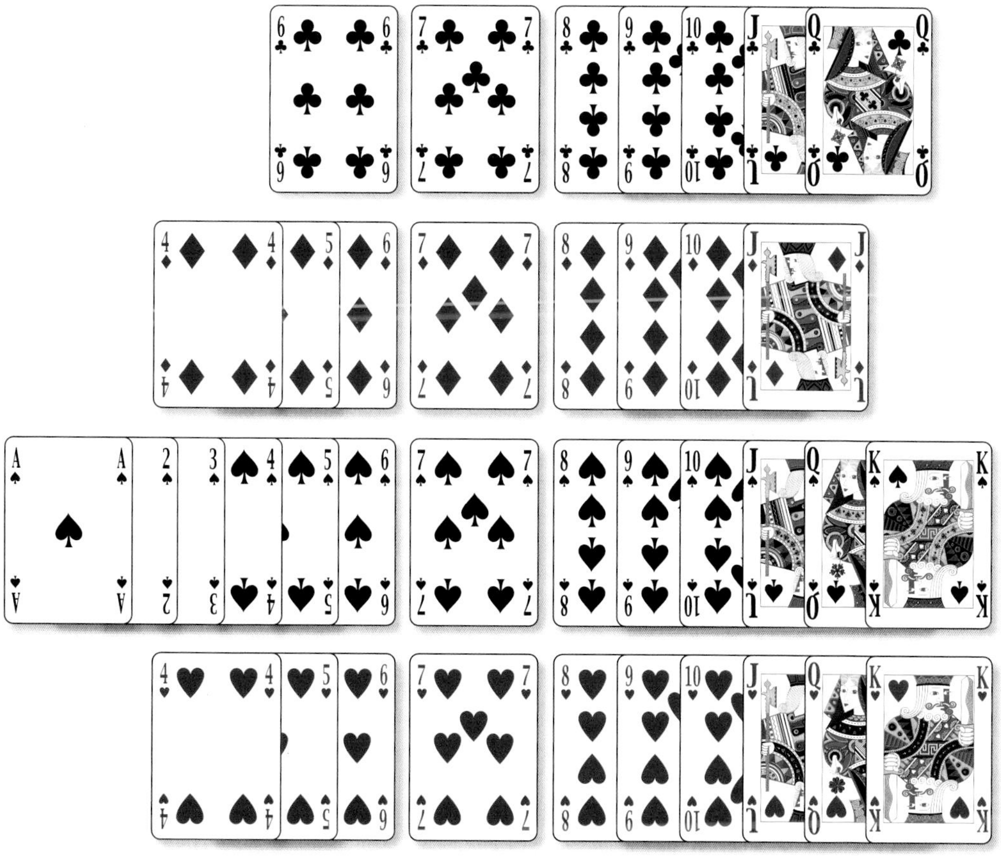

Left: The rows are all well on their way to completion and it's a race now to see who can play their last card first.

Michigan

Also known as Stops, or Boodle, this game is probably descended from the gambling games enjoyed by the 17th-century French nobility, although it is far less serious and the stakes are by no means as high. In Newmarket, the original British version, Aces are low.

You will need: Two packs of cards; no Jokers; gambling chips/counters

Card ranking: None

Players: Three to eight

Ideal for: 7+

Left: Cardinal Mazarin, pictured here, was an avid card player, and was thought to have used gambling games to his advantage as a 17-century politician in France.

Object

To be the first player out, winning stakes by playing specific cards along the way.

Betting

Before the deal, players stake a certain number of chips on four cards, which are the only ones taken from a second pack, placed face up in the centre of the table to form a layout. The cards in question, A♥, K♣, Q♦ and J♠, are termed 'boodle' cards or 'pay' cards. The dealer stakes two chips on each card and the other players a single chip on each. (In one variant, each player is allowed to distribute his chips freely among the boodle cards, rather than having to stake a fixed amount on each one).

Above: The four 'pay' cards, or boodle cards, (those that pay out) in Michigan are the A♥, K♣, Q♦ and J♠.

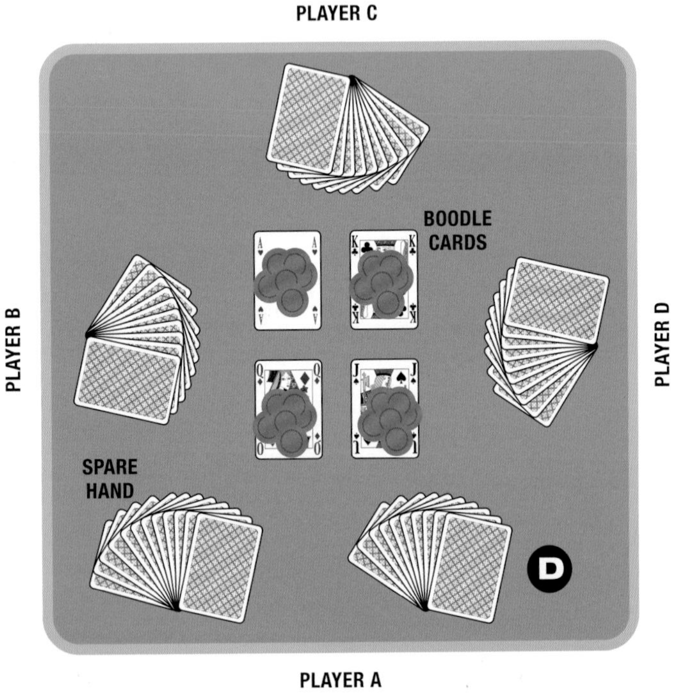

Above: If the dealer decides not to exchange the spare hand for his own, and no one else buys it from him in order to exchange it for his own hand, it is left face down on the table.

The Deal

Each player deals in turn, the deal passing to the left after a hand. All the cards are dealt one at a time, the last card of each round going to form a spare hand, left face down on the table. There are no fixed numbers of cards required to be dealt – the pack is simply dealt out one card at a time to each player. It does not matter if some players get one more card than others.

The dealer can exercise the option of exchanging the hand he was dealt for the spare one. He cannot look at the spare hand before deciding whether to make the exchange – this must take place sight unseen. If the decision is not to exchange, the dealer can auction the spare hand – again, sight unseen – to the highest bidder. Whichever player buys the hand must pay a fixed stake to the kitty. The dealer, however, can exchange his hand for the spare one for nothing. If no one wants to bid, the spare hand is left where it is and it takes no further part in the game. Evidently, whoever deals gets a slight advantage, so the usual practice is to end a game only after all players have had the chance to deal the same number of times.

Play

Starting with the player to the dealer's left, each player in turn plays a card face up to the table, announcing what the card is as it is played. Cards that have been played are kept in front of the person who played them until the end of the hand.

The suit that is led depends on which version of the game is being played. In some, any suit may be led, but others specify that Clubs or Diamonds must be played first. Whichever version is followed, the lowest card held in that suit must be led. Whoever holds the next highest card of the same suit must then play it, followed by the next highest and so on. A player holding more than one card in an ascending sequence may play them at the same time. If, for instance, a player holds the Three and Four of Diamonds, he can play both simultaneously.

During the course of play, any player who plays a card that matches one of the boodle cards wins all the chips staked on that card. The total number of chips staked is usually a set number, but how they are distributed varies. Play continues until either the Ace is played, or no one holds the next card in sequence, usually because the card needed has already been played or is in the spare hand. A stop card is one that no one can follow. The last person to play then starts a new round of play. Any suit can be played and the card played must be the lowest one held in that suit, followed by the next one in sequence, and so on.

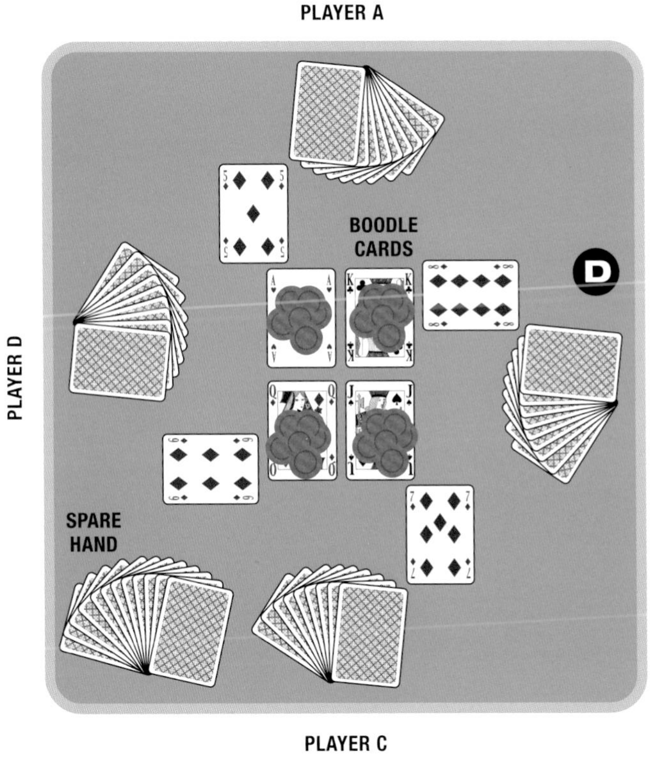

Above: The 8♦ is the last card laid, so the 9♦ is needed next.

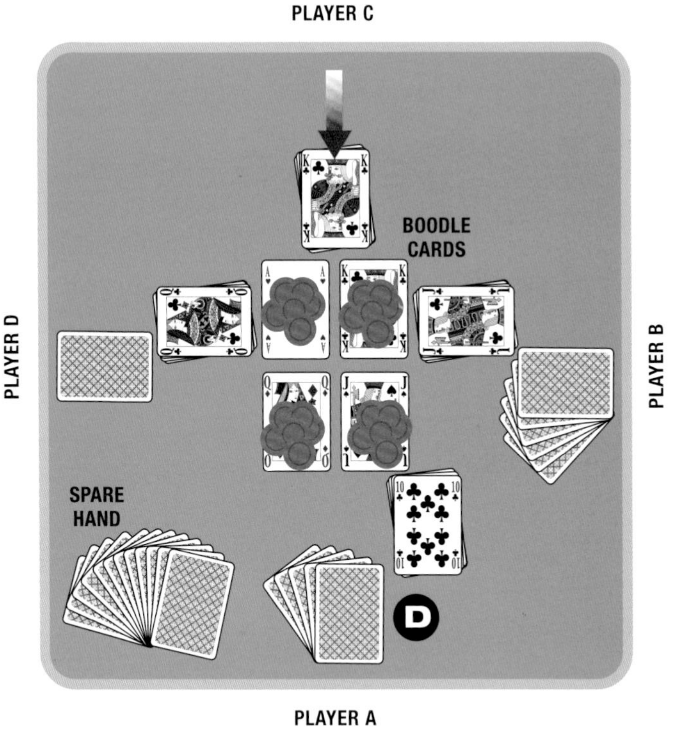

Above: Player C can lay his last card, the K♣, thus receiving gambling chips from other players for each card they hold in their hands – Player C receives two gambling chips if they are boodle cards.

In one variation of the game, the suit led to restart the game must be different to the previous one. Some versions insist on black after red and red after black. If the player who ended play in the preceding sequence cannot play a card with a different suit, the turn to play passes to the player to his left.

Conclusion

There are two possible conclusions. The first is when no one can play another suit, in which case the game ends in a stalemate and there are no forfeits for any cards left in hand. Otherwise, as soon as one player runs out of cards, play finishes. All the other players forfeit a chip for each card remaining in their hand – two chips if any of the remaining cards are unplayed boodle cards. The chips go to the winner. Any chips remaining on the table stay there, the stakes being carried forward to the next hand.

Crazy Eights

When it appeared in the 1930s, this game was called simply Eights. It developed its new name as it became more elaborate. Alternate names include Crates and Swedish Rummy. In Germany, it is Mau Mau (Mao in the USA), in Switzerland Tschausepp and, in the Netherlands, Pesten.

You will need: 52 cards; no Jokers	
Card ranking: None	
Players: Two to five (or more, using two packs combined)	
Ideal for: 7+	

Object

To discard as quickly as possible by matching the number or suit of the previous player's discard.

The Deal

The dealer deals five cards singly to each player (seven if only two are playing), the remainder being placed face down on the table to form a stock. The top card of the stock is turned up and placed beside it to start a discard pile. If it is an Eight, it is buried in the stock and the next card is turned up to take its place.

Play

The player to the dealer's left plays first. Each player in turn must discard a card on to the discard pile. To do so, the card has to match the rank or suit of the previous discard. If this is impossible, the player concerned must draw a card from the stock or, if the stock has run out, pass.

Eights are wild cards. An Eight can be played on any card, its player then nominating the suit that must be played next. It need not be the same suit as the Eight. Some other cards also have a special significance, depending on what form of the game is being played. Sometimes, for instance, playing a Queen means that the next player has to skip his turn, while playing an Ace reverses the direction of play from clockwise to anti-clockwise, and vice versa.

Scoring

If a player gets rid of all his cards, the others score penalties according to the cards they have left in hand. An Eight scores 50, a court card 10 and number cards count at face value. An Ace scores one. If no one can match the last card played, the player with the lowest combined value of cards in hand wins and the remaining players are penalized the respective difference between the value of the cards they hold and the winner's.

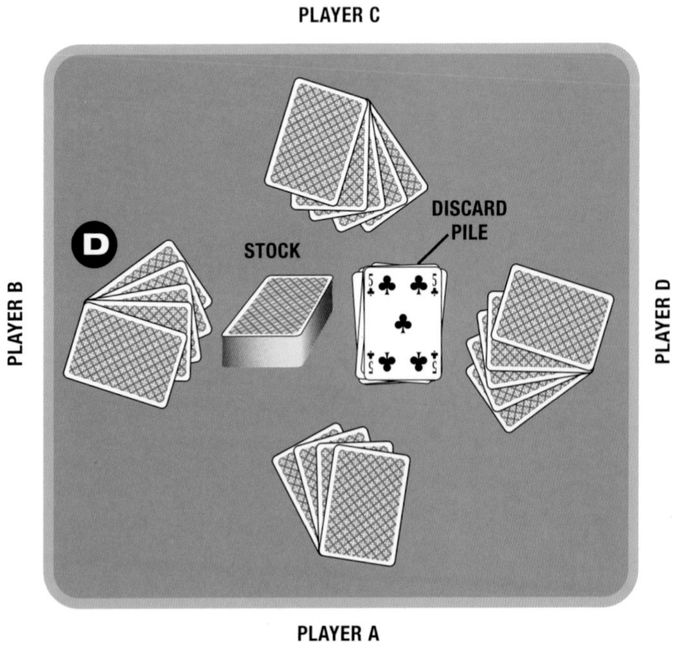

Above: Player B, to play, must lay a card of the same rank (another Five) or suit (another Club) or draw a card from the stock.

Conclusion

Play stops when one player has got rid of all his cards or no one can match the last card played, after which scores are calculated.

Above: If an Eight is turned up, it is buried in the stock and a new card turned up instead.

Left: In Crazy Eights, cards numbered Two to Six and Nine count against players at face value. Eights, however, count as 50, court cards as 10 and Aces as 1.

Switch

Also known as Two-Four-Jack or Black Jack, this elaboration of Crazy Eights became so popular in the 1960s and 1970s that it gave rise to a proprietary game called Uno, which is played with special cards of its own.

You will need: 52 cards; no Jokers
Card ranking: None
Players: Two to seven
Ideal for: 7+

Object

To be the first player to get rid of all your cards.

The Deal

Players receive 12 cards if two or three are playing, but otherwise the deal is 10 cards each. The remainder are stacked face down to form a stock, and the top card is turned face up and placed next to it to start the discard pile. This is the start card for the first sequence of cards.

Play

Starting with the player to the dealer's left and continuing clockwise, each player plays a card of the same rank or suit as the previous one face up on top of the discard pile. The alternative is to play an Ace. This is a wild card and its player can specify the suit that must be played next.

If a player cannot play with the cards in hand, he must draw from the stock until he can play. Once the stock is exhausted, all the cards that have been played, with the exception of the last hand, are gathered up, shuffled and laid down as a new stock.

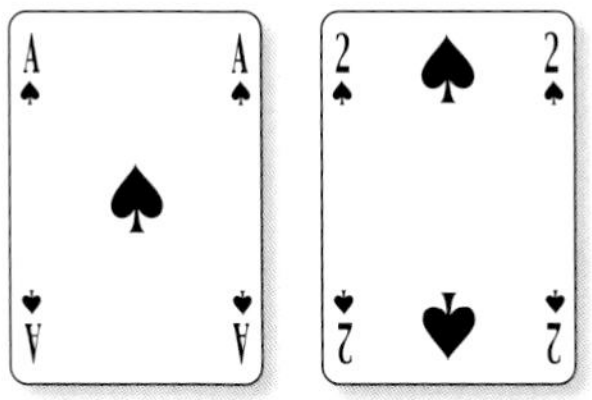

Left: Playing an Ace entitles a player to specify the suit to be played next. Playing a Two forces the next player to play another Two or draw two cards.

Left: A Four must be met with another Four, failing which, four cards are picked up. A Two on a Two or a Four on a Four doubles the penalty cards the next player must pick up, and so on. A Jack switches the direction of play.

Twos, Fours and Jacks

- Playing a Two forces the next player to either play a Two, or draw two cards from the stock and miss a turn. If the player after that also plays a Two, the fourth person must play a Two as well, or draw four cards and miss a turn. The maximum number of cards that a player can be forced to draw is eight.
- Playing a Four is the same, although the number of cards to be drawn goes up to four, eight, 12 or 16.
- Playing a Jack switches the direction of play.

A player with only two cards left must announce 'one left' as he plays the first of them. Otherwise, he misses a turn and has to draw a card from the stock.

Scoring

Aces score 20, Twos, Fours and Jacks 15, Kings and Queens 10. All other number cards count at face value.

Conclusion

The first player to get rid of all his cards wins, scoring the value of the cards left in the other players' hands.

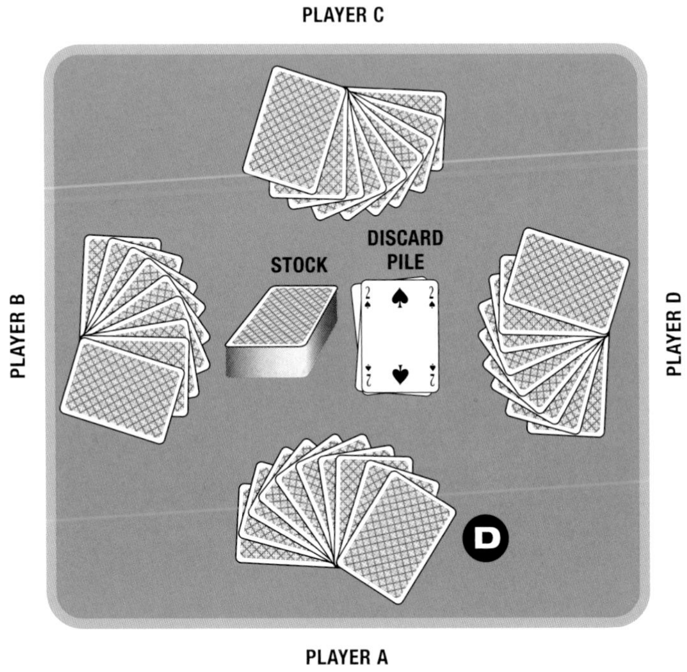

Left: Player D has laid a Two, meaning that Player A, the next to play, must pick up two cards and miss a turn. If Player A holds a Two, he can play it instead of picking up, meaning that Player B, if he does not have a Two, will have to pick up four cards and miss a turn.

Eleusis

This is certainly one of the most mind-bending card games around. Primarily, this is due to the fact that each hand of play is governed by a secret rule, chosen by and known only to, its dealer.

You will need: Three 52-card packs shuffled together; no Jokers

Card ranking: None

Players: Four to eight

Ideal for: 14+

Object

To decipher the dealer's rules and so be the first to get rid of all one's cards.

The Deal

The choice of dealer is random, although the convention is that no one deals more than once in the same session of play. Whoever deals receives no cards and does not take part in the game in the conventional way. Each of the other players is dealt 14 cards; then a card is dealt face up on to the table. The remaining cards are stacked face down as the stock.

The dealer's task is to devise a rule governing play that is not too easy or too difficult for the others to deduce and then to enforce it by declaring plays legal or illegal. The rule is never actually revealed during play, although the dealer may choose to give hints as to what it might be. A fairly typical rule would be as follows: if the last card played was from a red suit, the next card to be played must be from a black one, and, if the first card was even, the next card must be odd.

Play

The players' aim is to establish a 'mainline sequence' from the starter card across the table to the right, and to get rid of all their cards. A card can be played to the mainline only if it matches the card preceding it. Otherwise, it must be placed in a sideline extending at right angles from the mainline. What is a match varies, depending on the rule each dealer devises. Thus, play is more or less by trial and error until enough evidence has been obtained to suggest what the rule is most likely to be.

As each player plays a card, the dealer calls 'right' or 'wrong'. If the former, the card stays where it was played to the mainline. If the latter, the card is placed in a sideline and the dealer deals the offending player twice the number of cards played – a minimum of two up to a maximum of eight, if the player has tried to play a string of cards.

A player who believes he has discovered the rule, but who has no suitable card to play, can declare 'can't play' and expose the hand, so the dealer can check whether the declaration was right or wrong. If it was right, what happens depends on how many cards are left in hand. If it was wrong, the dealer plays any of the cards that will fit to the mainline and deals the mistaken player five cards. If there are five or more, the dealer places them at the bottom of the stock and deals the player in question four fewer cards than the number they previously held in hand. If there are four or fewer, the game ends.

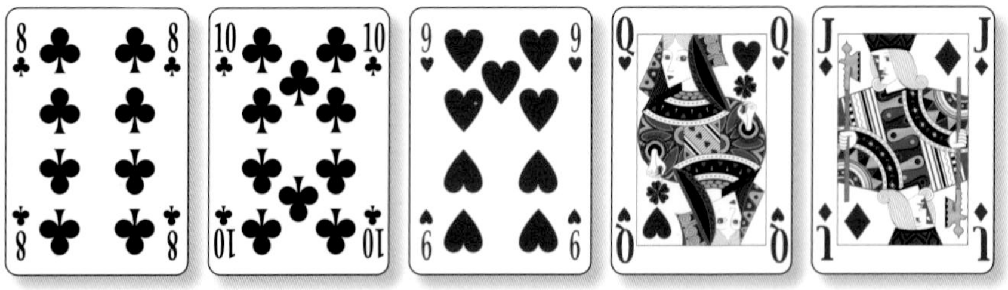

Left and Below: The dealer has devised a rule that cards must go up two in the same suit, then down one to a suit of the opposite colour, then up three in the same suit; then down one to the other red suit; then up four; then down one to the other black suit, and so on. This would make the sequence of cards in the top row unacceptable, but that of the row below, acceptable.

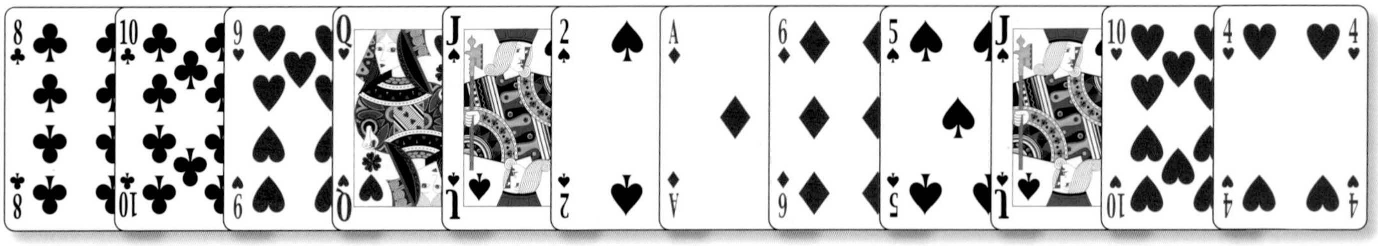

Becoming 'The Prophet'

A player believing he knows the rule may opt to declare himself the prophet in the hopes of bettering his score. There are four conditions:

- The declaration can be made only after successfully adding to the mainline (see 'Play') and before the next in turn starts to play.
- There can be only one prophet at a time.
- No one can be the prophet more than once in a deal.
- At least two other players must still be in play.

The prophet takes over the dealer's functions (telling players if moves are legal or not), and the dealer confirms or negates each decision. If a decision is negated, the prophet is deposed. If there is no prophet, an illegal play means expulsion from the game once 30 cards have been played to the mainline. If there is a prophet, expulsions start once 20 cards have been added to the mainline following the declaration.

Scoring

Every player scores a point for each card left in the hand of the player with the most cards and loses a point for each card in his own hands. A player with no cards in hand wins four points, while the prophet scores a bonus point for every card played to the mainline and two points for each card on any sideline since the declaration.

The dealer scores the same as the highest-scoring player, unless there is still a prophet. If so, the dealer counts the number of cards played since the declaration and doubles the total. If this is less than the highest score, the dealer scores that instead. If the game ends before all players have dealt, those concerned score an extra 10 points each.

Conclusion

Play ends and scores are calculated when a player is out of cards, or all, bar the prophet, have been expelled.

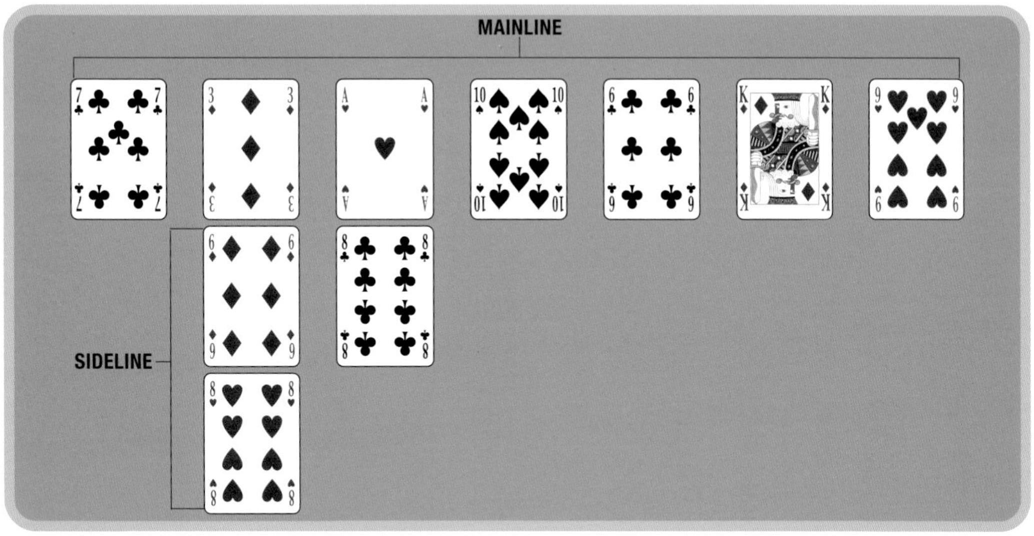

Left: An example of a very straightforward rule, soon cracked by the participating players. Cards must progress in the suit order of Clubs, Diamonds, Hearts, Spades.

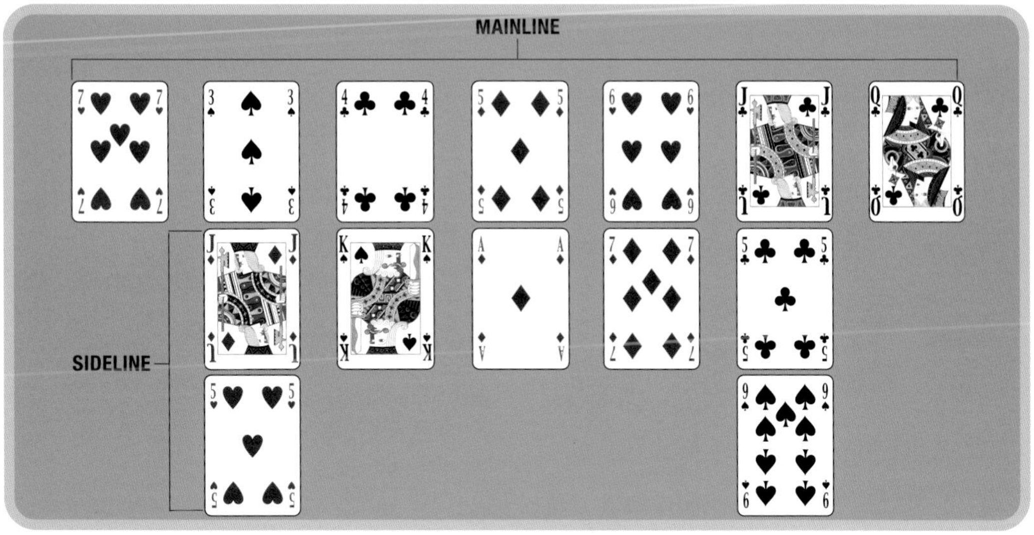

Left: A possible layout on the table during a game of Eleusis. The rule is that, after the first card, a card of the opposite colour must be played next, followed by one of the same colour in sequence. After this, any card of the opposite colour must be played, again followed by a card of the same colour in sequence. Cards breaking this rule are placed in a sideline until the correct card is laid.

Pope Joan

How this game came to be named after the legendary 13th century female pope is unknown. Traditionally, it was played with a special circular staking board with eight compartments labelled Ace, King, Queen, Jack, Game, Pope (9♦), Matrimony (King and Queen of trumps) and Intrigue (Queen and Jack of trumps). The layout is easy to replicate on paper. Each player starts with a specified number of chips or counters (at least 20).

You will need: 51 cards; no Jokers; 8♦ removed; gambling chips/counters; paper and pen

Card ranking: See 'Play and Scoring', below

Players: Three to eight

Ideal for: 10+

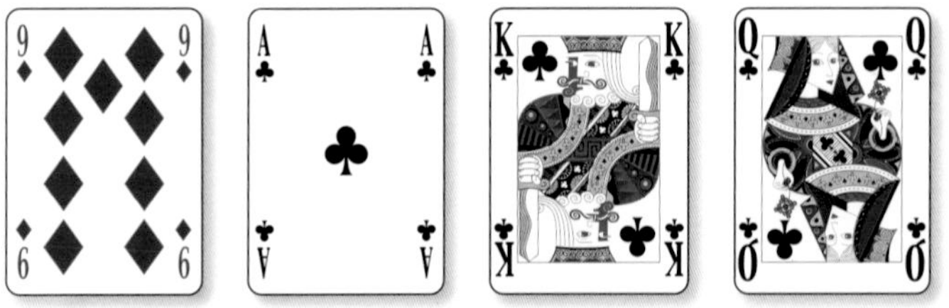

Above: Assuming Clubs are trumps, whoever plays the Ace wins the contents of the Ace compartment of the staking board. The same applies to the Queen and Jack, in their respective compartments. Whoever plays the 9♦ (the Pope) wins the contents of the Pope compartment. Playing the King and Queen of trumps in succession wins the chips in Matrimony, while playing a successive Queen and Jack wins Intrigue.

Object

To be the first player to run out of cards and also to win the most chips.

The Deal

The dealer starts by 'dressing the board' which means six chips must be put into the compartment that is labelled Pope, two chips are put into the compartments of Matrimony and Intrigue, and one in each of the other compartments. The cards are then dealt singly to each player, a spare hand also being dealt.

The last card of this hand is turned up for trumps. If it is Pope, Ace, King, Queen or Jack, the dealer wins the contents of the appropriate compartment. The hand plays no further part in the game.

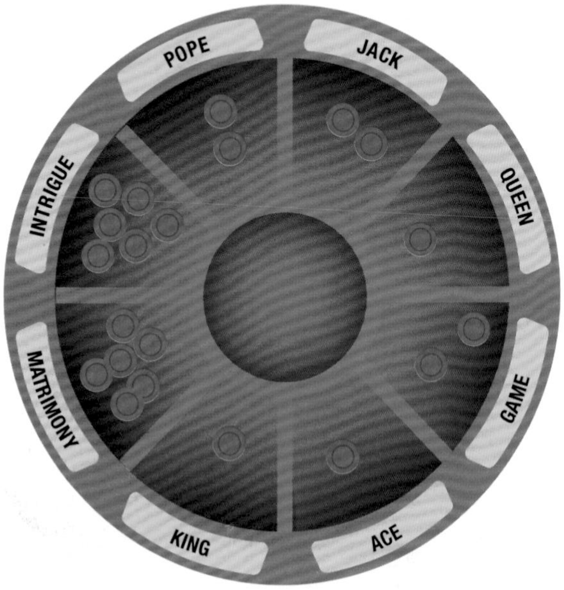

Above: Pope Joan is played on a special staking board with eight different compartments to accommodate the various betting chips, although a makeshift 'board' can easily be reconstructed using paper.

Play and Scoring

The player to the dealer's left leads with the lowest card of any suit in his hand. Whoever holds the next higher card of the same suit plays it, and so on, until the sequence cannot be continued. An Ace, for instance, is a natural stop card since it is the highest card in the game. Or, the card required may be in the spare hand, or may have been played already. The cards are played face up to the table, where they stay until the end of the game. The last to play starts a new sequence, again with the lowest card held of a suit of his choice.

Whoever plays the Ace, King, Queen or Jack of trumps, or Pope, immediately wins the contents of the relevant compartment. If the Jack and Queen of trumps are played in succession, their player wins Intrigue. Playing the Queen and King of trumps wins Matrimony, while playing all three wins both compartments.

Conclusion

The first person to play the last card from his hand, wins the game. The winner scoops the contents of the Game compartment and receives a chip for each card still held in hand from the other players, although a player holding an unplayed Pope (9♦) does not have to pay this. Any unclaimed stakes are carried forward to the next deal.

President

Possibly originating in China, President has several names and many variations. The aim is to be the first player to get rid of all one's cards, so becoming the President. The last player left in is the Donkey. The game's peculiarities include rules governing not only where players should sit, but also what they sit on. In most versions of the game, suits are irrelevant.

You will need: 52 cards, in some versions two Jokers are added as wild cards

Card ranking: Two, highest, then Ace down to Three. If the Jokers are added, they outrank all other cards

Players: Four to seven

Ideal for: 14+

Object

To get rid of all one's cards before anyone else.

The Deal

All the cards are dealt singly and the game proceeds clockwise around the table.

Play

The player to the dealer's left leads, or, alternatively, the player holding the 3♣. This person leads either a single card or a set of cards of equal rank (for example, three Fives). The others can either pass or play the same number of cards as the preceding player – and all of the same rank, which must be be higher than the ones previously played (for example, three Sixes).

The round continues until, after a play, the other players all pass. The last to play may not play again, but must turn, face down, all the cards that have been played, and then lead to the next round. If he has no more cards left, the lead moves round to the next player who has not run out of cards. Play stops when all bar one of the players have run out of cards.

The first player to run out of cards becomes the President, the next player the Vice-President and so on. The player who is left with a card or cards still in hand is the Donkey. At this point, the President shifts to the most comfortable seat, and the Vice-President to the next most comfortable one. Other players sit according to their winning or losing status, while the Donkey sits to the President's right (on the least comfortable chair) and the Vice-President to the left.

The Donkey now becomes dealer, dealing the first card to the President. Once the deal has been completed, the Donkey and the President exchange a card, the Donkey giving the President the highest card in his hand and getting back an unwanted one. The President leads to the next round.

In other versions of the game, the names given to players vary. At one time in Europe, King, Nobleman, Poorman and Beggar were popular, as were Boss, Foreman, Worker and Bum. In other versions, players are meant to wear appropriate items of headgear.

Scoring and Conclusion

Two points are scored for becoming the President, one for becoming Vice-President; other players score nothing. The first person to score 11 points is the overall winner.

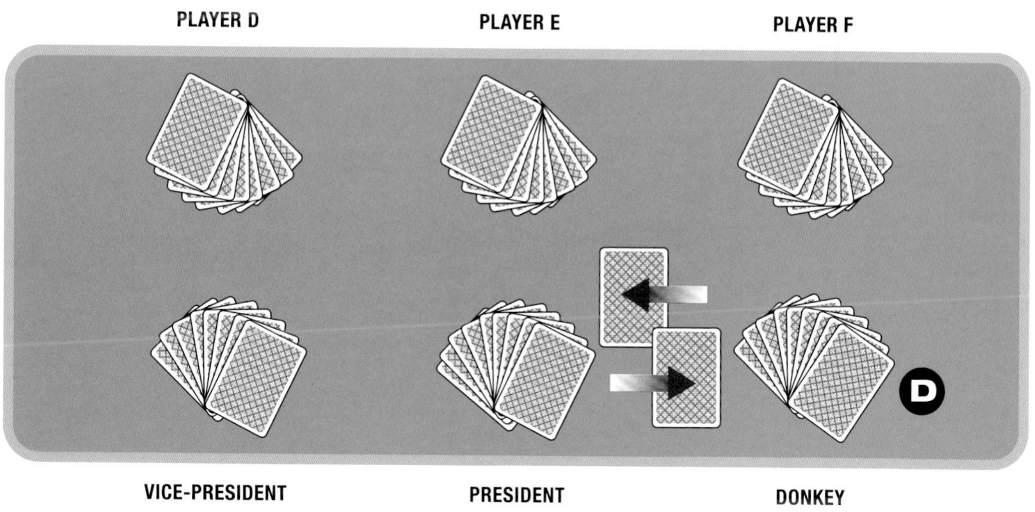

Above: In this scenario, the 7♦ has been laid, so the next player must lay an Eight or higher.

Left: After a deal, the Donkey gives his highest card to the President, in exchange for an unwanted one.

Zheng Shangyou

In Chinese, this name roughly means 'Struggling Upstream', but in Britain it has been christened Pits, since the losing players become 'pit dwellers'. It is related to several other Eastern games, such as Big Two, also from China, the Japanese game of Dai Hin Min, and Tien Len from Vietnam.

You will need: 52 cards and two distinguishable Jokers

Card ranking: When laying single cards or a set, the red Joker is highest, followed by the black, the Twos, then Ace down to Three. For single and multiple sequences, Ace is highest, Three lowest. For Twos and Jokers, see below under 'Wild Cards'

Players: Four or more play as individuals. There is also a partnership version

Ideal for: 14+

Object

To be the first or second player to get rid of all one's cards. Players drop out as they lose their cards until only the losing player remains with cards in hand.

The Deal

The first player to deal is chosen at random, the next to deal being the loser of the previous hand. The dealer shuffles the cards, places them face down on the table and draws the top card. This is followed by the player to the right. The process continues anti-clockwise around the table until the pack is exhausted.

Play

The dealer leads the first of a number of rounds of play. He may lead using any of the following patterns:

- A single card.
- A set of two or more cards of the same rank.
- A single sequence of three or more cards of consecutive rank.
- A multiple sequence (this consists of equal numbers of cards of each of three or more consecutive ranks – for example, 55, 66, 77 or JJJ, QQQ, KKK).

Although suits are generally irrelevant, any single suited sequence is better than any mixed suited one of the same length. If two sequences are mixed, the higher ranking one is the better.

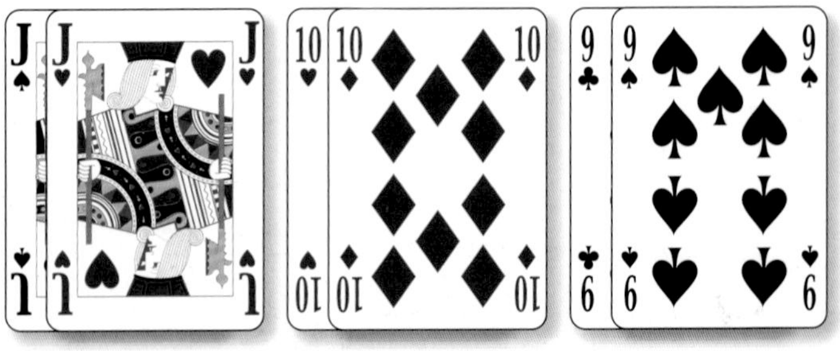

Above: A multiple sequence – three paired cards of consecutive rank. This combination would beat any pair, set or single sequence.

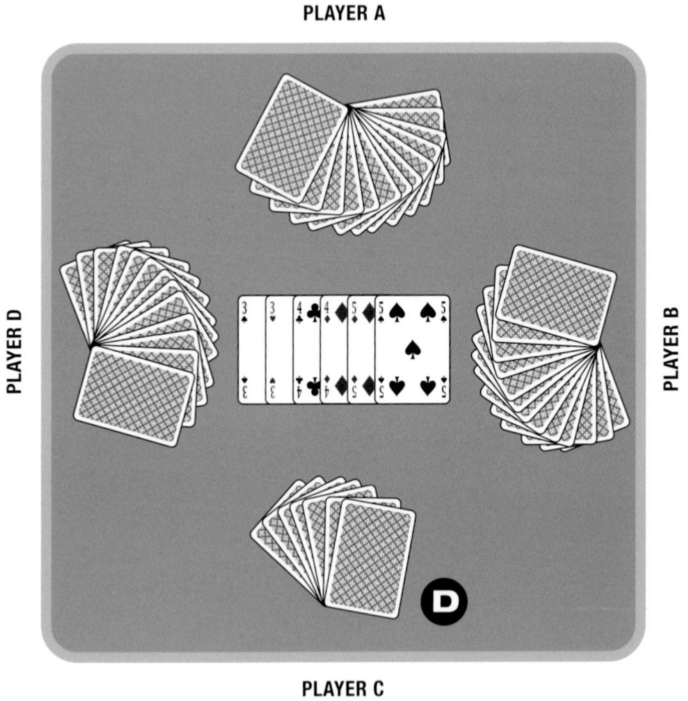

Above: The dealer has laid a multiple sequence – three paired cards of consecutive rank – thus getting rid of six cards.

Each player now has to decide whether to pass or to play. There is no penalty for passing even if a play could be made – a player can re-enter the game when his turn to play comes round again. The next player must play the same number of cards as there were in the original lead. The cards must also form the same pattern and have to outrank the cards that were in the preceding play. For example, a pair can be followed only by a higher pair, a single sequence by a single sequence of the same length, but with a higher-ranking top card, and so on.

Tactically, the highest priority is to get rid of the low cards as quickly as possible. It is probably best to avoid leading high cards unless, by doing so, a player can see a sure, safe way of getting rid of all his cards. Often, players holding long sequences find it better to split them up and play them as two or more sequences.

Play goes on until all, bar one, of the players opts to pass in turn. At this point, the last to play turns down all the played cards, which are gathered up and set aside. He then starts the game again by leading with a new playable combination. If that player has no cards left, then the lead passes to the right.

Wild Cards

Subject to certain restrictions, Jokers and Twos can be played as wild cards to stand for any lower cards. A set containing wild cards loses to an equally ranked natural or pure set. Twos cannot be played in single sequences at all. Jokers can stand in for any card from Three to Ace, but a single sequence reliant on a Joker or Jokers can be beaten by a natural or pure sequence. This also applies to multiple sequences. Although Twos are valid wild cards, they cannot stand for all the cards of a particular rank. At least one must be a natural card or a Joker. For example, 55, 62, 77 is legal, but 55, 22, 77 is not.

Scoring and Conclusion

The first player to run out of cards wins that particular hand and scores two points, while the second player to run out of cards, the runner-up, scores one point.

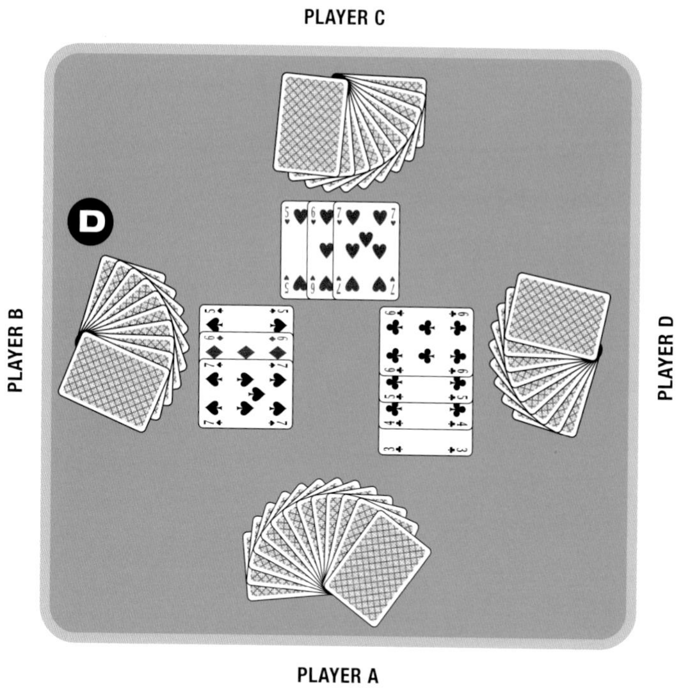

Above: Player B has a mixed sequence of three cards, but Player C beats this with a three-card sequence in the same suit. Player D, however, tops this in turn with a four-card sequence, putting the onus on Player A to lay a higher combination or pass.

No other player can score, although play continues until only one player is left with cards in hand. The last two players become what are known as 'the pit dwellers'. Immediately after the new deal, they must toss their highest-ranking card face up onto the table. If they hold cards of equal rank, they can decide which one of them they prefer to discard. The previous hand's winner is first to pick whichever card he prefers, leaving the second one for the runner-up. Both players then discard one unwanted card each. The second-to-bottom player picks up one of the cards first, leaving the other one for the bottom-placed loser. Play then continues.

The first player to score a total of 11 points wins a rubber. This is card parlance for the match. Typically, it consists of three games and is therefore won by the first player or partnership to win two games.

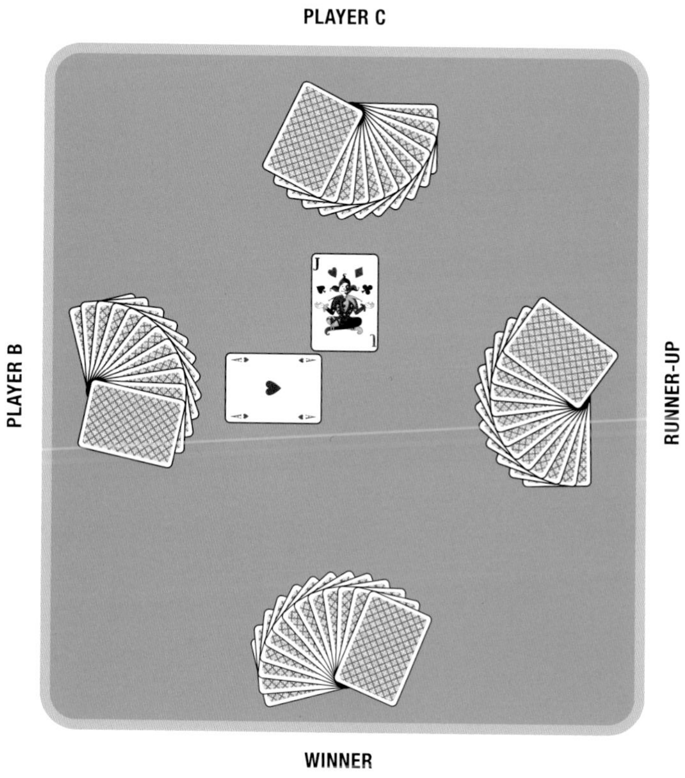

Above: The players who came last and second to last in the previous deal must toss their highest-ranking card face up on to the table. The winner of the previous hand can choose which to pick up, leaving the other card for the runner-up. Both winners discard, and the roles are now reversed, with the second-to-bottom player choosing a card first, followed by the losing player.

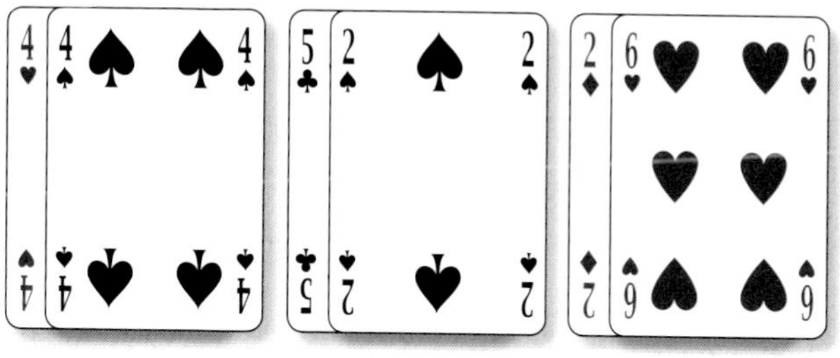

Above: A Two may represent any natural card to accompany an existing card (here Twos represent Five and Six). A Joker may represent any desired card.

Tieng Len

During the Vietnam War, the Vietnamese national card game reached the USA, where, in a slightly adapted version, it became known as Viet Cong or VC. It is a climbing game, in which Twos rank as the highest card. The highest-ranked suit is Hearts, followed by Diamonds, Clubs and Spades. Rank, however, takes precedence over suit, for example, the 8♠ would beat the 7♥.

You will need: 52 cards (two packs if more than four players)

Card ranking: Two (highest), then Ace down to Three

Players: Best for four, although it can be between two and eight

Ideal for: 14+

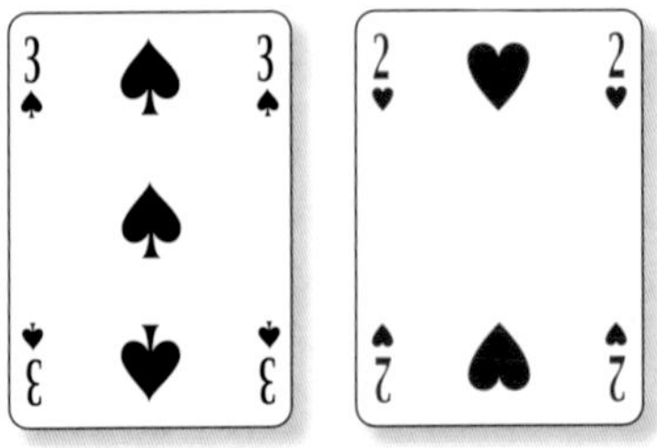

Left: The lowest single card that can be played in Tieng Len is the 3♠. The 2♥ is the highest.

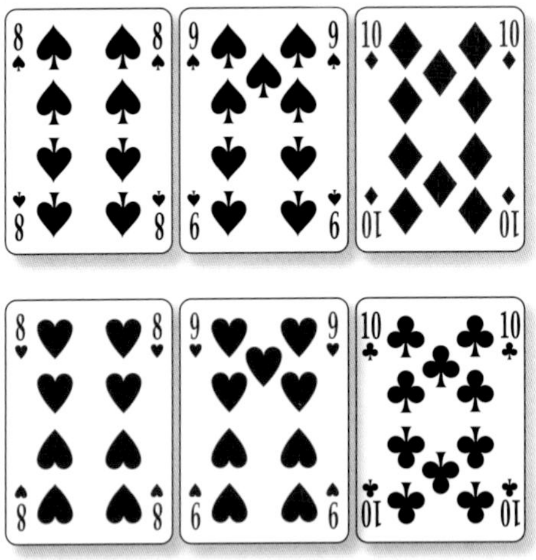

Left: The top three-card sequence would beat that on the bottom, since, when adjudicating between matching sequences, it is the highest-ranking, or top, card that is compared, and Diamonds rank higher in Tieng Len than Clubs.

Object

To get rid of your cards as quickly as possible by beating combinations of cards played by other players. The aim is to avoid being the last player with cards remaining in hand.

The Deal

The first dealer is chosen at random, after which the loser of each deal deals the next game. Cards are dealt one by one, the number depending on the number of players. When there are four, each receives 13 cards; two receive 26; and three receive 17 (the remaining card is left out of play). If more than four play, two packs are used, and the dealer must take care to ensure that an equal number of cards are dealt, and that any left over are discarded.

Play

Initially, the player holding the 3♠ plays first – if no one holds this card, it is the player holding the lowest-ranked card. The 3♠ must be played either on its own or as part of a combination. There are six valid 'combinations' that may be played:

- A single card: the lowest card is the 3♠, while the highest is the 2♥.
- A pair (two cards of the same rank).
- A triplet (three cards of the same rank).
- A quartet (four cards of the same rank).
- A sequence (three or more cards of consecutive rank).
- A double sequence (three or more pairs in which the cards rank consecutively, for example, 33, 44, 55). A sequence cannot 'turn the corner' between Two and Three because Twos are high and Threes low.

In two combinations of the same type, the highest-ranked card in them determines which of the two is the better. Each player now has to play to beat the previously played card or combination. If a single card is led, only single cards can be played; if a pair, only pairs; and so on. Playing a triplet, therefore, will not beat a pair. Nor will playing a five-card sequence beat a four-card one. A pair consisting of the 7♥ and 7♠ beats one consisting of the 7♣ and 7♦, because Hearts are ranked higher as a suit than are Diamonds. Similarly, 8♠, 9♠, 10♦ beats 8♥, 9♥, 10♣, because it is the Tens that are being compared and Diamonds rank higher than Clubs.

Generally, a combination can only be beaten by one of the same type. However, there are four specific exceptions involving beating Twos, as indicated on the opposite page.

Passing is allowed, even if a player, in fact, could play a card or cards. However, if a player passes, he must continue to pass throughout that round of play. Play continues around the table, omitting players who have passed until another player makes a play that no one else can beat. When this happens, all played cards are set aside and the player whose play was unbeaten starts play again.

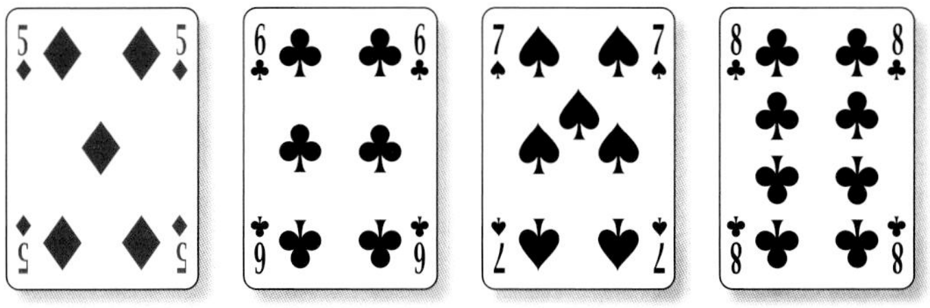

Above: If a four-card sequence is laid, then the next player must also lay a four-card sequence to beat it, topped either by the 8 (Hearts being the highest-ranked suit) or by a Nine.

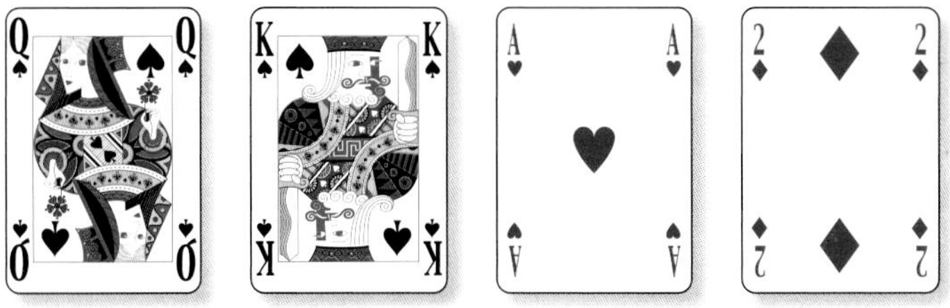

Above: A four-card sequence, topped by a Two, is the highest-ranking denomination in Tieng Len.

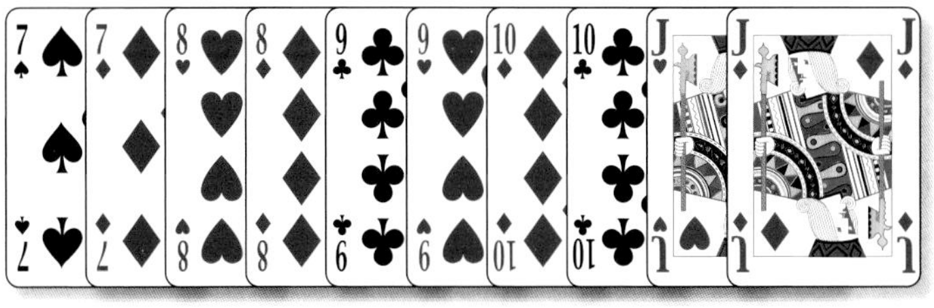

Above: To beat a triplet of Twos requires a double sequence of five, such as the above, a very rare combination.

Beating Twos

There are four exceptions to the rule concerning the play of similar combinations. These all involve beating the play of one or more Twos, the highest-ranked card, as follows:

- A single Two is beaten by a quartet.
- A single Two is beaten by a double sequence of three (for example: 55, 66, 77).
- A pair of Twos is beaten by a double sequence of four (for example: 33, 44, 55, 66).
- A triplet of Twos are beaten by a double sequence of five (for example: 33, 44, 55, 66, 77, 88).

Conclusion

As players run out of cards, they drop out of play. When it comes to their turn to lead, this passes to the next player to the left around the table still with cards in hand. Play ends when only one player has any cards remaining. He is the loser and has to pay a previously agreed stake to each of the other players.

Variants

Variants of Tieng Len are played in the USA under the name of Viet Cong. The rules vary slightly, as follows:

- A player with four Twos automatically wins the game.
- The player who holds the 3♠ initially must play a combination including that card.
- Twos can be included only in double sequences.
- The highest permissible card in a single sequence is an Ace. Single sequences are called straights and run from Three up to Ace.

There are also special combinations, termed slams, which can beat Twos. The rules for these are:

- A double sequence or a quartet beat one Two.
- A double sequence of five or two consecutive quartets beat a pair of Twos.
- A double sequence of seven or three consecutive quartets beat three Twos.

Another variant involves trading cards before the first lead is played. Any player can exchange any number of cards with another by mutual agreement. If there is no such agreement, the trade does not take place; if it does, a quartet of Twos does not automatically win the game.

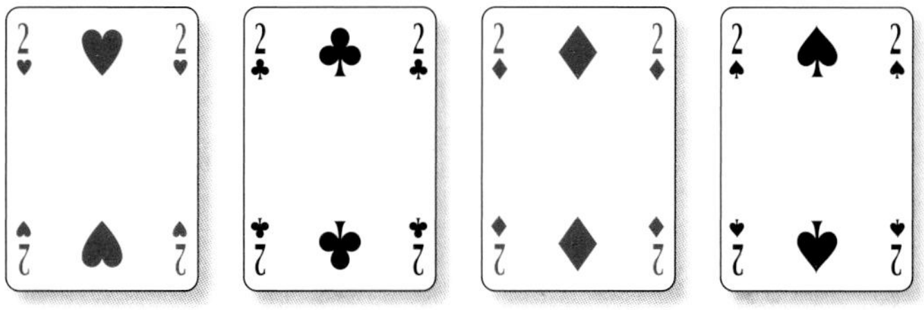

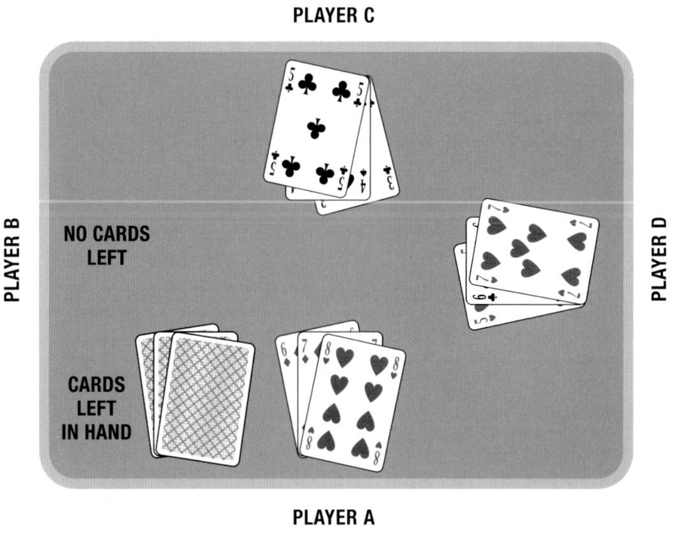

Above: Player B has got rid of his cards so sits out the rest of the hand. Player C lays down a sequence of three, which is topped by Player D and topped in turn by Player A. Players C and D now have no cards left, so Player A is the loser and has to pay an agreed stake to each of the other players.

7 | Beating Games

As a rule, games of this genre are more complex than those discussed so far in this book. In them, players generally take it in turns to be attackers and defenders. Failure to beat an attack means picking up the attacking cards, sometimes others as well, and adding them to your hand. While striving to get rid of one's cards. the primary object is usually to avoid being the last player in, rather than the first one out.

Perhaps the most celebrated example of a game of this kind is Durak, Russia's national card game since Tsarist times. It can be either a multiple or a continuous attack game, in which players take it in turn to attack and defend in what is called a bout. *Durak* means 'fool' and the title is awarded to the player left with cards in hand after all the other players have got rid of their cards.

Shed's origins are uncertain, and it has infinite variations and alternate names. It appears to be closely related to the Finnish game Paskahousu, but unlike the latter, has travelled and is now a favourite in most parts of the Western card-playing world. In all variants, the loser becomes the Shed. He has to perform any menial tasks the other players assign him until someone else succeeds to the role. Elsewhere in Europe, the beating games Rolling Stone and Sift Smoke are both popular.

Mustamaija, is another classic beating Finnish game where there is no winner, only a loser. This is the player left holding the Queen when all the other players have run out of cards. A player with the Queen also has to be careful not to play this card too early, or he may be forced to pick it up again. Its holder must therefore carefully judge the best time to play it, which is usually when he thinks that the game is about to end.

Above: An 18th-century Russian woodcut print of two card players. Russia's national card game, Durak, is the most elaborate of the beating games group.

Rolling Stone

The proverb says that 'a rolling stone gathers no moss', but the opposite can occur here. Players accumulate more cards as the game is played.

Object

To be the first player to run out of cards.

You will need: 52 cards
Card ranking: Standard
Players: The game is best for three to six
Ideal for: 7+

The Deal

Each player receives eight cards. All remaining cards are left unused.

Play

The player to the dealer's left leads. Players must follow suit, for example, with Clubs; the first player who is unable to do so takes the played cards and leads to the next round. If everyone follows suit, the highest card wins. The winner discards the trick and leads to the next one.

Scoring and Conclusion

The first player to run out of cards is the winner. He scores the value of all the cards held by other players. Number cards and Aces count at face value and the court cards count as 10 each. When playing with young children, you may prefer to start a new game after each hand.

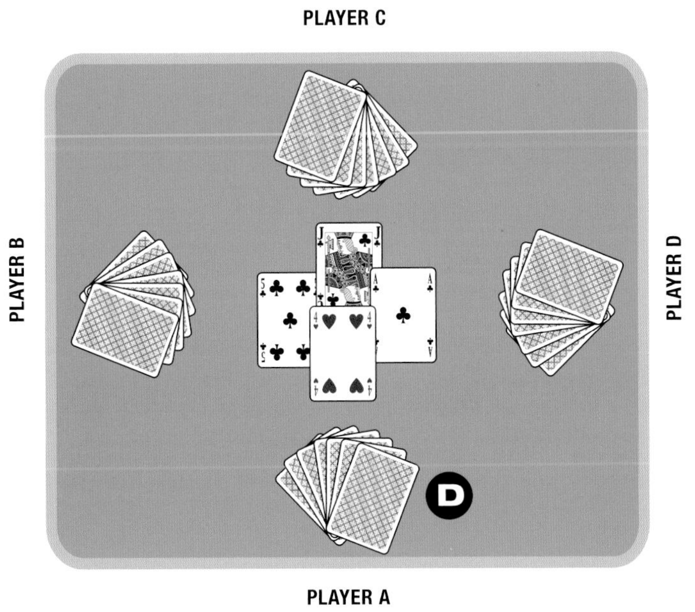

Above: Unable to follow suit after the preceding players have laid Clubs, Player A must pick up the played cards and lead to the next round.

Sift Smoke

Also known as Linger Longer and Lift Smoke, this game can be accurately classed as the negative version of Rolling Stone.

Object

To be the last player in, not first one out.

You will need: 52 cards
Card ranking: Standard
Players: Three to six
Ideal for: 7+

The Deal

Players are dealt 10 cards if three are playing, seven if four, six if five, and five if six. The last card establishes trumps.

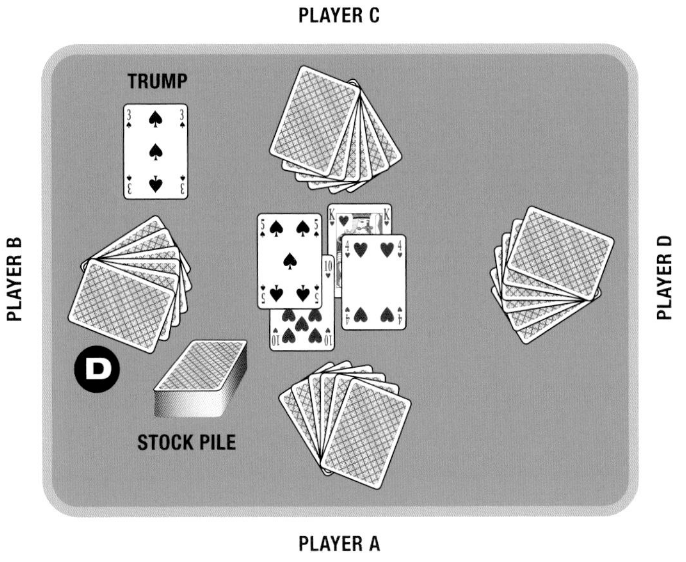

Above: Unable to follow suit, Player B can play a trump and win the trick. The cards in the trick are laid down on the table and will only be used again if new stock is needed.He picks up a card from the stock pile and adds this to his hand, which means he will have a card more than the other players.

Play and Scoring

The rules of play are the same as those of Rolling Stone, except that, if trumps are played, the highest trump wins, not the highest card of the same suit. The trick's winner draws a card from the stock. As players run out of cards, they drop out. The winner scores a point for each card in hand.

Conclusion

The last player with cards in hand wins. If the stock runs out before this, previous rounds are shuffled to form a new stock. If all players play their last card to the same round, the round's winner wins the game.

Durak

There are many versions of this celebrated Russian game, which has no winner – only a loser, or a losing side if the game is played with partnerships. One of the most popular versions of this game is Podkidnoy Durak, a game involving a rule which allows other players to join in an attack after it has started by 'throwing in' more cards of matching ranks to those that have been played.

You will need: A 36-card pack, Twos to Fives removed
Card ranking: Ace highest, down to Six, lowest
Players: Two to six; or four playing in partnerships of two
Ideal for: 10+

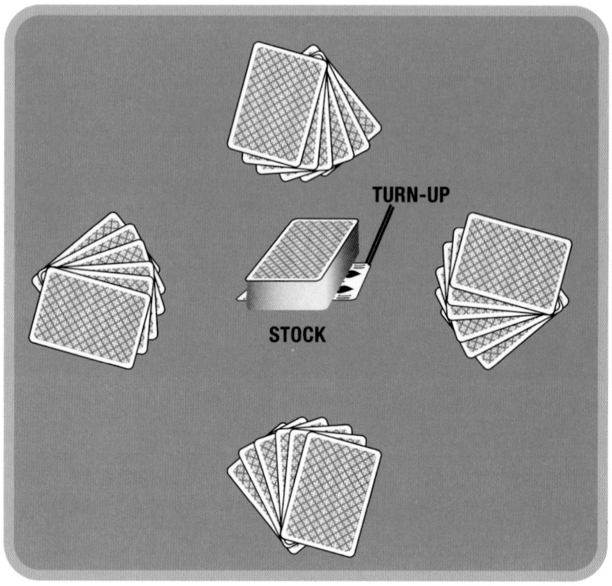

Above: Each player is dealt six cards face down, with the next card turned face up to determine trumps. The remaining cards are placed in a pile face down crosswise over the turn-up card and serve as the stock.

Object

To be the first player out of cards once the stock is exhausted, but, most importantly, to avoid becoming the *Durak*, or 'fool' with the remaining cards.

The Deal

Each of the players is dealt six cards one at a time, the next card being turned face up to determine trumps. The remaining cards are placed face down crosswise over the turn-up, so that its rank and value remain clearly visible. These cards form the stock.

Play

Initially, the player with the lowest trump (the Six of trumps or, failing a Six, the Seven, and so on) starts play. This consists of a series of bouts, in which there is an attacker, who, in this version, may be aided by the others, and a defender, who plays alone.

Below: This player has been tricked by the *Durak* (fool) into cutting the pack, so must take on the *Durak*'s role, which involves dealing and cutting cards.

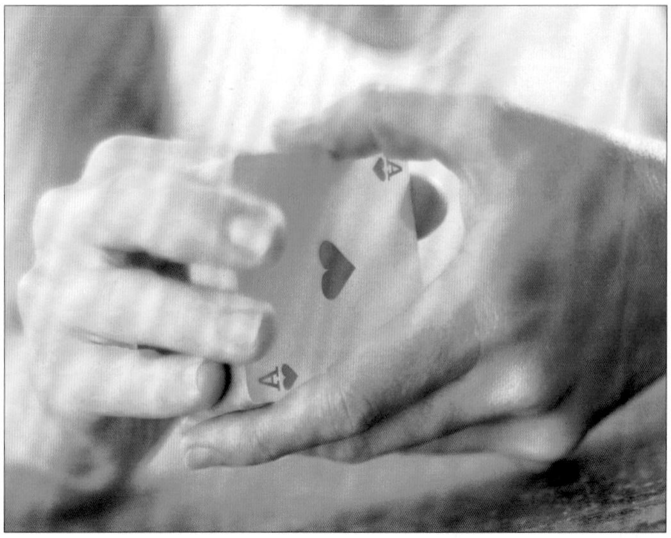

Attackers and Defenders

The first player is always the attacker, while the player to the attacker's left is always the defender. Although other players can join in an attack, they may do so only with the main attacker's permission, who must indicate whether to go ahead and play, or wait. Before deciding whether to continue with an attack, alone or with others, an attacker also has the right to ask questions regarding another player's proposed attacking cards.

The attacker starts by playing any card face up in front of the defender. To beat off the attack, the defender must play a higher card of the same suit, a trump, or a higher trump if a trump is led. If the defender cannot do this, he must take all the played cards into his hand.

Multiple Attacks

If this attack is beaten, more attacks can still be launched, subject to the following stipulations: each subsequent attack card played must be of the *same* rank (it doesn't need to be higher) as a card that has already been played by either the attacker or the defender. The maximum number of attack cards that can be played in any one bout is six. If a defender holds less than six cards before a bout starts, the maximum number of attack cards is the same as the number of cards in the defender's hand.

If a defender cannot beat an attack, he picks up the attack card, together with all the other cards played in the bout until then. All the players entitled to take part in the attack also give the defender the cards they could have played had the attack continued.

Each attack card is placed separately face up in front of the defender, who places each card played in reply on top of it, taking care to position it so that the values of both sets of cards can be seen. A successful defender becomes the new attacker. If the defence is unsuccessful, the role passes to the player to the defender's left, the next player in rotation becoming the next defender.

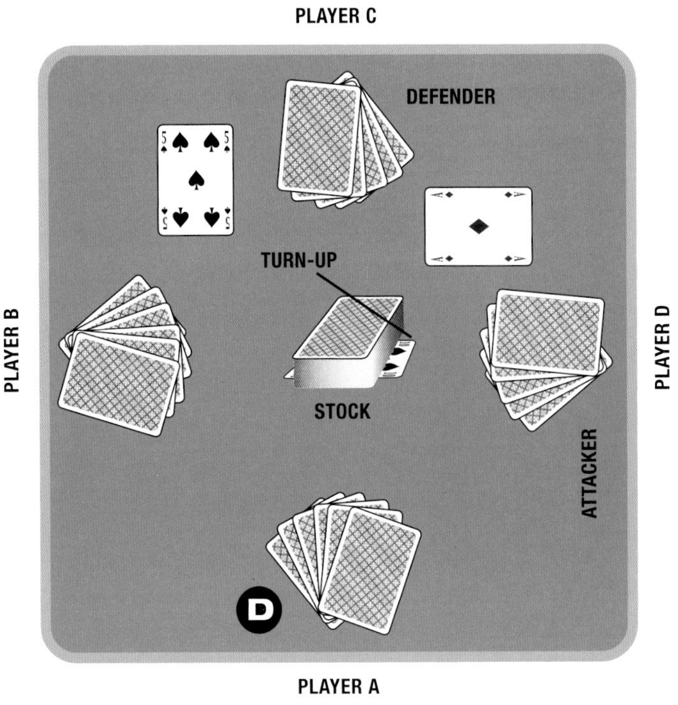

Above: The only defence against Player D's attack (A♦) is to play a trump.

Drawing From Stock

After each bout, any player left with fewer than six cards in his hand must replenish it by drawing cards from the stock. Each player in turn, starting with the attacker, takes a card from the stock until either he has six cards or the stock is exhausted with the taking of the trump turn-up. The defender draws last and does not draw if he holds six or more cards. After the stock runs out, play continues without drawing.

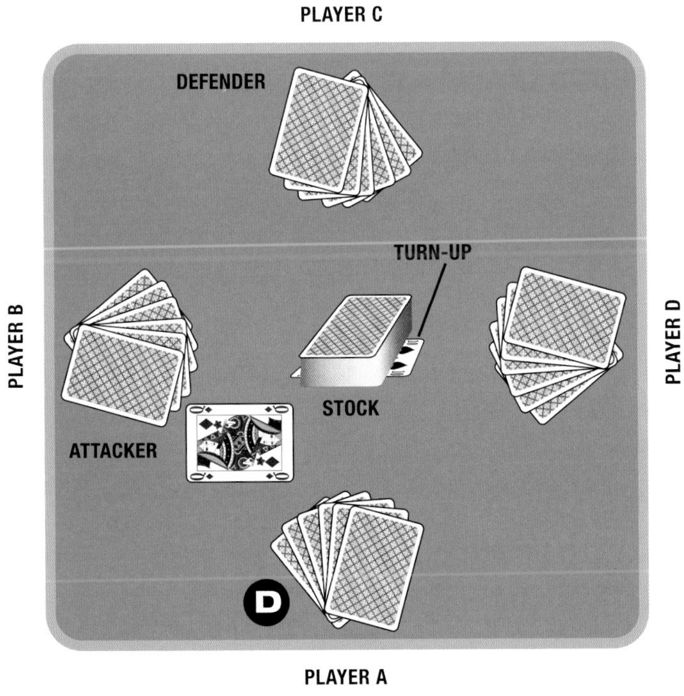

Above: A single attacker, Player B, has led the Q♦. The defender, Player C, must play a K♦ or A♦ or a trump, in this case, a Spade, to beat the attack.

If a player draws the Six of trumps, this card can be exchanged for the turned-up trump, even if another player has already drawn the turn-up, provided that play in the next bout has not yet begun.

Ending

In the individual version, as each player runs out of cards, he drops out of the game. If the defender's last card beats the attacker's last card, the result is a draw.

In a partnership, if one partner drops out, the other takes over the turn. They decide between themselves which of them will deal the next hand and become the *Durak*, or 'fool'. The other partner will then be the defender. In this scenario, it is often advantageous for the weaker player to deal first, so that the stronger one defends. He may also be able to take advantage of card etiquette.

According to the rules, only the dealer can handle the cards, which is deemed a menial task. If another player can be tricked into touching them – by cutting them, say, after the initial shuffle – that player must take over the dealer's, or *Durak's*, role.

Conclusion

Play continues until the last player remains with cards. This player still holding cards is the loser, also known as the *Durak*, or 'fool'.

Svoi Kozyri

This Russian single-attack beating game seems to have been around since the beginning of the 19th century. Its name means 'one's own trumps', which gives an immediate clue to its chief peculiarity. Before the game, each player chooses a different trump suit, cards of which can trump any other cards of any other suit.

You will need: A 36-card pack with Twos to Fives removed

Card ranking: Ace highest, down to Six, lowest

Players: Best for four

Ideal for: 14+

Object

Using trumps to avoid being the last to hold any cards.

The Deal

Before the cards are dealt, the players select their trump suits. Each player receives nine cards, dealt singly.

Play

Before play starts, the players check their hands to see if they are holding any Sixes of suits other than their personal trump suit. If they are, they give them to the player whose trump suit they belong to, which means that all the players hold at least one trump.

The player to the dealer's left leads any card face up to the table to start a play pile. The other players try to beat the top card of the pile by playing a higher card of the same suit or a personal trump, followed by a second card of their own choosing. It is not necessary to follow suit.

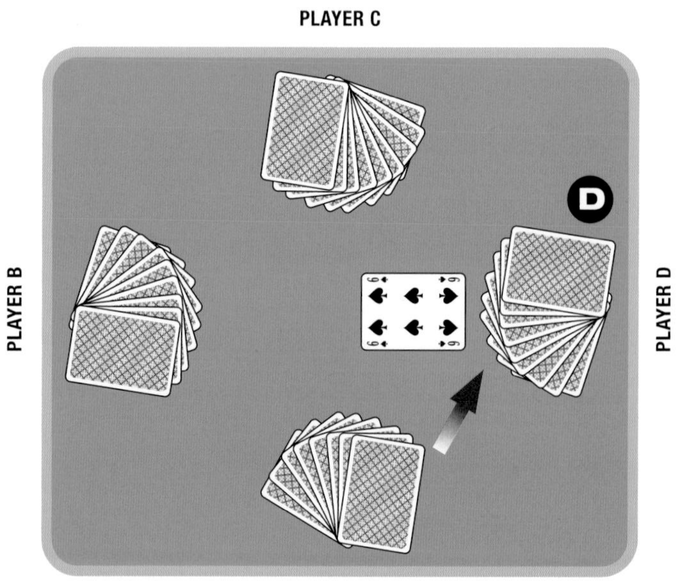

Above: At the start of play, each player who holds a Six that is not of his chosen trump suit must hand it over to whomever has chosen that suit.

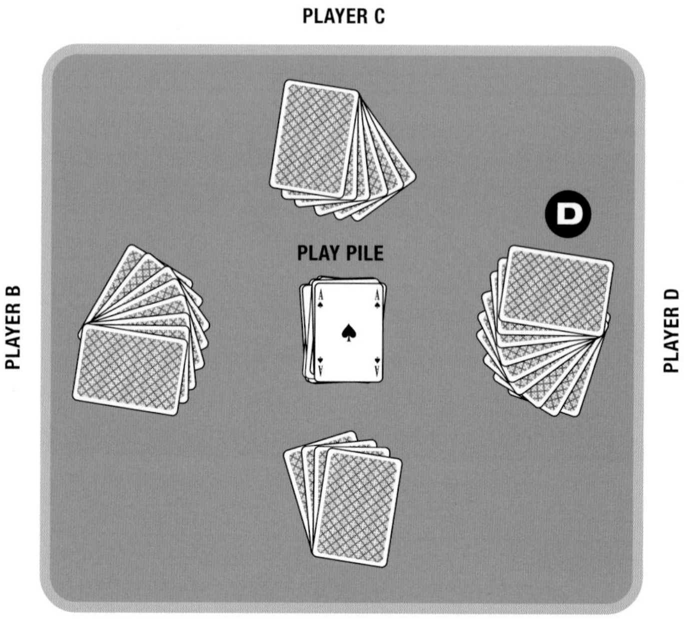

Above: The play pile is topped by an Ace, led by Player A. If this suit happens to be Player B's personal trumps, he must pick up the entire play pile. Players here hold different-length hands, having had to pick up penalty cards during play.

If a player cannot beat the top card, or elects not to do so, he has to pick up from the pile. If the top card is not one of that player's trumps, the pick-up is three cards, or the whole pile if there are fewer than three cards in it. If it is that player's trump other than the Ace, the pick-up is five cards. If it is the Ace of that player's trump, he must pick up the entire pile.

Before deciding whether to play, the player concerned is allowed to look at the cards that would have to be picked up, including the card that the next to play would have to beat. If the previous player takes the whole pile, the next to play starts a new pile. As players run out of cards, they drop out of the game.

Conclusion

The last player left holding any cards is the loser. If that player, however, has only one card left and can beat the last top card with it, the game is a draw.

Dudak

This Czech favourite (translated 'bagpipe') can trace its origins back to Durak and Svoi Kozyri, since it incorporates elements from both games. It is fairly straightforward to play, which is presumably why many children in its Bohemian homeland are said to be addicted to it.

You will need: A 32-card pack, Twos to Sixes having been removed

Card ranking: Ace highest, to Seven, lowest

Players: Best for four

Ideal for: 14+

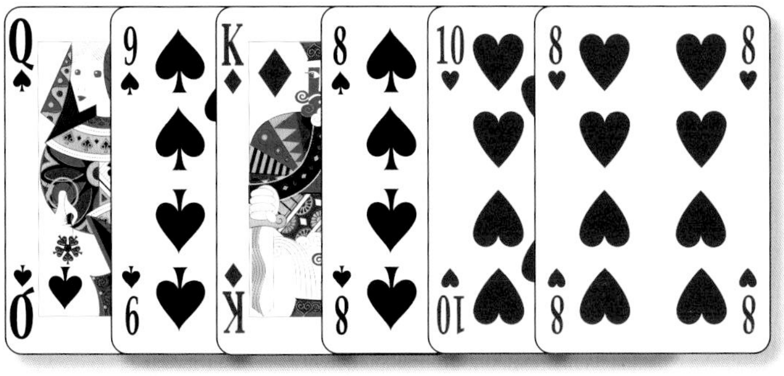

Above: With Clubs as trumps and the Q♥ topping the pick-up pile, a player holding this hand would be unable to beat or trump it. He would therefore have to pick up all the cards from the pick-up pile.

Object

The aim is to play out all of one's cards. The last player left holding a card or cards in hand is the loser.

The Deal

Each player is dealt eight cards singly from a 32-card pack.

Play

The player to the dealer's left leads, playing any card face up to start a play pile. Subsequently, each player in turn may, if possible, play two cards to the play pile. Before doing so, a player may opt to declare a suit to be personal trumps for the rest of the game. Each player will normally choose a different suit, but it is possible for two or more players to choose the same trump. However, having nominated a trump suit, a player may not change his suit for the rest of the game.

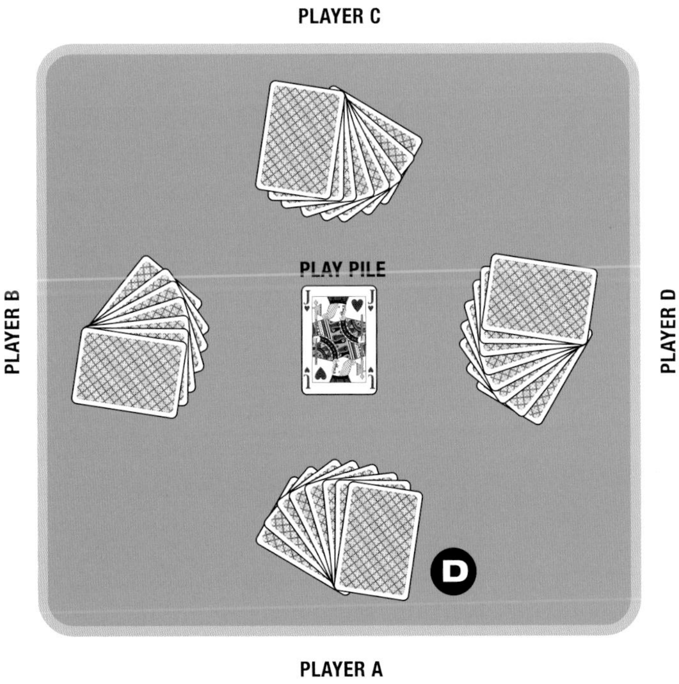

Above: Player B here, the first to play following Player A's deal, has led the J♥. Player C now must lay Q♥, K♥ or A♥, or a trump if trumps have been declared, after which he can lay a second card of his choice.

The first card to be played must be a higher card of the same suit as the top card of the pile, or a trump, if trumps have been declared. The choice of the second card is up to each player. If a player cannot beat the top card, or elects not to, he must pick it up and continue to pick up cards until one that he can beat or one which he is willing to beat, is uncovered. If the whole pile is taken, that player's turn ends and the next player starts a new pile.

If a personal trump suit has been declared, the procedure is slightly different. Rather than pick up cards one by one, the player is given no option other than to pick up the entire pile. The next to play then starts a new one.

As players play their last cards, they drop out of play. If a player goes out by playing two cards, play continues as normal. If he has only one card left and goes out by beating the top card of the pile with it, the pile is turned face up and put to the side. The next player starts a new one by playing one card, and play continues as before.

Conclusion

A round ends when just one player is left with cards in his hand. The overall winner is the one who loses fewest of an agreed number of games. Alternatively, it is the player who has not lost a game when everyone else has lost at least one.

Mustamaija

This interesting game from Finland is related to several other Scandinavian beating games, in particular the Norwegian game of Spardame ('Spade Queen'), which it closely resembles. In both games, the aim is to avoid being the player left holding the Q♠ (known as 'Black Maria') when all the other players have successfully managed to get rid of their cards.

You will need: 52 cards; no Jokers
Card ranking: Standard, except for the Q♠, which cannot beat, or be beaten, by any other card and doesn't count as a spade
Players: Two to six
Ideal for: 10+

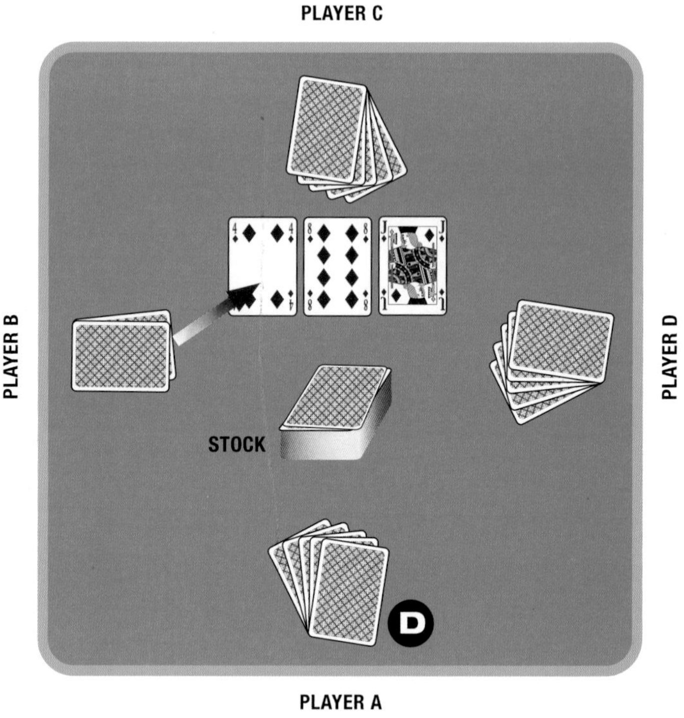

Above: Player B (the player to the dealer's left) launches the first attack. Player C must beat each of the cards with higher Diamonds or trumps in order to defend successfully. If so, all the cards are discarded. Otherwise, Player C must pick up any unbeaten cards.

Object

To avoid becoming 'Black Maria', or the loser who is left holding the Q♠.

The Deal

Each player is dealt five cards, one at a time. Those remaining are placed face down on the table as the stock.

Play

The player to the dealer's left starts the first round by playing between one to five cards of the same suit face up to the table. He may draw the necessary replacements from the stock. The cards may include the Q♠ if the other cards are spades.

Next, the dealer turns the top card of the stock face up to determine trumps. The usual convention is that Spades may not be trumps, so, if the turn-up is a Spade, the dealer places it in the middle of the stock and turns up the next card until another suit appears.

Attackers and Defenders

The player to the dealer's left is designated as the initial attacker and the player to the attacker's left as the first defender. The latter must beat as many of the attacker's cards as possible by playing a higher card of the same suit, or, if the card is from a non-trump suit, playing a trump.

The attacker's beaten cards, and the ones used to beat them, are discarded and take no further part in the game. Any of the attacker's unbeaten cards must be picked up by the defender and taken into his hand. If the defender beats all of the attacker's cards, he becomes the next attacker. If not, he forfeits the chance to attack, which passes to the player to his left, who otherwise would have been the next defender. The Q♠ can neither beat nor be beaten by any other card, and must therefore always be taken up.

Once the stock is exhausted, a new rule states that an attacker cannot lead more cards than there are in a defender's hand. As players run out of cards, they drop out of play.

Left: The Queen of Spades – a dreaded card in many betting games since the player left holding it loses the game. Known in Mustamaija as 'Black Maria', it can never be beaten, meaning that a defender is forced to pick it up and add it to his hand.

Conclusion

The last player left in, who invariably ends up holding the Q♠, is the loser, or 'Black Maria'.

Kitumaija

This unusual Finnish game is a cross between Durak and Mustamaija. The chief differences are that there are two classes of card, known as 'bound cards' and 'free cards', and permanent trump suits. Diamonds trump Spades and Hearts, but not Clubs, which are invulnerable.

You will need: 52 cards; no Jokers

Card ranking: Standard, except for the Q♠ (see under 'Play', below)

Players: Three to five

Ideal for: 10+

Object

To avoid being the player left with cards in hand, and thus the holder of the Q♠.

The Deal

Players are dealt five cards each, in packets of three and two. The dealer then deals a card face up to the table, to start the first spread. The remainder are placed face down to form the stock.

Play

Each player in turn, starting with the person to the dealer's left, must play as follows:

- If the topmost card of the spread is the Q♠, the next player must take it into hand, along with the top five cards of the spread (or as many as there are, if there are fewer than five), and end his turn.
- Otherwise, he must play a bound card – a higher card of the same suit – as the top card of the spread. If this top card is a Spade or a Heart, a Diamond can be played as trump, even if its player could have followed suit.

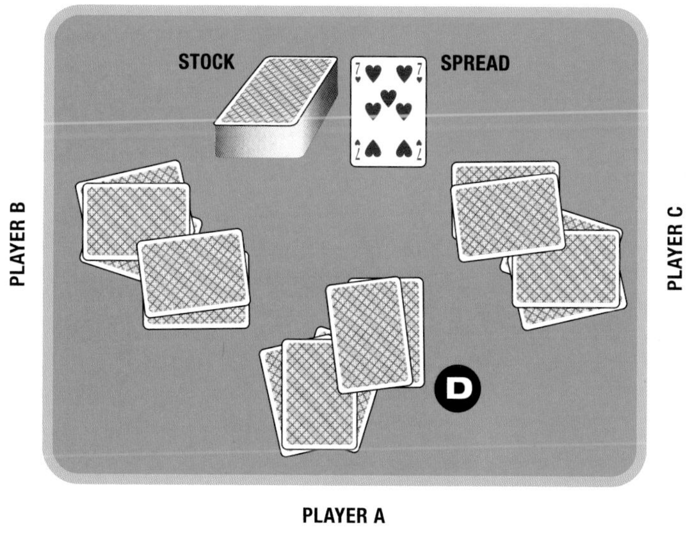

Above: Five cards are dealt to each player, first in packets of three, then in packets of two. The next card is turned face up in the centre, to start what is known as the spread (i.e. the play pile). It is placed beside the stock.

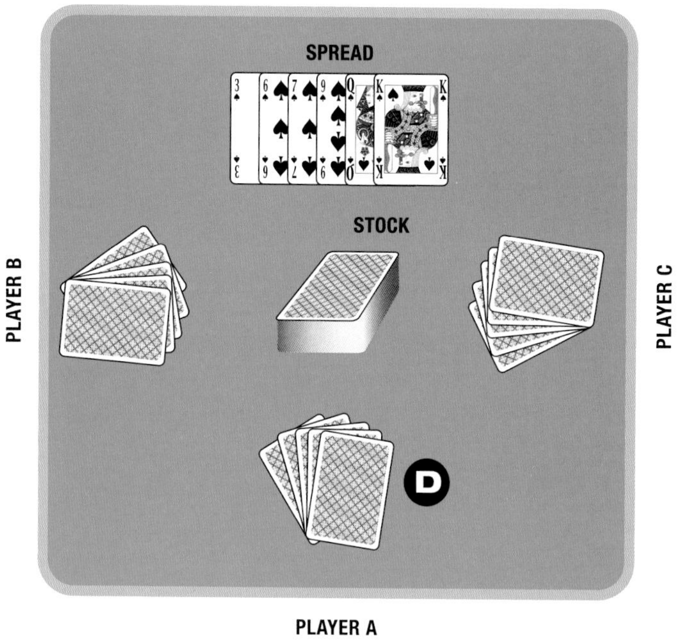

Above: The next player must beat the King with an A♣, or a trump (Diamond) of any rank. If not, he must pick up the spread's first three cards.

- The bound card must be followed by a free card – this is a card of its player's choosing. The Q♠ can be played only as a free card, not as a bound one. Any player who cannot beat the top card has to pick up the first three cards of the spread and take them into hand.
- Until the stock run outs, the players replenish their hands from it, so they always have five cards in hand.

Once the stock has run out, no further free cards may be played. However, to give the Q♠ holder the chance to get rid of it, many players opt to ignore this rule and continue playing bound and free cards, as before. The alternative is to make an exception in the case of the Q♠. Players drop out as they run out of cards.

Conclusion

The last player left in, who invariably will be the player left holding the Q♠, is the loser.

Hörri

This game is the Finnish equivalent of Durak. Many Finnish card games are related to Russian ones, owing to the fact that Finland was a province of the Tsarist Empire up until the 1917 Revolution.

You will need: 52 cards; no Jokers

Card ranking: Standard, except for the Q♠, which has no rank

Players: Two to five

Ideal for: 14+

Object

To avoid being the player left with cards in hand, and thus the holder of the Q♠.

The Deal

Instead of dealing cards as normal, the entire pack is placed face down in the centre of the table to form the stock. The dealer then takes the top eight cards of the stock and arranges them face up around it.

The Draw

Each player in turn draws a card from the stock. Diamonds trump Spades and Hearts, but not Clubs, which are invulnerable. If a Spade, Heart or Club is drawn, and the turn-up cards include a lower-ranking card of the same suit, the player takes all these cards into his hand. If there is no such card, the drawn card is replaced and the next player draws. If the next player draws a Diamond, and the turn-up cards include a lower-ranking Diamond or any Spade or Heart, all of these are added to the player's hand.

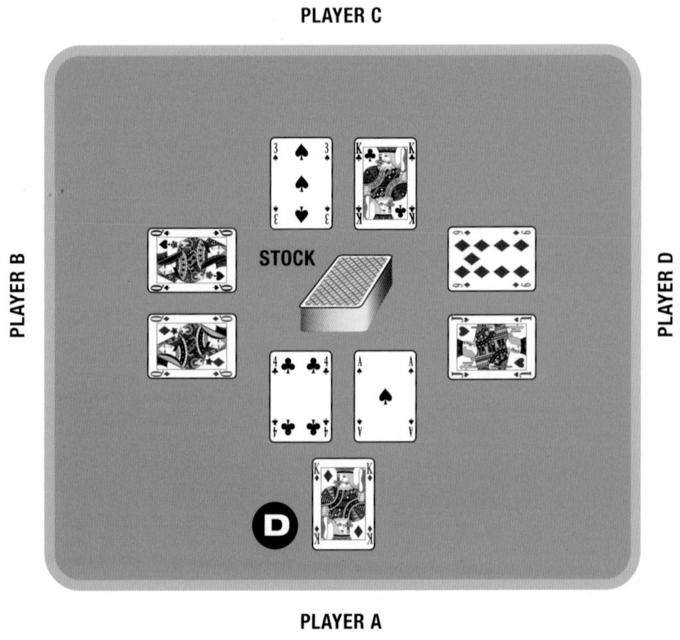

Above: Player A draws the K♦. It is higher than the 9♦ and, as Diamonds trump Spades and Hearts, he must also take the 3♠, the A♠ and the J♥.

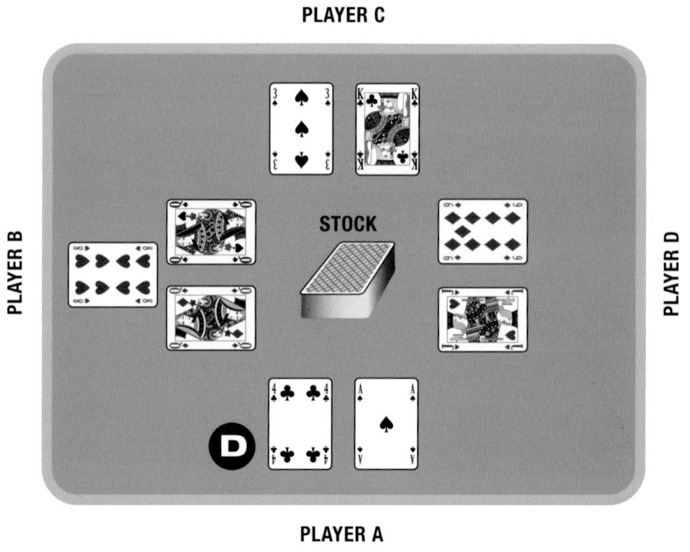

Above: Player B has drawn the 8♥. Since there are no lower Hearts among the turn-ups, the card is replaced and it is Player C's turn to draw.

Once the stock has been exhausted, the last player to take two cards adds any remaining turn-up cards to his hand. Naturally, the players end up with hands of varying length. Some may have no cards at all, in which case they have to sit out play.

Play

The player holding the 2♠ plays it face up to the table to start a spread of discards. Each player tries to lead a higher-ranking card of the same suit as the top card, or, if the top card is a Heart or Spade, trump it with a Diamond.

If unable or unwilling to play, the player concerned takes the bottom card of the spread and adds it to his hand. If a player 'completes' the spread – that is, plays a card that makes the number of cards the spread contains the same as the number of players – the spread is turned face down and a new one started.

Conclusion

The last player left in – who invariably will be holding the Q♠ – is the loser.

Skitgubbe

This is a popular Swedish game, originally for three players. Play is divided into two phases. Skitgubbe means 'dirty old man' (in the sense of unwashed), and is the name given to the loser.

You will need: 52 cards
Card ranking: Standard
Players: Three
Ideal for: 14+

Object

To collect, in the first phase of the game, cards that can be discarded as quickly as possible in the second phase.

The Deal

Each player is dealt three cards. The remainder are placed face down in a pile on the table to form the stock.

Play

This consists of tricks played by two players at a time, beginning with the two non-dealers. There is no need to follow suit – the highest card takes the trick. If the player who led wins the trick, he leads again with the same player; otherwise, the next trick is contested by the other two players, and so on. Cards from the trick are placed face-down in front of the player who wins them.

If the cards are equal, this is a *Stunza* (bounce). The cards are placed face up on the table, both players draw a card from the stock and the same player leads again. This continues until one of the players takes a trick.

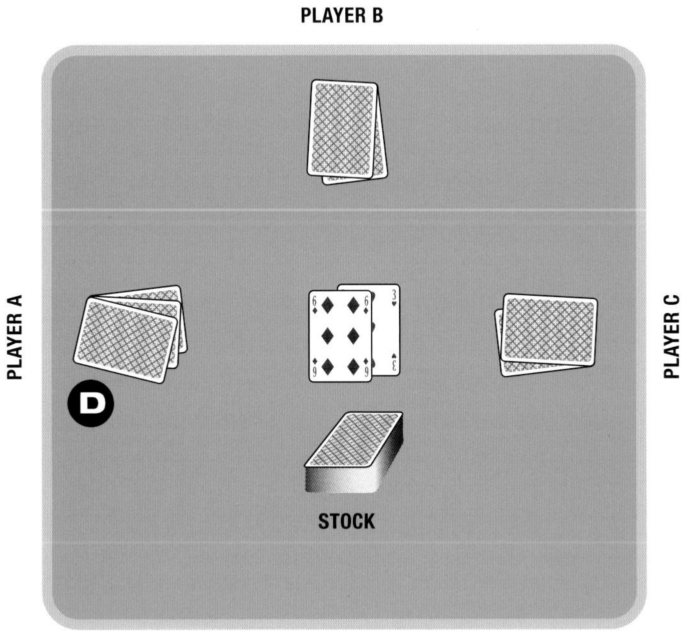

Above: Player B lays the 3♥, but Player C tops this with the 6♦. Player C must place both cards face-down on the table next to him and lay a fresh card to Player A.

The trick winner takes all the cards that have been played (including those in the *Stunza*), turns them face down in front of himself and leads to the next trick.

Each player draws a card from the stock after playing. Rather than playing from hand, a player can opt to turn up the top card of the stock and play that instead.

Left: If two cards of the same rank, such as these two Kings, are played in the first phase of the game, this is known as a *Stunza*. The cards are placed face up on the table, and both players draw a card from the stock, beginning a new trick. The trick winner takes all the played cards, and begins a new trick.

Once the stock runs out, play carries on for as long as possible. Then, all three players use the cards they have won, together with any cards they may have left in hand, as their playing hands. The aim is to play out all one's cards. The player who drew the last card from the stock leads, its suit determining trumps. Now all three players play in turn, not two at a time as in phase one.

The leader may play a single card, or a sequence of two or more cards in the same suit. For example, the player concerned could elect to lead a Two and a Three or a Three, Four and Five, and so on, provided that whatever cards he decides to play are all of the same suit.

In order to take the trick, the cards that the opposing players play must be better – of the same suit but higher in rank – or, if a non-trump suit has been led, they must be a trump or trump sequence. A player may play trumps even if he is able to follow suit. The winner of the trick leads to the next.

A player who cannot play a better card picks up the last cards to be played. The player to the left then leads.

Conclusion

The last player left with cards in hand is the loser.

SHED

Also known as Karma and Palace, among other names, Shed's origins are a mystery. What is clear, however, is its international acceptance.

You will need: 52 cards, with two Jokers added	
Card ranking: Two (highest), then Ace down to Two again, since Twos rank both high and low	
Players: Two to six	
Ideal for: 10+	

OBJECT

To avoid being the last player left holding cards.

THE DEAL

The addition of two Jokers to the pack is optional for up to five players, but essential for six. The dealer deals three cards face down to each player. These are the down-cards. Three cards are then dealt face up – the up-cards – and finally three cards to hand. Any remaining cards are placed face down to form the stock.

Before play starts, each player has the option to exchange any of the cards in hand with the up-cards. No one may look at their down-cards until they are played.

PLAY AND CONCLUSION

The first player to declare a Three in his hand leads. He plays any number of cards of the same rank face up to start the discard pile and then replenishes his hand from the stock to keep a minimum of three cards. Each player in clockwise turn must then play a card or cards of equal or higher rank to beat the pile's top card. If a player cannot discard, he picks up the discard pile and the next player starts a new one.

A Joker may be played at any time, and simply reverses the direction of play. Twos rank high and low, so one or more may be played at any time – the next player in turn may play any other rank. Tens can be played on any card, in which case, the discard pile is removed from play and the same player gets another turn to start a new one. The discard pile is also removed from play if a set of four cards of the same rank is played.

As players' hands run out, they switch to playing from their up-cards. If a player is forced to pick up the discard pile, he reverts to playing from hand. Once the up-cards are played, the down-cards are played (blind) one at a time. If the flipped card does not beat the top card on the discard pile, the discard pile is picked up. As players run out of cards, they drop out of play.

The winner is the first to discard the last down card and the loser is the last left holding cards – 'the shed'.

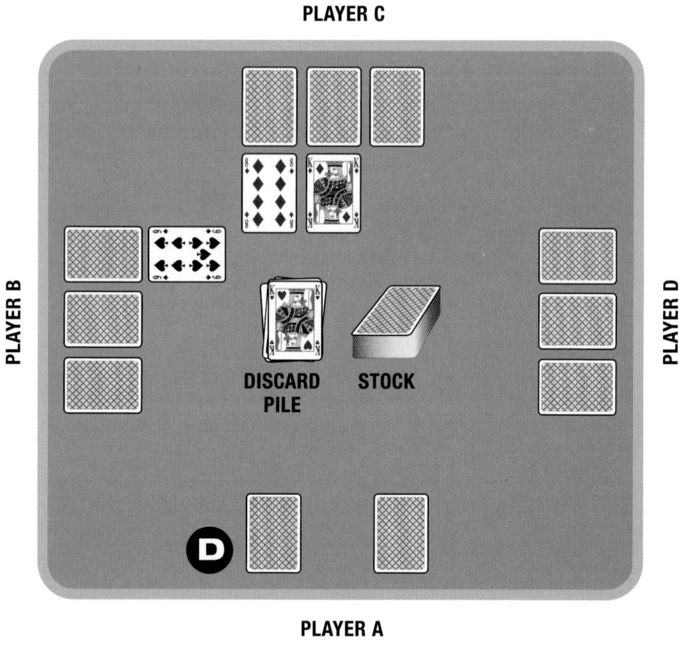

Above: Players B's up-card is not of equal rank or higher to Player A's K♥, so he must pick up the discard pile and revert to playing in hand.

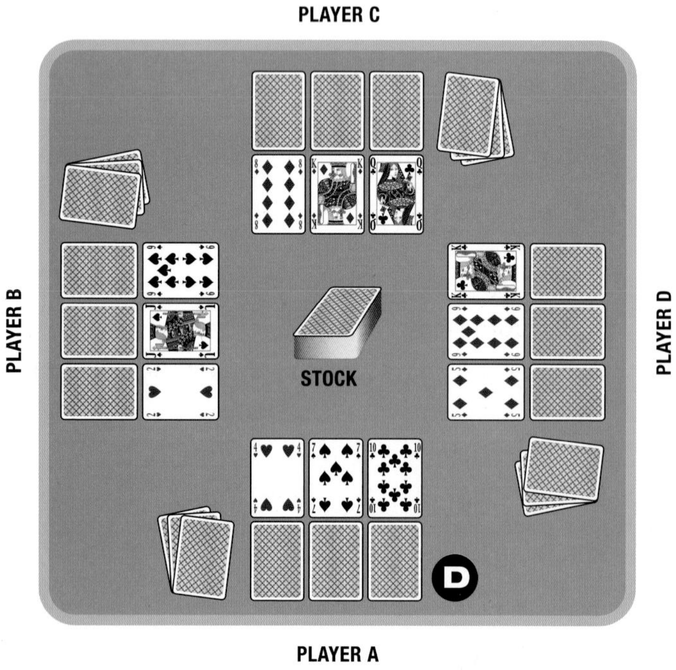

Above: Three cards are dealt face down and three face up to each player. Three are then dealt to each player's hands and the remainder of the cards are placed in the centre to form the stock.

Paskahousu

Verbal declarations and challenges are an integral part of play of this Finnish game. An ability to bluff successfully and a sharp card sense are essential qualities for would-be winners.

You will need: 52 cards
Card ranking: None
Players: Three or more, but ideally four or five
Ideal for: 14+

Object

To bluff, and avoid being the last left holding cards.

The Deal

Each player receives five cards, and the remaining cards are placed face down to form the stock.

Play

Starting with the player to the dealer's left, each player can pass, play a card face down claiming it to be a Three (whether or not truthfully), or draw the top card from the stock and play it sight unseen, making the same claim. If everyone passes, the process starts again, although the first discard is now claimed to be a Four.

Declarations and Challenges

Each player in turn plays a card or sequence of cards face down to the discard pile, declaring them to be of equal or higher rank than that of the cards previously announced. This may or may not be true. However, before the next player plays, the most recent declaration can be challenged, in which case, the cards in question must be turned face up.

If the declaration was true, the challenger must add the whole discard pile to his hand. If not, the challenged player must pick up. In either case, play passes to the player to the left of the player who was challenged.

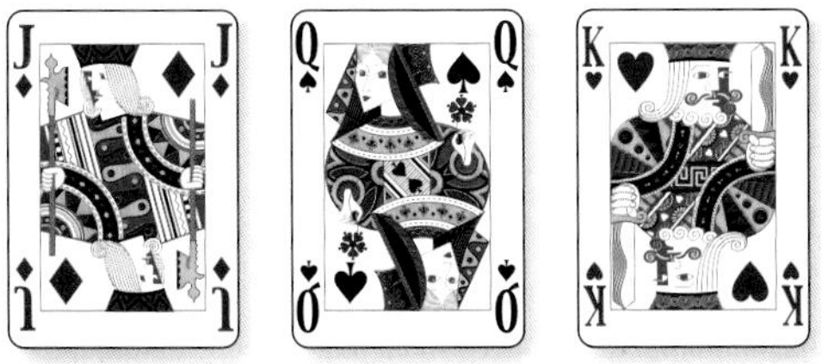

Left: Jacks, Queens and Kings cannot be declared unless the previous declaration was Eight or higher.

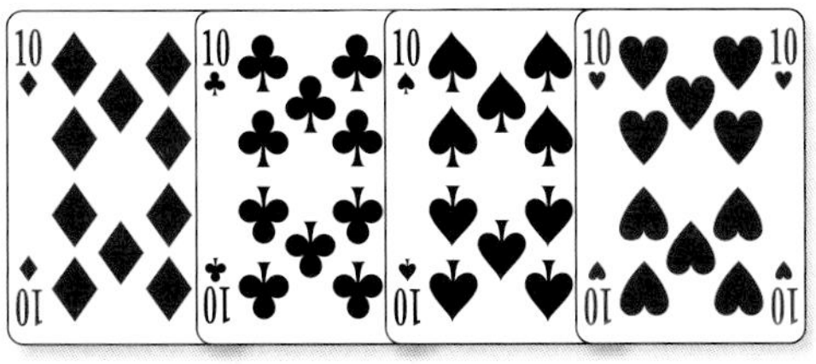

Left: If Tens are declared but unchallenged, the discard pile is moved out of play and a new one is started.

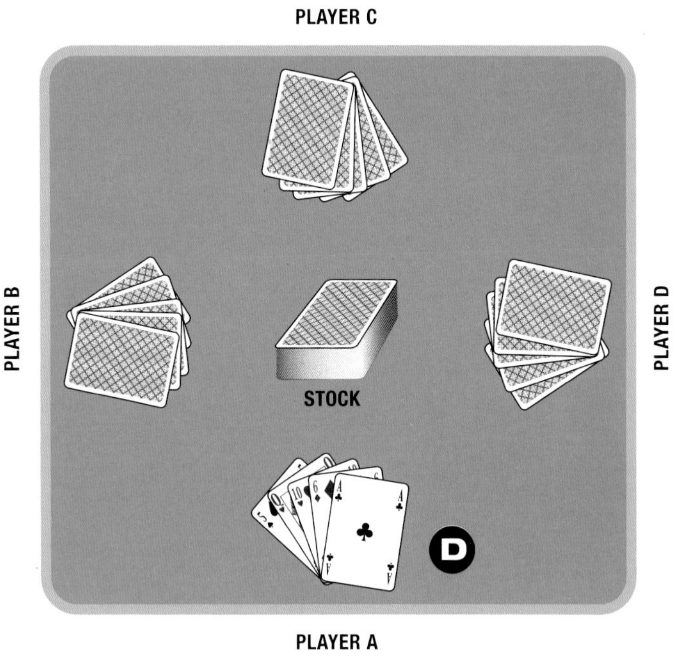

Above: At the start of the game, Players B, C and D have all passed. Having no Three (the card required as an opening lay), Player A can either pass as well or he can play a card from his hand (or the top card of the stock, sight unseen), claiming it as a Three. It's then up to the remaining players to challenge or leave the declaration unchallenged.

Special Rules

- A Jack, Queen or King may not be declared unless the previous declaration was Eight or higher.
- An Ace may not be declared unless the previous call was one of the court cards – or the discard pile is empty.
- A Two may be called at any time, but the next play must be another Two.
- If Tens are called unchallenged, a new discard pile is started. If a Ten is played to an empty table, the next to play must pick it up and miss a turn.
- A player may opt to draw the top card of the stock and add it to his hand (instead of playing from hand).

Conclusion

The game continues until all the players, bar one, are out of cards. That player is the loser.

Cheat

Known as I Doubt It, as well as another cruder title in the USA, this children's game remains popular with young people. There are many versions. It is an ideal game for larger groups to play, and 'cheats' or those who wrongly accuse can be given forfeits or dares.

You will need: 52 cards; no Jokers (two packs when more than five are playing)

Card ranking: None

Players: Two to 10

Ideal for: 7+

Object

To be the first player to get rid of all his cards (using false calls where necessary), but without cheating on the final play. To disrupt others by spotting cheats and making accusations.

The Deal

All the cards are dealt out singly to the players (some may end up with one card more than others).

Play

The player to the dealer's left plays first, play going clockwise around the table. Each player in turn discards from one to four cards face down, calling out their rank as they do so. The first to play calls 'Aces', the second 'Twos', the third 'Threes' and so on, up through the card ranks. After Tens come Jacks, followed by Queens and Kings, and then it is back to Aces again.

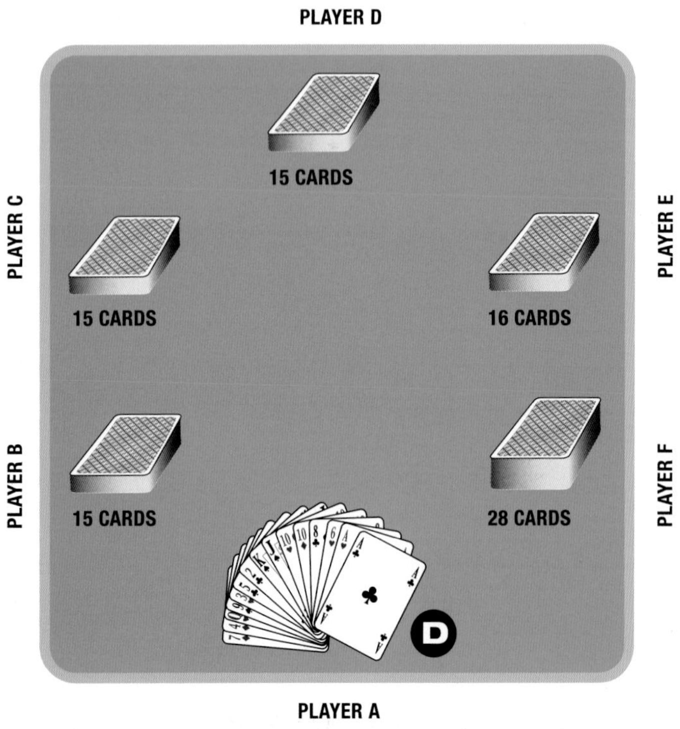

Above: Player F has been caught cheating and has had to pick up all the cards previously laid. Player A can legitimately lay the two Aces or Tens face down, announcing them as such, or add a card of a different rank to one of these, announcing 'Three Aces', for example. The onus would then be on one of the other players to make a challenge.

Challenging

The cards a player puts out supposedly belong to the rank that they are declared to be. In practice, however, a player may lie – in fact, lying may be compulsory since you must play at least one card even when your hand does not contain any cards of the required rank.

If any player thinks that call and cards do not match, he can challenge play by calling 'Cheat'. The cards that the player who is being challenged played are then turned face up. If the challenge is false, the challenger picks up the discard pile and takes it into hand. He may also be given a forfeit. If any played card is not of the called rank, the challenge is correct and the person who played the cards picks up the pile and adds them to his hand. The cheat may also be given a forfeit. If there is no challenge, play continues.

The winner of a challenge is the next to play, calling the next rank in sequence, although in some versions of the game, he can choose whichever rank he likes to call.

Variants

Other versions include making the sequence of ranks that have to be played run downwards (for example, Aces, Kings, Queens, Jacks etc.), and allowing players to play, or claim to play, the next rank above or the next rank below the one called by the preceding player.

Conclusion

The first player to get rid of all his cards and defeat a challenge arising from his final play wins the game. If there is a successful challenge, he must pick up the pile and play continues until there is a winner.

Verish' Ne Verish'

A cross between Cheat and Old Maid, another children's game, this Russian offering is slightly more complicated, but well worth the effort. The name itself translates as 'Trust, Don't Trust' or, more colloquially, as 'Believe It Or Not'.

Object

To avoid, through bluffs, becoming the last with cards.

The Deal

For two to three players, use a 32-card pack; for four to six players, use a standard 52-card pack. After the cards have been shuffled, one card is drawn at random and put face down to the side, after which the rest are dealt singly, face down to all the players in clockwise rotation.

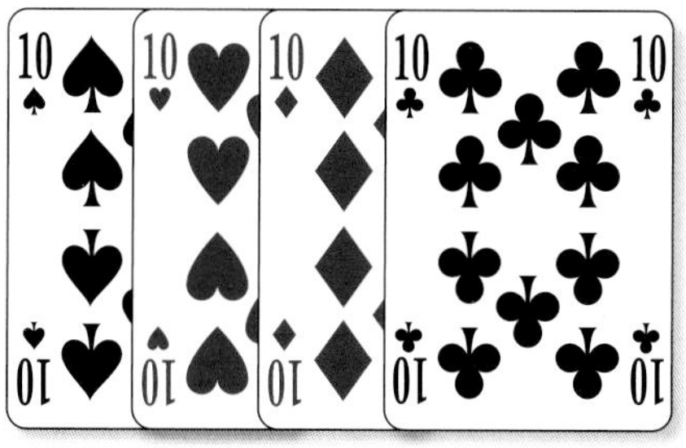

Left: A player starting a new round is allowed to discard any sets of four cards he has been dealt, such as these four Tens.

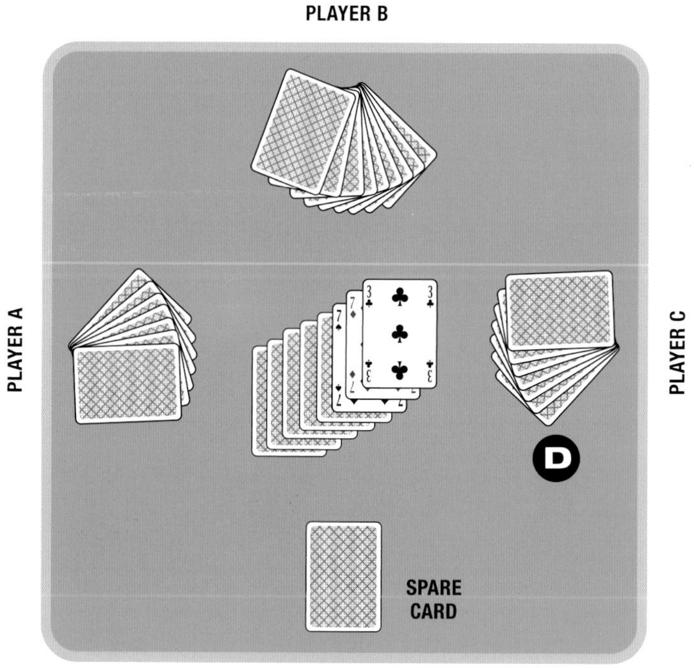

Above: Player C, the third to play, laid down three cards, claiming them to be three Sevens, but Player B challenged, saying '*Ne Verish*'. Player C must expose the cards, revealing that one is a Three, and pick up all the cards on the table. A new round then begins.

You wil need: 52-card deck withTwos to Sixes removed
Card ranking: None
Players: Up to six
Ideal for: 7+

Play

A game consists of several rounds and each round is made up of what are termed moves. It is generally played by up to six players. The player to the dealer's left makes the first move by playing up to four cards face down to the table and declaring their rank – although this declaration need not necessarily be true.

The next player has two options. He may say '*Verish*' ('I trust you'), or nothing, because trust is assumed, in which case he plays, face down, the same number of cards as the previous player and calls the same rank (truthfully or not), awaiting whether the next player will challenge him or not. Or, he may decide to challenge the previous player, and say instead '*Ne Verish*' ('I don't trust you'), and turn the previously played cards face up to discover the truth.

If the cards rank as declared, the unsuccessful challenger has to pick up all the cards so far played in the game. If, on the other hand, the challenge is correct, the player who was challenged must pick up the cards and take them into hand.

This ends the round, the next being started by the player to the left of the penalized player (this should be the challenger himself, if he was correct). Before play starts, that player is entitled to discard any set of four cards of the same rank, showing them to the others before setting them aside. This obviously decreases the number of cards in play.

As play continues, more and more sets of four cards are eliminated. However, because one card is removed from the pack before the deal, the other three cards of this rank necessarily remain in play until the end of the game.

Conclusion

The eventual loser is the player who is left holding one or more of the initially discarded ranked cards, while the other players have managed to get rid of all their cards successfully.

8 | Rummy Games

THERE ARE MANY DIFFERENT GAMES OF THIS TYPE, THE ORIGINS OF WHICH SEEM TO BE CHINESE. INDEED, THEY WERE UNKNOWN IN THE WEST UNTIL THE EARLY 20TH CENTURY. THEY ARE KNOWN TECHNICALLY AS DRAW-AND-DISCARD GAMES, IN WHICH THE OBJECTIVE IS TO COLLECT MATCHING CARDS, EITHER OF THE SAME RANK OR SEQUENCES IN A SUIT, AND MELD THEM INTO SETS, WHICH ARE THEN DISCARDED AND COUNTED UP AT THE END OF THE GAME.

In basic rummy games, such as Rummy itself, the aim is simple – to meld an entire hand into groups and then to discard the melds as quickly as possible. This sounds easy enough, but, as is often the case, there can be complications.

Loba (meaning 'she-wolf'), a South American version of Rummy much played in Argentina, can be either a positive or a negative game. In the former, Loba de Más, players score points for the melds they make and lose points for cards remaining in hand at the end of play. The objective is to score as many points as possible. In the latter, Loba de Menos, points are scored for cards in hand when play ends, but the objective is to score as few points as possible. Melds do not score.

In Three Thirteen, an American Rummy game, the number of cards dealt to each player differs from round to round, and there is a different wild card in each round. The number of cards dealt determines which card is the wild card.

What is termed Contract Rummy is played in much the same way as basic Rummy, the fundamental difference being that, in each round, the players' melds have to conform to a specific contract. Each player must also collect a particular combination of groups and sequences of cards before they can start to meld. The contract becomes harder with successive deals.

Contract Rummy is less a single game than a protracted contest: a typical game consists of seven deals.

Above: Tiles for Mahjong, a game that originated in China. The play in Rummy closely resembles that of the Chinese game, and probably derives from it.

Rummy

Straight Rummy, as it is sometimes called, first appeared in the early 1900s in the USA, where it also went under other names, such as Coon Can, Khun Khan and Colonel. How it originated is uncertain, though some think that it was derived from a Mexican game called Conquian, the earliest known Rummy game in the Western world, or from Rum Poker.

You will need: 52 cards; scorecards
Card ranking: See under 'Scoring', below
Players: Two to six, but best played with four
Ideal for: 7+

Left: In this hand, the four Fours make up a group and the three court cards form a sequence in Diamonds.

Object

To be the first to get rid of all one's cards by melding, laying off and discarding cards.

Melds, Lay Offs and Discards

There are two types of meld – sequences (runs) and groups (sets or books). Three or more cards of the same suit in consecutive order make up a sequence; a group is three or four cards of the same rank. Laying off means adding a card or cards to a meld you have played face up to the table. Players must discard one card onto the discard pile after each turn. No player may add to another's meld until he has laid down one of his own.

The Deal

The first dealer is chosen at random, the deal then passing to the left. If there are two players, each receives 10 cards, three or four get seven and more than four players receive six cards. The cards are dealt singly; then a card is turned face up to start the discard pile and the remaining cards put face down beside it to form the stock. Thorough shuffling is essential before each deal.

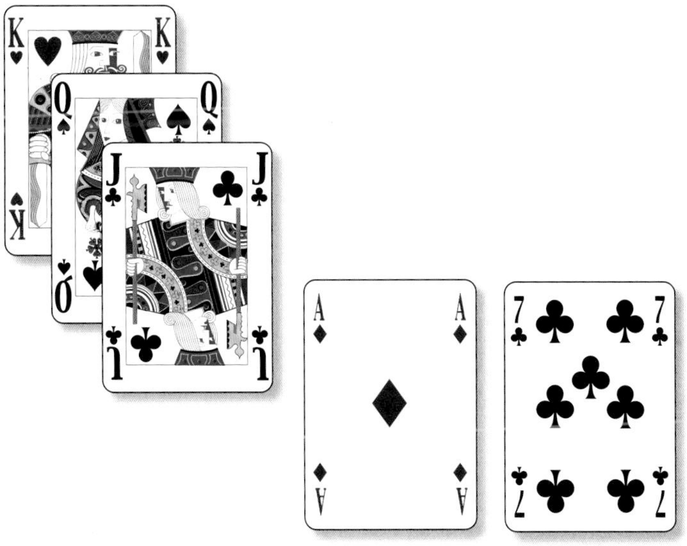

Above: The court cards score 10 points each, the Ace scores one point and the Seven scores its face value. These scores are added to the winner's total.

Play

The player to the dealer's left leads. Each player starts by drawing a card from the top of the stock, or the top card of the discard pile. Each can then play a meld, or lay off. Only one meld may be played per turn. The top card picked up from the discard pile cannot be discarded, but one drawn from the stock can. If the stock runs out, the discard pile is turned face down to form a new stock.

Scoring

In the version of Rummy given here, after a player goes out the remaining players add up the value of any cards that are not melded or that have not been declared and shown. Court cards are worth 10 points each, Aces one point and number cards face value. The cumulative total is added to the winner's score. In some versions, points count against players instead, one variation allowing them to wipe their score by collecting a sequence of seven cards of the same suit. The game should be played to a fixed number of deals or to a target score.

Conclusion

Play comes to an end when one player gets rid of all his cards. The winner is the player with the highest score.

Rummy Variants

Over time, many modifications have been made to the basic rules and structure of Rummy, so exactly which rules are being played should always be agreed before the start of the first deal. Some games, for instance, allow multiple melds; in others a player who has yet to meld or lay off wins a double score if he succeeds in going out in one turn. This is 'going rummy'.

House Rules

Practically every player favours a different set of house rules, the majority of which are optional. Some prefer, for instance, that no cards can be laid off on other players' melds unless the player wishing to do so has already laid down at least one meld of his own. In some games, though, a player may lay off cards only to his own or his partner's melds, while others allow cards to be laid off to any meld on the table.

Ace High or Low

Whether Aces are played high or low is a perennial debate. In the standard game of Rummy, they are low – so Ace, Two, Three is a valid sequence, while Queen, King, Ace is not. In some games, however, Aces are allowed to count as either, and are worth 11 points each in consequence. Such games are referred to as Round-the-Corner Rummy: this is because, if Aces are high, a sequence may 'turn the corner', as in High-Low Rummy.

Left: Examples of melds when the Ace counts high and low. Some variations allow only one of these options, others both.

Stock-pile Variations

Other variations specify how players can go out, what happens when the stock is exhausted, and how a hand is scored. In Discard Rummy, a player has to discard his last card – it cannot form part of a meld or be laid off. Alternatively, the discard pile is shuffled before being used as the new stock and limits may be placed on how many times this can happen.

Block Rummy

In Block Rummy, the discard pile is not reused at all. Assuming no one wants to pick up the top card of the discard pile, the hand ends once the stock is exhausted. Players score the value of the cards in hand, the winner being the player with the fewest points.

Boathouse Rum and Call Rummy

Both these variants are played much like basic Rummy, but with several important differences. In Boathouse Rum, a player drawing the turn-up from the discard pile must also draw the top card of the stock, or a second turn-up. Either way, he draws two cards. Cards may not be laid off and nobody can meld until one player goes rummy. At that point, the other players lay down as many melds as they can and the hand is then scored in the usual manner.

Call Rummy means just that. If any player discards a card that could be laid off against a meld, any other player can call out 'Rummy', pick up the discard, lay it off himself and replace it with one from his own hand. If two or more players make the call simultaneously, the one who is next in turn to play wins the call.

Right: A classic family game, Rummy has almost as many house rules as there are homes! All kinds of variations have sprung up, so players choose for themselves the conventions that fit them best.

Skip Rummy and Wild-Card Rummy

Both of these versions are played in much the same way as basic Rummy. In Skip Rummy, the principle difference is that sequences cannot be melded, only groups. In addition, once a player has laid down a meld, he is allowed to lay off the fourth card of a rank to his own or to any other player's three cards of the same rank. A player who is left with a pair in hand can go out without discarding as soon as he draws a third card of the same rank. Play ends when one player goes out, or when the number of cards in the stock equals the number of players. The discard pile is not reused.

In Wild-Card Rummy, Twos and Jokers – it is a further option whether the latter are played – are wild. They score 25 points each. Players can steal a wild card from any meld on the table provided that they can replace it with the card it represents, but no one may meld until one player has gone rummy. Scoring works in the normal way.

Right: In this wild-card version of Rummy, the 2♥ and Joker are wild cards so can count as anything. Here they represent Sevens, thus completing a winning meld.

Krambambuli

Other Rummy games adopting the same principle include Krambambuli, which hails from Germany. In this two- to three-player game, one of the options open to a player is to steal cards from another player's melds. You can do this provided that the theft does not invalidate the meld, that you can combine it with at least two cards from your own hand to make a new meld and that you do not steal more than one card a turn. The lowest score wins.

One-Meld and Two-Meld Rummy

The difference between these variants lies in the way players can go out in a hand. In the former, a player can go out only by going rummy, that is, by melding every card in hand at once, with or without the benefit of the discard. The player concerned scores the value of the meld multiplied by the number of players.

In Two-Meld Rummy, going rummy is forbidden. Any player able to do so must keep a meld in reserve to be laid down on his next turn.

Far right: In this One-Meld Rummy game, having picked up the Q♣, this player completes a second meld and wins the game.

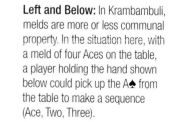

Left and Below: In Krambambuli, melds are more or less communal property. In the situation here, with a meld of four Aces on the table, a player holding the hand shown below could pick up the A♠ from the table to make a sequence (Ace, Two, Three).

Gin Rummy

Often referred to affectionately simply as Gin, its countless aficionados consider this to be the only form of Rummy worth playing. Best as a two-player game, it is far harder to master than it appears. When played well, it is a fast, exciting game, some players being expert enough to bring a hand to an end after only six or so draws.

You will need: 52 cards; scorecards
Card ranking: None
Players: Two
Ideal for: 10+

Two-Player Gin

Object

To end up with a hand in which most or all of the cards can be melded into groups – that is, three or more cards of the same rank – and sequences, which must consist of three or more cards in suit and sequence. Numerals count at face value, court cards 10 each and Aces one.

The Deal

In Two-Player Gin Rummy, each player receives 10 cards, dealt singly. After the deal, the next card is turned up to start the discard pile and the remaining cards are placed face down to form the stock.

Play

The non-dealing player always plays first. He must start by taking the turn-up or passing, in which case the dealer has the same option. If both players pass, the non-dealing player must take the top card of the stock. Subsequently, each player can take a card from either pile. At the end of his turn, each must discard a card face up on to the discard pile. If a player opts to take the turn-up, this cannot be discarded in the same turn.

Knocking

Either player can end play by 'knocking' – that is discarding one card face down to the discard pile and exposing the rest of the hand, arranged as far as possible into sequences and groups. For the knock to be valid, any deadwood (the value of unmatched cards) must not be worth more than 10 points. Knocking with no deadwood in hand is called 'going gin' and is worth an extra bonus. Play also stops if the stock is down to two cards and the player who took the third-to-last card discards without knocking. In this case, there is no score and the same dealer deals again. Once a player has knocked, the opposing player shows his cards. Provided that the knocker did not go gin, the opposing player can lay off unmatched cards by extending the melds laid down by the knocker. The reverse, however, is not allowed – the knocker is never permitted to lay off unmatched cards.

Scoring

Each court card is worth 10 points and Aces one, while the number cards count at face value. At the end of the game, both players count the values of their unmatched cards. If the knocker's count is higher than that of his opponent, he scores the difference between the two counts, plus a bonus of 20 points if he went gin, plus the opponent's count in unmatched cards, if any.

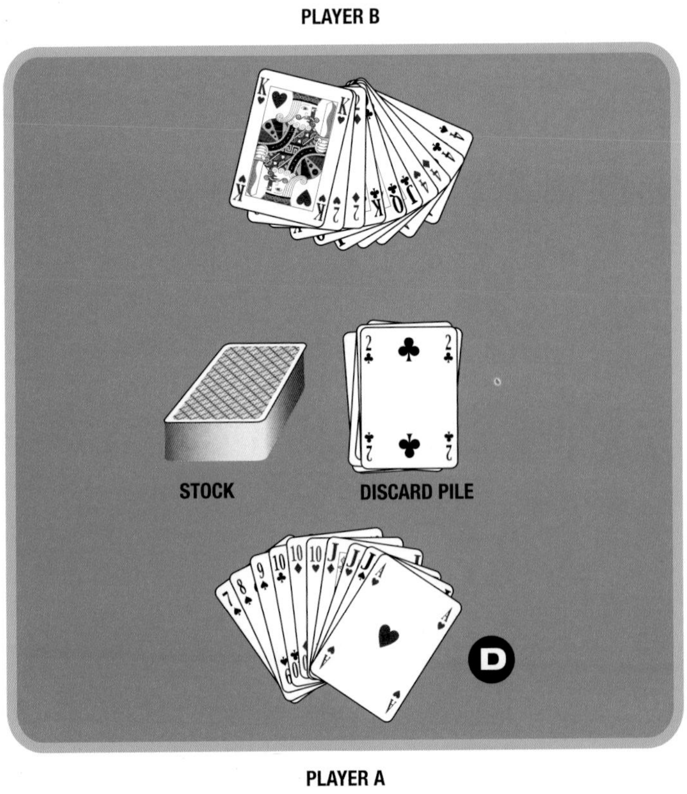

Right: Player A has here knocked and laid down his hand. With just one unmatched card (the Ace, counting for one point), this hand scores 13 points. Player B has unmatched cards worth 14 points. Had the hands been the other way round, Player B would have scored 13 points plus a bonus of 10 for what is known as the undercut.

If the knocker's count is lower than that of his opponent, or if the counts are equal, the opposing player scores the difference between the two, plus a 10-point bonus for what is termed the 'undercut'.

MELDS

Two types of meld (card combination) are used in Gin Rummy:

- A group or set – three or more cards of the same rank.
- A sequence or run – three or more cards of the same suit in consecutive order.

A card can be used only in one combination at a time. It is against the rules of the game to try to use the same card as part of a group and a sequence.

CONCLUSION

A player must reach a cumulative score of 100 points or more to win the game. Both players also receive a bonus 20 points for each hand they won, and the winner adds an extra bonus of a further 100 points for the game – 200 if the losing player failed to score at all. After all the points have been totalled, the player with the lower score pays the winner an amount related to the difference between the two scores, which is doubled if the loser failed to win a single hand.

PLAYER B

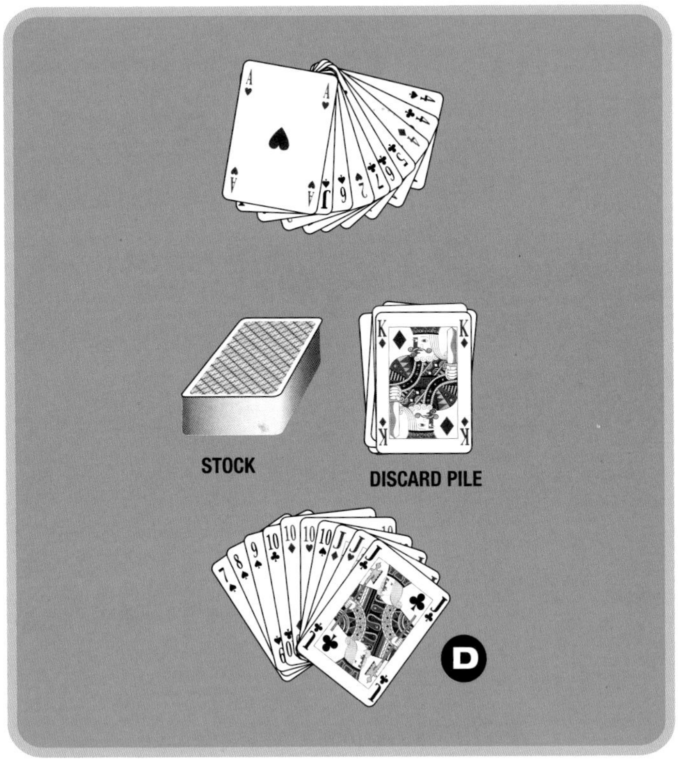

PLAYER A

Above: Had Player A not gone gin, Player B could have laid off the 6♠ on Player A's sequence and the J♠ on the group. As it is, no laying off is permitted, so Player A will score 19 points for Player B's unmatched cards plus another 20 points for going gin.

THREE- AND FOUR-PLAYER GIN

If three players are playing, the dealer deals to the other two players and then sits out the hand, with the loser of the hand dealing the next. There is also a three-player variant called Jersey Gin, in which the winner scores the difference between his hand and that of each opponent.

Four can play as two partnerships, each player in one team playing a separate game with one of the opposing pair. Players alternate opponents from hand to hand, but stay in the same partnerships throughout the game.

If both partners win at the end of a hand, they score their combined total of points. If only one player from a partnership wins, the partnership with the higher total scores the difference. To win the game, a partnership needs to reach a cumulative total of 125 points or more.

PLAYER B

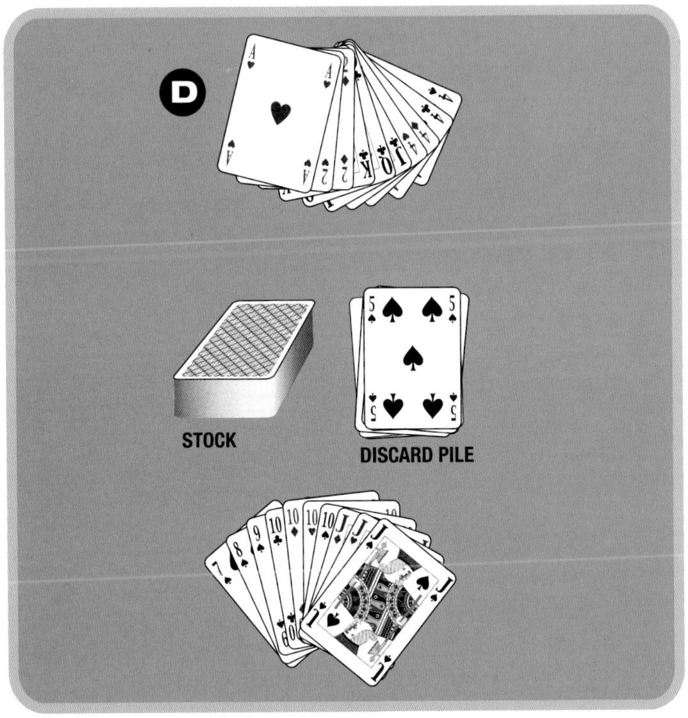

PLAYER A

Left: In this game Player A has melded every card before knocking and laying down his hand. Player B is still waiting for a Two. Although the difference between unmatched cards is only five points, Player A scores a bonus of 20 points for going gin.

LOBA

This Argentinian game can be played negatively (Loba de Menos), when the aim is to score as few points as possible, and positively (Loba de Más), when it is to score high. Both versions are played in much the same way, except in Loba de Más, Twos can be used as natural Twos or wild cards.

You will need: Two 52-card decks; four Jokers; scorecards; gambling chips/counters

Card ranking: See under 'Scoring', below

Players: Two to five

Ideal for: 10+

OBJECT

To be the first player to go out in the negative game, or the highest-scoring player in the positive version.

THE DEAL

Each player receives nine cards (11 in the positive version), the next being turned to start the discard pile. The remainder form the stock.

PLAY

Each player draws the top card of the discard pile or the top card of the stock. A card can be drawn from the former only if played immediately. In the positive game, the whole of the discard pile must be taken.

Melding follows. No player may add to another's meld until he has laid down one of his own. In Loba de Más (the positive game), players may add only to their own melds. Finally, a card is discarded face up. Jokers may be discarded only if they are the last cards held.

SCORING

In the negative game, the first to go out scores nothing, the other(s) scoring penalty points. Jokers, Aces and the court cards score 10 points each, number cards face value. Players scoring more than 101 points must drop out unless they elect to buy back in by paying a stake in chips into the pot. This is allowed twice.

MELDS

There are two types of meld (card combination) that are allowed in Loba:

- A *Pierna* – three or more cards of the same rank, but of different suits.
- An *Escalera* – three or more cards of the same suit in sequence.

Jokers cannot be used in *Piernas,* and *Escaleras* can contain only one. In the positive game, *Escaleras* can contain any number of wild cards, although these cannot all be Jokers.

In the positive game, melds score positive points, cards in hand negative ones. An Ace in a meld scores three points if high, one point if low, Kings to Eights two and Sevens to Threes score one. Jokers and Twos are worth three if substituting for Aces to Eights, otherwise one. The negative values are three for Aces, Jokers and Twos, two for Kings to Eights and one for Sevens to Threes.

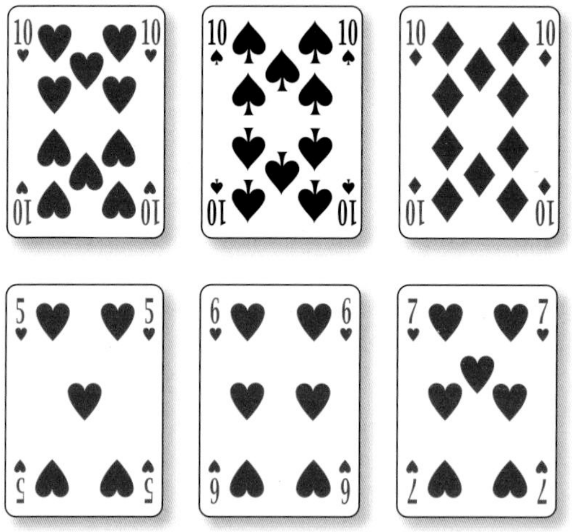

Left: In Loba, three of a kind (such as the three Tens) is known as a *Pierna*, or 'leg', while a same-suited sequence (such as the Five, Six, Seven) is called an *Escalera*, or 'ladder'.

CONCLUSION

A round ends when a player gets rid of all his cards. In Loba de Menos, the game is won when all other players have exceeded 101 points and are prohibited from buying their way back in again, and in Loba de Más when a player reaches 150 or more positive points. The winner takes the pot.

Above: An *Escalera* in Loba de Más can contain any number of wild cards, but they cannot all be Jokers. Here, the Jokers represent the 6♥ and 7♥.

THIRTY-ONE

Also known as Scat and Blitz, this is a straightforward draw-and-discard game. One of the oldest known gambling games, it has been popular in Europe since the 15th century.

You will need: 52 cards; gambling chips/counters
Card ranking: See under 'Scoring', below
Players: Two to nine, although probably best with three
Ideal for: 7+

OBJECT

To collect cards of the same suit totalling 31 points, or as near 31 as possible.

THE DEAL

The first dealer is chosen at random. After the deal of three cards to each player, the remaining cards are stacked face down to form the stock, the top card being turned up and placed separately to start a discard pile.

Left: An example of the highest possible hand in Thirty-One: two court cards and an Ace of the same suit, together worth 31 points.

PLAY

The normal practice is to start off with three chips each and all the players deciding which will be their particular points suit. The maximum hand value possible is 31, which would mean holding the Ace and two court cards of the same suit. If a player holds cards of three different suits, the value of the hand is that of the highest card. Play rotates to the left. Each player in turn draws the top card from the discard pile or the stock and throws away a single card on to the discard pile. If the top discard is taken, it cannot be thrown away in the same turn, but a card drawn from the stock can be.

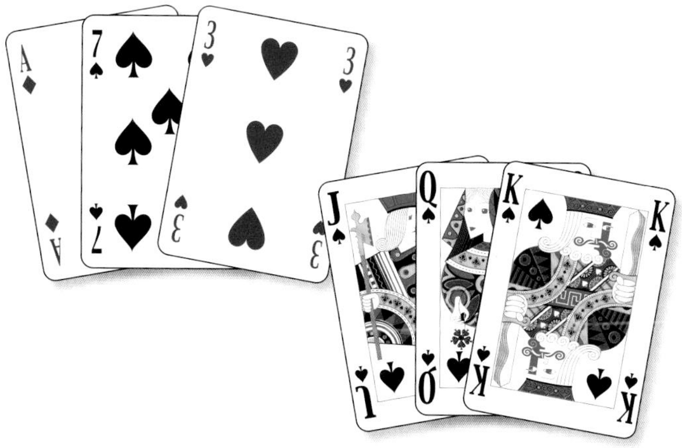

Above: Here, the A♦, 7♠, 3♥, which scores 11 for the Ace but nothing for the other two cards, is beaten by the J♠, Q♠, K♠ (scoring 30).

SCORING

Aces are worth 11 points, court cards 10 points each and number cards their face value. Winning the game depends on the number of lives lost. (In variations of the game a player scores $30^{1}/_{2}$ points for three of a kind).

Left: This player may hold an Ace and two court cards, but the hand's value is only 11 points, corresponding to the Ace, the highest-ranked card of the three.

CONCLUSION

The game continues until a player succeeds in scoring 31 points, in which case the cards are shown immediately. All the other players lose a life and pay a chip into the pool. The alternative is to knock before reaching 31 points. The knocker stops playing, the others getting one last chance to draw and discard. Then all the players show their hands. The player with the lowest hand value loses a life. If scores are tied, the knocker is safe, but the other player or players involved also lose a life each.

If the knocker is the loser, which can happen because he scores the lowest, or because another player declares 31 after the knock, he forfeits two lives. Players who have lost three lives can play on, but if they lose again, they are out of the game. The last player left in wins.

Three Thirteen

This is Rummy with a difference. In each of its 11 rounds, there is a different wild card, while a differing number of cards, three to 13, is dealt to each player. The number of cards determines which is the wild card. At the end of a round, players arrange as many of their cards as they can into groups, and any cards left over score penalties.

You will need: 52-card deck for two players; two 52-card decks for three or more; scorecards
Card ranking: See under 'Scoring', below
Players: Two or more players
Ideal for: 7+

Object

To form the cards in hand into groups, preferably of high-scoring cards. Groups consist of three or more cards of the same rank, or consecutive sequences of three or more cards in the same suit.

Wild Cards

There are different wild cards in each round: Threes in the first, Fours in the second and so on up to Kings. Aces, which are ranked low in this game, are never wild cards. A wild card can stand in for any other card – it can even be used to make up a complete group.

The Deal

The first dealer is chosen at random, after which the deal passes to the left after each round. In the first of these, three cards are dealt to each player, in the second four, and so on up to the final round, when, instead of 11 cards, 13 are dealt. The remaining cards are placed face down on the table to form the stock, the top card being turned up and put beside it to start a discard pile.

Play

The player to the dealer's left starts and play progresses clockwise around the table. Each player draws a card from the top of the stock or the discard pile and discards a card face up on to the latter. Players arrange as many cards as they can into groups, with penalty points being scored for any unmatched ones. A player can announce that he is out (has matched all his cards into groups) only when discarding, and the other players each get one more turn before the round ends and the scores are calculated.

Scoring

Any unmatched card counts against players. Aces score a point, Tens and the court cards 10 points and other number cards their face value.

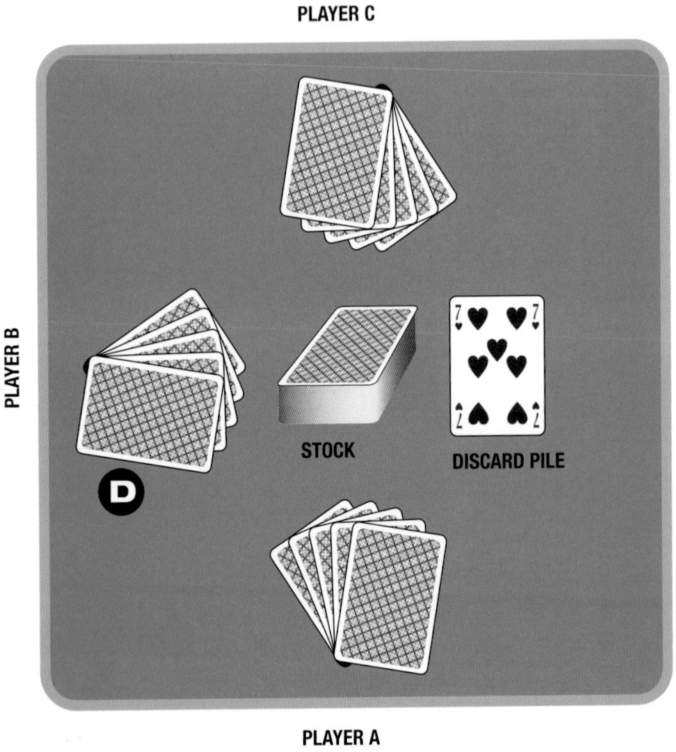

Left: As well as wild cards changing in each round, so too does the number of cards dealt. It starts at three and increases by one at a time, until 13 cards are dealt in the 11th round. In the third round, players receive five cards, as here.

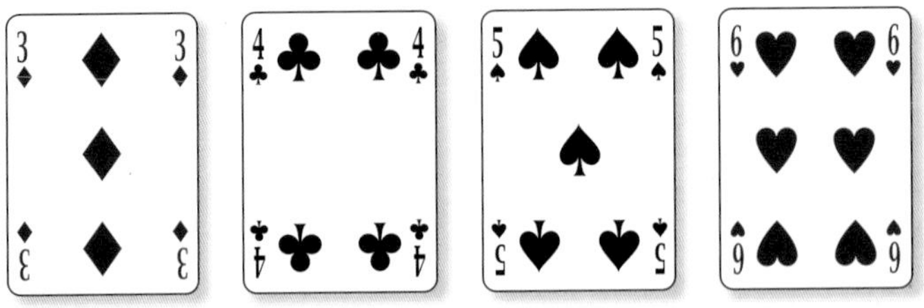

Above: Wild cards in Three Thirteen change round by round, ascending one rank after each deal. The cards shown here, therefore, are possible examples of wild cards in each of the first four rounds of the game.

Conclusion

The player who has the lowest cumulative score at the end of the game is the winner.

Conquian

Dating from the 1880s, this two-player game is thought to have originated in Mexico. It is considered by some to be the ancestor of all subsequent Rummy games devised in the West, although others say their origin is Chinese.

You will need: 40 cards (52-card deck with Eights, Nines and Tens removed)

Card ranking: Ace, lowest, up to Seven and then Jack, Queen and King (highest)

Players: Two

Ideal for: 7+

Object

To be the first player to go out by melding 11 cards – that is, the 10 cards that are being held, plus the top card of the stock.

The Deal

Each player gets 10 cards dealt singly, the remainder being placed face down to form the stock.

Melds

There are two types of meld (card combination) in Conquian:

- A group or short – three or four cards of the same rank.
- A sequence or straight – three to eight consecutive cards of the same suit.

During play, both players are allowed to rearrange their melds to create new ones, provided that their existing melds still contain the minimum three cards they need to be valid. Melds always have to include a turn-up from the stock. They also must be kept entirely separate. It is against the rules for a player to lay off cards on the other's melds.

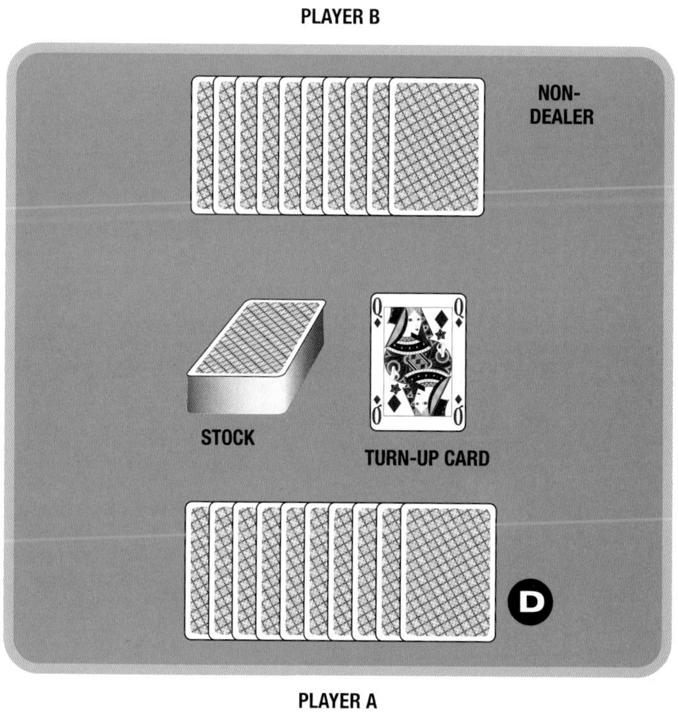

Play and Conclusion

The non-dealer starts by turning up the top card of the stock and then exercises one of two options. The turn-up must be melded immediately with at least two cards held in hand, after which another card must be discarded face up to serve as the next turn-up. Otherwise the player must pass, after which the dealer must decide whether to do the same or meld with the turn-up.

If he chooses to pass, a new turn-up is drawn from the stock and the process begins again. If a player declines to play a turn-up that could be added to an existing meld, the opposing player can force the meld to be made. A shrewd tactician can take advantage of this to destroy the opposing player's position.

Play continues until a player goes out by melding the turn-up with all 10 cards held in hand. It also stops when the stock runs out. If neither player can make the final meld, the game is a draw and the stakes for the next one are doubled.

Above: Examples of melds in Conquian: first a sequence of six Diamonds; second, a group of Aces followed by a group of Sevens.

Left: Ten cards have been dealt to each player and, having turned up the Q♦, the non-dealer can pick it up if he is able to meld it with two cards in his hand. Otherwise, he must pass, allowing the dealer the opportunity to meld or pass. If the dealer also passes, a new turn-up card is drawn from the stock.

Contract Rummy

The oldest known game of this type is called Zioncheck, which dates from the 1930s. Many other variants, such as Hollywood Rummy, Joker Rummy and Shanghai Rummy, have been devised since then. In each game, players contract to make certain melds, dictated by which deal is in progress. Contracts get harder from round to round.

You will need: Two decks of 52 cards with single Joker for three to four players; three packs of 52 cards plus two Jokers for five to eight players; scorecards

Card ranking: Standard, Aces low or high; Jokers serve as wild cards; Twos can also count as wild cards

Players: Three to eight players

Ideal for: 14+

Object

To make the required contract in a given round and end up, after seven deals, with the lowest score.

The Deal

There are seven deals in total. In the first three rounds, players receive 10 cards each, and then from the fourth round onwards, 12 cards. The first dealer is chosen at random, after which the deal passes to the left after each round. The deal is also clockwise, each player receiving one card at a time. The remaining cards are placed face down on the table to form the stock pile, the top card of which is turned face up and put alongside to start the discard pile. If the stock is exhausted before any player goes out, the convention is to turn the discard pile down, shuffle it, and use it as a replacement stock pile.

Contracts

The contracts specifying which melds (card combinations) have to be laid down by each player differ in each of the seven rounds, as follows:

- First round – two groups of three cards.
- Second round – a group of three and a sequence of four.
- Third round – two groups of four.
- Fourth round – three groups of three.
- Fifth round – two groups of three cards and one sequence of four.
- Sixth round – one group of three and two sequences of four.
- Seventh round – three sequences of four.

Above: An example of the melds required in the final round of Contract Rummy, when three sequences of four cards have to be laid down. Note that the third sequence actually contains five cards, since the 'discard' must be played in addition to the cards in hand in order to go out.

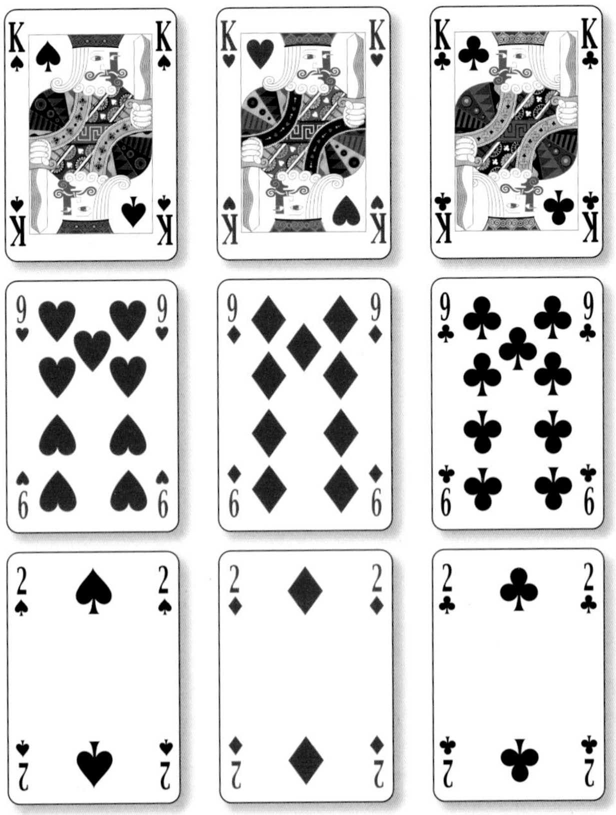

Above: In the fourth round of Contract Rummy, the card combinations needed are three groups (that is, cards of the same rank) of three. The groups shown here are of Kings, Nines and Twos.

Play

The player to the dealer's left plays first. Each player in turn starts by taking the top discard or drawing the top card of the stock. A player deciding to do the latter must wait until the others have had a chance to indicate whether they want to take the discard. A player does this by simply saying 'May I?' If more than one player makes the call, the discard goes to the next to play. Taking the discard like this means drawing an extra card from the stock as a penalty.

The first melds are then laid down. This can be done only once per round, although this does not necessarily have to be during the initial play. The melds must be the ones required by that round's contract (see box left).

Once players have melded, they are free to begin laying off the cards remaining in hand by adding cards to each other's melds, although this process cannot start until the turn after the initial meld has been laid. It is now within the rules to extend sequences, the longest possible one being 14 cards, with an Ace (one low and one high) at either end. To extend a group, players add more cards of equal rank to it.

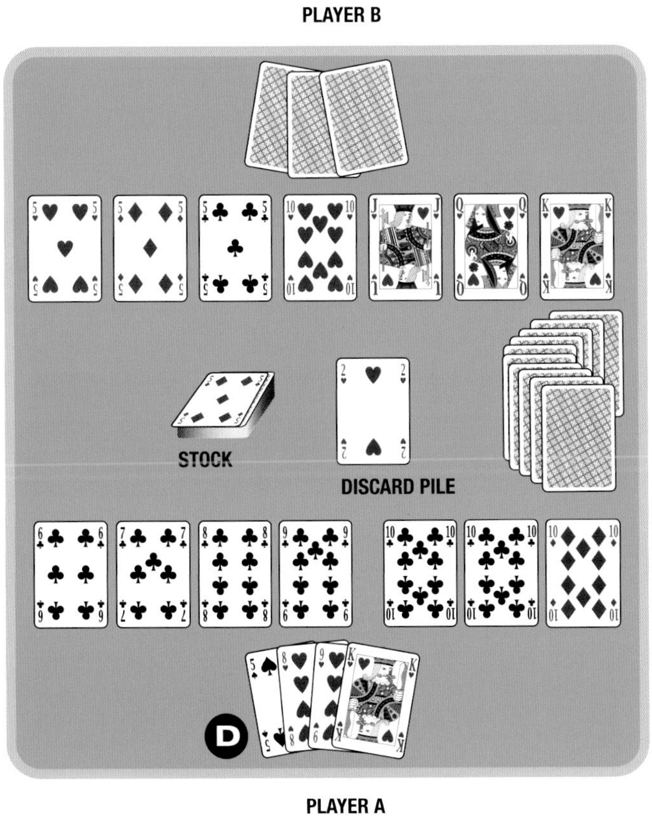

Above: Players A and B have both laid down the required melds for the second round (a group of three and a sequence of four). Player A has picked up the 5♠ from the stack, which can be laid off on to Player B's group of Fives. Similarly, his 8♥ and 9♥ can be added to Player B's sequence, but the K♥ cannot be laid.

Right: This sequence of cards would be legal because the two four-card sequences within it are in a different suit.

Right: This sequence of cards in the same suit needs a gap between the Five and Six to be legal. Only one of the four-card sequences within it is valid.

Scoring

The first player to go out wins the round with a score of zero. The others score penalty points for the cards left in hand. Aces and Jokers score 15 points, the court cards 10 points each and the number cards are worth their face values. The scoring is cumulative, the player with the lowest score at the end of the final round winning the game.

Melds

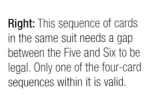

As in other forms of Rummy, there are two types of meld: sequences and groups. In this game, sequences must consist of at least four consecutive cards of the same suit.

- An Ace can count as low or high, but not both at the same time. Ace, Two, Three, Four would be a valid sequence, but Queen, King, Ace, Two would not.
- A group consists of three cards of the same rank irrespective of suit.
- Players may not meld two sequences in the same suit that are continuous. To be valid, they must either have a gap between them or overlap: for example, 2♠, 3♠, 4♠, 5♠ and 4♠, 5♠, 6♠, 7♠ would be valid, as would 2♠, 3♠, 4♠, 5♠ and 7♠, 8♠, 9♠, 10♠ but not 2♠, 3♠, 4♠, 5♠, 6♠, 7♠, 8♠, 9♠.
- All the cards held in the last round must be melded simultaneously, and a five-card sequence is allowable, since, in order to go out, the discard must be played as well as the cards in hand.

Conclusion

Play ends after the seventh deal, final scores then being calculated.

Push

This is the partnership version of Contract Rummy. Although it is played in much the same way, there are differences, notably in the way cards are drawn and discarded.

You will need: Two 52-card decks; four Jokers; scorecards
Card ranking: Standard, Aces high and low; Jokers and Twos are wild cards
Players: Four, in partnerships of two
Ideal for: 14+

Object

To make, as a partnership, the required contract for each deal. The aim during the game is to get rid of all wild cards and valuable cards from your hand during play so that you do not accrue lots of penalty points if you lose the round. The partnership with the lowest number of penalty points at the end of the final round is the winner.

The Deal

In each deal there is a minimum requirement for each player's initial meld. There are five rounds: in the first, six cards are dealt to each player and so on until a final deal of 10 cards. The first dealer is chosen at random, after which the turn to deal passes to the left. Once the cards have been dealt, the next card is turned face up to start the discard pile and the remaining cards placed face down to form the stock. If the first face-up card is a wild card (a Two or a Joker), the dealer will bury it in the stock pile and turn up a replacement card to start the discard pile.

Contracts, Melds and Wild Cards

The contracts specifying which melds (card combinations) have to be laid down by each player differ in each round as follows:

- First round – two groups of three equally ranking cards.
- Second round – one group of three cards and one sequence of four consecutive cards of the same suit.
- Third round – two sequences of four cards.
- Fourth round – three groups of three.
- Fifth round – two sequences of five.

Since two packs of cards are used, there are two of each card, which is why a group cannot contain two identical cards of the same suit. However, it is permissible to meld two groups of the same rank – an 8♣, 8♥ and 8♠ and an 8♥, 8♠ and 8♦, for instance, would be legal.

A sequence consists of three or more cards of the same suit in consecutive order. Aces can be either high or low, but not both at the same time. Once melded, sequences cannot be split up or joined together, but only extended by players laying off cards.

As wild cards, Twos and Jokers can be used to represent any card in any group or sequence. If a meld consists entirely of wild cards or has only one natural card in it, its player must state whether it is meant to be a group or a sequence. If the latter, what each card represents has to be specified, but, in the case of a group, it is necessary only to state the rank.

Below: In Push, the melds that are required change in each of the five rounds, examples being shown here.

ROUND 1

ROUND 2

ROUND 3

ROUND 4

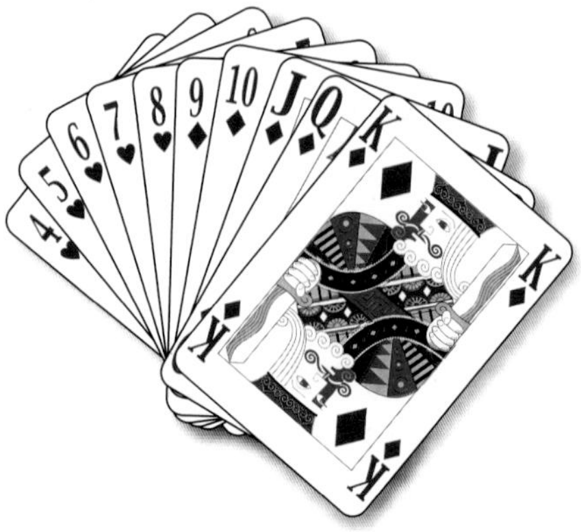

ROUND 5

Play

The player to the dealer's left plays first, play continuing clockwise around the table. Each turn consists of three elements: drawing, melding and discarding.

Drawing

As far as drawing is concerned, there are two options. If a player wants the top card of the discard pile, he may take it and add it to his hand. If a player does not want the top card, he can take a face-down card off the top of the undealt stock cards. The way this is done gives the game its name. The player takes a card from the stock, places it on the top card of the discard pile and then 'pushes' these two cards to the opposing player to the left, who must take these cards into hand. The first player then draws the next card from the stock pile. Because of the pushing, players can sometimes accumulate quite a large number of cards in their hands.

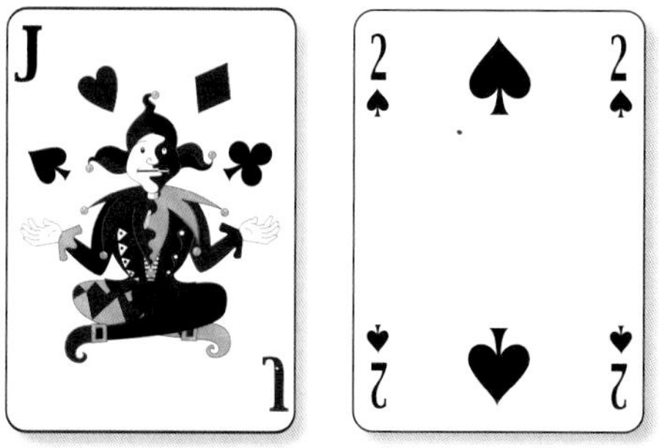

Left: If a wild card is turned up after the deal, it is buried in the stock and the dealer turns up a replacement.

Melding and Discarding

Having drawn, players have the opportunity to lay their first melds face up on the table. Not only must these meet the terms of the contract for the round, but both players in a partnership must meld individually before they can go on to lay down further melds or lay off cards to any meld already on the table made by themselves or by their opponents.

If a player holds a card that is represented by a Joker in any meld, he may exchange it, as long as the Joker can be laid off on to another meld immediately, or used as part of a new one. It cannot be taken into hand. Players end their turns by discarding a card on to the discard pile.

Scoring

The losing partnership counts the value of the cards that both of them are still holding. Each Two or Joker counts for 20 penalty points, each Ace 15, each of the court cards and Tens 10 and the remaining cards five points each. Scoring is cumulative from round to round.

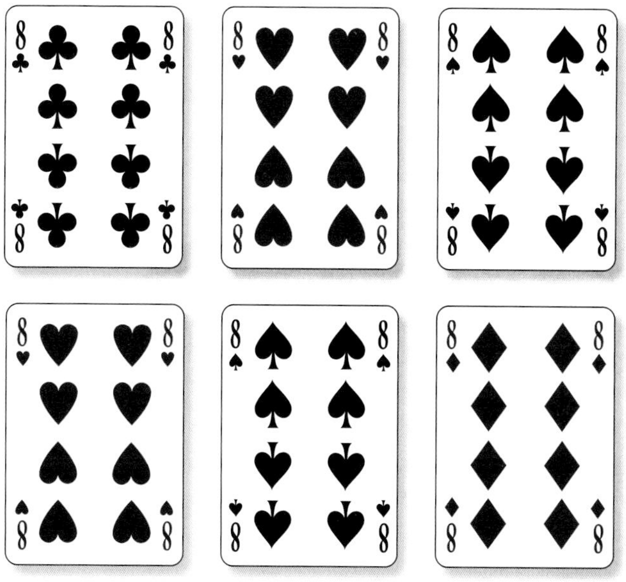

Above: Because two packs of cards are used in Push, it is possible to have two groups of the same rank, as shown here.

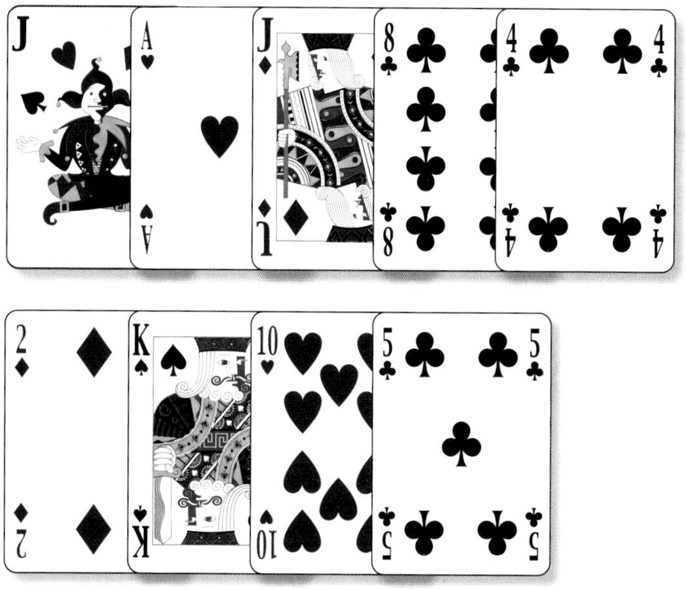

Above: A partnership left holding these cards would lose 100 points: 20 each for the Joker and Two, 15 for the Ace, 10 for the King, Jack and Ten, and five each for the Eight, Five and Four.

Conclusion

Play continues until a player succeeds in going out by getting rid of all the cards in hand. This involves melding or laying off the entire hand, or melding all bar one of the cards, which is then the last card to be discarded. It is at this point of the game that the penalty points are counted. The successful player and his partner score nothing – even though that partner will have cards remaining in hand.

Kaluki

Another version of Rummy with a difference, Kaluki, or Kalookie, is always played with a double pack, plus four Jokers as wild cards. The exact rules of play differ from place to place, but the ones detailed below are typical.

You will need: Two 52-card decks; four Jokers; gambling chips/counters

Card ranking: Standard, Aces high and low; Jokers are wild

Players: Two to five

Ideal for: 14+

Object

To combine all cards in hand into groups and sequences. Stakes are agreed beforehand. The call-up is the amount the losers pay to the winner of each hand, while a kaluki is paid to a player who melds all 13 cards simultaneously. An initial stake is paid into the pool. Players may decide to set the stakes as follows: one unit (chip) for a call-up; two for a kaluki; three for the initial stake and five for a buy-in (see below under 'Scoring and Conclusion').

The Deal

The dealer shuffles the pack, after which the player to his right cuts the cards. These are then dealt singly to the players until each player has 13. The next card is turned up to start a discard pile. The remaining cards are stacked face down beside the turn-up to form the stock.

Play

The player to the dealer's left draws a card from the top of the stock or the top discard. He can then meld or pass before discarding a card to the discard pile. (A meld is three or four cards of the same rank, or three or more cards in suit and sequence. No meld may contain two identical cards). If the top discard is taken, it must be melded on the first play. Play ends when a player melds all bar one of the cards in hand and discards that card. Each player's first meld must be worth at least 40 points.

Jokers can be used as wild cards, that is, they can represent any other card, in which case they take on that card's value. Once an initial meld has been laid down, its player can build on it by adding cards, or do the same with any other meld on the table. Jokers can also be exchanged for the cards they represent. If the stock runs out, the discard pile is shuffled to form a new one. If this, too, is exhausted, the game is declared void.

Scoring and Conclusion

Losers score penalty points for the cards that remain in their hands. Aces count for 11 points, the three court cards and Tens count for 10, Jokers score 15 points and all other number cards score at face value.

At the end of each hand, the stakes are paid and the losers' penalty points calculated. Players with more than 150 penalty points are eliminated unless they choose to buy in. This involves paying a buy-in stake (the amount must be agreed by all the players at the start of the game) to the pool so that a player may remain in the game. They are allowed to do this twice, but only if there are at least two other players left in the game. The winner is the last player left and he is entitled to scoop the contents of the pool.

Above: A player picking up the 3♦ or 4♦ could exchange them for the Jokers, enabling him to then use the Jokers in another meld.

Above: This meld could be laid down by a player with another meld on the table, but not as a player's first meld as it is worth only 32 points, which would be eight points short of the required 40.

Above: A player left holding these cards at the end of a round would score a total of 44 penalty points: 15 points for the Joker, 11 points for the Ace, 10 points for the Jack, and 8 points for the Eight.

VATICAN

No one knows exactly where this game originated, though some card authorities think that it was probably a Czech or Central European invention some time in the mid-20th century. What makes it different from other Rummy games is the way in which melds are treated as communal. They can be arranged and rearranged more or less as the players please.

You will need: Two 52-card packs; two Jokers
Card ranking: Standard, Aces high and low; Jokers are wild
Players: Two to five, though the experts say that it is at its best with three or four
Ideal for: 10+

OBJECT

To be the first player to go out by playing all the cards in his hand to card combinations (melds) on the table. Melds are sequences or groups of three or more cards of the same rank, or in suit and sequence. In a group, the cards must all be of different suits. In a sequence, the Ace can be high or low, so King-Ace-Two is allowed.

THE DEAL

In the initial deal, the two packs of cards are shuffled together with two Jokers, and each player receives 13 cards. The rest are stacked face down on the table to form the stock. There is no turn-up and no discard pile.

PLAY

Each player, in turn has the option of drawing a card from the stock or playing at least one card from his hand to any melds that have already been laid on the table. If the stock has run out and a player cannot play, he has no alternative but to pass.

Jokers are wild cards: they can be substituted for any other card, provided that, when one is played, its player states what card it represents. This cannot be changed unless the actual card is substituted for the Joker. After this, the Joker must be used immediately in a new meld.

It is illegal to draw and meld in the same turn. The first time players meld, they must begin by laying down a sequence of three cards of the same suit, all taken from their existing cards. Once they have done this, they can then add more cards and rearrange melds to form groups and sequences at will. The one thing that matters in this game is that every meld laid on the table must consist of at least three cards of the same suit, or three or four cards of the same rank, all of which must come from different suits. More than four of a kind is not allowed.

FIRST MELD

SECOND MELD

THIRD MELD

Above: The first meld here is legal in Vatican, but not the second or third. Five cards of the same rank cannot be melded, nor two of the same rank and suit.

Right: In Vatican, the first time that players meld, they must begin by laying down a sequence of three cards in suit, all taken from hand.

CONCLUSION

If the stock is exhausted, players must continue to play if they can. Otherwise, they must pass. There is no system of scoring. The first player to run out of cards wins the game.

9 | Banking Games

WHAT MAKES BANKING GAMES DIFFERENT FROM OTHER VYING GAMES IS THE NATURE OF THE VYING THAT TAKES PLACE. INSTEAD OF ALL THE PLAYERS COMPETING AGAINST ONE ANOTHER TO SEE WHO HAS THE BEST HAND, ONE PLAYER, THE BANKER, TAKES ON EACH OF THE OTHER PLAYERS INDIVIDUALLY. FOR THIS REASON, MANY BANKING GAMES ARE CONSTRUCTED TO GIVE THE BANKER A SLIGHT ADVANTAGE.

Many banking games require specialist equipment, such as a betting table marked with a staking layout or a shoe – a long oblong box with a tongue – from which the cards are dealt. To save time and effort, it is also customary to play with several packs of cards shuffled together, rather than just a single deck. Some games, however, can equally well be played off the cuff with a single pack of cards. Also, such games do not necessarily have to be played for money at all.

Banking games are quick to play and are essentially numerical, as suits are often irrelevant. Their widespread popularity is due to the combination of chance and skill. They are mostly defensive, not offensive, and there are two basic categories: turn-up games and point-card games. In turn-up games like Yablon, players bet on winning or losing cards as determined by a card or cards turned up by the dealer, and the bet is on whether a certain card will turn up before another. In point-card games, such as Blackjack, players draw cards one by one, with the aim of creating a hand of a given value, or nearest to that value. The objective in Blackjack is to achieve a hand with a total value of 21 or closer to 21 than the hand held by the dealer, but which does not exceed that figure. To achieve this straight off means being dealt a Ten, Jack, Queen or a King plus an Ace.

Above: Napoleon is known to have played Pontoon, among other card games, while he was held in exile on St Helena, from 1815 until his death in 1821.

Pontoon

This is the long-established British version of the internationally popular banking game Vingt-et-Un, or Twenty-One. Its origins go back at least to the early 19th century – when, to while away the time on the lonely island of St Helena, Napoleon's British captors taught him the game.

You will need: 52-card deck; gambling chips/counters
Card ranking: See under 'Scoring', below
Players: Five to eight is considered best
Ideal for: 7+

Object

To get a hand that adds up to 21, or as close as possible without going over, preferably with just two cards.

Scoring

Number cards count at face value, while the court cards are worth 10 points each. An Ace can be worth one or 11 points. The best possible hand is a Pontoon, which is 21 points in two cards, followed by Five-card Trick, which is five cards worth 21 or less. A hand of three or four cards totalling 21 points beats everything but a Pontoon or a Five-card Trick, while hands of fewer than five cards and worth 20 points or less rank in order of point value. A player with a hand worth more than 21 points is bust.

The Deal and Play

The banker deals a card face down to each player. All players bar the banker may examine their cards, then place their initial bets. Players can bet as many chips as they like up to an agreed maximum. When the players have made their bets, the banker looks at his card, and has the right to double. In this event, the players must double their bets. The banker deals another card face down. If any player has a Pontoon it must be declared, in which case the player turns the Ace face up and stakes nothing more. If a player has two cards of equal rank, they can be split into two hands by placing them face up and doubling the existing stake. A player with cards worth 16 points or more may now stick, i.e. keep his cards and stake as they are, and the turn passes to the next player. Otherwise, he may buy another card, which is dealt face down, by adding a chip to his initial stake or he can twist without adding to his stake, when another card is dealt face up. This continues until all the players stick or bust.

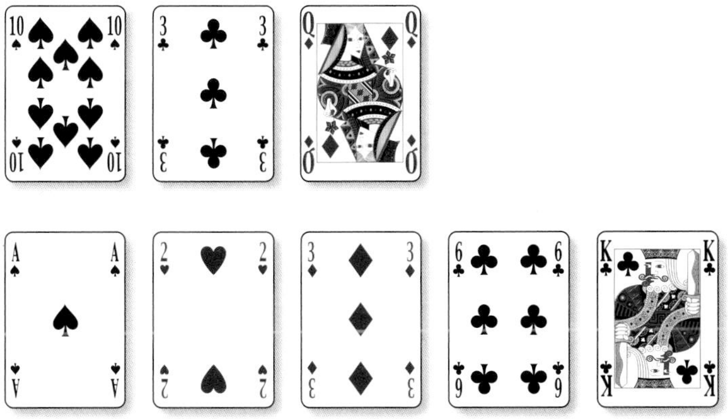

Above: Two examples of hands that have gone bust. In the first hand, an Eight was needed to make 21 points, but the Queen took the total to 23 points. In the second hand, a Five-card Trick looked like it was a real possibility, but the King takes the total just one point too high, at 22.

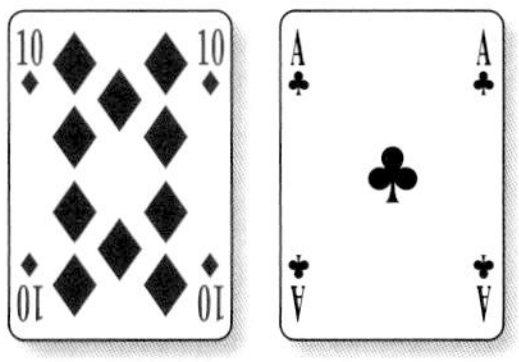

Left: Just one example of the best possible Pontoon hand, comprising 21 points.

Above: An example of a Five-card Trick which, in this case, adds up to 21 points, and is the second-best possible hand a player can have.

Conclusion

When all players have either stuck or bust, the game ends with the 'pay-off'. The banker's cards are turned face up, and the banker is free to add more cards to them, dealt face up one at a time, to attempt to bring his score to 21. At any point, the banker can elect to stick. If the banker has a Pontoon, the bank wins outright. If he sticks on a lesser hand, any player with cards worth more wins, and Pontoons and Five-card Tricks are paid double. If the banker goes bust, the bank pays players whose cards add up to 16 or more, the amount that they staked. If no one has a Pontoon, the used cards are added to the stock and a new hand is dealt. If there was a Pontoon, the cards are shuffled and cut before the next deal.

Blackjack

This is an extremely popular game, played in casinos around the world. Its origins go back as far as the 17th century to the French game called Vingt-et-Un. After the French Revolution, Vingt-et-Un migrated across the Atlantic to the USA, where it eventually took its current form.

You will need: 52-card deck; gambling chips/counters
Card ranking: See under 'Scoring', below
Players: Any number, each playing alone against the House (dealer)
Ideal for: 7+

Object

To beat the dealer by building up a hand worth as close as possible to 21 points, but not over that total. If the player busts he loses, even if the dealer also busts.

Scoring

Number cards count at face value, while the court cards (known in Blackjack as face cards) are worth 10 points each. An Ace can be worth one or 11 points. A hand consisting of an Ace plus a court card or a Ten is a Blackjack, or 'natural'. It can win its holder a bonus, since he receives one-and-a-half times the original bet. All other winnings are equal. If, however, the dealer also holds a Blackjack, the hand is tied – this is termed a 'push'. No one wins or loses, and the stakes are carried forward to the next hand.

The Deal and Play

Any number can play the game. The rules require all players to place their initial bets on the table before the hand can be dealt. Players simply put the chips they want to bet in front of them inside what is termed the betting circle. After the initial bets have been staked, the dealer deals two cards face up to each player and one card face up and one face down for himself. If a player is dealt a Blackjack and the dealer's turn-up is a number card between Two and Nine, that player is paid off immediately and his cards collected. If the dealer's turn-up is an Ace, court card or Ten, nothing can happen until the dealer's second card is turned.

If the dealer's turn-up is an Ace, a player can bet up to half the original stake that the down card is worth 10 points. In other words, he is betting that the dealer has a Blackjack. This is termed an 'insurance' bet, since it is worth double if it is correct. Similarly, if, after receiving the first two cards, a player thinks that he cannot beat the dealer's hand, he is allowed to 'surrender' – that is, immediately concede half the amount that has been bet. The exception is if the dealer has a Blackjack, in which case the entire stake is forfeit.

Standing and Hitting

Players dealt any combination of cards other than a Blackjack have two options. They can either stand (take no more cards) or call for a hit and be dealt additional cards. If the latter, these cards are dealt face up one at a time until the player either stands, or busts by exceeding 21 points. A player who busts loses cards and stake.

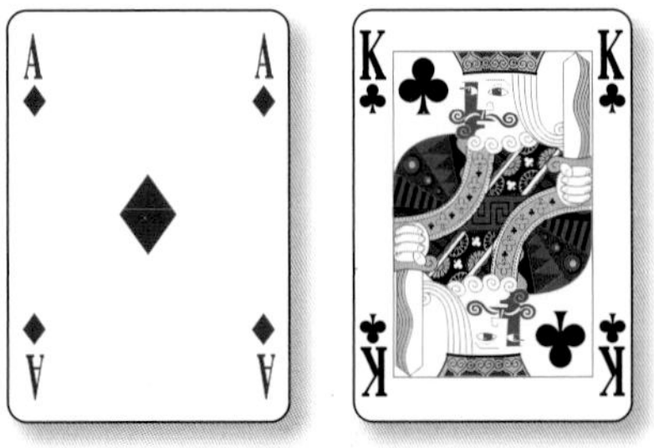

Left: Known as a 'natural' in Blackjack, this hand of 21 points wins its holder a bonus. The player receives one-and-a-half times the original bet.

Left: A player dealt two cards of the same rank can split them and play both as independent hands, an option often considered if the dealer has a poor turn-up showing.

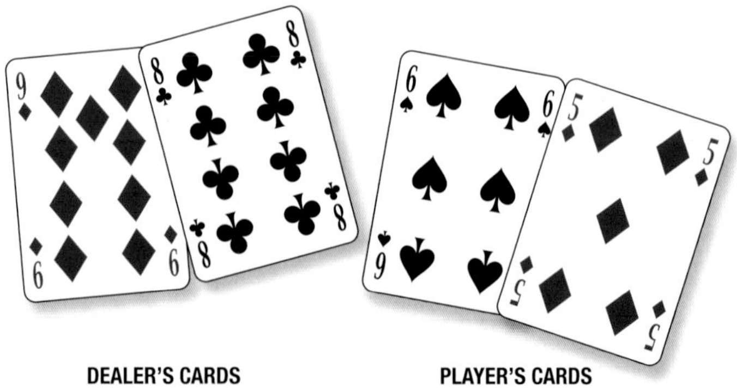

Above: The dealer's cards total an unpromising 17 points, while his opponent has 12 points. The player should hit for a further card here, in the hope of being dealt a card that takes his total closer to 21 than that of the dealer.

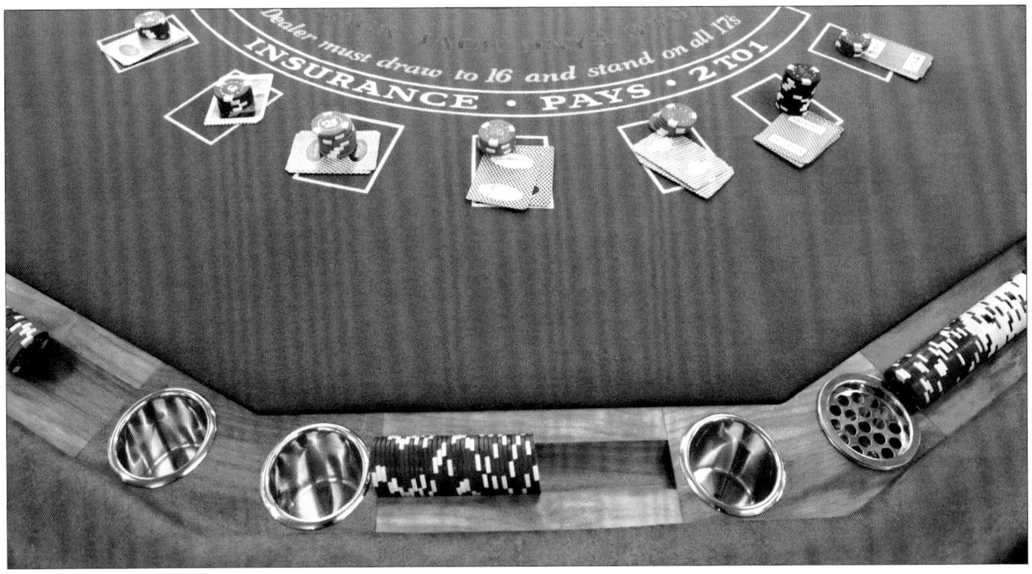

Left: Blackjack is one of the most popular casino card games in the world. Enthusiasts are attracted to the fact that success in the game requires a mix of chance with elements of skill. A lot of attention is given to card counting (keeping track of which cards have been played since the last shuffle).

Deciding when to hit or stand is key, as it can improve the odds of winning by more than 3 per cent. The basic rules are to stand on a hand of 17 or more and to hit on a hand of eight or less. If the dealer's turn-up is neither an Ace, nor a Ten or court card, he cannot make Blackjack. If it is a high card (an Eight or Nine), there is an increased chance he will go bust should he draw further cards.

Splitting

Players dealt two cards of the same rank have the option of splitting them and playing both cards as independent hands, though the same stake has to be wagered on the second hand as on the first. The player is then dealt a second card face up to each of them, and thereafter plays them as separate hands. There are two restrictions: if Aces are split, the player concerned can only receive one more card, while, in a split, a two-card 21 does not count as a Blackjack. Despite this, many players consider splitting to be worth doing if the dealer has a poor turn-up showing. In this situation, there is also the option of 'doubling down' (doubling the original bet). Players can also double down on any two cards.

Card Counting

Blackjack can be more rewarding than most casino games since it offers innumerable probability situations and choice of play. By keeping track of the cards that have already been played, a player can make a good estimate of the odds that apply to all the cards left in the deck. For example, the player can increase the starting bet if there are many Aces and Tens so far unseen, in the hope of hitting a Blackjack. If few Ten-cards have appeared to date, the fact the dealer must draw to 16 or less would mean that his chances of busting are relatively great. Card counting is helpful when used in conjunction with sound basic playing strategy and a good betting technique.

Hard and Soft Hands, or Pairs

Any hand without an Ace, or any with one where the Ace must be counted as one to avoid busting, is defined as a hard hand. Experienced players always hit a hard eight or less and stand on a hard 17 or better. Soft hands are hands that include an Ace, which can always be counted as one. They are so-called because the chances of going bust are reduced. Players should almost always stand on a soft 18 or higher and hit a soft 17 or lower.

Pairs are two cards of the same rank. A player holding one has to decide whether to split the pair and play two hands rather than just one, or to play the hand as dealt as a hard hand. Aces and Eights are always split.

Conclusion

Once all the players have ended their turns by standing or going bust, the dealer turns his face down card face up. If the result is Blackjack, the bank wins the stakes of all the other players. If not, provided that the two cards now on display count for 16 points or less, the dealer can draw more cards, face up and singly. He must stand when the cards are worth 17 points or more.

If the dealer busts, all the players still in the game win. If a player's card count is closer to 21 than that of the dealer, that player wins. If it is less, that player loses. The only way a player can lose without busting is when the dealer is closest to 21.

BACCARAT

Anyone who has read Ian Fleming's *Casino Royale* will be familiar with the climactic game of Baccarat played between James Bond and the chief villain. The game probably originated in Italy in the 1490s. Its name comes from the word *baccara*, meaning 'zero', which refers to the fact that court cards and Tens are worth nothing.

You will need: 52-card deck; gambling chips/counters

Card ranking: See under 'Play', below

Players: Any number, each playing alone against the bank (dealer)

Ideal for: 7+

OBJECT

To beat the banker with a higher hand, the best possible being worth nine points.

THE DEAL

In Baccarat proper, the house is always the bank; in Chemin de Fer, a popular variant, it passes from player to player. Either way, the banker shuffles the cards and passes them to each player in turn, who deals two cards face down separately. The banker finally takes two. Players examine their cards and bet against the bank, which plays against each of them separately.

Right: It is the practice in Baccarat to deal from a shoe, but this is not essential.

PLAY

Number cards count at face value. Aces are worth one point. A two-card total of nine points is termed a 'natural' and cannot lose. A two-card total of eight is the second-best hand. No further cards may be drawn if a player is holding a two-card draw of six or seven. In hands adding up to more than nine, only the second digit counts, i.e. five plus seven is worth two, not 12.

If the count is less than five, a player must call for another card, which is drawn face up, but, if the count is exactly five, he may stand (take no more cards) or draw (call for another card). If the banker's hand is worth less than five points, he must draw. If it is worth three points, the banker draws if the opponent's third card is anything between an Ace and a Ten. If the banker's hand is worth four points, he draws to an opponent's third card between Two and Seven and, if it is worth five points, he draws to a third card which is between Four and Seven. If the third card is worth six or more, the banker draws only to a Six or a Seven.

Even with a hand worth just three points, the banker stands if the opposing player's third card is an Eight. If the banker has four points, the bank stands if the player's third card is an Ace, Eight, Nine or Ten, while, if the bank's cards are worth six points, the bank stands to an Ace or Ten. If the bank's cards are worth seven points or more, the banker always stands, regardless of the value of the third card a player may hold.

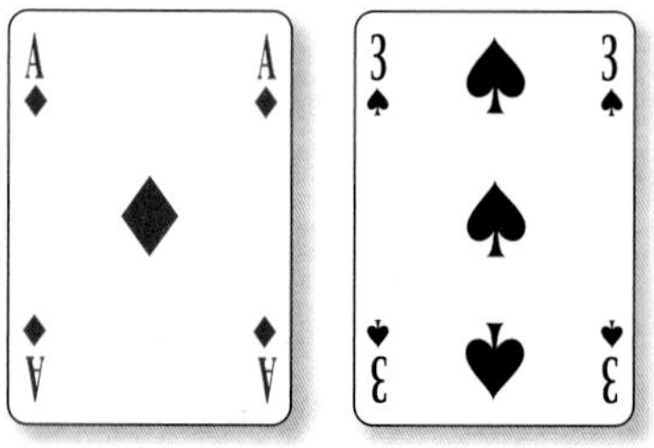

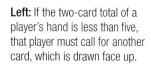

Left: If the two-card total of a player's hand is less than five, that player must call for another card, which is drawn face up.

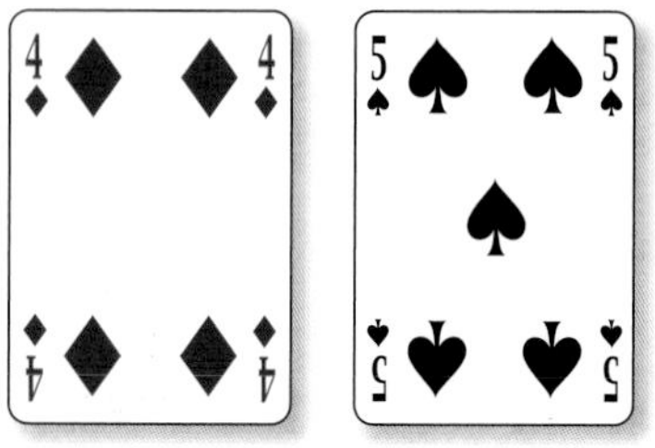

Left: A two-card total of nine, such as that shown here, is termed a 'natural' in Baccarat, and cannot lose.

CONCLUSION

The hand with a value of nine points, or the one closest to nine, wins. If the hands are tied, there is no winner or loser, and the stakes are carried forward to the next deal.

YABLON

Also often known as Acey-Deucey and In Between, Yablon is a simple gambling game in which suits are irrelevant and only three cards are played per hand. In the USA the game has been recently rechristened Red Dog, which is confusing because there is another gambling game of the same name. Casino play involves anything up to eight packs dealt from a shoe.

You will need: 52-card deck; gambling chips/counters

Card ranking: See under 'The Deal and Play', below

Players: Any number, each playing alone against the bank (dealer)

Ideal for: 10+

OBJECT

To bet on whether a third card dealt by the dealer will rank between the first two cards.

THE DEAL AND PLAY

Cards from Two to Ten count at face value, Jacks score 11, Queens 12, Kings 13 and Aces 14. In Yablon, players bet that the third card dealt from the top of the pack will be intermediate in rank between the first two cards. All players make an initial stake, after which the dealer deals them two cards face up on the table with enough space between them for a third.

The dealer then places a marker to indicate the spread, the difference between the card values of the cards that have been dealt, and the odds being offered on an additional bet. If a player bets no further, but wins the hand, he wins the original stake at even money.

If they wish, players can now raise their bets, but not by more than the initial bet, the odds being determined by the 'spread' – that is, the number of ranks intermediate between the first two cards. For example, if the 5♠ and the 7♣ are dealt then the spread is one, and the players are allowed to place a 'raise' bet up to the size of the original bet. If the two cards are consecutive (such as the 5♠ and the 6♣), it is a tie. If they are identical, then the players are not allowed to raise. The number of players is irrelevant, since all players win or lose simultaneously. The only strategy decision that the player is allowed to make is whether or not to double the bet.

SCORING

The odds paid to successful players vary with the 'spread' – the number of ranks between the first two cards. A spread of one has odds of 5:1, a spread of two has odds of 4:1, and a spread of three has odds of 2:1. For spreads of between four and 11, the odds are even.

CONCLUSION

The dealer deals a third card face up. If the card is intermediate, the players win. If not, the bank does. Players who have raised and won get the original stake back, plus the raise at the appropriate odds.

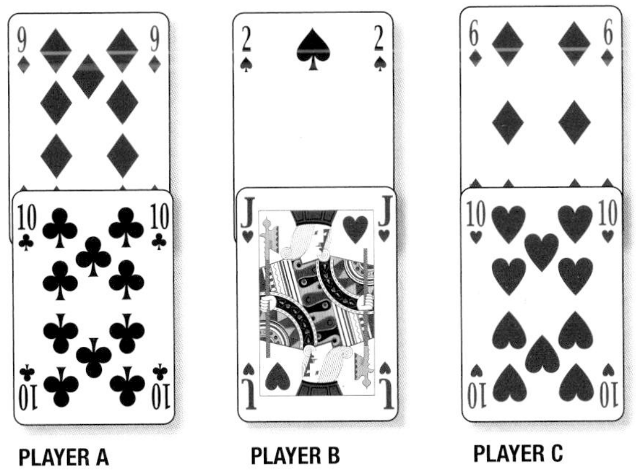

Above: Players bet that the third card from the top of the pack will be intermediate in rank between the first two cards. For Player A, this is impossible, so he will fold. Player B has every chance of success, so he is likely to bet heavily. Player C's chances are limited, so betting will be more circumspect.

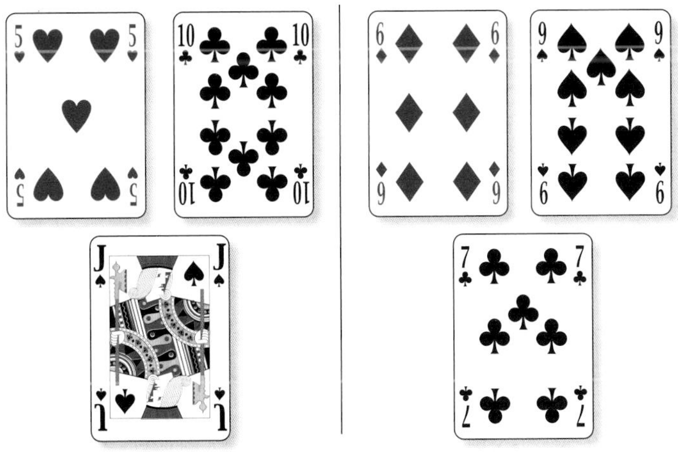

Above: On the left, the dealer has turned up a Jack outside the spread of the two cards dealt. All bets placed are lost. In the example on the right, the dealer's card falls in between the table cards, so any player who placed a bet and raised will retrieve his original stake plus the raise at appropriate odds.

Speculation

Mentioned by Jane Austen and Charles Dickens in their novels, this, according to the 1847 edition of *Hoyle's Games*, is 'a noisy round game that several may play'. In his *The Card Player*, published 20 years later, Charles Pardon described it as an ideal 'merry game for Christmas parties'. Though it dropped out of favour at the end of the 1800s, it is well worth reviving.

You will need: 52-card deck; gambling chips/counters
Card ranking: Standard
Players: Any number, each playing alone against the dealer
Ideal for: 7+

Object

To end the game holding the highest trump card when all the cards being played have been revealed.

The Deal

All players begin with the same number of chips, each anteing one to start the pot. (The ante is the stake that each player must put into the pot before receiving a hand or new cards.) The dealer deals three cards face down in front of each player in a stack, turning the next one up in front of him to establish the trump suit. If it is an Ace, the dealer wins the game immediately.

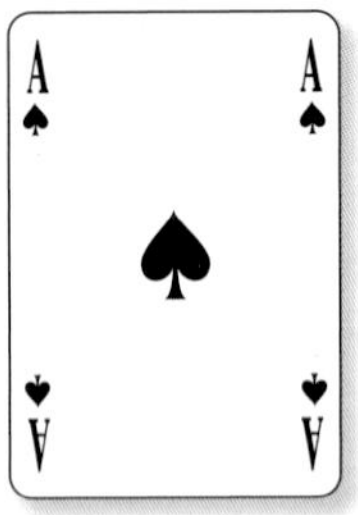

Left: If the dealer turns up an Ace, he wins immediately.

Right: In some variations of Speculation, a player turning over a Jack has to pay an extra chip into the pot.

Play

Assuming the dealer hasn't already won, players turn up their top cards, starting with the player to the dealer's left. If a trump card is turned up that is higher than the previous player's, its holder may offer it for sale or retain it. The holder of the highest trump card sits out play until a higher one is turned up. Any player may offer to buy any face-down card or cards sight unseen – they can be revealed only when turned up during play. If no trump card is turned up, the pot carries over to the next round.

Conclusion

The game ends when all the cards have been exposed or if a player turns up the Ace of trumps. Whoever holds the highest trump is the winner.

Left: Writer Jane Austen (1775–1817) mentioned the game Speculation in her novel *Mansfield Park*, as did Charles Dickens (1812–70) in his novel *Nicholas Nickleby*.

Let it Ride

This banking game is a variation of the poker game Five-Card Stud. In Let it Ride, players do not have to beat anyone else's hand. It is popular with beginners because it is very easy to learn.

You will need: 52-card deck; gambling chips/counters
Card ranking: See 'Hand Ranking' below
Players: Any number
Ideal for: 7+

Object

To construct a winning Poker hand, the minimum hand being a Pair of Tens. Players win according to how good a Poker hand is made by their three cards combined with the dealer's two cards.

The Deal and Play

Each player places three equal stakes before the deal, although subsequently one or two of them may be withdrawn. Each player is then dealt three cards face down, while the dealer takes two.

After the cards have been examined, each player can either withdraw one of the three initial stakes, or let it ride – stay with their stake. The dealer then exposes one of the two cards he has been dealt and the other players get the same opportunity. This means that, at the most, players will have three stakes in front of them when the dealer's second card is turned and, at the least, one.

The skill lies in knowing when to let a bet ride. It is the best strategy it to let it ride on the first bet if you hold a high-card Pair, Three of a Kind, three consecutive cards of the same suit valued Three, Four, Five or better, three of a Straight Flush with one skip – a missing card – and at least one high card, or with two skips and at least two high cards. On the second bet, in addition to the above, let it ride if you have Two Pairs, four of any Flush, four of a Straight or four High Cards.

Hand Ranking

Hands rank from highest to lowest as follows:

- Royal Flush – A Straight Flush up to Ace; i.e. J♦, Q♦, K♦, A♦.
- Straight Flush – A combined Straight and Flush; i.e. cards in sequence and of same suit.
- Four of a Kind – Four cards of the same face value ('quads').
- Full House – Three of a Kind (also known as 'trips') and a Pair. When two players hold a Full House, the one with the highest-ranking trips wins.
- Flush – Five cards of the same suit. If another player holds a Flush, whoever holds the highest card wins.
- Straight – A sequence of five cards in any suit; e.g. 5♦, 6♣, 7♠, 8♥, 9♣. The highest Straight is one topped by Ace, the lowest starts with Ace. Should two players hold a Straight, the one with the highest cards wins.
- Three of a Kind – Three cards of the same face value; e.g. Q♠, Q♣, Q♥.
- Two Pairs – Two sets of Pairs; e.g. 10♦, 10♥ and Q♠, Q♣. If two players hold Pairs of the same value, whoever holds the highest cards in the two hands – the 'kicker' – wins.
- One Pair – Two cards of the same value, Ten or above; e.g. 10♦, 10♥ or Q♠, Q♣. Should another player hold a Pair of the same value, then whoever holds the kicker wins.
- High Card – A hand with no combinations, but having within it the highest-ranking card among the hands in play.

Scoring

All players with a Pair or better are paid at the following fixed odds, according to their stakes.

- A Pair – evens
- Two Pairs – 2:1
- Three of a Kind – 3:1
- Straight – 5:1
- Flush – 8:1
- Full House – 11:1
- Four of a Kind – 50:1
- Straight Flush – 200:1
- Royal Flush –1,000:1

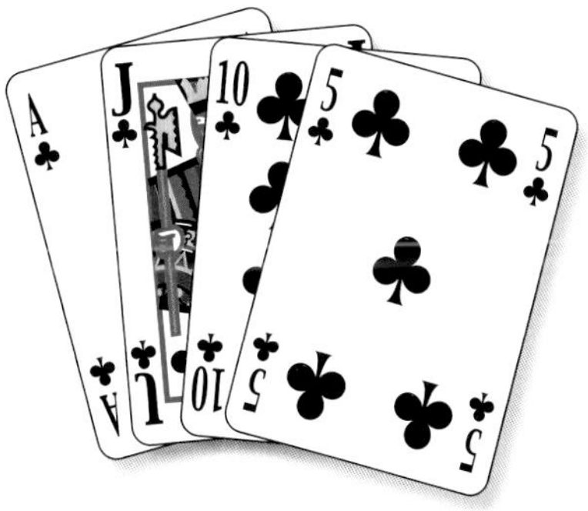

Left: On the second bet, it is best to let it ride if you have four of any flush.

Conclusion

The game ends after the dealer's second card has been turned with what's known as the payout. Players show their hands, and the dealer collects the stakes from any players whose three cards plus the dealer's two do not form a Pair of Tens or better. The others are paid according to their stakes at the appropriate odds.

10 | All Fours Games

Some of the most interesting card games in the English-speaking world can trace their ancestry back to the time of Charles II's reign in the 17th century, specifically to a game called All Fours. This game introduced the term 'Jack' for 'Knave', although it took many years for this name to be universally adopted. When All Fours reached the USA 200 years later, this soon spawned variants.

Despite its origins as a low-class game played mostly in alehouses or by servants and the lower ranks of the British Navy, All Fours rapidly became one of the most popular games in the USA in the 19th century. Despite subsequent competition from other games, notably Euchre and Poker, All Fours has survived, partly by developing more elaborate forms to compete with them for interest. It is the national card game of Trinidad and is still played in the Yorkshire and Lancashire regions of its British homeland.

Over time, quite a few variants of All Fours have developed including Pitch, Smear, Cinch and Don, all of which incorporate some system of bidding.

Pitch originated in the USA, where it is also called Setback or High-Low-Jack. There are two varieties: partnership and cut-throat. In the former, four players play in partnerships, and in the latter players are out for themselves. Smear is also American in origin and uses Jokers as extra trumps. Cinch comes from Colorado, and the aim is to play a trump high enough to beat the Five of Trumps.

Don is yet another version of the all-fours partnership game played in various forms in Ireland, from where it crossed the Irish Sea to reach Britain some time in the late 19th or early 20th century.

Above: The use of the term 'Jack' was considered rather vulgar when first introduced. In *Great Expectations*, Dickens has the character Pip divulge his social status when Estella says snootily 'He calls his knaves *Jacks*, this boy!'

All Fours

The earliest reference to All Fours dates from 1674, when it was recorded in Charles Cotton's *Complete Gamester* as being a game played in Kent, England. From there, it migrated to the USA under the names Seven Up and Old Sledge.

You will need: 52-card deck; scorecards

Card ranking: Standard

Players: Normally four, playing for themselves or in partnership, though two or three can play as well

Ideal for: 14+

Object

To win as many points as possible, thus being the first player to score seven.

The Deal

Players cut the pack for the deal: the one with the highest card becomes the first dealer. The deal passes to the right after each hand. Each player is dealt six cards, either singly or in two packets of three, and the next card is turned face up to indicate the putative trump suit for the hand. If the turn-up card is an Ace, Jack or Six, the dealer or the dealing partnership scores a bonus point.

Establishing Trumps

The player to the dealer's right has the option of accepting the trump suit, in which case he says 'Stand', or requesting a change by saying 'I beg'. If the dealer overrides the request, he says 'Take One', in which case the opposing player or partnership scores a point and play begins. If the dealer agrees to change trumps by saying 'Refuse the gift', the turn-up is set aside, each player is dealt three more cards and the next one is turned up to find a new trump. The procedure is repeated until a new trump suit is established. If the deck is exhausted before this happens, the cards are 'bunched', that is, thrown in, shuffled and then dealt again. The entire process is termed 'running the cards'. Following it, players discard enough unwanted cards face down to reduce their hands to six cards again.

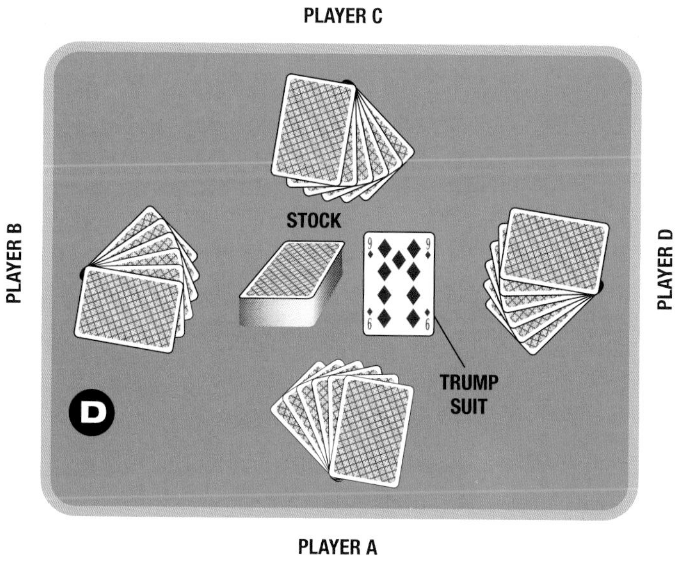

Above: In this scenario after the cards have been dealt, the player to the dealer's right can accept the turned-up trump suit or request a change, in which case it is down to the dealer to make the final decision.

Play and Scoring

The player to the dealer's right leads, and the other players must follow suit, or they must trump. If they cannot do either, they can play any card. The highest card of the suit led or the highest trump wins the trick. There are penalties for playing a card of a different suit to the card that was led when one could have followed suit, or failing to play a trump when one could have been played (termed a revoke or renege). If the offending player failed to follow a trump, despite holding one or more of the five top trumps, the penalty is to forfeit the game. For a revoke on a non-trump lead or failing to play a low trump to a trump lead, the opposing players win a penalty point and the revoking player cannot win the point normally awarded for game. Points are won in each hand as follows:

- One point for High (being dealt the highest trump).
- One point for Low (being dealt the lowest trump).
- One point for capturing the Jack of trumps.
- One point for turning up a Jack (if applicable).
- One point for Game (ending up with the highest total of point-scoring cards). Aces count four, Kings three, Queens two, Jacks one and Tens 10. Each partnership adds up the value of any such cards they have won in tricks, and whichever has the most scores the game point. In the event of a tie, no Game point is scored.

Conclusion

Play in each round continues until all cards have been laid. The first player to score seven points wins.

Pitch

This game, which is also known as Setback or High-Low-Jack, is played like All Fours, but with a round of bidding added. Instead of turning a card to establish trumps, the player who wins the auction chooses the trump suit, which is confirmed by 'pitching' – leading a card from the chosen suit to the first trick.

You will need: 52 card-deck; scorecards
Card ranking: Standard
Players: Two to seven (four usually play in partnerships of two; six can also play in pairs)
Ideal for: 14+

Object

To win a specified number of tricks (rounds of the game) or to score bonus points.

The Deal

Each player is dealt six cards three at a time, and the remainder of the pack is placed face down out of play. The deal rotates clockwise after each hand.

Bidding

Following the deal, there is a round of bidding in which each player can bid up to the maximum number of points that can be won in each hand for High (being dealt the highest trump), Low (being dealt or having captured the lowest trump), Jack (having captured the Jack of trumps) and Game (ending up with the most point-scoring cards). The bids are two, three and four, plus smudge, a bid to win all six tricks. Each bid must be higher than the one before it, though the dealer, who bids last, can 'steal the deal' by matching the previous bid. If, however, the other players all pass, the dealer is obliged to bid at least two.

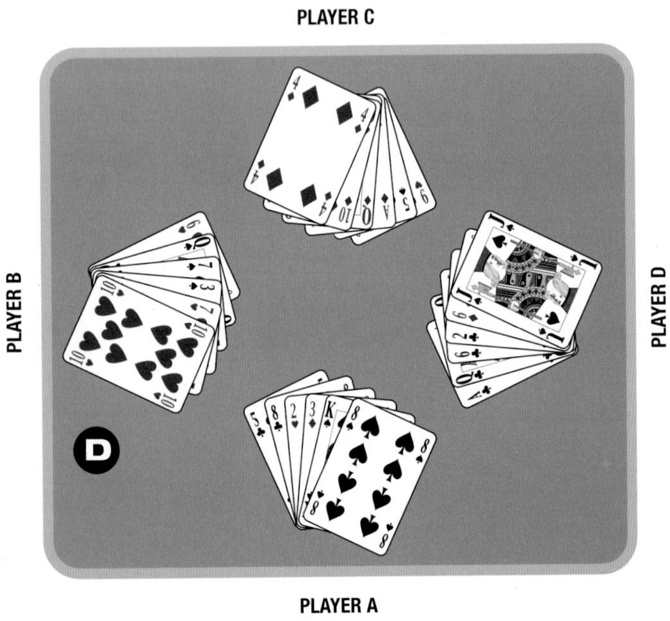

Above: A scenario after the deal. Player C bids two in an attempt to win a point for High (highest trump) with his Ace. Player D bids three for the same reasons, plus he is hoping to win a point for Low (lowest trump) with his Two. Players A and B decide to pass. As the highest bidder, Player D pitches the Ace, thereby making Clubs trumps.

Play and Scoring

The winning bidder becomes the pitcher, with the right to choose the trump suit and lead to the first trick. The highest trump played wins each trick, or the highest card in the suit led. Players may use a trump on any trick even if able to follow suit. The trick's winner leads to the next.

A player or partnership that fulfils their bid scores the number of points they have won. Bidding two and making four, for example, scores four points. If they fail to make their bid, they are 'set back' by that amount, that is, they lose the value of their bid.

The opposing player or partnership makes whatever points they earn. If, for instance, the pitching partnership bid two, but their opponents take the Two of trumps, they score a point for Low. Likewise, High, Jack and Game are also worth one point.

Left: Assuming Spades are trumps, if a partnership has bid two but its opponents capture the 2♠, the opponents score a point for Low (having captured the lowest trump).

Conclusion

The game is won by the first player or partnership to reach a previously agreed total of points – this can be as low as seven or as high as 21 – but this can be achieved only at the end of a hand in which the partnership made its bid. Paradoxically, this means that the game can be won by a partnership with fewer points than the losing partnership.

Smear

This game has four distinguishing features. First, two Jokers can be used as lowest trumps. Second, Low is always won by the holder of the lowest trump other than a Joker, not the winner of the trick containing it. Third, the Jick (the other Jack of the same colour as the trump suit) can be played as an extra trump. Finally, all players must discard after bidding is over.

You will need: 52-card deck; two Jokers; scorecards

Card ranking: Standard

Players: Four, in partnerships of two

Ideal for: 14+

Object

To be the first partnership to score 52 points by winning tricks containing scoring cards.

The Deal

Players are dealt 10 cards each.

Bidding

The deal is followed by a round of bidding, starting with the player to the dealer's left. Players can pass or bid the number of points (the minimum is four and the maximum 10) that they undertake to win in exchange for the right to name the trump suit. Each bid must be higher than the last.

Play

Once trumps have been called, the highest bidder picks up the 14 remaining cards, adds them to his hand and then discards 18 of them. The other players discard four cards from the hands they hold, so that everyone ends up with a six-card hand. A player with more than six trumps must play the excess number to the first trick: he may not include more than one point-scoring trump. The highest bidder plays first. The other players must follow suit if they hold any cards of the suit that was led. A player with no card of the suit led may play any card.

Above: With Diamonds as trumps, a player taking a trick with the Three in it scores three points for Trey.

Above: Players score one point for playing either of the Jokers.

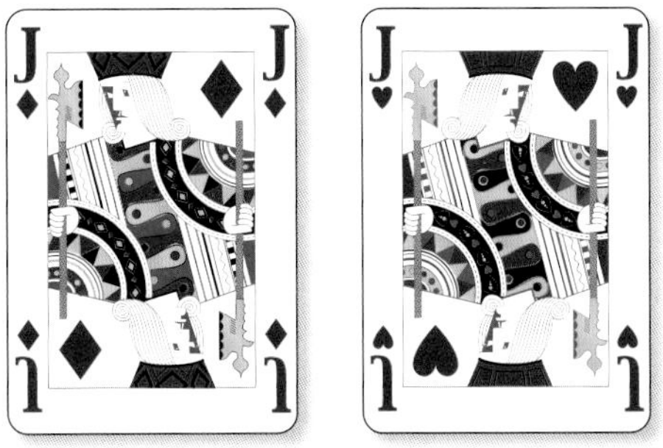

Left: The Jack of the same colour as trumps is called the Jick. So, if Diamonds are trumps, the J♥ is the Jick.

No trump may be played until all such cards have been played. The highest card of the suit led or the highest trump wins the trick.

Scoring and Conclusion

Points are won as follows:

- One point for High, won by the highest trump.
- One point for Low, won by the lowest trump.
- One point for capturing the Jack of trumps.
- One point for taking the Jick.
- One point for playing either of the Jokers.
- One point for Game.
- Three points for Trey, won by the Three of trumps.
- One point for Game (determined by card rankings).

The game point goes to the team taking the highest total in scoring cards. Aces count four, Kings three, Queens two, Jacks and Jokers one and Tens 10. Each partnership adds up the value of any such cards they've won in tricks, and whichever has the most scores the game point.

Some variations do not recognize the Trey point, in which case the maximum bid would be seven, not 10. If the winners of the bid make as many or more points as they bid, they score all the points they made. If not, the amount of the bid is deducted from their score, which may leave them with minus points. The non-bidding partnership scores all the points they take in either case.

The first partnership to score 52 points wins; in the event of a tie, the bidding partnership wins.

Cinch

This All Fours game, otherwise called Pedro, originated in the USA as a variation of Pitch. Though it's popularity has declined, it is still widely played in various parts of the USA and Central America, with variants in Finland and Italy.

You will need: 52-card deck; scorecards
Card ranking: See under 'Play and Scoring'
Players: Four in partnerships of two
Ideal for: 14+

Object

To be the first partnership to reach 62 points through taking tricks containing scoring cards.

The Deal

Players are dealt nine cards, three at a time.

Bidding, Discarding and Drawing

Each player has one chance to pass or to bid. The minimum bid allowed is seven points and the maximum 14. If the first three players pass, the dealer is obliged to bid seven. The highest bidder announces which suit will be trumps, after which everyone bar the dealer discards their non-trump cards face down and is dealt enough replacements to give them six.

The dealer then discards, goes through the remaining cards and picks up all the trumps they contain. This may mean that he ends up with a hand of more than six cards, in which case more than one card must be played to the first trick, the card on top being the only one that counts.

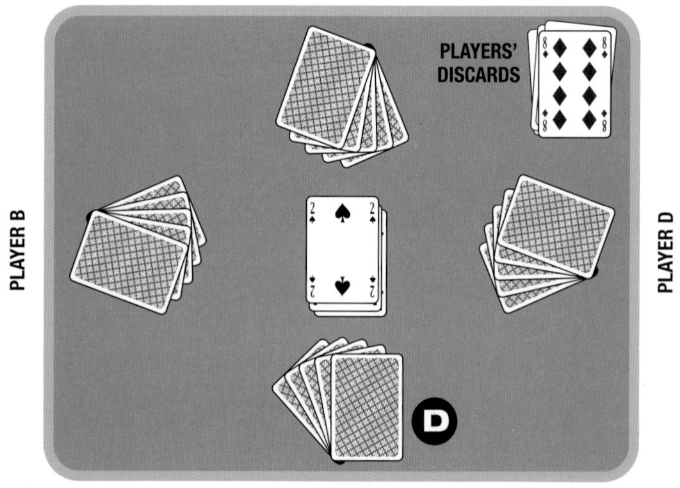

Above: As the dealer has the choice of taking any trumps from those cards left after the deal, he may have to play several cards to the first trick. Only the top card of those played by the dealer is considered to be in play, and he should end up with just five cards left in his hand.

The others are 'buried', that is, discarded and do not count. It is against the rules, however, to bury any of the scoring trumps.

Play and Scoring

The highest bidder leads to the first trick. Players follow suit if they can or they can play a trump. If unable to do either, they can play any card. In the trump suit, cards rank Ace, King, Queen, Jack, 10, 9, 8, 7, 6, 5 (the Pedro), the other 5 of the same colour (the Low Pedro), 4, 3, 2. In non-trump suits the ranking is Ace, King, Queen, Jack, 10, 9, 8, 7, 6, 5 (when the opposite colour to trumps), 4, 3, 2. The highest card of the suit led or the highest trump takes the trick, its winner leading to the next.

If the bidding partnership makes their bid, they score all the tricks they take. If unsuccessful, they must deduct the amount of the bid from their score. The Ace, Jack, Ten and Two of trumps each score one point, while the two Pedros score five points each.The non-bidding partnership scores for everything they make. With the exception of the point for the Two of trumps, which goes to the partnership of the player who was dealt it, the partnership capturing the cards in tricks takes the points.

Left: In Cinch, the Five of trumps is called the Pedro and the Five of the same colour the Low or Left Pedro. So, if Diamonds are trumps, the 5♦ is the Pedro and the 5♥ the Left Pedro.

Conclusion

If both teams score 55 points or more, the situation is termed 'bidder goes out'. If the bidding team make their bid on the next hand, they win. If not, the hand is scored normally, the result being that the opposing team can often snatch the victory. The winners of the game are the first team to reach or exceed 62 points.

Don

Related to All Fours, this game probably descended from the 19th-century game Dom Pedro, which became popular in Ireland and America, where the name was abbreviated to Don.

You will need: 52-card deck; Cribbage board for scoring
Card ranking: Standard
Players: Four, in partnerships of two
Ideal for: 14+

Object

To be the first to reach a predetermined score through wining tricks that contain scoring cards.

The Deal

Players cut to establish 'first pitch' – that is, who will lead first and set trumps. In the Irish variant, the player holding the 2♦ pitches or 'pucks out' to the first trick. The player to the pitcher's right then deals nine cards singly in the English version of Don or 13 cards in the Irish version. The remainder are stacked face down.

Play

All players now examine their hands, except the pitcher's partner, who cannot touch his cards until after the first card has been led. This is to avoid the risk of the player signalling to the pitcher the suit to make trumps. As in the majority of partnership card games, a player may not signal what cards he holds or what a partner should play.

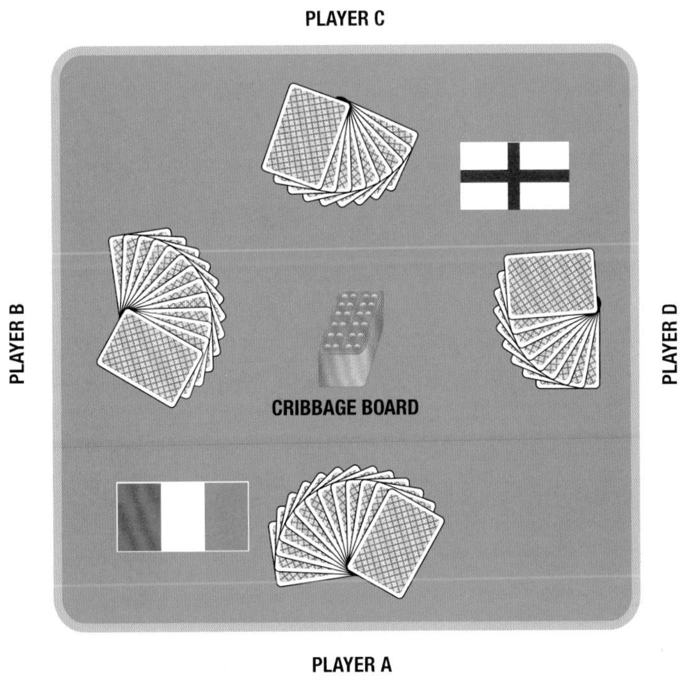

Above: In the English version of Don, players receive nine cards; in the Irish version, 13 cards are dealt.

The pitcher pitches a card to the first trick to start play, its suit establishing trumps. Players must follow suit if they can, trump or otherwise play any card. The highest card of the suit led or the highest trump played wins the trick. The winner of each trick leads to the next.

Scoring and Conclusion

Because the scoring system is somewhat convoluted, it is the custom to keep score by pegging on a Cribbage board. Firstly, each side sorts through its tricks, when all cards have been played. They add up the points scored for winning tricks containing specific trumps or any five, and peg the amount on the board. In nine-card Don, they are scored accordingly: trump Ace = four, trump King = three, trump Queen = two, trump Jack = one, trump Nine = nine, and trump Five = 10. Non-trump Fives are worth five points.

Next, they add together the card values of the Aces, Kings, Queens, Jacks and Tens they hold in each of the four suits, to decide which team scores the extra points for 'Game' at the end of the play. The side that wins the majority of card points in that deal wins eight points. Here, Aces score four points, Kings three, Queens two, Jacks one and Tens 10. If both partnerships tie, then neither scores for Game. The first partnership to score an agreed total of points, customarily 91 or 121, wins.

In the Irish variant, scoring is the same except that the trump Nine ('Big Don') = 18 points; the trump Five ('Little Don') = 10 points and non-trump Nines score nine. The first partnership to score 80 wins.

Above: The scoring trumps in Don are Ace, King, Queen, Jack, Nine and Five; the score is usually pegged on a Cribbage board.

11 | Solo Games

This type of game differs from other plain-trick games, such as Bridge and Whist, because the individual players are ultimately out for themselves and finish the game with a score of their own. There are no fixed or set partnerships, although if four players are involved, temporary alliances can be formed for convenience – sometimes three players against one, but more often two versus two.

Typically, the highest bidder in each deal names trumps and then sets out to win a specified number of tricks. The object of the other players is to prevent this. The bid is termed a solo. Its bidder is often known as the soloist and he leads.

Leading is often advantageous, since it determines the suit that the other players, if able, have to play. Playing last, however, has its merits as well, since the final player can react to what the previous players have played and, in theory, can compute the outcome of the trick for each of his possible plays. The contents of each trick are irrelevant – only the number of tricks taken by the individual players matters.

Some games have a remarkable historical pedigree. Ombre dates back to a 16th-century Spanish card game called Hombre, in which the term was used to denote the solo player. It is thought to be the most significant ancestor of subsequent bidding games, including Whist and Bridge. Boston, although its name suggests a link with the American War of Independence, probably started in France at the end of the 18th century.

Other noteworthy alliance games are Belgian Whist or Wiezen and Colour Whist or Kleurenwiezen, its more complex relation. Solo Whist, which developed in Britain into a popular game by the end of the 19th century, was derived from a Belgian game.

Above: An English engraving entitled *A game of Whist* (c.1821), a classic trick-taking card game that was played widely in the 18th and 19th centuries.

Solo Whist

Also known as English Solo, this game became popular in the 1890s, when it reached Britain from Belgium, where it was known as Whist de Gand (Ghent Whist). Players play for themselves, but they form temporary alliances – one against three or two against two – for each hand. There is no running score. Each deal is complete in itself.

You will need: 52-card deck; no Jokers; scorecards or counters
Card ranking: Standard
Players: Four
Ideal for: 10+

Object

To make at least as many tricks (or, in the case of *Misère* bids, at least as few) as bid.

The Deal

Whichever player cuts the lowest card deals first. The deal, bidding and play run clockwise around the table. The cards are dealt in four batches of three with the last four cards being dealt singly to each player until every one has 13 cards. The last card is turned face up to indicate the prospective trump for the trick.

Bidding

The auction starts with the player to the dealer's left, each player having the chance to bid a contract, or to pass. From lowest to highest, the possible bids are:

- Proposal (or Prop) – a bid to win at least eight tricks in partnership with another player with the suit of the upturned card as trumps (scores one point per trick).
- Cop – an acceptance of another player's prop.
- Solo – a contract to win at least five tricks on his own (scores one point per trick).
- *Misère* or *Mis* – an undertaking to lose every trick (scores two points).
- Abundance – a contract to win at least nine tricks, with trumps of one's own choosing (scores three points per trick).
- Royal Abundance – a contract to win at least nine tricks, with trumps being the suit of the turned-up card (scores three points per trick).
- *Misère Ouverte* – a contract, with one's cards turned face up after the first trick, to lose every trick (scores four points).
- Abundance *Declaré* (or Slam) – a bid to win all 13 tricks solo (scores six points).

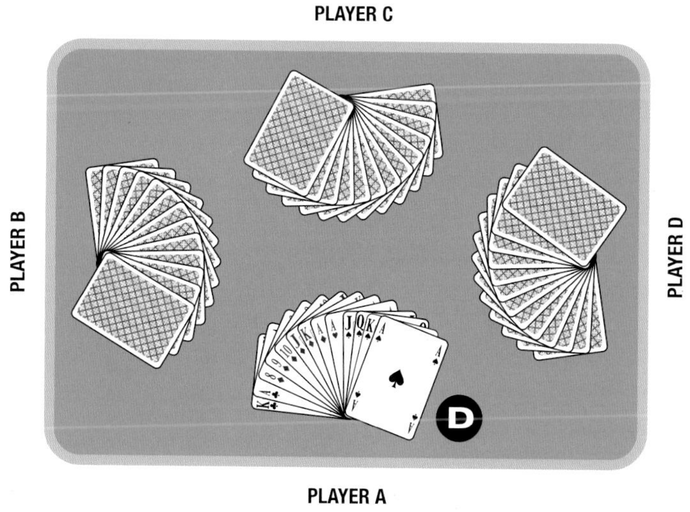

Above: This very strong hand, with Diamonds as trumps, is ideal for a bid of Slam: a contract to win all 13 tricks playing solo.

Play

Once the contract is established, the player to the left of the dealer leads to the first trick, except if a Slam has been called, in which case the lead passes to the soloist. In the *Misère Ouverte* bid, the soloist's hand must be spread face up on the table at the end of the first trick and before the second is led. Players must always follow suit if possible, otherwise any card may be played. The highest card of the suit that has been led takes the trick, unless trumps have been played, in which case the highest trump wins. The winner leads to the next trick.

Conclusion and Scoring

Generally, players settle up in counters or total scores at the end of each hand, when all 13 tricks have been won.

In Prop and Cop, each member of the winning partnership receives a counter for making the bid from both of the other two players, plus a further counter from both for each overtrick. If the contract is broken, each of the bidders pays five counters to the two other players for the failed bid, plus an extra counter to both per undertrick.

In all other bids, the successful soloist is paid by all three opponents, but pays them if the bid fails. The soloist wins three units in total (one from each opponent), for instance, if he makes a Solo, and nine if he makes an Abundance.

Belgian Whist

Otherwise known as Wiezen, the Flemish for Whist, Belgian Whist is a descendant of Boston and is similar to Solo Whist. It is closely related to Colour Whist (Kleurenwiezen in Flemish, Whist à la Couleur in French). The difference between them is that in Belgian Whist the trump suit is established by turning up the last card to be dealt. In Colour Whist, it is determined by the bidding.

You will need: 52 cards; no Jokers; gambling chips/counters
Card ranking: Standard, Aces high
Players: Four
Ideal for: 10+

Object

To make at least as many tricks (or, in the case of *Misère* bids, at least as few) as bid.

The Deal

Before the deal, each player puts an agreed number of chips or counters into a pool. The cards are then dealt four, four and five to each player. The last card to be dealt is turned face up to indicate the trump suit. The dealer picks it up when bidding is over.

Bidding

In the bidding, each player can make a proposal, accept a proposal, bid higher or pass. The various bids, from lowest to highest, are as follows:

- Proposal – a contract to win at least eight tricks with the help of a partner (the caller has to take five of these tricks and the partner three).
- Acceptance – agreeing to a proposal, and thus to score eight tricks (at least three oneself) in partnership with the proposer.
- Solo – a bid to take five or more tricks.
- Abundance – a bid to take at least nine tricks, with trumps of one's own choice.
- Abundance in trumps – a bid to take at least nine tricks, where trumps is the suit of the upturned card.
- *Troel* – open only to a player holding three Aces, this is an undertaking to win at least eight tricks with a partner – either the player holding the fourth Ace or the holder of the highest Heart not held by the bidder.
- *Misère* – an undertaking to lose every trick, playing solo with no trumps.
- Solo Slam – a contract to take all 13 tricks.

Play

The player to the dealer's left leads, except in Slam or Abundance when the lead is with the soloist. Players must follow suit if they can, otherwise play a trump or any other card. In *Troel* with three Aces, the fourth Ace's holder must lead it to the first trick. If the bidder holds all four Aces, the highest Heart must be played.

Scoring and Conclusion

The scores are totalled at the end of each hand when all 13 tricks have been won. A successful soloist wins the pool, plus a varying amount from the other players depending on the contract. The minimum is three times the contract's value. Partners divide the pool and win a set amount from their opponents. A losing soloist doubles the pool and pays the appropriate amount to each opponent. Losing partners double the pool between them and each pays the appropriate amount to one opponent.

Proposal, Acceptance and Solo bids score one for each trick, plus one for each overtrick. The scores are doubled if all 13 tricks are taken. Abundance scores eight points, *Misère* 10 points, *Troel* two points plus two per overtrick and Solo Slam scores 24 points.

Left: Comprising almost exclusively low cards, this hand is ideal for a bid of *Misère*: a contract to lose every trick, which is played in no trumps.

Left: With all four Aces, long Clubs, and only a slight weakness in Diamonds, this hand is worth a bid of Solo Slam, naming Clubs as trumps.

Solo Variants

Several solo variants exist, which are all fun to play and present a real challenge. Crazy Solo, of American origin, is a multi-player game – the number of players can vary from three to 12, which affects how it is played. A 36-card deck is used, but sometimes fewer cards are employed, depending on how many play. Knockout Whist is British in origin and it consists of seven hands of diminishing size.

Crazy Solo

You will need: 36-card deck, Twos to Fives removed

Card ranking: Ace, Ten, King, Queen, Jack (scoring 11, 10, four, three and two points respectively), followed by Nine, Eight, Seven and Six (each scoring no points)

Players: Four is ideal

Ideal for: 10+

Object

To make more tricks than one's opponents, either in partnership with another player or alone.

The Deal

All the cards are dealt singly, starting with the player to the dealer's left, who also leads the first trick.

Bidding

A round of bidding follows the deal to decide who will be the solo player, each bid having to be higher than the last. Players can bid Pass, Solo, Solo in Hearts, Go Alone or Go Alone in Hearts. In Solo in Hearts and Alone in Hearts, Hearts are the trump suit. Otherwise, the successful bidder calls the trumps.

Play

If the bid is Solo or Solo in Hearts, the successful bidder calls a card to choose a partner. The player holding that card does not need to reveal his identity until the time comes for the card to be played. The partnership is called the 'solo players' and their opponents are the 'gang'.

The player to the dealer's left leads to the first trick. Suit must be followed if possible or a trump played but there is no requirement to beat the previous card. A player who cannot follow suit or trump may play any card.

The highest card of the suit that has been led takes the trick, unless trumps have been played, in which case the highest trump wins. The winner leads to the next trick. The Ten ranks second, below Ace.

Scoring and Conclusion

At the end of the game, points won by the caller and his partner are totalled to establish the margin of the win or loss. There are 120 points to be won, so scoring 61 or more of them wins the game.

The solo players receive points from (or pay) each member of the gang, the payout being calculated according to which suit was selected as trumps. If trumps are Spades, Clubs or Diamonds, then the payout is two points for every point over 60. However, if Hearts are trumps, it is three points. Each hand ends when all nine tricks have been won.

Knockout Whist

You will need: 52-card deck; no Jokers

Card ranking: Standard, Aces high

Players: Any number from three to seven

Ideal for: 7+

Object

To be the player who wins the trick in the final hand.

The Deal

Each player receives seven cards. The uppermost of the undealt cards is turned face up to indicate what the trump suit will be. The player on the dealer's left leads the first trick.

Play

Players must follow suit if they can, otherwise they may play any card. Each trick is won by the highest trump in it; otherwise by the highest card of the suit led. The winner of the most tricks in subsequent hands chooses the trump suit for the next. The second hand consists of six cards and so on until in the final hand, one card is dealt to each player.

A player who fails to take any tricks in a hand is knocked out of the game. If this occurs in the first hand, he is awarded a 'dog's life' – that is, he is dealt one card and can choose when to play it. If he is successful, he is reinstated into the game.

Conclusion

The game is won by the winner of the one trick on the final hand, or before that if one player wins all the tricks in an earlier round.

Boston

There are many versions of Boston, which won widespread popularity despite its extremely complicated system of calculating payments for bids, overtricks and undertricks. The game is a hybrid of Quadrille and Whist and may have originated in France in the late 18th century.

You will need: 52-card deck; no Jokers; scorecards
Card ranking: Standard, Aces high
Players: Four
Ideal for: 14+

Object

To gain the most points by making no less and no more than the number of tricks bid.

The Deal and Bidding

Each player is dealt 13 cards. The player to the dealer's left opens the bidding, the highest bidder becoming the soloist, playing alone against the other three players unless one of them agrees to become an ally or supporter. The bids can be positive – an offer to win a stated number of tricks – or negative, in which case the contract is to lose them.

Positive Bids and Scoring

Five is the lowest positive bid. This is an undertaking to win at least five tricks with a named suit as trumps. The supporter must win at least three out of the five tricks. If the bid is six, seven or eight, the supporter must take four tricks, that number remaining the same if the bid is nine, 10, 11 and 12. The highest bids are a Boston and a Boston *Ouverte*. In both, the contract is to win all 13 tricks, in the latter with cards face up on the table. The former scores 100 points and the latter 200. Otherwise, starting from Five, the points that can be scored for each positive bid are: four (plus one for each overtrick or undertrick), six (plus two), nine (plus three), 12 (plus four), 15 (plus five), 18 (plus six), 21 (plus seven) and 24 (plus eight). Overtricks score if the contract is won. Undertricks score if the contract is lost.

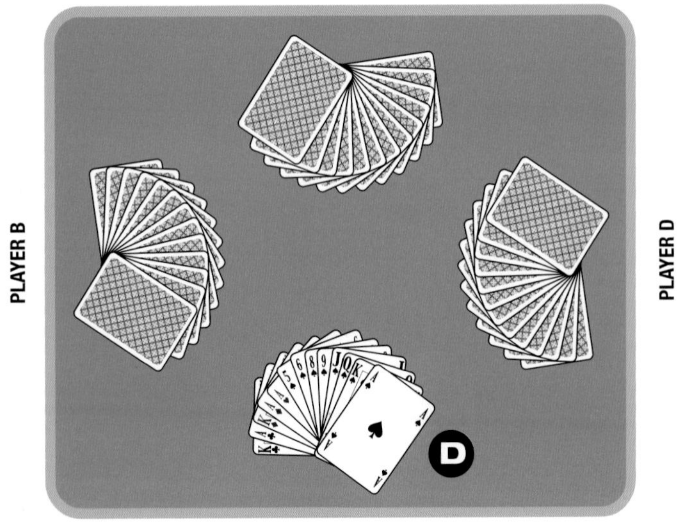

Negative Bids and Scoring

The lowest negative bid is *Petite Misère*, in which the contract is to lose 12 tricks with one discard at No Trumps. It is worth 16 points, while a *Grande Misère* is a bid to lose all 13 tricks and is worth 32. A bid of *Piccolissimo* is a contract to take only one trick and scores 24. If the bidder holds all four Aces, the bid is Four-ace *Misère* and scores 40.

Play

The player to the left of the dealer plays the first card. Subsequent players must follow suit, if possible, or play a trump. Otherwise, they can play any card. The highest card of the suit led or the highest trump takes the trick, its winner leading to the next one.

Conclusion

In a solo contract, bonuses are added for overtricks and undertricks, plus the equivalent of two overtricks if the soloist holds three honours and four if four. The total is doubled if trumps are Clubs, trebled if Diamonds and quadrupled if Spades. The honours are Ace, King, Queen and Jack of Trumps. If the contract is supported, the total for each partner is halved. If only one member of the partnership makes the contract, he scores zero, while the losing partner loses half the value of his contract plus half the value of that part of the contract that has been won. Play ends when the final trick has been won or lost.

Left: This hand, which is strong both in top cards and Spades, is perfect for declaring a bid of Boston *Ouverte*, naming Spades as trumps. The contract will be played with the bidding player's cards laid face up on the table, and will score 56 points if it is successful.

Quadrille

A four-handed adaptation of Ombre, Quadrille ousted Ombre in popular affection, only to be replaced by Partnership Whist. At least 160 chips of four different colours are needed to play it.

You will need: Standard pack with Eights, Nines and Tens removed; at least 160 gambling chips/counters of four colours

Card ranking: See below under 'Bidding'

Players: Four

Ideal for: 14+

Object

To win at least six tricks after nominating trumps, either solo or in alliance.

The Deal

From the 40-card deck, the deal is 10 cards per player, usually dealt in batches of four, three and three.

Bidding

Card rankings vary depending on the colour of each suit and whether the suit is plain or trumps. The top three trumps are *Spadille* for the A♠ (top trump), *Manille* (the Two if the trump suit is black or the Seven if the trump suit is red) and *Basta* (the A♣). They are collectively known as *Matadors*. The two black Aces are always trumps, regardless of what trump suit has been declared.

Each player takes it in turn to bid, pass or overcall – that is, to outbid a previous bid. In the simplest version of the game, the bids start with an alliance, in which the aim of the declarer is to take at least six tricks after nominating trumps and calling the holder of a specified King into a partnership.

If Solo is bid, the declarer proposes to win at least six tricks playing alone against the other three. *Vole* (slam) is a bid to take all 13 tricks without any support from a partner. A solo bid overcalls an alliance.

Play

The player to the dealer's left leads. Players follow suit if possible, otherwise they can play any card. However, a player holding a *Matador* (trump) need not play it to a trump lead unless it is lower in value than the led card.

Scoring

A successful soloist wins the pot, plus bonus chips paid to him by each opponent – four for the solo, one if he held three *Matadors*, two for double *Matadors*, one for *Premiers* (winning the first six tricks straight off) and two for *Vole*. If the contract is lost, the soloist forfeits the same number of chips to the other players.

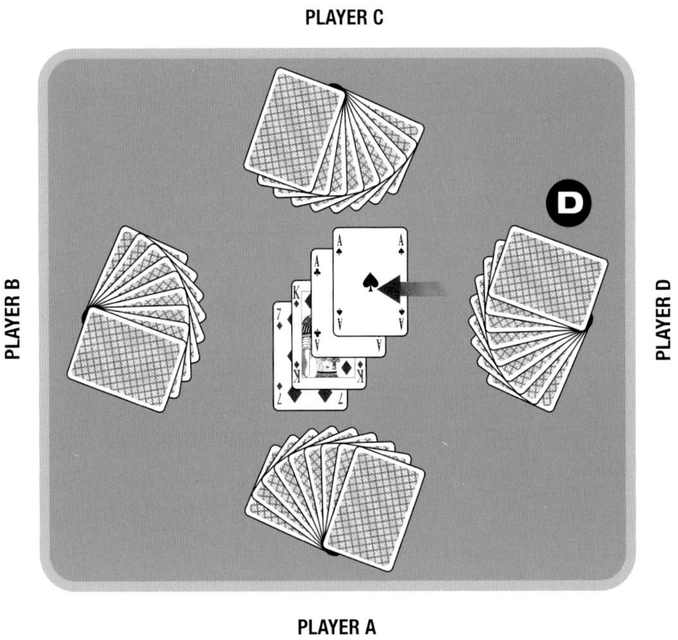

Above: Here, Player C looked set to win the trick after trumping with the A♣ before Player D played the highest trump of all, the A♠, and took the trick.

Losing partnerships divide losses according to how many tricks each partner won. If the declarer wins less than three tricks, he has to pay the total loss. The same goes if a player calls a partner.

If the declarer wins only five tricks, this is called *Remise*. If four or less, it is *Codille*. In the first instance, the declarer must double the stake and pay the opponents for any *Matadors* held. In a *Codille*, the stake is divided between the opposing players.

Conclusion

If the declarer wins the first six tricks, or *Premiers*, he has won the game. Alternatively, the declarer can decide to lead a seventh trick, in which case the bid becomes a *Vole* and all players must pay three more chips into a second pool. If the contract fails, the other players split this, but the declarer still gets paid for the *Premiers* and for winning the game.

Ombre

This fast-moving trick-taking game was originally for four players – even though the player opposite the dealer took no active part in the game. It was therefore as a three-hander that the Ombre craze swept Europe until it was superseded by Quadrille. It was one of the first card games to introduce the notion of bidding, in which one player tries to fulfil a contract while the other two players try to prevent this.

You will need: 40-card deck, Eights, Nines and Tens removed from a standard pack; gambling chips/counters
Card ranking: See under 'Card Ranking'
Players: Three
Ideal for: 14+

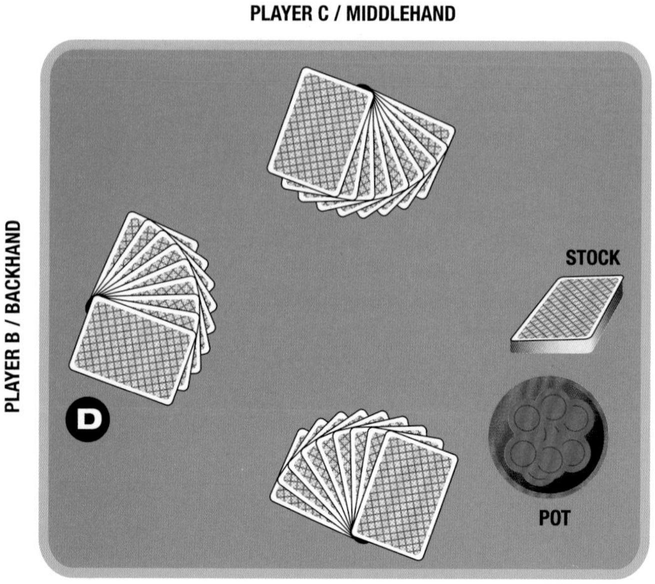

Above: The dealer in Ombre is called 'backhand', the player on the left 'middlehand' and the player on the right 'forehand'.

Object

The successful bidder aims to fulfil his contract by winning more tricks than any of his opponents. Their aim is to stop him by winning a majority of the tricks themselves, or to draw, in which case the bidder still loses.

Card Ranking

The ranking of the cards varies with the colour of their suit and whether they are trumps. The top three trumps are called *Matadors:* the *Spadille* (the A♠), *Manille* (the Two of a black trump suit or the Seven of a red trump suit) and *Basta* (the A♣). The two black Aces are always trumps, regardless of what trump suit has been declared.

The Deal and Auction

Before the deal, the dealer puts five chips in the pot. Each player is then dealt nine cards in packets of three. The remaining cards form the stock pile, which is placed face down on the table and used for exchanging cards.

Ombre has a language all of its own. The first dealer, chosen at random, is called backhand, the player to the right is forehand and the one to the left is middlehand.

Each hand begins with an auction. The winner of the bidding becomes the declarer (*Ombre*), and plays alone against the other two players (defenders) in partnership. The three calls that can be made in the auction are:

- Pass, in which case a player can take no further part in the bidding, and gives up his chance of being declarer.
- Bid, when a bid is made that outranks any bid previously made in the auction.
- Self, in which a player can equal a bid made previously by a player who is after him in rotation. Forehand can call self over the other two players, but middlehand can call self only over backhand.

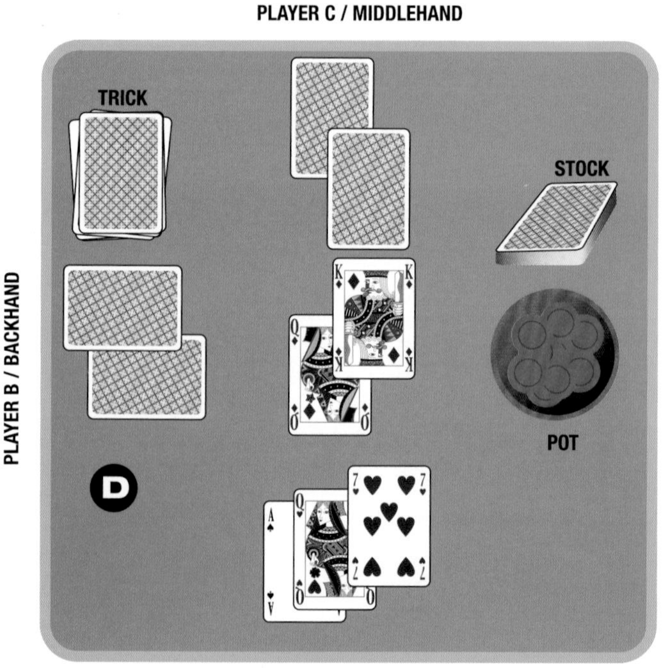

Above: Player A here can either trump by laying the *Spadille* (A♠), or renege with the 7♥. Doing the latter will leave the Queen a bare singleton, significantly reducing its chances of winning a trick.

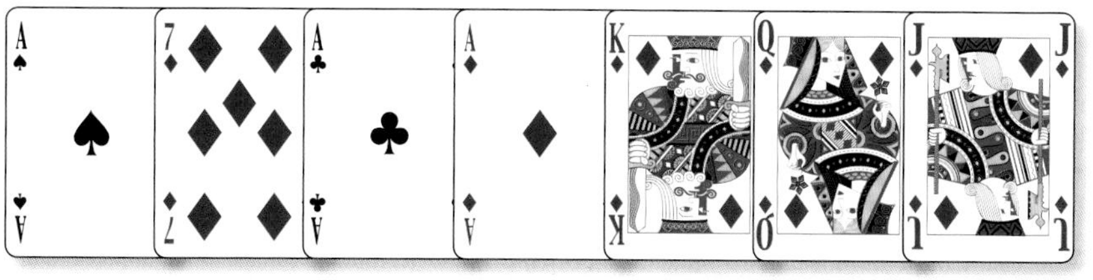

Left: With Diamonds as trumps, the top-ranking card is the A♠ *(Spadille)*, followed by the 7♦ *(Manille)* and A♣ *(Basta)*. In a red trump suit, the fourth highest is its Ace A♦ *(Punto)*, but it is not a *Matador*. The remaining Diamonds follow in rank in descending order.

Left: With Spades as trumps, the top-ranking card is the A♠ *(Spadille)*, followed by the 2♠ *(Manille)*, A♣ *(Basta)*, and then the remaining Spades in descending order, beginning with the King.

Only forehand and middlehand are involved initially in the auction, which ends when both players have called and one of them has passed. Backhand can then join in and the auction continues until the contract is settled.

Bidding and Contracts

The final bid by the declarer determines the contract. He plays either a Game or *Nolo* contract. In the former, he aims to take more tricks than either defender, and in the latter, he aims not to take any tricks at all. The players take turns exchanging cards with the stock pile, subject to restrictions relating to bids and corresponding contracts as follows:

- A simple game: the declarer names trumps, by naming the suit or turning the top card of the stock pile face up. All players can change their cards; the declarer goes first.
- A Spade game: Spades are automatically trumps.
- A *Tourné* or *Grand Tourné:* both game contracts, in which the top card of the stock pile is turned up. If *Grand Tourné* is bid, the bidder must hold *Spadille* (the A♠) and *Basta* (the A♣) in his hand.
- Solo: game contract where the declarer has to play his hand as dealt, but the defenders can exchange up to eight cards with the stock pile.
- Spade Solo: like Solo with Spades as trumps.
- Simple *Nolo*: *Nolo* contract. Only the declarer can exchange cards.
- Pure *Nolo*: like Simple *Nolo*, but neither the declarer nor defenders exchange cards with the stock pile.
- *Nolo Ouverte*: like Pure *Nolo* but when the declarer plays his first card, he also turns his hand face up for both defenders to see.

Play

Following the card exchange, the nine tricks are played. Forehand always leads the first trick, regardless of who was the dealer. Players have to follow suit if they can, unless one of them is holding a *Matador,* in which case he may choose whether to play it or keep it back and play a card from another suit. If the lead card is a higher *Matador*, a player holding a lower one must play it. The trick is taken by the highest card of the suit led or by the highest trump, the winner of the trick leading to the next.

Scoring and Conclusion

Play continues until all nine tricks have been won. If the declarer wins, he receives the contents of the pot, and from each of the other players:

- One chip for simple games and *Tourné*.
- Two chips for *Nolo*, *Grand Tourné* and Solo.
- Three chips for Pure *Nolo* and Spade Solo.
- Five chips for *Nolo Ouverte*.

In Game contracts, the declarer wins outright if he takes the first five tricks. The alternatives are:

- *Bête,* in which the declarer scores the same number of tricks as one of the other players.
- *Puesta,* where no one wins a majority of tricks.
- *Codille,* when the declarer takes fewer tricks than one of his opponents.
- *Tout,* when the declarer takes all nine tricks. In this case, he has to declare the decision to try to do so in advance before leading for the sixth trick.

Winning *Tout* means the others have to pay the declarer an extra chip each. In the case of *Bête,* the declarer pays the other players according to which contract was bid. In the case of *Codille,* there is an extra penalty. This is one chip for low contracts, two for Pure *Nolo* and Spade Solo and three for *Nolo Ouverte* with only the higher-scoring opponent being paid. If the declarer fails to win a *Tout,* he has to give both the others a chip, but still gets chips for winning.

In solo contracts, the declarer wins outright when he takes no tricks. The alternatives are:

- *Bête,* when one trick is taken.
- *Codille,* when the declarer takes two tricks or more.

Preference

This three-handed game is played in various parts of Europe, notably in Austria, Russia and the Ukraine, where it used to be the national game. Hearts is the highest suit, followed by Diamonds, Clubs and Spades. The game is played with either German-suited cards – a 32-card pack, the suits of which are Hearts, Bells, Acorns and Leaves – or a standard pack stripped of Sixes down to Twos. The main version of the game described here is called Austrian Preference.

You will need: 32-card deck (Sixes down to Twos removed from a standard pack); gambling chips/counters

Card ranking: Ace, King, Queen, Jack, Ten to Seven

Players: Three

Ideal for: 14+

Object

To win at least the predetermined number of tricks. In each hand, one player (the declarer) chooses trumps and tries to take six out of the possible 10 tricks. The other two players (the defenders) try to stop this happening, but they are also obliged to take two tricks each. If a defender believes it will be impossible to do this, he is allowed to drop out of the hand.

The Deal

Players cut to decide who will be the first dealer, after which the deal passes to the right. The cards are dealt clockwise, three to each player, two face down on the table to form a stock, four to each player and then a final three. All three players put the same stake into the pot – in Austrian Preference, it is the custom to use money, rather than chips or counters. At the outset, each player contributes an equal sum to the pot.

Bidding

The player to the left of the dealer opens the bidding. Players can either bid or pass, but if they pass they can take no further part in the auction. The possible bids are:

- One, two, three, four, representing Clubs, Spades, Diamonds and Hearts respectively.
- Game, which indicates that the bidder does not want to pick up and use the cards in the stock.
- Hearts, which is a Game bid in Hearts.

Players are only allowed to bid one higher than the previous bid or pass, so the first player to bid can only bid one, Game or Hearts. The other players can then bid two over the one, followed by three and then four.

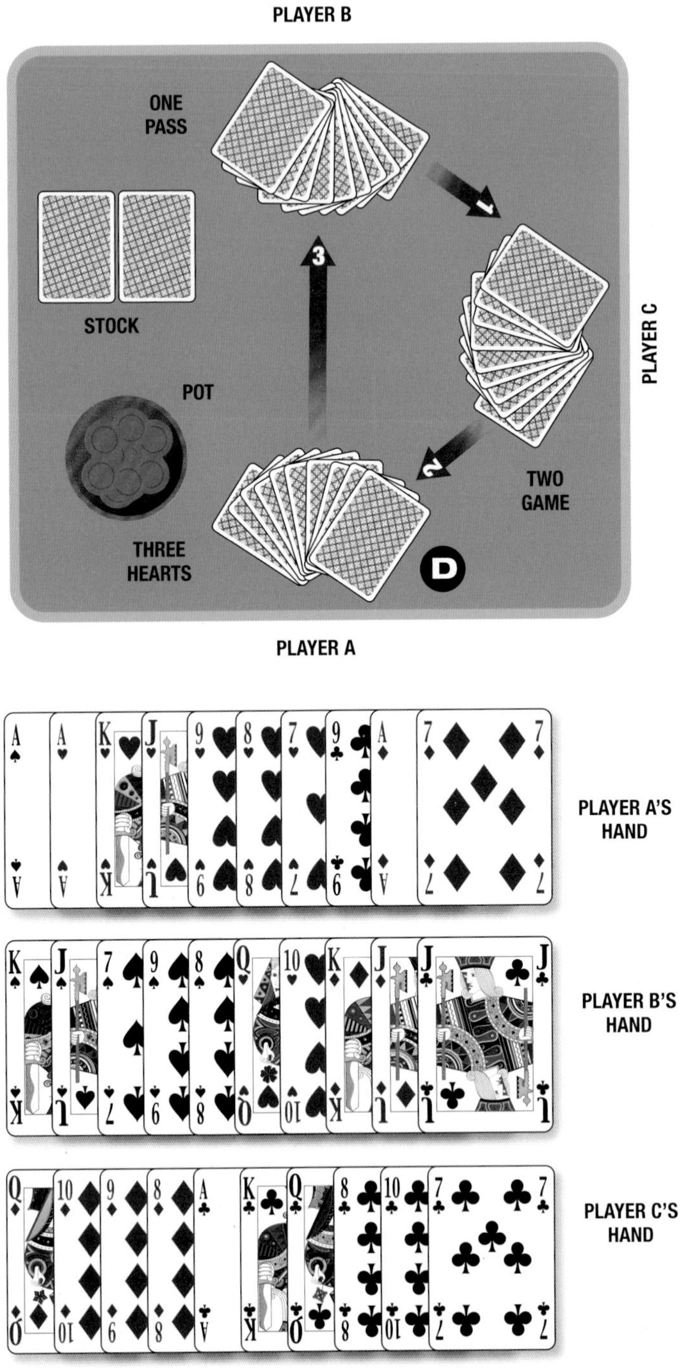

Above: A possible bidding sequence in Preference. Player B begins by contracting to make six tricks, but Player C bids higher, only to be outbid by Player A who goes higher again. After Player B makes the decision to pass, Player C then bids Game, forgoing the right to pick up the stock, but Player A contracts for Game in Hearts, the highest bid.

Above: A player holding all four Aces is paid an extra 10 points by each of his opponents if he wins the first six tricks.

Once game has been bid, only another bid of game or Hearts can outbid it. In the first instance, both bidders must declare what they are proposing as trumps. The one declaring the higher suit wins. If a player bidding a number is outbid, he can opt to hold. This is the equivalent to matching the other player's bid. If the second bidder does not raise the bid, the initial bidder wins.

A bid of one, if successful, means that the declarer can name any suit as trump. Two means that Clubs cannot be nominated, Three stops Clubs and Spades from being trumps, and Four means that Hearts are trumps.

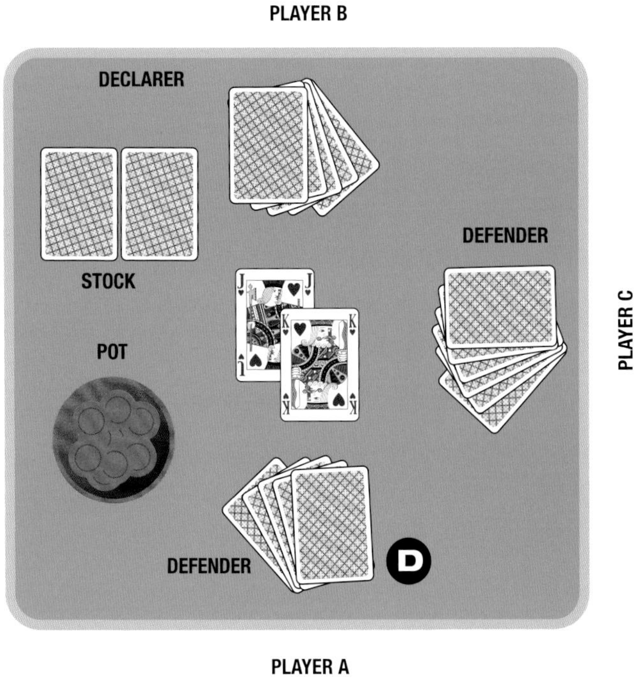

Above: With the declarer having led Hearts, the first of the two defenders, Player C, is obliged to beat the card if he can. Called 'indulging', it gives the defending partner the opportunity to take on the two tricks he needs to make.

Play

In a numerical contract, the declarer picks up the stock, adds it to his hand and then discards two cards face down. He then says what will be trumps, following which each opponent must decide whether or not to play the hand. If only one of them decides to play, he has the option of inviting the other to play with him, though it is his responsibility to win the four tricks the partnership needs, not that of his partner.

If both defenders concede, the declarer automatically wins all 10 tricks. If not, play proceeds with the declarer playing the first card of the first trick. The others must follow suit, playing a higher card, if possible. If not, they must trump or discard. The highest card of the suit led takes the trick, or the highest trump if any are played.

If, when both of the other players are defending, the first of them can beat the lead, he must do so with the lowest suitable card in his hand. This is termed 'indulging' and it provides the opportunity for the defending partner to take the two tricks he needs.

Failing to indulge when able to do so constitutes a revoke, when play stops and settlements are made without recourse to the pot. A revoking declarer pays the other players the equivalent of three-tenths of the pot, or five-tenths if only one defender was playing. If a defender revokes, he pays the declarer the full amount of the pot and four-tenths of its value to his partner.

Russian Preference

There are four types of Russian Preference – Sochi, St Petersburg, Classic, and Rostov or Moscow. Other versions of the game are played in Croatia, Serbia, Slovenia and Trieste.
The main difference between Russian and Austrian Preference is that, as well as being more complicated, the declarer in the former can contract to win more than six tricks.

Scoring and Conclusion

When 10 tricks have been played, the players are paid from the pot according to the number of tricks they have made. First the declarer takes 10 points and pays any defender who did not drop out one point for each trick taken. If a declarer has taken less than six tricks, he pays a penalty of 20 points to the pot. The following bonuses apply, depending on the bid:

- Hearts bonus: in a Hearts game, a successful declarer receives an extra 10 points from each of his opponents, although he has to pay 10 to each of them if the bid fails.
- Four Aces bonus: a declarer who held four Aces receives a bonus of 10 points from each opponent if successful, but does not pay anything if he fails to fulfil his contract.
- No Ace bonus: a declarer who held no Aces and declared the fact before leading to the first trick, receives a bonus of 10 points from each opponent if successful, but pays them an extra 10 each if not.

Asszorti

This compelling three-player game was invented in Hungary. In many respects, it is similar to Preference, but it is simpler to play. Like many other Hungarian card games it uses a German-suited 36-card pack, the suits of which are Hearts, Bells, Acorns and Leaves, but a standard pack can be used when stripped of Fives down to Twos.

You will need: 36-card deck – standard pack with Twos, Threes, Fours and Fives removed; scorecards

Card ranking: Ace down to Six

Players: Three

Ideal for: 14+

Object

To win at least the specified number of tricks bid. A bid is an offer to win at least six tricks after exchanging three, two, one or no cards with the stock.

The Deal

Players cut the pack to establish who deals first. Each player receives 11 cards, three each first then four batches of two. A further three cards are dealt face down on to the table to form a stock.

Bidding

After the deal, players bid or pass in turn, starting with the player to the left of the dealer. If a player bids, he is undertaking to win at least six tricks after exchanging three, two, one or no cards with cards from the stock. Players are only allowed to bid one higher than the previous bid, or pass, so the first player to bid can only bid three. The next player can bid to exchange two and so on. The highest bidder becomes the soloist, drawing as many cards as were bid (if any) from the stock, discarding the same number and naming the trump suit or deciding the hand will be No Trumps.

Below: Examples of the Hearts and Acorns suits in a German-suited pack of cards. The other two suits are Bells and Leaves.

Arrivázs and Doubling

If trumps are to be played, the soloist can also bid *Arrivázs*. This is an undertaking to win the last three tricks of the hand, for which he gets a bonus of eight points. This is doubled if the hand is No Trumps or if the tricks are captured without a trump being played. Game and *Arrivázs* are scored separately. Either or both can be doubled and redoubled up to five times, the levels being announced as *Kontra* (two), *Rekontra* (four), *Szubkontra* (eight), *Hirskontra* (16) and *Mordkontra* (32). If the soloist announces *Rekontra*, only the partner of the player who announced *Kontra* can respond by calling *Szubkontra*.

Play

Players must follow suit if they can, or trump if unable to follow suit. They may renounce, that is, play any other card, only if they are unable to do either. The player to the right of the soloist leads, the trick falling to the player of the highest card of the led suit, or to the highest trump if any are played.

Scoring

The basic scores for bids of three, two, one and hand are two, four, six and eight points respectively, the scores being doubled if the hand is No Trumps. Obviously, doubling and redoubling affects these basic scores. Overtricks count for half the above values, while undertricks score minus the full values in the first and second possible bids and half values in the remainder.

Conclusion

Play continues until all the tricks have been won or the soloist has won six or more tricks.

Oh Hell!

In this popular game, also known as Niggle, the objective is to bid to win an exact number of tricks – a player winning more or less is penalized. There are various ways of playing and scoring.

You will need: 52-card deck; no Jokers; scorecards
Card ranking: Standard, Aces high
Players: Three to seven players
Ideal for: 10+

Object

To win an exact number of tricks, no more or less.

The Deal

Players draw to establish who will deal first. If there are three or four players, the initial deal is 10 cards, if six play it is eight, while if seven play it is seven. (In the USA, each successive hand is dealt with one card fewer down to one, then one card up again back to the starting number. In Britain, the reverse happens, with the initial deal being just a single card.) The next card is turned face up to establish trumps and the remaining cards are stacked face down with the turned-up trump on top of the pile. The turn to deal passes to the left.

Bidding

Bidding starts with the player to the dealer's left – the dealer always bids last. No player can pass, though a bid of *Nullo* (zero) is allowed. The dealer, however, cannot bid a number that would enable all players to fulfil their bids.

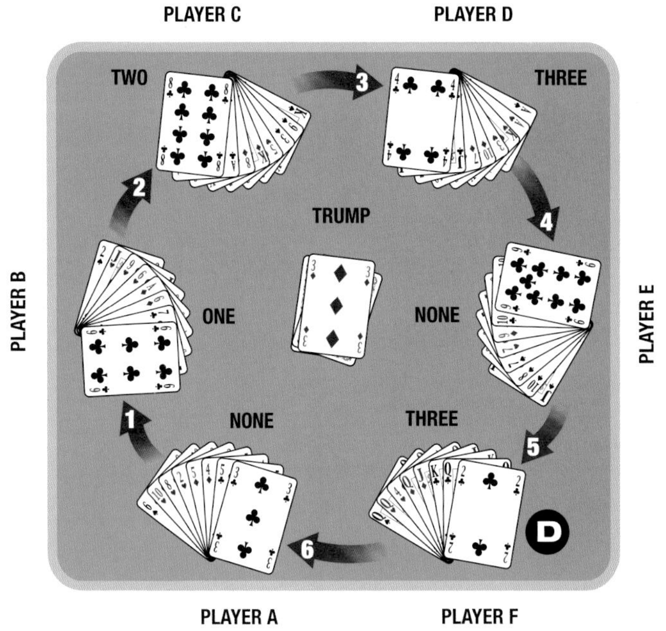

Above: A possible bidding sequence in Oh Hell! With six players involved, each receives eight cards, meaning that the final total of bids must not equal eight. Player F therefore, who is the last to bid here, cannot bid Two, so contracts instead to make three tricks. At least one player will fail to make the number of tricks he bids.

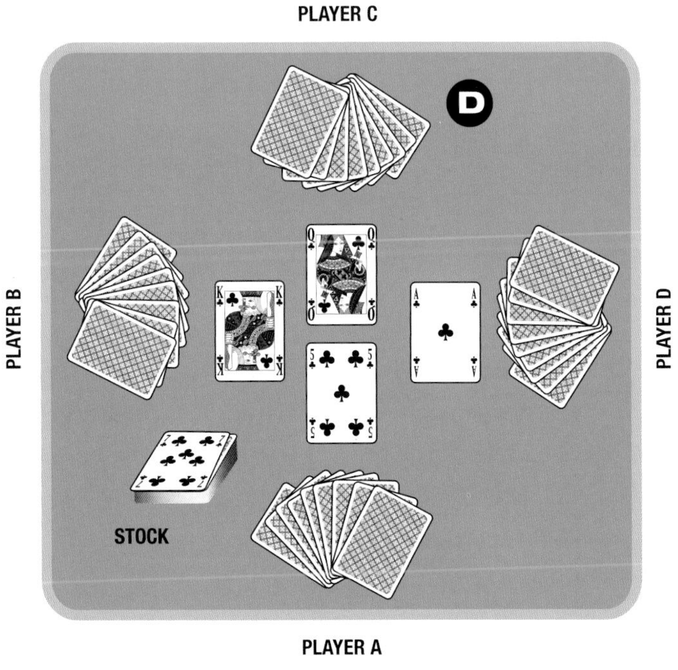

Above: Player D lays the A♣ to take the first trick in a round of Oh Hell! The game is also known by the name Niggle.

Play

The player to the dealer's left plays the first card, the other players following in turn. They must follow suit if they can, or, if they cannot, play a trump, assuming that they are holding trumps in their hands. Only if neither is the case can they play a card from any other suit.

Scoring

For making a bid, a player scores 10 points for each trick bid and won – just 10 points in total for a bid of zero. A player failing to make his bid has to deduct 10 points for each trick under the total.

Conclusion

Play continues until all tricks have been played and won. The final cumulative score decides the winner.

NINETY-NINE

Devised by British card authority David Parlett in 1967, this ingenious game revolves around its players bidding secretly, using bid cards, to win an exact number of tricks by removing cards from their hands. The suit of each bid card represents a different number of tricks: for example, Clubs represents three tricks.

You will need: 36-card deck, Fives to Twos removed; scorecards

Card ranking: Standard, Aces high

Players: Three ideally, although can be two to five

Ideal for: 14+

OBJECT

To win exactly the number of tricks bid by discarding three cards representing that number. Players use the suits to represent the number of tricks bid as follows: ♣ = 3 tricks, ♥ = 2 tricks, ♠ = 1 trick, ♦ = 0 tricks. For example, a player bids nine tricks by laying aside ♣♣♣ (3 + 3 + 3 = 9), or three tricks by laying ♣♦♦ (3 + 0 + 0 = 3).

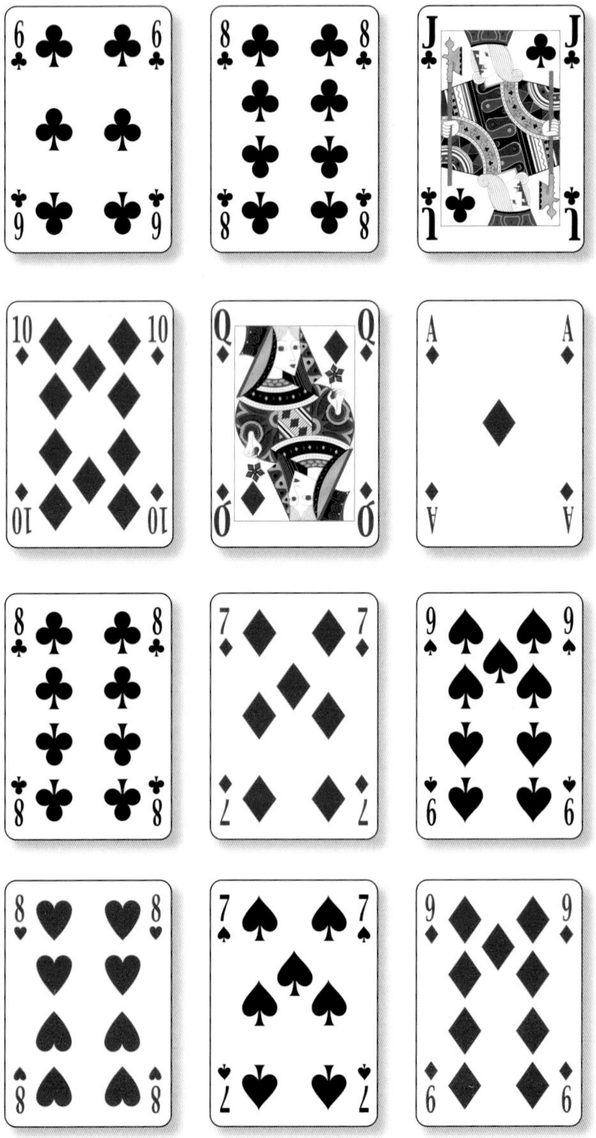

THE DEAL

Assuming there are three players, each player is dealt 12 cards, three of which become bid cards. Normally, the bid cards are left face down until play ends. However, a player can decide to up the stakes by offering to 'declare' by exposing these cards at the start of play, or 'reveal' – that is, to also play with his actual hand exposed.

Only one player is allowed to declare or reveal at a time. If more than one player wishes to declare, the player nearest to the dealer's left has priority. An offer to reveal always supersedes an offer to declare.

PLAY

The first deal is played without trumps. Subsequent deals are played with a trump suit, which is determined by the number of players who fulfilled their previous contract. If all three did, the trump suit is Clubs, Hearts if two, Spades if one, or Diamonds if none. The player to the left of the dealer plays first. Players must follow suit, if possible, or otherwise trump or play any card. The highest card of the suit led or the highest trump takes the trick, its winner leading to the next.

SCORING AND CONCLUSION

Each player scores a point for each trick taken regardless of his bid, 10 points if all three players make their contracts, double if two players succeed and treble if only one does. A successful premium bidder scores an extra 30 for a declaration and 60 for a revelation. If the bid fails, the other players score the appropriate premium.

Play continues until all the tricks have been played and won. A game is 100 points with a further 100 being added to the winner's score. A rubber is three games.

Left: Players lay down three cards (bid cards) to show the number of tricks they aim to make with the nine cards in their hands. Each card in Clubs indicates three tricks, in Hearts it indicates two, in Spades one, and in Diamonds none. These four sets of cards from the top down, therefore correspond to: nine tricks (3 + 3 + 3 = 9); no tricks (0 + 0 + 0 = 0); four tricks (3 + 0 + 1 = 4) and three tricks (2 + 1 + 0 = 3).

12 | Piquet Games

Various factors make this interesting family of card games stand out. Points can be scored for various combinations of cards (which, in Piquet, is termed making melds). In addition, players make additional scores by taking tricks. Piquet itself is the oldest of these games, with a history that dates back to at least the 16th century, and a strong following among card game aficionados.

Though Piquet has a long and venerable history, its exact origins are somewhat obscure. What seems the most likely is that it originated in France, where its unknown inventor devised it to entertain Charles VI. It later became an English game by adoption from the time of Charles I onwards. Piquet is regarded by many as one of the best card games for two players, but its association with the aristocracy and literate upper classes, and the complexity of its rules may partly explain why it has lost its popularity since the end of the First World War.

In France, Imperial emerged in the 16th century as a two-player hybrid of Piquet and another old game dating back to the 15th century, known as Triomphe. It still has its adherents, particularly in the Midi region of the southern part of the country, and offers many points of interest to card game enthusiasts. Variants for three players or more became popular as well.

One of the earliest three-player variants is 'the noble and delightful game' of Gleek, an English game that reached the height of its popularity between the 16th and the early 18th centuries. Its name may be related to the German word *gleich*, meaning 'equal' or 'alike', for Gleek is the term used in the game to describe a set of three Aces, Kings, Queens or Jacks. Individual cards have unusual titles: the Ace is Tib, Jack is Tom, while Six, Five and Four are called Tumbler, Towser and Tiddy.

Above: *A Game of Piquet* (*c.*1861) by Meissonier. References to the game date back to 1534, making it one of the oldest card games still being played.

PIQUET

Modern Piquet can be played in two ways – American style and English style – though in practice there is little difference between the two. Two 32-card decks are usually used at a time – one in use and the other shuffled ready for the next deal. A game is known as a *partie* and usually consists of six deals.

You will need: Two 32-card decks, Sixes down to Twos having been removed from a standard deck (see below)

Card ranking: Ace down to Seven

Players: Two

Ideal for: 14+

OBJECT

To score the most points by capturing tricks and collecting card-scoring combinations.

THE DEAL

The players cut for first deal, after which it alternates between them. The dealer is called Younger and the non-dealer Elder. The former deals 12 cards for himself and 12 for the opposing player in packets of two or three, spreading the eight cards that are left over face down on the table to form a stock.

DISCARDING

The first stage involves the discarding and exchanging of cards, but, before this, a player can claim what is termed *Carte Blanche* if there are no court cards in his hand. This is worth 10 points. Otherwise, Elder discards up to five cards face down and replaces them from the stock. American rules say this is optional, but English ones state that at least one card must be discarded. Younger may then discard and exchange up to as many cards as are left in the stock, but he has the freedom to decline to do so. If Younger does discard and exchange any cards, he may then inspect any remaining cards in the stock, but this means Elder can inspect them as well. Both players may examine their own discards at any stage during play.

Below: A standard pack of 52 cards is used in Piquet, but all of the cards below seven are removed – with the exception of the Aces. Of the remaining 32 cards, the Aces count for 11 points, followed by Kings, Queens and Jacks, which score 10 points each, and then Ten, Nine, Eight and Seven.

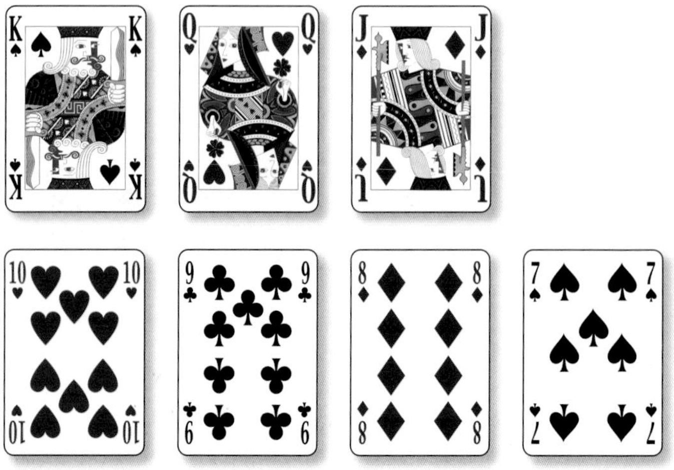

DECLARING COMBINATIONS

Depending on their cards, both players can declare three types of combination, namely:

- A point, which is a collection of cards all of the same suit.
- A sequence, which is a run of three or more cards in one suit in rank order.
- A meld, when a player holds three or four cards of the same rank but in different suits.

It is not obligatory to announce the best combination – or to declare a weak one – if the player concerned believes that such concealment will serve his tactics the better. This is termed 'sinking a declaration'.

Elder declares first, announcing his best combinations in each category, saying 'A point of...', 'A sequence of...' or, in the case of a meld, 'A three or four of...'. After each announcement, Young says 'good', meaning that Elder's hand is better and can be scored, 'not good' if Younger has a better combination, or 'equal', in which case the points go to the player with the higher-ranking cards. Aces score 11; the court cards and Tens 10 each; and Nines, Eights and Sevens their face value.

PLAYING

Once the declarations have been completed, Elder announces the score he has made thus far and leads the first trick, scoring an extra point for leading. Younger responds by announcing his total score. If he has failed to score anything and Elder's score reaches 30 as the result of leading the trick, the Elder wins a *pique*, a bonus of 30 points. Elder then plays the first card to the next trick. Younger responds by following suit, if possible, or otherwise discarding. He cannot play a trump, as trumps do not feature in Piquet. Players must follow suit. Each trick is worth a point if the player who led to it wins it, but otherwise it is worth two. A player taking between seven and 11 tricks gets a bonus of 10 points 'for cards', while taking all 12 tricks means a bonus of 40 'for *Capot*'. Winning the last trick wins an extra point.

Right: Piquet became a popular card game among the aristocracy in England during the reign of Charles I (1625–49).

Scoring

In a point combination, the player with the longest suit scores a point for each card in it. Thus:

- Point of three scores three.
- Point of four scores four.
- Point of five scores five.
- Point of six scores six.
- Point of seven scores seven.
- Point of eight scores eight.

Scoring for sequences is as follows:

- A *Tierce* (three cards) scores three.
- A *Quart* (four) scores four.
- A *Quint* (five) scores 15.
- A *Sixième* (six) scores 16.
- A *Septième* (seven) scores 17.
- A *Huitième* (eight) scores 18.

Scores for melds are as follows (sets of Nines, Eights and Sevens do not count):

- *Quatorze* (four Aces, Kings, Queens, Jacks or Tens) scores 14.
- *Trio* (three Aces, Kings, Queens, Jacks or Tens) scores three.

If a player scores 30 points before the other has scored, he is awarded a bonus of 60 points. This is a *repique*.

Above: An unbeaten set of four Queens is known as a *Quatorze* and is worth a total of 14 points to its holder.

Above: Elder's starting and finishing hands before and after discarding his cards. Elder has so many weak cards in his hand that it is worth exchanging the maximum five cards for five new ones.

Conclusion

At the end of the sixth deal, the scores are totalled. If a player has scored under 100 points, he is deemed to be 'Rubiconed.' His opponent wins and scores 100 plus the two final scores. If a player has scored more than 100 points, he 'crosses the Rubicon' and wins the game, scoring 100 plus the difference between the two final totals. In a tie, two more deals are played as a tiebreaker.

Above: Younger's starting and finishing hands. After Elder discards five cards, Younger is left with three cards to exchange with those from the stock in the hope of picking up some better ones.

Imperial

In this game, players use counters to keep score. Each player starts with five red counters and six white to their left, moving one of the white ones to the right to signify each point won in play. Six points equals an imperial. This is marked by a red counter and the six white counters are moved back again to the left.

You will need: 32-card deck, Sixes down to Twos having been removed; red and white counters

Card ranking: Ace down to Seven

Players: Two

Ideal for: 14+

Object

To score the most points by capturing tricks and collecting point-scoring card combinations.

The Deal

The dealer deals two hands of 12 cards each in packets of two, three or four. The next card is turned face up to establish trumps. The remaining cards are placed face down across it. If the turn-up is an 'honour card' (an Ace, King, Queen, Jack or Seven) the dealer scores a point for it. If it is an Ace or a King, the dealer can exchange a Seven for it, assuming that he holds one in his hand.

Play and Scoring

Before play starts, both players work out and announce how many points they have according to the values of the cards they hold in any one suit. An Ace scores 11, the court cards 10 each and the Ten, Nine, Eight and Seven are at face value. The player with the higher score wins a point, but, if the scores are tied, the point goes to the non-dealing player. Both players also score any *Impériales* they may be holding in their hand, which can be:

- An *Impériale d'Alout* (King, Queen, Jack and Ten), worth 12 points if they are trumps, six points if they are non-trumps.
- An *Impériale d'Honneur* (all four of one of the following ranks plus one of the other cards: Ace, King, Queen, Jack or Seven), worth six points.
- An *Impériale Blanche* (all four cards of any rank other than court cards with one other card, again not a court card), worth 12 points.

HAND 1

HAND 2

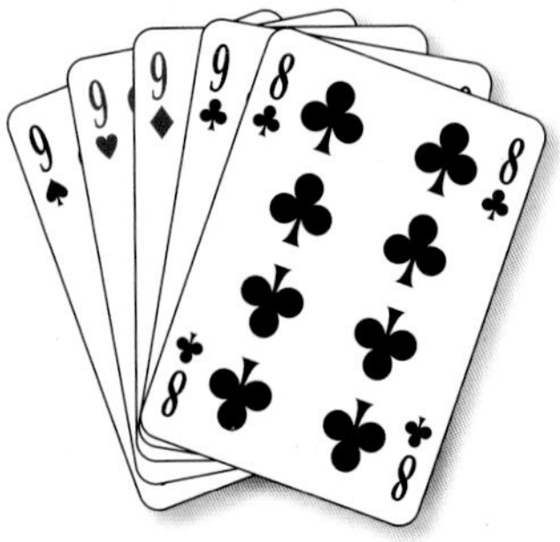

HAND 3

Above and left: Examples of scoring Imperials: (1) An *Impériale d'Alout*, worth 12 points in trumps or otherwise six points (2) an *Impériale d'Honneur*, worth six points and (3) an *Impériale Blanche*, worth 12 points.

They must be declared strictly in the above order and shown if the opposing player requests it.

After the *Impériales* have been declared, play begins with the non-dealing player leading. The dealer must follow suit with a higher card, play a trump or revoke if unable to do either. The trick is taken by the highest card of the suit led or the highest trump if any are played. The winner of each trick leads to the next.

A player scores a point for leading an honour to a trick and one for capturing a trick containing one. At the end of play, a player winning more than six tricks scores a point for each of them. If one player takes all 12 tricks, this is *Capot*, which is worth 12 points, but, if the tricks are divided, neither player scores.

Whenever a player scores six points, the opposing player's points are forfeited. The sole exception is when an *Impériale Blanche* is declared, when the opposing player's points are not forfeited. Scores can be written down but counters are preferable.

Conclusion

Game is 36 points. The first player to shift all 11 counters from left to right is the winner.

GLEEK

This is a somewhat elaborate game in which there are four main stages. In the first, players bid for the chance to improve their hands by discarding cards and replacing them with ones from the stock. They then bet as to who holds the longest suit, followed by declarations of Gleeks (three of a kind) and Mournivals (four of a kind) before getting down to the final stage of trick play.

You will need: 44-card deck, Threes and Twos having been removed; scorecards; gambling chips/counters

Card ranking: Ace down to Four

Players: Three

Ideal for: 14+

OBJECT

To score the most points by capturing tricks and collecting certain cards or card-scoring combinations.

THE DEAL

The players cut the pack to establish who will be the dealer. The lowest card wins. Each of the players is dealt 12 cards in packets of four, the remaining cards being placed face down to form the stock. Players put an equal number of chips into a pot. The dealer turns up the top card of the stock to establish trumps.

BIDDING

All players start with the same number of chips. After the deal has been completed, they bid for the right to discard seven cards in exchange for the stock, although the turned-up trump is excluded. The player to the dealer's left bids first, starting the bidding with 10 chips. The other players can either raise the bid by two chips or pass, so dropping out of the bidding. When two players have passed, the winning bidder pays half the final bid to each of them. Without showing any cards, he discards seven cards and replaces them with the stock.

VYING

The players now bet to see who holds the best 'ruff' – the highest card value in a single suit. This is determined by adding up the cards. Aces count 11, Kings, Queens and Jacks 10 each and all the other cards at face value. The players start by putting two chips each into a pot, after which they have several options. They can pass, decide to match the previous bet, or raise it by a further two chips. The process continues until two players pass or there is a showdown. The holder of the best hand wins the pot.

Finally, all the players declare and score for any Gleeks and Mournivals they may hold, each opposing player paying the holder the appropriate number of chips. In Gleeks, Aces are worth four chips, Kings three, Queens two and Jacks one. In Mournivals, Aces are worth eight chips, Kings six, Queens four and Jacks two.

PLAYING THE TRICKS

The player to the left of the dealer leads. Players must follow suit if possible, trump or otherwise play any card. The highest trump or the highest card of the suit led wins the trick, and the winner leads to the next.

Every trick taken scores three points for its winner, plus bonus points for the top trumps. These have their own names and special point values. An Ace is Tib and worth 15 points, Kings and Queens score three points each, a Jack is Tom and worth nine points, while Six (Tumbler), Five (Towser) and Four (Tiddy) score six, five and four points respectively. Tumbler and Towser are optional inclusions. If the turned-up card is an Ace or any of the court cards, the dealer counts it in as part of his total score.

CONCLUSION

A game consists of 12 tricks. At the end, any player scoring less than 22 puts a chip into the pot for every point of the shortfall, while any player scoring more than 22 takes a chip out of the pot for every point scored in excess of that figure.

Left: The top trumps won in tricks (here, assuming trumps are Spades) have their own names and special point values. An Ace is known as Tib and is worth 15 points, Kings and Queens are each worth three points, a Jack (Tom) scores nine points, while Six, Five, Four, known as Tumbler, Towser and Tiddy respectively, score just their face value.

Advanced Card Games

Dedicated card players are always on the lookout for games they have not played before. The card games in this section of the book require more skill than the average, and so will appeal to the more sophisticated player rather than the complete beginner. This is not to say that a novice should never experiment – only that it is a good idea to master the principles of simpler trick-taking games, such as Whist, before trying to tackle a more complicated bidding game such as Contract Bridge.

Excellent Contract Bridge players have almost always started off with Whist, its 17th-century antecedent. Indeed, many experts believe that, while any good Whist player can become a good Bridge player once the elements of bidding have been mastered, many who pass as good Bridge players could be quite out of their depth at Whist. In fact, the British card authority David Parlett is of the opinion that 'nobody should learn Bridge without prior experience of Whist', going as far as to say that 'many Bridge players would improve their game by going on a crash diet of Whist only'.

Quick-trick Games

Quick-trick games can also be very challenging. As in Bridge, many of these games include an element of bidding, but the element that makes them particularly demanding is that, as opposed to many other card games, not all the cards are dealt. Naturally, this makes it harder for players to deduce what cards their opponents may be holding.

Above: A fashionable group play a game of Bridge, 1912.

Above: Well-dressed players taking part in a Whist drive, *c.*1906. The players change tables every few deals and face several different pairs of opponents.

Euchre, for which the modern Joker was invented, is the most sophisticated of these games, although Nap, or Napoleon, a simplified version, is probably more popular, being played throughout northern Europe under different guises. The author Jerome K. Jerome mentioned the game in his comic masterpiece *Three Men in a Boat*, when he described his three leading characters – J, the book's narrator, George and Harris – settling down to indulge in a game of 'Penny Nap after supper'. The game was probably named after the French emperor Napoleon III, who is thought to have played a version of it.

Hearts and its Relatives

Games in the Hearts family stand the usual scoring conventions of card games on their head. The aim in these games is to *avoid* winning tricks, and so amass points. This makes Twos and Threes as valuable as Aces and Kings often are in other card games, while holding middle-ranking cards, such as Sevens and Eights, can mean positive danger, if not complete disaster.

Playing games like Hearts well means cultivating a special kind of card sense. Often, it is best to aim not to take any tricks at all, especially in games where holding or winning certain cards means incurring a penalty. Two variants (not included in this book) illustrate this point well. In Black Maria, the player ending up with the

Above: An international Bridge tournament in New York in 2005. Played socially by many, Bridge is also a seriously competitive game, with championship matches held across the world.

Queen of Spades scores an extra 13 points, and each Heart counts for a single point, although a player with the Jack of Diamonds deducts 12 points from his score. In Pink Lady, the other variant, ending up with the Queen of Hearts means a 13-point penalty.

In Jacks and its close relative Polignac, the Jacks, as might be expected, are the high-scoring danger cards.

Aces, Tens and Other Cards

Some card games give specific cards particular values. In games such as Skat, Germany's most popular card game, Aces count for 11 points, Tens 10, Kings four, Queens three and Jacks two. The aim is to win at least 61 card points in tricks (the number of tricks taken is in itself immaterial). So-called King-Queen games are governed by the same principles, and, in them, declaring the 'marriage' of a King and Queen of the same suit in the same hand wins bonus points. This makes games like Sixty-Six exciting because it introduces an element of unpredictability into the game. Declaring a 'marriage' can transform the scoring situation, turning a losing player into a winning one.

Games like Bezique, Marjolet and Pinochle use the same principles, with an extra 'marriage' being allowed between a specified Queen and a Jack of a different suit. They differ in the fact that players win most of their points by collecting and melding certain sequences and combinations of cards. In Jack-Nine games, the Jack is promoted to become the highest trump, followed by the Nine. The three classic examples of this type of game are Belote, Klaverjas and Schieber Jass, the national card games of France, the Netherlands and Switzerland, respectively.

Poker and its Origins

Of all these more advanced games, Poker stands alone. This is a five-card vying game in which players bet money or gambling chips into a communal pot during the course of a hand; the player who has the best hand at the end of the betting wins the pot, in a 'showdown'. It is also possible for the pot to be won by a hand that is not the best, by bluffing the other players out of play.

It is believed that Poker emerged early in the 19th century, probably in New Orleans, on board the great Mississippi paddle steamers. It seems likely that its immediate ancestor was a French game called Poque, which itself was a version of the German game Poch. According to American card authority Louis Coffin, 'the French name was pronounced 'poke' and Southerners corrupted the pronunciation to Pokuh or Poker'. Brag, a vying game based on three-card hands, is also thought to have been an influence.

By Victorian times, Draw and Stud Poker had emerged. Then came further variants in which the notion of one or more communal cards was introduced. By that time, Poker had become what American card historian Allen Dowling aptly termed 'the great American pastime'. It is now a favourite throughout the card-playing world.

Right: Classic image of a joker or court jester, wearing a cap and bells, carrying a ninny stick, or jester's wand, from a 15th-century manuscript.

13 | Bridge and Whist Games

Bridge and Whist belong to trick-taking card games, in which the objective is to win a specified number of tricks; as many tricks as possible; or occasionally a specified one, such as the last trick of a hand. In some games, the aim is to lose rather than win tricks, while in point-trick games, the total point value of the cards taken determines the result, rather than the number of tricks.

As far as most trick-taking games are concerned, the rules clearly state what can be led and when. The most common requirement is the need to follow suit. In certain games, players are required to ruff – that is, to play a trump – if they are unable to follow suit and hold a trump card or cards in their hands.

In trick play, each player is normally dealt the same number of cards and plays a card in turn face up to the table. The player with the best card, usually the highest-ranking card of the suit that has been led or the highest trump, wins all the others. These constitute a trick which the winner places face down in a winnings pile; he then plays the first card of the next trick. Who leads initially is normally decided by cutting the cards. The other players play in order according to their positions around the card table, typically clockwise in games from English-speaking countries. In positive trick-taking games, players aim to take as many tricks as possible. Exact prediction trick-taking games, such as Bridge, involve a contract, in which players aim to win a set number of tricks. There are two scoring systems. In what are termed plain-trick games, it is only the number of tricks taken by each player that matters. The points on the cards making up the tricks are irrelevant. In point-trick games, however, players are rewarded or penalized for capturing certain cards, each of which has a pre-assigned value.

Above: Harold Vanderbilt (1884–1970), American multi-millionaire, revised the rules of bridge in 1925, thus turning auction bridge into contract bridge.

Contract Bridge

Love it or loathe it, Bridge has long been one of the most popular card games in the world: its origins date back to the 1880s. Auction Bridge made its debut in 1904 and Contract Bridge in 1925. The latter soon became the dominant form of the game, thanks largely to two Americans – Harold Vanderbilt, who codified its rules, and master player Ely Culbertson, the great popularizer of the game.

You will need: 52-card deck; no Jokers; scorecard
Card ranking: Standard, Aces high
Players: Four, playing in partnerships of two
Ideal for: 14+

Above: Ely Culbertson (1891–1955) built on the efforts of the founders of Contract Bridge by developing the game's first comprehensive bidding system. The vast publicity campaign he orchestrated for Bridge was instrumental in establishing its popularity.

Object

To make, in tandem with one's partner, a specified number (contract) of tricks – or more – scoring enough points over a sequence of deals to make game and then win a rubber without giving away a greater number of points in doing so. A rubber is card parlance for a match. It usually consists of three games and is won, or taken, by the first partnership to win two of them.

Special Features

Establishing Partners

Partners are determined by social agreement, or by a cut, in which the cards are fanned out face down on the table. Each player in turn draws a card. The two players with the highest-scoring cards become the lead partnership; the player with the higher card becomes the dealer. The convention is to sit around the table according to the points of the compass – North and South form one partnership and East and West the other.

Dummy

After the first card of a hand has been led, the cards of the declarer's partner are laid face up on the table and he takes no active part in that particular hand. The declarer is the highest bidder at the auction (see page 135).

Ruffing

In Bridge, playing a trump is termed ruffing. Usually the declarer and the dummy (see above) control the majority of trumps between them since they chose the suit to be played. Thus, one of the declarer's aims is to draw off the opposing partnership's trumps, leaving them with none. The declarer normally has enough trumps left to make sure that the defending partnership is not given the opportunity to win tricks with what are termed long cards, as these will simply be trumped. Long cards are the cards remaining in a suit after all the cards of the other players have been exhausted.

Scoring

Both partnerships keep running scorecards, which are divided into two columns headed 'US' and 'THEM' with a horizontal line partway down each sheet. Points can be scored 'above the line' and 'below the line'.

If a partnership wins a contracted number of tricks or more, it is deemed to have fulfilled its contract and a score is awarded accordingly. If not, the contract is said to be defeated and points are awarded to the defending partnership. Each partnership aims to win the most points in the best of the three games that make up a rubber.

Points per Trick

Trick points (only given for each trick over 'the book', which consists of the first six tricks) are entered below the line. Only the declaring partnership can score them and then only if it has fulfilled the contract for the deal. If trumps are Clubs or Diamonds, the partnership scores 20 per trick, and 30 per trick if trumps are Hearts or Spades. If there are no trumps, it scores 40 for the first trick after the book and 30 for each subsequent one. Clubs and Diamonds are termed minor suits, while Hearts and Spades are the major suits.

Doubles and Redoubles

If the contract is doubled, scores are doubled in turn. If it is redoubled, points are multiplied by four. If the declaring partnership succeeds in winning a doubled contract, it wins an extra 50 points above the line. This is sometimes known as '50 for the insult'. The bonus above the line for a redoubled contract is 100 points.

Scores at Contract Bridge

Contract made: the declarer scores below the line for each trick bid and won

Suit bid and won	**Points**	**Doubled**	**Redoubled**
Minor suit (♦ ♣)	20	40	80
Major suit (♠ ♥)	30	60	120
No Trump (NT) for 1st trick	40	80	160
NT for subsequent tricks	30	60	120

Declarers may also score above the line
(TV= trick value, V=Vulnerable)

For each overtrick	TV	100	200
For each overtrick (V)	TV	200	400
For making a doubled/ redoubled contract	50	100	
For making a small slam	500/750 (V)		
For making a grand slam	1000/1500 (V)		

Contract defeated: the defenders score above the line

Undertricks	Points	Doubled	Redoubled
First	50	100	200 (if not vulnerable)
or	100	200	400 (if vulnerable)
Second/Third	50	200	400 (If not vulnerable)
or	100	300	600 (if vulnerable)
plus for each subsequent trick	0	100	200 (if not vulnerable)

Honours: scored above the line

Any four of A, K, Q, J, 10 of trumps	100
All five of A, K, Q, J, 10 of trumps	150
All four Aces at No Trumps	150

Rubber scores at the end of play

Winning the rubber, opponents winning one game	500
Winning the rubber, opponents winning no games	700
Winning the only game in an unfinished rubber	300
For the only part-score in an unfinished game	100

Bonus and Penalty Points

Bonuses for tricks made in excess of a contract, or points awarded to a defending partnership if the contract is defeated, are also recorded above the line. These are termed overtricks and undertricks. Overtricks are scored the same as bid tricks. If, however, a declaring partnership wins fewer tricks than it bid, neither side scores anything below the line, but the defending partnership scores above the line for the number of tricks by which the declaring partnership falls short of its target. The value of such scores varies, depending on whether a partnership is what is termed 'vulnerable'. If it is, the scores are increased. A partnership is deemed vulnerable once it has won a game towards a best-of-three rubber. Once the two partnerships have each won a game, they are both vulnerable.

Slams

A contract to make all 13 possible tricks is termed a Grand Slam, while a contract to make 12 is a Small Slam. If a declaring partnership is vulnerable, it wins a bonus of 750 points above the line for making a Small Slam and 1,500 for a Grand Slam. If it is not vulnerable, it wins 500 points or 1,000 points.

Honours

Bonus points are awarded to players holding honours in their hands before any cards are played, although these are not actually scored until the end of the hand. Honours are the top five trumps: Ace, King, Queen, Jack and Ten. If a player holds all of these, he scores a bonus of 150 points above the line for the partnership. Four honours in one hand score 100. If there are No Trumps, but a player holds four Aces, the partnership scores 150 points for honours.

Points when Vulnerable

A partnership that has won a game is deemed vulnerable, meaning that any penalty points incurred against it are significantly increased (see scoring table, left). Both partnerships can be vulnerable at the same time.

Game and Rubber

A rubber typically consists of three games, so is won by the first side to win two. If a partnership wins two games without reply, it scores 700 bonus points for the rubber, this being reduced to 500 points if the opposing partnership has won a game. Victory in the rubber, however, goes to the partnership with the highest total after trick and premium points have been added together.

HAND A

HAND B

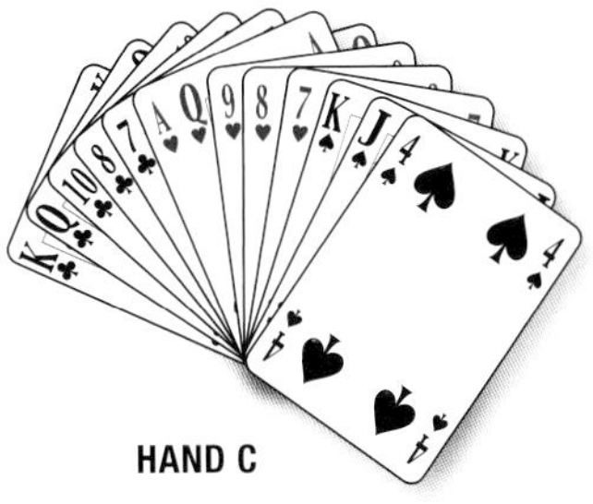

HAND C

Above and left: In adding up the value of hands, Aces are worth four points, Kings three, Queens two and Jacks one. An extra point is added in Hand A for the doubleton (just two cards in a suit), two points for Hand B for the singleton (just one card), and three points for Hand C for the void (where one suit is absent).

The Deal

Each player is dealt 13 cards, the dealer distributing the cards clockwise, one at a time. After each hand, the deal passes to the player to the left of the previous dealer.

A hand needs to contain at least 12 points to be worth an opening bid, i.e. to be considered a winning hand. An Ace is worth four points, a King three, a Queen two and a Jack one. Some players allow an extra point for a five-card major suit, or for a 'doubleton' (two cards in a particular suit), adding two points for a 'singleton' (just one card in a suit) and three for a 'void' (where one suit is absent).

The Auction and Contract

After the deal, the starting point is an auction, often termed bidding, which ends with the establishment of a contract. By this, the winning partnership commits itself to taking a minimum number of tricks, either with a specific suit as trumps or with No Trumps. The auction is started by the dealer when all the players have evaluated the cards in their hands, other players calling, in clockwise order.

There are four types of call – bid, double, redouble and pass. A bid indicates the aim of making six tricks, the book, with one's partner, plus a stated number of extra ones, from one to seven, 'the levels'. A bid of 3♦ would mean that the bidder anticipates the partnership can take nine tricks in all (the book plus three), with Diamonds – the denomination – as the trump suit. An alternative would be 3NT (No Trumps), in which case the target is still nine tricks, but the hand is played without a trump suit.

A player can double the last bid by an opponent and redouble if the opponent's last bid was a double. If a doubled bid becomes the contract, the score for making it, plus any overtricks, is doubled, but penalty points are doubled likewise if the contract is not made. A pass means no bid. The auction is over if three passes in succession follow a bid, double or redouble, or if all four players pass in the first round of bidding. In the latter case, all the cards are thrown in and the player to the dealer's left shuffles and deals again.

When first bidding, the key aim is to find the strengths and weaknesses of other players' hands as well as trying to making a contract. All kinds of bidding systems have been devised to this end. Players must state which system they are using at the start of a rubber before play begins.

There are 35 possible bids in all. Each bid has to be higher than the previous one. The level – that is, the number of tricks the bidding partnership undertakes to win – can obviously be increased, in which case any denomination can be specified, or the denomination can be changed to a higher one, with the level remaining the same. Denominations are ranked, from lowest to highest, as Clubs, Diamonds, Hearts, Spades and No Trumps (NT). The lowest possible bid is 1♣, while 7NT is the highest.

Play

Once the auction is over and the contract established, the player in the contracting partnership who first bid No Trumps or a trump suit becomes the declarer, playing his partner's hand (the dummy) as well as his own. The partner lays his cards down face up on the table, trumps to the right and other suits ranked in rows, as soon as the first card is played, and this player takes no further active part in the hand. The defending player to the declarer's left leads, followed by the other players clockwise round the table. The dealer plays a card from the dummy hand followed by one from his own hand after the opponent to his right has laid a card. Players must follow suit unless unable to do so, in which case a card from another suit, or a trump, may be played. The highest card of the suit led, or the highest trump, wins the trick.

Conclusion

Winning a game in bridge does not mean the contest is over. Game is awarded to a partnership that amasses 100 points or more below the line (either in a single contract or by adding together the scores of two or more). Partnerships must then score again from scratch in another game. The first partnership to win two out of the three games, takes the rubber.

Partnership Bridge Variants

Various forms of Bridge have developed over the years, including Duplicate Bridge, the game normally played in clubs, tournaments and competitions, Chicago Bridge, where a game is completed in four deals, and Auction Bridge, the precursor of Contract Bridge. Although the rules of bidding and play are the same in Auction and Contract Bridge, the scoring system is different.

Auction Bridge

In Auction Bridge, the notion of vulnerability does not exist, so there is no extra penalty for failing to fulfil a contract if your partnership has won a game already. Odd tricks – that is, tricks over the book – are scored below rather than above the line and count towards winning a game.

Clubs count for six points, Diamonds seven, Hearts eight and Spades nine. If the contract is doubled, so is the number of points. If it is redoubled, Clubs are worth 24 points, Diamonds 28, Hearts 32 and Spades 36. Undertricks are scored above the line, as are bonuses for completing the contract and making a Grand or Small Slam. The first partnership to score 30 points below the line wins that game and the first one to win two games takes the rubber, and is awarded another 250 bonus points.

Chicago Bridge

The advantage of Chicago Bridge is that it is complete in four contracts. Vulnerability (whereby a side, having won a game towards the rubber, is subject to increased scores or penalties) varies from hand to hand in a fixed pattern. In the first hand, neither partnership is vulnerable. In the second, North and South are vulnerable and in the third, East and West are vulnerable. In the final hand, both partnerships are vulnerable.

To determine the score for a successful contract, players first work out the score for the number of tricks made, including overtricks and taking any doubling into account. If the value of the contract was less than 100 points, 50 points are added for a part-score. If it was more than 100, 300 points are added if the partnership is not vulnerable, 500 are added if it is. The score for defeating a contract is the same as in Contract Bridge. There is no score for honours, nor extras for the rubber.

At the end of the fourth and deciding deal, if either side has a part-score – that is, points greater than zero but less than the magic 100 below the line – it receives a bonus of 100 points above the line.

Variants

In Duplicate Bridge, rather than trying to win more points than the opposing partnership, the aim is to do better than others playing the same cards.

In Rubber Bridge, each hand is freshly dealt at random, and scores depend as much on the run of the cards as on the skills of the players.

Each partnership is known as a pair and the final scores are calculated by comparing each pair's result with those of the others playing the same hand. At times, players are split into teams of four. Special four-way card holders called bridge boards are used to pass each player's hand to the next table to play it, while so-called bidding boxes, invented in Sweden in the 1960s, are also often used.

Other forms of Bridge include Reverse Bridge, where all cards rank back to front (in other words, Twos are the highest cards, followed by Threes, Fours and so on down to Aces, which are the lowest); Nullo Bridge, in which partnerships bid to lose tricks rather than to win them, and Brint, a variant of Bridge devised in the late 1920s, which is distinguished by its extremely elaborate – some would say over-sophisticated – scoring system. Basically, the higher the bid, the more each trick is worth. These three Bridge variants are rarely played.

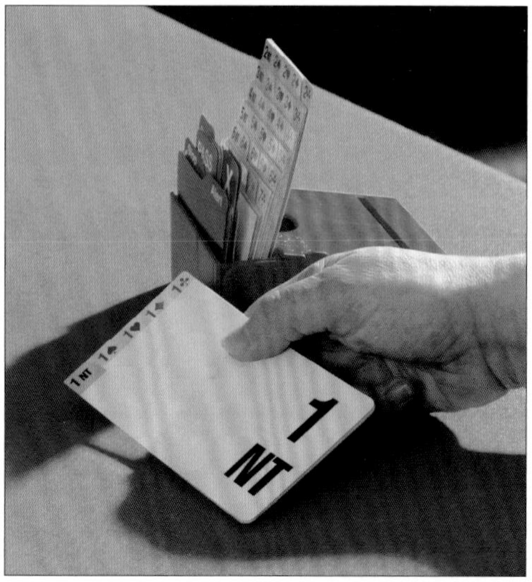

Left: Bidding boxes carry a set of cards, each bearing the name of a legal call in Bridge. This allows the player to make a call by displaying the appropriate card from the box, rather than speaking aloud and chancing others hearing the bid.

Pirate Bridge

This type of Bridge certainly seems to be a contradiction in terms, since, instead of playing in fixed partnerships, players switch alliances between deals.

Bridge authorities claim that Pirate Bridge was developed by R. F. Foster in 1917, but it seems likely that the occultist Aleister Crowley (1875–1947) devised it and Foster put the rules into definite shape. Crowley thought that what he had devised was 'such an improvement on the ordinary game', but it suffers from the fact that players with the best-matched hands inevitably manage to identify each other and make their contract easily as a result.

Pirate replaces fixed partnerships by floating alliances made from deal to deal. The dealer is the first to bid. Each player in turn has the choice of whether to accept the bid, so signalling his willingness to become dummy in partnership with the bidder, or passing. If all players pass, the hands are thrown in and the deal starts again. The player to the left of the previous bidder takes up the bidding. If the bid is accepted, each player in turn from the acceptor's left around the table may bid higher, pass, double or, if a double has been bid, redouble. If all players pass, the bid becomes the contract. A player may choose to make a new bid, which can be accepted or rejected by the previous bidder or acceptor. The latter can also try to break an alliance by naming a new contract when it is his turn to play, but, if no higher bid is accepted, that alliance must stand.

A double reopens the bidding. Making this bid gives sometime allies the chance to bid themselves out of their alliance by naming another bid in the hopes that another player will accept it. Or, if they are sufficiently confident, they can choose to redouble the accepted bid.

Once the contract is established, the declarer leads the opening trick, his partner laying down his hand as dummy. Play then proceeds in strict rotation around the table, even if declarer and dummy are seated next to rather than opposite one another. Scores are recorded below or above the line for each player. The game is scored in the conventional way (see scores at Contract Bridge), with individual scores noted above or below the line by each player involved.

Above: Aleister Crowley, occultist and probable inventor of Pirate Bridge.

Three-Handed Bridge

Aficionados of Bridge have ways of playing, even without the regulation four players. Three-Handed Bridge is has many devotees, particularly to the following two games.

Cut-Throat Bridge

In this simple version of Three-Handed Bridge, the dealer deals four hands, leaving one hand face down on the card table to eventually form the dummy. The declarer is the person who bids the highest. He turns the dummy face up between the two defenders after the left-hand opponent has led. Alternatively, players can mutually agree to turn one or more of the dummy cards face up after each bid.

Towie and Booby

In Towie, a three-handed variant that two American players devised in 1931, six of the dummy cards are dealt face up. The highest bidder becomes the declarer, turning up and playing the whole of the dummy hand.

In Booby, each player is dealt 17 cards, with one extra card being dealt face down. Each makes four discards face down to complete the dummy. Bidding follows the conventional pattern, with the addition of a *Nullo* bid. Ranking between Hearts and Spades, this is a bid to lose a specified number of tricks, playing at No Trump. A bid of two *Nullos* is a bid to win no more than five tricks, while seven *Nullos* corresponds to a *Misère*, i.e. losing all tricks. *Nullo* bids are valued at 30 points per trick.

Whist

Whist was the game of choice for many serious card players until Bridge took over from it in the early 20th century. Its popularity dates from the mid-1700s, when Edmond Hoyle described it in the first-ever rulebook of card games that was published in 1746. There is no bidding in classic Whist, but there are sufficient nuances in the play to make it a fascinating game.

You will need: 52 cards; no Jokers; scorecards
Card ranking: Standard, Aces high
Players: Four, in partnerships sitting opposite each other
Ideal for: 10+

Object

To win as many of the 13 tricks as possible.

Conventions

Like Bridge, Whist has its own accepted conventions, or 'conventional leads' as they are strictly termed, worked out when the game was most in vogue. These have been condensed and simplified in the table below. Leading to the first trick gives the player the advantage of setting the pace and being able to make the best use of the cards in hand to try to signal to a partner which cards are held. This signal is used if the player concerned does not hold the Ace or King of that suit.

Conventions include finessing (playing the third highest card of a suit while also holding the highest, to draw out opponents' highest cards); leading with a trump (to indicate that you are holding five or more in your hand), and forcing (leading with a suit you believe one of the other players does not hold).

Conventions

In plain suits

When holding	1st lead		2nd lead
• A, K, Q, J	K	then	J
• A, K, Q	K	then	Q
• A, K–J	K	then	A
• A, K	A	then	K
• K, Q, J, x	K	then	J
• K, Q, J, x, x	J	then	K
• K, Q, J, x, x and more	J	then	Q
• A, x, x, x, x and more	A	then	4th highest of remainder
• K, Q, x and more	K	then	4th highest of remainder
• A, Q, J	A	then	Q
• A, Q, J, x	A	then	Q
• A, Q, J, x, x	A	then	J
• K, J, 10, 9	9	then	K (if A or Q fails)
• Q, J, x	Q		
• Q, J, x, x and more	4th highest		

In trump suits

When holding	1st lead		2nd lead
• A, K, Q, J	J	then	Q
• A, K, Q	Q	then	K
• A, K, x, x, x, x and more	K	then	A
• A, K, x, x, x, x	4th highest		

The Rule of Eleven

A further convention – leading the fourth best of your longest suit (counting from the top down), enables a player to apply what is termed the 'rule of eleven' to gauge the lie of the cards. Assuming your partner has led his fourth highest card, you subtract its face value from 11, to establish (in theory), how many of the higher cards are lacking from his hand. By further subtracting the number you hold yourself, you can deduce the number of higher cards held by the opposing side.

To show that he is holding an Ace, for instance, a player will lead a King. If a player leads the Seven of a suit in which his partner holds the Jack and King, this means that there are four cards above the Seven against him, of which his partner holds two. The partner cannot hold the Ace, or he would have played it, so his hand must include any four cards from Queen and Ten down to Seven, while the opposing partnership must hold the Ace and any one of Queen, Ten, Nine and Eight between them.

Revokes

If a player does not follow suit when able to do so, a penalty is imposed. The cost of this (known as a revoke) is three game points, which can either be added to the opponents' score or subtracted from that of the revoking partnership. If both partnerships revoke, the hand is abandoned and a new one dealt.

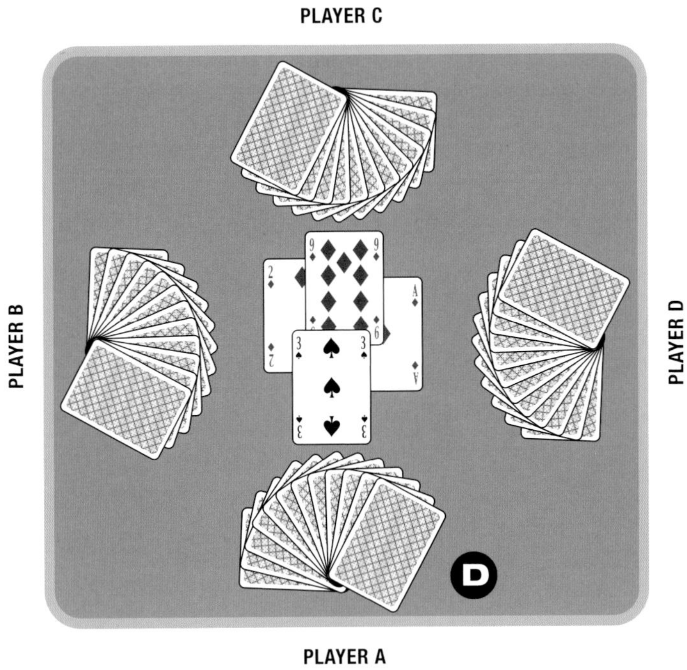

Above: With Diamonds having been played by Player B, Players C and D follow suit. The A♦ seems set to win the trick, but Player A is out of Diamonds, so wins the trick with a low trump.

The Deal

Who deals first is determined by cutting the pack. The player to the dealer's left shuffles and the one to the right cuts the cards before the deal is made. Each player is singly dealt 13 cards face down except for the last card, which is turned up to denote trumps for that hand. The dealer claims the card when the trick is led. Otherwise, players can agree trumps in advance, in which case the convention is to follow a fixed sequence: Hearts, Diamonds, Spades and Clubs. No Trumps can also be introduced, so every fifth hand is played without trumps. Subsequent deals pass clockwise to the next player, who shuffles as before.

Play

Play starts with the person seated to the dealer's left, moving clockwise around the table. The first card becomes the suit for the trick. The other players must follow suit if they can. If they cannot, they can play a trump or discard any card. The player playing the highest card of the suit that has been led or the highest trump, if any are played, takes the trick. To claim it, he turns it face down in front of him. The winner leads play for the next trick.

Right: Player D, the first to lead, played the K♠, indicating that he also holds the A♠. His partner, Player B, lays the Q♠, almost certainly indicating he holds either a singleton (just one card) or doubleton (just two cards) in Spades.

Scoring

The partnership that gets to or exceeds five game points first – seven game points in the USA – wins the game. A rubber is a match that consists typically of three games, and is therefore won by the first side to win two. The match is won by the partnership with the highest number of game points at the end of the rubber.

In a five-point game, points can be won from tricks, honours and revokes. The first six tricks do not score, while tricks from seven to 13 are worth one game point each. If a partnership holds all the honour cards, the Ace, King, Queen and Jack of trumps, it gains four game points. If three honour cards are held, two extra game points are given. The winning partnership is also given a game point if its opponents make three or four tricks, two points if they make only one or two, and three points if they fail to score at all. In the seven-point system, players who revoke concede two game points to the opposing partnership. The final score is the difference between seven and the number of game points, if any, won by the losers. The final hand is played even after seven points have been won, and the points are added to the final score.

Conclusion

The game continues until all 13 tricks have been won. If one partnership takes all tricks, it is termed a Slam.

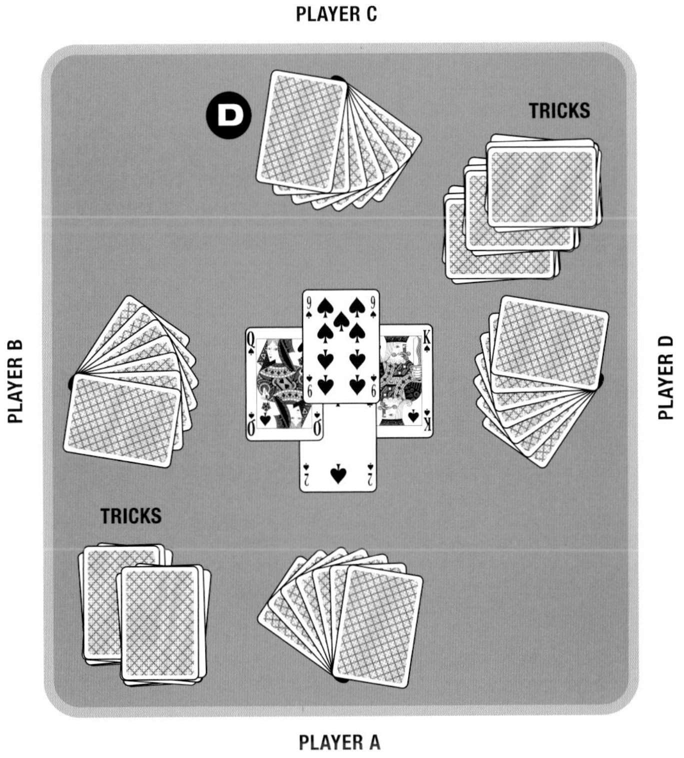

Bid Whist

Many other games have developed from Whist, often with some element of bidding added. Perhaps the most significant of these is Bid Whist, which is widely played by the African-American community in the USA. Other interesting bidding variants include Norwegian Whist, in which the aim can be to lose tricks rather than win them, and Contract Whist, which is much like Bridge but without the dummy.

You will need: 52 cards plus two Jokers, marked (or differentiated) the 'Big' Joker and the 'Little' Joker; scorecard

Card ranking: In high bids ('uptown'), cards rank Ace down to Two. In low bids ('downtown'), cards rank Ace up to King. In trump bids, cards rank Big Joker, Little Joker, Ace down to Two (uptown) or up to King (downtown)

Players: Four in partnerships, sitting opposite each other

Ideal for: 14+

Object

To fulfil the contract as bid and so score the points that are necessary to win the game.

The Deal

The player who draws the first Diamond deals first. Each player is dealt 12 cards, the remaining six being placed face down on the table to form a kitty.

Taking the Kitty

What happens after the deal depends on whether trumps are being played. If they are played, the successful bidder 'sports' the kitty, turning it up so the cards can be seen, and adds it to his hand before discarding six cards. Once sported in this way, the kitty counts as the first book to be won by the partnership. If there are No Trumps, the kitty is not shown to the other players.

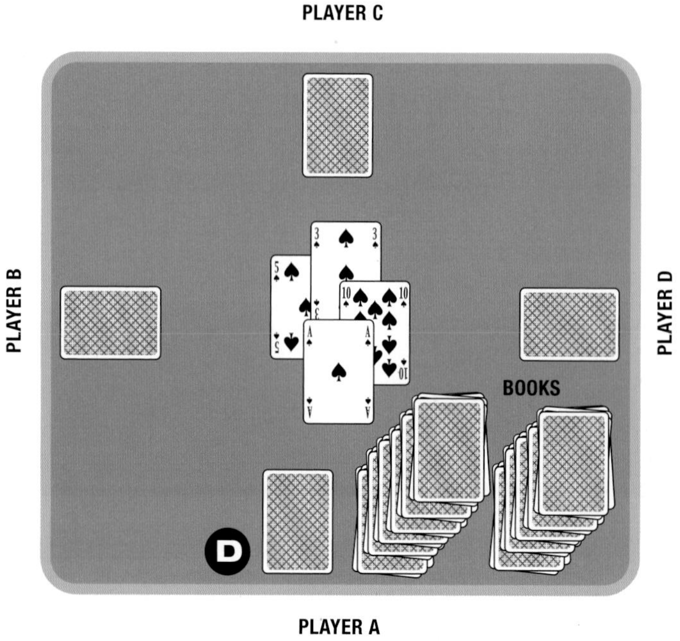

Left: This trick takes the A–C partnership to 12 tricks (or books, as they are called in Bid Whist). If they can win the last trick, they will have made a 'Boston', in which case, scores are quadrupled.

Bidding

Each player can bid only once, or pass. Each bid must be higher than the last. If the first three players pass, the dealer must bid. A bid consists of a number from three to seven, indicating the number of tricks (called 'books') above six that the bidder's team contracts to make.

Adding 'uptown' to a bid means that a trump suit will be named once the bidding is over and that high cards will win, while adding 'downtown' means that low cards will. When bidding No Trumps, a player waits until the end of bidding before specifying whether high or low cards count for more.

Play

Any card may be led, players following suit if possible. If not, they can play a trump or a card from a different suit. The ranking of the cards depends on what has been specified in the bid. If a player fails to follow suit despite holding an appropriate card, this is a renege and the reneging side is penalized. If it has won enough books, three are taken away from it. If not, the non-reneging team is deemed to have won 13 books.

Scoring and Conclusion

Players score points by bidding for and winning books. A game consists of 13 books, and each book won above six is worth a point, but, in order to score, the bidding side must make at least as many points as it has bid. If it fails, the points that were bid are subtracted from the score. If the winning bid is No Trumps, scores are doubled. Winning all 13 books is termed a 'Boston', in which case, scores are quadrupled. The game continues until all 13 tricks have been won.

Spades

Devised in the USA during the 1930s, Spades came of age globally with the coming of the Internet and the mushrooming of online card rooms. It is a plain-trick game (that is, one in which the winner or loser is determined solely by the number of tricks scored) in which Spades are always trumps. There are numerous variations in the rules, but what follows is the most generally accepted one.

You will need: 52-card deck; scorecard
Card ranking: Standard, Aces high
Players: Usually four, in fixed partnerships of two, although it can be adapted to suit two, three or six players
Ideal for: 10+

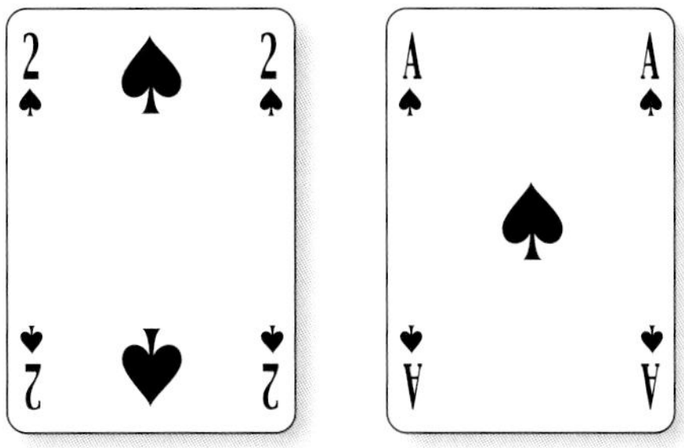

Left: The lowest and highest trumps in Spades. The A♠ will always win whatever trick it is laid to, while the 2♠ will win only when used to trump and no higher Spade is played to the trick.

Object

To win at least as many tricks as bid for, or no tricks at all.

The Deal

The first dealer is chosen at random, after which the deal rotates clockwise. The cards are dealt singly, starting with the player to the dealer's left. Each player receives a total of 13 cards.

Bidding

Players contract to win a specified number of tricks, the non-dealer partnership declaring first. Each pair's bids are added, the total being the number of tricks that partnership must win in order to make the contract. Once made, bids cannot be changed. Nor are players allowed to pass, although a player who believes that he can lose every trick may declare 'nil'. If that is the case, his partner must state how many tricks he is prepared to win.

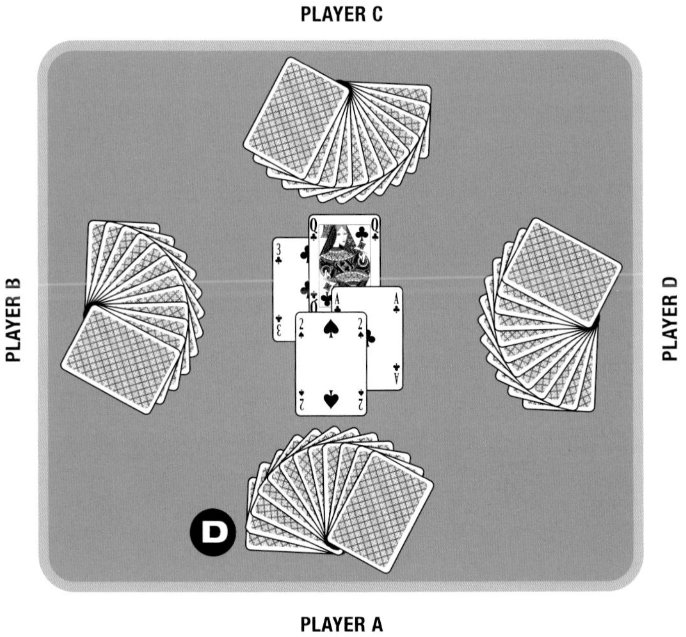

Above: Some versions of Spades stipulate that players must lead their lowest Club, as here. Surprisingly, the last player to play has won the trick with the 2♠, meaning that he must be void in Clubs. Laying the first spade like this is known as 'breaking Spades'.

Play

The player to the dealer's left leads. Any card, except a Spade, can be led, and other players must follow suit if they can. Some versions of the game stipulate that players must lead their lowest Club on the first trick and that anyone void in Clubs must discard a Diamond or a Heart.

Spades may not be played until either a player plays one because he cannot follow suit – this is known as 'breaking Spades' – or until the leader has nothing but Spades left. If no Spades are played, the player of the highest card of the suit that has been led wins the trick. Otherwise, the highest Spade wins.

Scoring and Conclusion

The side scoring 500 points first wins the game. Taking at least as many tricks as were bid means that the bidding partnership scores 10 times what it bid, and an extra point for each overtrick. These overtricks are known as 'bags'.

If a nil bid succeeds, the bidding players' side scores an extra 50 points, which are added to the score his partner makes for tricks taken. If the bid is unsuccessful, the partnership forfeits 50 points, but any tricks taken by the unsuccessful bidder count towards fulfilling their partner's contract. The game continues until all 13 tricks have been won.

Kaiser

Although Kaiser is German for 'emperor', this intriguing trick-taking game did not originate in Germany. Ukrainian immigrants to Canada are thought to have developed it half a century or so ago, although whether they brought it over from their homeland or devised it for themselves is a mystery. The side that bids highest chooses the trump suit, unless playing No Trumps.

You will need: 32 cards including Sevens to Aces, but with the 3♠ replacing 7♠ and 5♥ replacing 7♥; scorecards

Card ranking: Standard, Aces high

Players: Four, in partnerships of two

Ideal for: 14+

Object

To win at least as many tricks as bid, or to bring down the opposing partnership's bid.

The Deal

The deal and play are both clockwise. The first dealer is chosen at random, with the deal passing to the left after each hand. All the cards in the pack are dealt singly, so that each player ends up with a hand of eight cards.

Bidding

Once the deal has been completed, each player, starting with the player to the dealer's left, has one chance to bid or to pass. The possible bids are from five to 12 points.

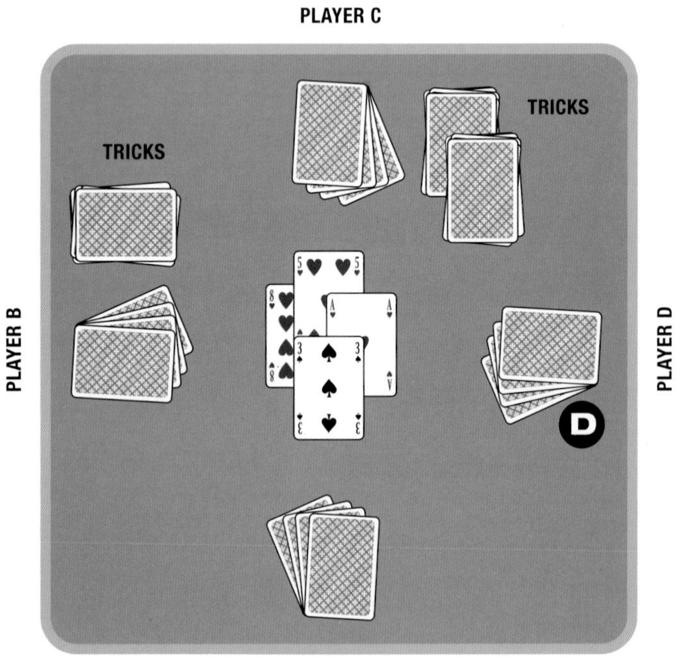

Above: Player C here looks to be on target to score a five-point bonus for his partnership by winning a trick containing the 5♥. However, Player A, unable to follow suit, plays the 3♠, thus reducing the trick's value to three points (one for the trick, plus five for the 5♥, minus three for the 3♠).

Each must be higher than the one before it, although the dealer only needs to equal the highest bid to win the bidding. It is unnecessary to specify a trump suit in a bid, but a player who wants to play No Trumps must say so. If all the players pass, the hands are thrown in and the deal passes to the next player.

Play

The highest bidder chooses trumps and leads to the first trick, the other players following suit if possible, or playing any other card. The trick is taken by the player of the highest card of the suit that has been led, or by the player of the highest trump, if trumps are being played.

Scoring and Conclusion

When all the cards have been played, the tricks are counted and scored. Each team gets one point for each trick it takes, plus five points for winning a trick containing the 5♥.

If it wins a trick containing the 3♠, it loses three points. If the side that chose trumps makes as many points as it bid, it adds that number of points to the score. If it took fewer, the bid is subtracted. If No Trumps was played, the figures are doubled.

If the bidding team's opponents have a cumulative score of less than 45 points, they score what they took. If it is 45 or more, the score is pegged, unless they end up with a negative score. In that case, the points are deducted from their total. Fifty-two points are needed to win the game.

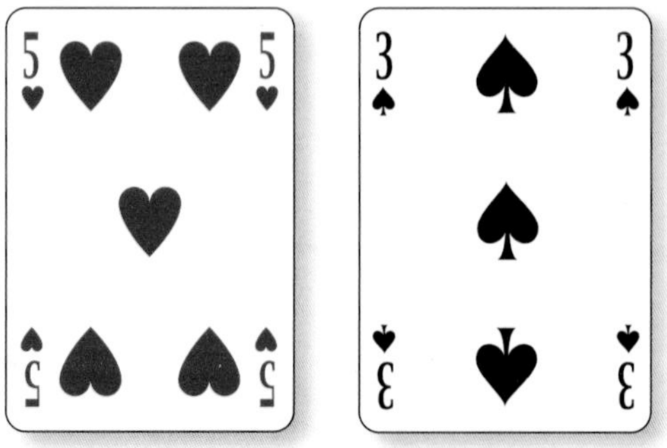

Left: Winning a trick containing the 5♥ scores the player concerned an extra five points. One containing the 3♠ loses three points.

Forty-One

This game originated in the Middle East, where it is a favourite among Syrian and Lebanese card players. Players partner each other as in Bridge; North and South play against East and West. Hearts is the permanent trump suit.

You will need: 52-card deck; no Jokers; scorecards
Card ranking: Standard, Aces high
Players: Four, in partnerships of two
Ideal for: 14+

Object

For one member of a partnership to win 41 points or more, and for all players to retain a positive score. A running total score is kept for each individual player.

The Deal

Each player gets 13 cards, dealt anti-clockwise around the table. The deal also rotates anti-clockwise. The first card is dealt singly, but others are dealt in twos.

Right: Forty-One is a much played card game in Syria, and to some extent in Lebanon. Even though it is a parnership game, a running total score is kept for each individual player.

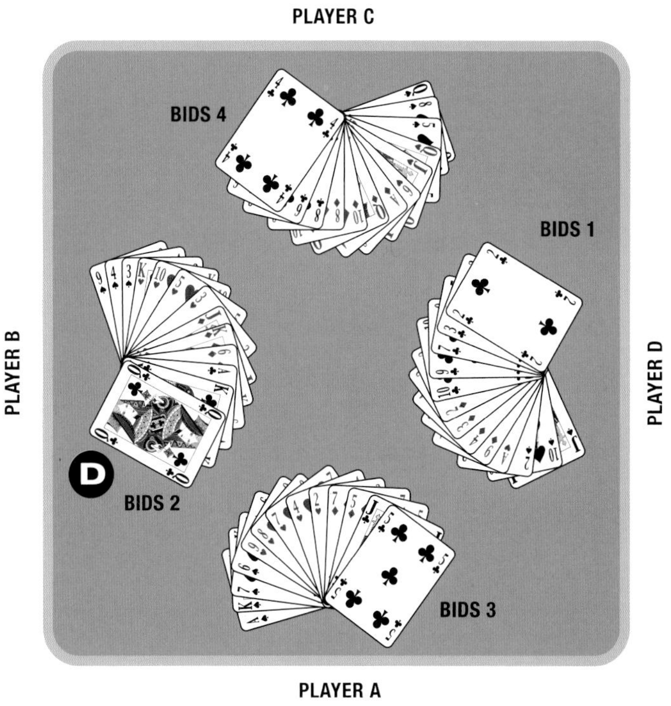

Above: The bidding shows that Player A aims to make three tricks, Player B two, Player C four and Player D one. As this falls one short of the minimum 11 tricks needed, the hands must be thrown in and the cards dealt again.

Bidding

The bidding starts with the player to the right of the dealer. Each player gets one chance to bid, stating the minimum number of tricks he expects to make. When added up, the bids must reach a minimum total of 11. Otherwise, the hands are thrown in and there is a new deal.

Bids of one to six score a point per trick if successful, otherwise they lose one point per trick. Bids of seven or more win or lose two points per trick bid. The common practice is to bid between two and six tricks. The dealer then decides whether to play the hand or not, and can bid to take the total up to the 11 needed for play to commence or he can over or under bid for a new deal.

Play

The player seated to the dealer's right leads. Any card of any suit may be led, but subsequent play must follow suit if possible. If not, a player can discard from another suit or trump with a Heart. If no trump is played, the highest card of the suit that has been led wins the trick. Otherwise, the highest Heart played wins. The winner of each trick then leads to the next.

Scoring and Conclusion

Each player's score is recorded cumulatively. A player who takes as many tricks as he bid scores the value of the bid. There is no bonus for taking tricks over and above the bid. A player who bids and takes seven or more tricks scores twice the number of tricks bid. If that player fails to take enough tricks in a subsequent hand, he loses the doubled points, i.e. 14. This can be important. Although it is only one player who has to reach the magic total of 41 points or more, the partnership can win the game only if the other partner's cumulative score is positive rather than negative. Play continues until all 13 tricks have been won.

VINT

This game originated in Tsarist Russia. It is thought to be an ancestor of Bridge, although there is no dummy and the tricks taken by both partnerships count towards a game. Vint in Russian means 'screw', which alludes to the way in which players force bids up by outbidding each other in the first of the two auctions that start off the game.

You will need: 52 cards; no Jokers
Card ranking: Standard, Aces high
Players: Four, in partnerships of two
Ideal for: 14+

OBJECT

To make as many tricks as bid for and to score 60 below the line for game. The first partnership to win two games scores a bonus of 400 points, the winners of the remaining four deals scoring 600, 800, 1,000 and 1,200 points, respectively.

THE DEAL

After the players have cut, the pack is dealt out to each player one card at a time.

BIDDING

The dealer begins the bidding. A bid is the number of tricks a player aims to take above six. A suit must be specified. If a player's bid is overcalled, he can make a higher one in the next bidding round, even at the expense of a partner.

The highest bidder becomes the declarer and starts the second auction, which ends when both partners have passed twice. The suit named in the highest-ranking bid becomes trumps unless the winning bid is No Trumps.

PLAY

The declarer leads, with each of the other players following with a card of the same suit. If a player cannot follow suit, he can play a trump or discard. The winner of the trick leads the next one.

Scores are recorded above and below the line, but the scorecard is split into four columns as opposed to two. The higher the bid, the more each trick is worth, with both partnerships scoring for the value of the tricks they take. On a bid of one, a trick is worth 10 points, on a bid of seven, it is 70 points. The total score is termed the game score and is entered below the line. Once a partnership scores 500 below-the-line points, the game is over.

SCORING AND CONCLUSION

All undertricks – tricks fewer than the numbers bid – incur a penalty of 100 times the trick value, entered above the line as a minus score. So, too, are bonus points for winning a game, rubber, Grand Slam (every trick) or Little Slam (every trick bar one), and honour points, which, in Vint, are the four Aces and top five trumps – there are nine in all, since the Ace of trumps counts twice.

They can be scored by either partnership, regardless of winning or losing, but whichever one holds the majority of them scores the number held multiplied by 10 times the value of the contract. For example, assuming that the contract is five, a partnership holding the Ace of trumps, two other Aces, and the King, Queen and Ten of trumps between them scores for the seven honours and five for the contract. They multiply this total by 10, so ending up with a score of 350 points. In No Trumps, they score 25 times the trick value.

If a player holds three Aces or a same-suited sequence of three, he scores 500 points, known as a coronet. If the sequence is in trumps, the score is doubled, and this is known as a doubled coronet. Play continues until all 13 tricks have been won.

Below and Right: Three Aces, or a same-suited sequence of three, is termed a coronet and scores 500 points. If the sequence is in the trump suit, it is termed a doubled coronet and scores 1,000 points.

QUINTO

In the early 1900s, Angelo John Lewis, better known as the stage magician 'Professor Hoffman', invented this imaginative variant of Whist. Quinto derives its name from the 'quints' that feature in the game – that is, the Joker, the Five of each suit, and two cards of the same suit totalling five. Points are gained for winning tricks, and especially for any quints that they may contain.

You will need: 52-card deck; one Joker; scorecards

Card ranking: Standard, with suits also ranked, Spades (lowest), Clubs, Diamonds, Hearts (highest)

Players: Four, in partnerships of two

Ideal for: 14+

OBJECT

The object of the game is to score 250 points in as many deals as it takes.

THE DEAL

Each player is dealt 12 card singly, the remaining five being left face down on the table. Hoffman referred to these as the '*cachette*'.

Above: Also known as the Quint Royal, the Joker has no trick-taking value. However, it is worth 25 points to the partnership that wins it.

BIDDING

Once the cards have been dealt, and before play begins, each player has the opportunity to pass, double or redouble an opponent's double. Doubling, as the name suggests, doubles the value of each trick won from 5 to 10 points, while redoubling raises it still further to 20 points. If this happens, the relative value of quints to tricks is reduced. Quints can be the Joker, which is worth 25 points, the Five of each suit or two cards of the same suit totalling five in the same trick. A quint in Spades is worth five points, Clubs 10, Diamonds 15 and Hearts 20.

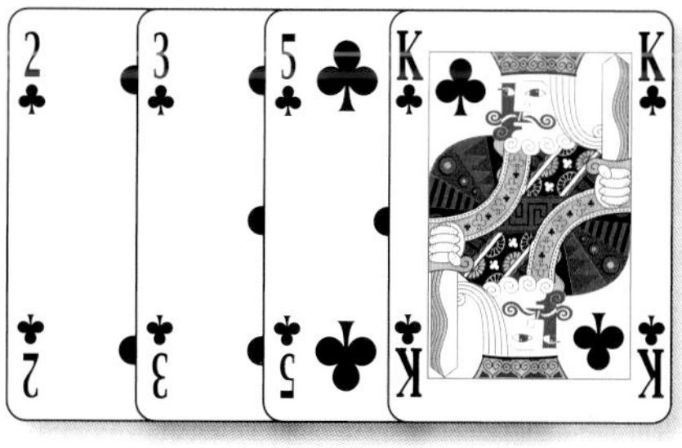

Left: This trick would be worth 20 points: 10 points for the 2♣ and 3♣ (making a quint in Clubs) and another 10 for the 5♣ (another quint). The points are scored immediately after the trick is taken.

Left: This trick also has two quints within it: the 5♥ as well as the 4♥ and A♥. Here, though, because the suit is Hearts, each quint would score 20 points, making 40 points in total.

PLAY

Play starts with the player to dealer's left, partnerships competing to win tricks containing quints. The winner of a trick leads to the next. If possible, players have to follow suit, although if they cannot, they can play any card from their hands.

The game is played without trumps. The suits, however, are ranked, from low to high, starting with Spades followed by Clubs, Diamonds and Hearts. A player may discard from a lower suit if unable to follow the suit led. Equally, he may win the trick by playing a card from a higher suit. This inevitably means that the highest card of the highest suit played takes the trick. A player whose hand contains the Joker at the 11th trick must play it if the only other option is to win the trick.

SCORING

Each trick is worth five points, with bonuses for any quints in it. The top-scoring quint is the Joker – the Quint Royal. It is worth 25 points. It cannot be led to a trick, nor can it win a trick, but otherwise it may be played at any time. If a partnership wins a trick with a quint in it, it scores the quint immediately. Its value depends on its suit.

CONCLUSION

If scoring a quint means that the partnership has reached the 250-point target, play stops. If not, the side taking the final trick also wins the *cachette*, which counts as a 13th trick and scores for any quint or quints it may contain. All the tricks are then scored to ascertain if there is a winner. If not, or if the two sides are tied, there is a new deal.

WIDOW WHIST Whist for Three Players

Whist is flexible enough to be adapted to suit three or even two players. This classic version of Three-handed Whist is aptly termed Widow Whist. It gets its name from the extra hand that is dealt just to the left of the dealer. This is the widow, which players are given the chance to play rather than their own hands. In Widow Whist, Clubs are always trumps and each player is out for himself – there are no partnerships.

You will need: 52 cards; no Jokers; scorecard
Card ranking: Standard, Aces high
Players: Three
Ideal for: 10+

Object
To win as many tricks as possible by playing the highest card of the suit led, or the highest trump.

The Deal
To establish who deals first, the players cut the deck for the highest card. The dealer then deals 13 cards each to the active players plus 13 cards face up for the widow.

Play
The player to the left of the dealer has first choice of playing the widow rather than his hand. If he decides not to play the widow, it is passed to the next person on the left, and so on, around the table. If a player takes the widow, the original hand is passed on.

Scoring and Conclusion
If the player to the dealer's left decides to play the widow, he has to take only three tricks to break even – in other words, a point is awarded for every trick taken over three. Any other player taking the widow has to take four tricks before he starts scoring. Play continues until all 13 tricks have been won.

GERMAN WHIST Whist for Two Players

Two-handed versions of Whist include German Whist, in which players start with either 13 or six cards each. Despite the name, the game is thought to have originated in Britain.

You will need: 52 cards; no Jokers; scorecard
Card ranking: Standard, Aces high
Players: Two
Ideal for: 7+

Object
To win high-ranking cards in the first phase of the game in order to win the majority of the tricks in the second.

The Deal
Thirteen cards are dealt to each player; the remaining cards are placed face down on the table to form the stock. The top card of the stock is turned up for trumps.

Play
The non-dealer leads and the dealer must follow suit. If unable, he may discard any card or play a trump. The highest card of the suit led wins the trick unless it is trumped. The trick's winner picks up the face-up card from the top of the stock and adds it to his hand. The loser takes the next face-down card. The trick's winner leads, turning up the top card of the stock. Players aim to add as many good cards from the stock to their hand as they can, which means they try to win tricks only if they think that the exposed card on top of the stock is likely to be worth more than the one beneath. Once the stock is exhausted, the two players aim to win the majority of the remaining 13 tricks.

Scoring and Conclusion
The only tricks to score are those won in the second phase of the game, after the stock has run out. Whoever wins the most tricks (seven or over) wins the game, or, if a succession of games are being played, the difference between the two totals at the end of the last trick. Play ends when all of the final 13 tricks have been won.

Calypso

Invented in the West Indies in the early 1950s, this is a partnership game in which each player uses the cards he wins to form 'calypsos' – all 13 cards of a given suit. Who partners whom is established by cutting the deck. Players with the highest cards partner each other against the ones with the lowest. Whoever cuts highest of all becomes the dealer and chooses where to sit, thus determining his own and the other players' personal trumps. In Calypso, North's trumps are always Hearts, South's are Spades, East's are Diamonds and West's are Clubs.

You will need: Four 52-card packs; scorecard
Card ranking: Standard, Aces high
Players: Four, in partnerships of two
Ideal for: 10+

Object

To build calypsos – all 13 cards of a given suit – in one's own trump suit, to help one's partner build his own, and to hinder the opposing partnership's attempts at calypso building.

The Deal

The player who cut the highest, deals first. There are four deals in all, one by each player. Each player is dealt 13 cards singly, the rest of the pack (containing all four packs shuffled together) being placed face down to one side of the table. These cards are gradually used up in subsequent deals.

Play

Tricks are played for, with players following suit where possible. If not, they can discard or trump each player using their personal trump suit. The only cards that can be used to construct a calypso are those won in tricks. Each calypso must be complete before a player can start building another, the process being made harder by the fact that any cards within a trick that duplicate ones already in a calypso cannot be retained for building any future calypsos.

The player who wins a trick takes the cards he needs from it and hands over any his partner requires. The remaining cards – those played by the opposing partnership and those unusable cards from the winning partnership's hands – are stacked face down in a winnings pile. When complete, the calypso is laid face up in front of the player who made it.

Scoring

Each partnership scores points as follows:

- 500 for each partnership's first calypso.
- 750 for each partnership's second calypso.
- 1,000 for each partnership's subsequent calypsos.
- 20 per card in an unfinished calypso.
- 50 for each card in the winnings pile.

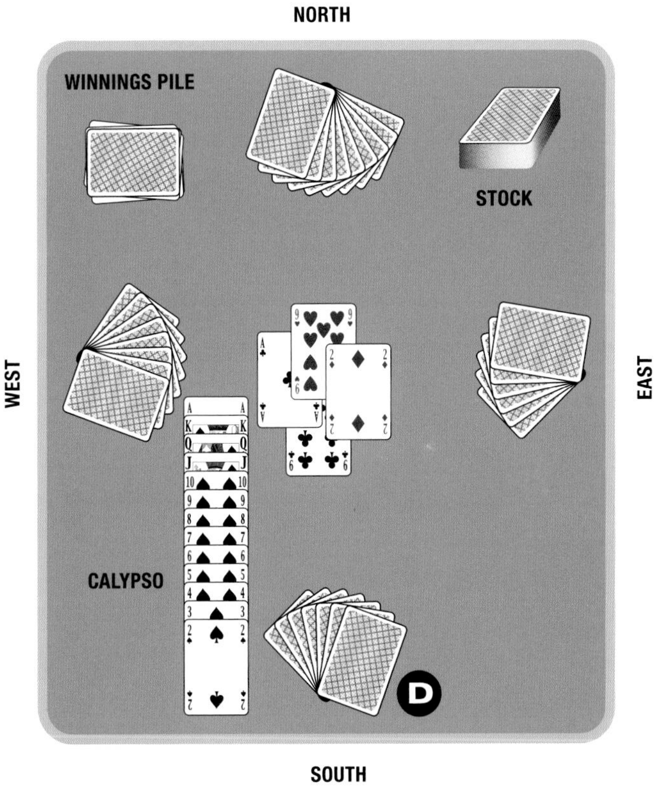

Above: South has just laid down a calypso in the appropriate personal trump suit (Spades) and led to a new trick. West seemed on course to win this, until North laid a personal trump, only to be trumped again by East, whose personal trump suit is Diamonds.

Conclusion

After 13 tricks have been taken, the deal passes to the player to the left of the previous dealer and new hands are then dealt. The procedure continues until four deals have been completed, after which the game is scored.

14 | Quick-trick Games

What distinguishes most quick-trick games is that not all the cards are dealt out, thus making it hard for players to deduce what their opponents are holding. The games range from sophisticated ones with an established historical pedigree, requiring an advanced level of skill, such as Euchre, to Truc, a Spanish and Provençal game in which tricks are won by bluff rather than by calculation.

Most quick-trick card games involve gambling. In most of them, each player is dealt three cards, the aim being to win a single trick; or five cards, in which case he has to take at least three tricks; or bid a minimum number. Bidding is the hallmark of games of skill such as Euchre, Five Hundred and Napoleon (or Nap as it is more commonly known). In their day, all three games attracted a fanatical following.

Although it is French by origin, and thought to descend from a game called Juckerspiel that was formerly played in Alsace, Euchre was, at one time, the most popular trumps game in the USA. Originally brought to Pennsylvania by German immigrants known as the Pennsylvania Dutch, Euchre has the distinction of being the first game to use the Joker. This was introduced at some time during the 1850s, to serve as the highest trump. The Joker started to appear in the well-known guise of the court jester around 1880.

The origins of Napoleon or Nap are particularly interesting. Some authors suggest that it derived its name from the French Emperor Napoleon III, the nephew of the great Napoleon, who popularized a version of it in the mid-19th century. Others trace its roots back even further, to the First French Empire (1804–14), pointing out that the names of Wellington and Blücher, Napoleon's successful adversaries at the Battle of Waterloo in 1815, feature in it as possible bids, as does Napoleon himself.

Above: This classic image of a jester playing a flute, with a ninny stick attached to his belt, appeared on cards around 1880.

Euchre

This popular partnership game is played widely in Canada, the north-eastern USA and in England's West Country. Although the essentials are fairly consistent, the game has a wide range of variations. In North America, it is customary to play with a 24-card deck, but in British Euchre, a Joker, known as Benny or Best Bower, is added.

You will need: 24-card deck, Eights and below having been removed; one Joker; scorecard

Card ranking: See under 'Card Ranking' below

Players: Four, in partnerships of two

Ideal for: 14+

Object

To win at least three of the five tricks, in which case the score is one point. If the same partnership takes all five tricks, they score two points.

Card Ranking

Aces are the highest-ranking cards and Nines the least valuable ones, but there are two exceptions. The Joker (Benny or Best Bower) is the highest trump, followed by the Jack of the trump suit, the so-called Right Bower, and the other Jack of the same colour, which is the Left Bower.

The Deal

Each player is dealt five cards, the remaining cards being placed face down on the table. The dealer, chosen at random, turns the top card face up to set the trump suit.

Bidding

Starting to the left of the dealer, players bid to establish which side will win at least three tricks with the face-up card's suit as trump. As soon as a player says, 'I accept', taking the face-up card and replacing it with one of his own face down, the bidding is over. The alternative is to pass. If everyone passes, a new bidding round ensues.

The partnership that chooses trumps is known as the 'makers' and the other as the 'defenders'. However, a player with a strong hand may bid to 'go alone' – that is, to play the hand without a partner. This means that the other player places his cards face down on the table and sits out the hand.

Play

The player to the dealer's left leads, unless someone has decided to go alone, in which case the lead passes to the player on that person's left. If two players go alone, the player of the team that did not choose trumps leads.

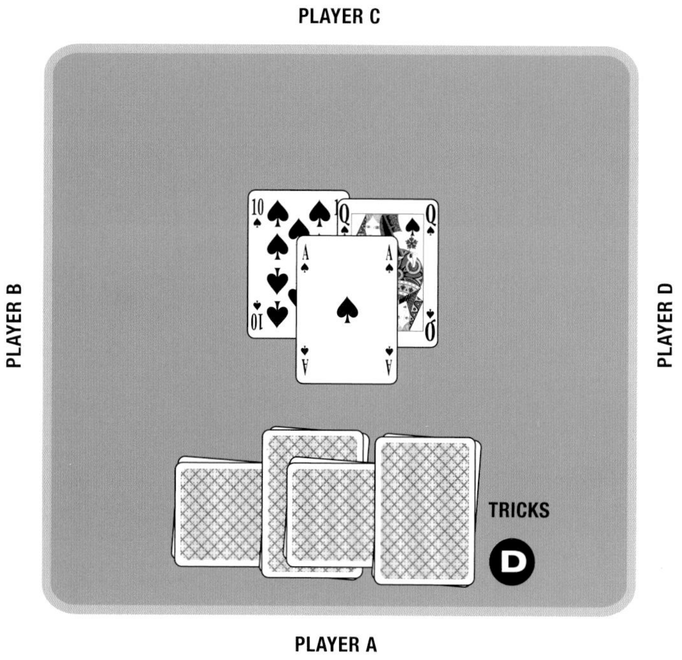

Above: Player A, going alone, wins the final trick, thus taking all five tricks (a march). His partnership scores five bonus points.

Players must follow suit if possible, otherwise they may play any card. The highest card played in the led suit wins the trick, unless trumps are played. If so, the highest trump wins, and the winner leads to the next trick.

Scoring

If all four players take part, the makers score a point for taking three or four tricks. If they take all five – termed a 'march' – they get a bonus point. If they fail to win three, they are 'euchred' and the defenders score two points.

If a maker goes alone and wins all five tricks, the partnership scores five points, or one point if the score is three or four tricks. If a defender does so and wins three or more tricks, that partnership scores four points.

Conclusion

The winning partnership is the first to score an agreed number of points (such as 10, 11 or 21).

Pepper

The modern descendant of a game called *Hasenpfeffer* (Jugged Hare), this fast-paced game is closely related to Euchre. The chief differences are that, in Pepper, all the cards are dealt, and an element of bluffing is also encouraged. As in Euchre, the top trumps are the Right and Left Bowers (Jack of trumps and Jack of the same colour), but there is an additional No Trumps bid in which the Ace in every suit ranks the highest.

You will need: 24 cards, Twos to Eights having been removed; no Jokers; scorecard

Card ranking: See under 'Card Ranking' below

Players: Four, in partnerships of two

Ideal for: 10+

Object

To make at least the number of tricks bid and to score 30 or more points. If both sides reach this total in the same hand, the result is a draw.

Card Ranking

The Jack of the trump suit, the so-called Right Bower, is the highest trump, followed by the other Jack of the same colour (the Left Bower). Aces are the next highest-ranking cards and nines the least valuable. In a No Trump bid, cards rank Ace to Nine in all suits.

The Deal and Bidding

Six cards are dealt to each player singly, after which the player to the dealer's left bids, or passes, first. Players have one chance to bid, the choice being to pass or to raise the bidding. Bids can be for one, two, three, four, or five tricks. The highest bids are Little Pepper and Big Pepper. Both are bids to take all six tricks, but the former is more conservative than the latter. A bid of Little Pepper means that the score for taking all six tricks is six. A bid of Big Pepper doubles the score to 12 points for winning all six tricks, but the penalty for failing to do so is also doubled.

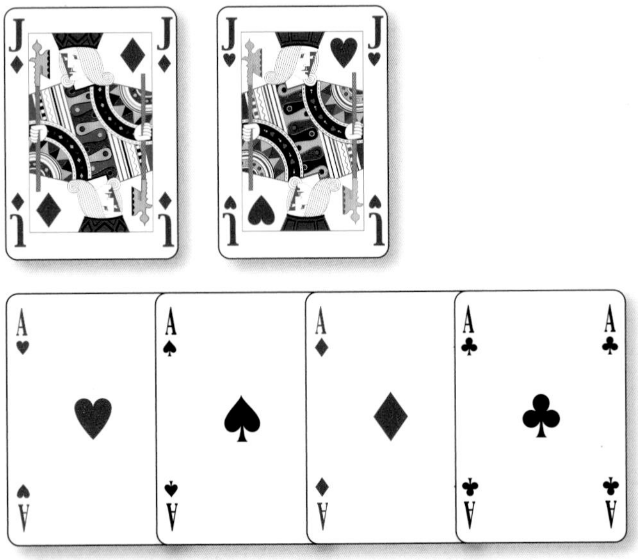

Above: As in Euchre, the Jack of trumps (here, it is Diamonds) is the top-ranking card and the other red Jack ranks second. The two Jacks are called the Right and Left Bowers, respectively. In a No Trumps contract, Aces are the highest cards, with Jacks ranking below Queens.

Play

Players must follow suit, if possible, or otherwise play a trump or any card. The highest card of the suit led takes the trick, or the highest trump if trumps are played. The winner of each trick leads to the next.

Scoring and Conclusion

The bidding side scores a point for each trick it takes if it makes its contract, but is set back (loses) six points if it fails. If the bid is Big Pepper, the bidders are set back 12 points. Their opponents score a point for each trick they take. The first partnership to score 30 or more points wins.

Variants

Some enthusiasts favour a different version of the game, in which the defenders can challenge or concede the hand at the end of bidding. If the decision is to challenge, actual play is restricted to the winner of the bidding and the two defenders, the remaining player sitting out the hand. If the defenders concede, the bidders score the value of the bid.

There is only one round of bidding, with the two highest bids becoming Pepper and Pepper Alone. They are worth seven and 14 points, respectively. Unless the bid is Pepper Alone, the successful partners exchange a card. Neither is allowed to look at the card until the exchange is completed. The main difference in the scoring system is that the defenders lose points if they fail to take any tricks, the amount varying with the bid's value, as do the penalties for not making the contract.

Five Hundred

Related to Euchre and Pepper, this fascinating game was originally devised and copyrighted by the United States Playing Card company in 1904. While still played in the USA, it has since become extremely popular in Australia and New Zealand.

You will need: 32-card deck, Sixes and below having been removed; one Joker; scorecard

Card ranking: See under 'Card Ranking' below

Players: Three is optimal

Ideal for: 10+

Object

To achieve a score of 500 points or more as a result of winning a contract.

Card Ranking

The rank order for trumps is Joker, Right Bower (Jack of trumps), Left Bower (Jack of the same colour suit) and then Ace down to Seven. In No Trumps hands, there are no Bowers. The Joker becomes the highest-ranking card in whatever suit is chosen by the player holding it and so will win any trick in which it is played.

The Deal

Who deals first is established by cutting the pack, Kings ranking highest, Aces second to lowest and the Joker the lowest. The player making the lowest cut wins the deal. Each player is dealt 10 cards in packets of three, two, three and two, or three, three, three and one. The three cards left over are placed face up to form a kitty.

Bidding

Starting with the player to the dealer's left, each player bids in turn. The options are to name a contract with a higher value than the preceding one, or to pass. Each step upward in the bidding is termed a 'jump'.

When bidding, players must state how many tricks they expect to make, (the highest number that can be bid is 10 and the lowest six), and nominate trumps or

Left: Although holding the Ace, this player's long suit in Spades makes this an excellent hand for bidding *Open Misère* – a contract played out with the declarer's cards face up on the table.

No Trumps. A No Trumps bid ranks the highest, followed by one in Hearts, Diamonds, Clubs and Spades. This makes the most valuable contract 10 No Trumps and the least valuable one six Spades. If the bid is *Misère*, the contract is to lose every trick at No Trumps. An Open *Misère*, the same bid but with cards exposed, scores double.

Scores for Contract Made

	♠	♣	♦	♥	No Trumps
Six	40	60	80	100	120
Seven	140	160	180	200	220
Eight	240	260	280	300	320
Nine	340	360	380	400	420
Ten	440	460	480	500	520
No tricks/No trump	Misère 250		Open misère 500		

Play

The winning bidder, the contractor, starts by picking up the kitty and discards three cards face down to take its place. He can discard any three cards, including the ones he has just picked up. What happens next depends on the nature of the contract. If it is *Misère* or Open *Misère*, the contractor's partner takes no part in play, simply putting his hand face down on the table. The contractor leads to the first trick. The other players must follow suit if they can or, if they cannot trump, must play any card. The highest trump or the highest card of the suit led takes the trick, its winner leading to the next.

Scoring and Conclusion

If the bidder wins the contract, the score is the value of the bid. A contract of 10 No Trumps scores 520 points, while one of six Spades is worth 40 points. If the contract fails, its value is deducted from its bidder's score.

The opposing players score 10 points for every trick they take. At *Misère*, they score 10 for each trick taken by the bidder. If a player contracted to take eight tricks or fewer manages to win all 10, a Grand Slam, the bonus is 250 points, or double the value of the contract. Play continues until all 10 tricks have been taken.

Ecarté

This elegant two-hander, derived from a French 15th-century game called Triomphe, was once extremely popular in casinos, largely because onlookers placed sizeable side-bets on the outcome. It is fast, skilful and extremely enjoyable to play, despite a somewhat convoluted scoring system involving whether cards are exchanged or not after the deal.

Object

To score five points in order to win a game.

You will need: 32 cards, Sixes and below having been removed; scorecard

Card ranking: Kings highest, then Queens, Jacks and Aces down to Sevens

Players: Two

Ideal for: 14+

The Deal

The deal alternates, and each player is dealt five cards in packets of three then two, or two then three. The remaining cards are placed face down on the table to form a stock, and the dealer turns the top card up to determine which suit will be trumps. If the card is a King, the dealer scores a point. If this takes his total from previous games to five points, he wins automatically and there is no actual play.

Exchanging of Cards

If the non-dealer believes that he can make at least three tricks, he leads to the first trick, or otherwise can 'propose' that both players exchange some of their cards. What happens next is for the dealer to decide: he can accept the proposal or refuse it. If the dealer accepts, the non-dealer, followed by the dealer, discards at least one card and draws the same number of replacement cards from the top of the stock.

If the dealer's decision is to refuse the proposal, the hand is played without any exchange of cards. However, the dealer is now obliged to take at least three tricks and a failure to do so is reflected in the scoring.

The process can continue until the non-dealer decides to lead, the dealer refuses a proposal, or the stock is exhausted, in which case play must start immediately with the non-dealer leading to the first trick. Neither player may discard more cards than remain in the stock and the trump card may not be taken in hand.

Showing the King

If either player holds the King of trumps, he may show it before play and score a point, provided that he has not already played some other card to the first trick.

Play

At the start, the non-dealer plays first. The other player must follow suit and win the trick if possible, either by leading a higher card of the same suit or by trumping a non-trump lead. If he can do neither, he can play any card. The winner of each trick leads to the next.

Scoring

Taking three or four tricks wins a point, while taking five, a '*Vole*', wins two points. If the player who rejected an exchange fails to take three tricks with the hand he was originally dealt, two points go to the opponent. Further deals ensue until one player scores 5 points. At the end of a game, if one player ends up with only one or two points, the other wins a double stake, which becomes a treble if the loser's score is zero.

Conclusion

The first player to score five points wins a game.

Left: A strong Ecarté hand. With the top card (King) in two suits, and strong cards in the others, it is likely to win at least three tricks unless the opponent's hand is almost all trumps. A player with these cards would have no need to countenance exchanging cards.

Right: If either player holds the King of trumps, he may show it before play and score a point. If the turn-up after the deal is a King, the dealer scores a point.

TWENTY-FIVE

The national card game of Ireland, Twenty-Five was originally called Spoil Five or Five Fingers, since the aim is to prevent anyone from winning three of the five tricks played. It is descended from a game called Maw, reputedly the favourite of James VI of Scotland (later James I of England). What makes the game unique is its peculiar card ranking, although this is soon mastered with a little practice.

OBJECT

To win at least three tricks – better still, all five – and sweep the kitty, or to stop opposing players from doing so (known as 'spoil five').

You will need: 52-card deck; no Jokers; gambling chips/counters
Card ranking: See under 'Suits and Ranking' below
Players: Five considered ideal, although can be two to ten
Ideal for: 14+

SUITS AND RANKING

The game is always played with a trump suit, the highest trumps being the Five of trumps (Five Fingers), Jack of trumps, A♥, and Ace of trumps if a trump other than Hearts is being played. The remaining cards rank according to the colour of their suit. Hearts and Diamonds rank from King and Queen down to Two and Ace, while Spades and Clubs rank King, Queen, Jack, Ace and from Two to Ten.

THE DEAL

Each player starts with a total of 20 chips and puts one into the kitty. Players then cut for the deal: the one to cut the lowest wins. Starting with the player to the dealer's left, five cards are dealt face down to each player in packets of two and three. The remaining cards are stacked face down, the dealer turning the top one up to determine trumps.

If the turned-up card is an Ace, the dealer may pick it up and exchange it for any unwanted card in his hand. This is termed 'robbing the pack'. Similarly, if a player is dealt the Ace of trumps, he may declare it, then rob the pack, by taking the turn-up and discarding an unwanted card face down, before playing to the first trick.

Above: In Twenty-Five, the highest-ranking trump (here, Diamonds) is the Five, known as Five Fingers. The Jack of trumps ranks next, followed by the A♥ and Ace of trumps if a trump other than Hearts is being played.

Right: Descended from a game called Maw, Twenty-Five was reputedly the favourite card game of James VI of Scotland.

PLAY

The player to the dealer's left leads. If the lead is a plain suit, the other players must follow suit or trump. If they cannot, they may discard. If trumps are led, the same ruling applies, unless the only trump a player holds is one of the top three – a Five or Jack of trumps or the Ace of Hearts. In this case, assuming that the trump that was led is lower in value, the player can choose to discard from another suit rather than play the trump.

CONCLUSION

A player taking the first three tricks can choose to take the kitty or 'jinx' – that is, try to win the two tricks that remain. If successful, as well as taking the kitty, each player pays the jinxer a chip. If not, the jinxer loses the kitty and the tricks are 'spoilt'. The same applies if no one takes three tricks: the kitty is carried forward to the next hand, each player raising it by one chip.

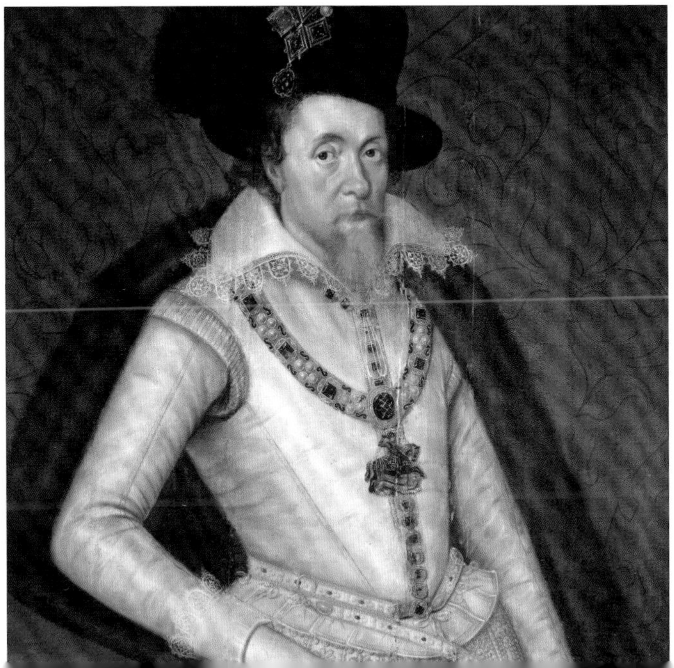

Auction Forty-Fives

This variant of Twenty-Five is a Canadian favourite, the ranking of the cards, the way in which tricks are played and the right to renege being the same as in the Irish original. The difference is that a bidding element is introduced, in which bids are made in multiples of five up to 30 without a suit being declared. The winning bidder names trumps.

You will need: 52 cards; no Jokers; scorecard

Card ranking: See under 'Suits and Card Ranking' below

Players: Four to six, in partnerships of two (in alternating seats)

Ideal for: 14+

Object

To win, as a partnership, the requisite number of tricks to score 120 and so take the game, or, if not, to prevent the opposing partnership from doing so.

Suits and Card Ranking

The game is always played with a trump suit, the highest trumps being the Five of trumps (Five Fingers), Jack of trumps, A♥, and Ace of trumps if a trump other than Hearts is being played. The other cards rank according to the colour of their suit. Hearts and Diamonds rank from King and Queen down to Ace, while Spades and Clubs rank King, Queen, Jack, Ace and from Two to Ten.

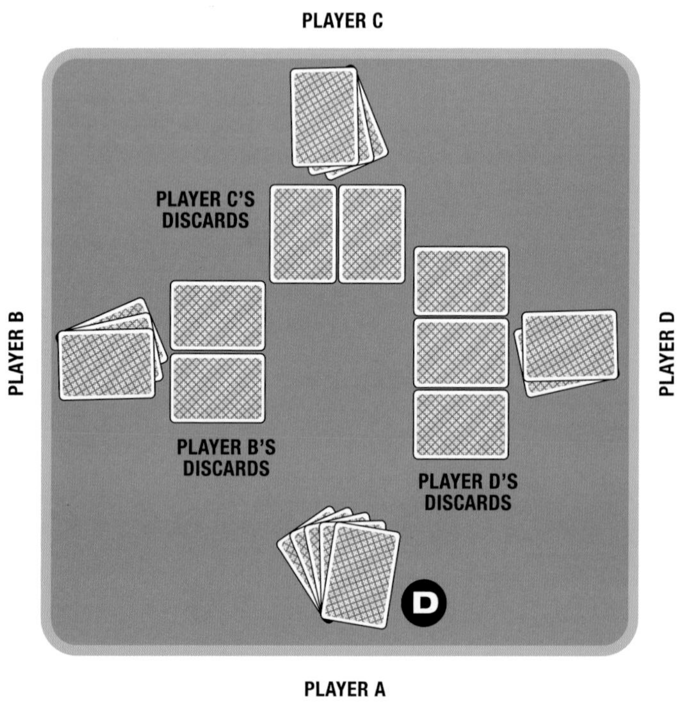

Above: Once bidding is over and trumps have been declared, each player in turn, starting with the player to the dealer's left, can discard as many cards as he wishes from his hand. Before dealing the required number of replacements, the dealer has the option of 'robbing the pack' – that is, examining all the cards that have not been dealt and adding any he wants to his hand.

The Deal

Each player is dealt five cards in packets of three and two or two and three. Once bidding is over and trumps have been declared, each player in turn, again starting with the player to the dealer's left, may decide to discard as many cards as he wishes from his hand face down on the table. Before dealing the required number of replacements, the dealer has the option of 'robbing the pack' – that is, to examine all the cards that have not been dealt and pick out whichever ones he wants in his hand.

Bidding

The bidding starts with the player to the dealer's left and continues clockwise around the table. Each player in turn may bid or pass, although the player who passes may not re-enter the bidding at a later stage. Each bid must be higher than the one that preceded it, although the dealer has the privilege of opting to say, 'I hold'. This means that the last bid is equalled. The next player to bid must therefore raise the bid or decide to pass.

Play

The player to the left of the winning bidder leads. If the lead is a plain suit, other players must follow suit or trump. If they cannot, they may discard. If trumps are led, the same rule applies, unless the only trump a player holds is one of the top three and ranked higher than the led trump. In this case, the player may discard from another suit.

Scoring and Conclusion

Each trick taken scores five points, as does the highest trump in play. If the bidding partnership takes at least the amount of the bid, it scores all the tricks won, but, if not, the amount of the bid is deducted from the score. The other partnership always scores what it has taken in tricks. If a partnership bids and makes 30 (the maximum number of possible points in a hand) the score is doubled to 60. A partnership that has won 100 or more points is not allowed to bid less than 20. The game is over when a partnership reaches 120 points.

NAPOLEON

In spite of its name, this is a British card game, which was extremely popular in Victorian times. A straightforward trick-taking game, the convention is to play Nap, as it is usually known, for small stakes and settle up after each hand. Although usually played with a standard deck, some players prefer to strip out the low cards of each suit to increase the skill factor. A Joker can also be added, in which case it becomes the highest trump or in *Mis* – a bid to take no tricks – the only trump.

You will need: 52-card deck (occasionally with lower ranks removed or a Joker added)

Card ranking: Standard, Aces high

Players: Four to five is best

Ideal for: 14+

Left: The author Jerome K. Jerome mentions Victorian favourite Penny Nap in his celebrated book *Three Men in a Boat.*

OBJECT

To make at least the number of tricks bid or to stop another player from doing so.

THE DEAL

It is standard practice to shuffle the cards only at the start of a game and after a successful bid of five. Otherwise, they are simply cut by the player to the dealer's right before each deal. Each player is dealt five cards in packets of three and two or two and three. The deal passes to the left after each hand.

BIDDING

Each player bids to win a number of tricks if given the lead and choice of trumps, starting with the player to the dealer's left, moving clockwise round the table. There is only one round in which each player must bid higher than the last one, or pass. The lowest bid is two, which is worth two points, followed by three, which scores three, *Mis* (lose every trick), also worth three, four, worth four, and Nap, which is worth five. A Wellington is worth five for doubled stakes and, if a Blücher follows, this is redoubled. A Wellington can be bid only if another player has already bid Nap and a Blücher can only follow a Wellington.

PLAY

The highest bidder leads to the first trick. The suit of the card that is led automatically becomes trumps, except in a *Mis* if it has been agreed that the bid should be played at No Trump. Players must follow suit, if possible, or trump or, otherwise, play any card. The highest card of the suit led, or the highest trump if any are played, takes the trick, the winner leading to the next.

SCORING AND CONCLUSION

If the bidder is successful, each of the opposing players has to pay him the value of the bid. If the bidder wins insufficient tricks, or, in the case of *Mis*, takes any at all, he must pay each opponent the same amount that would have been won had the contract been successful.

In some games, the payments for Nap, Wellington and Blücher are doubled if they are won, but not if they are lost. The game continues until all tricks have been played.

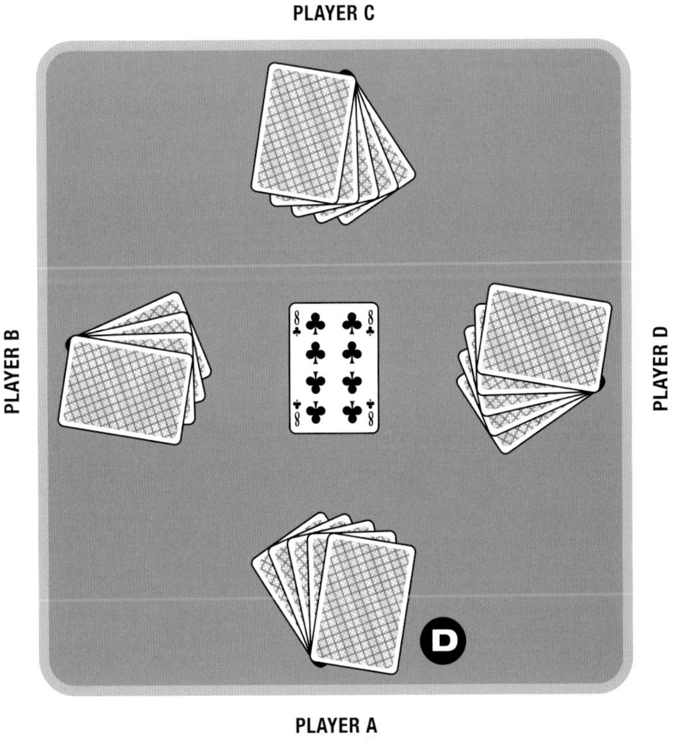

Above: Player B leads to the first trick, so Clubs automatically become trumps.

Brandeln

This attractive game is the German equivalent of Nap. Its name in English means 'to smoulder'. Two of the bids – *Bettel* and *Herrenmord* – are for No Trump games. In the others, the successful bidder nominates trumps before he leads.

You will need: 28 card-pack, Eights, Sixes and below having been removed; scorecard

Card ranking: Ace, King, Queen, Jack, Ten, Nine, Seven in every suit except trumps (Jack, Seven, Ace, King, Queen, Ten, Nine)

Players: Four

Ideal for: 14+

Object

To take at least three tricks, the lowest possible bid, up to a maximum of seven. There is no bonus for overtricks.

Bidding and Play

Players are dealt seven cards. They may bid or pass. Each bid must be more than the previous one, unless an earlier bidder decides to 'hold' the bid of a later one, forcing that player to raise or pass. Bidding a *Brandeln* means taking three tricks and a score of a point. Four tricks wins two points, five wins three, and six wins four, while *Bettel*, (a *Mis* bid), *Mord* and *Herrenmord* score five, six and seven.

The successful bidder announces trumps on leading to the first trick. The others must follow suit, trump or overtrump or otherwise play any card. The highest card of the suit led or the highest trump wins the trick. If successful, the bidder wins the value of the bid from each opponent; if unsuccessful, he deducts it from his score.

Left: In plain suits (left), card ranking is standard, Ace high. In the trump suit, (right, here ♣), the Jack and Seven are the top trumps.

Rödskögg

This is the Swedish version of Nap, the name of which translates as Redbeard. It is also known as Fem Opp (Five Up), probably because of the five-point penalties that feature in various stages of the game. It is played without trumps.

You will need: 52 cards; scorecard

Card ranking: Standard, Aces high

Players: Three to seven

Ideal for: 14+

Object

To shed enough points to end up with a score of zero from an opening score of 12.

The Deal

Players are each dealt six cards in two packets of three, after which the dealer 'knocks' with the words 'Knock for cards and misdeal'. Any player picking up his cards before the dealer knocks goes five up – that is, has five penalty points added to his score.

Bidding, Play and Scoring

Players, who each start with scores of 12, can bid from one to six, or pass. A bid of six can be overcalled by a bid of Redbeard, which is an all-or-nothing bid and cannot be overcalled. The successful bidder becomes the soloist and leads to the first trick. Other players must follow suit, or otherwise play any card. The highest card of the suit led takes the trick, the winner of each trick leading to the next.

A successful bidder of Redbeard sheds as many points as the bid, or, if unsuccessful, goes five up. The other players shed one point per trick. If they take no tricks at all, they go five up, unless they take the option the soloist must give them to drop out after the fourth trick. If they do so, no penalties are incurred, but if they play on, they must take at least one of the final two tricks.

Conclusion

The player who is the first to reach zero wins. If he fails to announce this by saying 'Knock for going out' and another player subsequently makes the announcement, he goes five up.

Bourré

This game owes its present popularity in the American South to its successful revival as a Cajun game in Louisiana. It probably descends from a French three-card game, which, in turn came from the Spanish game Burro, meaning donkey.

You will need: 52-card deck; no Jokers; gambling chips/counters
Card ranking: Standard, Aces high
Players: Two to eight, but five and over is optimal
Ideal for: 14+

Object

To win as many of the five tricks as possible. A player who wins three tricks scoops the pool.

The Deal and Play

Each player puts the same number of chips into the pot, and is then dealt five cards singly face down. The dealer's last card is dealt face up to indicate trumps. The player to the dealer's left now decides whether to pass or play. This is announced in turn around the table. Players who have decided to play undertake to win at least one trick. They state how many cards – if any – they want to discard, the dealer dealing the replacements from the stock.

The player to the dealer's left leads. Tricks are played for as in Whist, with players having to follow suit, discarding or trumping if they cannot do so. Any player holding the Ace, King or Queen of trumps is obliged to play it as soon as possible.

Scoring and Conclusion

Holding cards that will ensure winning three tricks is termed a 'cinch' and guarantees winning the pot. A player who does not take any tricks is *bourréd* and must pay into the pot the same number of chips as is already there. If two players win two tricks each – this is a split pot – the hand is tied and the pot is carried forward to the next deal.

Julep

Originally from Spain, this game is firmly established throughout South America. The name literally means 'a sweet drink'.

You will need: 40 cards, Tens, Nines and Eights having been removed; gambling chips/counters for juleps
Card ranking: Ace, Three, King, Queen, Jack, Seven, Six, Five, Four, Two
Players: Three to seven, five to six being ideal
Ideal for: 14+

Object

To take at least two tricks to avoid having to pay sweeteners, *juleps*, as forfeits of chips to other players or into the pot.

The Deal

Each player is dealt five cards, the dealer turning up the topmost undealt card to establish trumps. The remaining cards form a stock.

Play and Scoring

Each player can choose to pass, in which case he throws in his hand, or bid to play. This means taking at least two tricks. Players must follow suit or trump. Only if they can do neither can they discard. The highest card of the suit led, or the highest trump, takes the trick. Players who bid to play can discard as many cards as they like, drawing replacements from the stock. If only one player bids, any one player who passes may offer to 'defend the pack' by drawing six new cards from the stock and discarding one of them. The player to the dealer's right leads.

Any player who fails to take a minimum of two tricks has to pay an agreed forfeit, the *julep,* into the pot. If only one player succeeds, he wins the pot plus a *julep* from the other players. If two players win two tricks, they split the pot and *juleps*.

Conclusion

If the pack was defended unsuccessfully and lost, the lone bidder wins the pot, but no *julep*. If the defender wins, he gets the pot and a *julep* from the lone player.

Five-Card Loo

This is a typical example of a plain-trick game in which players who think they will be unable to take a single trick or reach a minimum quota of tricks can drop out of the hand before play begins. There are five- and three-card versions, the latter being covered later. The J♣ is known as Pam. It always belongs to the trump suit and beats every other card in the pack, including the Ace of trumps. As well as Loo, other games of this kind include Rams in France and Blesang in Switzerland.

Object

The object is to win at least one trick, each trick earning the player taking it a fifth of the pot.

The Deal

Players cut to see who deals first, the player with the lowest card winning – Aces are low for this purpose. The dealer puts five chips into the pot and deals five cards to each player in packets of three and two. The remaining cards are stacked face down to form the stock, the topmost being turned face up to indicate trumps.

Flush

A Flush is five cards of the same suit – a plain suit or trumps – or four of a suit plus Pam. The highest Flush is four of a suit plus Pam, followed by a Flush in trumps and then by a plain-suit Flush containing the highest top card. Whoever holds the best Flush 'looes the board', taking all five tricks by default and so winning the game.

Scoring

All the players have the opportunity to stay in or to drop out. Any player who stays in wins a share of the pot in proportion to the number of tricks he takes, but a player failing to win a single trick is deemed to be 'looed' and has to double what is already in the pot.

You will need: 52 cards; no Jokers; gambling chips/counters
Card ranking: J♣ highest, then standard, Aces high
Players: Three to eight
Ideal for: 14+

Bidding, Play and Conclusion

Each player in turn announces whether to pass or to play. All the active players then have the right to discard as many cards as they choose in exchange for replacements from the stock. The player to the dealer's left leads. The others must follow suit, if they can, or otherwise play a trump. Only if they can do neither are they permitted to discard. The highest card of the suit led or the highest trump, if any trumps are played, wins the trick.

If the Ace of trumps is led, its leader may say 'Pam, be civil', in which case anyone holding Pam may not play it if there are any other trumps in his hand. Each trick a player takes wins a fifth of the pot, but anyone failing to take a trick must pay a forfeit into it. The winner of each trick leads to the next and must lead a trump if possible.

Below: The J♣ in Five-Card Loo is known as Pam, and beats every other card in the pack, including the Ace of trumps. In this case, if Clubs were trumps, the player holding Pam would beat the A♣.

Left: A Flush is five cards of either a plain suit or trumps, or four of a suit and the J♣ (Pam). The best Flush is four of a suit plus Pam, then a Flush of trumps, then a plain-suit Flush with the highest top card. The player with the best Flush (if any), wins all five possible tricks without play.

Norrlandsknack

The name of this game from the far north of Sweden means 'North Country Knock'. It is related to Ramina, which is played in Finland.

You will need: 52-card deck; gambling chips/counters
Card ranking: Standard, Aces high
Players: Three to five
Ideal for: 14+

Object

To lose tricks rather than to win them. The winner is the first player to reach zero points.

The Deal

The dealer deals three cards to each player, turns up the next card to establish trumps, and then deals the final two cards. Each player can either knock, so undertaking to take at least one trick, or, on the first deal, say 'I lurk'. This means he won't be penalized for failing to win a trick. Subsequently, the choice is to knock or pass. In the opening deal, a draw follows the initial knock. Every player, except the dealer, who has to take the turned-up trump, can discard and exchange as many cards as he likes. After that, players choose whether to drop out or play.

Play, Scoring and Conclusion

Each player puts a chip into the pot and is given a score of 10 points, which goes down a point for every trick a player takes. The player to the left of the dealer leads, playing the Ace of trumps if he holds it. Otherwise, the lead can be any card. In the opening hand, if a knocker fails to take any tricks, he is 'loafed'. This means either adding five to his score, or raising it to 10 if that would make the score more. In subsequent hands, the same penalty applies to all players. They must also put a chip into the pot. The player who reaches zero first, takes the pot.

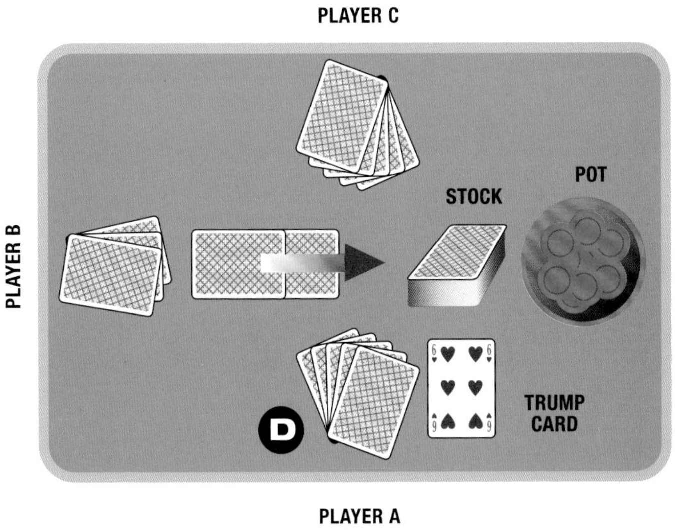

Above: After the deal and knock, every player, except the dealer, who has to take the turned-up trump card, can discard and exchange as many cards as he likes. Here, Player B exchanged two cards.

Femkort

The name of this Swedish game translates as Five Cards. It is unusual, as it does not matter how many tricks are won until the last trick is played, and any player may call for 'better cards' during the course of play. There are no trumps.

You will need: 52-card deck; no Jokers; gambling chips/counters
Card ranking: Standard, Aces high
Players: Two to ten
Ideal for: 14+

Object

The object is to take the final trick and so win the pot.

The Deal

Each player puts an equal number of chips into the pot; this is agreed prior to the start of the game. They are then dealt five cards each in packets of two and three.

Play and Conclusion

Each player plays to a trick by laying a card face up on the table. The card is left like that for the remainder of the game, so that all the players can see who has played what. The player to the left of the dealer leads first, play following suit if possible. The highest card of the led suit takes the trick, the winner leading to the next.

If a player calls for 'better cards' and no other player objects to the call, the hand is void and a new deal follows. Otherwise, play continues with the cards as held. The game is won by whoever takes the final trick.

Three-Card Loo

This is the older version of Loo, which can trace its origins back to the 17th century. It was a notorious gambling game in the 19th century, when, unless stakes were deliberately limited, fortunes were quickly lost on the turn of a few cards. The rules, conventions and card etiquette are broadly the same as in Five-Card Loo, but there are some important differences. Initially, the dealer puts three chips into the pot – this is termed a 'single'. If the pot contains chips left over from a previous hand, it is a 'double'.

Object

To win at least one trick. A player who fails to win a trick is said to be 'looed' and, as a penalty, must add three chips to the pool.

You will need: 52 cards; no Jokers; gambling chips/counters
Card ranking: J♣ highest, then standard
Players: Up to 17, but five to seven is optimal
Ideal for: 14+

The Deal

Everyone starts with an equal number of chips. Each player receives three cards, which are dealt singly, while a spare hand, called Miss, is also dealt. The remaining cards are stacked face down, and the top one is turned up to indicate trumps.

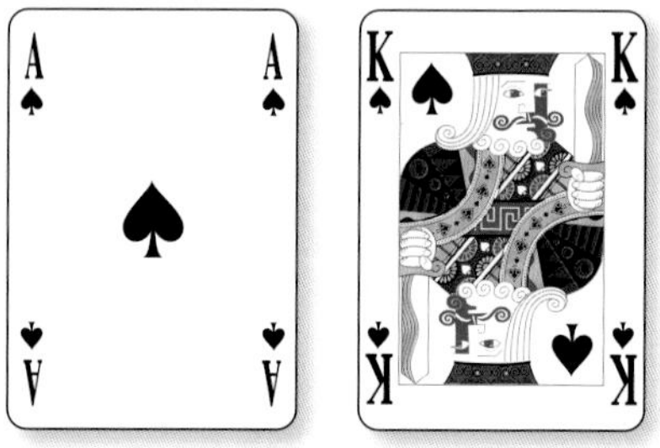

Right: In Three-Card Loo, the first to lead must play the Ace of trumps (here, Spades) if he holds it. If the Ace is the turned-up trump, he must, if possible, lay the King of trumps instead.

Passing and Exchanging

Each player decides whether to play, in which case the undertaking is to take at least one trick, or to throw in the hand. Any player offering to play is entitled to ask if he can exchange the hand he has been dealt for Miss, but only the first player to request this can actually do so. He does this without looking at Miss (sight unseen) and afterwards cannot drop out or exchange back again.

Above: Although Three-Card Loo had a bad reputation for being a vicious gambling game, it was also played in the 19th century as a mild domestic pastime, and appeared frequently in the novels of Jane Austen.

If every player passes, the dealer scoops the pool, as does the exchanging player if everyone else passes. If only one player plays before the dealer without exchanging, the dealer must either play for his hand – exchanging or not – or elect to 'defend Miss'. In this case, he must still play, but cannot win or lose.

Play, Scoring and Conclusion

The leading player must lead the Ace of trumps if he holds it, or, if the Ace is the turned-up trump, the King of trumps, if he has it. Otherwise, he must still lead a trump if he holds more than one in hand. The other players must follow suit and play a higher card if they can. If not, they must trump. Only a player holding no cards of the suit led and no trumps can discard. The highest card of the suit led or the highest trump wins the trick. The winner leads to the next trick, which he must lead with a trump, if possible.

Each trick earns the player who took it a third of the pool. A player who is 'looed', i.e. one who takes no tricks at all, pays three chips into the pot (or an amount agreed in advance before play starts), which is then taken forward as a double. Otherwise, a player who is looed must put in whatever the pool contained at the start of the deal.

Tomato

This Spanish equivalent of the game Loo is extremely popular in its homeland.

You will need: 40-card deck, Eights, Nines and Tens having been removed; gambling chips/counters

Card ranking: Ace, Three, King, Queen, Jack, Seven, Six, Five, Four and Two

Players: Three to ten

Ideal for: 14+

Object

The first player deciding to play after the cards have been dealt must take two tricks, while the others must take at least one trick each to avoid being 'tomatoed'. Each trick taken wins a third of the pot.

The Deal

The dealer puts three chips into the pot, after which each player is dealt three cards. Before looking at his hand, the dealer must say 'pass' or 'play'. If the latter, the next card is turned up to establish trumps, after which the dealer discards a card (sight unseen) and picks up the upturned one. This commits him to taking two tricks, and only then does the dealer look at his hand. If the dealer passes, the first to say 'play' goes through the same procedure, though only one trick has to be taken. If all pass, the hands are scrapped and the pot is carried forward. The other possibility is for a player to 'defend the pack', which he does by drawing a new hand from the stock. If he takes a trick, the pot is carried forward to the next hand.

Play, Scoring and Conclusion

The first active player to the right of the dealer leads. Players must follow suit and beat the card if posssible or, if unable to follow, must trump or overtrump. They may pass only if unable to do either. Each trick taken wins a third of the pot, while a player who wins no tricks is 'tomatoed' and has to double it.

Zwikken

This is the Dutch version of an old Austrian game, Zwicken, once widely played throughout the old Hapsburg Empire until it was banned. Players can decide whether to play for the entire pot or just for part of it, or to pass. Anyone holding a *Zwikk,* three of a kind, automatically wins the game.

You will need: 20-card deck, Nines and under having been removed; no Jokers; gambling chips/counters

Card ranking: Ace, King, Queen, Jack, Ten

Players: Three

Ideal for: 14+

Object

To win by either getting the highest *Zwikk*, or taking two tricks, or winning a trick that is worth more card points than those of the other two players added together.

The Deal

Players each put a chip into the pot and are dealt three cards – first one, then two – from a 20-card pack. The next card is turned up to set trumps.

Play, Scoring and Conclusion

The player offering to play for the highest amount becomes the shooter, the person who undertakes to win by either of the three ways detailed under Object. Before play, a player holding the Ten of trumps may exchange it for the turned-up card. Any player holding a *Zwikk* declares it, and wins the pool. If there are two *Zwikks*, the higher-ranking one wins. If no one has a *Zwikk*, the player to the dealer's left leads. Players must follow suit if possible, otherwise trump, or overtrump. The highest card of the suit led or the highest trump, wins the trick.

An Ace is worth four points, a King three, a Queen two and a Jack one. A successful shooter wins the stake he played for, but, if not, the same amount must be added to the pot, probably because of the high stakes involved.

Left: One of the aims in Zwikken is to secure three of a kind, the highest being three Aces.

Toepen

This noisy cheating game is very popular in Dutch cafés and bars, as the loser has to pay a forfeit, which is usually a round of drinks.

You will need: 32 cards, Twos to Sixes having been removed
Card ranking: Ten (highest), Nine, Eight, Seven, Ace, King, Queen and Jack (lowest)
Players: Three to eight
Ideal for: 10+

Object

To lose as few lives as possible, starting with 10, and to take the last trick. The winner of that trick becomes the next dealer.

The Deal

Four cards are dealt two at a time. Any player with a hand consisting of an Ace and the three court cards may elect to exchange it for a new one, but this opens up the possibility of a challenge from another player, who can insist on turning up the discarded hand.

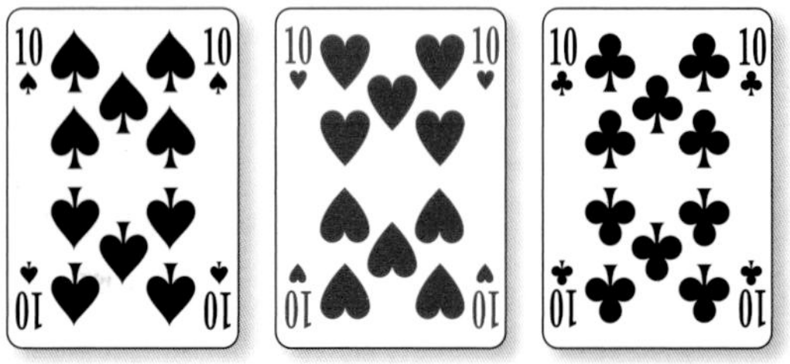

Left: A player in Toepen with three Tens in his hand must whistle or sing, while one with four Tens must stand up.

If the discarded hand contains cards other than the ones specified, the discarder loses a life for cheating. If not, the challenger loses one. A player with three Tens must whistle, or sing, or, if holding four, stand up. For a player holding three or four Jacks, both conventions are optional.

Play and Conclusion

The player to the dealer's left leads and the winner of the final trick deals the next hand; each other player losing a life. Play then follows convention, but a player may knock the table to raise the stakes by an extra life at any stage. Once a player has knocked, he may not do so again until someone else has done so. The others can stay in at the risk of losing a further life for each subsequent knock, or fold.

The game ends when a player loses 10 lives and has to pay an agreed forfeit.

Agurk

This Danish game is popular throughout the Baltic region – *agurk* is Danish for cucumber. Suits have no significance; what counts is the face value of each card. The twist comes in the last trick, when the player taking the trick is penalized.

You will need: 52 cards; no Jokers; gambling chips/counters
Card ranking: Ace is 14, King 13, Queen 12, Jack 11 and the other cards as marked
Players: Three to seven
Ideal for: 10+

Object

To end up with the lowest number of penalty points.

The Deal

Players pay the same stake into the pot and are each dealt six cards.

Play

The player to the dealer's left leads. Each player after that can play a card with a rank that is at least as high as the highest card previously played, or play his lowest-ranking card. Whoever plays the highest card or, if the cards are of equal value, whoever is the last to play, leads to the next trick.

Scoring and Conclusion

The player taking the final trick is penalized according to its face value (the sum of the cards that make up the trick). Once a player has accumulated 30 penalty points, he is 'cucumbered' and drops out of play. The player can elect to come in again, but, if so, starts with the same number of penalty points as the player with the next highest total. This can be done only once. The pot goes to the player with the lowest total of penalty points when only two players are left in the game.

Truc

There are several versions of this Spanish game, the one played in Catalonia being the most popular. It is also played with slight variations in the south of France. Played with a Spanish pack, the cards in each suit run from Ace to Seven and Ten to Twelve – the Ten is the Valet, the Eleven is the Horse and the Twelve the King. Suits are Coins, Cups, Swords and Batons. The dealer and the player to the dealer's left are the captains of their respective partnerships, which sit opposite each other at the table.

Object

In each deal, the aim is to win two tricks, or, the first if both sides win one. The first partnership to reach 12 points wins.

Betting and Signalling

The hand, and the bets associated with it, is won by the partnership taking two out of the three possible tricks. If there is a tie, the non-dealing partnership wins. While a hand is in progress, players are allowed to talk freely and even signal to their partners. Winking, for instance, means that the player holds a Three, pouting means a Two, and showing the tip of the tongue means an Ace.

The Deal

The deal passes to the right after every hand. Three cards are dealt to each player singly. Provided that neither partnership has yet scored 11 points from previous hands, the non-dealing one may propose a one-card deal, in which there is no raising of the stakes. The partnership's captain requests this by tapping on the pack instead of cutting it after shuffling. The dealer can accept or reject the proposal.

Below: Played with a 40-card Spanish pack, the cards used in Truc in each suit run from Ace to Seven and Ten to Twelve, with the Ten called *Sota* (Valet), the Eleven *Cavall* (Horse) and the Twelve *Rei* (King).

You will need: Spanish 40-card deck

Card ranking: Three (highest), Two, Ace, King, Horse, Valet, Seven, Six, Five and Four (lowest)

Players: Four, in partnerships of two

Ideal for: 14+

Play

The player to the dealer's right leads. The highest card takes the trick, unless both teams play two or more cards of equal value. In this case, the trick is drawn and goes untaken. The winner of a trick leads to the next.

Scoring and Conclusion

Each hand is initially worth a point, but any player can double this to two by calling '*truc*' either before or after playing a card. The captain of the opposing partnership decides whether to accept the call, or concede. The alternative is for either player in that partnership to call '*retruc*', so raising the stakes by a further point.

When a partnership reaches 11 points – the game is 12 points – the players must decide whether or not they want to play the next hand. If they play, the hand is automatically worth three points and no raising is allowed. If not, the opposing partnership scores a point.

Treikort

Treikort is a three-player game that was at one time widely played in Iceland, where it originated. It is closely related to Alkort, another Icelandic card game.

You will need: 27 cards, consisting of Aces, King of Diamonds, Queen of Clubs, Jacks, red Nines, Eights, Sevens, Sixes, Four of Clubs, Two of Spades and Two of Hearts

Card ranking: Sevens win if led, otherwise they lose, followed by Q♣, 2♠, K♦, 2♥, 4♣, 8♠, 9♥ and 9♦. Aces, Jacks, Sixes and the remaining Eights are worthless

Players: Three

Ideal for: 10+

Object

To win as many tricks as possible and take the title of Pope. This means winning 13 tricks over three games.

The Deal and Play

Each player is dealt nine cards, three at a time. The player to the dealer's left leads to the first trick. Whichever player plays the highest card takes the trick and leads to the next. Any card may be led at any time with the exception of a Seven. A player cannot lead a Seven until he has taken a trick. The first player to take five tricks scores a point.

Left: The Sevens in Treikort are unusual in that they cannot be beaten if led but otherwise are worthless.

Becoming Pope

A player who wins 13 tricks over three games takes the title of Pope. This gives him the right to get one of the two other players to give up his highest card and to take a Seven from the third player – if that player has one in his hand – in exchange for any cards he elects to discard. If the first player has no Seven, the Pope must do without.

The title of Pope is lost as soon as its holder fails to take 13 tricks in any further three consecutive games.

Conclusion

The highest cumulative trick taker at an agreed point wins the game.

Put

This English version of Truc traces its origins back to the 16th century. Its name derives from the call 'put', made when a player is about to play a card.

You will need: 52 cards; no Jokers

Card ranking: Three (highest), Two, Ace, King, Queen, Jack and Ten down to Four (lowest)

Players: Two

Ideal for: 10+

Object

To be the first player to score five points.

The Deal and Play

Both players contribute the same stake before they cut for the deal, which subsequently alternates. Each player receives three cards, which are dealt to them singly.

The non-dealer leads, the higher ranking of the two cards played winning the trick. If both cards are of equal rank, the trick is tied and the cards discarded.

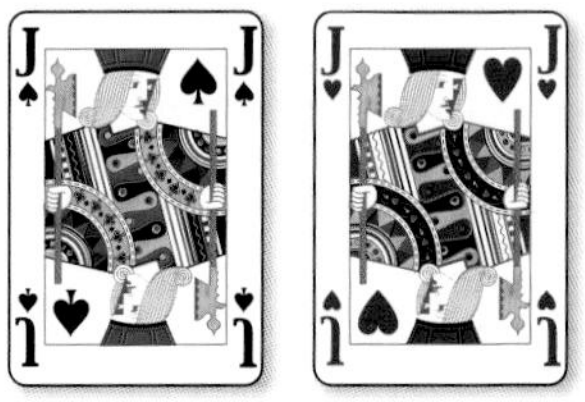

Scoring and Conclusion

A player winning two tricks or one trick to two ties scores a point. If the score is one trick each and the third is tied – this is termed 'trick and tie' – the hand is a draw, as it is if all three tricks are tied. The first player to score five points wins the game. A player can call 'put' while playing a card, in which case the opposing player may either resign and concede the point or play on, in which case the winner of the trick automatically scores five points and so wins the game. If the call of 'put' is made and the result is a tie, no one scores any points.

Left: In Put, any card may be played to a trick, which is taken by the higher-ranking of the two. If both are equal, the trick is tied and discarded.

Aluette

Otherwise known as Le Jeu de Vache (The Cow Game), Aluette is played along the French Atlantic coast, where its likely cradle was Nantes. It has many unusual features, including the way cards are ranked and the signalling system employed to indicate which cards individual players hold.

You will need: 48-card Spanish-style pack, or conventional pack with the four Tens removed

Card ranking: See under 'Ranking and Signalling' below

Players: Four, in partnerships of two

Ideal for: 14+

Object

To ensure that just one partner takes more tricks than any other single player.

The Deal

Each player is dealt nine cards three at a time, the rest being stacked face down on the table.

Ranking and Signalling

The card rankings in Aluette are complex. Eight individual cards rank the highest. The first four are termed *Luettes* and consist of the 3♦ (*Monsieur*), the 3♥ (*Madame*), the 2♦ (The One-eyed Man) and the 2♥ (The Cow). Players signal that they are holding these cards by looking up, placing a hand on the heart, closing one eye and pouting respectively. *Doubles* consist of the 9♥ (Big Nine), the 9♦ (Little Nine), the 2♣ (Two of Oak) and the 2♠ (Two of Script). The signals are lifting a thumb, raising a little finger, raising an index finger and pretending to write.

These cards are followed in order by Aces, Kings, Queens, Jacks and Nines down to Threes. Suits do not feature in the game. This means that all Aces are equal in value and will beat Kings, which beat Queens and so on.

Above: 19th-century playing cards from the Aluette deck. Aluette is also called Le Jeu de Vache, from the picture of a cow depicted on the Two of Cups.

Play

The player to the left of the dealer leads, after which any card can be played since there is no compulsion to follow suit. The highest card takes the trick and the winner leads to the next. If a trick is tied, it is discarded.

Mordienne

This is not compulsory, but is a commonly played extra. If a player is confident that he will not only win the most tricks, but also take them in unbroken succession, he signals this by biting his lip. If his partner nods back, the bidder says '*Mordienne*' and the contract is made. A successful bid wins its bidder two game points, but, if it fails, they are awarded to the opposing partnership.

Scoring and Conclusion

The player who takes the most tricks individually scores a game point for his partnership. In a tie, the partnership to reach that number of tricks first scores a game point. The first side to score five game points wins the game.

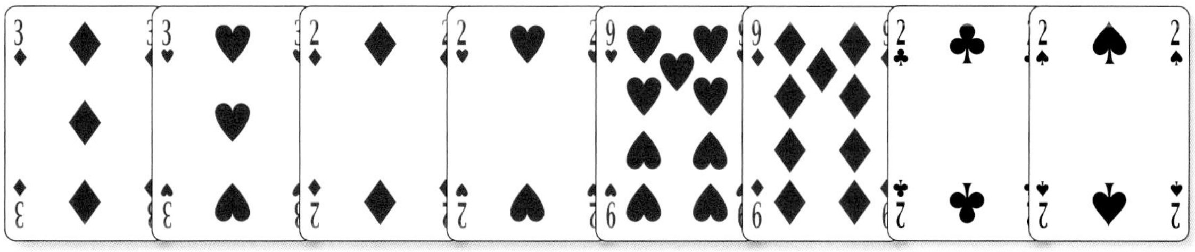

Left: The highest-ranked cards in Aluette are *Luettes* and consist of the 3♦, 3♥, 2♦ and 2♥. These are followed by the *Doubles*, the 9♥, 9♦ and the 2♣ and 2♠.

15 | Hearts Games

What makes games of this family unique is that the basic aim is to not win tricks, or at least to not win those that contain cards carrying a penalty. The skill lies in knowing when to play your high cards and win safe tricks, leaving the bogus cards for your opponents to take. Penalty cards are usually Hearts plus the Q♠, although in Jacks and Polignac, Jacks are the cards to avoid.

It takes a particular type of card sense to successfully play Hearts and other games in this fascinating family. Cards such as Twos and Threes are as valuable as Aces and Kings in many of these games, and the middle ranks such as Sevens and Eights can be quite dangerous. Most of these games seem straightforward enough on the surface, and all of them are fun to play, but many have an added sting that can sometimes take an unwary player by surprise.

Generally, the best strategy is to aim to take no tricks at all, or at least avoid winning tricks that contain penalty cards. However, this is not necessarily always the case. In some Hearts games, it can pay a player to try to take every trick because if he is successful, his score is reduced rather than increased.

In the Italian game Coteccio ('reverse' in Italian), for instance, the aim is either to avoid taking the greatest number of card penalty points or to win all five tricks. In the latter case, the successful player wins outright. Hearts, the classic trick-avoidance game, has an interesting possible twist. If a player wins all the scoring cards, termed 'hitting the moon', his penalties are reduced by 26 points, or all the other players' scores increase by the same amount.

Above: In Hearts, capturing all the scoring cards, plus the Q♠, is known as 'hitting the moon', and reduces a player's penalties by 26.

Hearts

First recorded in the USA in the 1880s, Hearts is an extremely popular game with literally dozens of possible variations. Thanks to its success as a computer game, the four-handed version may reasonably be regarded as standard. There are no partnerships as such, although sometimes it pays for two players to collaborate informally. There are no trumps.

Object

To avoid taking any tricks containing penalty cards (the entire Hearts suit and the Q♠) or to capture all 14 of them (termed 'hitting the moon').

You will need: 52-card deck; no Jokers
Card ranking: Standard, Aces high
Players: Three to eight, but four most commonly
Ideal for: 10+

The Deal

Each of the players receives 13 cards dealt singly.

Passing of Cards

After the first deal, each player passes three cards face down to the player to the left and gets the same number from the player to the right. Each player must place the cards to be passed – there is no restriction on what these can be – face down on the table, ready to be picked up by the receiving player. Only then may players pick up the cards that have been passed to them.

The process is repeated on the second and third deals, the difference being that, on the second deal, the cards are passed to the right and received from the left. On the third deal, the players seated opposite each other exchange them. The cycle is repeated until the game is over.

Play

Any player holding the 2♣ must lead it to the first trick. If possible, players must follow suit, otherwise playing any card. The person playing the highest card of the led suit takes the trick and leads to the next.

It is against the rules to lead a Heart until one has been discarded – this is 'breaking Hearts' – unless a player holds nothing but Hearts or the only alternative is to lead the Q♠. Nor can any penalty card be played to the first trick unless there is no alternative. Normally, all non-penalty cards won in tricks are discarded on to a waste pile, and penalty cards are turned face up on the table and laid in front of the players who won them. This allows players to work out which penalty cards are still to be played.

Scoring

Every Heart is worth one penalty point, while the Q♠ scores 13 points. If a player manages to 'hit the moon', he can either deduct 26 points from his total, or elect to have all the other players' scores increased by 26 points.

Conclusion

The game continues until one player reaches or exceeds a score of 100 penalty points at the end of a hand. The player with the lowest score is the winner.

Left: A typical trick in Hearts. Unable to follow suit, Player C gleefully discards the Q♠. Player D also cannot follow suit, so discards the A♥. Player B unexpectedly finds he has 14 penalty points counting against him.

Below: The cards to avoid in Hearts games are usually Hearts and the Q♠.

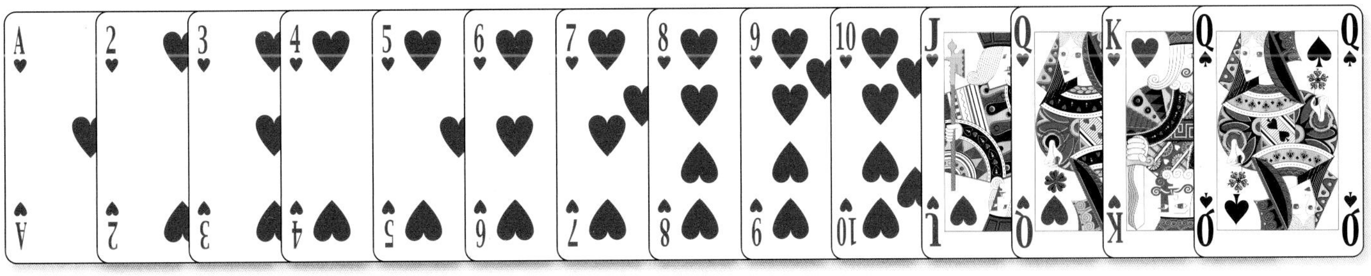

Jacks

Sometimes called Knaves, this penalty-trick game is best described as a cross between Hearts and Polignac. In this game, tricks with Jacks in them score minus points, while tricks without Jacks win plus points.

You will need: 52 cards; no Jokers
Card ranking: Standard, Aces high
Players: Three, easily adaptable for more
Ideal for: 10+

Object

To take as many tricks as possible without Jacks in them.

The Deal and Play

Each player gets 17 cards, the remaining card being turned up to establish trumps. The player to the dealer's left leads, the others following suit if possible. A revoke – that is, not following suit nor playing a trump when able to do so – costs the player concerned three plus points. The trick goes to the player of the highest trump, or the highest card of the led suit.

Scoring

At the end of a hand, each player scores one plus point for every trick he has taken. If, however, he has any Jacks in his tricks, he scores minus points – one for the J♠, two for the J♣, three for the J♦ and four for the J♥.

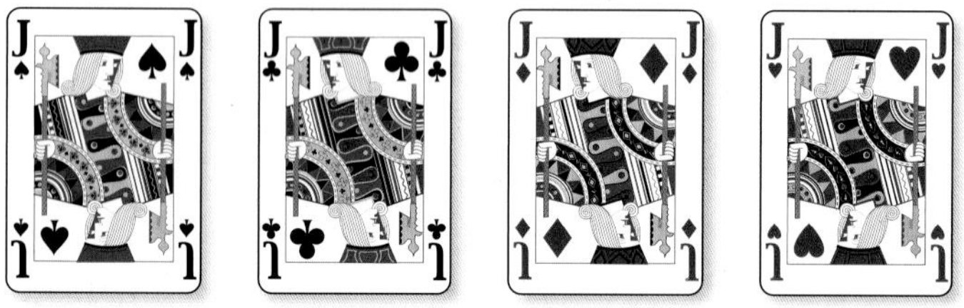

Left: In Jacks, there is a penalty for each Jack taken in tricks, so the aim is to avoid winning tricks with Jacks in them.

Conclusion

The first player to score 20 plus points wins.

Polignac

The French version of Jacks, Polignac dates back to the early 19th century. Its German equivalent is Slobberhannes (Slippery Hans).

Deck: 32 cards for four players, Twos to Sixes removed; 28 cards for five or six players, Twos to Sevens removed
Card ranking: Standard, Aces high
Players: Four to six
Ideal for: 10+

Object

To avoid taking any tricks with Jacks in them – especially the J♣ (the Polignac).

The Deal and Play

The cards are dealt evenly in batches of two or three. The player to the dealer's left leads, the others following suit if they can, otherwise playing any card. The highest card of the led suit takes the trick.

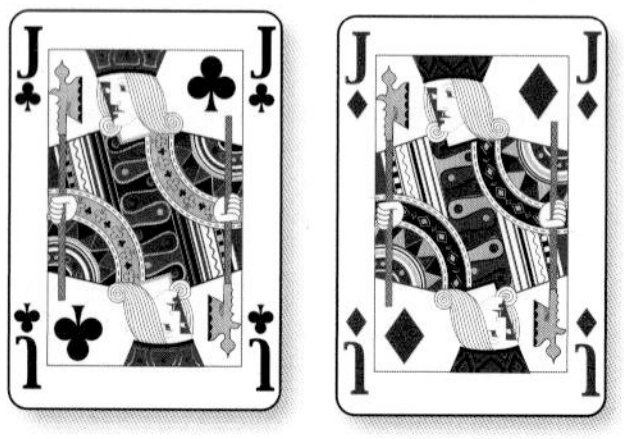

Left: In Polignac, the aim is to avoid taking tricks containing Jacks. The J♣, known as the Polignac, incurs two penalty points, while other Jacks, such as the J♦ here, incur just one penalty point.

Scoring

After each hand, each player scores penalty points for any Jacks taken. If a player takes Polignac, the score is two penalty points. The other Jacks score a point each.

If a player decides to take all the tricks – which is known as 'general' – this must be declared before play. If successful, the other players are penalized five points each. If not, the 'general' gets the penalty and the Jacks are scored as usual.

Conclusion

The player with the fewest points after an agreed number of hands wins. Alternatively, the first person to score ten points is the loser.

Barbu

In this complex and skilful game, players take it in turns to be dealer and declarer, each playing seven possible contracts once. This means 28 hands must be played in all to make up a game.

You will need: 52-card deck; no Jokers; scorecard
Card ranking: Ace down to Two
Players: Four
Ideal for: 14+

Object

To make one's contract, or prevent other players from making theirs.

The Deal and Contracts

The dealer deals 13 cards to each player, then declares which of the seven contracts (see box) is to be played. It takes some experience to decide when to declare each contract. It is best to play No Tricks close to the last hand, when playing it with a weak hand is unlikely to prove a disaster. Trumps is best left to last, so that the declarer can be sure of having a hand with four trumps in it.

Doubling and Redoubling

After a contract has been declared, each player in turn may double all or some of the other players, or elect not to do so at all. It is what amounts to a side-bet between two players in which one of them is confident that he will outscore the other, though in the two positive contracts, players are only allowed to double the declarer.

The declarer can only double players who have doubled him, though, over each sequence of seven deals, each player has to double the dealer at least twice. A player who is doubled can redouble the player who doubled him. Saying 'Maximum' means that the player making the announcement is doing that and at the same time doubling any players who have not already doubled him.

Negative Contracts

The five contracts (all in No Trumps) are as follows:

- No Tricks – each trick is worth minus two points.
- No Hearts – each Heart scores minus two with the exception of the Ace, which scores minus six. The declarer cannot lead a Heart unless there is nothing else but Hearts in his hand.
- No Queens – each of the four Queens scores minus six points and the hand ends when the last one has been taken.
- No King – the K♥ scores minus 20.
- No Last Two – taking the last trick of the hand scores minus 20, while the penultimate trick is worth minus 10.

Positive Contracts

The two contracts are as follows:

- Trumps – the declarer selects a trump suit.
- Dominoes – the declarer announces a starting rank – e.g. Dominoes from Eights – and plays a card accordingly. The next player must play either a card of the same rank from a different suit or a card of the same suit and adjacent rank to the one that has already been played. These cards are placed face up in a pattern on the table. So, if the card that is led is the 8♠, the next player places a 7♠ or 9♠ to the appropriate side of it or an Eight of a different suit above or below it. A player without such a card has to pass. The first player to lay down all of his cards scores plus 40, the second, plus 20, and the third plus 5. The final player scores minus five.

Play and Scoring

The declarer starts play. Players must not only follow suit but also play a higher card than the preceding one if possible. If unable to follow suit, any card can be played in a negative contract, or trumps in a positive contract. The highest card played takes the trick, its winner leading to the next. At the end of each hand, all players record the points they have taken in plus or minus columns.

Following this, the results of any doubling are calculated pair by pair, doubles having been recorded on the scorecard as they were made. By convention, the declarer's doubles are ringed to make it easier to check that each player has made the two doubles required by the rules. If neither of the two players doubled the other, there is no side-bet. If only one of a pair doubled the other, the difference between their scores is calculated and then added to the score of the player who did better and subtracted from the score of the one who did worse. If one player doubled and the other redoubled, the procedure is the same, but the difference is doubled before being credited to the one and subtracted from the other.

Conclusion

Play continues until every trick has been taken. The highest cumulative score at an agreed point wins.

TËTKA

Also known as Tyotka, this game hails from Russia and is widely played throughout eastern Europe. The word *tëtka*, which means 'auntie' in Russian, refers to the Queen of the 'bum suit' in each hand. Both the card and the suit are best avoided or penalty points are incurred. It is virtually impossible to escape all of them, particularly as the game progresses.

You will need: 52-card deck; scorecard
Card ranking: Standard
Players: Four
Ideal for: 10+

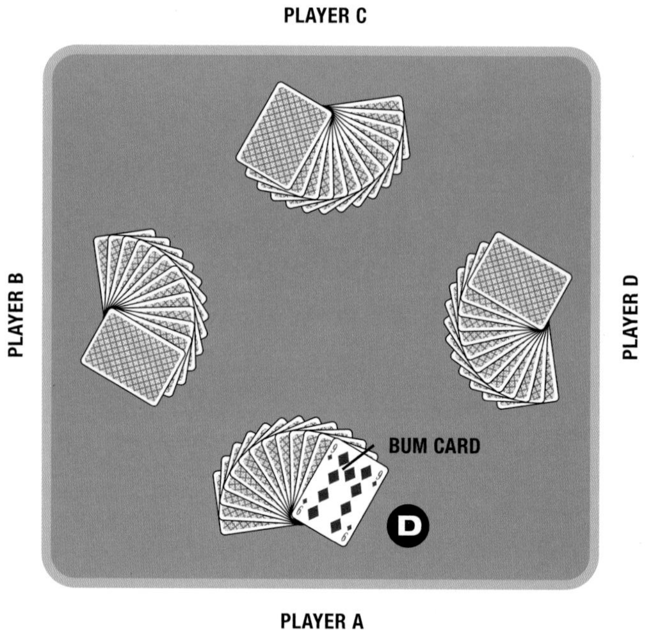

Above: The last card, turned up by the dealer, becomes the 'bum card', meaning that its suit is the 'bum suit' for that particular deal and its rank the 'bum rank'. Here, then, Diamonds are the bum suit and Nine is the bum rank.

OBJECT

To play your hand tactically so that you win only tricks that contain no 'bum cards'. The lowest score (which is the lowest number of penalty points) wins.

THE DEAL

Each player takes it in turn to deal. The first is chosen at random by cutting the pack; and the player with the highest card wins. Four players are dealt 13 cards each singly, the last card being turned up before the dealer adds it to his hand. This becomes the so-called 'bum card'; its suit is the 'bum suit' for that particular deal, and its rank is the 'bum rank'. Play proceeds to the left and a game is any agreed multiple of four deals.

PLAY AND SCORING

The player to the left of the dealer leads, and the other players follow suit if possible. Otherwise, any card may be played. There are no trumps involved. The player of the highest card of the suit that was initially led takes the trick and then leads to the next.

Each penalty incurred scores one point. Penalties are given for the following: for taking a Queen; for taking the Queen of the bum suit (*tëtka*); for taking the bum card in a trick; for winning the 'bumth trick' (i.e. the first if the bum card is an Ace, the second if it is a Two, and so on); for taking the last trick; and for winning the most tricks.

Tactically, it is well worth remembering that several different penalties may be incurred during the course of a single deal. This is a common feature of many so-called compendium games in the Hearts family, of which Tëtka is a classic example. Each of the four Queens, for instance, is worth one penalty point. If more than one Queen is played in a trick, the penalties soon start to mount up. Equally, if a King is the bum card, for example, and a player leads a King at trick 13 (the bumth trick), he would incur two penalty points.

CONCLUSION

Play continues until every trick has been taken. The lowest cumulative score at an agreed point wins the game, a game being any agreed multiple of four deals.

Left: Taking a Queen of any suit incurs a penalty. If a player takes a Queen of the 'bum suit' (*tëtka*), he incurs an extra penalty point.

Schieberamsch

This is a trick-avoidance game, the name of which comes from the German word *Schieben* (shove) and *Ramsch* (rubbish). Its complex scoring is similar to that of Skat. Here, however, the undesirable cards (*Skat*) are 'shoved' round from player to player. Jacks are the trump suit.

You will need: 32-card deck, Sixes down to Twos having been removed; scorecard

Card ranking: J♣ is the highest trump, J♠, J♥ and J♦, then Ace to Seven

Players: Three

Ideal for: 14+

Object

To avoid winning the most card points in tricks. However, before play begins, each player has the chance to bid 'grand hand', whereby he undertakes to win at least 61 points in tricks and without picking up the *Skat.*

The Deal

Each player is dealt 10 cards as follows: one batch of three (then two extra cards are placed face down on the table to form the *Skat*), then batches of four and three.

Discarding and Calling

The player to the dealer's left may pick up the *Skat*, add one or both cards to his hand, and discard an equal number of cards face down in its place to form a new one. Each player in turn may repeat the process. A player with sufficient confidence in his hand can pass the *Skat* on unseen, in which case the loser's eventual score is doubled.

If a player calls 'grand hand', he becomes the soloist, playing against the other two players in partnership. In this case, the *Skat* is not used, but is turned up and added to the soloist's won tricks at the end of play. Either opponent may call '*Kontra*' to double the contract and the soloist can respond with '*Rekontra*', redoubling it.

Play

The player to the dealer's left plays the first card. The others follow suit if possible. The highest card of the suit led or the highest Jack wins the trick. The winner of each trick starts the next round. If a non-trump suit is led, a player cannot follow suit by playing its Jack but may trump with another Jack if unable to follow. The player who wins the last trick must take the *Skat.*

Scoring

Each Jack is worth two points. Aces score 11 points, Tens are worth 10, Kings four and Queens three. Nines, Eights and Sevens score zero. The number of points scored by each player is divided by 10, and fractions are rounded down. If all take tricks, the player with the most card points scores that number as a penalty score, increased by as many doubles that apply, then rounded down to the nearest 10. For example, if two players doubled by not taking the *Skat*, and the loser took 64 card points, he scores 4 x 64 = 256 ÷ 10 = 25 (ignoring the remainder). If one player takes no tricks, the player with the most card points scores double (before rounding down). In the event of a tie, both players count the same penalty. If one player takes all the tricks, his penalty score is then reduced by 120.

Grand hand is scored with the 'base value' set at 24 points and multiplied by a 'multiplier' calculated as follows: each Jack is worth a point; two are added for game; and one point for either side getting 90 or more card points (a *Schneider*) or taking all the tricks (a *Schwarz*).

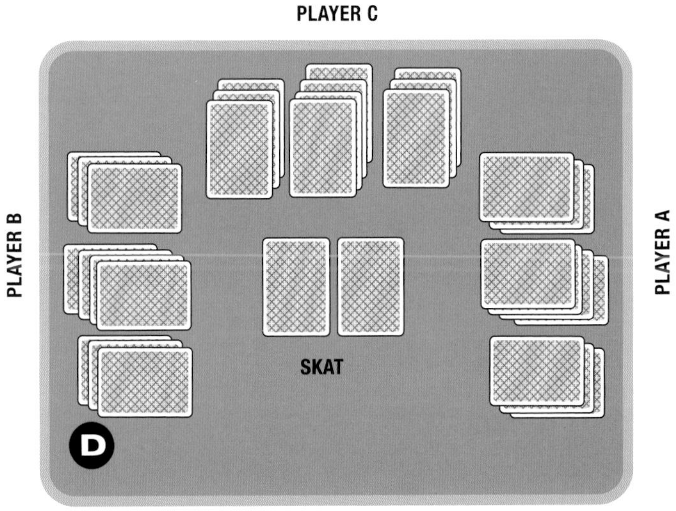

Above: The layout of the cards after the deal, with two cards for the *Skat.*

Conclusion

The player with the cumulative lowest score over an agreed number of hands wins the game.

Bassadewitz

Originating in Germany, this uncomplicated game is thought to be a precursor to Ramsch, itself the original version of Schieberamsch. It is still played in parts of German-speaking Europe.

You will need: 32-card deck (Sixes down to Twos having been removed from a standard pack); gambling chips/counters

Card ranking: Jacks (in descending order J♣, J♠, J♥, J♦), followed by Ace, Ten, King, Queen, Nine, Eight and Seven

Players: Four

Ideal for: 10+

Object

To take as few as possible of the 120 card points available in each hand, and win the pool.

The Deal

The dealer puts 12 chips into the pool (or all four players contribute three) and deals eight cards to each player.

Play

The player to the dealer's left leads to the first trick, the other players following suit if they can. Otherwise, they play any card. The highest ranked card or highest card of the led suit takes the trick. The winner of each trick leads to the next. There are no trumps.

Scoring and Conclusion

Cards rank and score as follows: each Jack is worth two points, Aces score 11 points, Tens are worth 10, Kings four and Queens three. Nines, Eights and Sevens score zero.

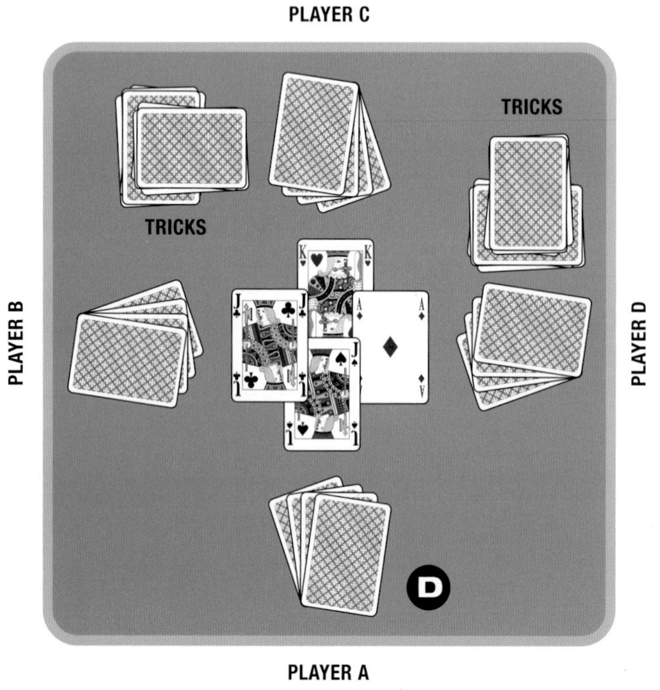

Above: Player C, having just won a second trick, leads the K♥. Player D tops it with the A♦, Player A tops it again with the J♠, but Player B takes the trick with the J♣, the highest-ranked card.

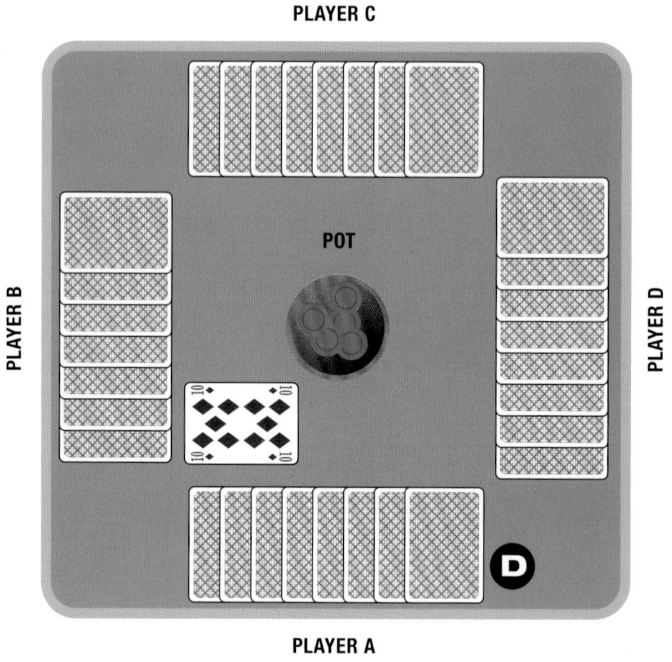

Above: Before dealing eight cards to each player, the dealer has to put 12 chips into the pot (or, upon agreement, each player can put in three).

The player with the lowest number of card points wins five chips from the pool, the second lowest four chips and the third lowest three chips. In the event of a tie, the player who led to the trick wins. A player taking no tricks can beat a player who scores no card points.

If a player takes every trick, he receives four chips from each of the other players. If a player scores 100 card points or more and fails to take all the tricks, he pays four chips to each of his opponents. In both cases, the pool is carried through to the next hand and the same player deals again. This also happens when everyone takes the same number of card points.

Variant

In an earlier version of the game, an Ace would count for five penalties instead of 11, and each player would add one per trick to his card-point total. This meant that the maximum score would be 88 when four played.

Coteccio

The name Coteccio or Cotecchio is applied to various negative point-trick games in Italy. The version that is described here is played in Trieste. It uses the card-points system that is associated with the ancient game of Trappola.

You will need: 40 cards (Tens, Nines and Eights having been removed); gambling chips/counters

Card ranking: Ace down to Jack, then Seven down to Two

Players: Two to seven

Ideal for: 14+

Object

To avoid taking the most card points in tricks; but if a player takes all the tricks, he wins the contents of the pot.

The Deal and Play

All the players pay agreed equal stakes into the pool and start the game with a notional four 'lives'. Five cards are then dealt to each player in turn, and the remaining spare cards are put to one side.

The player to the dealer's right leads to the first trick. Play proceeds anti-clockwise. The other players must follow suit if possible, or they may play any card. The player who places the highest card of the leading suit wins the trick. The trick is then placed face up in front of the player taking it. The winner of each trick leads on to the next. There are no trumps.

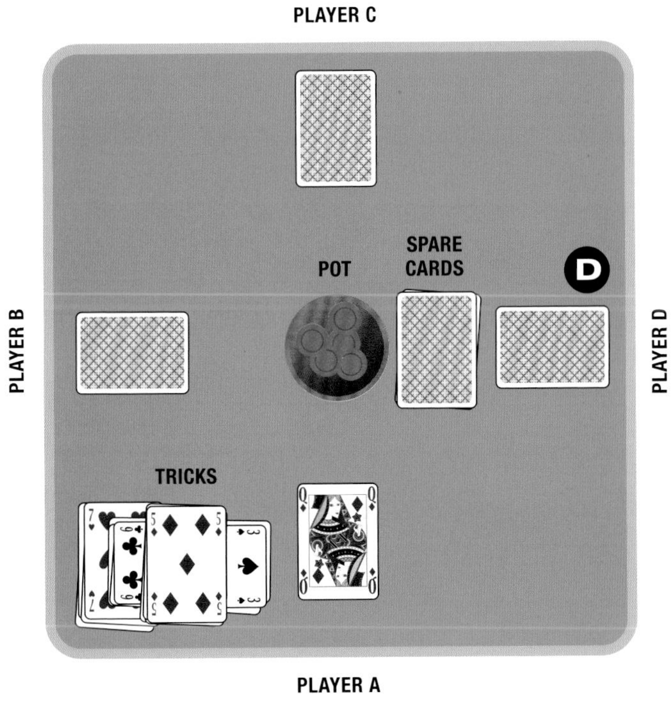

Above: Player A, having taken the first four tricks, can annul the hand, in which case no one loses a 'life', or he can lead the last card. If this wins, he gains a life and the other players lose one. If not, he loses a life and the trick's winner gains one. Here, he gambles on winning the final trick.

Scoring

Aces score six points, the Kings five, the Queens four and the Jacks three. The remaining cards, from the Sevens downwards, score zero. The winner of the last trick scores six. The player with the most points at the end of a hand normally loses a life. If two or more players tie for the most points, they each lose a life. If one player takes all of the first four tricks, he has two options. He can elect to annul the hand, in which case no one loses a life, or he can try to win the fifth trick by leading to it. If his card wins the trick, he gains a life and the other players each lose one. If not, he loses a life and the winner of the trick gains one.

If all four players tie for most of the tricks, which means that they will 'die' at the same time, the entire game is anulled. Players re-start the game with four lives each, and a new pool is added to the old one.

Conclusion

In theory, players drop out once they have lost four lives. By agreement, though, a player in this position can opt to 'call the doctor' after paying an extra stake into the pool (provided at least two other players remain alive) and receive as many lives as remain to the player who has the second fewest. Those left alive continue until only one player remains. The last player wins and collects the contents of the pot.

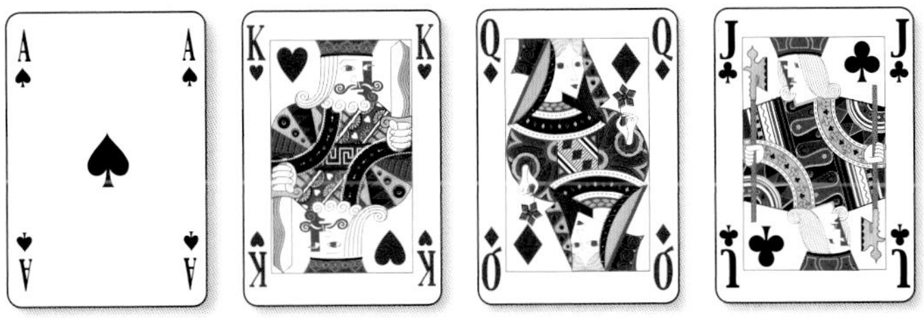

Above: Coteccio is unique among Italian card games for its points system. Of the top four cards, Aces score six points, the Kings score five points, the Queens four points and the Jacks score three.

16 | Ace-Ten Games

Many of Europe's best-known card games are termed Ace-Ten games, that is, ones in which Aces count for 11 points, Tens score 10, Kings four, Queens three and Jacks two. The other cards are usually valueless, as are tricks. It is scoring card points that counts. Games are usually won by taking at least 61 card points in tricks, and players are almost always penalized for taking fewer than 31 points.

The first Ace-Ten game in card-playing history is Brusquembile, recorded as being played in France as early as 1718. The most celebrated of all is Skat, Germany's national card game. There are many others, each with unique characteristics. In games such as Schafkopf, for instance, some of the Queens and Jacks are permanent trumps whereas in Klaverjas, which originated in the Netherlands, Jacks and Nines, rather than Aces and Tens, are the highest trumps. Players holding the King and Queen of the same suit, four of a kind, or sequences of three or more cards in a suit score bonuses. In southern European countries, most notably in Italy and Spain, local packs do not include a Ten. This has not stopped games like Briscola and Madrasso, the latter being a favourite in Venice and the surrounding area, from becoming widely popular. Another card, which is usually the Three, but sometimes the Seven, takes the Ten's place.

All these games are played with stripped-down packs, containing 40, 36, 32, 24 or 20 cards. Reducing the size of the pack has several advantages. It obviously speeds up the game, and has led to the invention of new games ideally suited to three players.

Having fewer cards also introduces variety into trick play and trick taking. Some tricks are worthless, while others may contain enough high-scoring cards to win the game outright after only a few tricks have been played. Some of these games are extremely complicated to play but are worth the effort.

Above: Skat, which was invented in 1810 in Germany, is now the country's national card game and one of the most celebrated of all Ace-Ten games.

Schafkopf

Widely played in southern Germany, notably in Bavaria where it was invented in 1811, this three- or four-player game exists in many forms. It is played with a 32-card German-suited pack, but here French suits have been substituted.

You will need: 32 cards, Sixes and below having been removed; scorecard

Card ranking: Queens and Jacks (*Wenzels*) are the highest trumps, ranked Q♣, Q♠, Q♥, Q♦, J♣, J♠, J♥, J♦. Other trumps and non-trumps: Ace (highest), Ten, King, Nine, Eight and Seven

Players: Three or four, with ad hoc partners from deal to deal

Ideal for: 14+

Object

The aim of the game is to win at least 61 card points of the 120 available. A bonus is awarded for taking 90 or more (*Schneider*), or winning all eight tricks (*Schwarz*).

The Deal and Play

Each player is dealt eight cards four at a time. Each in turn says 'Pass' or 'Play'. If all pass, the deal is annulled. If one or more bids, they declare their contract (see box). The player to the left of the dealer leads to the first trick. Players must follow suit if possible, otherwise they may play any card. The highest card of the led suit wins the trick, or the highest trump if played. The winner of each trick leads to the next. Whoever holds the called Ace (see below) must play it when its suit is led, or must lead with it the first time he leads from its suit, unless he holds four or more other cards of the same suit.

Contracts and Bidding

After the deal, players either pass or compete for bidding. From lowest to highest, the bidding contracts are:

- Call-Ace – Hearts and *Wenzels* are trumps. The bidder 'calls the Ace' by naming the Ace of a suit other than Hearts (which must be a suit of which he holds at least one card, other than the Q, J and A) and the player holding it becomes the bidder's partner (which is only revealed by play).
- *Wenz* – Jacks are trumps, ranking in their normal order.
- *Suit Solo* – the bidder can nominate a trump suit, which, headed by all the *Wenzels*, forms a series of 14 trumps. The bidder cannot hold any trumps other than *Wenzels.*
- *Solo-Tout* – a bid to take all eight tricks.
- *Sie* – a bid to take eight tricks, using all the *Wenzels.*
- *Kontra* – an opponent may double a contract by saying '*Kontra*' at any time up to the playing of the opening trick's second card. The soloist or soloist's partner, can in turn redouble. In both cases, the side concerned must score at least 61 in order to beat the contract.

Left: If a player bids Call-Ace, and asks for the A♦, the holder of this hand will become his partner for the deal, assuming that no other player bids higher. The bidder's hand must contain a Diamond, other than a Q, J or A.

Scoring and Conclusion

Aces are worth 11 points, Tens score 10, Kings four, Queens three and Jacks two. 'Runners' are the top three trumps held in one hand, or by one partnership, together with any more trumps held in downwards succession. They score 10 points each, and this is increased if there is any doubling.

In Call-Ace, the losing players pay 10 points to each of their opponents, or 20 points if they are *Schneidered* (their opponents have taken 90 or more), or 30 points if they are *Schwarzed* (their opponents have won all eight tricks).

In *Wenz* and *Suit Solo*, the soloist can win or lose 50 points or get a bonus of 60 points for *Schneider* and a bonus of 70 points for *Schwarz*. Winning or losing *Solo-Tout* is 100 points, *Sie* is 200 points. Play continues until all the tricks have been played. A game is any multiple of four deals.

Left: German-suited double-headed picture cards. Queens and Jacks are permanent trumps, ranking above Aces.

Skat

Invented in around 1810 in Germany, Skat has spread across the world. Basically it is a three-handed trick-taking game. Each hand begins with an auction, the winner becoming the declarer and playing alone against a partnership of the other two players. The player to the dealer's left is called Forehand, the one to Forehand's left Middlehand, and the player to Middlehand's left Rearhand.

You will need: 32 cards, Sixes and below having been removed; scorecard

Card ranking: Trumps (except in a Grand game, see below): J♣ (highest), J♠, J♥ and J♦, Ace, Ten, King, Queen, Nine, Eight and Seven. Non-trumps: Ace, Ten, King, Queen, Nine, Eight and Seven

Players: Three (or four, with dealer sitting out hand)

Ideal for: 14+

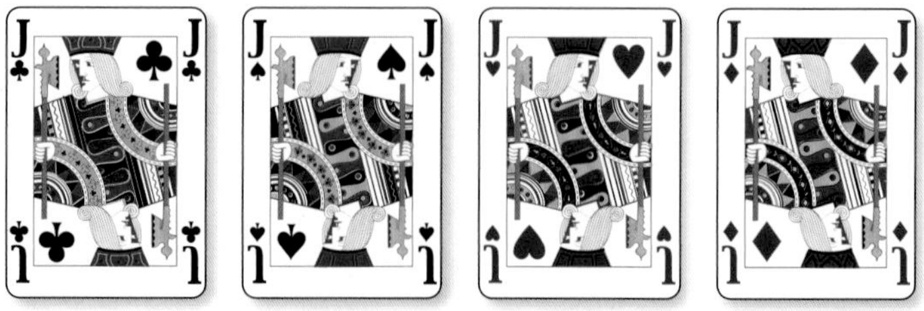

Above: In a Suit game, the four Jacks are the highest trumps, ranking from high to low according to suit ♣, ♠, ♥, ♦. In a Grand game, only the Jacks are trumps, whereas in a Null game there are no trumps at all.

Object

Usually to win at least 61 card points. There are options to take at least 90 points, or to win or lose all 10 tricks.

The Deal

Each player receives 10 cards in packets of three, four and three. The last two cards of the deck, the *Skat*, are placed face down on the table. This takes place after the players receive their first three cards and before the second and third packets of four and three cards are dealt to them.

Types of Game

Which player will be the declarer, playing alone against the other two players in partnership, is determined by an auction. The declarer's aim is usually to win at least 61 card points, although there are the options of aiming to take at least 90, or to win or lose all 10 tricks. It all depends on which type of game the declarer elects to play – Suit, Grand or Null. In a Suit game, the four Jacks are the highest trumps regardless of suit, followed by the remaining seven cards of the chosen suit. In a Grand game, only the Jacks are trumps, while Null is a bid in which there are no trumps, to lose every trick.

The declarer can also elect to play with the *Skat* or without it. No one else may examine the *Skat* until after the last trick has been played, but any card points it may contain count for the declarer.

Game Values

Players bid by announcing the minimum score of the contract they wish to play (and *not* the name of the contract), which they calculate in advance as follows.

In Trump games, what is termed the 'base value' of the suit chosen as trump is multiplied by additional factors known as 'multipliers'. The base values are nine for Diamonds, 10 for Hearts, 11 for Spades and 12 for Clubs. The base value for a Grand – that is, when only the four Jacks are trumps, is 24.

The multipliers are always taken in the following order, all being added together as you go. *Spitze* (Tops) is based on the number of consecutive top trumps (*Matadors*), from the J♣ downwards, held or not held in hand. If a player holds the J♣, he is 'with' as many *Spitze* as there are in hand. The maximum possible holding is 'with 11' in a Suit game and 'with four' at Grand. If the J♣ is not held, that player is playing 'without' as many of the top trumps that rank above the highest trump in hand. If that trump is the J♠, the player concerned is 'without one' and so on up to a possible maximum of 'without 11' in a Suit game or 'without four' at Grand.

A point is then added for game – 'one for game' – by which the player undertakes to win at least 61 card points. Another point can be added if the intention is to reach *Schneider* (90 points or more) and another point for *Schwarz* (winning every trick).

If a player intends to play from hand without taking the *Skat*, he adds another point – 'one for hand'. If this is the case, then he can also increase the game value by adding one or two extra points for declaring he will win *Schneider* or *Schwarz* as well as the points gained for actually winning either. If declaring *Schwarz*, game value can be further increased by a point for playing *Ouvert* – that is, with the hand exposed on the table.

The lowest possible game value is 18, the highest valued Suit game 216 and the highest Grand is 264. Null games, by contrast, have set values, which never vary. These are 23 for Null with *Skat*, 35 for Null hand, 46 for Null *Ouvert* and 59 for Null *Ouvert* from hand.

Bidding

Middlehand starts by bidding against Forehand, by announcing successive game values, starting with 18, to which the response is 'Yes' until either Middlehand decides not to bid higher or Forehand passes. Jump bids are allowed (jumping from 18 straight to 33, say), but it is illegal to announce anything but a specified game value.

With the first stage of the auction concluded, Rearhand takes over the bidding. The last player not to pass becomes the declarer. If using the *Skat*, the declarer picks it up, discards two cards and announces what the game is to be. If playing from hand, the word 'hand' is added, together with any other declaration, *Schneider*, *Shwarz* or *Ouvert*. In the last instance, the declarer lays his hand face up on the table before leading the trick.

Conceding the Game

The declarer has the right to concede the game at any time before he plays to the first trick. There are various reasons for this, the commonest one being that, when playing with *Skat* exchange without two or more *Matadors*, the declarer finds one or more higher *Matadors* in the *Skat*. Suppose, for instance, there is a successful bid of 30, its bidder intending to play in Hearts (Hearts 'without' two, game three, x 10 = 30). If the *Skat* includes the J♣ or J♠, this revalues the bid at 20 ('with' or 'without' one, game two, x 10 = 20).

The declarer now has three choices. He can announce Hearts, as he intended, and attempt to win *Schneider* for the extra multiplier that will increase the game value to 30. He can choose a different game – Spades (22), Null (23), Clubs (24) or Grand (48). If none of these options is playable, then the game is conceded without play.

Play and Scoring

The player to the dealer's left (Forehand) leads and the winner of each trick leads to the next. Suit must be followed if possible, but otherwise any card can be played. The highest card of the suit led or the highest trump, if any are played, takes the trick. All the cards won by the partners should be kept together in a single pile. All 10 tricks have to be played – except if the declarer wins a trick and the contract is Null. Once all the tricks have been completed, the *Skat* is turned face up so the game can be valued correctly.

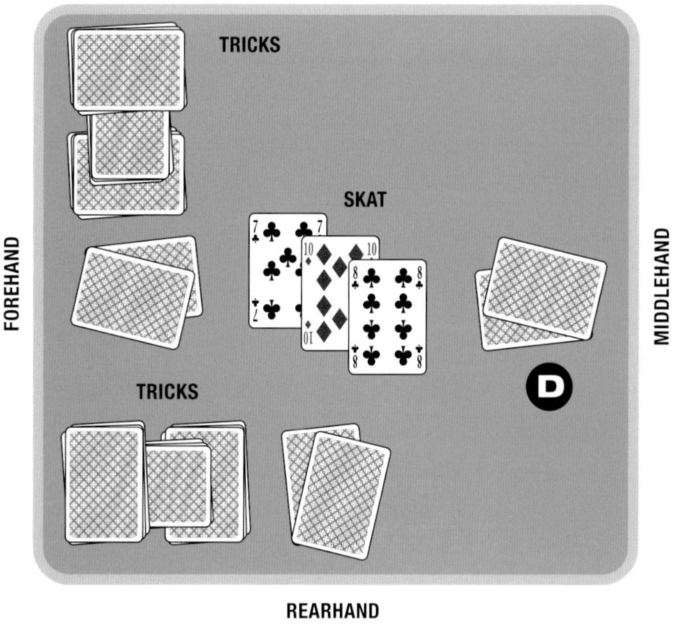

Above: Middlehand here, going for a Null contract, is caught out when the dealer leads the 7♣ and Forehand discards, as he is unable to follow suit. Middlehand's 8♣ wins the trick, meaning that the contract is lost. There is no need to play out the remaining two tricks.

For the declarer to win the game, he must take at least 61 card points – 90 points if the bid was *Schneider*, every trick if the bid was *Schwarz* or no tricks at all if the bid was Null – and the game as revalued after the end of play is worth at least the amount that he bid.

Assuming all these conditions are satisfied, the declarer adds his actual game value to his aggregate score. The *Skat* counts as part of the hand for the purposes of game valuation. This means that it is possible to be 'with' or 'without' 11, even though only 10 cards are actually held in hand.

If the declarer loses a game worth at least the amount bid, its full value is doubled and deducted from his aggregate score. If the value of his game is less than the amount bid, the value to be doubled is defined as the nearest appropriate multiple of the relevant base value that exceeds the bid or equals it, i.e, if his bid was 36, and the game was 30, he loses 40, doubled to 80. If he is *Schneidered*, no extra penalty is applicable.

Conclusion

Play continues until all the tricks have been played.

Doppelkopf

The north German equivalent of Schafkopf, Doppelkopf is played with a double pack and has an unusual system of 26 trumps. There are a number of somewhat arcane variations.

You will need: Two 24-card decks (Eights and below having been removed from two standard packs); scorecards

Card ranking: Trumps: 10♥, 10♥, Queens, Jacks, A♦, A♦, K♦, K♦, 10♦, 10♦, 9♦, 9♦. Clubs and Spades: Ace, Ten, King, Nine. Hearts: Ace, King, Nine

Players: Four, in variable partnerships

Ideal for: 14+

Object

To take at least 121 card points by capturing valuable cards in tricks.

The Deal

Each player is dealt 12 cards each in batches of three. Any player dealt five or more Kings, eight or more Aces and Tens or just one trump, may demand a redeal.

Above: The first hand here has five Kings, while the second has four Tens and four Aces. In each case, the player holding such a hand can demand a redeal.

Bidding

Players announce '*Gesund*' ('healthy'), meaning that they are happy to play a normal game in which players with the Queens of Clubs ('the grannies') partner each other, or '*Vorbehalt*' ('reservation'), meaning that they want to play some other type of game. In *Vorbehalt,* the first two options are *Hochzeit* (Marriage) or *Armut* (poverty), in both of which the player seeks a partner. A player who, despite holding both grannies, is not confident of playing solo, bids *Hochzeit*. The first player other than the bidder to take a trick becomes the bidder's partner. A player holding three or fewer trumps, which must be placed face down on the table, can bid *Armut*. The partner is the player who picks up these discards and exchanges the same number of cards with the bidder.

The third option is to choose one of eight types of solo. In Trump Solo, the bidder names the trump suit, while in Queen and Jack Solo only Queens or Jacks are trumps. Ace Solo is a No Trumps bid. In Hearts, Spades, Clubs and Diamonds Solo, the respective suits are trumps.

Play, Scoring and Conclusion

In a *Gesund* game, the partnership with the Queens of Clubs is dubbed the Re team; in a *Vorbehalt* game, it is the partnership or soloist specifying the game that is Re. The opposing players are know as the *Kontra* team. Announcing '*Re*' or '*Kontra*' doubles the amount of points to be won.

Once a double has been announced, there can be further announcements. 'No 90' is an undertaking to win at least 151 card points, 'No 60' at least 121 and 'No 30' at least 211. *Schwarz* means the players intend to win every trick that is played. If successful, each member of the announcing team wins an extra game point, but if they fail they lose the game. *Re* team players each score a game point for winning at least 121 card points. If the *Kontra* team takes 120 card points, each player wins two game points.

'Catching a fox', won by the team capturing the A♦ (the fox), is worth one game point for each player. *Karlchen Müller* (Charlie Miller),which is winning the last trick with the J♣, scores the same, as does *Doppelkopf*, which is taking a trick where all the cards are Tens and Aces. Note that neither catching a fox or *Karlchen Müller* can be scored in Solo contracts.

Above: Two players holding the Q♣ have the option of partnering with each other, in which case they are dubbed the *Re* team.

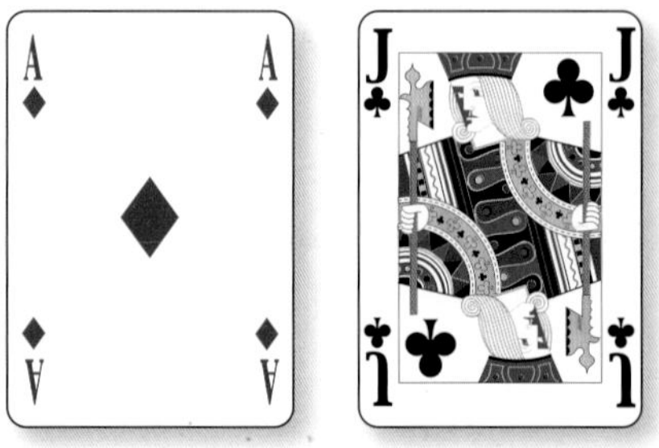

Above: Winning a trick containing the A♦ is termed 'catching a fox', and is worth one game point for each player in a partnership. Winning the last trick with the J♣ is termed *Karlchen Müller* (Charlie Miller) and, again, scores a point for both players.

Avinas

This partnership game hails from Lithuania. It is played in two ways, depending on whether or not Sevens are exposed during the deal.

You will need: 32-card deck, Sixes and below having been removed; scorecard

Card ranking: Q♣ (highest), Sevens, Q♠, Q♥, Q♦, J♣, J♠, J♥, J♦, Aces, Tens, Kings, Nines, Eights

Players: Four, in partnerships of two

Ideal for: 14+

Object

The aim of the declaring side is to take at least 61 of the 120 card points available.

The Deal

Each player is dealt eight cards in batches of four, and the dealer exposes everyone's fourth and eighth cards. If no Seven is turned up, the player to the dealer's left chooses a trump suit and states how many trumps he holds without revealing the name of the suit. The other players either pass or quote a higher number of cards held in a suit of their own choosing. The player stating the greatest number of trumps becomes the declarer and leads to the first trick. This is a No Sevens game.

If one of the exposed cards is a Seven then its suit is trumps; if more than one card is a Seven, then the last one dealt becomes the trump suit for that deal. The player who was dealt the Seven of trumps is declarer and will lead to the first trick. This is a Sevens game.

Play

In a No Sevens game, the declarer must lead a trump to the first trick. If a Queen or Jack is led and it is unclear what the trump suit is, the player at his left must ask and be answered. The first trick's winner must lead a trump to the second if one is held. All other tricks can be led by any card, and players must follow suit if possible. The declarer may stop play when he realizes he has won or lost.

In a Sevens game, the declarer knocks the table if he aims to take all eight tricks, doubling the value of the game. Opposers can knock to redouble. All the tricks are played, but, if the game is doubled, the declarer loses as soon as his opponents take a trick.

The declarer leads to the first trick. Players must follow suit if possible. The highest card of the suit led, or the highest trump, wins the trick. Normally all eight tricks are played. The declarer wins if he scores more than 61 points, and his opponents are penalized. If not, he is penalized.

Right: As no Sevens feature in the dealt cards, the player to dealer's left chooses a trump suit. The other players can pass or announce a trump suit in turn. He who bids the longest suit sets trumps and becomes the declarer.

Scoring and Conclusion

Aces score 11, Tens 10, Kings four, Queens three and Jacks two. Both games are scored negatively, i.e. marking or cancelling penalties against the losers and winners.

A Sevens game is scored by means of circles called *Avinas* (Rams). If the declarers win, their opponents are penalized by as many *Avinas* as there were Sevens in the deal. If the declarers lose, they are doubly penalized. In subsequent hands, *Avinas* are scored by cancelling those of the opposing side.

A No Sevens game is scored in Pips, written down as a running total. Pips cannot be cancelled. If the declarers win, opponents are penalized one Pip if they score between 31 and 59 card points, two Pips if they take 30 or fewer, and three if they score zero. If the declarers score between 32 and 59, they are penalized two Pips; if they score between two and 31, they are penalized four four Pips, and they are penalized six if they score zero.

Play lasts until one side has 12 Pips, while the other has none. If both sides have scored Pips, the game goes to the side with fewer penalty *Avinas*.

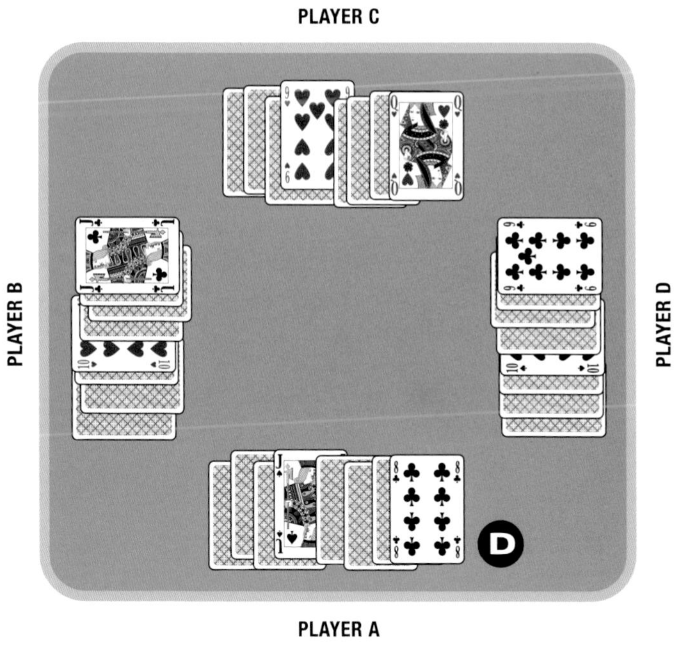

Six-Bid Solo

This is one of three American games – the others are Crazy Solo and Frog – derived from Tappen, which first appeared in southern Germany, western Austria and Switzerland in the early 1800s.

You will need: 36-card deck, Fives and below having been removed; scorecard

Card ranking: Ace (highest) down to Six

Players: Three

Ideal for: 14+

Object

The player who bids the highest value game plays solo against the other two players, competing to win tricks containing valuable point-scoring cards.

Bidding

There are six possible bids, the bidding starting with the two players to the dealer's left. Only after one of them has dropped out is the dealer allowed to participate.

The Deal

Each player is dealt seven cards in packets of four and three, then three are dealt to the table to form a widow, or stock, then each player gets a final four. The widow is left untouched until the end of the game.

Play

Except in Spread *Misère*, when it is the player to the right, the player to the bidder's left always plays the opening lead. Players must follow suit or play a trump card if they can. The highest card of the led suit or highest trump played takes the trick and the winner leads to the next.

Scoring

Aces score 11, Kings four, Queens three, Jacks two and Tens 10. The Eight, Seven and Six are valueless. If the bid is Solo, a successful soloist wins two points from each opponent for every card point taken over 60, but loses two points for every card point taken short of that total if the contract fails. A Heart Solo scores three points, *Misère* 30, Guaranteed Solo 40, Spread *Misère* 60, Call Solo 100 and Call Solo in Hearts 150. Except in *Misère* bids, any card points the widow may contain are added to the soloist's final score.

Conclusion

Play stops once all the tricks have been taken, at which point the player with the highest score wins.

Bidding

The bids, from lowest to highest, are as follows:

- Solo – an undertaking to win at least 60 card points. with any suit other than Hearts as trumps.
- Heart Solo – the same as Solo but with Hearts as trumps.
- Guarantee Solo – an undertaking to win at least 74 points if playing in Hearts, or 80 if in another suit.
- Call Solo – an undertaking to win 120 points, the soloist having the right to name any card, upon which the holder must surrender it in exchange for a card of the soloist's choice.
- *Misère* – an undertaking to lose every trick (there are no trumps).
- Spread *Misère* – the same as *Misère*, but with the soloist's cards exposed.

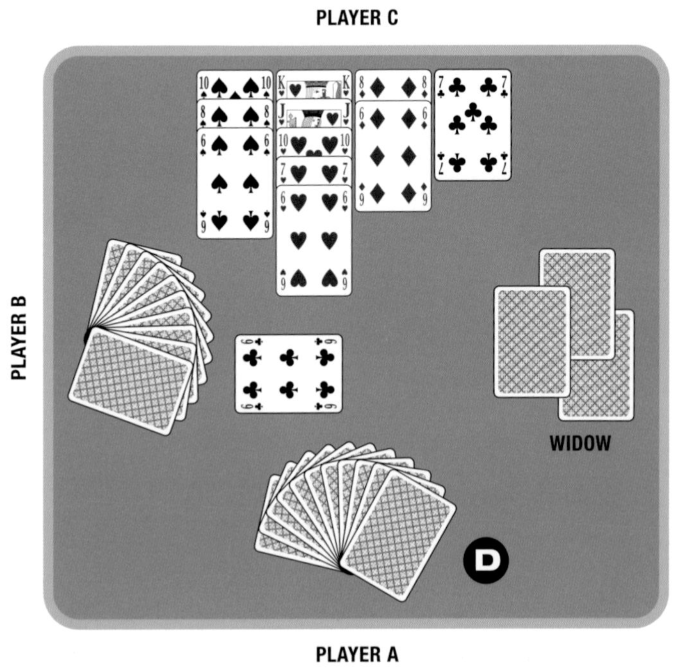

Above: Player C has bid Spread *Misère* (undertaking to lose every trick with his hand exposed). Player B has led the 6♣. Player C will have to play the 7♣ to this, but Player A will have to play higher unless unable to follow suit.

HAFERLTAROCK

This is one of several German games that are obviously derived from Tarock, as Tarot is termed in German-speaking countries, but with the 22 *tarocks* that make up the fifth suit in true Tarot left out. It is definitely not as old as its venerable Italian ancestor, the origins of which date back to the 15th century, but it is a stimulating game to play in its own right.

You will need: 36-card deck (Fives and below having been removed from a standard pack); gambling chips/counters

Card ranking: Ace, Ten, King, Queen, Jack, Nine down to Six

Players: Three

Ideal for: 14+

OBJECT

To win at least 61 of the 120 card points available after naming trumps and playing alone against the other two players.

THE DEAL

Each player gets 11 cards in packets of four, three and four, with three cards being placed face down on the table as a widow (stock) before the final packet is dealt.

BIDDING

As a preliminary, the three players each contribute 100 chips into the pot. Starting with the player to the dealer's left, each player decides whether to pass or say 'Play'.

PLAYER A

PLAYER B

PLAYER C

Above: With poor cards, Player A passes immediately, but Players B and C indulge in a bidding battle. Player B's strong Clubs, however, coupled with support in other suits, provides enough incentive to outbid Player C, who finally passes as well.

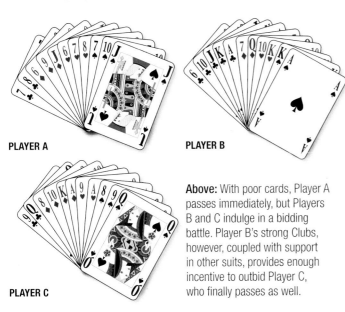

Player A	**Player B**	**Player C**
Pass	Play	Play/Hand
—	And Five	And Ten
—	And Fifteen	And Twenty
—	And Twenty-five	Pass

The latter is a bid to take at least 61 of the 120 card points, playing solo against the other two players and nominating trumps. The next player can take the game off him by bidding 'Hand'. The first bidder can then bid 'Hand' to reassert his bid, or pass. 'And Five', which raises the bid to 66 points, then 'And Ten' and so on, raises the bidding in multiples of five.

This continues until there is a winning bid. The soloist now declares whether the intention is to play a Pick-up or a Hand game. In the former, the soloist picks up the widow and discards three cards before naming trumps. The latter means he will play his dealt hand.

PLAY

The player to the left of the dealer leads to the first trick and play follows convention, with the highest card of the led suit (or the highest trump if any are played) taking the trick. The winner of the trick leads to the next.

SCORING

The scoring cards are Aces, worth 11 points, Tens 10, Kings four, Queens three and Jacks two. The other cards are valueless. Any points in the widow go to the soloist, whether he fulfils his contract or not.

If successful, the soloist wins a basic five chips, plus five chips for every five points in excess of the contract. If the contract fails, the soloist loses five chips for every five points of the shortfall.

If successful in a Pick-up game, the soloist takes the appropriate number of chips from the pot. In a Hand game, the opponents each pay the soloist one chip per point, plus five points for every five points the contract was raised above 61 during the bidding.

CONCLUSION

The game ends when the pot is empty, or by mutual agreement. The winner is the one with the most chips.

EINWERFEN

Einwerfen is a long-established German partnership game and a good one to start with if you are new to Ace-Ten games.

You will need: 32 card-deck (Sixes and below having been removed from a standard pack); scorecard

Card ranking: Ace down to Seven

Players: Four, in partnerships of two

Ideal for: 10+

OBJECT

To win a single game by taking 61+ card points, a double game (90+ points) or a treble for taking every trick.

THE DEAL

Players are dealt eight cards each, the dealer turning up the last one for trumps. The player to the dealer's left leads to the first trick.

SCORING

Aces score 11, Kings four, Queens three, Jacks two, and Tens score 10. The other cards do not score. A partnership scoring 61+ card points wins a single game, a double for 90+, a treble for every trick. If the scores are tied, the value of the next deal is doubled. Any subsequent deal that has the same trumps as the first is doubled in value.

Right: This trick scores four points for the King, 11 for the Ace and three for the Queen, used as a trump: 18 points in all.

Right: This trick scores 10 for the Ten, two for the Jack and 11 for the Ace: 23 points in total.

PLAY AND CONCLUSION

Players must follow suit if they can, play a trump or else play any card. The trick is taken by the highest card of the suit led or the highest trump. The trick's winner leads to the next. Play ends once all tricks have been chased.

YUKON

This Canadian game is a curious blend of elements drawn from Skat and Scotch Whist.

You will need: 52 cards; no Jokers; scorecards

Card ranking: Grand Yukon (J♠), the other Yukons (Jacks), Tens, Aces, Kings, Queens and then Nine to Two

Players: Four, in partnerships of two

Ideal for: 10+

OBJECT

To become the first side to score 250 card points.

THE DEAL

The players receive four cards each. The rest of the pack is placed face down to form the stock, from which players draw the top card after each trick to replenish their hands.

PLAY

The player to the dealer's left leads to the first trick. Players must follow suit if possible or otherwise trump. The Yukons (Jacks) are permanent trumps and they all rank higher than the other cards.

The J♠, the Grand Yukon, takes any trick in which it is played, as does the first played of two or more Yukons (i.e. if two Yukons are played to the same trick, the first one laid wins). Otherwise the highest card of the suit led wins.

SCORING AND CONCLUSION

The highest-scoring card is the J♠, worth 15 points, followed by the other Jacks, which score 10, as do Tens. Aces score five, Kings three and Queens two.

The game ends when a partnership scores 250 points. If the stock is used up, play continues until players run out of cards, when the side with the most points wins.

Scotch Whist

In this straightforward partnership point-trick game, players cut the deck to determine partners – the two high cuts play the two low cuts.

You will need: 36-card deck, Fives and below having been removed; no Jokers; scorecard

Card ranking: Standard, Aces high

Players: Four

Ideal for: 10+

Object

To score points by winning tricks, especially those including the top five trumps.

The Deal

The person with the lowest cut deals a hand of nine cards to each player. The last card is turned up and its suit is trumps. It belongs to the dealer, but it stays face-up on the table until the dealer plays to the first trick.

Play

The player to the dealer's left leads the first trick. Players must follow suit if they can, or trump or discard. The highest card of the suit led wins the trick. If a trump is played, the highest trump wins. The winner of the trick sets it aside and leads the next trick. Each trick taken after a team 'makes book' (wins six tricks) counts for one point.

Scoring and Conclusion

The Jack of trumps scores 11 card points, followed by the Ace, worth four, King three, Queen two and Ten scores 10. No other cards count. Players score the point value of any top trumps that they may take in tricks, plus an extra point per card for each card they end up with in excess of the number they were dealt. The first partnership to score 41 points wins the game.

Left: Also known as Catch-the-Ten, this interesting game has a venerable history. In his biography of Samuel Johnson, author James Boswell (pictured) referred to Scotch Whist as Catch-Honours.

Reunion

This 18th-century game from the Rhineland consists of three deals – one by each player.

You will need: 32 cards, Sixes and below having been removed; gambling chips; scorecard

Card ranking: Jack of trumps (Right Bower), the other Jack of the same colour (Left Bower), Aces, Tens, Kings, Queens, non-trump Jacks, Nines, Eights and Sevens

Players: Three

Ideal for: 10+

Object

To win the most card points and to avoid ending up with a score of less than 100, as this carries penalties.

The Deal

The player who cuts the lowest deals 10 cards in packets of three, four and three, turning up the second of the final two cards for trumps. The dealer discards two cards – not a Bower or an Ace – face down. Any card points they may be worth go to the dealer at the end of the game.

Play

The turn-up is left in place until the second trick has been played. The player to the dealer's left leads. Players must follow suit, if possible, or otherwise trump if possible.

Scoring and Conclusion

Each Bower scores 12 card points, Aces 11, Tens 10, Kings four, Queens three and the other Jacks two. The last trick is worth an extra 10 points. If both Bowers are taken in the same trick, the Left Bower's holder immediately pays a chip to the Right Bower's player.

Play continues until the third deal has been completed. Any player with a score of between 100 and 150 pays the winner a chip. If the score is under 100, the penalty is two chips and, if under 50, three.

Madrasso

A cross between Tressette and Briscola, Madrasso is the most popular card game in Venice and its environs. It is usually played with the Venetian patterned 40-card Italian pack, with suits of Swords, Batons, Cups and Coins, equivalent to ♠, ♣, ♥, ♦.

You will need: 40 cards, Tens to Eights having been removed; scorecard

Card ranking: Ace, Three, King, Queen, Jack and Seven to Two

Players: Four, in fixed partnerships

Ideal for: 14+

Object

A game consists of at least 10 *Battutes* (deals) and the winning partnership is the first to reach the target score of at least 777 points.

The Deal

For the first hand, the dealer is chosen at random; in subsequent hands, the deal passes to the right. Each player is dealt 10 cards, starting with packets of three and two. The next card is turned face up on the table to establish trumps. Three cards each are then dealt to the players, the dealer taking only two, followed by a packet of two cards.

The dealer's face-up card stays on the table until it is played to a trick. However, a player holding the Seven of trumps has the option of exchanging it for the turn-up before playing a card to the first trick.

Scoring

At the end of each deal, each side calculates its score, totalling the point value of the cards it has taken in tricks. The scoring cards are Aces, which are worth 11 points, Threes 10, Kings four, Queens three and Jacks two. In the event of a revoke (that is, if a player fails to follow suit when holding a card of that suit), play stops and the revoking partnership is penalized 130 points. The winners of the last trick receive a 10-point bonus.

Play and Conclusion

The player to the dealer's right leads the first trick. Players must follow suit if possible, otherwise any card can be played. Each trick is won by the highest trump in it, or, if no trumps are played, by the highest card of the suit led. The winner of each trick leads to the next. Each hand is played until all 10 tricks have been won.

After 10 hands have been played, any player can make a declaration claiming to have reached the 777-point target immediately after taking a trick. Play stops immediately, the claim is checked, the score of the non-scoring partnership being calculated by subtracting the scoring side's total from 1,300. If the claim is upheld, the declaring partnership wins. If it is not upheld, it loses. If neither has reached that total, the game resumes until one does, or one partnership declares that it is out.

Another way of winning is termed *Cappotto*, which means taking all of the 10 tricks in a hand. This is why declarations are not allowed until 10 hands have been played. Even if one partnership has scored 777 points by the eighth or ninth hands, the other could still make *Cappotto* and so steal the game.

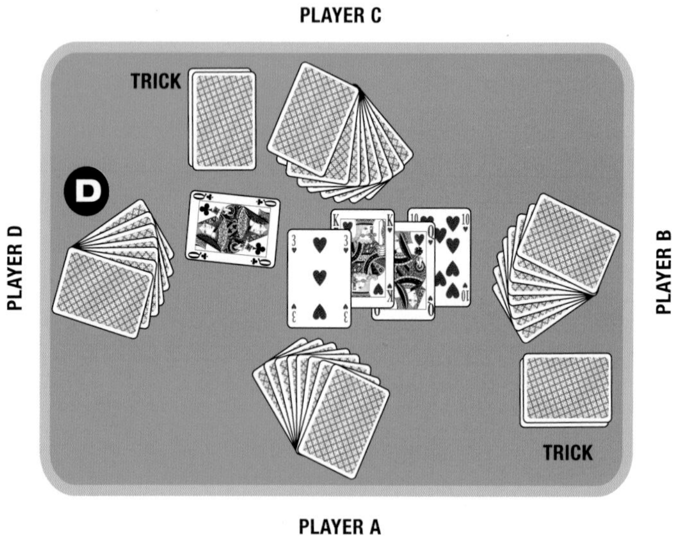

Above: Players B and C here have both won a trick. The dealer's turn-up card (used to determine trumps), the Q♣, is still exposed on the table. Player B lays the 10♥, which is topped by the Queen, King and Three in succession. Player A wins the trick, as Three is highest.

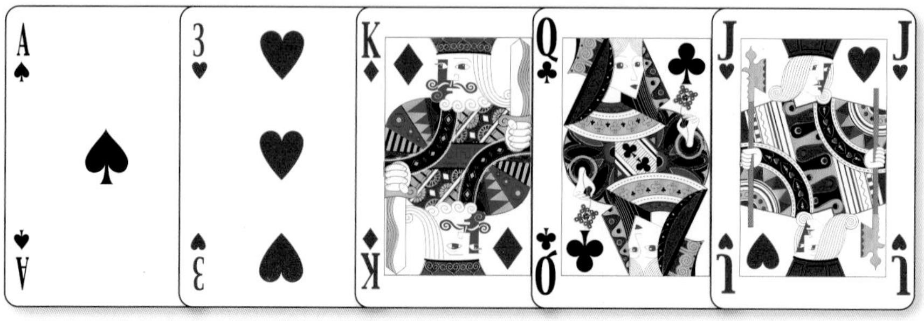

Right: The scoring cards in Madrasso are Aces (worth 11 points), Threes (10), Kings (four), Queens (three) and Jacks (two).

Briscola

One of Italy's most popular card games, Briscola is most notable for the various facial expressions that are allowed as a way of signalling between partners.

You will need: 40 cards, Tens to Eights having been removed; 39 cards, with a Two also removed if three are playing; scorecard

Card ranking: Ace highest, then Threes, Kings, Queens, Jacks and Sevens to Twos

Players: Two to three playing solo, or four in partnerships

Ideal for: 10+

Object

To be the first player or partnership to score a game (at least 61 cards points) or a rubber (three games).

The Deal

The player cutting the lowest card is the first to deal – the deal subsequently passes to the right. Each player is dealt three cards face down, the next card being turned face up to set trumps. The remaining cards are placed face down on the table to form the stock.

Play

The player to the dealer's right leads to the first trick. Unlike other card games, there is no obligation to follow suit for as long as any cards remain in the stock. The winner of each trick takes the top card from the stock to replenish his or her hand, followed by the other players.

When the stock is exhausted, the next to play draws the turn-up and the game continues until all the cards have been played.

Above: A group of men playing cards in Palermo, Sicily, 2004. Briscola remains one of Italy's most popular card games.

Scoring and Conclusion

Aces score 11 points, Threes score 10 points, Kings four points, Queens three points and Jacks score two. The remaining cards are valueless. A two-way or three-way split of card points at the end of a game is a draw. A rubber is the best of five games, a game equating to at least 61 points.

Play continues in each hand until all the tricks have been won. The player or partnership taking the majority of the 120 card points available wins a game.

Signals

When four people play, certain signals are allowed in Briscola so that partnerships can signal certain trump holdings to each other, when neither opponent is looking. These conventional signs are codified as follows:

- Ace – go tight lipped.
- Three – twist the mouth sideways.
- King – raise eyes upwards.
- Queen – show the tip of the tongue.
- Jack – shrug shoulders.

Variant

A chief five-player variant of Briscola is Briscola Bastarda. The chief differences are the introduction of a round of bidding and a secret partnership between the winning bidder and another player.

In the bidding, players estimate the number of points they will take in the game. The highest bidder names a specific card to establish the trump suit and who his partner will be. This is the holder of the specified card. The scores of the caller and holder count together. If the total equals or exceeds the bid, the caller wins two points, the holder a point and each opponent is penalized a point. If the bid is lost, each opponent wins a point, the holder is penalized a point and the caller two.

17 | King-Queen Games

As the saying goes, marriages are made in heaven. In King-Queen games any player declaring the 'Marriage' of the King and Queen of the same suit in the same hand wins bonuses. Typically, a non-trump Marriage scores 20 points, while a trump (Royal) one scores 40. Such games are exceptionally fascinating because, as every experienced card player knows, their outcome is so unpredictable.

There are several games that share the same basic system of trick-taking and card values, although some introduce an extra element of bidding. Of these intriguing games, the German game Sechsundsechzig (Sixty-Six) – and its Austrian equivalent Schnapsen – is probably one of the best known. It is an exciting game because nearly every card in the deck counts. This means that a player who looks sure to lose can suddenly turn a game on its head and emerge as its winner.

The basic aim is to win points by capturing the most valuable cards and to score bonuses by melding Marriages (matching Kings and Queens). However, there are specific features that make play even more challenging and stimulating. For instance, in many games, players are not allowed to keep scorecards, so they need really clear heads in order to keep track of what is going on as well as good card sense to make the most of the cards.

In Spain and some Latin American countries, Tute is a popular card game. In it, declaring a Marriage is referred to as 'singing' it. A player is only allowed to 'sing' immediately after he has taken a trick. Mariás is the most popular card game in the Czech Republic and Slovakia. Tysiacha, an Eastern European game, is less well known than it should be. Its peculiarity is that bidding must start at 100 points, which means that higher bids can only be fulfilled by declaring King-Queen marriages.

Above: Melding Marriages of the King and Queen of the same suit gains a player bonuses in this group of games.

Sechsundsechzig (Sixty-Six)

This is one of the best card games for two players. Although there is some doubt as to when and where it was invented, Sixty-Six has probably been played at least since the 17th century.

You will need: 24 cards, Eights and below having been removed
Card ranking: Ace (highest), Ten, King, Queen, Jack and Nine
Players: Two
Ideal for: 14+

Object

To make Marriages of King and Queens in the same suit or score tricks containing certain cards, and thus to be the first player in each deal to take 66 points.

The Deal

Each player gets six cards, dealt in two packets of three. The next card is turned up to establish trumps and half covered with the rest of the cards (the stock) face down.

Play

Initially, suit need not be followed, the winner of each trick being the higher card of the suit led or the higher trump. Once a trick has been played, both players (starting with whoever won the trick) replenish their hands with a card from the stock.

After the stock has run out, suit must be followed and no more Marriages may be melded. The stock is often closed before this by a player who thinks 66 points can be won with the cards as they stand. Either player may close when it is their turn to lead by flipping over the turn-up and placing it face down on top of the stock.

Trumps and Marriages

A player with the Nine of trumps can exchange it for the turn-up, provided it is still covered by at least two cards and he has taken a trick. If a player is dealt a Marriage or melds one with a card from the stock, he can claim 20 points for a non-trump Marriage and 40 for a trump one, provided that he has taken a trick, is about to lead to a trick, and at least two cards remain in the stock. The declaring player must lead one of the Marriage cards to the trick. If a player declares a Marriage but fails to take any subsequent tricks, its score is cancelled.

Scoring and Conclusion

Players must keep a mental note of their running score. The Ace, Ten, King, Queen, Jack and Nine count for 11, 10, four, three, two and zero points, respectively. After the last trick, or earlier if either player claims to have reached 66 points, the hand is scored. In the first case, the player with the most points wins. In the second, if 66 points have been scored , the declarer scores a game point if the opposing score is 33 points or more, two if under 33, and three if zero. If the claim is incorrect, the other player scores two game points, or three if he has not taken a trick. If a player closes and subsequently fails to score 66 points, the penalties are the same. The first player to take seven game points wins the game.

Play in each hand continues until all tricks have been played or until a player claims to have scored 66 points.

Above: The scoring cards are Aces (worth 11 points), Tens (worth 10), Kings (worth four), Queens (worth three) and Jacks (worth two).

PLAYER B

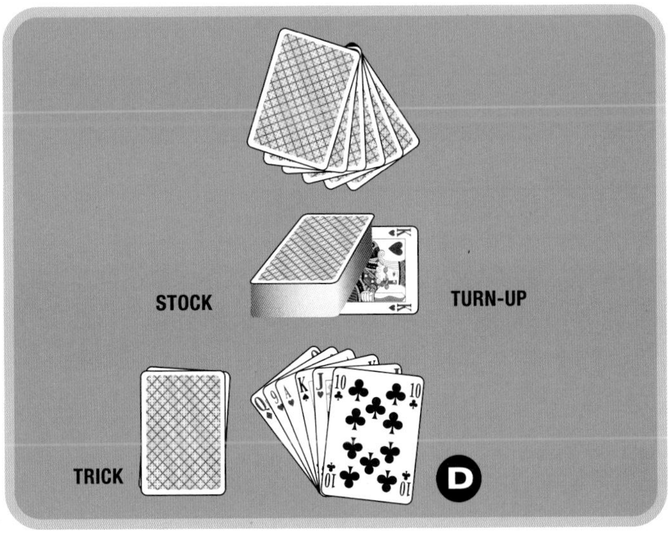

PLAYER A

Above: A player who is holding the Nine of trumps (the 9♥) can exchange it for the turned-up card, provided he has already taken a trick and that the stock contains at least three cards.

Bondtolva

This is a traditional Swedish favourite, the name of which translates as 'farmer's dozen'. Roughly speaking, it is the Swedish equivalent of Sixty-Six, but with a few quirks of its own. The simplest version is for two players.

You will need: 24 cards, Eights and below having been removed
Card ranking: Ace, Ten, King, Queen, Jack and Nine
Players: Two
Ideal for: 14+

Object

To be the first to get to 12 points by melding Marriages (King and Queen of same suit), winning *Matadors* (Aces and Tens) and taking the last trick.

The Deal

The two players are dealt six cards each, three at a time, the other cards being stacked face down to form the stock.

Play

The first player to declare a Marriage establishes which suit is trumps. The non-dealer leads. Each trick is taken by the higher card of the suit led, or by the higher trump once trumps have been fixed, but players do not have to follow suit or trump. The winner of each trick draws the top card of the stock, followed by the other player, and leads to the next trick. Once the stock is exhausted no Marriages are allowed; the second to play must follow suit, playing a higher card if possible, or play a trump.

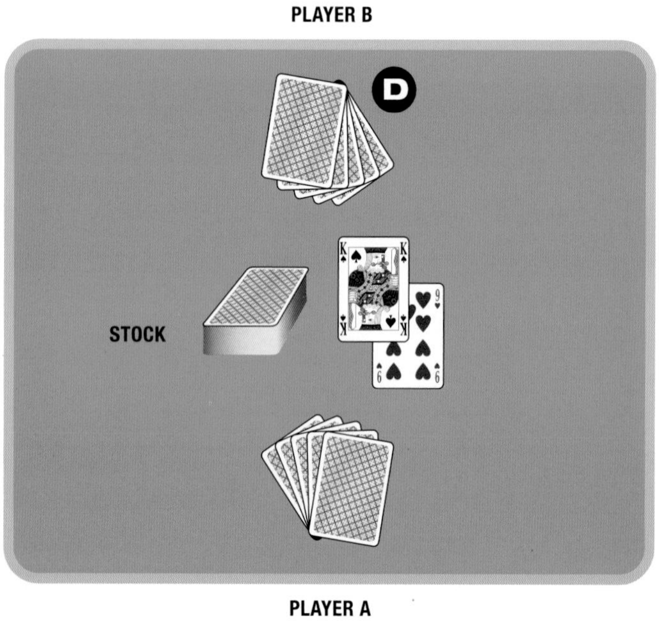

Above: Player A has led the 9♥ to the first trick. Since no Marriages have been melded yet, there are no trumps, so Player B, unable to follow suit, discards the K♠. Player A therefore wins the trick and picks up a card from the stock, followed by Player B.

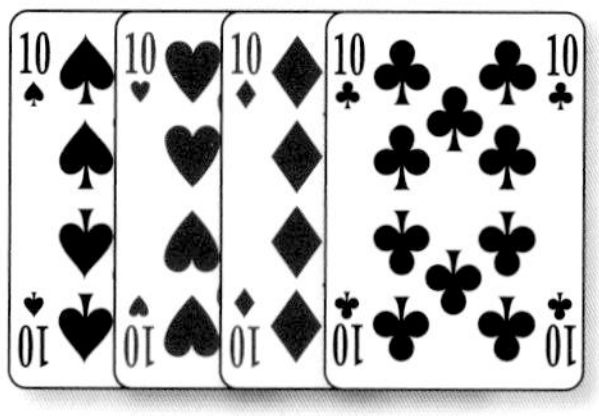

Above: In Bondtolva, Aces and Tens, the top- and second top-ranking trumps, are known as *Matadors*.

Scoring

Aces score four points, Kings three, Queens two and Jacks one. The Nine is valueless. The first Marriage to be declared scores two points; subsequent Marriages score a point. The bonus for winning the last trick is a point, as is the bonus for taking the majority of Aces and Tens. If the scores are equal, the point for the latter goes to the player with the most card points. If the scores are still equal, neither player scores the bonus point. To win the game, a player needs to score exactly 12 points.

Conclusion

Play in each hand continues until all tricks have been played or until a player scores 12 points. A player scoring over 12 must deduct the excess from his previous total.

Variants

There are three- and four-player versions of the game, which are played in much the same way with a few minor differences. The four-player version is played in partnerships. Before trumps are established, the player leading the trick can ask if his partner holds a Marriage, or, if holding one card of a Marriage, if the partner can pair it. The next trick must then be started, if possible, from the declared Marriage. Once trumps are fixed, a player can ask the first question again, in which case that suit must be led to win the point, or lead a King or a Queen and ask the partner to wed it.

Tute

One of the most popular card games in Spain and in Spanish-speaking Latin America, Tute exists in many forms. The two-player version called Tute Corriento is the oldest form of the game and is the one described here.

You will need: 40 cards, Tens to Eights having been removed
Card ranking: Ace, Three, King, Queen, Jack and then Seven to Two
Players: Two
Ideal for: 14+

Object

To be the first to score 101 points by winning tricks, declaring Marriages and taking the last trick.

The Deal

The two players deal in turn, six cards to each player. The next card is placed face up on the table to determine the trump suit. The remaining cards are placed face down across it to form the stock.

Play

The non-dealer leads to the first trick. Until the stock is exhausted, there is no need to follow suit or trump. The winner of a trick draws the top card of the stock and the loser draws the next. The face-up trump forms the last card of the stock. When the stock runs out, the second to play must follow suit, playing a higher card if he can, or, if possible, trumping.

Exchanging and Singing

A turned-up Ace, Three or court card (a King, Queen or Jack) can be exchanged for the Seven of trumps. If a Four, Five, Six or Seven, it can be exchanged for the Two of trumps. To signal an exchange, a player places the appropriate card under the turned-up one, and the exchange occurs when that player takes a trick. If the stock runs out before then, the original card is reclaimed.

A player who holds the King and Queen of the same suit can score extra points by declaring ('singing') them, and showing the two cards. This can only be done immediately after winning a trick and before leading to the next. A player having more than one such combination must win another trick before being allowed to declare it. However, if a player holds four Kings or Queens (a *tute*), he can sing them after winning a trick and immediately wins the game. If a player has a Marriage in a trump and a non-trump suit, the trump suit must be declared first. When declaring a Marriage in a non-trump suit, the suit should be named.

Scoring

Aces score 11 points, Threes 10, Kings four, Queens three and Jacks two. Ten points are awarded to the player taking the last trick. A non-trump Marriage (King and Queen of same suit) scores 20 points and a trump Marriage (King and Queen of trump suit) scores 40.

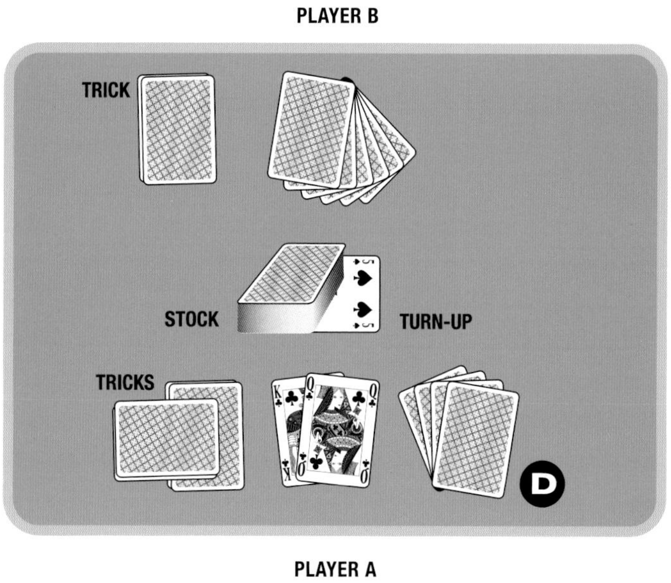

Above: Player A here, having just won a second trick to Player B's one, sings a Marriage by showing a King and Queen of the same suit. Trumps being Spades, this is a non-trump Marriage, which scores 20 points.

Conclusion

Declaring a *tute* wins the game outright. Otherwise, after the last trick, both players count the points they have won for cards in tricks, singing Marriage and for taking the last trick. If neither has scored 101 points, there is a second deal, the points won in that being added to those taken in the first. If either player thinks that he has scored 101 points, this can be declared and play stops. Such a declaration must be made immediately before leading a trick. If the claim is correct, the declaring player wins; if not, he loses.

Tysiacha

In Russian-speaking countries, this three-player game is known by the above name. In Poland, it is called Tysiac. Both words mean '1,001' – the target score needed to win the game, and are basically the same game, but with slight variations.

You will need: 24 cards, Eights and below having been removed; scorecard

Card ranking: Ace, Ten, King, Queen, Jack and Nine

Players: Three (or four with dealer seating out the hand)

Ideal for: 14+

Left: If a player holding this hand is passed a fourth Nine by the soloist, he can call for a new deal.

Object

To be the first to score 1,001 points or more.

The Deal

Seven cards are dealt singly to each player. Three cards, termed the *prikup*, are then dealt face down on the table.

Bidding

Following the deal, players bid to determine who will be the soloist against the other two players. The first bid must be at least 100 points, following which bids go up in fives. Bids over 120 are not allowed unless the player making the bid has a Marriage in hand.

The soloist takes the *Prikup*. He can increase the bid, or, if he decides there is little likelihood of honouring it, he can declare *Rospisat* (that he concedes). In this case, each opposing player scores 60 points. A player declaring *Rospisat* is not penalized on the first two occasions, but on the third, and every third time thereafter, 120 points are deducted from his score.

The soloist passes a card face down to each opponent, so that all three players have eight cards in hand. Any player holding the four Nines can now opt to show them and ask for a new deal.

Play

Trumps are established when the first Marriage is declared, although they can be changed by the declaration of a subsequent Marriage. Declaring a Marriage involves showing both cards, announcing their suit and leading either of them to the next trick.

Scoring and Conclusion

An Ace scores 11, Ten 10, King four, Queen three, Jack two and Nine zero card points. A Marriage (King and Queen of same suit) scores 100 points in Hearts, 80 in Diamonds, 60 in Clubs and 40 in Spades. If the soloist scores at least the value of the bid, this is added to his score. If not, the value is subtracted from it. The other players score the full value of card points taken in tricks, rounding them up or down to the nearest five, plus the value of any Marriages they may have made.

Scoring between 880 and 1,000 is against the rules. If this happens, the player is said to be 'on the barrel', a fact indicated by drawing a box on his scorecard. The score is pegged at 880 and the player is given three chances to score 120 points and win the game. In the event of failure, the player 'falls off the barrel' and is penalized 120 points. If either opposing player fails to take any points in tricks three times, he is penalized 120 points on the third occasion. From that point onward, he loses 120 points every third time this occurs. Play continues until all the tricks have been played.

Right: In Tysiacha, a Marriage of the King and Queen of Spades scores 40 points, in Hearts 100 points, in Diamonds 80 points and in Clubs 60 points.

Gaigel

This game has spread from southern Germany and Switzerland to the USA, where it has been adapted for two players. It is a three- or four-player game, the latter played in partnerships. There is no universally accepted set of rules, and the game is played differently from place to place. The partnership version is described here.

You will need: Two 52-card decks, each with Nines, Eights and cards below Seven removed; counters

Card ranking: Ace (highest), Ten, King, Queen, Jack, Seven

Players: Three, or four playing in partnerships. The partnership version is explained here

Ideal for: 14+

Object

To be the first side to win or exceed 101 points in counters and Marriages, or to detect that the opposing side has done so and failed to claim their win before leading to the next trick.

The Deal and Play

After shuffling the two 24-card packs together, each player is dealt five cards, and the next card is turned up to establish trumps. The cards left over form the stock. As long as there are cards left in the stock, there is no necessity to follow suit, but when it is exhausted, players must do so, head the trick if possible (play a higher card than any so far played to the trick), or otherwise trump and overtrump. A trick's winner draws the top card of the stock, the other players then drawing in turn.

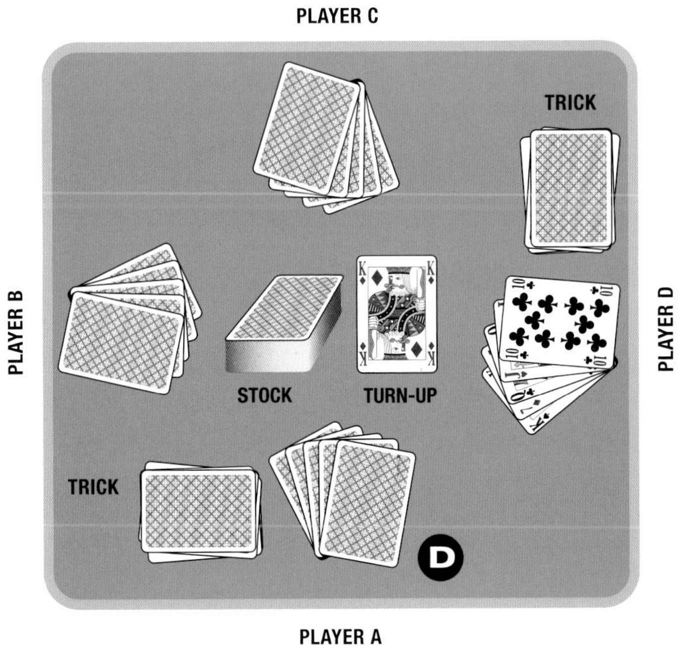

Above: Holding the Seven of trumps (known as the *Dix*), Player D can exchange it for the turn-up at any time, provided the partnership has taken at least one trick and the stock contains at least three cards.

When players play to a trick, they are allowed to declare a Marriage (King and Queen of same suit) if they hold one, but no more than one Marriage in the same deal. Such a declaration can be made only if the declaring partnership has already taken a trick, or if the card to be played takes the trick for them. The declaring player shows both cards and then plays one of them. A non-trump Marriage scores 20 points, a trump one 40.

Taking the Turn-up

A player with the Seven of trumps, the *Dix*, can exchange it for the turn-up at any time, provided that the partnership has taken at least one trick and at least three cards remain in the stock.

Alternatively, the player can place the Seven under the turn-up for his partner to pick up if he holds the other Seven. His partner may decide to take the turn-up and pass across the other Seven. If he is not holding the other Seven and one of the opposing partners then plays it, the first player can pick up the turn-up immediately.

Scoring

Aces score 11 points, Tens 10 and the court cards – Kings, Queens and Jacks – score four, three and two points respectively. Sevens are worthless and count for nothing.

Conclusion

Play stops when either side claims to have taken 101 or more points, or when the opposing partnership has done so but neglected to declare it before leading to the next trick. If correct, the claiming partnership wins a single game. If its opponents have not taken a trick, they win a double game or *Gaigel*. If the claim is wrong, the other side wins a *Gaigel*. Claiming a win incorrectly is known as 'overgaigling' and failing to claim a win is 'undergaigling'.

Mariás

Closely related to the Hungarian game Ulti, the most popular version of Mariás is for three players, although four can play it. In the three-player game, one player becomes the soloist, playing against the other two in partnership. In its Czech homeland, Mariás is customarily played with a 32-card German-suited pack, but here a reduced standard pack has been substituted.

You will need: 32 cards, Sixes and below having been removed

Card ranking: Aces, Tens, Kings, Queens, Jacks, Nines, Eights and Sevens

Players: Three, or four with the dealer sitting out the hand

Ideal for: 14+

Object

To win a clear majority of the points available. This is at least 90, but can rise as high as 190 when Marriage declarations are taken into account.

The Deal

The first dealer is chosen at random, after which the deal passes to the left for each subsequent hand. Before the deal, the player to the dealer's right must cut the cards. The dealer then gives a packet of seven cards face-down to Forehand (the player to the dealer's left) and continues dealing clockwise in packets of five, so that after two rounds of dealing, Forehand has 12 cards and the other two players each have 10. At this stage, Forehand is only allowed to pick up and look at the first seven cards dealt; Forehand's other five cards are left face down on the table until trumps have been chosen. The other players may look at all 10 of their cards.

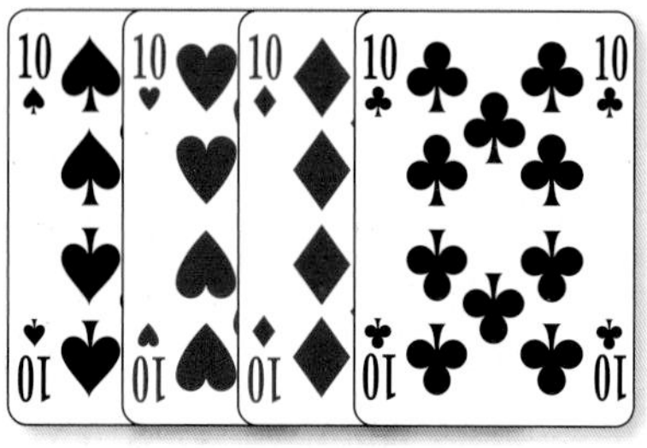

Right: In Mariás, Aces and Tens are the only scoring cards. Known as 'sharp cards', they are worth 10 points each. Points are also scored for melds and winning the last trick.

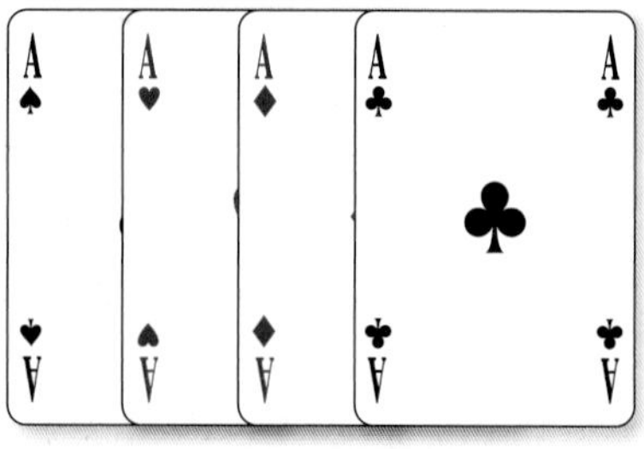

Below: After the deal, Forehand can only look at the first seven cards he has been dealt and choose a trump suit from them should he wish. The strong Diamond suit looks a good bet.

Choosing Trumps

Forehand proposes a trump suit, bids first and leads to the first trick, the next being Middlehand and the third Rearhand. To choose trumps, Forehand examines the first seven cards in his hand. If he elects to choose the trump suit from them, he turns up the appropriate card. If not, he can 'choose from the people' – that is, by selecting any card from the five remaining ones sight unseen, turning it up as before. He then takes all the cards except for the turn-up and discards two, face down. An Ace or Ten cannot be discarded and if the discards include a trump, Forehand must say so.

Choosing the Contract

Forehand starts by bidding Suit, a game with trumps, that only he can play as soloist. Either opponent can veto this by bidding *Betl* or *Durch*. Both are no-trump bids. In *Betl*, the opposing players win if they can force the soloist into taking a trick. In *Durch*, the soloist loses if his opponents win a trick. There are open options for each bid in which players' cards are placed face up on the table after the first trick has been played. Such bids double the score. In Suit, the soloist has to win more points than the combined scores of the opposing players.

Various bonuses augment scores. For the soloist, Seven is an undertaking to win the last trick with the Seven of trumps; Hundred is one to win 100 points or more without melding more than one Marriage.

Both bids can be combined. A Double Seven is an undertaking to win the last trick with a Seven and the trick before that with another one. The opposing players can make identical announcements by adding 'Against' to the bids.

Doubling and Redoubling

To double, either of the opposing players can call '*Flek*', the soloist having the option of redoubling by calling '*Re*'. The opponents can then double again by saying '*Tutti*', which the soloist can redouble by announcing '*Retutti*'. How this is done depends on the type of contract.

If *Betl* or *Durch* is to be played, the option to double goes hand in hand with the final determination of the contract. There are three possible responses to its announcement: 'Good', which means that it is accepted as it stands; 'Bad', which means that the player making the call is prepared to play higher; and '*Flek*', which doubles the contract's value as explained above. In a Suit contract, the opponents simply answer 'Good' or 'Bad'. As well as starting the doubling processes, players can now announce for which bonuses they intend to play.

Play

In Suit contracts, following suit, playing a higher card of the same suit to lead to the trick or playing a trump is obligatory, if possible. In non-trump contracts, the first two conditions apply. In a Suit contract, any player announcing a Marriage (King and Queen of same suit) must play the Queen and announce the appropriate score before playing the King. The cards of a Marriage are kept separate from the trick and left face up in front of the player scoring them, so that they can be checked afterwards when scores are totalled.

Above: An example of 18th-century German playing cards showing the four suits of Acorns, Leaves, Hearts and Bells. In its Czech homeland, Mariás is traditionally played with a 32-card German-suited pack.

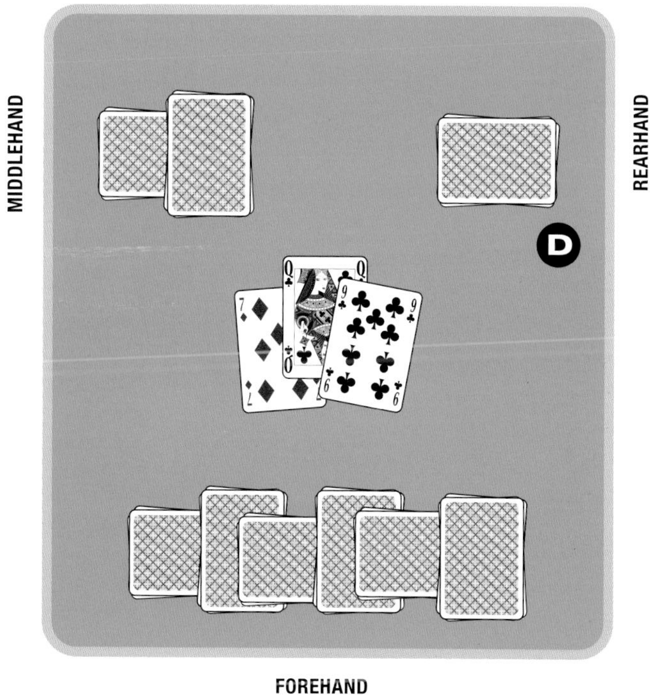

Above: Forehand not only takes the final trick (winning seven to his opponents' combined total of three) but does so with the Seven of trumps (in this case, Diamonds). If he had announced during the bidding the intention of winning the last trick with the Seven of trumps, he would have scored two bonus points. Unannounced, he scores a single extra point.

Scoring and Conclusion

Play continues until all tricks have been played. Aces and Tens, known as the 'sharp cards', are the only cards to score and are worth 10 points each. Melding a non-trump Marriage scores 20 points, and melding a trump Marriage scores 40. A further 10 points are awarded for taking the last trick. A successful Suit contract scores a point for game, while *Betl* scores five points and *Durch* scores 10 points.

Unannounced bonuses are worth a point for Quiet Seven and Killed Quiet Seven – that is, when the Seven of trumps is beaten on the last trick – and two for Quiet Hundred. In this, every extra 10 scored over 100 is worth another two points. Announced bonuses – Seven, Seven Against, Killed Seven, Hundred and Hundred Against – score double. All bonus scores are also doubled if the trump suit was Hearts. Revoking costs the offender 20 points – 10 to each of the other players – or the value of the contract plus bonuses, whichever is more. If Forehand bids the basic game and no extras are added or doubles made, it is taken that the opposing players have conceded, and Forehand scores accordingly.

18 | Queen-Jack Games

Games such as Bezique and Pinochle stand the concept of Marriage on its head by allowing melds (sets of matching cards) between the Q♠ and the J♦. These are known as beziques and can be either single or double. There are also scores for holding Four of a Kind, or same-suit sequences. In Bezique, even if a player starts with poor cards, skilful building of melds means that he may well end up a winner.

Although originally conceived for only two players, other versions of Bezique for more players developed, while the size of the deck, originally 32 cards, also increased to make games last longer. Two-pack Bezique was all the rage in Paris in the 1840s, while Rubicon Bezique, which is played with four decks totalling 128 cards, originated in London slightly later. Chinese Bezique, which was Sir Winston Churchill's favourite card game, is played with six packs.

Pinochle, the American counterpart of Bezique, remains one of the country's most popular card games. Its basic form is Two-handed Pinochle, although Partnership Pinochle, Partnership Auction Pinochle and Double-Pack Pinochle are all games for four players, two against two as partners. Auction Pinochle is the most popular form of the game for three. In general terms, players score for melds and tricks that contain specified scoring cards. The game can seem over-complex, particularly in the second stage of the game, when players have to take back the cards in the melds they have previously declared, but it more than repays the effort of learning it.

Marjolet is an elegant game for two players that is popular in southwest France. As in other games of this genre, part of the excitement comes from the balancing of the cards that are played to tricks against those that are kept in hand in the hopes of making melds. To heighten the tension, some players allow the scoring of only one meld after winning a trick.

Above: Original boxed set of the Royal game of Bezique, which was manufactured by Godall & Son, London (1910).

Bezique

A game called Hoc, played at Louis XIV's court at Versailles, may be the origin of Bezique. The improved two-pack version then became the height of fashion in Paris in the 1840s.

You will need: 64 cards, two packs with all cards below Seven having been removed

Card ranking: Ace, Ten, King, Queen, Jack, Nine, Eight and Seven

Players: Two

Ideal for: 14+

Object

To be the first to reach 1,000 points over as many deals as necessary, dealing alternately.

The Deal

Eight cards are dealt to each player in packets of three, two and three. The next card is turned up to establish trumps and the remaining cards are placed face down to form the stock. If the turn-up is a Seven, the dealer scores 10.

Play

The non-dealer leads. The trick is taken by the higher-ranking card of the suit led, or by a trump. At this stage, there is no need to follow suit. If both players play the same card, the leading card takes the trick. The winner of the trick can declare a scoring combination, laying the cards face up. These can still be used to take future tricks and to help to form new combinations, although they cannot be used twice in the same combination. The declaring player draws the top card of the stock followed by the opposing player, and leads to the next trick.

A player with the Seven of trumps may exchange it for the trump turn-up after taking a trick as an alternative to declaring a combination.

Above: Scoring combinations in Bezique, assuming Hearts as trumps.

Scoring

Brisques (Aces and Tens) taken in tricks score 10 points. Scoring combinations, from highest to lowest, are:

- Double Bezique (two Q♠ and two J♦): 500 points.
- Same-suit sequence of Ace, Ten, King, Queen and Jack of trumps: 250 points.
- Any four Aces: 100 points.
- Any four Kings: 80 points.
- Any four Queens: 60 points.
- Any four Jacks: 40 points.
- Single Bezique (between Q♠ and J♦): 40 points.
- Royal Marriage (between the King and Queen of trumps): 40 points.
- Common Marriage of a non-trump King and Queen: 20 points.

Also, any player may show a Seven of trumps and win 10 points. There are 10 bonus points for winning the last trick.

Conclusion

Once the stock is exhausted, suit must be followed and trumps played if this is impossible. The player taking the final trick wins a bonus 10 points. No further declarations are allowed. Play continues until one player has reached or exceeded a total of 1,000 points. If the losing player has scored under 500 points, he is 'rubiconed', and the winner scores a double game.

Marjolet

Simpler to play than Bezique, Marjolet allows the Jack of trumps – the Marjolet – to be melded (matched) to the four different Queens. Indeed, a Queen may be melded to the Marjolet and to her matching King at the same time.

You will need: 32 cards, Sixes and below having been removed
Card ranking: Ace, Ten, King, Queen, Jack and Nine to Seven
Players: Two
Ideal for: 14+

Object

To score points by taking Aces and Tens, so-called *Brisques*, in tricks and by declaring melds (sets of matched cards).

The Deal

Both players receive six cards. The next card turned up sets trumps; the remainder of the pack forms the stock.

Play

There is no need to follow suit. The trick is taken by the higher card of the suit led, or by a trump played to a non- trump lead. Both players take a card from the stock. The player who won the trick leads to the next. Before this, the winner can declare any meld. All melds are placed face up in front of the declaring player. His cards can still be used in trick play and to make other melds.

Once the stock runs out, both players take their melds into hand. For the last six tricks, suit must be followed and a higher card played, if possible. Otherwise, a trump must be played, again if possible. Melds may still be declared.

Scoring

If the Seven of trumps (the *Dix*) is turned up at the start of play by the dealer, he wins 10 points, while a player holding it can exchange it for the turn-up after taking a trick. The score for the exchange is 10 points. If the player opts not to exchange, the *Dix* still scores 10 when it is played, regardless of whether the trick is won or lost.

Winning the last trick is worth a bonus of 10 points, while, should a player succeed in taking all six tricks, he receives a bonus of 50 points. Each player then sorts through the cards he has won and scores 10 for each *brisque* he has taken.

Melds

The winner of a trick can declare any of the following melds:

- Four Aces – 100 points.
- Four Tens – 80 points.
- Four Kings – 60 points.
- Four Queens – 40 points.
- Marriage between the King and Queen of trumps – 40 points.
- Marriage between the King and Queen of a non-trump suit – 20 points.
- Marriage between the Jack of trumps and any trump or non-trump Queen – 20 points.

Above: in Marjolet, it is possible to meld the Jack of trumps (in this example, Clubs) with any of the four Queens.

Above: Scoring combinations in Marjolet, assuming Hearts as trumps.

Conclusion

Play continues until all tricks have been taken. The winning score can be either 500 or 1,000 points.

Pinochle

Closely related to Bezique, Pinochle started life in the USA as a two-player game, but there are now three- and four-handed versions, plus ones for five or more players. Auction Pinochle, described here, is the most popular three-handed form.

You will need: Two packs of 24 cards, Eights and below having been removed

Card ranking: Ace, Ten, King, Queen, Jack and Nine

Players: Three in this version, although can be two to five

Ideal for: 14+

Object

To make as many points as bid from melds (matches) declared from hand after taking the widow. Card points are made in tricks, with extra for winning the last trick.

The Deal and Bidding

Each player is dealt 15 cards three at a time. Three cards are placed face down to form the widow (stock). The player to the dealer's left bids first. All bids must be multiples of 10 and the opening one must be at least 300 (unless agreed otherwise). The highest bidder takes the widow, discarding three cards face down, announces trumps and declares any melds. If these fulfil his bid, there is no play and he scores the value of his game.

The bidder can also concede if he doubts he can fulfil his bid in play. He loses only his game value, as opposed to twice the game value if he plays and fails.

Play

The bidder leads to the first trick. Suit must be followed and, if possible, a player has to 'kill', that is, play a higher card of the same suit. If not, a trump must be played. Otherwise, a player can 'slough' or discard any card. The highest card of the suit led, or the highest trump if any are played, wins the trick. The trick's winner leads to the next.

Melds

All versions of the game employ the same standard melds:

- Flush (Ace, King, Queen and Jack of trumps) – 150 points.
- Royal Marriage (King and Queen of trumps) – 40 points.
- Plain Marriage (non-trump King and Queen) – 20 points.
- Aces around (four Aces, one of each suit) – 100 points.
- Kings around (four Kings, one of each suit) – 80 points.
- Queens around (four Queens, one of each suit) – 60 points.
- Jacks around (four Jacks, one of each suit) – 40 points.
- Pinochle (Q♠ and J♦) – 40 points.
- *Dix* or *Deece* (Nine of trumps) – 10 points.

Scoring

There are two ways of scoring points, through melding combinations and winning scoring cards in tricks. Aces, Tens and Kings are called counters and are worth 10 points each, while Queens, Jacks and Nines count for nothing. The winner of the last trick scores an extra 10 points.

If the bid is made, the bidder scores the points taken in melds and play. If not, the bidder 'goes out' with the bid being deducted from his score. The other players score the same way, provided that they have captured at least one counter. If not, they score nothing. All scores are doubled when Spades are trumps. Frequently, although not always, Hearts as trumps triple the scores.

150 POINTS

100 POINTS

80 POINTS

40 POINTS

40 POINTS

40 POINTS

20 POINTS

10 POINTS

Above: The above are all standard scoring melds or cards, where Hearts are trumps. Other scoring melds can be included by prior agreement.

Conclusion

Play continues until all tricks have been taken. The first player to score 1,500 or more points wins.

19 | Jack-Nine Games

What differentiates these games from others of the Marriage family is the promotion of the Jack to the highest-ranking trump, with a value of 20, followed by the Nine with a value of 14. Belote is the national game of France, and Klaverjas the favourite in the Netherlands, while in Switzerland and Austria, Jack-Nine games are universally popular. The games are so similar that if you master one it is easy to learn another.

Although authorities on the history of card games agree that the first Jack-Nine games probably originated in the Netherlands, it was undoubtedly the Swiss who honed them until they reached their present sophisticated status. Indeed, these so-called Jass games have become so popular in Switzerland that others which have nothing to do with them have been classified as kinds of Jass, while Swiss cards have come to be known as Jass cards.

A standard Jass pack consists of 36 cards in suits of Bells, Shields, Acorns and Flowers. The French-suit equivalents are Hearts, Diamonds, Clubs and Spades. The name Jass (pronounced 'yass') is thought to originate from Jasper, which was the Dutch name for the knave in the 18th century.

The French version, Belote, became the most popular card game in the country in the mid-20th century. A close relative of Klaberjass and of Klaverjas, the Dutch national card game, it has spawned many variants of its own. Of these, the most interesting is probably Coinche, which now rivals its precursor in the popularity stakes. It has one particularly novel feature. In order to make a declaration during the bidding stage of the game, players have to bang their fists on the table. Schieber Jass, a long-established Swiss game for four players playing in partnerships, also has an unusual feature – an elaborate scoring system, in which, at least traditionally, scores are chalked on a slate painted with two Zs.

Above: A Swiss card deck, also known as Jass cards, which consist of 36 cards in suits of Bells, Shields, Acorns and Flowers.

Klaberjass

This popular two-hander is known in Britain as Clob, Clobby or Clobiosh, while in the USA it is known as Klob, Kalabriasze or Klabber. It is also sometimes called Bela. In trumps, the Jack and Nine – the *Jass* and the *Menel* or *Mi* – are promoted over the Ace. As well as the two-player version, there are three- and four-player variants.

You will need: 32-card deck (Sixes and below having been removed from a standard pack); scorecards

Card ranking: Ace, Ten, King, Queen, Jack, Nine, Eight, Seven, except in trumps, where the *Jass* (Jack of trumps) ranks highest, followed by the *Menel* (Nine of trumps)

Players: Two (though three to four versions exist)

Ideal for: 14+

Object

To reach or exceed a total of 500 points.

The Deal

Each player receives six cards three at a time. The next card is turned up to establish a possible trump suit and the remainder placed face down to form the stock. Once trumps have been decided (see below), three more cards are dealt to both. A player holding the Seven of trumps, the *Dix*, can then exchange it for the trump turn-up.

Bidding

The bidding that follows establishes whether either player accepts the turned-up suit as trumps. The non-dealer can either pass, say 'Take it' or say '*Schmeiss*'.

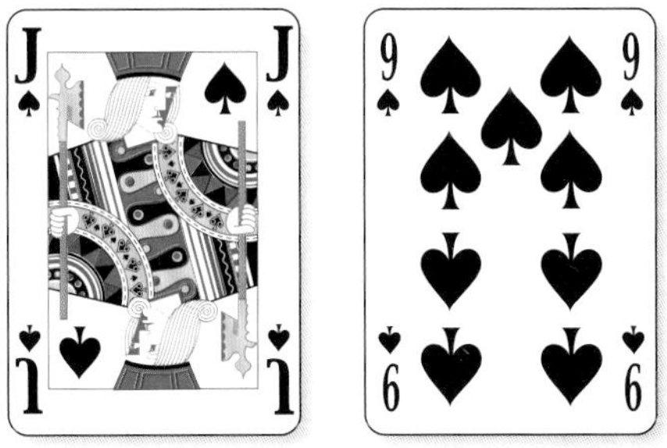

Left: In trumps (here, assumed as Spades) the Jack (known as the *Jass*) and Nine (known as the *Menel*, or *Mi*), rank above the Ace.

Below: A same-suit sequence of three in Klaberjass is a *Terz* and scores 20 points, but it would score nothing if the other player holds a better sequence. This could either be one of three cards running Queen, King or Ace, or a sequence of four cards or more, known as a *Halbe*, which counts for 50.

Schmeiss is an offer to become the Maker with the turned suit as trumps and has to be agreed by the dealer. Otherwise, the deal is annulled. If the non-dealer passes, the dealer has the same choices.

Play and Scoring

Before the trick is led, either player holding a sequence of three or more cards must announce the fact. A *Terz*, a sequence of three cards, is worth 20 points, while a *Halbe*, a sequence of four or more, counts for 50. It is only the player with the best sequence who can score. Any *Halbe* beats a *Terz*, a *Terz* with a higher top card beats one with a lower top card, and a *Terz* in trumps is better than one in a plain suit. To determine who has the best sequence, the non-dealer announces 'Twenty' or 'Fifty' on leading to the first trick. The dealer replies 'Good' if he cannot match the number, or 'Not Good' if he can beat it. The questions 'How many cards?', 'How high?' and 'In trumps?' can also be asked.

A *Belle*, the King and Queen of trumps, is worth 20 points. Unlike the preceding melds, or matches, it is not announced until one of its cards is played to a trick. A 60-*Terz* is the term applied to describe a *Terz* of the King, Queen and Jack of trumps. It is worth 60 points.

Winning the last trick scores 10 extra points. The *Jass* is worth 20 points, Nines 14, Aces 11, Tens 10, Kings four, Queens three and the other Jacks two.

Conclusion

At the end of the hand, both players declare their totals. If the Maker has scored higher, both players score the points they made. If not, his opponent scores the total made by both players. If equal, the Maker scores nothing and the opposing player scores what he took. The first to score 500 or more points in melds and card points wins.

Belote

Although it came to France only in about 1914, Belote is now the country's most popular card game. Two, three or four players can play it, but the four-player partnership version described here is the one most often played.

You will need: 32 cards, Sixes and below having been removed

Card ranking: Trumps: Jack, Nine, Ace, Ten, King, Queen, Eight and Seven. Plain suits: Ace, Ten, King, Queen, Jack and Nine to Seven

Players: Two to three, or four in partnerships of two, as here

Ideal for: 14+

Object

To score as many points as possible through taking tricks and making melds (matches).

The Deal

Five cards are dealt to each player three and two at a time. The next card is turned face up. The player to the dealer's right can now 'take' (that is, choose the suit of the turned-up card as trumps) or pass. If the latter, each player gets the same option. If all pass, each has another chance to 'take', this time, naming a trump suit other than the turn-up. If everyone passes again, there is a new deal but the pack is not shuffled. The player who 'takes' becomes the Taker and picks up the turn-up. The others are dealt three more cards, with the Taker getting two.

Play

The player to the dealer's right leads. Players must follow suit, trump, over- or undertrump, or discard any card.

Scoring and Conclusion

The Jack of trumps is worth 20 points, the Nine of trumps 14, Aces 11, Tens 10, Kings four, Queens three and the other Jacks two. The other Nines, Eights and Sevens are valueless. When declaring *Belote* and *Rebelote*, *Belote* is declared first, followed by *Rebelote* when the Queen is played. Apart from this, only the partnership with the highest declaration can score.

The last trick scores an extra 10 points, the *Dix de Der*, for the partnership winning it. If the taker's partnership wins at least as many points as its opponents, both sides score all the points they have made. If not, they are *dedans* (inside). Their opponents score 162 points to which they add the value of the taking side's declarations plus their own. If the taker's partnership wins all nine, it scores *Capot* (100 points) not *Dix de Der*.

Play continues until one partnership has scored 1,000 or 1,500 points (as agreed before play starts).

Melds

Various types of meld score, namely:

- *Carré* (Four of a Kind – can consist of all four Jacks, Nines, Aces, Tens, Kings or Queens) – four Jacks scores 200 points, four Nines 150 and the others 100 points each.
- *Cent* (a sequence of five or more cards of the same suit) – 50.
- *Cinquante* (a sequence of four cards of the same suit) – 50.
- *Tierce* (a sequence of three cards of the same suit) – 20.
- *Belote* and *Rebelote* (the King and Queen of trumps) – 20.

200 POINTS

100 POINTS

100 POINTS

100 POINTS

100 POINTS

50 POINTS

50 POINTS

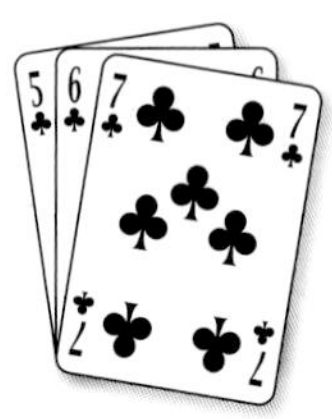

20 POINTS

20 POINTS

Left: Standard scoring melds or cards in Belote, assuming Hearts as trumps.

Coinche

This is a popular version of Belote, with the unique feature that players have to bang the table to signal a declaration. Its name derives from the twist that players can *coincher* (double) and redouble each other's bids.

You will need: 32 cards, Sixes and below having been removed

Card ranking: Trumps: Jack, Nine, Ace, Ten, King, Queen, Eight and Seven. Plain suits: Ace, Ten, King, Queen, Jack and Nine to Seven

Players: Four, in partnerships of two

Ideal for: 14+

Object

To score points through taking tricks, holding the King and Queen of trumps, or achieving the highest meld.

The Deal

The players are dealt eight cards before bidding starts.

Bidding

Whether or not there is a trump suit depends on the contract to be played – a suit contract, a no trump contract or an all trump one. In the bidding, the aim is to take more than half the trick points available and to score more points in tricks and melds (matched set of cards) than the other partnership. The convention is to bid a number followed by a contract, the lowest permissible number being 80. Subsequent bids go up in multiples of 10. Bidding ends when the other players all pass, or when an opponent doubles the bid, unless the bidding partnership redoubles. The traditional way of signalling a double is to bang a first on the table – in fact, *coinche* means 'fist' in French.

When declaring *Belote* and *Rebelote, Belote* is declared first, followed by *Rebelote,* when the Queen is played. Apart from this, only the partnership with the highest declaration can score. If two declarations appear equal, the second to declare asks 'How high?' and the previous declarer must give a clearer and truthful indication accordingly.

Left: An unusual feature of Coinche is that players have to bang the table to signal a declaration.

Melds

On playing to the first trick, players announce their highest meld – the possible combinations are the same as in Belote, namely:

- *Carré* (Four of a Kind) – four Jacks scores 200 points, four Nines 150, and four Aces, Tens, Kings or Queens 100 points.
- *Cent* (a sequence of five or more cards of the same suit) – 50.
- *Cinquante* (a sequence of four cards of the same suit) – 50.
- *Tierce* (a sequence of three cards of the same suit) – 20.
- *Belote* and *Rebelote* (the King and Queen of trumps) – 20.

Play

If the lead is a trump, players must follow suit, playing a higher card if possible. If a plain suit is led, it is not necessary to head the trick (play a higher card). If an opponent is winning with a trump, a higher one must be played, but if it is a partner any card can be discarded.

Scoring and Conclusion

At the end of play, both partnerships calculate how much they have won in trick-points and melds. Aces are worth 200 points, Tens 150, and Kings, Queens, Jacks 100 each. Taking the last trick is worth 10 points, while announcing *Belote* and *Rebelote,* the King and Queen of trumps, scores 20 points, except in a non-trump contract.

If the declaring partnership is successful, both sides score the points that they have made and the declarers add the value of the contract to their total. If not, they score zero, their opponents winning 160 trick points, the value of their melds and the value of the lost contract. All scores are affected by any doubling. Game is 3,000 points.

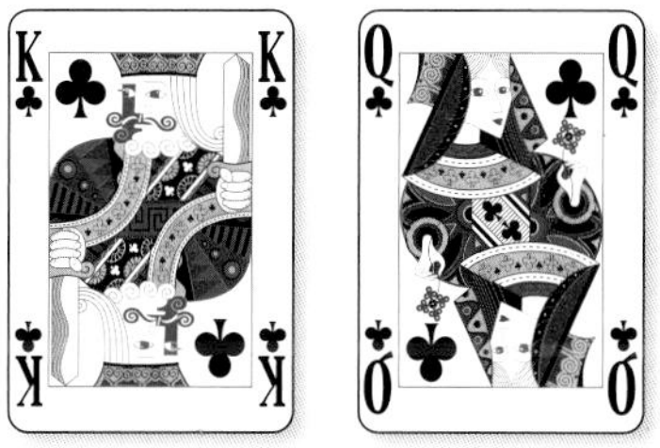

Left: When declaring *Belote* and *Rebelote* (the King and Queen of trumps, which here are Clubs), *Belote* is declared first, followed by *Rebelote* when the Queen is played.

Boonaken

Closely related to another Dutch game called Pandoeren, this is faster, less complicated and decidedly less serious. In all probability, it gets its name from the Dutch for the three highest trumps – *Boer, Nel, Aass,* or Jack, Nine, Ace.

You will need: 32 cards, Sixes and below having been removed; scorecard

Card ranking: Trumps: Jack (highest), Nine, Ace, King, Queen, Ten, Eight, Seven. Plain suits: Ace (highest) down to Seven

Players: Five is optimal

Ideal for: 14+

Object

To find a loser, who has to pay for a round of drinks.

Bidding

The player to the left of the dealer bids first. A number bid is an undertaking to win that many points in tricks and *Roem*, which are specific card combinations (see Scoring). *Misère* is a no-trump bid to lose every trick and *Zwabber* a bid to take them all. *Boonaak* is the same as *Zwabber* but with trumps. *Boonaak* plus a number is a bid to win all the tricks plus that score in *Roem*. Bidding continues until three players pass in succession.

The Deal

Six cards each are dealt three at a time, and two cards are placed face up on the table, one after each packet has been dealt. The successful bidder uses these cards to improve his hand by exchanging and discarding. If the bid is a number or a *Boonaak*, he also chooses the trump suit.

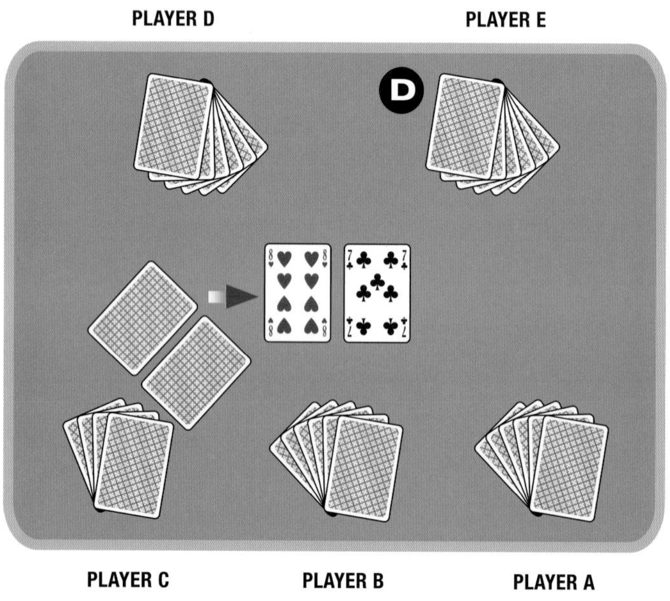

Above: The declarer (Player C), can improve his hand by exchanging up to two cards with the two in the centre. Having bid *Misère*, Player C in this instance discards two high cards and picks up the 8♥ and 7♣.

Play

The successful bidder leads to the first trick. If the bid is a number bid, he must also announce *Roem* at this stage. The amount announced must be equal to or more than the number bid. If an opposing player has *Roem* in hand worth at least as much as the *Roem* the successful bidder has announced, he announces it as well. If it is worth more than the bidder's, the latter's *Roem* is cancelled and does not count towards winning the contract.

If a trump is led, the other players must follow suit, unless the only one held is the Jack of trumps, when any card can be discarded. When a plain suit is led, that suit must be followed or a trump played. A player is allowed to trump even though suit could have been followed.

Scoring

In the trump suit, Jack scores 20, Nine 14, Ace 11, King three, Queen two, Ten 10, while Eight and Seven score zero. Plain suits (those that are not trumps) score 11 for the Ace, three for the King, two for the Queen, one for the Jack and 10 for the Ten, cards below Ten not scoring. There are no bonus points for taking the last trick.

Roem also scores, provided that the *Roem* held by any opposing players are not higher. A sequence of three cards in a suit scores 20, four 50, five 100 and six 200. Four Jacks are worth 200 points, Aces, Kings and Queens 100 points and the King and Queen of trumps (*Stuk*) 20 points.

Conclusion

In a number contract, the declarer wins if trick-points and *Roem* equal or exceed the amount of the bid. Other contracts are scored as might be expected. All scores are entered on a scorecard, a win being marked by a plus and a loss by a minus. A player with two pluses is a winner and can sit out the game. A player with two minuses is the loser.

Klaverjas

Extremely popular in its Dutch homeland, Klaverjas is distinguished from other games of this genre because melds (matched sets of cards) are scored as they occur within individual tricks.

You will need: 32 cards, Sixes and below having been removed

Card ranking: Trumps: Jack, Nine, Ace, Ten, King, Queen, Eight, Seven. Plain suits: Ace, Ten, King, Queen, Jack, Nine, Eight and Seven

Players: Four, in partnerships of two

Ideal for: 14+

Object

To win more than half of the available points in each hand if your partnership has chosen trumps, otherwise to prevent the opposing partnership from scoring these points. Ultimately, the aim is to score as many points as possible over 16 hands.

The Deal

Each player is dealt eight cards in packets of three, two and three.

Choosing Trumps

Trumps are determined in either of two ways. Free choice means that the player to the dealer's left can either nominate a trump suit or pass. If he passes, the next player has the same choice. If all four players pass, the player to the dealer's left must decide.

The alternative is to choose trumps at random by turning up the top card of a second deck. The player to the dealer's left either accepts this card as trumps or passes. If he passes, the next player chooses. If everyone passes, a second card is turned up. Its suit automatically becomes trumps.

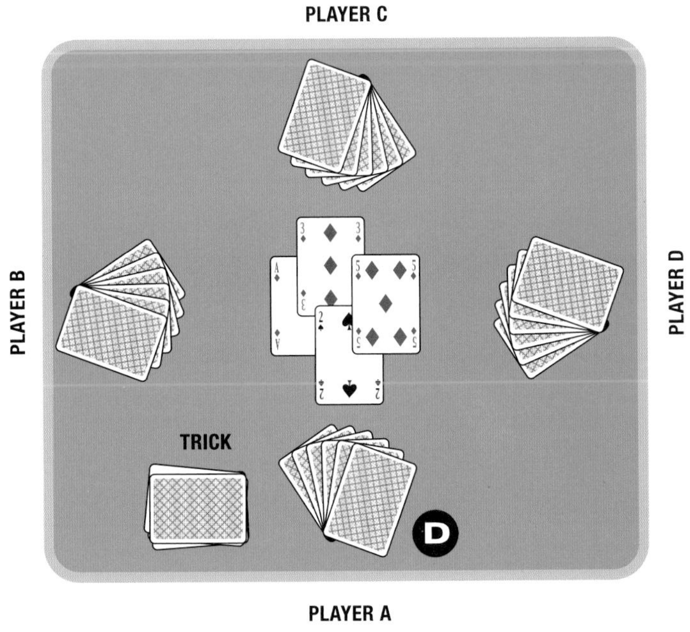

Melds

Melds score as follows:

- Three consecutive cards of the same suit – 20 points.
- Four consecutive cards of the same suit – 50 points.
- Four of a Kind (except Jacks) – 100 points.
- Four Jacks – 200 points.
- A Marriage of the King and Queen of trumps (known as *Stuk*) – 20 points.

Play

The player to the dealer's left leads to the first trick. The others must follow suit if possible. If no trumps are played, the highest card of the suit led takes the trick. If the trick contains trumps, the highest trump wins. Before leading to the next trick, the winner of the previous one scores the value of any *Roems* (melds).

Signalling between partners is accepted. Discarding a low card of a particular suit, for instance, means the player holds its Ace, while discarding a court card (King, Queen or Jack) is a warning not to lead that suit.

Scoring and Conclusion

In the trump suit, the Jack is worth 20 points, the Nine 14, Ace 11, Ten 10, King four and Queen three. In non-trump suits, Aces score 11 points, Tens 10, Kings four, Queens three and Jacks two. If the partnership choosing trumps wins more than half of the available points, both sides keep the points they have taken. If not, the partnership scores nothing and its opponents take all the points, including bonuses. The winner of the last trick gets a 10-point bonus. Play continues until 1,500 points have been scored.

Left: Signalling through discards is a feature of Klaverjas. A low discard, such as the 2♠ played here, is used by Player A to show he holds an Ace of that suit (A♠). Discarding a court card is a warning not to lead that card's suit.

Handjass

Like its Swiss and western Austrian counterparts, this Jass game revolves around points, which can be scored for three features known as *Stöck, Wys* and *Stich* (Marriages, melds and tricks). In its homeland, it is played with a 36-card Jass pack with its suits of Acorns, Shields, Bells and Flowers.

You will need: 36 cards, Fives and below having been removed

Card ranking: Jack of trumps (highest), Nine of trumps, Aces, Kings, Queens, the other Jacks, Tens, Nines, Eights, Sevens and Sixes

Players: Two to five, although four is optimal

Ideal for: 14+

Object

To score at least 21 game points for melds (matched sets of cards) in hand and counting cards captured in tricks.

The Deal

Each player gets nine cards in batches of three. If two are playing, two extra hands of nine are dealt. One of these is spare. This means that each player in turn, starting with the one to the dealer's left, has the right to replace the hand he has been dealt with the spare. The other hand is dead and its top card is turned up for trumps.

If three play, the remaining cards are laid down as a spare hand, but the top card is turned for trumps. If four play, there is no spare hand and the dealer's last card is shown to determine trumps. If five play, each deals in turn and then sits out that hand.

Left: The highest-scoring cards in Handjass are the Jack of trumps (known as the *Puur* and worth 20 points) and the Nine of trumps (known as the *Näll* and worth 14 points). Here, Diamonds are trumps.

Melds

Same-suit sequences are allowed, as are groups. Only the player with the best meld in hand can score for melds. Four Jacks are worth 200 points, four Nines 150 and four of any other numbered card 100. If there are two quartets of cards worth 100, a higher-ranking one beats a lower-ranking one. A three-card sequence is worth 20, a four-card one 50, five 100, six 150, seven 200, eight 250, nine 300. The sequence order – Ace, King, Queen, Jack, Ten, Nine, Eight, Seven and Six, is the same in every suit, including trumps. A longer sequence beats a shorter one. If equal in length, a higher-ranking one beats a lower-ranking one. A Marriage between the King and Queen of trumps, a *Stöck,* is worth 20.

Play

The player to the dealer's left leads to the first trick. If the lead is a trump, the other players must follow suit, unless the only trump a player is holding is the Jack of trumps. In this case, any card may be played. If a plain suit is led, the others are free to follow suit or trump. In neither case can a lower trump be played if a higher one has already been led, unless a player's hand consists of nothing but trumps, in which case any card can be played.

Scoring

The highest-scoring card is the Jack of trumps (the *Puur*), worth 20 points, followed by the Nine of trumps (the *Näll*), which scores 14. Aces score 11, Kings four, Queens three, the other Jacks two and Tens 10. The other Nines, together with the Eights, Sevens and Sixes, do not score.

At the end of a hand, the two players taking the most meld points each score a game point. If scores are drawn, the pack is cut to break the tie. A player scoring less than 21 meld points is penalized by having a game point taken away. Game points are sometimes called 'sticks' and minus points are 'potatoes'.

Left: If two players tie at the end of a hand for the second-best score in meld points, the players concerned cut the pack and whoever draws the highest card scores the game point.

Conclusion

A player drops out on reaching either five game points or seven sticks, depending on which version of the game is being played. The last player left in is the loser.

Schieber Jass

Schieber is probably the most popular member of the Swiss Jass family of card games. The game itself is a variant of Handjass, although its precise rules vary. It is played with a 36-card Jass pack, but here the suits of Acorns, Flowers, Shields and Bells have been substituted with the English counterparts Clubs, Spades, Hearts and Diamonds, respectively.

You will need: 36-card deck, Fives and below removed

Card ranking: *Obenabe* ('top-down') no-trumps contracts: Eights (highest), Sevens, Sixes, Nines, Tens, Jacks, Queens, Kings and Aces. *Undenufe* ('bottom-up') no-trumps contracts: Sixes (highest), Sevens, Eights, Nines, Tens, Jacks, Queens, Kings and Aces. Plain suit contracts: Jacks (highest), Nines, Aces, Kings, Queens, Tens, Eights, Sevens and Sixes

Players: Four, in partnerships of two

Ideal for: 14+

Object

To win 3,000 points in total, by melding (matching sets of cards) and winning tricks.

The Deal

Each player gets nine cards dealt in threes. In the first trick, the player with the Seven of Spades starts the bidding, leads to the trick and deals the second hand.

Bidding and Contracts

The player holding the 7♠ can choose which contract is to be played, or can decide to *schieben* (shove) the responsibility over to his partner. The choice is between suit contracts in Clubs and Spades, which score single; Hearts or Diamonds, which score double; and the no-trumps contracts (*Obenabe* – meaning literally 'top-down' – and *Undenufe* – meaning 'bottom-up'), which score treble.

Play

The player to the dealer's left leads. If the lead is a trump, the other players must follow suit, unless the only trump a player is holding is the Jack of trumps. In this case, any card may be played. If a plain suit is led, the others are free to follow suit or trump. In neither case can a lower trump be played if a higher one has already been led, unless a player's hand consists of nothing but trumps, in which case any card can be played.

In a no-trump contract, players must follow suit if they can. Each player announces the highest *Weis* (meld) he holds when he plays to the first trick. The partnership with the highest *Weis* scores for it, and for any other *Weis* that it may hold, the score being multiplied by the factor for the contract. Their opponents score nothing. A player holding the King and Queen of trumps may announce *'Stöck'* ('Marriage') as the second card is played.

Scoring

In *Obenabe*, contracts Aces are worth 11 points, Kings four, Queens three, Jacks two, Tens 10 and Eights eight. Nines, Sevens and Sixes count for nothing. In *Undenufe* contracts, Sixes score 11, Eights eight, Tens 10, Jacks two, Queens three and Kings four. Sevens, Nines and Aces do not score. In plain suit contracts, Jacks score 20, Nines 14, Aces 11, Kings four, Queens three and Tens 10. The other cards are valueless.

After each hand, both partnerships multiply their totals by the factor for the hand. The first partnership to score 3,000 points wins. If the losing partnership has failed to score more than 1,500, the winners are awarded a bonus game. If a side claims a win during the first trick of a hand, their opponents can counter-claim. *Stöck* (Marriage) is scored, followed by *Weis* (meld) and *Stich* (first trick), to establish who won first. Twenty points are awarded for *Stöck* (Marriage), which again is multiplied by the factor for the contract. The winner of the last trick scores a bonus of five points. If either side manages to take all nine tricks, a bonus of 100 for 'match' is awarded.

Left: In an *Undenufe* contract, the meld that contains higher trick winners is the winning three-card sequence. In this instance, 6-7-8 is the higher and Queen-King-Ace the lower meld.

Conclusion

A hand continues until all tricks have been taken. The game lasts until one partnership or the other scores at least 3,000 points – this typically takes 12 hands.

20 | Canasta Games

Although they are members of the Rummy genre, Canasta games have one important difference. Instead of using melds (matches) simply as a tool for getting rid of cards in hand, players score positively for the melds themselves. Canasta itself was the most popular American card game of the 1950s. It reached the USA from Latin America in about 1948, and is still played by millions around the world.

In fact, Canasta – the word is Spanish for 'basket' – was not the first game to introduce a positive scoring system for melds. The honour belongs to a game called Michigan Rum and another called 500 Rummy, both of which were widely played in the 1920s and 1930s. However, Canasta certainly has been the most influential worldwide. Although it is invariably regarded as a partnership game, perhaps because Bridge players invented it, it works just as well for two players.

The story of Canasta goes back to 1939, when well-to-do attorney Segundo Santos and his architect friend Alberto Serrato met in the Jockey Club of Montevideo, Uruguay, to devise an alternative to Bridge. The new game quickly spread throughout South America and then, after the Second World War, to the USA. It was soon played everywhere, from smart resorts on the eastern seaboard to highly fashionable clubs in California. American forces overseas spread the game to Asia, Europe and even the Soviet Union, and for a time in the early 1950s, it came close to displacing Contract Bridge as the world's most popular card game.

The various games Canasta has spawned over the years all have their individual quirks. In Samba, for instance, three packs of cards are used. Hand and Foot is another interesting variant, in which each player is dealt two sets of cards: the hand and the foot.

Above: Originating in Uruguay, Canasta reached dizzying heights of popularity in the USA in the early 1950s.

Samba

There are seemingly countless variations on classic Canasta. Some are simple adaptations to suit differing numbers of players, while others have developed into interesting games in their own right. Of these, Samba – also known as Samba-Canasta and, in the Netherlands, as Straat-Canasta (Sequence Canasta) – has been the most influential.

You will need: Three 52-card decks; six Jokers; scorecards

Card ranking: Ace down to Four, with Twos and Jokers serving as wild cards, and Threes having special rules attached to them (see 'Play' for wild cards and Threes)

Players: Two to six. If there are two, three or five, they play independently; if four or six, they play in partnerships

Ideal for: 14+

Object

To be the first player to score 10,000 points by melding (matching sets of cards) in order to win the game.

The Deal

With two to five players, the deal is 15 cards to each player; six players get 13 cards each. The remaining cards form the stock, the top card of which is turned up to start the discard pile.

Left: Samba is characterized by allowing same-suit sequences as melds, as well as groups. A sequence, however, is not allowed to contain any wild cards.

Melds

Same-suit sequences and groups are allowed. A group of seven or more cards is a *Canasta* and a seven-card sequence is a *Samba*. To go out, a player or partnership must have melded at least two *Canastas*, two *Sambas* or one of each. Wild cards – Jokers and Twos – cannot be used in a sequence, while a group may contain only two.

Aces and wild cards count for 20 points, Kings to Eights 10, and Sevens to Fours and black Threes five. Red Threes can be melded only if two *Sambas* or *Canastas* have already been laid, in which case each is worth 100 bonus points (1,000 if all six are melded).

If any are left in hand, they count as 750 penalty points. Black Threes can be melded in groups, but only when going out. Wild cards and Threes block the discard pile if discarded. Using the top card, which is blocking it, to start a new meld, unblocks it.

Play

Each player draws two cards from the stock, melds if he can, and discards a card. To use the discard pile, players must hold two natural cards of the same rank as the top discard, or, if they have not yet melded, meet the initial meld requirements. For scores under 1,500 points, this means the cards must be worth 50 points; for up to 3,000, 90 points; for up to 6,000, 120 points and for 7,000 or more 150 points.

Scoring and Conclusion

Scores are calculated by taking the value of the cards that have been melded and deducting from that the value of cards left in hand. Any bonus points are then added. Each *Samba* is worth 1,500 points. A pure *Canasta* – one made up solely of natural cards – scores 500 and a mixed one 300. Going out is worth 200 points. The first to score 10,000 points wins outright.

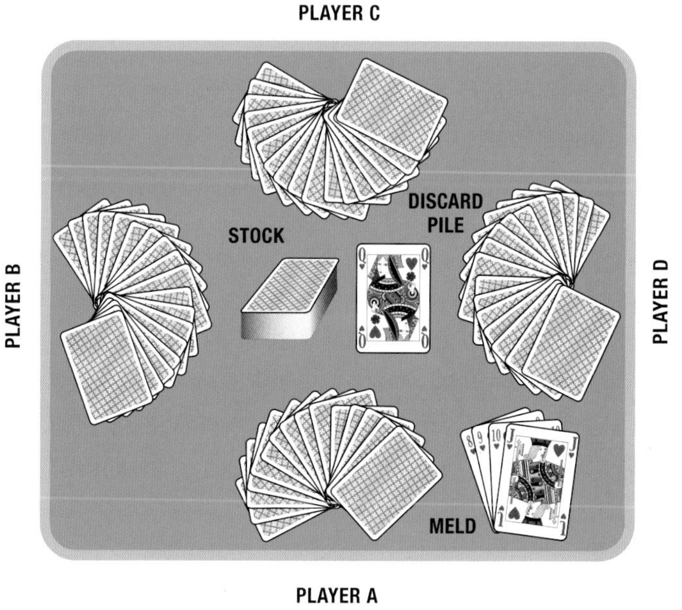

Above: Having already laid down a meld in Hearts, Player A can pick up the discard pile and add the Q♥ to the meld. Had the meld been in hand rather than laid to the table, Player A could not then have picked up the discard pile.

Canasta

Invented in 1939 in Uruguay, Canasta is one of the great successes of modern card games. The rules vary, but always include laying at least one seven-card meld (matching set) or *Canasta*.

You will need: Two standard packs plus four Jokers

Card ranking: Ace down to Four, with Twos and Jokers serving as wild cards, and Threes having special rules attached to them (see 'Play' for wild cards and Threes)

Players: Four, in partnerships of two

Ideal for: 14+

Object

To make melds – three cards or more of the same rank other than Jokers, Twos and Threes – and build them up into *Canastas*, which are melds of at least seven cards.

The Deal

Each player is dealt 11 cards singly, after which the remaining cards are placed face down to form the stock. Its top card is turned face up to start the discard pile. If the turn-up is a Joker, Two or a red Three – Jokers and Twos are wild cards (that is, they can represent any card) – another card is turned up and placed on top of it. A player dealt one or more red Threes must place them face up in front of him and draw replacements from the stock. They are bonus cards that take no part in play.

Left: When a red Three tops the discard pile it is placed at right angles over it, meaning it is frozen and no player can take the pile. To unfreeze the pile, a player needs to have two natural cards of the same rank as the turn-up in hand.

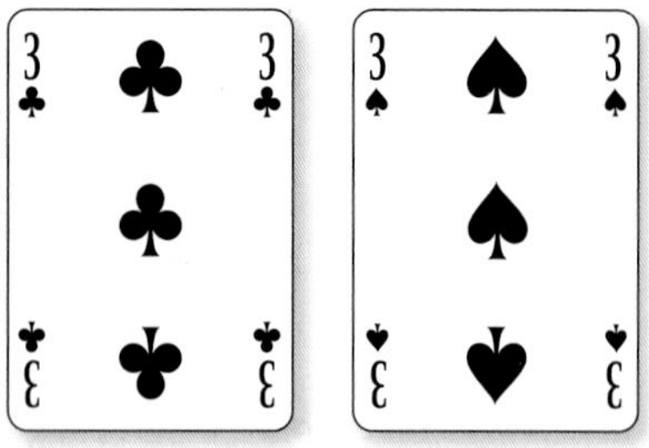

Right: Black Threes are stop cards. When one tops the discard pile, the pile cannot be picked up until the Three is covered by another card. They cannot be melded unless a player is 'going out', (getting rid of all cards in hand).

Melds

Suits are irrelevant in Canasta, so melds consist of three or more cards of the same rank. At least two of these cards must be natural cards as opposed to wild ones. No meld can contain more than three wild cards, although there is no limit to the number of natural cards in one.

If a seven-card meld is all natural, it is termed a natural *Canasta*. If it contains wild cards, it is mixed. Adding a wild card to extend a natural *Canasta* will turn it into a mixed one, but a wild card cannot be shifted from meld to meld. Nor is a partnership allowed to run more than one meld of a given rank or to add cards to a meld laid by the opposing side.

The first meld laid by a partnership must meet or beat a specific points requirement, which is calculated according to that partnership's current score. At the start of play, it is 50 points. If a partnership's score is 1,500 or over, it is 90 points and, if 3,000 or more, it is 120.

Individual Card Scores:

- Red Threes – 100 points each.
- Jokers – 50 points each.
- Aces and Twos – 20 points each.
- Kings, Queens, Jacks, Tens to Eights – 10 points each.
- Sevens, Sixes, Fives, Fours and black Threes – five points each.

Left: At the start of play, the value of cards in a first meld must be at least 50 points. The first meld is unacceptable, as Jacks are only worth 10 points. Aces score 20, so the second meld could be be laid.

Right: Twos and Jokers in Canasta serve as wild cards, that is, they can represent any card.

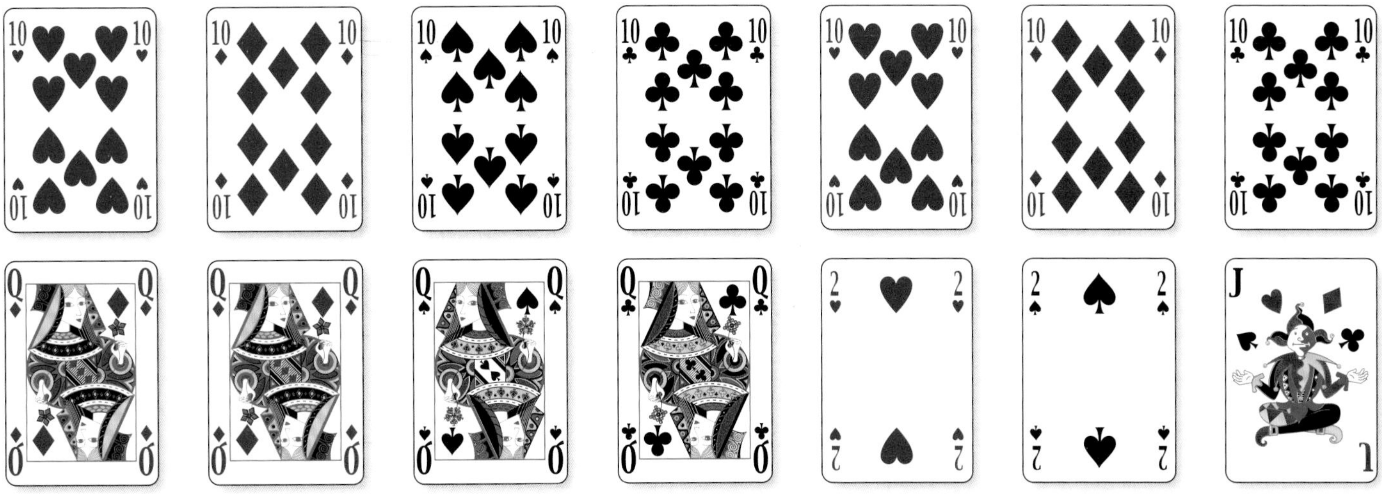

Above: The natural *Canasta* is worth 500 bonus points, plus 70 points as it is comprised of Tens. The mixed *Canasta* is worth 300 bonus points plus a further 130: 10 each for the Queens, 20 each for the Twos and 50 for the Joker.

Play

At the start of a turn, the player concerned can draw the top card of the stock or take the discard pile in its entirety. If the player chooses the first option, the card can be added to hand, melded or, if desired, discarded at the end of the turn. The second option applies only if the top discard can be melded at once. Nor may the discard pile be taken if the top discard is a wild card or a black Three. The latter is a stop card. By discarding one, a player can stop an opponent taking the pile until the Three is covered by another card. Moreover, black Threes cannot be melded unless a player is 'going out' – that is, getting rid of all cards in hand.

If the turn-up is a wild card or a red Three, no player can take the pile. It is what is termed 'frozen'. Nor may a partnership take it if it has yet to meld. To unfreeze the pile, a player needs to have two natural cards of the same rank as the turn-up in hand. The three cards can then be used to make a new meld, or be added to an existing one. Players end their turns by making a discard face up to the discard pile. This can be any card except a red Three.

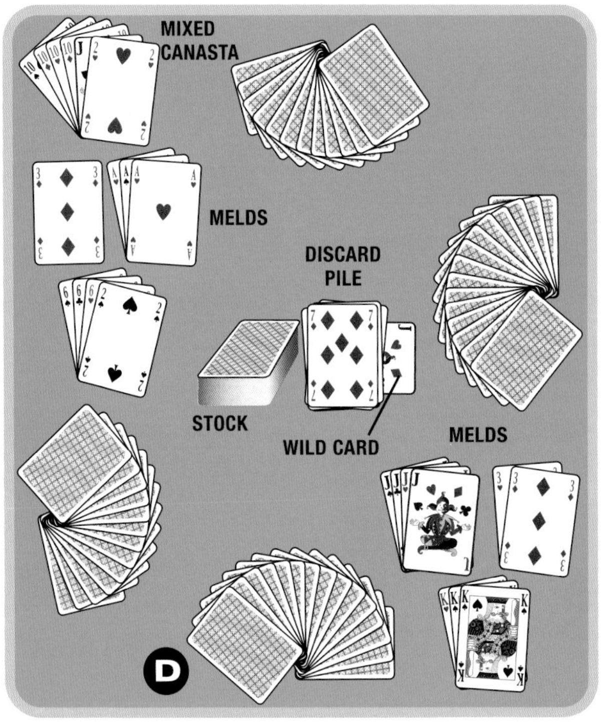

Above: A game of Canasta in progress. The North–South partnership is well on its way to a mixed *Canasta* in Tens, and also has melds in Sixes and Aces, together with a red Three. East–West has two red Threes, and melds in Jacks and Kings. The discard pile is currently frozen by a wild card, meaning that no player can pick up the pile unless he holds in his hand two cards of the same rank as the card topping the discard pile (here, a Seven).

Conclusion and Scoring

Play ends when a player goes out, which can be by melding, laying off, or discarding the last card in hand, provided that the partnership concerned has laid at least one *Canasta*. Each partnership scores the value of the cards it has melded, plus bonuses of 500 points for each natural *Canasta*, 300 for each mixed one and 100 for each red Three declared (800 if all four red Threes are held). There is a further bonus of 100 points for going out, which is doubled if the player is going out 'concealed' – that is, without having previously made any melds or lay-offs and doing so by playing a complete *Canasta*.

The value of cards left in hand is subtracted from both totals. If a partnership has failed to lay a single meld, or failed to declare a red Three, each red Three it may hold counts for 100 points against it (800 points if all four are held). The cumulative score needed to win the game is 5,000 points, the margin of victory being the difference between the scores of the two partnerships.

Hand and Foot

Invented in North America, this fascinating game has several features that set it apart from other games of its ilk. It uses one more pack than the number of players – up to five can play – plus Jokers. Each player is dealt two separate hands simultaneously and there are three types of combinations – natural, mixed and wild. The last of these consists entirely of Jokers and Twos.

You will need: Five standard packs plus ten Jokers, for four players

Card ranking: Ace down to Four, with Twos and Jokers serving as wild cards (see 'Play', opposite, for rules on this and Threes)

Players: Ideally, four, in partnerships of two

Ideal for: 14+

Object

To meld (group) as many cards as possible and either to go out first or to be left with as little 'deadwood' (cards that are not in any meld) as possible. You score points for cards you have melded, and lose points for any cards left in your hand at the end of the play.

The Deal

Once it has been agreed which partnership is to deal first and after the cards have been thoroughly shuffled, one partner takes part of the deck and deals four stacks of 13 cards face down from it. This is the Hand. Meanwhile, the partner of the hand dealer does the same with the other part of the deck until each player has a second stack, known as the Foot. The remaining cards are placed face down to form the stock, the top card of which is turned up and placed next to it to start the discard pile. If the turn-up is a red Three or a wild card – a Two or a Joker – it is buried in the stock and the next card turned up.

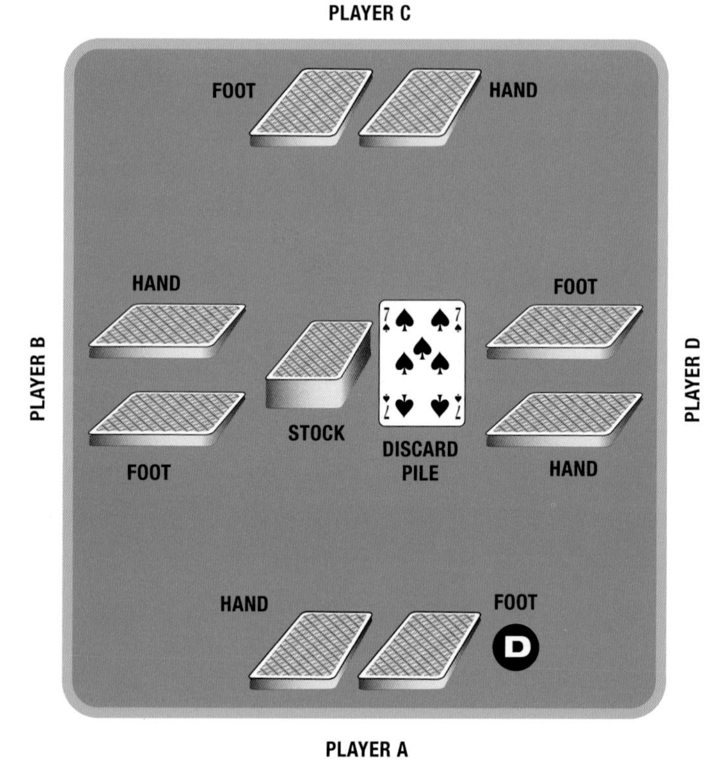

Above: After shuffling the packs, one partner takes part of the deck, deals four face-down stacks of 13 cards and passes them around the table in a clockwise direction until each player has a stack – the Hand. Meanwhile, the dealer's partner takes another part of the deck and deals a further four stacks of 13 cards each, once again passing these in a clockwise direction until each player has a second stack – the Foot.

Above: A feature of Hand and Foot is that matching combinations, known as melds, can consist entirely of wild cards, which are Twos and Jokers.

Melding

Players score points for the cards that they have melded and lose points for any cards left in hand at the end of play. In this game, a meld is a set of from three to seven cards of the same rank. Once such a meld has been started, either partner is at liberty to add more cards to it until there are seven in place.

There are three valid melds. A natural (or clean) meld contains no wild cards, while a mixed (or dirty) meld contains one or two. There must be at least six cards in such a meld for two wild cards to be included. A wild meld, as its name implies, consists entirely of wild cards. A complete meld of seven cards is called a pile.

Play

Players pick up and play the Hand first. The Foot stays face down sight unseen until its owner has played the last card from the Hand. Before each player plays, he must place any red Threes held in the Hand face up and draw replacements from the stock. The player to the left of the person who dealt the hands plays first.

Each player starts by drawing the top two cards from the stock. He then melds some cards or adds to his partner's melds and finally discards one card face up to the discard pile. An alternative to drawing from the stock is to pick up the top seven cards from the discard pile. This option is open only if the top discard is not a Three, and the player is holding two cards of the same rank as the top discard that can be melded with it immediately.

The first meld each partnership makes in each round must meet the minimum meld requirements. Several melds may be made at once to achieve this. In the first round, the requirement is at least 50 points, in the second 90, in the third 120, and in the fourth 150. Jokers are worth 50 points each, Twos and Aces 20, Kings down to Eights 10, and Sevens to Fours score five points.

Neither red nor black Threes may be melded. Red Threes, if declared, are worth a bonus 100 points each, but any left in hand count for 100 penalty points. If discarded, black Threes block the discard pile, so they are often used tactically. Any left in hand count for five penalty points. This means discarding any Threes held in hand one at a time on to the discard pile as quickly as possible.

Below: An excellent, if unlikely, opening hand. The red Three can be declared, earning a bonus of 100 points, while the black Three can be saved to block the discard pile at an opportune moment. The wild Twos and Jokers can be used towards a wild meld, or towards a mixed meld in Queens or Aces.

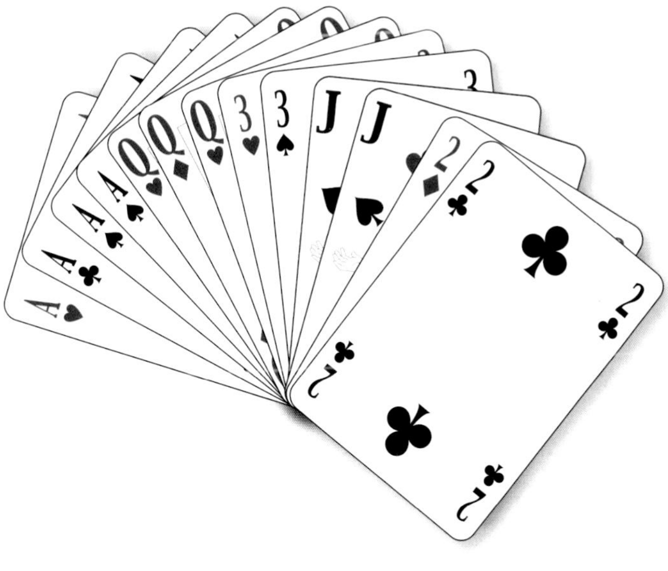

Scoring and Conclusion

For a player to be allowed to go out, the partnership concerned must have melded two natural, two mixed and one wild meld between them. The other partner must have picked up his Foot and played at least part of a turn from it. The player seeking to go out must also have obtained his partner's permission to do so.

Scores are then totalled, points deducted for cards left in hand, and bonuses awarded. Each natural pile is worth 500 points, a mixed one 300 and a wild pile 1,500. This is why most players, if possible, try to complete this particular pile as soon as they can. There is an additional 100-point bonus for going out.

If the stock is depleted to the point where no player can draw from it, play also ends, although it may be possible to continue for a time as long as each player is able to take and meld the previous player's discard. In this case, both partnerships score for the cards that they have melded, less the points for the cards they have remaining in their Hands and Feet. Obviously, the bonus for going out is not awarded.

The game ends when a partnership has made 10,000 points, or the four rounds have been played. In that case, the partnership winning the most rounds wins the game.

Below: Here, only Player A's hand is shown, along with the table cards. Players A and C have a natural meld of Aces and are well on the way to completing a mixed meld in Queens. Their opponents have nearly completed a wild meld and have started a mixed meld in Nines. Player A, whose turn it is to play, can pick up the discarded J♠ or pick up two cards from the top of the stock.

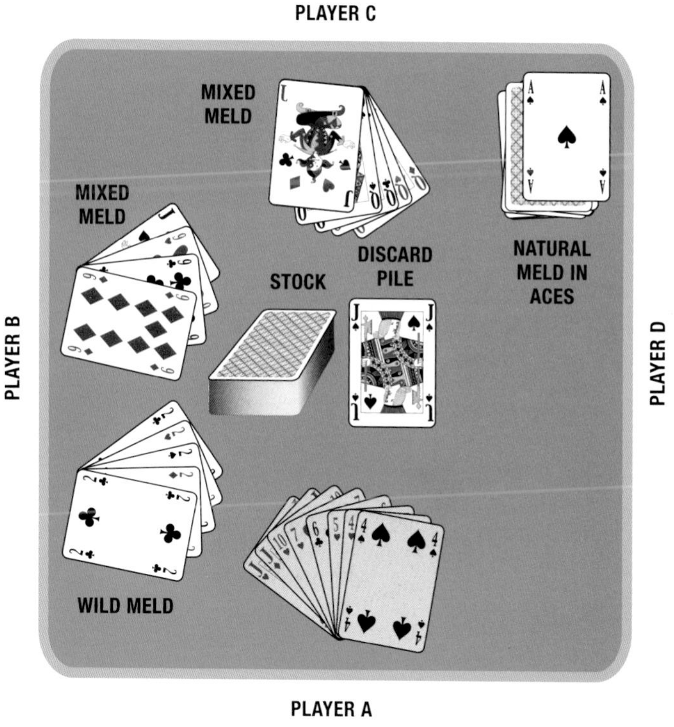

Pennies From Heaven

This variant of Canasta is notable for the highly unusual role played by Sevens. They may not be discarded until each partnership has grouped seven or more cards consisting solely of Sevens. Nor may they be discarded when going out. There are also two deals in this game.

You will need: Four standard packs plus eight Jokers

Card ranking: Aces down to Eights, then Sixes, Fives and Fours, with Twos and Jokers serving as wild cards, and Threes and Sevens having special rules attached to them (see 'Play' for wild cards and Threes)

Players: Four or six, playing in partnerships

Ideal for: 14+

Object

To score points by melding (grouping) cards into four types of *Canastas* (a meld of seven or more cards): natural, mixed, wild and sevens. A team needs one of each of these types to go out.

Left: A *Canasta* of Sevens in Pennies from Heaven scores 1,500 points.

The Deal

Each player receives 13 cards, dealt singly, and followed by a packet of 11 cards, which is kept face down until a player has personally completed a *Canasta* by laying the requisite seventh card from his hand.

The second hand, the so-called 'pennies from heaven', can then be picked up and taken into hand. The remaining cards form the stock, the top card of which is turned up to start the discard pile.

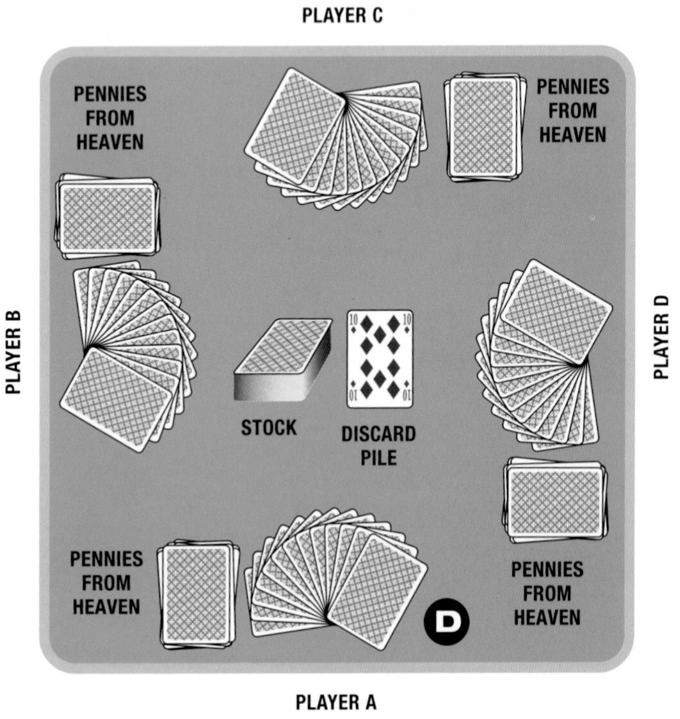

Above: Each player is dealt a batch of 11 cards in addition to his main hand of 13 cards. The second hand cannot be picked up until a player has personally completed a *Canasta* by laying the requisite seventh card from hand.

Melds and Canastas

A natural *Canasta* – consisting of seven cards of the same rank with no wild cards – is worth a bonus of 500 points. A mixed one, containing up to three wild cards with all the others of the same rank, counts for 300. A *Canasta* of seven wild cards scores 1,000 points and a *Canasta* made up of Sevens scores 1,500 points.

A meld must consist of a minimum of three cards and a maximum of seven. Depending on a partnership's cumulative score, the first meld to be laid must meet a minimum points requirement. For a minus score, this is 15 points; for a score from zero to 4,995, it is 50 points; and for one from 5,000 to 9,995, it is 90 points. If the score is between 10,000 and 14,995, the requirement is 120 points and 150 thereafter.

A mixed meld in process of construction must contain at least two natural cards and not more than three wild ones. A natural meld can be turned into a mixed one by adding wild cards to it, while, once a meld has been completed, the partnership that melded can start another meld of the same rank.

Play

Each player in turn has the option of drawing the top two cards from the stock or taking the entire discard pile. He can then start a new meld or add cards to melds his

Above: The meld at the top is acceptable, containing no more than three wild cards. The second of the two contains four, so would not be allowed.

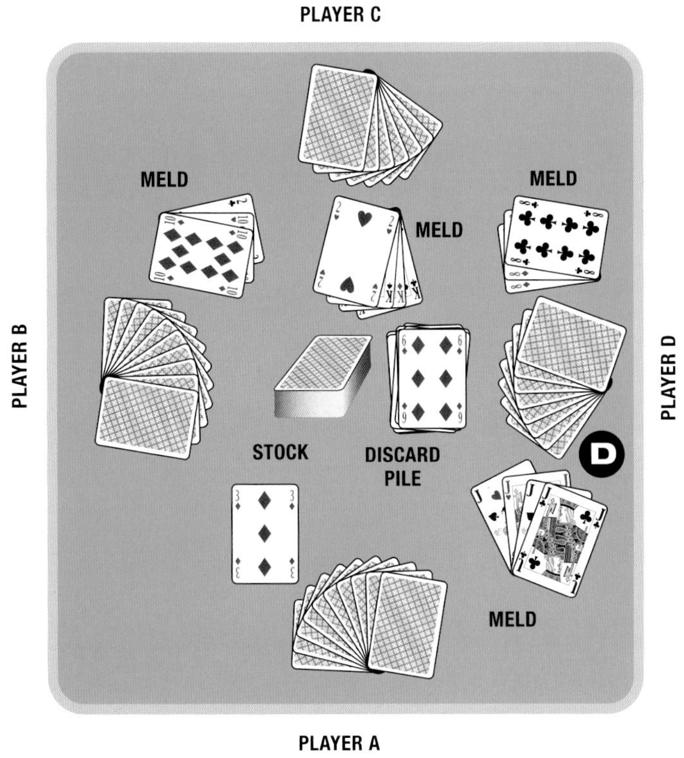

Above: An example of play in progress. Player A has laid down a red Three (and drawn a replacement from the stock) and a meld of Jacks. Player B has begun a meld in Tens, Player C one in Kings, and Player D has, so far, a natural meld in Eights.

partnership has already started constructing. To end a turn, one card from hand is discarded face up on to the discard pile. Whether the discard pile can be taken or not is subject to certain conditions. If its top card is a natural one and the player concerned holds two matching natural cards in hand, the pile may be taken, always provided that the three cards are melded immediately and that the minimum meld requirement has been satisfied previously. It can also be taken if its top card matches an existing meld of fewer than seven cards, provided that it is added immediately to that meld. A discarded wild card freezes the pile.

Twos and Jokers are wild cards. Jokers are worth 50 points each, Twos and Aces 20 points, Kings down to Eights 10, and Sevens to black Threes score five points. Red and black Threes have the same properties as in regular Canasta. Any player who is dealt or draws a red Three must place it face up on the table immediately and draw a replacement from the stock.

Each declared red Three counts for 100 bonus points (1,000 if the same partnership lays out all eight of them). Any left in hand score 100 penalties each (1,000 if all eight are held). Black Threes cannot be melded, except by a player going out. If one is discarded, it blocks the discard pile, as does a red Three if that is the first card to be turned up after the deal.

Scoring

A partnership must have completed all four types of *Canasta* before one of its players can go out by melding all of the remaining cards in hand, or all bar one of them, which is the final discard. This must not be a Seven. It is customary to ask a partner's permission to go out before doing so, in which case the player concerned must abide by that partner's decision.

The partnerships each score all the cards they have melded, plus any bonuses for *Canastas* and a further 100-point bonus for the side that went out first. From this, they deduct the value of any cards left in hand. Scores for red Threes are added or debited as appropriate.

Conclusion

If the stock is exhausted, play can continue as long as the players are willing to pick up discards. If not, it ends and the hand is scored as above, although the bonus for going out is obviously not awarded. The first partnership to score 20,000 or more points wins the game. If the scores are tied, a deciding hand is played.

PINÁCULO

This game originated in Spain and is regarded by some as a forerunner of Canasta. Jokers and Twos are wild cards. As well as scoring for groupings (melds) in the same way as Canasta, there are additional scores for specified melds.

You will need: Two standard packs plus four Jokers
Card ranking: Standard, with Twos and Jokers being wild
Players: Four, in partnerships of two
Ideal for: 14+

OBJECT

To score 1,500 points over as many deals as it takes, scoring extra for melds and conceding penalties for 'deadwood', or cards not in a meld.

THE DEAL

After the initial shuffle, the player to the dealer's left cuts the cards. Each player is then dealt 11 cards singly from the bottom half of the cut pack. The remaining cards are stacked face down to form the stock, and the top card is turned up to start the discard pile. If exactly the right number of cards (44) is cut for the deal, the cutter scores a 50-point bonus.

MELDING

A meld contains three or more cards of the same rank, or three or more in suit and sequence. The latter is an *Escalera* and must contain at least two natural (not wild) cards. In addition, Aces count as high and Threes low.

Melds are the property of the player or partnership that played them, and must be kept separate. No two melds may be combined, even if their ranks match or such a combination will complete a sequence.

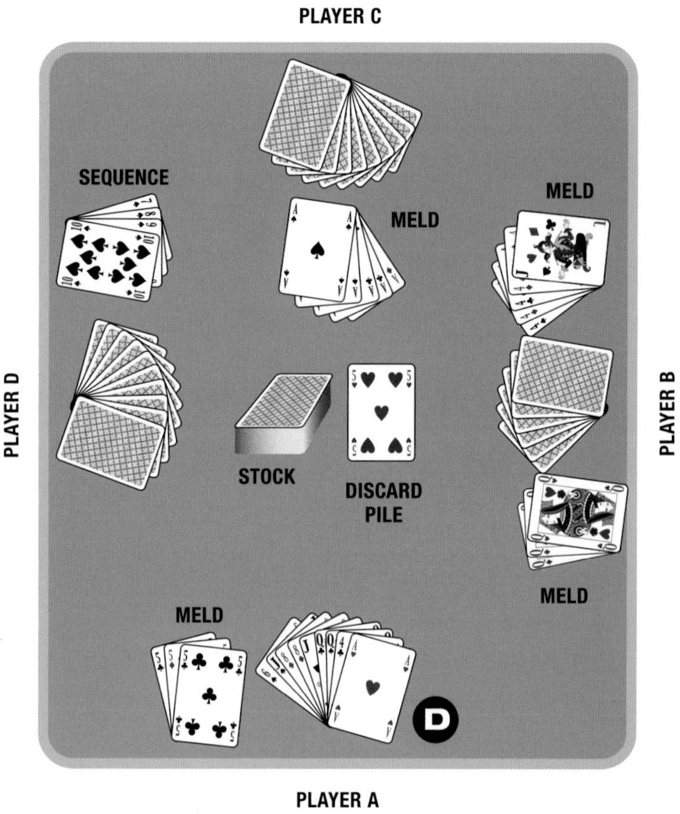

Above: Player A can play the J♠ and 6♠ on to Player D's sequence, the A♥ on to Player C's meld and the 4♣ and Q♣ on to Player B's melds. But first, he must decide whether to pick up the 5♥, together with the rest of the discard pile, adding the Five to his existing meld, or to pick up from the stock.

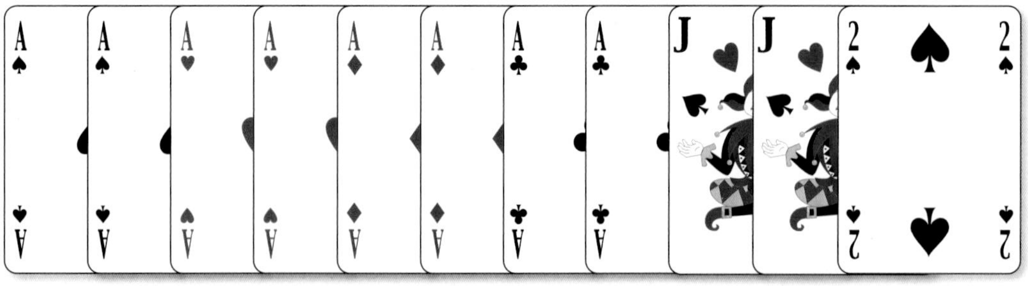

Left: The highest-scoring meld in Pináculo, 11 of a kind, is called a *Pinnacle* and scores either 3,000 points or 1,500 points, depending on whether it was constructed gradually or not.

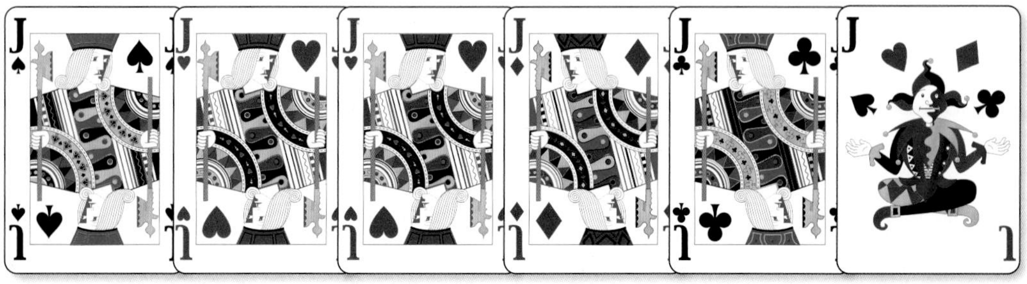

Left: The lowest-scoring meld in Pináculo is five court cards and a wild card, which scores 120 points.

Play

The player to the right of the dealer leads and play proceeds in an anti-clockwise direction. Each player in turn draws a card from the stock or takes the whole discard pile. The player then goes on to start a meld or to lay off cards to a meld that has already been started by the partnership. At the end of each turn, a card is discarded face up to the discard pile.

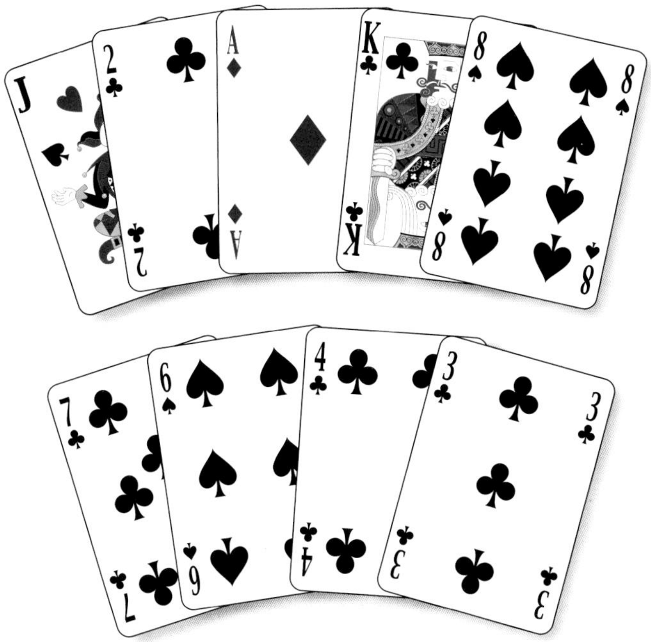

Above: The penalty points for being left with these two sets of cards contrast sharply. In the first set, the Joker would count for 30 points, the Two for 20, the Ace for 15, and the King and Eight for 10 each, making a total of 85. In the second, each card counts for just five points, making a total of 20.

If a player is holding a natural card that is being represented by a wild card at either end of an incomplete *Escalera,* he may substitute a natural card for the wild one. The wild card is not taken into his hand, but is placed sideways at one end of the *Escalera* as a reminder to score it at the end of play. There is an added twist. A partnership or player with 750 points is said to be *barbelé* (French for caught in the barbed wire). This means that the next meld they lay must be worth at least 70 points. Any meld lower than this must be withdrawn and the offending partnership has to concede a 50-point penalty.

Scoring

Players score positively for cards in melds but lose points for cards left in hand at the end of the game. Jokers score 30 points either way, Twos 20, Aces 15, Kings to Eights 10 and Sevens to Threes five points each.

Scores are calculated at the end of the game. There are points for melds and bonus or penalty points scored during play: there is a bonus of 20 for going out; going out without the use of a wild card doubles the values of all the cards in the final meld; going out 'concealed' (melding all 11 cards) similarly doubles their face values; if they are all natural cards, their values are quadrupled.

Scoring Melds

Specific melds score a premium number of points, rather than their face value, as follows:

- A *Pinnacle* (a meld of 11 of a kind, declared simultaneously) scores 3,000 points; a *Pinnacle* constructed gradually in one hand, scores 1,500 points.
- A clean *Escalera* (a sequence of 11 natural cards in suit) scores 1,000 points.
- An unclean *Escalera* (containing a Two of a matching suit) scores 800 points.
- An unclean *Escalera* (containing two Twos of a matching suit) scores 750 points.
- A dirty *Escalera* (that is, one containing one or more non-matching Twos) scores 550.
- A meld of eight natural Aces scores 1,000 points.
- A meld of eight natural Kings, Queens or Jacks scores 750 points.
- A meld of seven natural Aces scores 400 points.
- A meld of seven natural Kings, Queens or Jacks scores 300.
- A meld of six natural Aces scores 300 points.
- A meld of six natural court cards scores 200 points.
- A meld of six Aces that includes a wild card scores 180 points.
- A meld of six court cards that includes a wild card scores 120 points.

Eight natural number cards score their total face value plus 50. Each Joker replaced by a natural card during the course of play scores an extra 30 points. Each Two that was similarly replaced scores an additional 15 in an *Escalera* or twice face value in a meld of cards of the same rank.

Conclusion

When a player has one card left in hand, he must call '*Pumba!*' or be penalized 50 points. The game ends when a player goes out by melding or laying off the remaining cards in hand, with or without discarding. It also ends if the stock is exhausted.

CONTINENTAL RUMMY

There are many different versions of this attractive game, which can be played by up to 12 at a time. What makes Continental Rummy different from other games of its ilk is that no groupings (melds) can be laid until a player can go out by doing so. No cards may be laid off, nor can natural cards be exchanged for wild ones.

You will need: Two packs or more, with Jokers. Five players or fewer use a double pack plus two Jokers; six to eight use a triple pack with three Jokers; more than nine use a quadruple pack with four Jokers; gambling chips/counters

Card ranking: Aces rank high and low, the remaining cards ranking from Kings down to Threes; Twos and Jokers are wild cards

Players: Two to 12

Ideal for: 10+

OBJECT

To meld all one's cards in sequences of the same suit and in only one of the specified patterns, which are 3–3–3–3–3, 3–4–4–4 or 3–3–4–5 (see picture, below).

THE DEAL

If two packs are used, the dealer shuffles. Otherwise, the dealer and another player each shuffle parts of the pack – the dealer has the right to shuffle second, and these packs are then combined. Each player is dealt 15 cards three at a time, the remainder being placed face down to form the stock. In some versions of the game, the dealer is awarded a bonus of 15 chips for lifting off exactly the right number of cards to complete the deal. The top card of the stock is turned up to start the discard pile. Players are given an agreed number of gambling chips.

PLAY

Each player in turn draws either the top card of the stock or the turn-up from the discard pile and then discards one of his cards. Only same-suit sequences count, not matched sets. To go out means melding five three-card sequences, three four-card and one three-card sequences, or one five-card, one four-card and two three-card ones. Two or more of these sequences may be of the same suit, but a sequence must not 'go round the corner' – that is, an Ace can count as high or low, but not as both.

SCORING

If a player goes out without drawing a single card, there is a bonus of ten chips; for going out after only drawing once, seven chips; and for doing so without playing a Joker or a Two, 10 chips. Melding all 15 cards of the same suit is also worth 10 extra chips.

CONCLUSION

The game ends when a player melds 15 cards in one of the specified patterns and makes a final discard. The winner collects a chip from each of the other players for winning, two for each melded Joker and one for each Two.

Above: The sequences in Continental Rummy must conform to specified patterns, comprising: five sets of same-suit sequences of three; three sets of four and one of three; or two sets of three, together with one of four and one of five. Sequences must be of the same suit, and they must not 'go round the corner'; in other words, a sequence could not run from King through to Two.

500 Rum

This variant of Rummy dates from the 1930s. In it, points are scored for grouped (melded) cards and lost for unmelded ones. Unlike similar games, players are not limited to only taking the top discard: more cards may be drawn, but at least one must be laid off or melded straight away.

You will need: 52 cards (two packs for five or more players); no Jokers

Card ranking: Aces high or low, then Kings down to Twos

Players: Two to eight, but three is optimal

Ideal for: 10+

Above: To calculate scores, the point values of the cards each player has melded are added up and that of any cards left in hand are subtracted. The first hand here scores 40 points for the meld of four Jacks, but loses 25 points for the number cards, making a total of 15 points. The second hand scores 22 points for the same-suit sequence in Hearts, but loses 22 points for the two Queens and 2♠, meaning that no points are scored.

Object

To score points by melding cards, the game being won by the first player to score 500 or more points.

The Deal

Players draw for deal, and the person with the lowest card deals first. Each player is dealt seven cards. If only two are playing, the deal is 13 cards each, and the remaining cards form the stock. The top card of the stock is then turned face up to start the discard pile. As play progresses, this should be spread sufficiently for players to see all the cards in it.

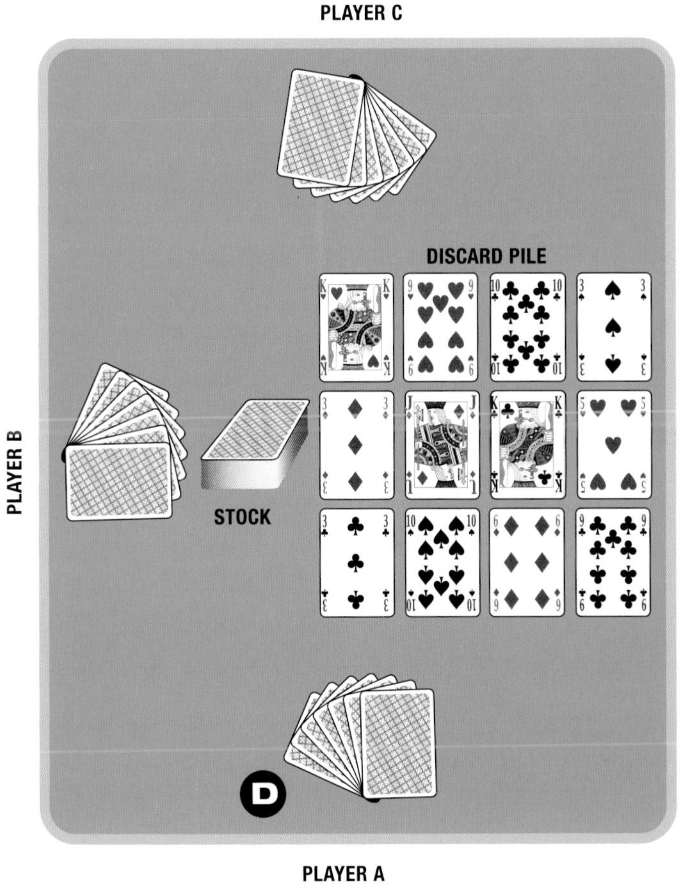

Above: The discard pile in 500 Rum should be spread out, so that all the cards in it can be seen by every player.

Play

Each player in turn draws the top card of the stock or any card from the discard pile. In the latter case, the desired card must be played immediately, and all the cards lying above it must be taken. The other cards may be melded or laid off in the same turn or added to the hand.

Melds consist of sets of three or four cards of the same rank and sequences of three or more cards of the same suit. Sequences may not 'go round the corner', in other words, a sequence of Ace, King, and Queen is valid, but King, Ace, and Two is not. Each player finishes by discarding a card.

Scoring and Conclusion

Play ends when a player goes out – that is, gets rid of all the cards in his hand, or the stock is exhausted. To calculate scores, the point values of the cards each player has melded are added up and that of any cards left in hand are subtracted. An Ace is worth 15 points if high and a single point if low. The court cards count for 10 points each and the number cards at face value.

The first player to score 500 points wins the game, the winning margin being the difference between that and the final scores of the other players.

21 | Vying Games

In this group of games, of which Poker in all its forms is unquestionably the best known and the most popular, players bet on who holds the best hand. Most games end with a 'showdown', in which the hands are compared to see which is the best. Vying games are unusual in that there is no actual card play, although players occasionally have the chance to improve their hands by discarding and drawing new cards.

As well as gambling, what these games have in common is that, to a greater or lesser extent, they all involve an element of bluff. This is why, although a player may be dealt a bad hand, he can still win by superior play. It means having the courage to bet on bad cards in the hope that the other players will lose their nerve and all drop out of play, so that you win by default. This happens when a player raises the stake and the others are not prepared to match the bet in case the stake-raising player has an unbeatable hand.

Vying can take either of two forms. In the first, the oldest type, players pay into a pot to back up the claim that they hold the best hand, or drop out, losing whatever they have staked. When only two players are left in the game, there is a showdown. The way to call this is by matching the previous player's stake. It does not have to be raised further.

In the second, newer form of vying, all the players in the game can force a showdown by matching the previous stake. This means that the player who previously raised the stake is unable to raise it further. The procedure for this can be quite complicated. In the Swedish game Chicago (not to be confused with the Bridge variant of the same name), there are two showdowns between the players before a final trick-taking phase.

Above: The film based on Fleming's *Casino Royale* features a game of no-limit Texas Hold 'em Poker between James Bond (Daniel Craig) and the chief villain.

Poker

It was in New Orleans in 1829 that the name Poker was first used for this game. Despite its somewhat insalubrious reputation, it has gone from strength to strength to become one of the world's most popular card games. What follows is an introduction to the basics, after which the most widely played Poker variations are covered individually.

Play

Any number of players from two to eight can play the game, but the experts reckon that five to eight is ideal. All players play individually and for themselves – there are no partnerships in Poker.

The game is played with a standard 52-card pack, sometimes with the addition of two Jokers, although some players prefer using two packs to speed up proceedings. If this option is preferred, the packs should be of contrasting colours.

The object is to secure the best hand and thus win the pot (which holds all the bets that players have made in any one deal). In most forms of the game, this is the top combination of five cards.

If two hands are identical card for card, the hands are tied, since suits have no relative ranks in Poker. In such a case, the pot is split between the tied players.

Scoring

Poker is traditionally a gambling game, so winnings are settled up in gambling chips, which can be exchanged for money. If you wish to play Poker as a family game, it is still best to play for stakes, as this helps to concentrate the minds of the players and reduces the temptation to indulge in unrealistic bluffs. You can keep the stakes small and use alternatives to money.

Poker Hands

From highest to lowest, poker hands rank as follows:

- Five of a Kind – Four Aces and Joker (obviously this can occur only in games where wild cards are being used).
- Royal Flush – A Straight Flush up to Ace.
- Straight Flush – A combined Straight and Flush; i.e. cards in sequence and of the same suit. A hand containing Ace, Two, Three, Four and Five is the second-highest Straight or Straight Flush, ranking between Ace, King, Queen, Jack and Ten and King, Queen, Jack, Ten and Nine.
- Four of a Kind – Four cards of the same face value (known as 'Quads').
- Full House – Three of a Kind ('Trips') and a Pair. When two players hold a Full House, the highest-ranking Trips wins.
- Flush – Five cards of the same suit. If another player holds a Flush, whoever holds the highest card wins.
- Straight – A sequence of five cards in any suit; e.g. 5♦, 6♣, 7♠, 8♥, 9♣. The highest Straight is one topped by an Ace, the lowest starts with an Ace. If two players hold a Straight, the one with the highest cards wins.
- Three of a Kind – Three cards of the same face value ('Trips'); e.g. Q♠, Q♣, Q♥.
- Two Pairs – Two sets of Pairs; e.g. 3♦, 3♥ and Q♠, Q♣. Whoever holds the highest card in the two hands (called the 'Kicker') wins, if two players hold matching Pairs of the same value.
- One Pair – Two cards of the same value; e.g. 3♦, 3♥ or Q♠, Q♣. If another player holds a Pair of the same value, then whoever holds the 'Kicker' wins.
- High card – A hand with no combination, but having within it the highest-ranking card among the hands in play.

Above: During a game, gambling chips are used to keep track of Poker winnings. Some argue it detaches players from the cash sums involved.

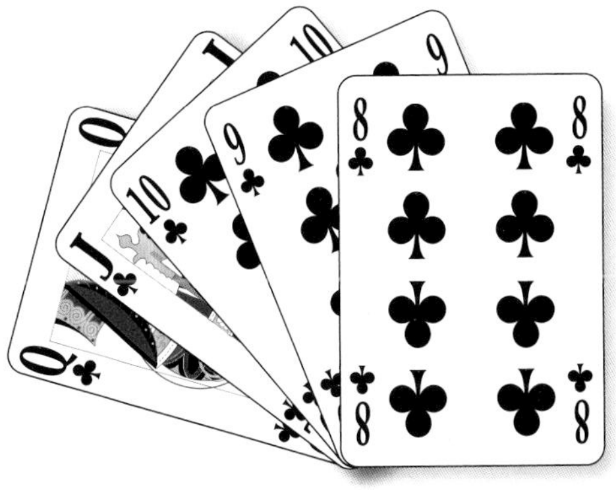

Above: A Straight Flush (five cards of the same suit) is a very strong Poker hand. If two players hold a Straight Flush, the highest card determines the winner.

HOW BETTING WORKS

The Banker

One player becomes the banker, issuing chips to each player before and during play. It is also his job to keep track of the bets.

The Ante

Depending on the game, players may have to put one or more chips into the pot to guarantee that there is something in the pot to generate competition. This is the ante.

The Stakes

To bet, players move chips from the stacks in front of them in turn towards the centre of the table, where they become part of the pot. These stakes, however, must be kept separate and not merged into a single pile, as it is essential to know exactly what each player has staked. Once a bet is made, it cannot be retracted.

Betting and Raising

There are normally two opportunities to bet – the first before the pot is opened and the second before a player opens the betting. Who is entitled to bet first varies between games, and depends on what rules are being played. It may depend, for instance, on what minimum card combination is required and on the smallest and highest amounts that are allowed as an opening bet. Regardless, the other players, starting with the player to the left of the one making the opening bet, have the chance to 'call' the bet by putting the same number of chips into the pot, or raising it.

A raise is one of the key elements of poker because it increases the cost to opponents of remaining in a hand, and also suggests that the player making one has a strong hand. Raising involves matching a previous bet and making an additional bet of at least equal value. For example, if the bet stands at 40 chips, anyone wishing to raise can expect to bet at least 80 chips – 40 to call the bet and a further 40 chips to increase the betting level.

Above: When betting, players should make their aims clear by announcing 'call' or 'raise' for example, and placing their chips immediately in front of them.

Folding or Checking

The alternative is to fold or to check. In the former case, the folding player discards his hand and is out of the betting until the next deal. As players fold, they 'muck their hand' by placing their cards face down with the other discarded cards.

By checking when it is his turn to act, a player effectively defers a decision to bet, but remains in the hand. A player may check provided that no compulsory or voluntary bets have already been made during a betting round. If an opponent subsequently makes a bet, then a player who previously checked must choose whether to fold, call or raise when the action returns to him; he no longer has the option to check at this stage. A player who checks may subsequently raise a bet that has been raised by another player. This particular practice is called 'sandbagging or 'check-raising'.

Final Bets

Betting ends if all the players check, or when all the bets have been equalized, after which play continues, or there is a showdown, the result of which is that the player with the best hand wins the pot. If all the players fold by not calling the last raise, the last raiser wins the pot without having to show his hand.

Left: A game of Texas Hold 'em is underway in Caesar's Palace casino, Las Vegas, which is marketed as 'the entertainment capital of the world'.

Wild-Card Poker

There are many different forms of Poker, but all of them can be played with one or more wild cards – that is, a card that its holder may count as any natural card missing from his hand. Their use increases the chances of making combinations, such as a Straight Flush or a Full House, and introduces an extra hand – Five of a Kind – into the game. Five of a Kind ranks the same as, or above, a Royal Flush.

The usual choices for wild cards start with Jacks, one or more of which may be added to the pack. If so, they are called 'bugs'. However, the extent of their wildness is limited by the rules. A Joker can stand for an Ace, a card of any suit for making a Flush, or a card of any rank or suit for making a Straight or Straight Flush.

Deuces and One-eyed Jacks

Twos are often played wild, especially in Deuces Wild, which is a popular form of Draw Poker. The J♠ and the J♥ – these are called One-eyed Jacks, because only one eye shows – are sometimes played as wild cards as well.

Which wild cards to use is down to prior agreement between the players. According to convention, if one wild card is agreed, it is a Joker and, for two, the One-eyed Jacks. For four, any four cards of a given rank are nominated and, for eight, any two ranks.

Variable Wild Cards

The more wild cards there are, the higher the winning hands. The game becomes even more complicated if variable wild cards are introduced.

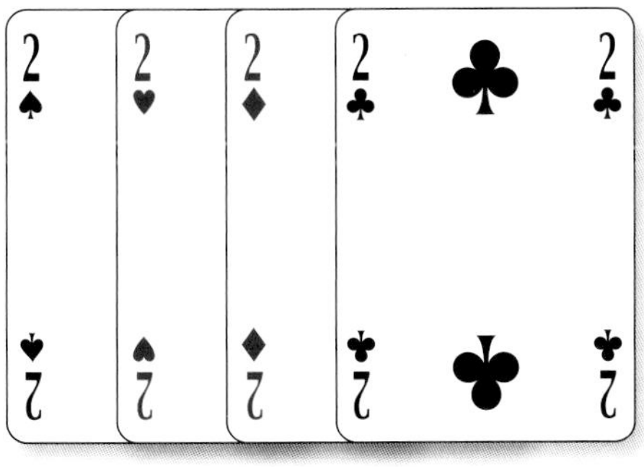

Left: Twos are often used as wild cards in Poker, especially in Deuces Wild, a popular form of Draw Poker.

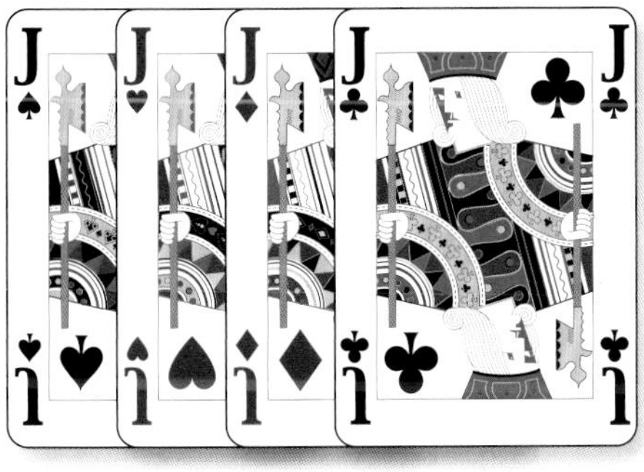

Left: When used as wild cards in Poker, Jacks are called 'bugs'. The J♠ and J♥ are called One-Eyed Jacks, because only one eye shows.

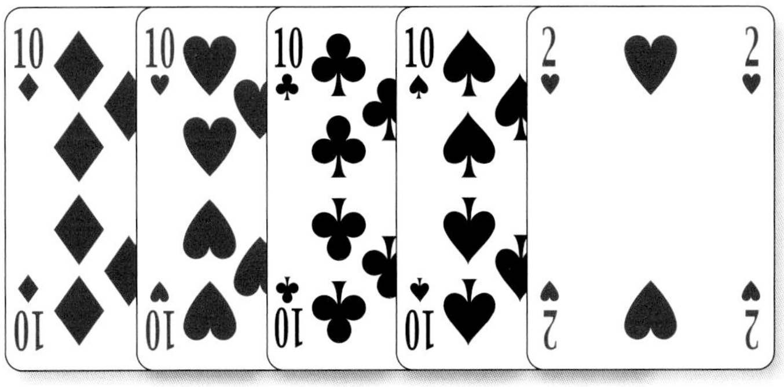

Above: If you are playing wild-card games, then an additional hand of Five of a Kind can come into play, which ranks the same as, or above, a Royal Flush and above a Straight Flush. Here, with Twos as wild cards, this hand counts as Five of a Kind.

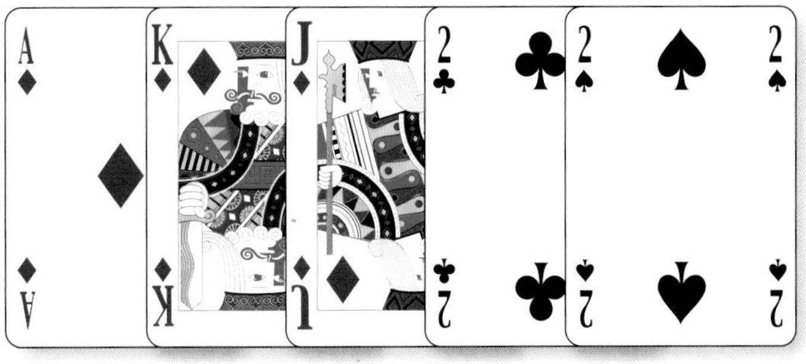

Above: It is wise to be clear on house rules when using wild cards. Here, for example, it ought to be decided whether a Royal Flush of an A♦, K♦ and J♦, plus any pair of Twos, substituting for the Q♦ and 10♦, count as the equal of a 'natural' Royal Flush or if it would be inferior to it.

In Five-Card Stud Poker, each player's hole card, that is the lowest card to be dealt face down, can be designated wild by its holder. In Seven-Card Stud, two cards are dealt face down and one face up. In Draw Poker, the hole card is the lowest card in a player's hand. If such a card is designated as wild, it means that every card of the same rank in its holder's hand is wild as well. It should be noted, though, that just because a card is wild in one player's hand, this does not make the same rank of card wild in the hands of other players.

Although wild cards do not alter the relative ranking of the hands, they do introduce a new one. This is Five of a Kind. In the event of two hands tying, the one with fewer wild cards in it wins. The most basic wild-card variant is Deuces Wild.

Draw Poker

Otherwise known as Five-Card Draw, this is the original form of the game. After the cards are dealt face down, players may decide to 'stand pat' or exchange cards. If the latter, they must discard the cards in hand before being dealt replacements.

You will need: Standard, sometimes with the addition of two Jokers (some players prefer using two packs to speed up proceedings, in which case they should be of contrasting colours); gambling chips/counters

Card ranking: See box opposite

Players: Two to eight (experts consider five to eight is ideal)

Ideal for: 14+

Object

The object is to secure the best hand and thus win the pot (which holds all the bets that players have made in any one deal).

Buying In and The Ante

Before play starts, players must buy in to the game by buying an agreed number of chips from the banker. There should be at least 200 chips on hand.

White chips are the lowest, red chips are worth five whites and blue chips are worth four or five red chips. Each player antes (puts in) a chip to start the pot, or the dealer antes chips on his behalf.

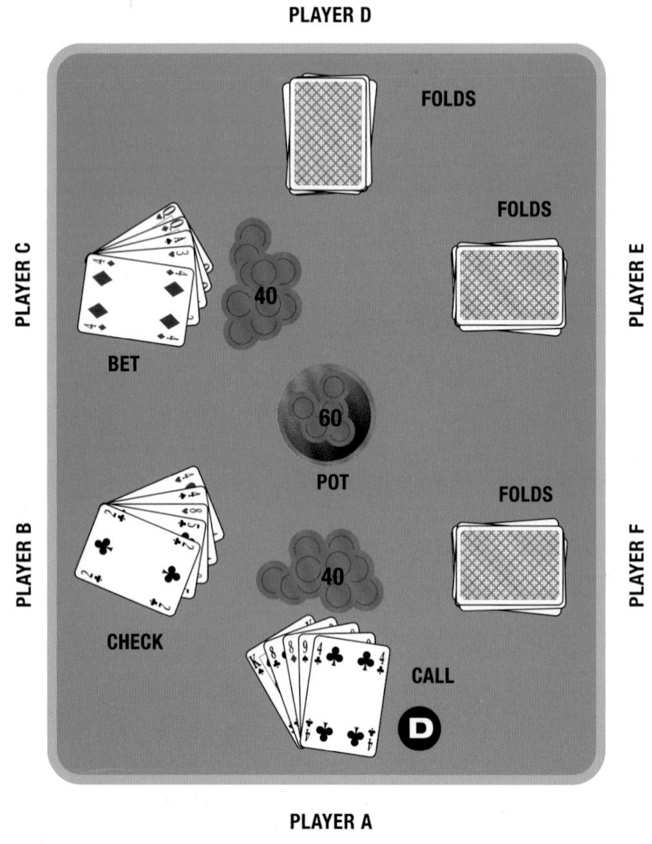

Above: After the deal, the player to the dealer's left (Player B) checks, since he does not hold a pair of Jacks. The option passes to Player C, who opens with a bet of 40 chips on the basis of his pair of Queens. Players D, E and F all fold, but Player A calls the bet.

The Deal

Once everyon has added an ante to the pot, players receive five cards, dealt face down singly clockwise around the table. Each player can discard up to three cards, after which the dealer deals the required number of replacements. Each player gets the chance to deal in turn.

Play

First Betting Round

Starting with the player to the dealer's left, each player has a chance to open the betting. A player must be holding a pair of Jacks or better to do this, a higher pair or a higher card combination. He must also be prepared to prove that he is entitled to open. The alternatives are to pass or to fold. If all players pass, the hands are thrown in and the pot is carried forward to the next deal.

Drawing

After the betting round is over, each player has the option of 'standing pat', that is, playing with the cards as dealt, or exchanging up to three cards. A player with an Ace may exchange four cards, provided that the Ace is first shown to the other players. The replacements are dealt from the top of the pack.

The cards are discarded face down, the player making the exchange announcing how many cards are being discarded. The dealer, who is always the last to draw, deals the requisite number of replacements immediately.

Second Betting Round

A second betting round follows, the first to speak this time being the player who initially opened the pot. Each player in turn may now check (which is indicated by knocking on the table) or bet. If all players check, the player who opened the pot originally must start the proceedings again. The other options are to call (that is, to match the previous stake), to raise or to fold.

Play ends when there are calls for a showdown, or if a time limit that has been agreed in advance is reached. If a player runs out of chips, he must buy more from the banker, or drop out. In the latter case, he forfeits any claim to the pot. The banker is nominated to keep the stock of chips and to record how many have been issued to each player, or how much each player has paid for his chips. A showdown may be called only after a raise.

Conclusion

In a showdown, the player with the best hand wins the pot. If all the other players have folded, however, the last player to have raised will automatically win without having to show his hand.

Variants

Hi-Low Draw is probably the most common variant that can be played, where the holder of the highest and the lowest hands split the pot. In Lowball, which is popular in the western USA, the lowest hand wins. Aces are always low, so that two is the lowest possible Pair, while Straights and Flushes do not count. The lowest possible hand, known as a 'wheel' or a 'bicycle', consists of a Five, Four, Three, Two and an Ace, regardless of suits. In Double Draw, there is a second exchange of cards after the first betting round and then a further betting round.

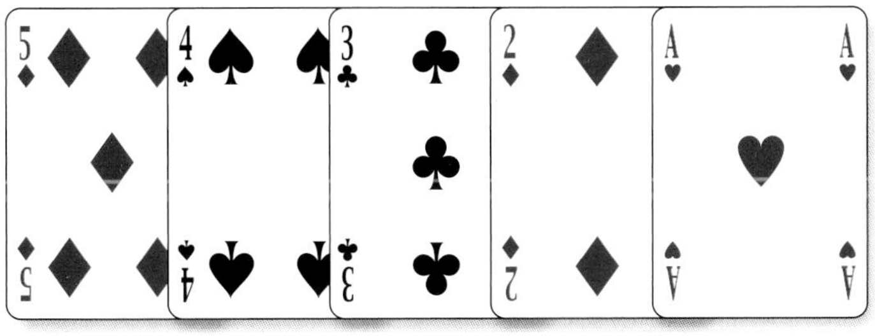

Above: In Lowball the lowest possible hand, known as a 'wheel' or a 'bicycle', consists of a Five, Four, Three, Two and an Ace, regardless of what the suit is.

Special Hands

As well as introducing variants like the ones detailed above, many players also favour allowing so-called special hands into the game in addition to the standard ones. A Skip Straight, also known as a Dutch Straight, for instance, consists of five cards in alternate sequence, such as Queen, Ten, Eight, Six and Four. It beats Three of a Kind, but loses to a conventional Straight.

Poker Hands

From highest to lowest, poker hands rank as follows:

- Five of a Kind – Four Aces and Joker (obviously this can occur only in games where wild cards are being used).
- Royal Flush – A Straight Flush up to Ace.
- Straight Flush – A combined Straight and Flush; i.e. cards in sequence and of the same suit. A hand containing Ace, Two, Three, Four and Five is the second-highest Straight or Straight Flush, ranking between Ace, King, Queen, Jack and Ten and King, Queen, Jack, Ten and Nine.
- Four of a Kind – Four cards of the same face value (known as 'Quads').
- Full House – Three of a Kind ('Trips') and a Pair. When two players hold a Full House, the highest-ranking Trips wins.
- Flush – Five cards of the same suit. If another player holds a Flush, whoever holds the highest card wins.
- Straight – A sequence of five cards in any suit; e.g. 5♦, 6♣, 7♠, 8♥, 9♣. The highest Straight is one topped by an Ace, the lowest starts with an Ace. If two players hold a Straight, the one with the highest cards wins.
- Three of a Kind – Three cards of the same face value ('Trips'); e.g. Q♠, Q♣, Q♥.
- Two Pairs – Two sets of Pairs; e.g. 3♦, 3♥ and Q♠, Q♣. Whoever holds the highest card in the two hands (called the 'Kicker') wins, if two players hold matching Pairs of the same value.
- One Pair – Two cards of the same value; e.g. 3♦, 3♥ or Q♠, Q♣. If another player holds a Pair of the same value, then whoever holds the 'Kicker' wins.
- High card – A hand with no combination, but having within it the highest-ranking card among the hands in play.

A Round-the-Corner Straight is a sequence such as Three, Two, Ace, King and Queen, while a Bobtail is a four-card Flush or Straight with both ends open. Thus, Eight, Seven, Six and Five is a valid Bobtail, but Ace, King, Queen and Jack is not because only a single card, a Ten, can complete the sequence. A Bobtail beats a Pair, but loses to Two Pairs. If Bobtails are allowed, the player opening the pot can count holding one as the necessary qualification to do so. A Zebra is five cards that alternate in colour when put in numerical order.

Above: An example of a Round-the-Corner Straight.

Five-Card Stud

After Draw Poker, Five-Card Stud is the another classic form of the game with which non-poker players are most likely to be familiar. It perceived benefits over the original draw or 'closed' form of the game, derives from the fact that players receive most of their cards face up, giving them more information upon which to make betting decisions.

You will need: 52 cards; Jokers optional; gambling chips/counters

Card ranking: See box below

Players: Any number up to eight

Ideal for: 14+

Object

To create the best-ranking hand, or bluff opponents into believing you have achieved this, so that at the showdown you take the pot.

The Deal

Players cut the pack to decide who deals, the role of dealer subsequently rotating on a clockwise basis. Participants in the game receive five cards during the course of each deal, hence the name given to this particular variety of the game. The dealer antes as many chips as there are players to the pot and then deals each player one card face down and another face up. The former is known as the hole card. Since the remaining cards to be dealt during the hand will also be face up, it is cricual that players keep their hole cards obscured from opponents.

Poker Hands

From highest to lowest, poker hands rank as follows:

- Five of a Kind – Four Aces and Joker (obviously this can occur only in games where wild cards are being used).
- Royal Flush – A Straight Flush up to Ace.
- Straight Flush – A combined Straight and Flush; i.e. cards in sequence and of the same suit. A hand containing Ace, Two, Three, Four and Five is the second-highest Straight or Straight Flush, ranking between Ace, King, Queen, Jack and Ten and King, Queen, Jack, Ten and Nine.
- Four of a Kind – Four cards of the same face value (known as 'Quads').
- Full House – Three of a Kind ('Trips') and a Pair. When two players hold a Full House, the highest-ranking Trips wins.
- Flush – Five cards of the same suit. If another player holds a Flush, whoever holds the highest card wins.
- Straight – A sequence of five cards in any suit; e.g. 5♦, 6♣, 7♠, 8♥, 9♣. The highest Straight is one topped by an Ace, the lowest starts with an Ace. If two players hold a Straight, the one with the highest cards wins.
- Three of a Kind – Three cards of the same face value ('Trips'); e.g. Q♠, Q♣, Q♥.
- Two Pairs – Two sets of Pairs; e.g. 3♦, 3♥ and Q♠, Q♣. Whoever holds the highest card in the two hands (the 'Kicker') wins, if two players hold matching Pairs of the same value.
- One Pair – Two cards of the same value; e.g. 3♦, 3♥ or Q♠, Q♣. If another player holds a Pair of the same value, then whoever holds the 'Kicker' wins.
- High card – A hand with no combination, but having within it the highest-ranking card among the hands in play.

Play

Having examined their hidden card, each player places it face down and half covered by the face-up card. The player showing the highest face-up card, known as the 'door card', has to make the compulsory open bet. Should two or more players hold a door card of the same rank, then the opening bet is made by the player nearest to the dealer's left.

Betting follows the standard form until all bets have been equalized (see the introduction to Poker), when a second face-up card is dealt, followed by a third and then by a fourth. After each face-up card is dealt, there is another round of betting, the opening bet being made by the player showing the highest card combination, or, if there are no combinations, the highest card or cards. It is the dealer's job to confirm this by announcing, for instance, 'First King bets' or 'Pair of Sixes bets'. After the third and fourth face-ups have been dealt, the dealer should indicate which of the players still contesting the pot might be holding a possible Straight or Flush. If the cards or combinations are equal, then the player nearest to the dealer's left makes the opening bet.

Conclusion

At the end of the final betting round, each player left in the game has one card face down and four cards face up. There is now a showdown, in which players turn up their hole cards and the best hand wins. Otherwise, the game ends when all but one player have folded; that player takes the contents of the pot.

Seven-Card Stud

This variant is played in much the same way as Five-Card Stud, except players receive seven cards and there are five betting rounds before the showdown.

You will need: 52 cards; Jokers optional; gambling chips/counters
Card ranking: See box on page 224
Players: Any number up to eight
Ideal for: 14+

Object

To create the best-ranking hand, or bluff opponents into believing you have achieved this, in order to win the pot.

The Deal

Players cut the pack to decide who deals; the role of dealer then rotates on a clockwise basis. Players receive seven cards during the course of each deal, but only the five cards they select from these determine the pot's winner. The dealer antes as many chips as there are players to the pot and then deals each player two cards face down and another face up. The former are known as the hole cards. Further cards are dealt at intervals during the game, as explained in the next section.

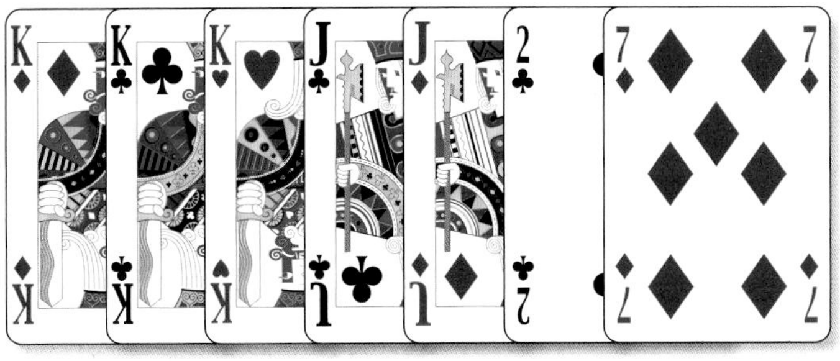

Above: In Seven-Card Stud, players use five cards of the seven ultimately available to make a viable poker hand. Here, the player would make a Full House of Kings over Jacks, making the 2♣ and 7♦ redundant.

Play and Conclusion

The player with the lowest turn-up opens the betting. If there is a tie, the lowest card is determined by suit, the ranks, from high to low, being Spades, Hearts, Diamonds and Clubs. Each player is now dealt another turn-up. This card is called Fourth Street. A further round of betting follows, and the player whose exposed cards have the highest Poker value either bets or checks first. The alternative is to fold. The same process continues with two more face-up cards, Fifth Street and Sixth Street, being dealt, each deal being followed by another round of betting. The final card is dealt face down, so its value can be known only to the player holding it.

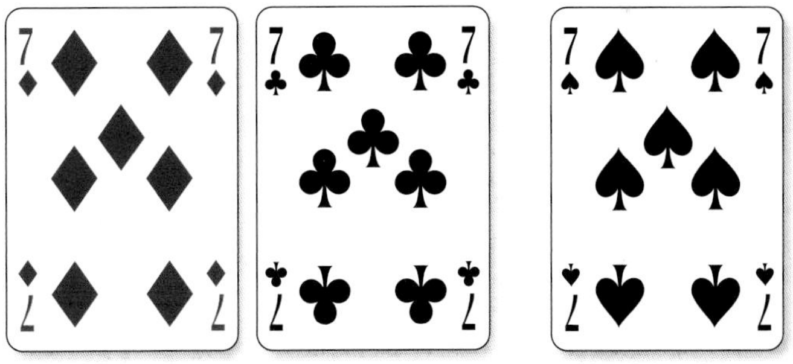

HOLE CARDS

TURN-UP CARD

Above: Being dealt Three of a Kind after the deal, in the form of two hole cards (dealt face down) along with a face-up card, presents a huge advantage. This hand is highly likely to win the pot even if further cards do not improve on it.

PLAYER A

PLAYER B

PLAYER C

PLAYER D

Above: In Seven-Card Stud, each player plays the best hand that he can make with the seven cards available. Player A has an Eight-high Straight, Player B has Three of a Kind, Player C an Ace-high Flush. Player D has the best hand, with a Full House.

A player who folds at any stage of the game must turn all of his cards face down immediately. If there is more than one player still in the game once the last betting round has been completed, all the remaining players turn up their hole cards and select five out of the seven cards as their hands. The other two cards must be discarded separately. They cannot be reclaimed. At the conclusion of each hand, known as the showdown, the highest hand wins the pot. If two hands are valued identically, the pot is split between those players.

Variants

While purists prefer to play without wild cards, others argue that their inclusion adds excitement. In Seven-Card Stud, each player's lowest hole card can be wild, but only in its holder's hand. Other variations include Baseball and Football, Seven-Card Flip, and Heinz.

Texas Hold 'em

Sometimes called Hold 'em, this fast-moving high-stakes game is the game of choice across North America, where it features in many top tournaments, such as the World Series of Poker and the World Poker Tour, both held annually in Las Vegas. There are four variants of the game, which are distinguishable by their betting limits.

You will need: Standard, sometimes with the addition of two Jokers (some players prefer using two packs to speed up proceedings, in which case they should be of contrasting colours); gambling chips/counters

Card ranking: See box below

Players: Two to eight (experts consider five to eight is ideal)

Ideal for: 14+

Object

To secure the best hand, or bluff opponents into believing you have achieved this, in order to win the pot (which holds all the bets that players have made in any one deal).

The Deal and Play

Each player receives two cards dealt face down. These are the hole or pocket cards. A first round of betting follows – this is referred to as the pre-flop – started by the player to the left of the two players who 'posted the blind'. These are the two players seated to the left of the dealer, who put a predetermined number of chips into the pot to get the game started. The player to the left of the dealer places a mandatory bet, known as the 'small blind', and the player to his left the 'big blind'. Typically, the 'big blind' is double the amount of the 'small blind'. As the deal moves clockwise around the table, each player faces the prospect of making these forced bets.

Much like most other Poker games, players can call, raise (match the previous bet and increase it) or fold. The amount players can bet varies, depending on what form of the game is being played. In fixed-limit games, this is predetermined, and the number of times each player can bet is limited to four. No limit is just what its name implies, while, in a spread-limit game, players have to bet within a specified range of amounts. In pot limit, a player can bet what is in the pot.

Poker Hands

From highest to lowest, poker hands rank as follows:

- Five of a Kind – Four Aces and Joker (obviously this can occur only in games where wild cards are being used).
- Royal Flush – A Straight Flush up to Ace.
- Straight Flush – A combined Straight and Flush; i.e. cards in sequence and of the same suit. A hand containing Ace, Two, Three, Four and Five is the second-highest Straight or Straight Flush, ranking between Ace, King, Queen, Jack and Ten and King, Queen, Jack, Ten and Nine.
- Four of a Kind – Four cards of the same face value (known as 'Quads').
- Full House – Three of a Kind ('Trips') and a Pair. When two players hold a Full House, the highest-ranking Trips wins.
- Flush – Five cards of the same suit. If another player holds a Flush, whoever holds the highest card wins.
- Straight – A sequence of five cards in any suit; e.g. 5♦, 6♣, 7♠, 8♥, 9♣. The highest Straight is one topped by an Ace, the lowest starts with an Ace. If two players hold a Straight, the one with the highest cards wins.
- Three of a Kind – Three cards of the same face value ('Trips'); e.g.Q♠, Q♣, Q♥.
- Two Pairs – Two sets of Pairs; e.g. 3♦, 3♥ and Q♠, Q♣. Whoever holds the highest card in the two hands (called the 'Kicker') wins, if two players hold matching Pairs of the same value.
- One Pair – Two cards of the same value; e.g. 3♦, 3♥ or Q♠, Q♣. If another player holds a Pair of the same value, then whoever holds the 'Kicker' wins.
- High card – A hand with no combination, but having within it the highest-ranking card among the hands in play.

The Flop

After the initial betting round ends, the dealer discards the top card of the pack. This discard is called a burn card and the reason for discarding it is to prevent cheating. The dealer then flips the next three cards face up on the table. These cards are the flop. They, together with the other flop cards that are dealt later, are communal property, and can be used by any of the players to make up a winning hand.

Bluffing

At this stage of the game, there are several things to take into consideration. The first is the number of players. The more there are, the greater the chances that someone else is holding a strong hand and the more the likelihood of another player's hand fitting the flop.

As far as individual hands are concerned, the best hand to hold is a Pair of Aces, while it also helps if the cards that are held are sequential in rank. The capacity of the flop to offer potential to several players generates many opportunities to practise the art of bluffing, but knowing the right time to bluff is particularly important. A bluff works best when there are only a few players left in the game. It is always a mistake to bluff when other players are expecting it, or when it is against a dangerous flop, especially one containing an Ace. If this is the case, it is more than likely that another player will be holding a Pair of Aces.

Further Betting Rounds – the Endgame

Another round of betting follows, this time started by the player to the left of the dealer. After this, the dealer burns another card and flips a fourth card onto the table. This is the turn card. It is added to the flop. A third betting round ensues, in which the amount that can be bet doubles, after which the dealer burns a card and flips a final turn-up. This is called the river and it is also added to the flop. After this, there is a final round of betting.

Conclusion

All the players still in the game reveal their hands, starting with the player to the left of the last one to call. Players are allowed to use both of their hole cards and three of the cards on the table (these are the board cards); one of their hole cards and four board cards; or neither of their hole cards but all of the board cards, which is termed 'playing the board'. If the hands are tied, the player with the highest-ranking card wins. If this does not produce a result or if no one can improve on the five-card flop, the pot is divided equally between the players who are left.

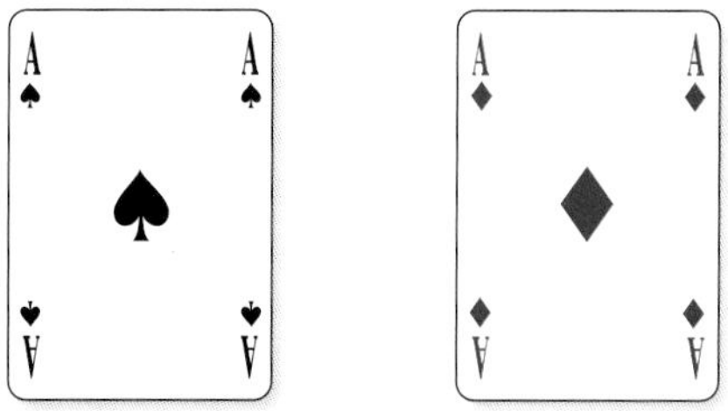

Right: A pair of Aces as pocket or hole cards, sometimes referred to as 'pocket rockets' is the strongest starting hand available in Texas Hold 'em.

Above and right: The pair of Aces (top) matched with these five board cards makes a Full House of Aces over Sevens. However, a player may be holding a pair of Sevens, giving him Four of a Kind, which beats Full House.

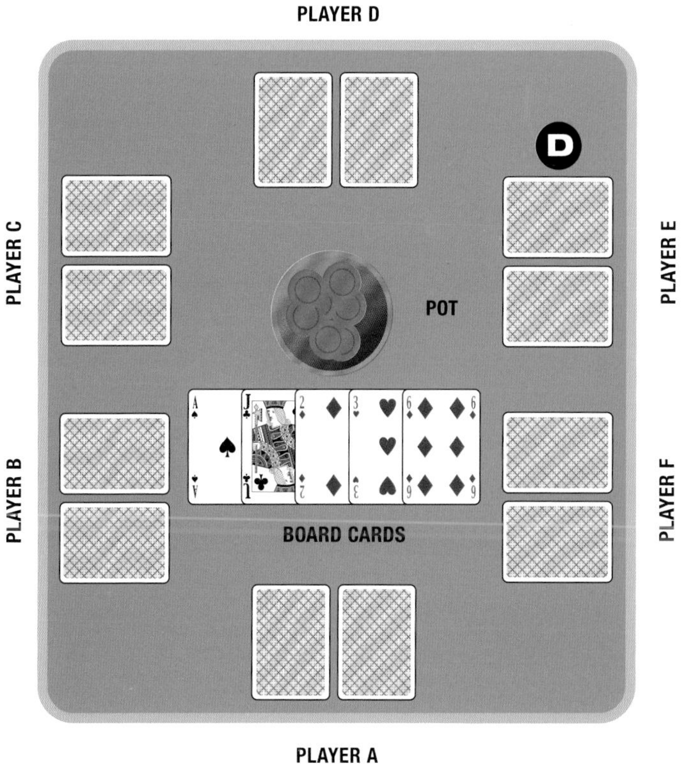

Above: Recognizing the best hand available is a fundamental part of Hold 'em strategy. Here, with all five board cards revealed, after the final turn up of the river card, a player holding 4, 5 as hole cards could bet knowing that the hand was unbeatable.

Left: Australian professional poker player Joe Hecham with his US$7.5 million winnings after claiming the World Series of Poker champion title in 2005. The top 12 players competing in this tournament, which takes place annually in Las Vegas, all become millionaires.

Pai Gow Poker

This enjoyable game is a cross between the Chinese domino game Pai Gow, and Poker, which has become popular in American casinos. A single Joker is used as a wild card, and can represent an Ace or any other card to complete a Straight, Flush or Straight Flush.

You will need: 52 cards; one Joker; gambling chips/counters
Card ranking: See box below
Players: Two to seven
Ideal for: 14+

Left: Players are dealt seven cards in Pai Gow Poker, such as here. Each player must split their cards into two hands, one of five cards and the other of two. The five-card hand must rank higher than the two-card one. Here, the cards could be divided into 7♣, 7♦ and 2♥, 5♥, Q♠, K♦, K♠, the pair of Kings in the five-card hand ranked higher than the pair of Sevens.

Object

To secure the best possible two hands from the seven cards that are dealt, which will beat those of the dealer when his turn comes to play.

The Deal

The dealer plays against the others on each deal. Before the deal, players each 'ante' (put in) the same stake to the pot and agree how the bank is to rotate between them. Each player should be given the chance to deal the same number of times during a session. The players are each then dealt seven cards face down, which the players have to split into two hands, one of two cards and the other of five cards.

The five-card hand must rank higher than the two-card one. If, for instance, the two-card hand was a Pair of Aces, then the corresponding five-card hand must be two Pairs or better. The Joker may replace an Ace or whatever card is needed to complete a Straight, a Flush or a Straight Flush, but nothing else. At this stage of the game, the dealer's cards remain untouched.

Poker Hands

From highest to lowest, poker hands rank as follows:

- Five of a Kind – Four Aces and Joker (obviously this can occur only in games where wild cards are being used).
- Royal Flush – A Straight Flush up to Ace.
- Straight Flush – A combined Straight and Flush; i.e. cards in sequence and of the same suit. A hand containing Ace, Two, Three, Four and Five is the second-highest Straight or Straight Flush, ranking between Ace, King, Queen, Jack and Ten and King, Queen, Jack, Ten and Nine.
- Four of a Kind – Four cards of the same face value (known as 'Quads').
- Full House – Three of a Kind ('Trips') and a Pair. When two players hold a Full House, the highest-ranking Trips wins.
- Flush – Five cards of the same suit. If another player holds a Flush, whoever holds the highest card wins.
- Straight – A sequence of five cards in any suit; e.g. 5♦, 6♣, 7♠, 8♥, 9♣. The highest Straight is one topped by an Ace, the lowest starts with an Ace. If two players hold a Straight, the one with the highest cards wins.
- Three of a Kind – Three cards of the same face value ('Trips'); e.g. Q♠, Q♣, Q♥.
- Two Pairs – Two sets of Pairs; e.g. 3♦, 3♥ and Q♠, Q♣. Whoever holds the highest card in the two hands (called the 'Kicker') wins, if two players hold matching Pairs of the same value.
- One Pair – Two cards of the same value; e.g. 3♦, 3♥ or Q♠, Q♣. If another player holds a Pair of the same value, then whoever holds the 'Kicker' wins.
- High card – A hand with no combination, but having within it the highest-ranking card among the hands in play.

Play

Players place their two hands face down, after which the dealer's seven cards are turned up and formed into two hands. All the players then expose their cards.

Conclusion

The winner and loser are determined by comparing the player's and dealer's hands. If a player wins both of these hands, the dealer pays out the amount staked by that player, and vice versa if the dealer's hands are better.

If the dealer wins one hand, but a player wins the other, it is deemed a 'push' and no stakes change hands. If either hand is tied, the dealer wins the hand.

Freak-Hand Poker

This form of Poker is aptly named, since, as well as the standard hands, it features others made up of unorthodox card combinations. Freak hands were originally devised to liven up games like Draw Poker, where, without them, the majority of hands were won on Two Pairs. Their use is now mostly confined to Lowball Poker.

Freak hands first made their appearance towards the end of the 19th century, when the Blaze – a five-card hand containing five picture cards other than Four of a Kind – became widely recognized, along with the Blaze Full, a Full House in picture cards.

Above: A hand of five picture cards is a Blaze. It often ranks below Four of a Kind, but above a Full House.

Above: A Full House composed of picture cards is known as a Blaze Full.

Other examples include a Dutch Straight (Alternate Straight) – which is a sequence of every other card, such as Two, Four, Six, Eight and Ten – Kilters and Skeets. A Kilter is a hand starting with an Ace, followed by cards of alternate value down to Nine, and a Skeet contains a Two, Five, Nine, either a Three or a Four, and a Six, Seven or Eight. The Eight is the Skeet. A Skeet Flush is when all the cards are of the same suit.

A Big Dog consists of cards ranking from Ace down to Nine with no Pair, while a Little Dog, which often ranks below it but above a Straight, consists of a Two to a Seven.

Above: A Little Dog, which can rank above a Straight.

Above: A Big Dog, which always ranks above Little Dog.

Above: A Little Tiger, which can rank above a Big Dog.

Above: A Big Tiger, which often ranks just below a Flush.

Little Tiger is a hand consisting of cards from Three up to Nine with no Pair, while Big Tiger is Eight to King. It ranks just below a Flush. A Bobtail Flush consists of four cards of the same suit and a Bobtail Straight one of four cards in consecutive order, both of which are open ended. A Flush House consists of three cards of one suit and two of another. The ranking of these combinations is often based on which of these hands are included in the game.

Above: A Bobtail Flush.

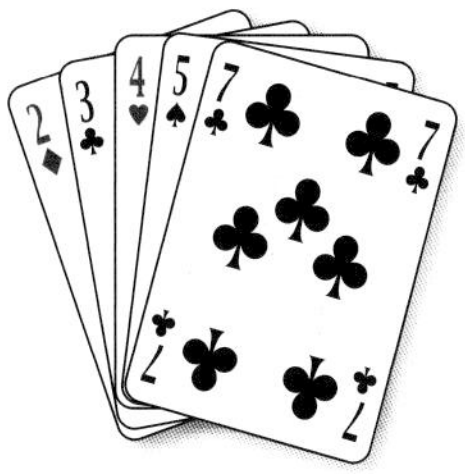

Above: A Bobtail Straight.

Left: A Flush House can rank between a Bobtail Straight and Bobtail Flush.

Freak Draws

As well as freak hands, Poker also sometimes features freak draws, although these are down to luck and usually greatly defy probability. In Lowball, drawing three cards and making a Six or better is a freak draw.

In Draw Poker, if a player draws three cards to two cards of the same suit to make a Flush, this, too, is regarded as a freak. The phenomenon is sometimes called a Gardena miracle, after the city of Gardena, in southern California, which was once the poker-playing capital of the USA.

Dealer's Choice Games

In Poker, dealer's choice means exactly what it says. The player dealing selects the game to be played on his particular deal, as opposed to playing one game exclusively for the entire playing session. In friendly games, the choice can be pretty well unlimited, but casinos usually restrict it to a small number of possibilities. Some, like Fifty-Two and Forty-Two, are variants of Draw Poker, where four or five cards are dealt face down, while others, such as Razz and Chicago, are played in the same way as Seven-Card Stud, where cards are dealt, face up and face down, at intervals throughout the game.

Draw Games

Fifty-Two

Each player is dealt five face-down cards, known as hole cards, with two more cards being placed face down on the table. After a round of betting, one of these cards is turned face up, followed by the other one after a second betting round. Players may draw up to three cards, but, to make their hands, they must use all their hole cards, or three hole cards and both board cards (the exposed cards dealt to the table). A combination of four hole cards and a single board card is against the rules. It is not recommended for more than seven players since you will often run out of cards.

Forty-Two

The key differences between this game and Fifty-Two are that only four hole cards are dealt, players may draw only up to two cards and any five cards can be used to make up their hands. Note that in both games, the dealer enjoys a significant advantage, since he knows how many cards other players have drawn before having to make a draw.

Stud Games

Razz and Chicago

In high-card Poker, the highest hand wins; in low-card Poker, the lowest one. Razz is played for low only. Chicago, on the other hand, can be played either high or low. In High Chicago, the holder of the highest Spade as a hole (face-down) card splits the pot with the holder of the highest hand. In Low Chicago, it is the holder of the lowest Spade who splits the pot. If no player has a Spade as a hole card, the highest hand wins the pot outright.

No Peek Stud

Here, each player is dealt seven cards, but no player is allowed to look at them. Instead, the cards must be placed face down in a pile. The player to the dealer's left turns over a card, after which there is a round of betting. The next player then turns over cards until he has the higher hand. Another betting round follows. The process continues round the table until all the players run out of cards, when the pot goes to the highest hand.

Below: Playing High Chicago, Player A has a seemingly stronger hand, with a Full House of Queens over Jacks, but Player B has the A♠ as a hole card, which means that he can claim half the pot.

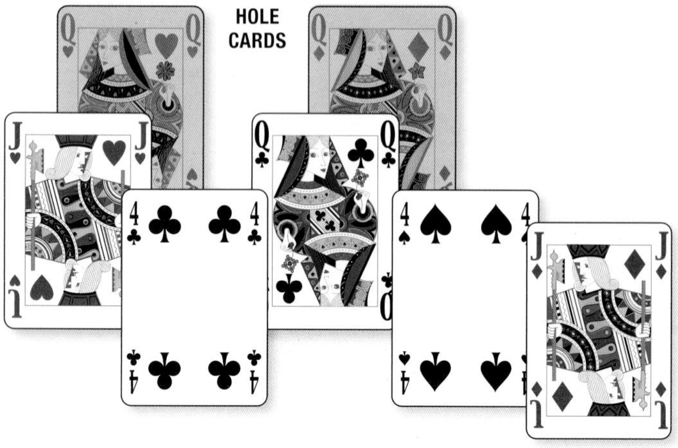

PLAYER A'S HAND

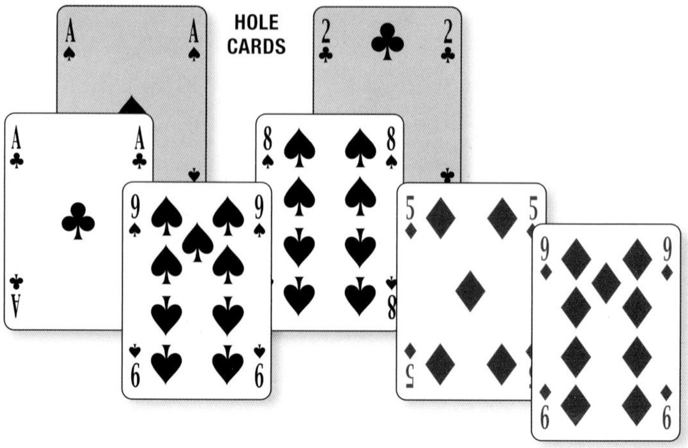

PLAYER B'S HAND

Poker Hands

From highest to lowest, poker hands rank as follows:

- Five of a Kind – Four Aces and Joker (obviously this can occur only in games where wild cards are being used).
- Royal Flush – A Straight Flush up to Ace.
- Straight Flush – A combined Straight and Flush; i.e. cards in sequence and of the same suit. A hand containing Ace, Two, Three, Four and Five is the second-highest Straight or Straight Flush, ranking between Ace, King, Queen, Jack and Ten and King, Queen, Jack, Ten and Nine.
- Four of a Kind – Four cards of the same face value (known as 'Quads').
- Full House – Three of a Kind ('Trips') and a Pair. When two players hold a Full House, the highest-ranking Trips wins.
- Flush – Five cards of the same suit. If another player holds a Flush, whoever holds the highest card wins.
- Straight – A sequence of five cards in any suit; e.g. 5♦, 6♣, 7♠, 8♥, 9♣. The highest Straight is one topped by an Ace, the lowest starts with an Ace. If two players hold a Straight, the one with the highest cards wins.
- Three of a Kind – Three cards of the same face value ('Trips'); e.g. Q♠, Q♣, Q♥.
- Two Pairs – Two sets of Pairs; e.g. 3♦, 3♥ and Q♠, Q♣. Whoever holds the highest card in the two hands (called the 'Kicker') wins, if two players hold matching Pairs of the same value.
- One Pair – Two cards of the same value; e.g. 3♦, 3♥ or Q♠, Q♣. If another player holds a Pair of the same value, then whoever holds the 'Kicker' wins.
- High card – A hand with no combination, but having within it the highest-ranking card among the hands in play.

Follow the Queen

Each player starts with two face-down hole cards, followed by a face-up card. In this game, a player with a Queen in his hand (either turned up or face down) treats the Queen as a wild card. If a Queen is dealt as a turn-up, the next turn-up dealt is a wild card, as are the other three cards of the same rank. The process is repeated each time a Queen is turned up, the previous wild card reverting to its original status. The best hand wins.

Left: A feature of most Lowball games is the fact that Straights and Flushes are not counted. In Razz, the lowest hand is a 'wheel', a Straight of 5, 4, 3, 2, A.

Three Cards or Fewer

Three-Card Drop

In Three-Card Drop, each player is dealt three cards face down. Players make an initial ante to the pot. Other than this, there is no betting, nor is there a draw, while there are also no common cards. (A common card is a card dealt face up to be used by all players at the showdown, when the highest hand wins the pot.) After examining their cards, players decide whether to drop out of or stay in the game. If the decision is to stay in, the player concerned takes a chip and places it in his hand. A player who wishes to 'drop', that is, not take part, indicates this by not taking a chip.

If all players drop, there is no winner. They ante again and the game is replayed. If more than one player stays in, there is a showdown. This, however, does not end the game. All the losing players must fund a new pot by putting in an equal number of chips to those in the pot that has just been won, and re-ante. After this, a new hand is dealt. The process goes on until only one player declares himself to be in, at which point he wins the final pot and the game ends.

Guts

In Guts, players are dealt only two cards and must announce if they are in or out simultaneously. A player may unclench a fist to reveal a chip if he is in, or players may all hold their cards just above the table, dropping them to indicate a fold. Those players still in now reveal their cards. The highest Pair wins – or the highest card if there are no Pairs. The winner takes the pot, the losers staking the amount it contained to form a new one ready for the next deal. Play goes on until only one player is willing to continue. He takes the final pot. If no one is prepared to play, the players keep going with the same cards until someone is prepared to bet. Otherwise, the hands are revealed and the player who would have won is penalized by having to match the contents of the pot.

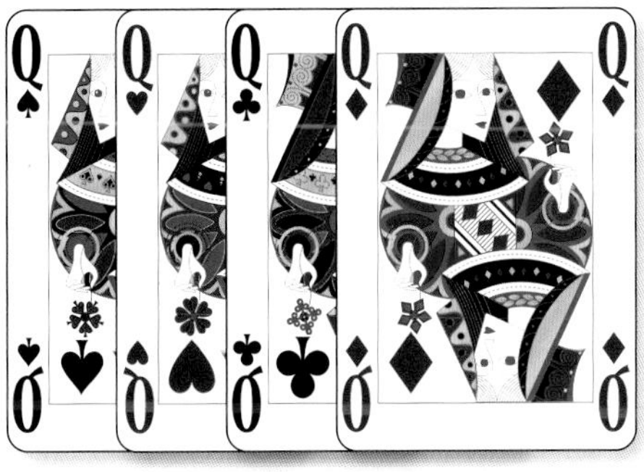

Left: In Follow the Queen, whenever a Queen is turned up, the next turn-up to be dealt is a wild card, as are the other three cards of the same rank.

Brag

Thought to be derived from a Tudor card game called Primero, which was popular in the days of Elizabeth I, Brag has a long and illustrious history. While it is similar to Poker, the way in which bets are made is different. In the classic game, hands consist of three cards and the highest hand is a Prial (Three of a Kind) of Threes. There are several varieties, but all are what are termed hard-score games – that is, those played for gambling chips or cash.

You will need: 52 cards; gambling chips/counters
Card ranking: Standard (except for wild cards – see below)
Players: Four to eight is optimal
Ideal for: 14+

Object

To finish with the best-ranked hand and scoop the pot.

Antes

Before play begins, players should agree on several points: the initial stake, or ante, to be put into the pot before each deal; the maximum and minimum initial bet and amount by which bets can be raised, and any variations to the basic rules such as whether or not wild cards are to be played.

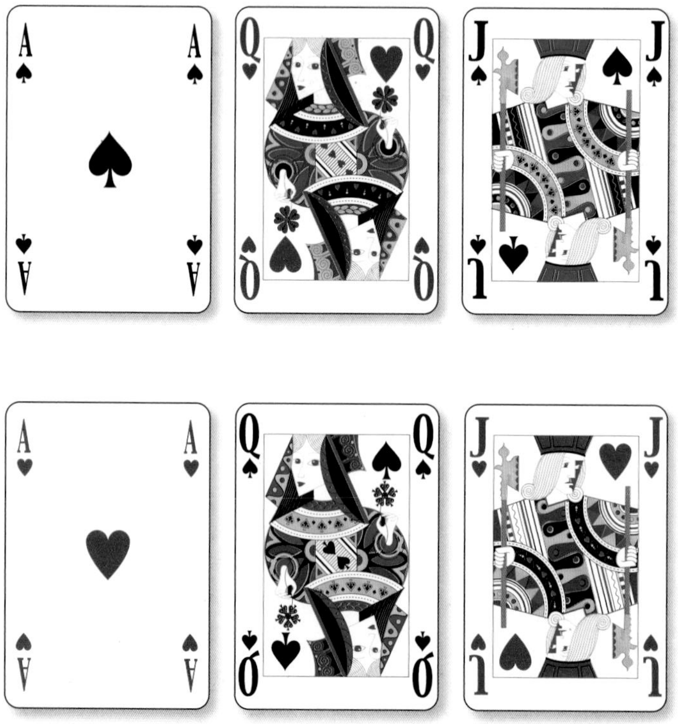

Above: The cards are ranked by suit in the conventional order of ♠♥♦♣, which means a Spade will beat a Heart of the same rank and a Diamond will beat a Club. This is only needed when two players have the same hands but in different suit combinations (as shown). In this case, the combination at the top wins, due to the Ace being a Spade.

Brag Hands

From highest to lowest, Brag hands rank as follows:

- Prial – A set of three cards of equal rank (a set of Threes is the best possible Prial, followed by a set of Aces down to Twos, the lowest).
- Running Flush – Three cards of the same suit (highest is an Ace, Two, Three).
- Run – Three consecutive cards of mixed suits (highest is an Ace, Two, Three).
- Flush – Three non-consecutive cards of the same suit.
- Pair – Two cards of equal rank.
- High Card – A hand consisting of three cards that do not fit into any of the above combinations. It ranks according to the highest card in it. There is no ranking of suits.

Wild Cards

In Brag, wild cards are known as floaters – they were once called braggers or turners. Either all Twos can be wild, or just the black ones. The One-Eyed Jacks, the J♠ and the J♥, (so called because only one eye shows), can also be wild – so can the K♥, known as the Suicide King because the sword the King carries appears to pass through his head.

A Joker or Jokers can be added to the pack to serve as extra wild cards. Such cards can replace any natural card in the pack. If, however, two hands are equal, a hand with no wild cards always beats one with wild cards in it, while a hand with fewer wild cards beats one with more of them. Thus, a hand of three Fives will beat a hand of two Sixes and a wild card, or a Seven and two wild cards.

The Deal

The cards are shuffled only for the first deal. In subsequent ones, this happens only if the previous deal was won by a Prial. Otherwise, the cards are simply added to the bottom of the pack as players fold. Each player receives three cards dealt singly face down to the table. However, each player is obliged to contribute one chip into the pot before any cards are dealt.

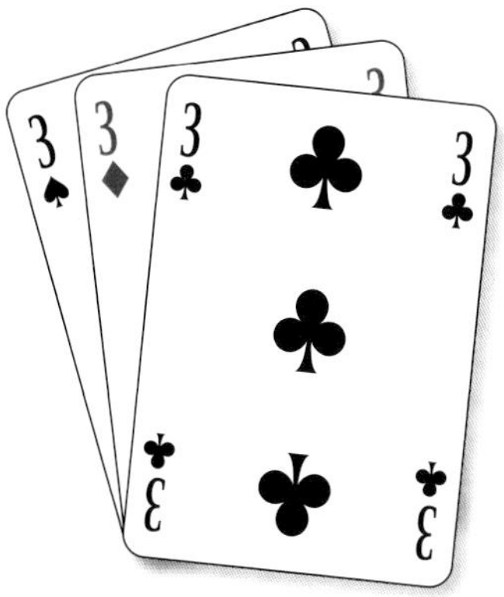

PRIAL

PRIAL

PRIAL

Left: A Prial of Threes is the highest possible hand, and a Prial of Twos is the least strong Prial possible. The second of the three hands, although ostensibly a Prial of Threes, would be beaten by a hand with no wild cards.

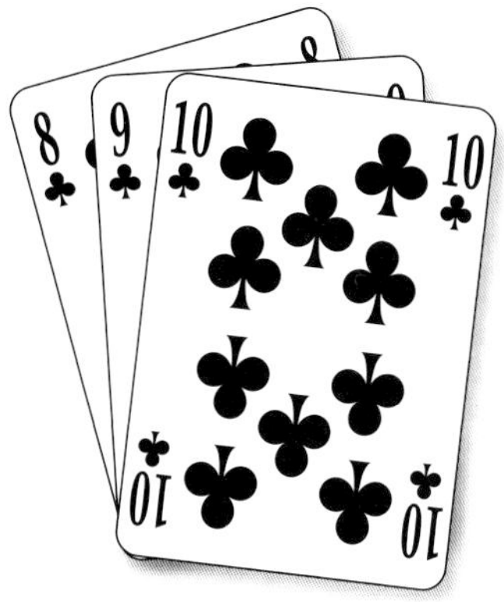

RUNNING FLUSH

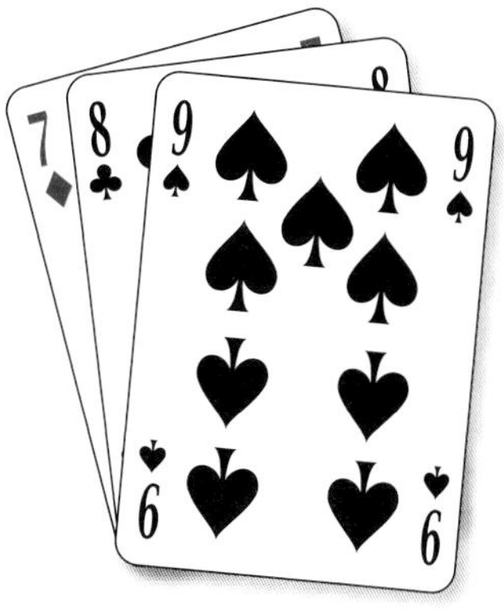

RUN

FLUSH

Left: Examples of a Running Flush, Run and Flush. After a Prial, these are, in descending order, the next highest hands in Brag.

Play and Betting

Once dealt, cards may either be examined or left as they are should their holder take the option of playing blind. If a player decides to do this, he takes part in the betting in the normal way, but any bets are worth double.

At any stage, when it is that player's turn to bet, he can decide to look at the cards before making the decision of whether to bet or to fold. In that case, he ceases to be a blind player.

The player to the left of the dealer has the chance to bet first. The options are to bet any amount between the minimum and maximum stakes that have been previously agreed, or to fold.

A player who runs out of chips during the betting, but who still wants to stay in the game, may 'cover the kitty' by placing his hand over the pot. The other players then start a new pot and continue playing.

The process continues until there are only two players left in the game. They carry on betting until one drops out, in which case the surviving player wins the pot without having to show his hand. The alternative is for either to 'see' the other by doubling the previous player's bet. Both players then expose their hands, the one who called for the showdown exposing his hand first.

Variants

In Five-Card Brag, each player receives five cards, discarding two face down before play starts. In Seven-Card Brag, anyone dealt Four of a Kind wins the pot automatically and there is a new deal. Otherwise, each player discards a card and forms the others into two hands, placing the higher one to the left and the lower one to the right. The higher hand is played first. The procedure is the same in Nine-Card Brag; each player ends up with three hands, ordered and played from highest to lowest.

Conclusion

The player with the highest hand wins the pot. If the two hands are equal, the player who paid to 'see', loses. If a player has covered the kitty, his hand is compared at the end of play to the hand of the 'winner', and the better of the two hands wins it. If one player is playing open and the other blind, the rules state that 'you cannot see a blind man'. The only options are to continue to bet or to fold. If both players are blind, betting twice the blind stake forces the hands to be compared.

Mus

A game from the Basque part of Spain, Mus is unusual: although its mechanics resemble those of Poker in that cards are drawn and each player then bets on his hand, it is played up to a fixed total of points. And unlike Poker, players are allowed to signal to their partners which cards they hold. Suits are irrelevant. What matters are the cards' ranks and values. In Mus, originally played with a 40-card Spanish pack, Threes count as Kings and Twos as Aces. The cards also have point values – a *Rey* (King), *Caballo* (Horseman) and *Sota* (Ten) are each worth 10 points, while the other cards score at face value. This becomes important in the final betting round of each deal.

Object

To score points through various card combinations. The game is not usually played for money.

You will need: 40-card Spanish pack; 22 stones or counters

Card rankings: *Rey* (King), *Caballo* (Horseman), *Sota* (Ten), and then Seven down to Ace

Players: Four players in partnerships of two

Ideal for: 14+

The Deal

The player to the dealer's right, known as the *Mano*, is the person who leads play, and all procedures pass to the right. All players are dealt four cards singly and the remaining cards are stacked face down to form the stock. Players can call '*Mus*' if they want to try to improve their hands by discarding, or can say '*No hay mus*' if happy with the cards as dealt. All four players must agree to the exchange, otherwise none can be made.

The players must then all discard from one to four cards, which are replaced by cards from the top of the stock. The process can be repeated until a player calls a halt to it. If the stock is exhausted before this, a new stock is formed from the shuffled discards.

Play and Betting

There are four rounds of betting, each for a particular combination of cards, carried out in strict order (see box below). In each round of betting, the *Mano* starts by deciding to pass or to bet. If the former, the next player to the right takes over. If no one bets, the *Mano* starts the next betting round.

If someone bets in the *Grande* and *Chica* betting rounds, the opposing players can fold, match the bet, or raise it. This is when signalling between partners becomes important. Closing the eyes means poor cards,

Mus Hands

There are four valid card combinations: *Grande*, *Chica*, *Pares* and *Juego*, on which players bet in strict order. They comprise the following:

- *Grande* – a bet that one or the other player in a partnership holds the highest hand.
- *Chica* – a bet that one or the other player in a partnership holds the lowest hand.
- *Pares* – a bet for the best-paired hand, a hand where two or more cards rank equally. Sub-rankings within *Pares* are:
  a. *Par Simple* (the lowest), two cards of equal rank.
  b. *Medias,* three cards of the same rank and one of a different one.
  c. *Dobles* (the highest), two pairs.

If no betting takes place, a *Par Simple* is worth one point, a *Medias* two and a *Dobles* three.

- *Juego* – a declaration that the cards in hand are worth at least 31 points. If no player can declare *Juego*, the alternative is *Punto*, denoting a hand worth 30 points or less.

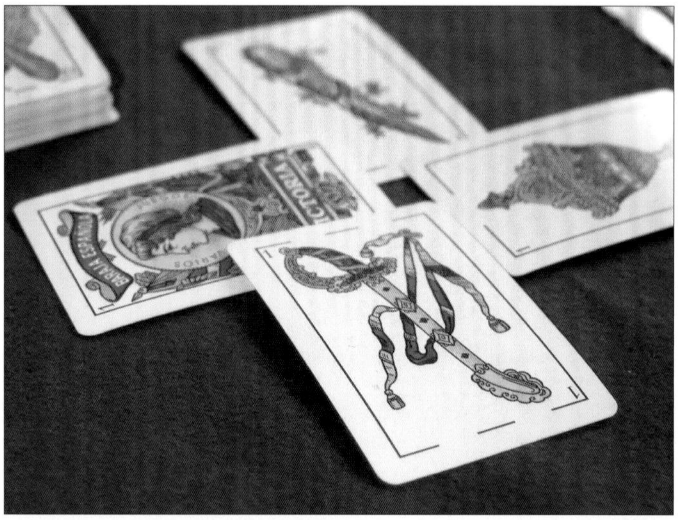

Above: Mus was originally played with a 40-card Spanish pack, organized into four suits, the Aces of which are shown clockwise from the top: *Bastos* (Clubs), *Copas* (Cups), *Espadas* (Swords) and *Oros* (Golds or Coins). The three distinctive court or face cards in each suit are the *Rey* (King), *Caballo* (Horseman) and *Sota* (Ten).

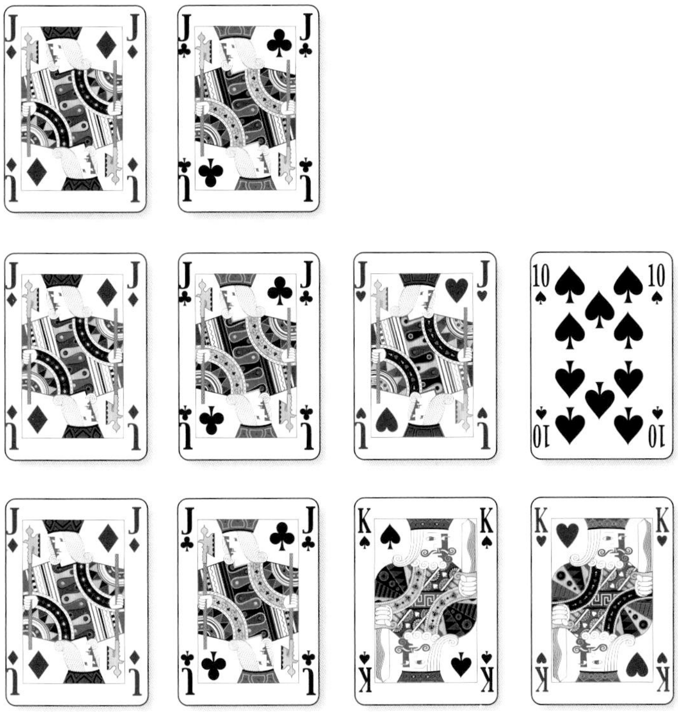

Left: Three examples of *Pares:* a *Par Simple* (the lowest, being two cards of equal rank; a *Medias* (being three cards of the same rank and one of a different one); and *Dobles* (the highest, being two pairs).

Below: After the last betting round, players lay down their hands. Player A has a *Par Simple* as does Player C. Players D has *Medias* (Three of a Kind), but Player B wins with *Dobles* (two pairs).

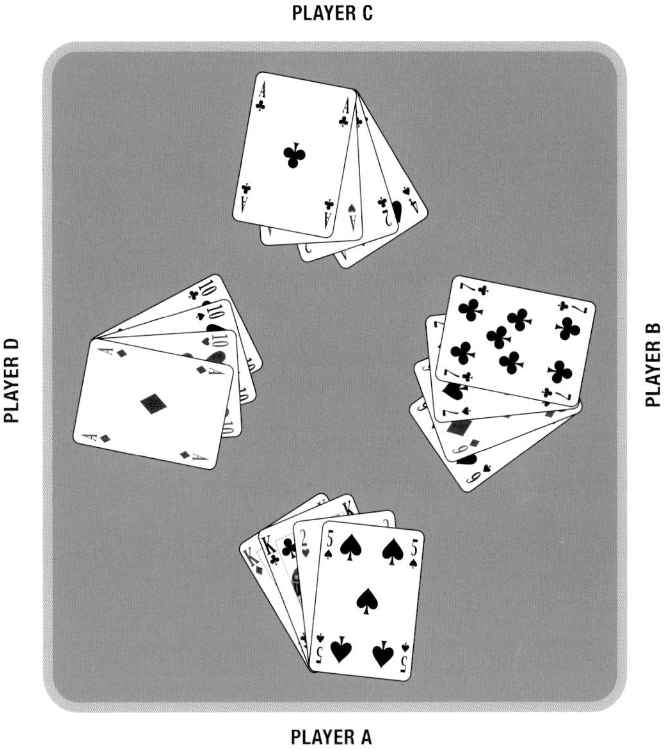

for instance, a hand of Four, Five, Six and Seven. In some versions, a player with these cards can expose them immediately and be dealt a replacement hand, provided that the declaration is made before calling "*Mus*".

Biting the lower lip means three Kings. Pouting the lips means that the player concerned would like to exchange some cards or it can mean that the player is holding three Kings and an Ace. Inclining the head to the right means that the player would prefer not to change cards. Shrugging the shoulder means that a player has a *Punto* of 30, while sticking out the tip of one's tongue means that the player is holding three Aces.

Betting continues until one side or the other folds, or sees the last raise. In the latter case, there is a showdown. Before any bets can be made in the *Pares* and *Juego* stages, each player must say if he actually holds the requisite cards. If at least one player from each partnership says 'Yes', a round of betting follows. If both players in one partnership say 'No', but either or both members of the opposing one say 'Yes', they can score the basic number of points for what they hold, but betting is disallowed. If all four players say 'No', there is no score. Instead, players then bet on who has the best *Punto*, that is, a hand worth 30 or fewer points

One final bet, an *Órdago*, is a call for an immediate showdown. The opposing players must either fold or see the bet. The outcome of the entire game is determined by who holds the best hand for that particular round.

Scoring

After the last betting round, players all show their cards, and the hand is scored round by round, although only for points that have not as yet been claimed and taken. These are represented by tokens called *piedras* (stones), 22 of which are placed in a saucer in the centre of the table. A minimum bet is two stones.

In each partnership, one player is responsible for collecting the stones. For every five stones won, four are returned to the saucer and one passed to the other partner. Each of these is worth five points.

When the player in charge of the *piedras* has collected seven such stones, he must call '*Dentro*' ('inside') to alert the opposing players to the fact that the team is within five points of winning the game.

Conclusion

A match is three games, the side winning two of them winning the contest.

Primero

This intriguing game, which is still played in parts of central Italy as Goffo, or Bambara, originated in Renaissance times. It is thought likely that a variant of it was favoured by Henry VIII of England. It has strong similarities to many aspects of modern-day Poker, although it is based on four-card, rather than five-card, combinations.

You will need: 40 cards, Eights to Tens removed; gambling chips/counters

Card ranking: King, Queen, Jack, Seven down to Two, and Ace

Players: Four to eight

Ideal for: 14+

Object

To score points through various card combinations and to finish with the highest-scoring hand.

The Deal

Before the deal, players each ante an agreed amount to the pot. The ante is the stake that each player must put into the pool before receiving a hand or new cards. Each player is dealt four cards, two at a time. The turn to deal and bet passes to the left.

Play and Betting

Any player dealt a winning hand can call for an immediate showdown, in which the best hand wins the pot. If no one wins outright, each player makes the necessary discards and is dealt replacements. There may be a further round of betting at this stage.

Otherwise, play starts with the player to the dealer's left, each player in turn having the choice of three options: to stake, bid or pass. In order to bid, the previous bet must be staked, that is, matched, before the new bid can be announced. Any bid must specify a points total, the type of hand and the amount being bid. The hand type must be higher than the one bid by the previous bidder, or the points total must be higher than the preceding one. A player who passes must discard one or two cards and draw replacements. Unlike Poker, it is impossible simply to fold.

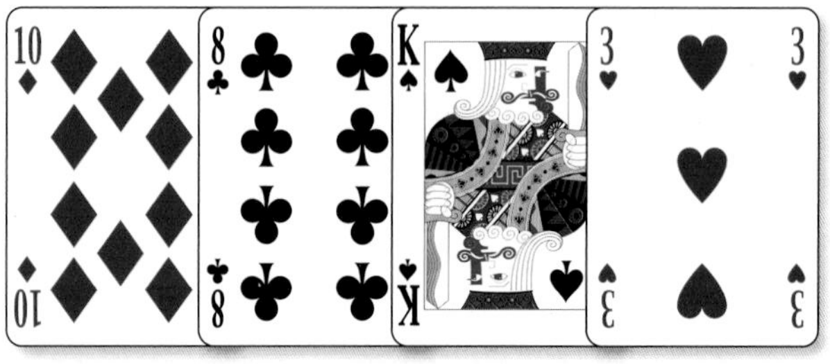

Above: A *Primero,* which is the lowest-ranking hand in the game, consists of one card in each suit.

Scoring

Ties are broken in favour of the hand with the highest point count. For this purpose, each rank scores a specific number of points. The court cards are worth 10 points each, and Aces 16. Sixes and Sevens count as three times their face value. Hence, a Six counts as 18 and a Seven as 21. Twos to Fives are worth 10 points plus their face value. Thus, a Four is worth 14 points and a Five 15.

Above: A Fifty-Five, the second-lowest-ranking hand in the game.

Above: Four of a Kind (Chorus), the highest-ranking hand in the game.

Primero Hands

There are four possible winning hands, which are detailed below from highest to lowest. Hand ranking wins over the highest score unless in a tie.

- Chorus – Four of a kind.
- Flush (or *Fluxus*) – A hand in which all four cards are of the same suit.
- Fifty-Five (or *Maximus*) – A hand consisting of Ace, Six and Seven of one suit plus one other card.
- *Primero* – A hand consisting of one card of each suit.

Conclusion

The game continues until a win is claimed. If there is a tie, the hand with the highest points wins.

Poch

This game is at least 500 years old. It has spread from its German homeland as far as North America, where variants of it are played under the names of Tripoli and Three in One. To play, you need a special board called a *Pochbrett*, which has nine compartments, each of which holds the chips bet on specific winning cards and combinations.

You will need: 32 cards, Twos to Sixes removed; gambling chips/counters; representation of a Pochbrett board (on paper)

Card ranking: Ace down to Seven

Players: Three to six

Ideal for: 14+

Left: A copy of a cover of a Poch boardgame (*c.*1897), with a picture of the Joker. It is currently on display at the Munich Municipal Museum.

Object

To be the first player to get rid of all his cards.

The Deal

Before the deal, players dress the *Pochbrett* board, each putting one chip into each of its nine compartments – Ace, King, Queen, Jack, Ten, Marriage, Sequence, Poch (marked with a Joker on the board) and the unlabelled centre pot. Players are then dealt five cards each, the next one being turned face up to determine the 'pay suit'. If a ready-made board is not to hand, it is fairly easy to make your own using paper.

Left: A *Pochbrett* board has nine sections for holding gambling chips, which are bet on specific winning cards and combinations.

Play and Scoring

In the game's first stage, holding the Ace, King, Queen and Jack of the pay suit means winning the chips in the matching compartment. Holding the King and Queen wins the Marriage compartment, while holding Seven, Eight and Nine of the pay suit wins the Sequence compartment; if no one declares these, or if an Ace, King, Queen, Jack or Ten is turned up as the pay suit card, the chips are carried forward.

In the second stage, players bet on who has the best combinations of cards. Any set of Four of a Kind beats any set of Three of a Kind, and any set of Three of a Kind beats any Pair. A set of higher-ranking cards always beats the same number of lower-ranking ones. If two players hold Pairs of the same rank, one containing a card from the pay suit is better. Four Eights, for instance, beats three Kings, which beats two Nines, which beats the Queens of Hearts and Diamonds, which beats the Queens of Spades and Clubs, if Diamonds or Hearts is the pay suit. Players bet by stating '*Ich poche*' and how many chips they are betting. The alternative is to pass. After the initial bet, players can either match it, raise or fold. The winner takes all the chips that were bet, plus the chips in the Poch compartment.

The previous stage's winner starts the final one by placing a card face up on top of the centre compartment on the board. Whoever holds the next higher card of the same suit then plays it, the process continuing until no one can play the next card required. The player of the last card of that sequence starts play again.

Conclusion

The first player to get rid of all his cards wins, taking the contents of the centre compartment. Other players forfeit a chip for each card they hold in hand.

Bouillotte

This game was invented at the time of the French Revolution as the official replacement for a game called Brelan, which the Revolutionary government decided to ban. It was popular in France until the late 19th and early 20th centuries, when it was slowly but surely supplanted in French affections by the newly fashionable game of Poker.

You will need: 20 cards comprising Aces, Kings, Queens, Nines and Eights; gambling chips/counters

Card ranking: Ace highest, Eight lowest

Players: Four

Ideal for: 10+

Object

To finish with the highest-ranking combination or suit, and so win the pot and/or bonus chips.

Straddling

Each player starts with a stack of 30 chips, known as the *cave* (stack). Players ante a chip to the pot, the dealer adding an extra chip. The ante is the stake that each player must put into the pool before receiving a hand or new cards. The player to the dealer's right can now elect to double the size of the pot. This is known as a straddle. The next player can do the same and so on round to the dealer. If a player chooses not to straddle, or does not have enough chips to do so, the straddling ends and the cards are dealt.

The Deal

Each player receives three cards, the dealer turning the next card face up to establish the trump suit.

Play

Players bet on who has the best hand, the first to bet being the player to the right of the last player to straddle. He can either open or pass. To open, a player must bet at least as many chips as the highest previous stake. The others may call (match) the bet, raise it or fold.

Scoring

Bonus chips from each of the opposing players are given to the holder of a *Brelan Carré* or *Brelan* (see box). If no one holds a *Brelan Carré* or a *Brelan*, the points for the cards held by all the players, including those who folded, are calculated suit by suit. Aces score 11 points, Kings and Queens 10 points each and the others score at face value. The suit with the highest total is the winning suit and the player with the highest card of it wins the pot.

Above: Bouillotte was invented during the years of the French Revolution.

Bouillotte Hands

From highest to lowest, Bouillotte hands rank as follows:

- *Brelan Carré* – Three of a Kind of the same rank as the turn-up. It is worth a bonus three chips.
- *Brelan* – Three of a Kind. It is worth one extra chip. If more than one player holds a *Brelan*, the highest wins.

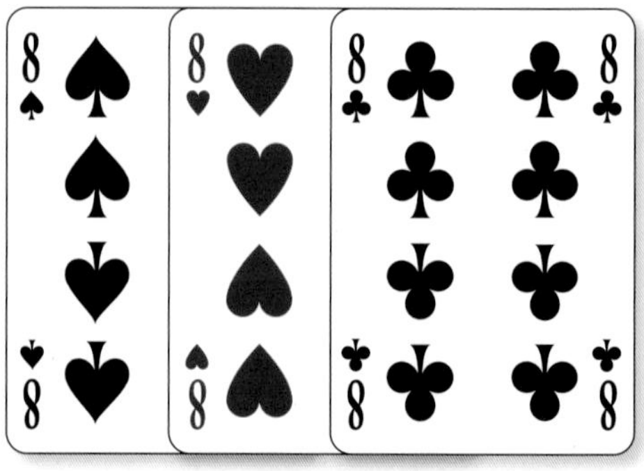

Right: Three of a Kind (*Brelan*). In the event of a tie, the best hand is one that matches the rank of the turn-up, making a *Brelan Carré*. If neither matches, the highest-ranked *Brelan* wins.

Conclusion

Betting continues until there are only two players left, when the first to call a bet forces a showdown.

Seven Twenty-Seven

In this American vying game, the court cards are worth half a point each and number cards their face values. Aces can count for either a point or 11 points, depending on whether they are being played low, high – or, indeed, both.

You will need: 52 cards; gambling chips/counters
Card ranking: Ace high or low, remaining cards Kings down to Twos
Players: Four to ten
Ideal for: 10+

Object

To end up with a hand that is as near to seven or 27 points as possible.

The Deal

Players ante their initial stakes to the pot. The ante is the stake that each player must put into the pool before receiving a hand or new cards. After this, one card is dealt face up to each player and another one face down. Once the face-down cards have been examined, each player, starting with the one to the dealer's left, may ask for an extra face-down card to be dealt.

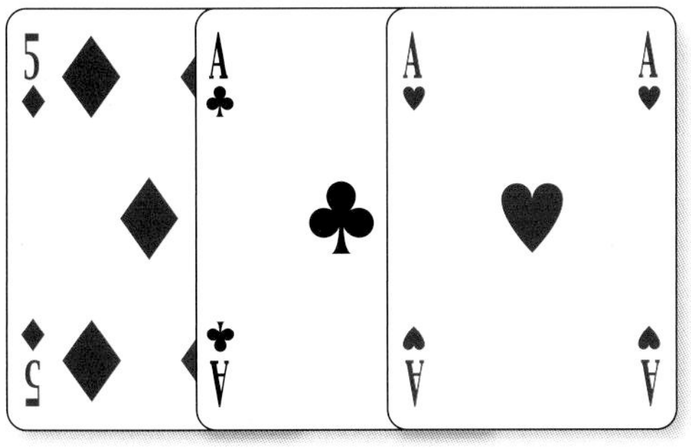

Left: The perfect hand in Seven Twenty-Seven: two Aces and a Five, the cards adding up to seven for Aces low and 27 for Aces high.

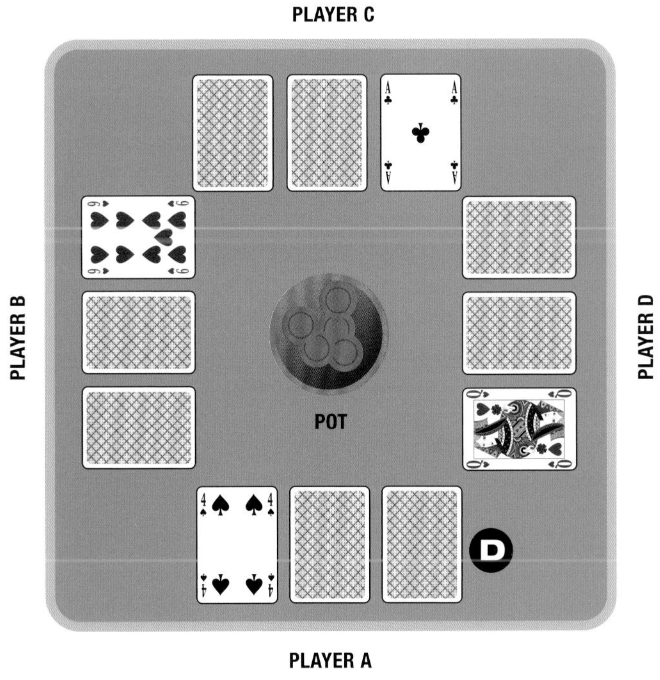

Above: Once players have examined the face-up and face-down cards they have been dealt, each player, starting with the one to the dealer's left, may ask for an extra face-down card.

Play and Betting

The first round of betting follows, initiated by the player to the dealer's left, who may either pass or bet any amount within the agreed maximum and minimum betting limits. If he passes, the chance to open the betting passes to the next player and so on round the table.

Following this, the other players can fold, or call (match) or raise the bet. If all the players but one fold, that player takes all the bets, the cards are thrown in and the next in turn deals. Otherwise, betting continues until the stakes are equalized – this happens, when, after one player has bet or raised, all the other players call or fold.

After each betting round, the remaining players can each ask for an extra card to be dealt to them face down. The alternative is to play the hand as it is. Another betting round follows.

Scoring and Conclusion

When no player asks for an extra card, there is a showdown. Everyone still in the game reveals his cards. There are two winners – the players whose totals are nearest to seven and 27, respectively. They split the pot equally. In the event of a tie, players split the relevant part of the pot. For example, if two players score 6 points and one scores 24, the player with 24 takes half the pot and the players with 6 take one quarter of the pot each. If no one has scored exactly seven or 27 (the perfect hand to do this is Five, Ace and Ace), the nearest wins.

To win, you have to be below or equal to the target. This means that you cannot win the seven pot if your score is more than seven, or anything at all if your score is over 27. Under beats over means that, if the differences are equal, it is better to be under the target, not over it. For example, if the four players have scored 5.5, 7.5, 26 and 28 respectively, the ones with 5.5 and 26 win.

22 | Quasi-trump Games

British card game authority David Parlett coined this phrase for a strange group of trick-taking games, each with its own idiosyncrasies. Players need not follow suit and instead can play any card they like. There is no conventional trump suit – certain cards, often with special names, act as quasi-trumps or have special powers of their own. This applies to Sevens, which always win the trick, but only when led.

Until Charles Cotton published *The Complete Gamester* in 1674, rules of card games were rarely written down and, when they were, they were almost always never complete. Generally speaking, they seem to have been transmitted orally. The French comic genius François Rabelais (*c.*1483–1553) noted the names of games, but these were not standardized and varied from place to place. Given all the variations, it is surprising that so many games managed to survive.

It is now accepted that the first trick-taking games probably first appeared in around 1400. Karnöffel is among the first, with reference to it dating back to 1426. Its rules were thought to be totally lost until it was discovered that a game called Kaiserspiel, which fitted Karnöffel's general description almost exactly, was still being played in a few places south of Lucerne in Switzerland. Judging by researchers' reconstructions, Karnöffel was an anarchic affair. Any card could be played to a trick, players could talk freely about the cards in their hand and what they wanted their partners to do. Also, only some of the cards in the suit designated as trumps had trick-taking powers: namely, the Jack, the Seven (if led), the Six and the Two. When it was introduced, Catholics were outraged that the Pope, as one trump is named, was outranked by the Devil, while royalty were not amused to see Kings being beaten by low cards.

Above: Charles Cotton, 17th-century author of *The Complete Gamester*, was one of the first to write down the rules of several quasi-trump games.

Watten

This eccentric game originated in Bavaria, from where it spread to the Tyrol. It started life as a four-player partnership game, but there are versions for two and three players. In Bavaria, it is played with a 32-card German-suited pack; the Tyrolean version introduces the 6♦ as an extra wild card.

You will need: Standard pack with Sixes and below removed

Card ranking: Non-trump ranking is Ace down to Seven; for trump ranking, see below

Players: Four, in partnerships of two

Ideal for: 14+

Object

To score two or more game points by taking three tricks, or for one partnership to bluff the other into conceding.

Trumps and Ranking

Watten is distinguished in having three permanent top trumps, the K♥, the 7♦ and the 7♣. Individually, these are known as *Maxi*, *Belli* and *Spritzer* and collectively as *Kritischen*. There is also a separate *Schlag* (trump rank) and trump suit. The cards of the trump rank are called *Schläge* (strikers), the highest being the *Hauptschlag* (chief striker) – the card that also belongs to the trump suit. The three other strikers rank immediately below it, followed by the remaining cards of the trump suit. The player to the dealer's left selects the trump rank and the dealer names the trump suit.

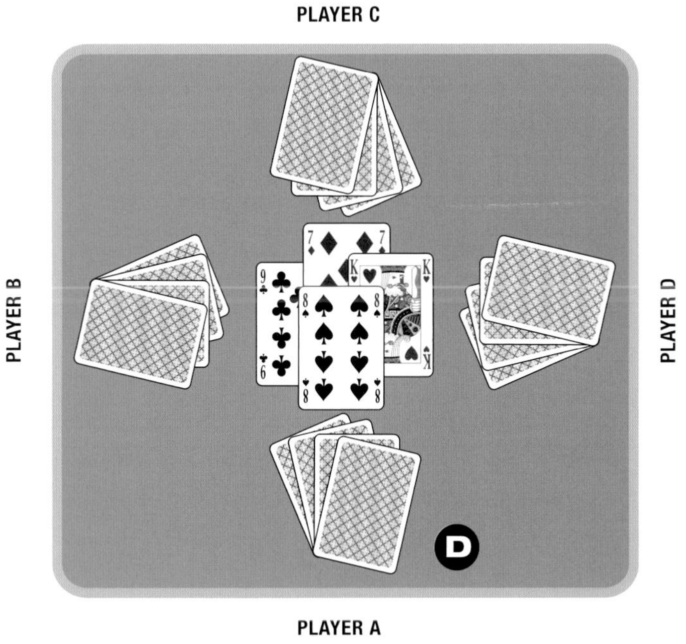

Above: In this hand of Watten, Player B has announced Nine as the trump rank, and the dealer has announced Clubs as the trump suit. Player B leads the *Hauptschlag* (chief striker – the card belonging to both the trump suit and the trump rank), forcing the next player to lay a top trump, another striker or a card from the trump suit. Player C lays the 7♦ (*Belli*), but Player D tops this with the K♥ (*Maxi*). Player A discards, allowing Player D to take the trick.

The Deal and Play

The dealer shuffles the 32 cards, which are then cut by the player to the right. If the cut card is a top trump, the cutter may take it. If the next one is the second-top trump, the dealer may take that and, if the next card is the third, the cutter can take it again. Each player is dealt five cards in packets of three and two, although the dealer and cutter get fewer if they have added to their hands.

After the deal, the trump rank and suit are announced, and the player to the dealer's left leads to the trick. If the chief striker is led, then a top trump, another striker or suit trump must be played if possible. Otherwise, there is no obligation to follow suit.

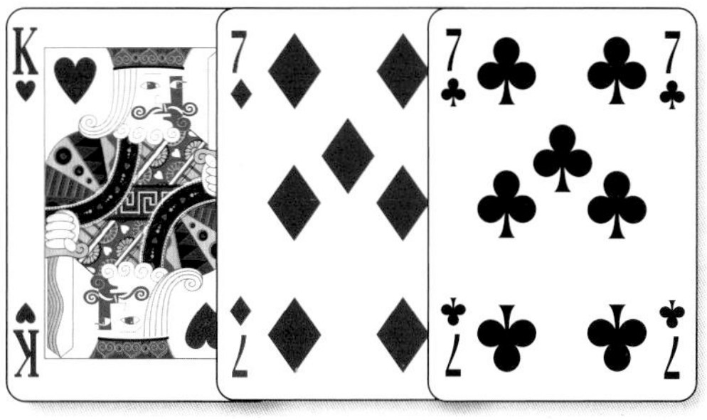

Left: There are three permanent top trumps: the K♥, 7♦ and 7♣, collectively called *Kritischen.*

Scoring

The score can be affected by any prior betting, which can take place at any time after the announcement of trump rank and suit by a player saying '*Gehen*' (go). If the opposing side respond with '*Schauen*' (see), the stakes are raised to three game points, or they can concede. Betting can continue indefinitely, although a team with nine or 10 game points is *Gespannt* (tight) and not allowed to bet further. Game is either 11 or 15 points.

Conclusion

Hands continue until three tricks are taken (if there is no betting, the team taking them scores two points) or a partnership is bluffed into conceding.

Karnöffel

Claimed to be the oldest trick-taking game in the Western world, Karnöffel was one of the first to have a trump suit, properly termed the 'chosen' suit. This reconstruction is based on the research of US card authority Glenn Overby.

You will need: 48 cards, Aces having been removed
Card reading: King down to Two, except in trumps (see below)
Players: Four, in partnerships of two
Ideal for: 14+

Object

To take the most tricks out of five to win a hand. Players agree how many hands make up a game at the start.

Trump Suit Rankings

The trump suit ranks differently, and certain cards have trick-taking powers. The Jack of trumps (*Karnöffel*) ranks highest, beating all other cards. The Seven of trumps, the Devil, comes second, but enjoys that status only if it is led. Following this is the Six of trumps (the Pope) and the Two of trumps (*Kaiser*), then the Three of trumps (the *Oberstecher*) and the Four of trumps (the *Unterstecher*). These last two cannot beat any of the above trumps. The Three of trumps cannot beat a King, and the Four of trumps cannot beat a Queen or King. A Five of trumps, the *Farbenstecher*, cannot beat any of the court cards or any of the above trumps.

The Deal

Each player receives five cards dealt singly, the first face up, the others face down. The lowest-ranking face-up card determines which suit is trumps. In the event of a tie, trumps are set by the first card of that rank to be dealt.

Play

The player to the dealer's left leads to the first trick. The person who plays the highest card of the suit led or the highest trump wins the trick and leads to the next. Subsequently, any card can be played, since there is no requirement to follow suit. During the course of play, players are allowed to communicate freely with one another. In fact, most of the important cards have signals linked to them. It is even legal to signal cards that are not held in order to try to confuse the opposition.

PLAYER C

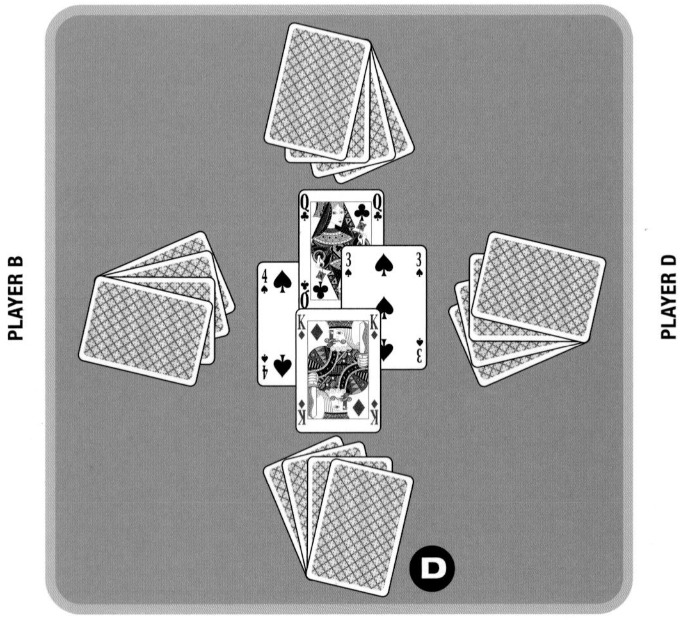

PLAYER A

Above: Here, Spades are trumps. Player B leads the 4♠ (*Unterstecher*) but this is not strong enough to beat the Queen played by Player C. Player D plays the 3♠ (*Oberstecher*), winning the trick until Player A tops it with a King.

Conclusion

The partnership taking the most tricks out of the five available wins the hand. The player who led to the first trick then deals the next hand. Partnerships agree at the start how many hands will make up a game.

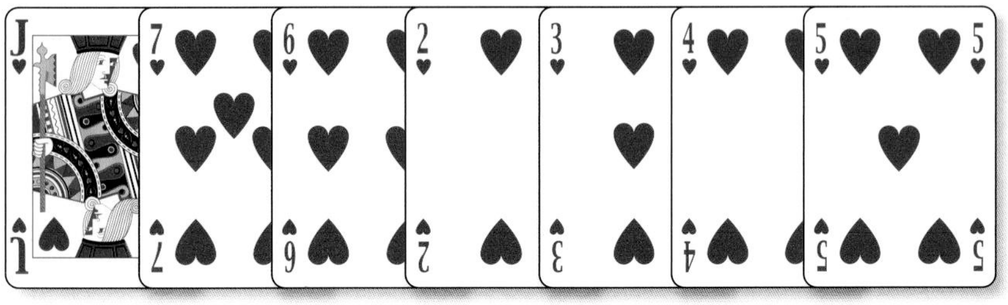

Left: Trumps (here assumed to be Hearts) have special ranks and trick-taking powers. The Jack (*Karnöffel*) ranks highest, followed by the Seven (the Devil), but only if this is led to a trick. Next comes the Six (the Pope), the Two (*Kaiser*), the Three (*Oberstecher*), the Four (*Unterstecher*) and the Five (*Farbenstecher*).

Brus

A Swedish partnership game, Brus is unique because it is played with a mixture of 18 playable and 14 unplayable cards.

You will need: 36 cards, Fives and below having been removed
Card ranking: See 'Playable and Unplayable Cards'
Players: Four or six, playing in partnerships of two or three
Ideal for: 14+

Object

To score six strokes (game points) over as many deals as it takes. In each deal, a game point is won by the partnership that wins six tricks.

Playable and Unplayable Cards

Playable cards are the only ones that can be played to tricks, while the unplayable ones are unusable, the exception being the K♣, which can score if a side that has taken five tricks holds it. For this reason, it is known as the 'outcome card'.

From highest to lowest, all playable cards are the J♣ *(Spit)*, the 8♠ *(Dull)* and the K♥ *(Brus)*. These cards are the *makadori* (matadors) and are followed by the Nines, Aces, the other three Jacks and Sixes of Clubs, Spades, Hearts and Diamonds, respectively. The 9♣ is commonly called *plägu* – literally, this means 'torture', because playing it may force the next player into leading a *makadori* he would rather have kept in reserve.

Unplayable cards are the remaining Eights, Tens, Queens and the other Kings, although the K♣ can score in a specific instance. Sevens have their own status. They are scoring cards and cannot be beaten, but they cannot beat other cards. They have no rank order.

The Deal

Each player receives nine cards each (or six cards each if there are six people playing), dealt one at a time. Play is to the left.

Play

The player to the dealer's left leads, but first he lays any Sevens he may hold face up on the table. Each of these counts by itself as a trick. He then leads a playable card to the first trick. Each of the other players in turn must subsequently play a higher card if they can. If not, they must pass. The highest card played wins the trick and its winner leads to the next, assuming that he holds Sevens or playable cards. If not, the lead passes to the next player in clockwise rotation.

Scoring

Winning six tricks is worth a stroke. Winning six tricks in succession is known as a lurch *(jan)* and is worth two strokes. A no-score draw is a possible outcome.

Conclusion

Play continues until a partnership has won a score by taking six tricks – five if they hold the K♣. The latter feature is often called into play when playable cards have been exhausted and neither side has managed to take six tricks. If neither partnership succeeds in taking six tricks, there is no score and the same dealer deals again. Six strokes wins the game.

Below: The so-called playable cards in Brus, ranked in order from the highest to lowest.

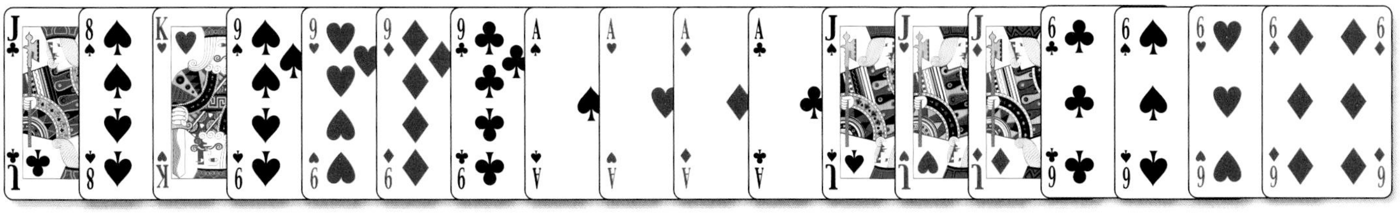

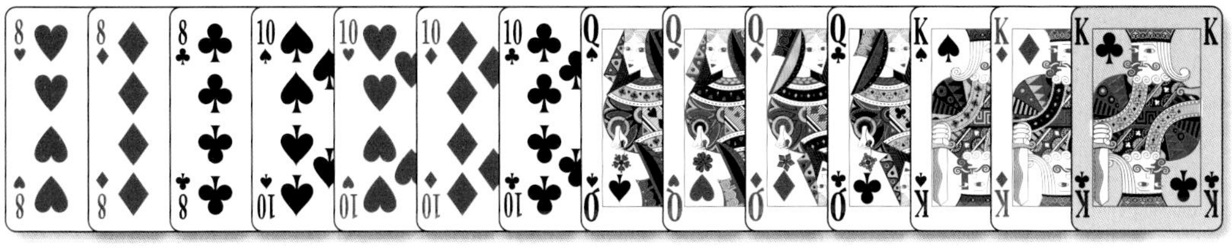

Left: The so-called unplayable cards in Brus. They are all unusable, except the K♣, which is the 'outcome card'. Possession of this decides some games which would otherwise be drawn.

Alkort

This was Iceland's national card game until its place was usurped by Bridge. What adds spice to this game, which can trace its origins back to at least the 18th century, is its unusual card rankings and the fact that, before play starts, it is perfectly legal to show your partner your highest card.

You will need: 44 cards, Tens and Fives having been removed
Card ranking: See under 'Card Ranking' below
Players: Two, or four in partnerships of two, as described here
Ideal for: 14+

Object

To take as many tricks as possible. Five or more tricks need to be taken in order to win a game.

Card Ranking

The cards rank as follows. The K♦ is highest, followed by a 2♥, 4♣, 8♠, 9♥ and 9♦, and then Aces, Jacks, Sixes and the remaining Eights, regardless of suit. The Queens, Threes, black Nines, and remaining Fours, Twos and Kings are valueless. The Sevens have a special status. When led to a trick, they are unbeatable, but otherwise they cannot beat another card. A Seven cannot be led unless its player has previously taken a trick.

The Deal

Players cut for partners and deal. Each receives nine cards three at a time, the remaining cards being placed face down to form the stock. If a player holds no card capable of beating an Eight, he may declare himself *friöufaer* (under eight). He shows all his cards, discards all but one and takes eight replacements from the stock.

Play

Before play, the partners secretly show each other the highest card in their hands. The player to the dealer's left leads to the first trick. The trick's winner leads to the next.

There is no need to follow suit, and the highest card played takes the trick. If two or more equally high cards are played, the one played first counts as highest.

Scoring

At least five out of the nine tricks need to be taken in order to score a game point. If a partnership takes five tricks before their opponents have taken one, they *múk* their opponents and score five points. If they win six or more tricks in this way, they make a stroke, scoring as many points as there are tricks in the stroke.

Conclusion

Play continues until all five tricks have been played for, unless one partnership has taken five tricks in succession. In this case, play continues for as long as it continues to win.

Left: This player holds no card capable of beating an Eight, so may declare himself *friöufaer* (under eight). To do this, he must show all his cards, and discard all but one of them, taking eight replacements from the stock.

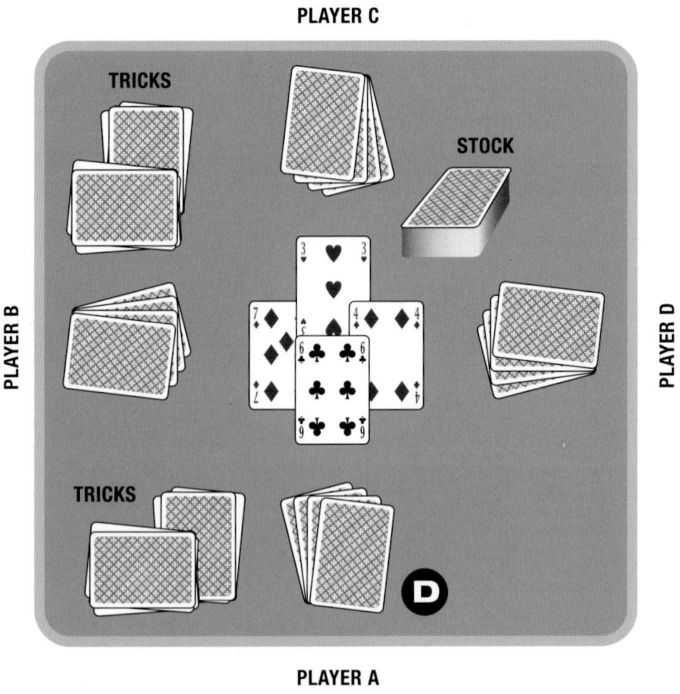

Above: Player B has led the 7♦. Sevens can only be led after having previously taken a trick, and, although worthless otherwise, when led they cannot be beaten, so Player B takes the trick.

23 | Tarot Games

Contrary to popular belief, Tarot cards were not originally invented for fortune telling. They were introduced into the Italian card world in the early 15th century as a means of pepping up trick-taking games by introducing a new ingredient into them – the notion of trumps. From there, Tarot games spread throughout much of Europe, and they are still popular there today.

The Italian idea was to add a fifth suit of 21 specially illustrated numbered cards called *trionfi* (triumphs) to the then standard pack of 56 cards bearing the standard Italian suitmarks of swords, staves, cups and coins, plus a special card called the Fool or *Excuse*. The original full pack therefore consisted of 78 cards. Despite appearances, the Fool is not the origin of the modern Joker. Originally, it was simply a card that could be played at any time, rather than following suit or trumping. It could not take a trick. Later, in Central Europe, its role changed and it became the highest trump.

The *trionfi* were trick-takers, and their original function was to act as cards that would beat any ordinary card played to the same trick. In English, *trionfi* was to become trumps, but Tarot games never really caught on in Britain in the same way as they did in Spain, Portugal and the Balkans, where they remain popular to this day. It was not until early in the 16th century that card players decided that it was simpler and more economical to pick a card at random from the existing pack and make its suit trumps, so doing away with the complexities of the separate *trionfi* suit. Slightly later, for reasons unknown, the Italians renamed *trionfi* as *tarocchi*. It is from this latter word however, that the German word *tarock* is derived and subsequently the French and English word tarot.

Above: Most people associate Tarot cards with fortune telling, but, contrary to popular belief, they were not invented for that purpose.

French Tarot

This, as the name suggests, is the most popular Tarot game in France. The 78-card *Tarot Nouveau* deck consists of the four standard suits, a suit of 21 *atouts* (trumps) and the *Excuse* (the Fool). The *Excuse*, the One and Twenty-one of trumps, are known collectively as *bouts* (ends).

You will need: 78-card *Tarot Nouveau* deck (see opposite)

Card ranking: The 21 numbered trumps (from Twenty-one to One); the *Excuse* (depicting a Fool or Jester); the 14 cards in the four suits: King, Queen, Cavalier, Jack and Ten down to One

Players: Four, in variable partnerships from hand to hand

Ideal for: 14+

Object

The soloist, the successful bidder, aims to win a minimum number of points, the amount of which depends on the number of *bouts* in the tricks he wins.

Bidding and the Soloist

The person who will play alone as the soloist against the three others is decided by an auction. Starting with the player to the dealer's right, each player in turn has one opportunity to bid to win a certain number of points with their hand, or to pass. Each bid must be higher than the one preceding it. If all four players pass, the cards are thrown in and the next to deal deals a new hand.

The soloist's objective is to win a set number of points, which varies depending on the number of *bouts* that are contained in the tricks he takes. Three *bouts* means that the soloist needs at least 36 card points to win, two *bouts* requires 41 points to win, and one *bout* 51 points. With no *bouts*, at least 56 card points are needed to win. Each *bout* and King is worth five points, Queens four, Knights three and Jacks two.

Declarations

Before play, each player in turn can make one or more declarations. The points these score do not count towards winning a bid. They are scored in addition to what is won or lost. A player holding 10 or more trumps can declare *Poignée* (bunch). A single bunch scores 20 points (10–12 trumps), a double (13–14 trumps) 30 and a treble (15 trumps) 40. Declaring *Chelem* (slam) is an announcement of the intention to take all 18 tricks. If successful, it is worth 400 points; there is a 200-point penalty for failure. An undeclared *Chelem* scores 200 points and no penalties.

The Deal

Each player receives 18 cards in packets of three, with six cards being dealt face down to form the *chien* (dog). They can be dealt at any stage of the deal, but the first and last three cards of the pack cannot be included. A player who has been dealt the One of trumps and no other trump must declare the deal void. The cards are thrown in and the next dealer deals.

Right: Cards from the Marseilles Tarot pack, one of the standard patterns for the design of tarot cards accepted today. There are 21 trump cards, the first of which is the Magician (*le Bateleur*); the House of God, or Tower (*la Maison Dieu*), is the sixteenth trump. At times, the Fool (*le Mat*), is unnumbered and viewed as separate and additional to the other 21 numbered trumps.

Above: 17th-century French tarot cards: *La lune* (moon), *Le chariot* (chariot), *L'ermite* (hermit) and *Ivsttice* (justice), by an unknown Parisian manufacturer.

The four possible bids are as follows:

- *Petite* (small): if successful, its bidder can use the cards in the *chien* to improve his hand
- *Garde* (guard): the same bid for a higher score. In both this and *Petite*, the soloist turns up and takes the cards in the *chien* and discards six cards from his hand face down. These discards may not include any trumps, Kings or the *Excuse*.
- *Garde Sans Chien* (guard without the dog): the taker plays without the benefit of the cards in the *chien*, although the card points in it still count towards his score
- *Garde Contre le Chien* (guard against the dog): the taker plays without the cards in the *chien*, and the card points in it go to the taker's opponents.

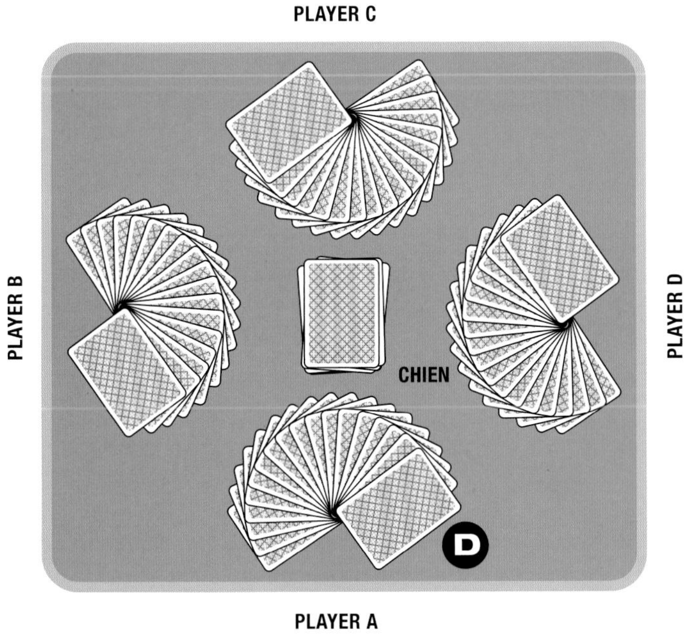

Play

The soloist takes the *chien* and discards, moving it to his side of the table if playing *sans le chien*, or, if the bid is *contre le chien*, moving it to the opposite player's side. The player to the dealer's right leads. Players must follow suit if they can, or trump or overtrump. If this is impossible, a trump must still be played even though it will not take the trick. The *Excuse* can be played at any time. It can also be retrieved from a taken trick and replaced by a worthless card. The *Excuse* cannot take a trick unless it is led to the last trick by a team that has won the 17 preceding ones.

Scoring and Conclusion

At the end of the hand, the opponents pool their tricks. The last trick is worth 10 points (*Petit au Bout*) if it holds a One of trumps. The cards are counted in pairs of two non-scoring cards or a non-scoring card and a scoring one. The first scores a point, and the second is worth the scoring card's value. The total is deducted from 91 for the soloist's score. In a *Petite*, the score won or lost is 25 for game, plus the difference between the card points the soloist won and the number needed. The *Petit au Bout* is added or subtracted. In a *Garde*, the total is doubled; in *Garde Sans Chien* quadrupled and in *Garde Contre le Chien* sextupled. The *Poignée* and *Chelem* bonuses are added or subtracted. The soloist wins, or loses, this number of points from all three opponents.

Left: The remaining six cards in the pack, the *chien*, can be dealt at any stage of the deal, but must not include the first and last cards of the pack.

Ottocento

Originating in Bologna in the 16th century, hence its other name Tarocco Bolognese, this partnership game is still played there with a special 62-card pack also known as the *Tarocco Bolognese*. It consists of four 10-card suits (Swords, Batons, Coins and Cups), 21 trump cards, and a wild card called the *Matto*, which is not a trump and has no ranking order.

You will need: *Tarocco Bolognese* 62-card pack
Card ranking: See box below
Players: Four, in partnerships of two
Ideal for: 14+

Object

To be the first to score 800 points. There are four ways to score points: for card combinations in individual hands; for card combinations from tricks captured by each partnership; for individual counting cards captured in tricks by each partnership; and for winning the last trick.

The Deal

Who deals first is decided randomly, after which the deal passes to the right. The dealer shuffles the cards, and the player to his left cuts them. Each player receives 15 cards five at a time, the dealer discarding two from the seven he would otherwise be left with at the end of the deal. The discards count for the dealing partnership as though they were in tricks, but if the partnership loses every trick, they too are lost. The only cards that may not be discarded are the *Tarrochi* (see box) and the Kings.

Play

Immediately before playing to the first trick, each player in turn has the opportunity to declare any scoring combinations by placing the appropriate cards face up on the table. Otherwise, after this, the cards are picked up and returned to that player's hand. The alternative is to score them at the end of the hand. It is not compulsory to make declarations, nor need they be made in full. A player may declare a sequence of four cards, for instance, while actually holding five, without penalty. If either side scores 800 points through declarations alone, the game ends then, without any further play.

Any card may be led, the other players following suit or playing a trump, unless a player holds the *Matto*. This can be played regardless of whether its player holds any

Card Rankings Suit by Suit

Card rankings differ from suit to suit, as follows:

- In Swords and Batons, the highest-ranking card is the King, followed by Queen, Knight, Jack, Ten to Six and Ace.
- In Cups and Coins, it is King, Queen, Knight, Jack, Ace and then Six to Ten.
- Of the 21 trumps, *Angelo* (Angel) is the highest, followed by *Mondo* (World), *Sole* (Sun), *Luna* (Moon), Sixteen down to Five, the four *Mori cards* (Moors), and *Bègato*.

The cards from Sixteen down to Five also have names. They are:

- *Stella* (Star)
- *Saetta* (Thunderbolt)
- *Diavolo* (Devil)
- *Morte* (Death)
- *Traditore* (Traitor)
- *Vecchio* (Old Man)
- *Ruota* (Wheel)
- *Forza* (Strength)
- *Giustitia* (Justice)
- *Temperanza* (Temperament)
- *Carro* (Chariot)
- *Amore* (Love).

The *Matto* is not a trump and has no ranking order. *Angelo*, *Mondo*, *Bègato* and *Matto* are collectively termed *Tarrochi*.

Left: Aces from an Italian playing card set, of the Batons, Cups, Coins and Swords suits. Italian playing cards most commonly consist of a deck of 40 cards (four suits from one to seven, plus three face cards). Since these cards first appeared in the late 17th century, when each region in Italy was a separately ruled province, there is no official Italian pattern.

cards of the suit led. It is always retained by the partnership playing it – if the opposing partnership takes the trick, it is simply exchanged for a worthless card. It can be lost only if the partnership playing it loses every trick.

Upon leading to a trick, a player can make three signals. *Vollo*, tossing a card in the air, means that this is the last card held in that particular suit. *Busso*, striking the table with the fist, is a signal to play the highest card held. *Striscio*, scraping a card on the table, is a request to lead trumps. It is acceptable to make more than one signal at the same time.

Scoring

The *Tarrochi* (*Angelo*, *Mondo*, *Bègato* and *Matto*) and Kings are worth five points, Queens four, Knights three, Jacks two and all other cards a point each. The winner of the last trick scores six extra points. The cards are counted in pairs, a point being deducted from each pair's value. Including the last trick, there are 93 points available in the pack.

To work out card points, a single one-point card is placed on top of each two-, three-, four-, or five-point one and the values scored. The remaining one-point cards are counted in pairs with the six-point bonus for taking the last trick being added, if appropriate. The other side's score is determined by subtracting the declaring partnership's total from the possible 93 points in the pack. The partnership to score 800 points first wins the rubber.

Combinations of three or more cards of the same kind are called *cricche*. A *cricche* of all four *Tarocchi* is worth 36 points, while any three scores 18. Kings score 34 and 17 for four or three respectively, Queens 28 and 14, Knights 26 and 13 and Jacks 24 and 12. If three or more different *cricche* are scored at the same time, the total score is doubled. Combinations of three or more cards in sequence also score. A three-card sequence scores 10 points, with each additional card adding five points to that score.

This is where the *Matto* and *Bègato* shine. As wild cards, they can be used to establish a sequence or to extend one, but can only be used in trump sequences. They can then be used consecutively, except at the end of a sequence. If they are not needed to establish a sequence, they can be added to its length – and increase the score.

Conclusion

If any combinations are announced during the first trick, they are scored then. Otherwise, scoring takes place at the end of the hand. Usually, one partnership starts by laying out all the cards it has captured face up on the table, so as to show all the significant cards of each suit, trumps and *Mori* in rank order.

The *cricche* are counted first, remembering to double the score if there are more than three of them, followed by those of the opposing partnership. Sequences are then scored, and the scores are again doubled if there are three or more. Finally, the individual card points are calculated.

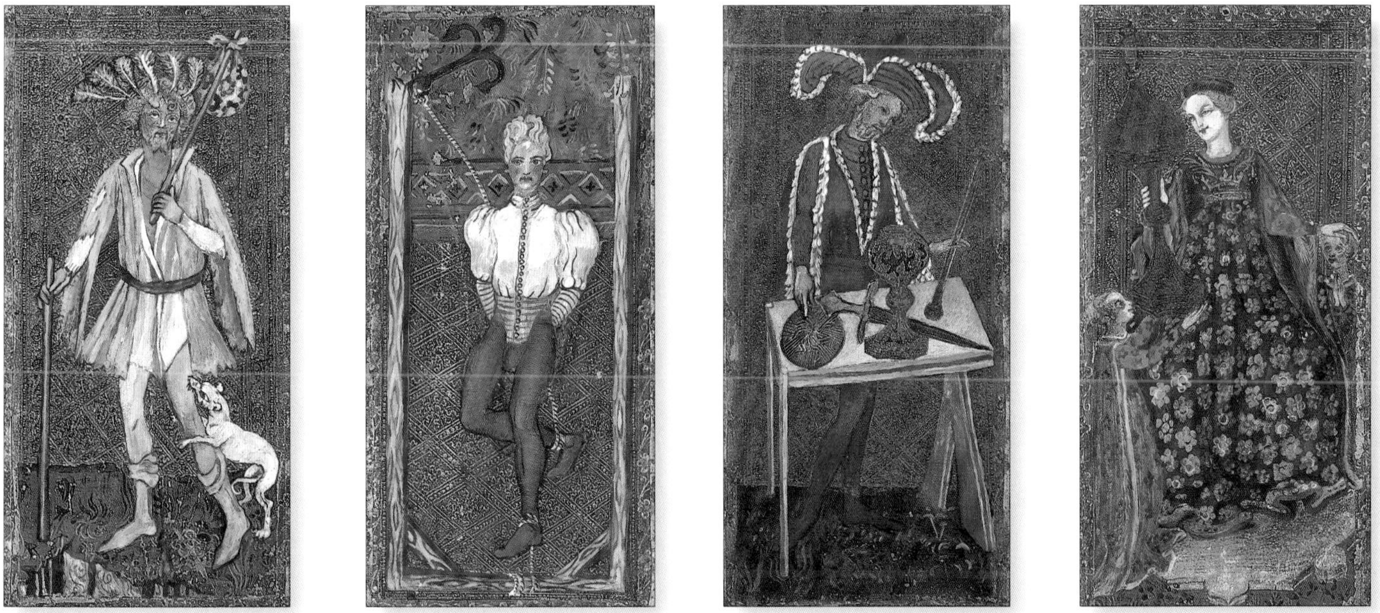

Below: Cards from the Visconti-Sforza deck, the earliest set of Tarot cards, which was produced in Italy in the mid-15th century. They were commissioned by Filippo Maria Visconti (1392–1447), Duke of Milan. The cards were then still called *trionfi* (trump) cards, From left to right, the cards are the Fool, the Hanged Man, the Magician, and the Empress.

GLOSSARY

A

Aces High The term used when the Ace is the highest-ranked card in each suit. When it is the lowest-ranked, the term is **Aces Low**.

Alliance A temporary partnership between players that lasts for only one deal.

Ante In gambling games, the opening stake that all players must make before or at the start of each deal.

Auction Bidding to establish which suit should be trumps, how many tricks the bidders undertake to win and other basic conditions of a particular game.

B

Bid The offer to win a certain number of tricks in exchange for choosing conditions of play, for example, what the trump suit will be. If a bid is not overcalled by a higher one, then it becomes a contract.

Blank A term used in card-point games to describe a card that is valueless.

Boodle In the game Michigan, cards from a separate pack placed on a layout on which bets (gambling chips or counters) are staked.

Book In Bridge and Whist, the first six tricks won by a side, which are recorded 'below the line'. In collecting games, a set of four cards of the same rank.

C

Card-points The point-scoring values of specific cards, principally in point-trick games. These points are different to the nominal face values.

Carte blanche A hand containing no court cards.

Carte rouge A hand in which every card counts towards a scoring combination.

Chip Counter which is used to represent money. Also called a gambling chip.

Combination A set of scoring cards that match each other in rank or by suit.

Court cards The King, Queen and Jack of each suit, as opposed to the numbered or 'pip' cards. They are also sometimes referred to as picture cards.

Cut To divide a pack of playing cards by lifting a portion from the top, to establish who deals first.

D

Deadwood Penalty cards remaining in opponents' hands when a player goes out.

Deal The distribution of cards to the players at the beginning of a game and the play ensuing between one deal and the next.

Declare To state the contract or conditions of play (for example, the trump suit or number of tricks intended, etc.). To reveal your hand and score for achieving a particular combination of cards.

Declarer The highest bidder in an auction, who then tries to fulfil his contract.

Deuce The Two of any suit.

Discard A card that a player has rejected and placed on a discard pile. To throw away a worthless or unwanted card to a trick

Draw To take or be dealt one or more cards from a stock or discard pile.

Dummy A full hand of cards dealt to the table, or, in Bridge, to one of the players (who has to spread them face up on the table at a certain point in the game), with which the declarer plays as well as with his own hand.

E

Elder/Eldest The player who is obliged to lead, bid or make the opening bet first, usually the person seated to the left of the dealer in left-handed games, or to the right in right-handed games.

Exchange To discard cards and receive the same number of replacements or to add cards to a hand and then discard the same number.

F

Flush A hand of cards that are all of the same suit.

Follow suit To play a card of the same suit as the last one played.

G

Game The whole series of deals, or the target score. for example, 'game is 500 points'.

Game points Card points that are won to make a particular bid.

Go out To play the last card of a hand.

H

Hand The cards held by each player or the play that takes place between one deal and the next.

Head To play a higher card than any so far played to the trick.

Hole cards The cards dealt face down to each player which remain unseen by the other players, until the end of the game.

Honours Cards that attract bonus scores or extra payments if they are held in hand and, occasionally, if captured in play.

J

Joker An extra card supplied with the standard 52-card pack that is often used as a wild card.

K

Kitty Another term for the pool or pot of chips that are being played for.

Knock In Rummy, a player uses this to signify that all his cards are melded. In Poker, knocking can be used to signify that a player will make no more bets.

L

Laying off The playing of cards to opponents' melds on the table in Rummy games.

Lead The first card to be played or the action of playing the first card.

M

Maker The player who names the trump suit.

Marriage A meld of the King and Queen of the same suit.

Meld A group of cards of the same rank or in sequence that attracts scores or privileges.

Misdeal To deal cards incorrectly, in which case they must be collected, shuffled and dealt again.

Misère A contract to lose every trick in a hand, otherwise termed a *Null*.

N

Null A contract to lose every trick in a hand, or a card carrying no point-value in point-trick games.

O

Ouverte A contract played with one's hand of cards spread face up on the table for everyone to see.

Overcall To bid higher than the previous bidder.

Overtrick A trick taken in excess of the number a player is contracted to take.

P

Pair Two cards of the same rank.

Pass To miss a turn when it comes to bidding or playing without dropping out of play.

Plain suit A suit other than the trump suit.

Pool/Pot This is a sum of money or an agreed equivalent, such as a number of chips, to which the players contribute before play starts or throughout play and which is taken by the eventual winner.

Prial Three cards of the same rank; a triplet.

Q

Quint In Piquet, a set of five cards. In Quinto, the Five of every suit, and every pair of cards in a suit that totals five. In this game, the Joker is known as the Quint Royal.

R

Raise In Poker, to increase the level of a bet, usually by calling the previous bet and then wagering at least the same amount again.

Rank A card's denomination and its relative trick-taking power (for example, 'Ace ranks above King').

Renege To fail to follow suit to the card led, but legally, in accordance with the rules of the game.

Revoke To fail to follow suit, when able and required to do so. It usually incurs a penalty if detected.

Round A division of play in which every player participates in dealing, bidding, playing a trick, etc. the same number of times (usually once).

Rubber In partnership games, a match usually consisting of three games and thus won by the side winning two.

Ruff In games of Bridge, playing a trump card on a trick that was led with a plain suit. In Gleek, it is the highest card value a player holds in a single suit

Run Another term for a sequence.

S

Sequence A run of three or more cards of the same suit in rank or numerical order.

Shoe A box from which cards are dealt in some card games.

Slam A bid to win every trick in a hand.

Solo A contract played with the hand as dealt without exchanging any cards, or, played alone against the other players. The soloist is the player who elects to play alone.

Stake The amount of money or chips a player is willing to play with during a game, or the amount a player needs to be included in a game.

Stock The cards that are not dealt immediately to the players, but may be dealt or drawn from later on during the game.

Suit The internationally recognized suits are Hearts, Clubs, Diamonds and Spades. There are also local ones found in German Italian and Spanish games.

T

Talon The undealt portion of the pack put aside for use later in a game; the same as the stock.

Three of a Kind Three cards of the same rank.

Trey The Three of any suit.

Trick A round of cards, consisting of one from each player in turn, played according to the rules of the particular game.

Trump A suit that outranks all the others. A trump card always beats any card from a plain suit.

Turn-up A card, also called the upcard, turned up at the start of play to determine which suit is trumps and, depending on the game, at other times during play for a variety of reasons.

U

Undertrick A trick which is less than the number bid or contracted.

Upcard Another term for the turn-up card.

V

Void Having no cards of a specified suit.

Vole The winning of every trick; same as slam.

Vulnerable In Bridge, this describes a partnership, which, having won one game towards the rubber, is subject to increased scores or penalties.

W

Waste pile A pile of unwanted cards, usually dealt face up.

Widow A hand of cards dealt to the table face down usually at the start of play which players may exchange cards with during the game.

Wild card A card that can stand in for any other card, either played freely or subject to certain restrictions, depending on the game.

Y

Younger/Youngest The player last in turn to bid or play at the beginning of a game.

INDEX

A
500 Rum 217
Accordion 16
Ace-Ten games 174–85
Aces Up 16
Acey-Deucey *see* Yablon
adding games 13, 46–53
Adders games 52–3
Agurk 162
Alkort 244
All Fives 106
All Fours 106, 107
  games 106–11
Aluette 165
Asszorti 122
Auction Bridge 133, 136
Auction Cribbage 50
Auction Forty-Fives 154
Auction Pinochle 197
Austen, Jane 104
Austrian Preference 120–1
Authors 30, 35
Avinas 179

B
Baccarat 13, 102
Bambara *see* Primero
banking games 13, 98–105
Barbu 169
Bartok 54
Basra 43
Bassadewitz 172
Beat Your Neighbour Out of Doors *see* Beggar-My-Neighbour
beating games 68–81
Beggar-my-Neighbour 31
Bela *see* Klaberjass
Belgian Whist 112, 114
Belote 23, 131, 198, 200
Bezique 131, 194, 195
Bid Whist 140
Black Jack *see* Switch
Black Maria 130–1
Blackjack 13, 98, 100–1
Blitz *see* Thirty-One
Block Rummy 84
Boathouse Rum 84
Bondtolva 188
Booby 137
Boodle *see* Michigan
Boonaken 202
Boston 112, 114, 116
Bouillotte 238
Bourré 157
Brag 131, 232–3
Brandeln 156
Bridge 46, 112, 130, 132–7
  Auction Bridge 133, 136
  Chicago Bridge 136
  Contract Bridge 130, 133–5, 206
  Cut-throat Bridge 137
  Duplicate Bridge 136
  Nullo Bridge 136
  Pirate Bridge 137
  Reverse Bridge 136
  Rubber Bridge 136
  Three-Handed Bridge 137
Brint 136
Briscola 174, 184, 185
Brus 243
Brusquembile 174

C
Cadogan, Lady 14
Calabresella *see* Terziglio
Call Rummy 84
Calypso 147
Canasta 206, 208–9
  games 206–17
Card Dominoes *see* Domino
card-catching games 31–4
Casino 13, 36, 37
Cat and Mouse *see* Spite and Malice
catch and collect games 13, 30–5
Cheat 80
Chicago 218, 230
Chicago Bridge 136
Chinese Ten 44
Churchill, Winston 194
Ciapanò 28
Cicera 42
Cinch 106, 110
Cirulla 42
Clob/Clobby/Clobiosh *see* Klaberjass
Coffin, Louis 131
Coinche 198, 201
collecting games 13, 35
Colonel *see* Rummy
Colour Whist 112, 114
Comet 54
Conquian 83, 91
Continental Rummy 216
Contract Bridge 130, 133–5, 206
Contract Rummy 82, 92–3
  Push 94–5
Contract Whist 140
Coon Can *see* Rummy
Costly Colours 51
Coteccio 166, 173
Cotton, Charles 51, 107, 240
court cards 8, 9, 10, 11
Crates *see* Crazy Eights
Crazy Eights 58
Crazy Solo 115, 180
Cribbage 13, 46
  Auction Cribbage 50
  Five-Card Cribbage 46, 50
  Four-Handed Cribbage 50
  Losing Cribbage 50
  Six-Card Cribbage 46, 48–9, 50
  Three-Handed Cribbage 50
Crowley, Aleister 137
Cuarenta 39
Culbertson, Ely 133
Cut-throat Bridge 137

D
Da Bai Fen 29
Dickens, Charles 104, 106
Domino 55
Don 106, 111
Doppelkopf 178
Dowling, Allen 131
draw and discard games 13, 82, *see also* rummy games
Draw Poker 131, 222–3
Dudak 73
Duplicate Bridge 136
Durak 68, 70–1

E
Ecarté 152
Einwerfen 182
Eleusis 54, 60–1
Enflé *see* Rolling Stone
English Solo *see* Solo Whist
Etoni 22
Euchre 11, 106, 130, 148, 149, 151

F
Fan Tan *see* Domino
Femkort 159
Fem Opp *see* Rödskögg
Fifteens 25
Fifty-Two 230
fishing games 13, 36–45
Five Fingers *see* Twenty-five
Five Hundred 148, 151
Five-Card Brag 233
Five-Card Cribbage 46, 50
Five-Card Draw *see* Draw Poker
Five-Card Loo 158
Five-Card Stud 105, 221, 224
Fleming, Ian 102
Follow the Queen 231
Forty for Kings 25
Forty-One 143
Forty-Two 230
Foster, R. F. 137
Four-Handed Cribbage 50
Four-Player Gin Rummy 86–7
Freak-Hand Poker 229
French Tarot 256–7

G
Gaigel 191
German Whist 146
Ghent Whist *see* Solo Whist
Gin Rummy 13, 86
  Four-Player Gin Rummy 87

Jersey Gin 87
Three-Player Gin Rummy 87
Two-Player Gin Rummy 86–7
Gleek 125, 129
Go Fish 30, 35
Go Stop 36
Goffo *see* Primero
Goofspiel *see* Gops
Gops 13, 30, 32
Guts 231

H
Haferltarock 181
Hand and Foot 210–11
Handjass 204
Happy Families 13, 30
Hearts 130, 166, 167
games 130–1, 166–73
High-Low-Jack 106, 108
Hi-Low Draw 223
history of playing cards 8–11
Hold 'Em *see* Texas Hold 'Em
Hollywood Rummy *see* Contract Rummy
Hörri 76
Hosen'runter *see* Schwimmen
Hoyle, Edmond 138
Huc 54

I
I Doubt It *see* Cheat
Idiot's Delight *see* Aces Up
Imperial 125, 128
In Between *see* Yablon

J
Jack-Nine games 131, 198–205
Jacks 131, 168
James I 153
Jass 131, 198
Jerome, Jerome K. 130
Jersey Gin 87
Le Jeu de Vache *see* Aluette
Joker 11, 130, 148
Joker Rummy *see* Contract Rummy
Jubilee 53
Julep 157

K
Kaiser 142
Kaiserspiel 240
Kalookie 96
Kaluki 96
Karma *see* Shed
Karnöffel 240, 242
Khun Khan *see* Rummy
King-Queen games 131, 186–93
Kitumaija 75
Klaberjass 199
Klaverjas 131, 174, 198, 203
Kleurenwiezen 112, 114
Klob/Kalabriasze/Klabber *see* Klaberjass
Klondike 15
Knack *see* Schwimmen
Knaves *see* Jacks
Knockout Whist 115
Krambambuli 85

L
Labyrinth 17
Laugh and Lie Down 45
Let It Ride 105
Lewis, Angelo John 145
Lift Smoke *see* Sift Smoke
Linger Longer *see* Sift Smoke
Literature 30
Loba 82, 88
Loba de Más 82, 88
Loba de Menos 82, 88
Long Stud *see* Seven-Card Stud
Losing Cribbage 50
Lowball Poker 223

M
Madrasso 174, 184
Manille 12, 22, 23
Manille à l'Envers 23
Manille Muette 23
Manille Parlée 23
Mariás 192–3
Marjolet 196
matching games 13
Mau Mau 54, 58
Maw 153
Memory 12, 31
Michigan 13, 54, 56–7
Mighty 22
Mus 234–5
Mustamaija 68, 74

N
Napoleon/Nap 130, 148, 155, 156
Nerts 20
Newmarket *see* Michigan
Niggle *see* Oh Hell!

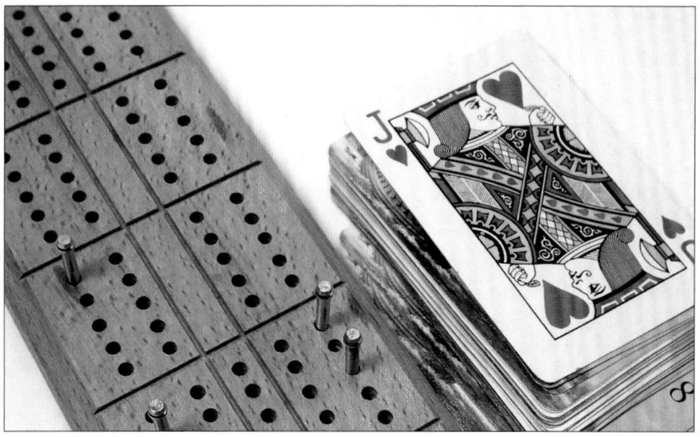

Nine-Card Brag 233
Ninety-Eight 52
Ninety-Nine 52, 124
No Peek Stud 230
Noddy 46, 47
Norrlandsknack 159
Norwegian Whist 140
Nullo Bridge 136

O
Oh Hell! 123
Old Sledge *see* All Fours
Ombre 12, 112, 117, 118–19
One Hundred 53
One-Meld Rummy 85
Ottocento 248-9
outplay games 12
Overby, Glenn 242

P
Pai Gow Poker 228
Palace *see* Shed
Pardon, Charles 104
Parlett, David 12, 14, 124, 130, 240
Parliament *see* Domino
Partnership Whist 117
Paskahousu 68, 79
Patience 12, 13, 14–21
Peanuts *see* Nerts
Pedro *see* Cinch
Pennies from Heaven 212–13
Pepper 150, 151
Perdivinci *see* Ciapanò
Pesten *see* Crazy Eights
Pig 30
Pináculo 214–15
Pink Lady 131
Pinochle 131, 194, 197
Piquet 12, 126–7
games 125–9
Pirate Bridge 137
Pitch 106, 108
Pits *see* Zheng Shangyou
Poch 237
point-card games 98
point-trick games 22–9
Poker 106, 131, 218, 219–20
dealer's choice 230–1
Chicago 230
Draw Poker 131, 222–3
Fifty-Two 230
Follow the Queen 231
Forty-Two 230
Freak-Hand Poker 229
Guts 231
Hi-Low Draw 223
Lowball 223
No Peek Stud 230
Pai Gow Poker 228
Razz 230
Stud Poker 131, 224–5
Texas Hold 'Em 226–7
Three-Card Drop 231
Whisky Poker 30, 34
Wild Card Poker 221
Poker Patience 21
Poker Solitaire *see* Poker Patience
Poker Squares *see* Poker Patience
Polignac 131, 168
Pontoon 99
Pope Joan 54, 62
Pounce *see* Nerts
Preference 120–1
President 63
Primero 236
Push 94–5
Put 164

Q
Quadrille 116, 117, 118
Quarante de Roi *see* Forty for Kings
quasi-trump games 240–4
Queen-Jack games 194–7
Quinto 145

R

Rabelais, François 240
Racing Demon *see* Nerts
Razz 131, 230
Red Dog *see* Yablon
Reunion 183
Reverse Bridge 136
Rödskögg 156
Rolling Stone 68, 69
Rovescino *see* Ciapanò
Rubber Bridge 136
Rummy 13, 82, 83
  500 Rum 217
  Ace high or low 84
  Block Rummy 84
  Boathouse Rum 84
  Call Rummy 84
  Continental Rummy 216
  Contract Rummy 82, 92–3
  games 13, 82–97
  Gin Rummy 13, 86–7
  One-Meld Rummy 85
  Skip Rummy 85
  stock-pile variations 84
  Two-Meld Rummy 85
  Wild-Card Rummy 85
Rumstick 125
Russian Preference 121

S

Samba 207
Samba-Canasta *see* Samba 207
Santos, Segundo 206
Scat *see* Thirty-One
Schafkopf 174, 175
Schieber Jass 198, 205
Schieberamsch 171
Schnapsen 186
Schnautz see Schwimmen
Schwellen see Rolling Stone
Schwimmen 30, 33
  see also Thirty-One
Scopa 40
Scopone 41
Scopone Scientifico 41
Scotch Whist 182, 183
Sechsundsechzig 131, 186, 187, 188
Serrato, Alberto 206
Setback 106, 108
Seven Twenty-Seven 239
Seven Up see All Fours
Seven-card Brag 233
Seven-card Stud 221, 225, 230
Shanghai Rummy *see* Contract Rummy
Shed 68, 78
shedding games 13, 54–67
Sift Smoke 68, 69
Six-Bid Solo 180
Six-Card Cribbage 46, 48–9, 50
Sixty-Six *see* Sechsundsechzig
Skat 131, 174, 176–7, 182
Skip Rummy 85
Skitgubbe 77
Slapjack 31
Smear 106, 109
Snap 13, 30, 31
Solitaire 12, 14–21
solo games 112–24
Solo Whist 112, 113
Spades 141
Spanish Solo 24
Speculation 104
Speed *see* Spit
Spit 19
Spite and Malice 18
Spoil Five *see* Twenty-Five
Spoof Sevens *see* Domino
Spoons 30
Squeal *see* Nerts
Stops *see* Michigan
'Stops' games 54
Stovkahra 22
Straat-Canasta *see* Samba
Straight Rummy *see* Rummy
Stud Poker 131, 224–5
Suckling, Sir John 46
suits 8, 9, 10, 11
Svoi Kozyri 72
Swedish Rummy *see* Crazy Eights
Switch 59

T

Tarocco Bolognese *see* Ottocento
tarot games 9, 181, 245–9
Terziglio 27
Tëtka 170
Texas Hold 'Em 226–7
Thirty-One 89
  see also Schwimmen
Three in One *see* Poch
Three Thirteen 82, 90
Three-Card Drop 231
Three-Card Loo 160
Three-Handed Cribbage 50
Three-Handed Whist 146
Three-Player Gin Rummy 86–7
Tieng Len 66–7
Toepen 162
Tomato 161
Towie 137
Trappola 22, 173
Traversone *see* Ciapanò
Treikort 164
Tresillo 24
Tressette 26, 184
Tressette a non Prendere *see* Ciapanò
trick-taking games 12, 131, 132–47
Tripoli *see* Poch
Truc 163
Tschausepp *see* Crazy Eights
turn-up games 98
Tute 189
Twenty-One 99
Twenty-Five 153
Two-Four-Jack *see* Switch
Two-Meld Rummy 85
Two-Player Gin Rummy 86–7
Tyotka *see* Tëtka
Tysiacha (*Tysiac*) 190

U

Uno 59

V

Vanderbilt, Harold 13
Vatican 97
Verish' Ne Verish' 81
Vierzig von König *see* Forty for Kings
Viet Cong 67
Vinciperdi *see* Ciapanò
Vint 144
vying games 218–39

W

Watten 241
Whisky Poker 30, 34
Whist 46, 112, 130, 131, 132, 138–9
  Belgian Whist 112, 114
  Bid Whist 140
  Contract Whist 140
  German Whist 146
  Knockout Whist 115
  Norwegian Whist 140
  Partnership Whist 117
  Scotch Whist 182, 183
  Solo Whist 112, 113
  Three-handed Whist 146
  Widow Whist 146
  Whist à la Couleur 114
Wiezen *see* Belgian Whist
Wild-Card Poker 221
Wild-Card Rummy 85

Y

Yablon 103
Yukon 182

Z

Zheng Shangyou 64
Zioncheck *see* Contract Rummy
Zwicker 38
Zwikken 161

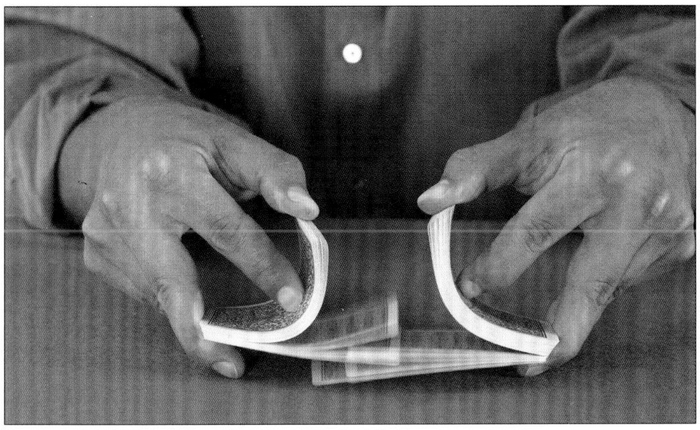

RECOMMENDED BOOKS

There are countless books on individual card games and aspects of card play. The following books are a personal selection. Some are more useful than others, but all of them are worth a read. David Parlett's website (*www.davidparlett.co.uk*) repays investigation, particularly if you are interested in more arcane historical games. Equally, the Pagat web site (*www.pagat.com*) is an indispensable, instant on-line reference. *Mentored* by John McLeod, a leading member of the International Playing Card Society, is also a treasure trove of information.

Andrews, Joseph P., *The Complete Win at Hearts* (Bonus Books, 2000)

Buttler, Frank, Buttler, Simon, *Cribbage* (Weidenfeld & Nicolson, 2000)

Frey, Richard L., Culbertson, Ely, *How to Play Canasta* (Kessinger Publishing, 2007)

Fry, Sam, *Gin Rummy* (Dover, 1978)

Gibson, Walter B., *Hoyle's Modern Encyclopaedia of Card Games* (Robert Hale, 1987)

Johnson, Herman, *Bid Whist* (Author House, 2003)

Kantor, Eddie, *Bridge for Dummies* (Hungry Minds Inc., 2006)

Klinger, Ron, Kambites, Andrew, Husband, Pat, *Basic Bridge* (Cassell, 2001)

Mendelson, Paul, *Texas Hold 'em Poker* (Elliot Right Way Books, 2005)

Morehead, Albert, Mott-Smith, Geoffrey, *Complete Book of Solitaire and Patience Games* (Foulsham, 1996)

Parlett, David, *A History of Card Games* (OUP, 1990)

Parlett, David, *A–Z of Card Games* (OUP, 2004)

Parlett, David, *Card Games for Everyone* (Hodder & Stoughton, 1983)

Pottage, Julian, *The Bridge Player's Bible* (Barron's Educational, 2006)

Regal, Barry, *Card Games for Dummies* (Hungry Minds Inc., 2005)

Robson, Andrew, *Bridge* (HarperCollins, 2007)

Scarne, John, *Scarne's Encyclopaedia of Card Games* (Harper Reference, 1995)

Scharf-Cohen, Leo E., Scharf-Cohen, Robert, *Cohen's Complete Book of Gin Rummy* (Ace Books, 1973)

Schüssler, Thomas G., *Skat* (Südwest Verlag, 2004)

Sharvik, Andrea, Sharvik, Dan, *Playing Poker to Win* (How To Books, 2006)

The Diagram Group, *Card Games* (HarperCollins, 1977)

Wilson, Greg, *Bezique* (Robert Hale, 1998)

PICTURE CREDITS

Anness Publishing would like to thank the following for kindly supplying photographs for this book: **Akg** 193 (tr); **Alamy** 14 (br), 31 (tr), 36 (br), 70 (bl), 131 (br), 148 (br), 166 (br), 174 (br), 186 (br), 198 (br), 220, 234 (br), 237 (tr, cl), 245 (br), 255 (br); **Bridgeman Art Library** 8 (bl, bc, br), 22 (br), 28 (cl), 30 (br), 68 (br), 98 (br), 125 (br), 183 (tr), 248 (br); **BBco** 2, 4 (l), 136 (br), 204 (br), 220 (tr), 246 (b), 249 (b), 256 (b); **Corbis** 12 (tr), 13 (tr), 101 (t), 102 (tr), 104 (bl, br), 127 (tr), 132 (br), 133 (tr), 143 (cl), 153 (br), 160 (bl), 201 (bl), 238 (tr), 255 (bl); **Dover Publications Inc.** 14 (tl), 22 (tl), 30 (tl), 36 (tl), 46 (tl), 54 (tl), 68 (tl), 82 (tl), 98 (tl), 106 (tl), 112 (tl), 122 (bl), 125 (tl), 132 (tl), 148 (tl), 165 (tr), 163 (b), 166 (tl), 174 (tl), 175 (br), 186 (tl), 194 (tl), 198 (tl), 206 (tl), 218 (tl), 240 (tl), 247 (t); **Getty Images** 130 (tr), 206 (br), 227 (bl); **iStockphotography** 49 (br), 82 (br), 84 (br), 219 (bl), 254 (t); **Mary Evans Picture Library** 9, 13, 130 (bl), 131, 137, 194, 195, 240; **Photos.com** 155 (tr); **The Kobal Collection** 218 (br); **The Picture Desk** 10 (bl, bc), 11 (tl, tc, br), 12 (bl), 13 (bl), 46 (br), 56 (tr), 106 (br), 112 (br), 127 (tr), 255 (tr), 256 (tr); **Robert Abbot** 54 (br); **Topfoto** 185 (bl).
Images are listed in clockwise order (t = top, c = centre, b = bottom, l = left, r = right, tr = top right etc.).

All artwork by Virginia Zeal

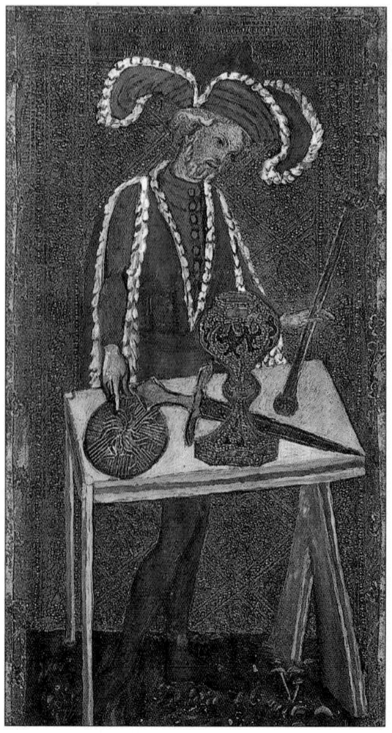

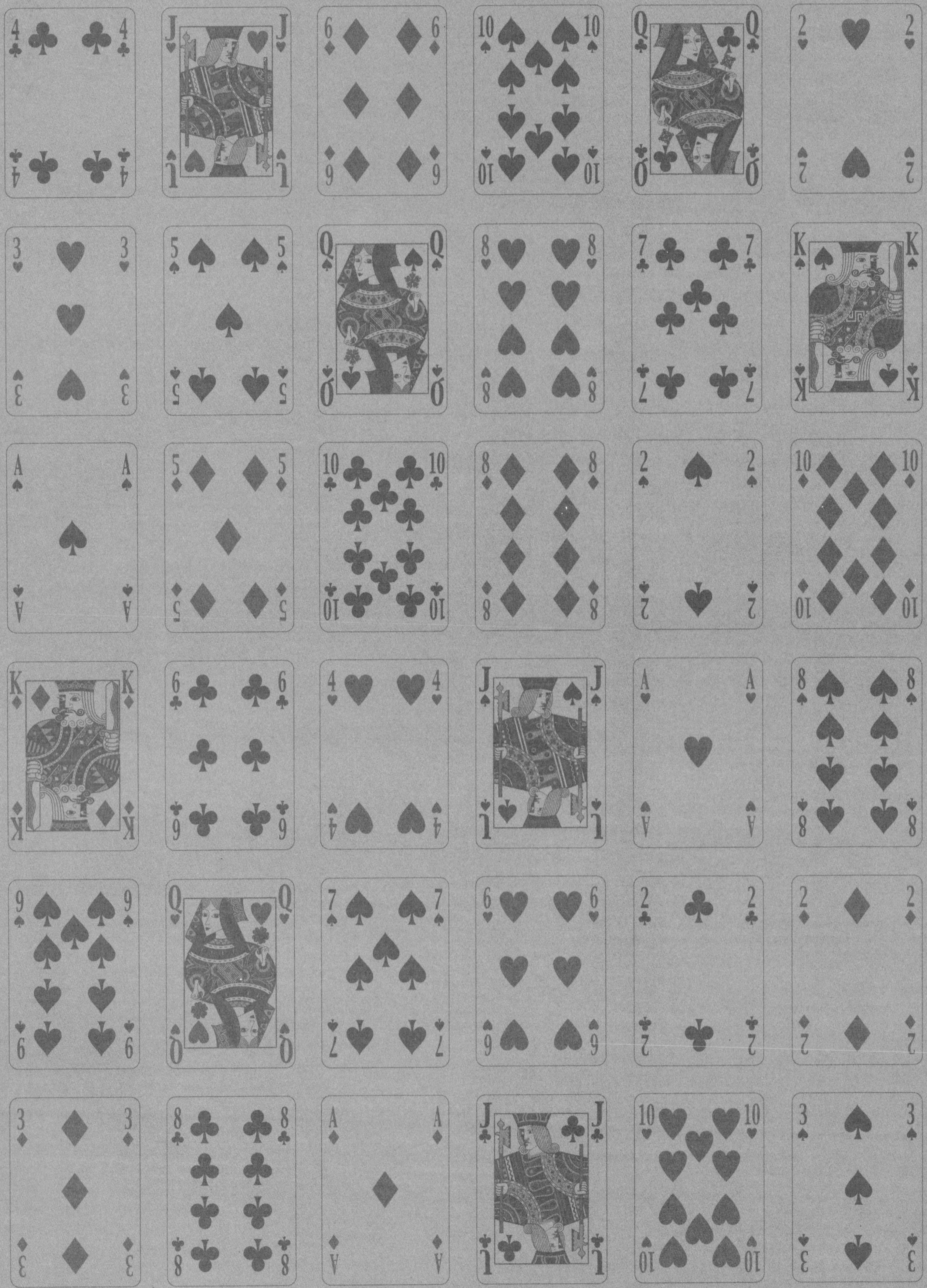